Third Edition

Youth Justice
A Canadian Overview

John Winterdyk
Kelly Gorkoff
Daniel Antonowicz
Russell Smandych

OXFORD
UNIVERSITY PRESS

OXFORD
UNIVERSITY PRESS

Oxford University Press is a department of the University of Oxford.
It furthers the University's objective of excellence in research, scholarship,
and education by publishing worldwide. Oxford is a registered trade mark of
Oxford University Press in the UK and in certain other countries.

Published in Canada by
Oxford University Press
8 Sampson Mews, Suite 204,
Don Mills, Ontario M3C 0H5 Canada

www.oupcanada.com

Library and Archives Canada Cataloguing in Publication
Title: Youth justice: a Canadian overview / [edited by] John Winterdyk, Kelly Gorkoff, Daniel
Antonowicz and Russell Smandych.
Other titles: Youth at risk and youth justice
Names: Winterdyk, John, editor. | Gorkoff, Kelly, editor. | Antonowicz, Daniel H., editor. |
Smandych, Russell, 1956- editor.
Description: Third edition. | Previous editions published under title: Youth at risk and youth
justice. | Includes bibliographical references and index.
Identifiers: Canadiana (print) 20190187301 | Canadiana (ebook) 2019018731X |
ISBN 9780199032723 (softcover) | ISBN 9780199038671 (looseleaf) | ISBN 9780199032730 (EPUB)
Subjects: LCSH: Juvenile delinquency—Canada—Textbooks. | LCSH: Juvenile justice,
Administration of—
Canada—Textbooks. | LCGFT: Textbooks.
Classification: LCC HV9108 .Y67 2020 | DDC 364.360971—dc23

Cover image: Caiaimage/Trevor Adeline/Getty Images
Cover design: Laurie McGregor
Interior design: Sherill Chapman

Oxford University Press is committed to our environment.
Wherever possible, our books are printed on paper which comes from
responsible sources.

Printed and bound in Canada

1 2 3 4 — 23 22 21 20

Contents

6 Youth Deviance and the Media: Mapping Knowledge and the Limits to Certainty 136

Chris McCormick

7 Canadian Girls and Crime in the Twenty-First Century 162

Lorinda Stoneman, Mandeep Mucina, Thais Amorim, and Sibylle Artz

8 Theoretical Perspectives on Youth Crime 196

Stephen W. Baron

9   Critical Criminology and Youth Justice in the "Risk Society": Issues of Power and Justice   229

Bryan Hogeveen and Joanne Minaker

Part III   Criminalized Youth in Canada: Selected Types and Problems   259

10   Issues of Substance Use and Related Crime in Adolescence   261

Jordan Diplock, Nick Pauls, and Gwendolyn Geuze

16   Juvenile Justice and Restorative Justice in British Columbia:
     Learning through the Lens of Community Praxis   436

Brenda Morrison, Muhammad (Asad) Asadullah, and Colleen Pawlychka

About the Editors

John A. Winterdyk is a professor of criminology and has been working at Mount Royal University for over 30 years. During his tenure, he has held several visiting positions at the Max Planck Institute in Germany, been the Endowed Chair at St Thomas University in Fredericton, New Brunswick, and has held several adjunct and visiting professorships at various Canadian and international universities. He has published over three dozen peer-reviewed articles, including being guest (co-)editor for five different journals; has over 35 academic books to his credit; and is the recipient of several academic awards. His research interests include youth justice, youth "at risk," crime prevention, human trafficking, comparative criminal justice, and adult corrections. Among other past academic awards, in 2019 he received the Outstanding Scholar Award in the Faculty of Arts. In his spare time, he enjoys travelling, riding his bicycle, and spending time with his grandson.

Kelly Gorkoff is an associate professor at the University of Winnipeg in the Department of Criminal Justice. Her research is focused on critical political economy and the corporatization of criminal justice practices and policies, including work in the areas of specialized courts, public inquiries, and the regulation of sex work. She teaches social theory, ethics, and advanced theory. For eight years, she was a research associate at RESOLVE, a tri-provincial research centre dedicated to studying violence against women, and she now sits on their board.

She is co-editor of *Being Heard: The Experiences of Young Women in Prostitution* (Fernwood 2003) and *Thinking about Justice* (Fernwood 2012).

Daniel Antonowicz is an associate professor of criminology at Wilfrid Laurier University in Brantford, Ontario. He has worked as a research officer for various Canadian federal government departments, such as the Correctional Service of Canada and the Ministry of Justice. His research interests include the essential characteristics of effective correctional treatment programs, offender assessment, and corporate wrongdoing. He teaches courses on offender rehabilitation, penology, white-collar crime, and global justice.

Russell Smandych is a professor in the Department of Sociology and Criminology at the University of Manitoba. His current research and teaching interests include global criminology and criminal justice, comparative legal history, and comparative youth justice. He is the author and editor or co-editor of 10 books and has published widely in leading Canadian and international journals in the fields of law, legal history, and criminology. He has held several honorary appointments as a distinguished visiting professor and scholar at universities in Canada, Ireland, Australia, New Zealand, and England, and continues to engage actively in research and teaching on topics including British colonial legal history, youth justice policy transfer, global crime, and international criminal justice.

About the Contributors

Thais Amorim is a sessional teacher in the School of Child and Youth Care at the University of Victoria. She teaches in the areas of law, mental health, substance use, and helping skills. Her doctoral research focuses on how proportional sentences consider and balance offenders' risks of reoffending and their needs (criminogenic or not). She received her master's degree in child and youth care from the University of Victoria in 2013, where she completed a thesis on the overrepresentation of female young offenders in custody for administrative offences in British Columbia. Thais graduated from the Faculdade Milton Campos in Nova Lima-MG in Brazil with a bachelor of laws in 2008.

Sibylle Artz is a professor in child and youth care at the University of Victoria. Her research focuses on youth aggression with an emphasis on girls' use of violence and on youth resilience to violence exposure. She has published more than 60 refereed articles and book chapters, co-edited four special journal issues, and authored two books. Since 2009, Dr Artz has been working with a team of researchers from six European countries and is currently working with a Swiss-based group on a research project that focuses on understanding the violence resilience pathways of adolescents with experiences of family violence.

Muhammad (Asad) Asadullah is a Ph.D. candidate at Simon Fraser University's School of Criminology and a criminology instructor at Kwantlen Polytechnic University. He has a master's degree in criminology from Simon Fraser University and a master's in conflict transformation from Eastern Mennonite University (Pennsylvania). His research interests include restorative justice, village court, youth justice, Indigenous justice, and contemplative justice. As a sessional faculty, Asadullah taught restorative justice at Simon Fraser University and peace and conflict studies at the University of the Fraser Valley for several semesters. He is the recipient of multiple awards and scholarships, including the Contemplative Social Justice Scholar Award, the ACJS Doctoral Fellowship Award, the C.D. Nelson Memorial Graduate Award, the Provost Prize of Distinction, and the Graduate Fellowship and Law Foundation Scholarship in Restorative Justice. Currently, he is a member of the board of both the Vancouver Association for Restorative Justice and the Salish Sea Empathy Society.

Harpreet Aulakh is an associate professor in the Criminal Justice program at Mount Royal University, in Calgary. Her research primarily focuses on the lived experiences of youth in gangs, with an emphasis on girls' involvement in gang activities. Her interests in youth behaviour also include youth "at risk" and youth resiliency. Her other research interests include issues of diversity in the justice system, Indigenous people and justice, and understanding Indigenous gangsta rap music. She co-authored the third edition of *Diversity and Indigenous Peoples in Canada* (2017). At Mount Royal University, she teaches a variety of criminology and criminal justice courses. For many years, she has been actively involved with the local youth justice committee and the Calgary John Howard Society.

Stephen W. Baron is a professor in the Department of Sociology at Queen's University. His research focuses primarily on homeless street youth and crime and substance abuse. He is concerned with how various criminological theories can be used to help us understand these forms of behaviour among the homeless street youth population. His work on these types of issues has appeared in a variety of academic journals, including *Criminology, Journal of Research in Crime and Delinquency, Justice Quarterly, Criminal Justice and Behavior*, and *Crime and Delinquency*.

Courtenay Bolton is enrolled at Mount Royal University, where she is completing a bachelor of arts in child studies, with a major in child and youth care counselling and a minor in psychology. She has experience working with vulnerable and "at-risk" youth through various organizations in Calgary. She is currently employed as a research assistant at Constellation Consulting Group and is passionate about pursuing a career in research and evaluation.

Raymond R. Corrado is a professor and director of the Institute on Violence, Terrorism & Security in the School of Criminology at Simon Fraser University (SFU) and was the associate director of research and an associate faculty member in the psychology department and the Faculty of Health Sciences at SFU. He is a visiting fellow at Clare Hall College and the Institute of Criminology, University of Cambridge, and he is a founding member of the Mental Health, Law, and Policy Institute at Simon Fraser University. Dr Corrado is also a former co-director of the BC Centre for Social Responsibility and former director of the Centre for Addictions Research British Columbia, SFU Site. He was also a visiting professor at the Faculty of Law, University of Bergen. He is on the editorial boards of eight major criminology and forensic mental health journals. He has co-authored nine edited books, including *Evaluation and Criminal Justice Policy* (1981); *Current Issues in Juvenile Justice* (1983); *Juvenile Justice in Canada* (1992); and *Multi-Problem Violent Youth* (2001), as well as having published over 200 articles, book chapters, and reports on a wide variety of theory and policy issues, including terrorism, youth/juvenile justice, violent young offenders, mental health, adolescent psychopathy, Indigenous victimization, and child/adolescent case management strategies. Currently, Dr Corrado is a principal investigator and co-principal investigator of several research projects, including three large-scale studies on incarcerated serious and violent young offenders, comprehensive risk management instruments for violent children and youth, and early childhood aggression. He has conducted policy research and advised governments at national and regional levels in Canada as well as Australia, Italy, and Norway. He received his Ph.D. from Northwestern University in Chicago.

Louis-Georges Cournoyer is currently an associate professor at the School of Criminology of the Université de Montréal. He has a Ph.D. in psychology, has been a psychologist for 30 years, and has worked with various clientele, especially with high-risk young people and families at Centre jeunesse de Montréal—Institut universitaire (CJM-IU) (now named Centre de recherche et d'expertise jeunes en difficulté du Centre intégré universitaire de services santé et services sociaux du Centre sud de l'Île-de-Montréal (CIUSSSS-CSDIM)), with which he is now affiliated as a researcher. His research interests focus on the rehabilitation processes and effectiveness of treatments for youth offenders and drug addicts.

Jacques Dionne has for over 20 years been an educator, psycho-educator, chief of unit, and program director. Since 2000, he has been a researcher and the professional staff-training director at Boscoville in Montreal (an institution for youth offenders). He was also a full professor at the Université du Québec en Outaouais, associate professor at UQO, and a researcher at l'Institut de recherche pour l'adaptation des jeunes du CJM-IU. Dr Dionne specializes in staff training, program development, and evaluation for youth offenders and adolescents in difficulty. Since 2000, he has also been the leader of several international collaboration projects on rehabilitation in such countries as Chile and Brazil.

Jordan Diplock is a research analyst with the Royal Canadian Mounted Police. He also teaches part time in the School of Criminology and Criminal Justice at the University of the Fraser Valley. He has co-authored numerous reports and articles relating to illicit drug production and use.

Marie-Michèle Dumas is currently a teacher's assistant in qualitative research methodology and a research assistant at the Université de Montréal. She has a bachelor's diploma in psycho-sociology and a master's degree in criminology. Her projects have addressed behaviours of opposition and resistance in youth offenders during the rehabilitation process.

Gwendolyn Geuze is a master of science student in the Crime and Criminal Justice program at Leiden University. As a former research assistant for the Centre for Public Safety and Criminal Justice Research at the University of the Fraser Valley, and former employee of the Royal Canadian Mounted Police, she has been involved in various criminal justice and public-safety-related research projects.

Sarah Gilliss has taken a leave of absence from her position as an instructor in the Social Sciences Department of the New Brunswick Community College to pursue graduate studies at the University of Ottawa. She has had experience on the front lines as a youth worker and correctional officer. As a facilitator for the Students Commission of Canada, she worked, through the Centre for Research on Youth at Risk at St Thomas University, to facilitate a youth-led group inside the New Brunswick Youth Centre.

Michèle Goyette is a consulting director at l'Association des centres jeunesse du Québec (Youth Centres Association of Quebec) and has been the director of specialized services for young offenders at Centre jeunesse de Montréal—Institut universitaire. For 35 years, she worked primarily as a criminologist or manager for young offenders' services. She participated in the development of different programs for young offenders and collaborated with Quebec's major research partners, working on the provincial organization and orientation of services. She is a member of the board of directors of Quebec's Society for Criminology and of the Child Welfare League of Canada. She uses every possible platform in Quebec and Canada to promote the rehabilitation and social reintegration of young offenders.

Hirsch Greenberg is the practicum coordinator in the Department of Justice Studies at the University of Regina, where he is also a member of the Research Ethics Board and chair of the Faculty Association's grievance committee. He has spent the past 45 years in Saskatchewan working for community-based organizations in Regina and File Hills (First Nations communities) in various roles: line staff, administrator, and volunteer. His research mostly engages community-based organizations and government projects dealing with homelessness, specialized courts, community policing, mental health, and substance abuse. He is an active board member of the Regina Alternative Measures Program. He received the Regina YMCA

Peace Medal in 2009 and was recognized by the Correctional Service of Canada in 2010 for his work in restorative justice. He has published chapters in several textbooks. Hirsch has a bachelor of arts in sociology and a master's in social work from the University of Regina.

Jana Grekul is an associate professor of sociology and director of the bachelor of arts Criminology program at the University of Alberta. Her research interests include street and prison gangs, Indigenous gangs, and the study of punishment within the criminal justice system. Gender and the "doing of gender" in these environments is an important component to her research. Other research interests include pedagogy in the university classroom and, more recently, reintegration of women, post-incarceration. She teaches a variety of sociology and criminology courses and is co-author of Sociology (McGraw-Hill Ryerson, 2009), and Criminology (McGraw-Hill Education, 2012).

Julius Haag is currently a doctoral candidate at the Centre for Criminology & Sociolegal Studies, University of Toronto. His research interests include youth justice, policing, terrorism, gangs, youth culture, crime prevention and intervention programming, and program design and evaluation. The focus of his research has been on the experiences of racialized and marginalized youth within the criminal justice system. Julius is currently co-investigator on an SSHRC-funded project with Scot Wortley examining police–youth relations within disadvantaged Toronto communities. He has also worked as a youth employment counsellor in Toronto's Jane and Finch community, as well as an evaluator and program design consultant for various youth-focused agencies. Julius graduated from the University of Waterloo with an honours bachelor of arts degree in sociology with a crime, deviance, and regulation specialization, and from the University of Toronto with a master's degree in sociology. Julius has been the recipient of both the SSHRC doctoral fellowship and the Ontario graduate scholarship.

Pierre Hamel worked as a lawyer for many years in the litigation department at the Centre jeunesse de Montréal– Institut Universitaire. Being a specialist in juvenile delinquency policy, he was responsible for the reference manual guiding the application of the Youth Criminal Justice Act (YCJA) for youth centres throughout Quebec. He also authored a 2009 book on the application of the YCJA in Quebec and, from 2011 to 2013, was director of the legal department of the Association des centres jeunesse du Québec, where he played a key role in preserving the philosophy of the Quebec model of juvenile delinquency intervention. In February 2013, he was appointed as judge of the Cour du Québec, chambre de la jeunesse (Provincial Court of Quebec, Youth Division).

Bryan Hogeveen received a Ph.D. in criminology from the University of Toronto. He is the vice dean of the Faculty of Graduate Studies and Research at the University of Alberta, where he is responsible for a portfolio that includes student awards; quality assurance; and equity, diversity, and inclusion for graduate students. His interdisciplinary scholarly work intersects at three distinct points: (1) sociological engagement with sport; (2) youth in/and society; and (3) social theory. He is co-author (with Joanne Minaker) of *Youth, Crime and Society: Issues of Power and Justice* (2009) and the edited collection of essays *Criminalized Mothers, Criminalized Mothering* (2015). Dr Hogeveen is a proud father of three children (Ayden, Taryk, and Maylah), has a Brazilian jiu-jitsu black belt, and can most often be found in one Edmonton arena or another.

Bruce MacLaurin is an assistant professor at the Faculty of Social Work, University of Calgary. He is a co-investigator on the four cycles of the Canadian Incidence Study of Reported Child Abuse and Neglect (1998, 2003, 2008, 2019), as well as the principal investigator for provincial studies in British Columbia, Alberta, Saskatchewan, and the Northwest Territories. His research and publishing have focused on child maltreatment, child welfare service delivery and outcomes, foster care, youth "at risk," and street-involved youth. He has collaborated with provincial and territorial governments over the past 20 years and has consulted on a variety of government initiatives, including front-end services, ongoing services, kinship care, and outcome-based service delivery. Bruce has also served as an expert panel member for a legislation review in the Northwest Territories, for the Office of

the Child and Youth Advocate in Alberta, for the Ministerial Panel on Child Fatalities, for the Ministerial Panel on Child Intervention, and as an advisor for the Auditor General of Canada Review of the Northwest Territories Legislative Assembly.

Chris McCormick is a professor and a co-founder of the Criminology and Criminal Justice Department at St Thomas University in Fredericton, New Brunswick. His research is in areas of cultural criminology, and he teaches courses on wrongful conviction, crime and media, and visual criminology. He has published in the areas of corporate crime, media studies, and deviancy theory, and his most recent book is *Constructing Danger: Emotions and the Mis/Representation of Crime in the News* (2010).

Anne Miller has a master's in public policy and public administration, with a focus on leadership and decision-making. She wrote her master's thesis on her experience working under the registrar at the International Criminal Court. Anne is a credentialed evaluator through the Canadian Evaluation Society and an accredited social return on investment (SROI) practitioner and licensed SROI trainer through Social Value Network International. Anne has conducted research, evaluation, and SROI analysis in fields such as crime prevention, youth "at risk," and housing. Anne runs her own research and evaluation consultancy called Constellation Consulting Group (for more information see www.constellationconsulting.ca).

Joanne Minaker received a Ph.D. in socio-legal studies from Queen's University. She is associate dean, academic in the Faculty of Arts and Science at MacEwan University. A sociologist, qualitative researcher, and ardent mother, Dr Minaker's corpus of work centres around care, human connection, and social (in)justice. An emphasis on knowledge for social transformation resonates deeply and underscores her scholarly, creative, and pedagogical contributions, which include the book *Youth, Crime and Society: Issues of Power and Justice* (2009), co-authored with Bryan Hogeveen; *Criminalized Mothers, Criminalized Mothering* (2015); and numerous articles that call into question marginalizing processes that exclude, silence, and dehumanize groups such as young women, criminalized youth, and survivors of sexual violence. In 2016, she spoke at TEDxUAlberta "The Power of Meaningful Connections," on the transformative power of relationships inside and outside academia.

Brenda Morrison is co-chair of the Safe Schools and Communities Special Interest Group of the American Education Research Association and a member of the Scientific Committee of the International Observatory of Violence in Schools. She has presented papers at the United Nations Educational, Scientific and Cultural Organization (UNESCO) in Paris, and for the House of Lords in London, and has chaired many panels on restorative justice and schools for the World Congress of Criminology as well as for several other associations. She is a research partner with PREVNET (Promoting Relationships and Eliminating Violence Network) within Canada's Networks of Centres of Excellence. In British Columbia, she is a member of the Working Group for Social Responsibility and Collaborative Learning in Education. In her home community, she is an active board member for the North Shore Restorative Justice Society.

Mandeep Kaur Mucina is an assistant professor in the School of Child and Youth Care at the University of Victoria. Mandeep has worked in the human services sector as a child and youth worker and social worker for more than 20 years, including work in child welfare, gender-based violence, and community engagement with immigrant/refugee/migrant women and families. Mandeep received her undergraduate degree from the School of Child and Youth Care, a master's in social work from the University of Toronto, and her Ph.D. in adult education and community development from OISE, University of Toronto. Mandeep has also worked as a practitioner, educator, researcher, and community educator in Victoria, Vancouver, Toronto, and Halifax, and has sat on various boards across Canada.

Nick Pauls is a graduate student in the School of Criminology at Simon Fraser University. He is also a researcher on the Incarcerated Serious and Violent Young Offender Study, the largest and longest-running study on young offenders in Canada. Nick has also worked as a youth

addictions counsellor in several rural areas of British Columbia.

Colleen L. Pawlychka, Ph.D., is a faculty member at Douglas College. Her areas of expertise include restorative justice, institutional corrections, prison reform, prisoners, punishment, masculinities, childhood psychological trauma, and trauma-informed correctional practices. Colleen's doctoral research focused on the impact of psychological trauma on the brain and behaviour, its role in the generation of criminal behaviour, and the role of trauma healing as an agent of rehabilitation for male federal prisoners in Canada. Specifically, Colleen's research examined the experiences of former federal prisoners to gain an in-depth understanding of healing from childhood psychological trauma while in prison and during community re-entry, from the men's perspectives. Community–prisoner connection was found to be integral to healing childhood psychological trauma, and reflected trauma-informed, gender-responsive care. The community–prisoner connection created turning points in participants' life trajectories, providing motivation and opportunities to increase emotional ability, especially empathy, and to develop skill-building capacity as well as pro-social values and behaviours. Colleen holds that the powerful and positive contribution of community should be encouraged as a rehabilitation strategy and an enhancement of prisoner reintegration.

Adrienne Peters is an assistant professor and police studies liaison/co-coordinator in the Department of Sociology at Memorial University. Her research areas include youth justice intervention programming; serious/violent offending; mental health and delinquency; youth and sexual offences; youth justice policy; rehabilitation and re-entry; police training and education; evidence-based policing; and collaborative crime-reduction strategies. Adrienne is the principal investigator of several projects on youth corrections and policing, and has delivered presentations and published on each of these themes. She is chair of the fasdNL Network and a member of 7th Step Society Newfoundland, and sits on a provincial alcohol action plan working group. She received her Ph.D. from Simon Fraser University.

James Popham is an assistant professor in the Department of Criminology at Wilfrid Laurier University, where he researches issues of cyber criminality, technology, and social empowerment. His background, both professional and scholarly, includes work with marginalized and criminalized youth from multiple backgrounds across Canada.

Susan A. Reid is a professor of criminology and criminal justice at St Thomas University in Fredericton, New Brunswick. She is also the director of the Centre for Research on Youth at Risk, which is the eastern hub of the Students Commission of Canada/Centre of Excellence for Youth Engagement. Her research interests include youth justice, youth "at risk," youth voice, and youth engagement, and she has several publications in these areas. Her work with youth in closed custody for over 20 years has informed her research and teaching. Her service to the community has been recognized with several awards for crime prevention, leadership, and community engagement.

Chloe Shepherd is a recent graduate of the University of Winnipeg in Winnipeg, Manitoba. Upon the completion of her four-year bachelor of arts degree in 2015, she was awarded the gold medal for achievement in sociology. Chloe also graduated with a three-year bachelor of arts in conflict resolution studies from Menno Simons College. Her research interests include, among others, deviance and social control, theories of penality, cultural conflict, and genocide studies. Going forward, Chloe plans to further her studies in the field of social work, with emphasis on the issues faced by newcomers and refugees in Canada.

Lorinda Stoneman received her Ph.D. from the School of Child and Youth Care at the University of Victoria in 2016. In her dissertation, Lorinda undertook a qualitative analysis of Canadian youth justice policy, with a focus on diversion and community-based alternatives to custody for young offenders. Prior to this, Lorinda received her master of arts degree in criminology from Simon Fraser University in 2008, where she became interested in the connections between the disciplines of criminology and child and youth care, and female young offenders. Other research interests include crime prevention and domestic violence. In addition to her academic work, Lorinda has worked for the BC provincial government since 2012, where she is currently a senior policy analyst in the Community Safety and Crime Prevention Branch of the Ministry of Public Safety and Solicitor General. Her portfolio includes program and policy development related to the areas of victim services, domestic violence, restitution, and youth online harassment.

Catherine (Cathy) Worthington is a professor and director at the School of Public Health and Social Policy, University of Victoria. She has a background in health services research, social work, and public health, and conducts research on community health and social services, particularly those for underserved populations. She was the principal investigator on the Canadian Institutes of Health Research (CIHR)-funded Calgary Youth, Health and the Street Study. Her current work in the HIV field focuses on services development for First Nation and Métis communities; social inclusion (housing, employment, stigma reduction, comorbidity/[dis]ability); training and mentoring; and innovations in community-engaged research methods. She is part of the leadership team for the CIHR HIV Clinical Trials Network (CTN) (http://www.hivnet.ubc.ca); is the BC co-lead for the CIHR Centre for REACH in HIV (http://www.reachprogramscience.ca); and is co-director for the CIHR REACH CBR Collaborative Centre (http://www.reachprogramscience.ca/cihr-cbr-collaborative-a-program-of-reach).

Preface

This third edition of *Youth Justice: A Canadian Overview* introduces two new editors to the team: Kelly Gorkoff and Dan Antonowicz. Russell Smandych, co-editor with John Winterdyk on the first two editions, has decided to slowly wind down his esteemed career. The new editors are incredibly pleased to have been involved in editing this edition of the book, and we hope that you will not only enjoy reading it but also learn and be inspired to inquire further. Gorkoff and Antonowicz have both taught courses on young offenders and youth justice as well as published nationally and internationally on the general subject of youth crime. In addition to lending our knowledge and experience to this book, we have assembled a substantial list of contributors who are all well-established experts in their chapter topics. This depth and variety of author experience brings a richness and an elevated level of comprehensiveness to the book that we could not have achieved otherwise. As a result, the readers are the beneficiaries of the collaborative effort that has allowed us to prepare this textbook.

Despite its long history, the study of youth crime and youth justice remains one of the most intriguing and invigorating, yet enigmatic, areas within criminology and criminal justice. For example, whether locally, provincially, or nationally (and even internationally), criminologists and social scientists, in general, have been intrigued by the challenges of youth crime and its prevention and control. At a more fundamental level, everyone reading this book has at one time or another likely wondered why young people commit delinquent or criminal acts and what we can, or should, do about it. While this book does not profess to provide answers to all possible questions, it does explore a wide range of topics and issues that will provide the reader with a thorough understanding of the richness and complexity of youth crime and youth justice.

To provide an appropriate overview of youth crime and justice, we have intentionally attempted to avoid endorsing any ideological agenda. However, we have asked all the chapter authors to be reflective and, where appropriate, critical about the topics they have covered. As the editors, we feel that by introducing learners not only to the history of youth justice but also to a variety of theoretical perspectives and a range of topical issues (e.g., young female offenders, substance abuse, Indigenous youth) that are framed in an informative but also reflective manner, readers will learn to reflect critically on the chapter topics and form their own observations and conclusions about the different issues being covered.

Given this perspective, we solicited chapters for the book with several key goals in mind. First, we wanted to ensure that the book was comprehensive in its coverage, substantial in content, and yet reader-friendly, to encourage learners to not only read but be challenged by the questions offered and intrigued by the additional sources identified. Although the book is divided into four main parts, each with its introduction, the sections and chapters do not need to be followed in sequence, nor do they necessarily all need to be covered. Collectively, they serve to provide a solid foundation for almost any undergraduate-level Canadian course on youth crime, young offenders, and the workings of the youth justice system.

Second, we were keen to include pedagogical materials and features that are intended not only to enliven the learners' understanding of the topic but also to stimulate further questioning, in-class discussion, and possibly a desire to take more advanced or specialized courses on one or more of the chapter themes. The chapter overview and key objectives, questions for review and critical thinking, and the key terms (and glossary) combine to make the book learner-friendly and to serve as a primary text at the undergraduate level. Where appropriate, chapters also include Youth Justice in Action boxes, as well as tables and figures that are intended to enrich the chapter content without detracting from the main message.

A third goal we had in mind was to ensure topical coverage. Each chapter devotes attention to a specific topic that is seen as fundamental to understanding the complexity of youth crime and youth justice. Also, we wanted to include essential topics that were timely but not commonly addressed in as much detail in other undergraduate textbooks. For example, street-involved youth (Chapter 13), sex work (Chapter 14), the Quebec approach to youth justice (Chapter 15), and restorative justice (Chapter 16) have received little to no attention in textbooks with a similar focus. Yet we also wanted to ensure that the core themes typically introduced in youth crime and justice courses were covered as well, and so have included chapters ranging from a historical overview of youth justice in Canada (Chapter 1) to examinations of current youth justice legislation (Chapters 3 and 4), young female offenders (Chapter 7), racialized youth in the youth criminal justice system (Chapter 12), substance use (Chapter 10), and Indigenous youth in conflict with the law (Chapter 11).

Organization of the Book

As indicated above, the textbook is organized into four parts. "Part I: History, Trends, and Legislation" presents four chapters that collectively serve to provide a foundation for a better understanding of the development of legislative and policy approaches taken in Canada over the last century to define, measure, and deal with "at-risk," delinquent, and criminal youth. Part I includes chapters aimed at accounting for historical and contemporary trends in delinquency and youth justice legislation (Chapter 1); understanding how we measure and use different data sources to describe and explain contemporary youth crime (Chapter 2); describing the current Youth Criminal Justice Act (YCJA) and some of its effects (Chapter 3); and examining the youth criminal justice system "in action," using the system operating in British Columbia as a specific example (Chapter 4). The chapters in this part follow a similar format to facilitate reading about, reflecting critically upon, and understanding these essential topics.

"Part II: Understanding Contemporary Youth Crime and Justice: Theories and Perspectives" shifts attention to the examination of the different ways a student can try to develop a broad understanding of youth crime and justice in today's society. Chapter 5 offers an evocative discussion as to why we need to maintain a separate justice system in which young persons' needs are recognized and supported. The authors also place the examination of Canada's youth justice system within an international context by discussing the United Nations Convention of the Rights of the Child, and they argue for changes in youth justice that give young people a voice in decisions that affect their well-being. Chapter 6 turns to a critical examination of the role of the media in creating public knowledge and awareness of youth crime and youth justice, while the subsequent chapters in this part focus more on the various theoretical approaches that have been developed to explain juvenile delinquency and youth crime. Because the behaviour of females is often influenced by different factors than those that influence the behaviour of young males, Chapter 7 focuses specifically on young female offending behaviour. The remaining two chapters address new theoretical perspectives on youth crime (Chapter 8) and the need for a critical criminological perspective on youth and crime that pays attention to issues of power and justice (Chapter 9).

Inevitably, when we think of young offenders we tend to categorize their behaviour as either that of offenders or that of victims. Within each category, we then attempt to refine our labelling based on the behaviour(s) the youth are engaged in. In "Part III: Criminalized Youth in Canada: Selected Types and Problems," the chapters focus on five areas that in addition to being topical also serve to reflect the complexity of young persons' behaviour. For example, Chapter 10 covers the age-old problem of substance use/abuse among youth to see what, if anything, has changed in addressing this issue and how well it is working. Chapter 11 focuses on the overrepresentation of Indigenous youth in the criminal justice system. Also included in this part is a chapter on the topical issue of racialized youth (Chapter 12). Chapter 13 covers the unfortunate plight of homeless youth, who, while commonly seen as victims of social and personal circumstances, often turn to crime to survive. In an era when awareness and resources have never been so plentiful, the question of whether we care takes centre stage here. The part concludes with a chapter on youth involved in sex work (Chapter 14). After reading some or all of the chapters in Part III, students will have a deeper appreciation of the diversity of what constitutes youth crime and of the complexity of trying to address the problem. For example, while young people may engage in an anti-social and illegal activity, such behaviour is not always a matter of choice. To this end, we might reflect on the chapters in Parts I and II and ask, again, if we are "doing the right thing."

What lies ahead for the administration of youth justice in Canada remains unclear. Notwithstanding this uncertainty, the chapters in Part IV, "Keeping Young Persons out of the System: Exploring Progressive Approaches to Youth Crime and Justice," show that diverse initiatives are being used with varying degrees of success and controversy. Collectively, Chapters 15 and 16 speak to public policy and legislative issues that show promise in the possible refinement (or overhauling) of the youth justice system. Specifically, Chapter 15 provides an overview of the multidisciplinary assessment and intervention approach as used in Quebec, while Chapter 16 explores the history and feasibility of restorative justice.

Finally, to paraphrase the esteemed American psychiatrist Karl Menninger (1883–1990), who once said that society gets the youth crime it deserves, it may be argued that if we fail to understand youth crime and if we respond with poorly informed evidence, then we cannot blame anyone but ourselves for the resulting state of affairs. As is conveyed throughout this textbook, over the past century we have seen a considerable transformation of youth justice policy and practices, from the introduction of the Juvenile Delinquents Act in 1908 and the Young Offenders Act (YOA) in 1984 to the implementation of the Youth Criminal Justice Act (YCJA) in 2003. During this history, we have shifted from a welfare model, which emphasized a social work approach that focused on diagnosing the problem and providing treatment under the premise of *parens patriae*—"the state knows best"—toward a justice model with the YOA, in which due process and accountability were emphasized but in measured ways (see Chapter 3). Arguably, the YCJA, with its revised objectives, is reflective of what Reid and Reitsma-Street (1984) referred to as a "community change model" or "modified justice model" that attempts to strike a balance between crime control and providing rehabilitative and restorative options for young offenders. According to this model, and as Christopher Anne Robinson-Easley (2012) concluded in her book on saving youth, we must "never give up on a child!" (p. 206).

We realize that despite our efforts to prepare a textbook that would span the spectrum of course curriculums that focus on youth crime and youth justice, we may have come up short in some areas. We debated at some length about including more content, but in part because of practical constraints, we had to make informed decisions about what to include and what not to. Should you have any constructive feedback, we would welcome hearing from you. We are always receptive to trying to improve the approach we have taken in our attempt to contribute to an understanding of youth crime and youth justice in Canada.

Cheers,
John Winterdyk, Kelly Gorkoff, and Dan Antonowicz

References

Reid, S.A., and Reitsma-Street, M. (1984). Assumptions and implications of new Canadian legislation for young offenders. *Canadian Criminology Forum, 7*, 1–19.
Robinson-Easley, C.A. (2012). *Our children, our responsibilities: Saving the youth we are losing to gangs*. New York: Peter Lang.

Acknowledgements

Although I did not know it at the time, my nearly 40-year involvement with writing and editing books on young offenders and juvenile justice dates to the late 1970s when I agreed to run a wilderness adventure program in Ontario for an eager and creative probation officer by the name of Rick Mazur (we are still dear friends to this day). My experience over those years eventually drew me back to school, intent on learning more about young offenders and youth at risk. Also, while much has transpired since the days of ACTION (Accepting Challenge Through Interaction with Others and Nature), my interest in young offenders and youth justice remains steadfast.

In the preparation of this third edition, little has changed. Co-editing this collection of original articles requires much teamwork and dedication by all involved. Although the process never seems to get any easier, it has also been a joyous experience to witness how well so many different ideas, agendas, and personalities can come together with dedication to a common cause. Therefore, for my part, I again would like to express my most profound appreciation to all the returning as well as several new contributors who were kind enough to prepare their chapters and who graciously worked with us as we finalized their submission for the book. Without their contribution, the book would never have been published.

While my previous co-editor, Russell Smandych, is slowly preparing for retirement, I remain deeply appreciative for his past involvement in co-editing this book. Our friendship dates to our days as graduate students in criminology at Simon Fraser University, and it has been a genuine pleasure and honour to have worked with him on two previous editions. Therefore, in the interest of preparing this new edition, I invited two aspiring young Canadian scholars who bring their enthusiasm and exceptional skill set to assist with this edition. In my estimation, they have not only heartily embraced the opportunity, but they've been extraordinary to work with.

I would also be remiss if I did not thank my past and current students, who diplomatically endured being subjected to portions of the new material and who regularly offered constructive feedback. It is for you that this book has been written and edited with the hope that it will inspire you to want to make a difference for our youth, especially those youths who are at risk in society today.

Finally, but most definitely not least of all, is my partner in life and happiness, Rosemary Buck. While she justifiably continues to question the sanity of my academic dedication, I am truly blessed to have a partner who has stood by me and been my confidante and best friend over the past few decades. And to our two sons, who, now as young men, still wonder at times why I do not take my own advice when it comes to understanding them, I say, thanks guys, for being who you are, and thank you, Michael, for being the father to our first grandson, Alex.

—John Winterdyk

When I was asked to contribute to this collection of authors, I was pleased. The collection encompasses essential scholars studying and seeking to understand the landscape of age as it intersects with issues of justice. Then, when asked by John Winterdyk to be a co-editor along with him and Dan Antonowicz, I was delighted. My long-term interest in the governance of youth via state practices and non-governmental organizations is longstanding, stemming from both non-academic and academic work, some of which began when I was a master's student of the former editor of this collection, Russel Smandych. Constant questioning of state practices and public discourse associated with youth, crime, and justice is paramount in a changing society, especially for those most vulnerable. It is clear the contributors to this volume share that concern, interest, and dedication. I am incredibly grateful for the tutelage and guidance of John Winterdyk. I have learned a tremendous amount from this process, and I am grateful. It was also a pleasant surprise to cross the path of Dan Antonowicz again. They have made a complicated process seem remarkably simple. I look forward to future editions. Many thanks to my colleagues at the University of Winnipeg who, for so many reasons, provide the best place to go to work. Personally, thanks to my children, Gabrielle and Mara, who, on the cusp of adulthood, remind me of the importance of understanding how age contours our lives. I also thank them for teaching me the language of youth, which I admittedly still don't completely understand. Also to Greg, my partner and best friend, who, through ups and downs, provides me with encouragement and love, and always acts as my favoured sounding board.

—Kelly Gorkoff

I would like to first thank John Winterdyk for providing this opportunity to be a co-editor for this edition. I have genuinely enjoyed working with you once again, John, and it has been a pleasure working with Kelly Gorkoff for the first time. Last but not least, I would like to thank my family, who has always been very supportive of my academic career.

—Dan Antonowicz

To the staff at Oxford—words cannot express our collective gratitude. A special thanks goes to David Stover, former president of Oxford University Press Canada, who embraced the initial project and encouraged us to follow through with it after incurring a number of stumbling blocks; to Amy Gordon, our developmental editor, who once again adeptly helped to get this project on track and keep us all within a reasonable timeframe; and to Ian Nussbaum, acquisitions editor, who skilfully helped to guide the project along. A special thanks to Tara Tovell, who provided invaluable copy editing.

Thanks to the reviewers, whose feedback informed this edition:

- Dale Ballucci, Western University,
- Irfan Chaudhry, MacEwan university,
- Chris Hay, MacEwan University,
- Jarkko Jalava, Okanagan College,
- Kirsten Kramar, University of Calgary,
- Voula Marinos, Brock Unversity,
- Evan McCuish, Simon Fraser University, and
- Temitope Oriola, University of Alberta,

as well as those who chose to remain anonymous.

Finally, the caveat that so often appears at the end of acknowledgement sections and remains true in this latest edition: any shortcomings within this text remain ours alone. Just as we must learn to have compassion for each other rather than sympathy, we hope you will see the intent in this edition and provide feedback so that the book can continue to evolve to serve its readers even better.

—John Winterdyk, Kelly Gorkoff, and Dan Antonowicz

Part I

History, Trends, and Legislation

In order to appreciate the current problems, issues, trends, and circumstances surrounding why some youth engage in anti-social or delinquent behaviour, as well as understand the scope and nature of the Canadian youth justice system that is largely responsible for handling and processing young offenders, there are three key steps we must first take: (1) develop a knowledge of youth justice history; (2) learn how we go about acquiring information about youth crime and youth justice; and (3) determine the objectives and purposes of youth justice legislation. The specific historical and comparative questions we need to include the following:

- Why do we have a youth justice system in Canada?
- How did that system develop?
- How well is it working and how does it compare to youth justice systems in other countries?

We also need to attempt to answer questions about how, over time, criminologists and governments have attempted to assess trends in "juvenile delinquency" and "youth crime" and respond to them in various ways.

One of the most common ways with which Western countries have responded to juvenile delinquency and youth crime since the late nineteenth century has been to enact and implement legislation to treat and punish young offenders. Since the beginning of the twentieth century, the Canadian federal government has followed this pattern by putting into place three succeeding legislative regimes: the Juvenile Delinquents Act (JDA) (1908); the Young Offenders Act (YOA) (1984); and the Youth Criminal Justice Act (YCJA) (2002). Collectively, the chapters in Part I help us to appreciate better how the approach taken in Canada to define, measure, and deal with criminalized youth—and/or youth who are exposed to certain risk factors and stand a greater chance of becoming involved in anti-social or deviant behaviour—has developed over the past century and evolved into its current practice.

In Chapter 1, Russell Smandych adopts a critical historical and comparative approach to explain the development of Canada's youth justice system. He argues that to answer the question of why we have a youth justice system, one must start by developing a knowledge of the factors that contributed to the creation of the early juvenile justice systems in Canada and the United States, beginning in the late nineteenth century. Similarly, in order to understand current developments occurring in the Canadian youth justice system—including the apparent trend toward a more punitive approach to dealing with youth crime—one needs to consider comparable cross-national developments that also may be influencing these changes. In addition to emphasizing the need for a broader comparative perspective, Smandych closely examines the historical literature on the development of early juvenile courts in the United States and Canada.

In doing so, he points to a variety of different accounts of reform in the youth justice system, including, most notably, Thomas Bernard's perspective on the cyclical nature of changes in juvenile justice. Smandych argues that although Bernard's cyclical theory of juvenile justice reform does not provide a specific explanation of the reasons underlying historical changes in Canada's youth justice legislation, the theory nonetheless provides a relevant perspective on youth-justice-system reform that can be applied to Canada. In particular, Smandych notes that Bernard's theory provides a useful starting point for explaining the ostensibly cyclical nature of the legislative shift from the JDA to the YOA and the YCJA.

In addition to understanding the social, political, and legislative context of youth justice, one must also have a clear understanding of how "youth crime" is defined and measured in Canada. The study of youth crime and/or delinquency poses many of the same challenges as the study of crime in general. For example, just as more general concepts and definitions of crime have changed over time, the concept of youth crime has only in recent years come to be used by governments, criminologists, and the media in most of the Commonwealth countries, including Canada, England and Wales, New Zealand, and Australia. On the other hand, the earlier popular concepts of "juvenile delinquency" and "juvenile crime" continue to be more commonly used in other countries such as the United States. While at first glance this might appear to be a negligible difference, these various concepts also imply different views about the level of culpability and responsibility that the legal system should attribute to young people who break the law, with juvenile "delinquency" implying less culpability than youth "crime." In Chapter 2, John Winterdyk provides an overview of the concepts and data-collection methods that criminologists have developed to study what we now commonly refer to in Canada as youth crime. Importantly, this discussion illustrates that one of the main purposes of governments' measuring and recording juvenile delinquency and youth crime has been to justify for the state to control and/or prevent "the problem." Consequently, as Winterdyk outlines, one must develop a thorough understanding of the strengths and weaknesses of the significant data-collection methods used to study and develop and/or inform government policy on the perceived contemporary problem of youth crime.

In Chapter 3, James Popham and Dan Antonowicz begin by offering a brief discussion about the influential social changes in relation to youth crime throughout the 1980s that served to trigger first the Young Offenders Act and then the Youth Criminal Justice Act (YCJA). From here, the authors provide a comprehensive overview of five major characteristics of the current YCJA and describe how and why they are relevant to the Act as well as how they relate to the Canadian Criminal Code. For example, Popham and Antonowicz note that the YCJA resembles a "modified justice model" that, while being grounded in due process, is designed to encourage informality by prioritizing diversion, individual-specific needs, and sanctioning. The balance of the chapter offers a detailed (but not exhaustive) overview of the implications and practical realities of the Act. Areas covered include, among others, the meaning and objective of the declaration of principles, the core administrative elements of the YCJA, how it provides for measures that balance restorative justice with accountability, as well as how it ensures that young offenders' (special) needs can, and should, be taken into consideration when administering justice. The authors conclude by emphasizing the fact that the YCJA was informed by several historical social environmental factors and several of the key cases are summarized. Yet, as well-intended and robust as the YCJA is, they observe that it is not without controversy.

In Chapter 4, Adrienne Peters and Raymond Corrado provide an overview of how the Canadian youth justice system works in action on a day-to-day basis in different Canadian provinces, territories, and municipalities. This includes, first, describing how young offenders are dealt with at various stages of the youth justice process—from the first contact with the police to court appearances—and, in the case of convicted young offenders, the way in which they experience community- and custody-based correctional sanctions. In addition, the authors address vital current challenges and issues faced by professionals working in the youth justice system, including net widening, police racial profiling, the changing scope of the work of probation officers, the increasing use of risk assessment tools in youth courts and corrections, and the challenges of dealing with young offenders who suffer from mental disorders. Overall, the authors observe that despite some of the controversies created by the original enactment and more recent amendment of the YCJA, for the most part, the Act has been successfully implemented across the country and has resulted in a reduced number of young offenders being formally involved in the justice system. Consequently, they conclude that for youth justice workers and professionals to continue to make progress in developing effective responses to youth crime, it is essential that they embrace the principles and goals of the YCJA at each stage of a young person's contact with the justice system.

From "Misguided Children" to "Criminal Youth"
Exploring Historical and Contemporary Trends in Canadian Youth Justice

Russell Smandych

1

Overview

This chapter offers a historical and comparative perspective on the development of juvenile justice legislation in Canada and other Western countries from the late nineteenth to the early twenty-first century. Particular attention is given to accounting for the development of early juvenile justice systems in the United States and Canada in the late nineteenth century and the more recent contemporary shift—referred to by some as the punitive turn in youth justice—that now appears to be occurring in a number of Western countries. The primary purpose of this chapter is to develop an understanding of the importance of historical and comparative research in helping to explain contemporary trends in youth justice in Canada.

Key Objectives

After reading this chapter, you should be able to:

- Explain how "deviant" and "dependent" children were typically dealt with in Western countries prior to the invention of juvenile courts.

- Understand the factors that led to the creation of early delinquency legislation and juvenile courts in the nineteenth and early twentieth centuries.

- Identify factors linked to changes in early juvenile delinquency and to more recent youth criminal justice legislation in Canada.

- Understand the role of historical and comparative research in helping to explain contemporary trends in youth justice in Canada.

Introduction

Over the past 120 years, Canada has seen the introduction of three different legislative regimes for administering juvenile justice: the Juvenile Delinquents Act (JDA) of 1908, the Young Offenders Act (YOA) of 1984, and the Youth Criminal Justice Act (YCJA) of 2003. In the course of this legislative history, Canada has followed a pattern of legislative change that appears similar to that of many other Western countries, including Britain, Australia, and the United States. In each of these jurisdictions, the 1980s and 1990s witnessed an earlier, predominately child welfare model of juvenile justice eroded and replaced with more legalistic, and arguably more punitive, due process and crime-control models of juvenile justice procedure (Bernard and Kurlychek 2010; Hogeveen and Smandych 2001; Trépanier 1999). As a result of these changes, specialized justice systems designed for "juvenile" or "young" offenders, but also sharing some of the characteristic features of adult criminal justice systems, remain largely in place in many Western countries today.

These historical developments around legislation and models of juvenile justice have been accompanied in some countries by changes in the terminology used to refer to young people who are caught up in the criminal justice system. Most notable among these is the shift in language that has occurred, from considering such young people as "misguided children" or "juvenile delinquents" who have committed acts of **juvenile delinquency** that are best dealt with in **juvenile courts**, to viewing them as "criminal youth" whose alleged anti-social and criminal acts are best dealt with through more formal **youth criminal justice systems**. Stating this somewhat differently, Bryan Hogeveen and Joanne Minaker (Minaker and Hogeveen 2009, pp. 12–18) have argued that in Western countries like Canada, discussions of how society should deal with troubled and/or troubling youth have oscillated over time between the two competing discourses. First, the discourse of the **reformable young offender**, which prevailed for much of the nineteenth and twentieth centuries, proposed that troubled youth "required intervention and could be rehabilitated." Second, that of the **punishable young offender**, which has been prominent in debates since the 1990s and proposes that "troubling" youth require "punishment first

juvenile delinquency
The legal term that came into popular use in the nineteenth century to describe violations of the law by persons who had not reached the legal age of adulthood.

juvenile courts
Specialized courts first created in the late nineteenth century to apply juvenile justice laws in the care of dependent and delinquent children.

youth criminal justice systems
A term often used today as a substitute for *juvenile courts*. Critical criminologists argue that it signifies a shift toward treating young offenders more like adult offenders.

reformable young offender
A term coined by Bryan Hogeveen (2005) to describe the discursive construction of some young offenders as "troubled" and therefore needing intervention in the hope they can be rehabilitated.

punishable young offender
A term coined by Bryan Hogeveen (2005) to describe the discursive construction of some young offenders as "troublesome" and therefore requiring punishment in order to make them accountable for their criminal acts.

punitive turn thesis
The argument that in recent decades the criminal justice systems of many Western countries have become more punishment oriented, with longer prison sentences and higher rates of incarceration.

and foremost, leaving reform and rehabilitative interventions as secondary measures." Indeed, Minaker and Hogeveen, among others, argue that recent decades have witnessed a "punitive turn" in youth jutice in Canada that parallels similar trends in both the adult and juvenile (or youth) justice systems of several other Western countries (Muncie and Goldson 2006). On the other hand, other prominent Canadian scholars disagree with this **punitive turn thesis**. They contend that there is very little evidence to support the claim that Canada's more recent approach to dealing with young people in conflict with the law (under the YCJA) is any more punitive in practice than it was in earlier decades (when the JDA and YOA were in effect) (Bala, Carrington, and Roberts 2009; Doob and Sprott 2006).

One of the aims of the current chapter is to evaluate the merits of competing views on historical and contemporary developments in Canadian youth justice, including the origins of Canada's early juvenile delinquency legislation and the alleged punitive turn in youth criminal justice since the 1990s. As we will see, this task is complicated because attempts to account for changes in Canadian youth justice must also take into consideration the way in which Canadian developments have frequently been tied to and influenced by similar changes in other countries. Indeed, a key argument made in this chapter is that the nature and direction of historical and contemporary trends in Canadian youth justice cannot be adequately understood without taking into account the connected experiences of other countries. The essential questions addressed in this chapter are as follows:

- Where did our modern (Western) juvenile or youth justice systems come from, and why did they come about when they did?
- What are the key changes that have occurred in juvenile justice administration over the course of the twentieth and early twenty-first centuries, and to what extent have Canadian developments been influenced by developments in other countries?

The essential point we will learn is that while there are many commonalities that link the historical development and current state of juvenile systems across various Western countries, there are also important historical, cultural, and political differences that make Canada's current approach to youth justice unique. In turn, as we will attempt to show, understanding these commonalities and differences can help us better appreciate how the Canadian public and Canadian youth justice law- and policy-makers can more fruitfully undertake the complicated task of improving the way we deal with the recurrently perceived problems of juvenile delinquency and youth crime.

The Development of Modern Juvenile Justice Systems

From "Little Adults" to "Misguided Children": The Changing Role and Status of Children in Western Society

In order to understand why young people are viewed the way they are by the criminal justice system today, we must begin by exploring the meaning of childhood and how the meaning has changed over time (Empey 1982). Of all of the historians who have written on the topic, criminologists have been most influenced by the work of Philippe Ariès. In his provocative book *Centuries of Childhood: A Social History of Family Life*, Ariès (1962) undertook a detailed historical study of the treatment of children in Western Europe from the Middle Ages to the nineteenth century. In doing so, Ariès was the first social historian to propose an argument explaining how children were viewed and treated by adults in earlier times and how these views and practices changed over the centuries.

Ariès argued that the modern concept of childhood was "discovered" in Western Europe in the seventeenth century, and that prior to this time few distinctions were made between individuals based on age, and young people were fully integrated into the mainstream of social life. In addition, he claimed that the very high infant mortality rate at the time discouraged parents from wanting to invest emotionally in their children. However, Ariès argued that despite the high mortality rate and the lack of emotional investment they received from parents, children living prior to the seventeenth century were probably happier than they were in later periods.

According to Ariès, because pre-seventeenth-century Western European society was not preoccupied with raising the young and severely restricting their lives, conditions for children were relatively good. In addition, he claimed that because of this much of the status ambiguity and intergenerational conflict that now exist because of the way children are treated in modern Western society did not exist before the "discovery" of childhood in the seventeenth century. Indeed, he concluded that "[r]ather than repressing, judging, or attempting to protect children with a special set of moral rules, adults shared all aspects of existence with them" and that "[t]he years of littlehood, as a consequence, were sociable and happy" (Empey 1982, p. 33).

The work of juvenile justice historians who have drawn uncritically on Ariès's thesis has been criticized for creating an oversimplified account of the invention of juvenile delinquency and the juvenile court. It has been pointed out that they problematically ignore the work of later historians of childhood and the family, including Pollock (1983), Gottlieb (1993), and Spagnoli (1981), whose studies raise serious concerns about the validity of Ariès's thesis on several grounds (Smandych 2001). Perhaps most damaging is the argued concern that Ariès allowed his personal religious and ideological beliefs about the role of parents in child rearing and the need to maintain traditional conservative family values to bias his historical analysis (Spagnoli 1981).

In addition, historians like Gottlieb (1993) show that it is misleading to talk about the "discovery of childhood" as having occurred at a specific point in time, since both historically and in more recent times adults have displayed a great deal of ambiguity in their thinking about the definition and treatment of children and youth. The currency of this continuing dilemma of parenting is captured in Box 1.1 in the discussion and quote from Gottlieb's (1993) study.

The lesson that stands out from studies like Gottlieb's is that parents have always found raising children to be a complicated and difficult task. The literature also adds credence to the argument that while changing adult sensibilities about childhood in seventeenth-century Europe may have had some influence on thinking about the need for a different way of dealing with juvenile delinquency, many other local, national, and more broadly international influences need to be considered. The following section describes and offers a critical analysis of the various explanations that juvenile justice historians have developed

Box 1.1 | Youth Justice in Action

Is It More Difficult Raising Children Today than in the Past?

In her study *The Family in the Western World from the Black Death to the Industrial Age*, Gottlieb provides many examples that illustrate how ambiguous the category of "youth" was in Western countries prior to the nineteenth century. Gottlieb (1993, pp. 156–7) notes that prior to the nineteenth century "[y]oung people were subject to full parental authority as long as they were under the parental roof, and the father's legal authority usually continued after they left home." Except for young men in Catholic countries who entered the celibate clergy, adulthood did not begin for males until they were married. Gottlieb (1993, p. 157) further notes that, not entirely unlike today, "[t]he adulthood of women was an even more ambiguous matter," since "[t]he only grown women who could function as full legal adults were widows in certain localities and under certain circumstances." In her discussion of the ambiguity of youth in pre-industrial Western society, Gottlieb makes another statement that probably sounds quite familiar to many parents of today's Canadian youth, who are usually under the age of 30 but are sometimes even older:

> Since most people did not marry until their middle or late twenties, it is plain that a sizeable chunk of the population drifted in a no-man's land between childhood and adulthood, the ill-defined territory called "youth." It was generally assumed that by fourteen, or at the latest sixteen, nobody could any longer be considered a little child. On the other hand, before being established in the religious life or as the head of a household, a male over sixteen was necessarily a dependent of some sort. . . . Youth of both sexes constituted a large mobile population that formed only temporary attachments to households. Some journeymen and maidservants spent years moving about before they finally settled into marriage, the only conceivable end to youth. (Gottlieb 1993, pp. 157–8)

Source: Smandych 2001, p. 9.

to account for the creation of late-nineteenth- and early-twentieth-century delinquency legislation and juvenile courts in the United States, in selected European countries, in Britain, and in Anglo white-settler colonies, including Canada. However, before turning to this comparative historical discussion, it is necessary to note some important common facts about the how juvenile delinquents were dealt with in the legal systems of Western countries before the creation of specialized delinquency legislation and juvenile courts. As well, the following section describes some common features of how juvenile delinquents were dealt with after early child welfare–model delinquency legislation came into force.

Precursors to the Creation of Delinquency Legislation and Juvenile Courts

The term *juvenile delinquency* was first used in the eighteenth century, primarily as a legal term to describe "violations of the law by persons below the community's legal age of adulthood" (Graebner 1994, p. 379). By the late nineteenth century, however, the term was in widespread use and new juvenile justice systems had begun to be put into place in order to deal with the special needs of perceived delinquent and dependent children. Although, as we will see in this chapter, it is clear that a transformation in the way young people were dealt with by the criminal justice system did occur in the nineteenth century, one must be careful not to exaggerate the extent of this transformation. In particular, it is not true that prior to the development of juvenile courts young offenders were dealt with in exactly the same way as adult offenders. Historians who have examined the operation of English-based criminal courts in common-law countries prior to the mid-nineteenth century have shown that the severity of the criminal law was often mitigated by sympathetic juries and paternalistic judges who showed mercy toward those accused of serious crimes (see Beattie 1986). Evidence also shows that young people who were accused of crimes that made them liable to the same punishment as adults were usually shown an even greater degree of mercy than adults who came before the courts (Carrigan 1998). It is also significant that under English common law, persons below the age of seven years could not be convicted of committing an offence, while "youths between the ages of seven and fourteen were subject to the doctrine of **doli incapax**, which involved a presumption of incapacity that could be contested by the Crown" (Griffiths and Verdun-Jones 1994, p. 597).

Common Features of Early Child Welfare–Model Delinquency Legislation

Before examining the development of delinquency legislation and juvenile courts in specific countries, it is also important to highlight a number of common features shared by juvenile justice systems. Although the timing of their establishment varied between jurisdictions, three common features came to characterize the operation of all newly invented juvenile courts and the laws that provided for their establishment.

First, the laws commonly recognized that there were three distinct age-graded levels of criminal accountability:

- no criminal accountability for youth under a certain legislatively determined age (e.g., under 10 years old);
- limited criminal accountability for youth who were subject to the jurisdiction of the legislation because they fell within a certain legislatively determined age range (e.g., 10 to 15 years old); and
- full criminal accountability for youth above a certain age (e.g., 16 years old). In other words, all late-nineteenth- and early-twentieth-century juvenile delinquency legislation came to be formally premised on the concept of **diminished criminal responsibility** for so-called juvenile delinquents.

A second general feature related to both legislation and the operation of early juvenile courts was that they were based on the principle of **parens patriae**—the idea that the state had a duty to intervene in the lives of children and assume the role of a substitute parent for those who were found to be either "delinquent" or "dependent."

A third feature of the delinquency legislation enacted in many jurisdictions—including the United States, France, Belgium, England and Wales, Australia, and Canada—was the extent to which it reflected the common belief that juvenile delinquents

doli incapax
A legal doctrine that, literally translated, means "incapable of doing harm" and refers to the English common-law presumption that children between 7 and 14 years of age could not be prosecuted for committing criminal offences, unless this presumption was contested by the Crown.

diminished criminal responsibility
The general view that individuals who are not adults should not be held fully responsible for their criminal behaviour.

parens patriae
The legal doctrine that the state has a duty to assume the role of a substitute parent in the case of delinquent or dependent children who do not have parents who are able to adequately control or care for them.

should be viewed as "misguided children" and treated with "friendly helpfulness" (Hogeveen 2001). Most commonly, the state made this operational in juvenile courts by giving judges wide discretionary power to deal with juvenile delinquents as they saw fit and by appointing probation officers to give individual attention to the cases of young people who were brought before the court. Indeed, throughout Western countries where new juvenile justice systems were created, probation officers came to assume a key role in the development and operation of those systems. While these were important common features of the way early delinquency legislation and juvenile courts were in theory supposed to operate (see below); across all the jurisdictions where they came into being the development of juvenile courts was also uneven and, in some cases, took many decades to evolve from inception to more uniform practical implementation.

The Invention of the Juvenile Court in the United States

A great deal has been written and continues to be written today about "the invention of the juvenile court" in the United States (Rothman 1980). One reason for this is that the United States, and more specifically the state of Illinois, was arguably the first jurisdiction where a juvenile justice system was created based explicitly on a child welfare model. Another reason for the attention US criminologists and juvenile justice historians have given to the topic may be that in the 1980s and 1990s the juvenile justice system in the US came under increasing and constant attack from critics. Many of the critics called for replacing the existing child welfare–oriented system with a more punitive one based on reforms, including the more frequent waiver of juvenile cases to adult court and the use of tougher "more adult-like" sentences for juvenile offenders; which Barry Feld (2017, p. vii) and others have described as the "get-tough era" (Tanenhaus 2013).

Some of the recent accounts of the original juvenile court movement in the US have been written with knowledge of, and concern about, these contemporary trends. They express misgivings about the punitive turn in juvenile justice in the US that characterized developments in the 1980s and 1990s. It is not possible in this chapter to review the extensive literature on the early development of the juvenile court systems in the US. However, it is important to develop an understanding of the evidence and arguments advanced by specific key authors, both for what they have to tell us about the invention of the juvenile court in the US and for what their studies reveal about the shortcomings of existing historical writing on the topic. As we will see, one of these weaknesses is the lack of attention most US historians have given to examining important cross-national connections that linked late-nineteenth-century juvenile justice reform movements in the US and other countries.

Much of the US historiography on the juvenile court has focused on histories of the circumstances and events that surrounded the creation of the first statewide juvenile court system in 1899, and its evolution, which began with the establishment of the Cook County Juvenile Court in Chicago, Illinois. The first scholar to undertake a detailed study of the origin and operation of the famous Chicago Juvenile Court was Anthony Platt, in his (also soon to be acclaimed) book on *The Child Savers: The Invention of Delinquency* (1969). Platt argued that the Illinois juvenile justice system and the Chicago juvenile court came about as a result of the child-saving movement that emerged in Chicago and many other US cities in the late nineteenth century. Platt portrayed the child-saving movement as a middle-class, Anglo-Saxon, Protestant movement dedicated mainly to attempting to control the moral behaviour of lower-class families and immigrants, who were perceived to pose a threat to moral values as well as to the economic interests of the more "respectable" middle class. In his study, Platt shows that rather than it being the product of an outpouring of genuine humanitarian concern for "saving children" from lives of poverty and parental neglect, the child-saving movement was an ideologically conservative movement that was influenced significantly by scientifically racist ideas associated with "social Darwinism and European [criminological] positivism" (Platt 1969, pp. 13, 19). While Platt does not extend his critical analysis in any way to take into account simultaneous developments occurring in Canada, it is notable that his interpretation (see Platt 1974) was later criticized by Canadian juvenile justice historians Hagan and Leon (1977, 1980). It was criticized for its inability to explain the factors surrounding the emergence of the child-saving movement and the juvenile court in Canada. As we will also see a little later, in their early comparative historical research, Hagan and Leon (1977, p. 240) did draw attention to the "cross-fertilization of ideas that occurred between Canada and the United States in the juvenile justice context."

David Rothman (1980) offers a second and quite different account of the invention of the juvenile court in the United States in his book on *Conscience and Convenience: The Asylum and Its Alternatives in Progressive America*. Unlike Platt (1969, 1974), who stressed the need to examine changes in the social structure and economy of American society to explain changes in juvenile justice, Rothman focused on examining the power of the ideas and rhetoric of social reformers involved in the late-nineteenth-century child-saving movement. Rothman linked the efforts of child-saving reformers and "the invention of the juvenile court" to a much broader range of social reform movements that emerged in the United States toward the end of the nineteenth century. According to Rothman (1980, p. 43), the "Progressive era" in American history (which continued through the first two decades of the twentieth century) "marked a major divide in attitudes and practices toward the deviant, creating new ideas and procedures to combat crime, delinquency, and mental illness." Rothman also importantly points out that in each of the areas of adult criminal justice, mental health, and child welfare and juvenile justice, the growing occupational and professional status of reformers and the increasing extent to which they relied on social-scientific knowledge about the causes and treatment of deviant behaviour were used to justify the introduction of new methods of treatment and control.

In Rothman's view (1980, pp. 207–11), the person who perhaps best epitomized the social-scientific approach that came to underpin the Progressive-era juvenile court movement was the psychologist G. Stanley Hall. Hall undertook "the first systematic studies of childhood in the United States" and introduced the term **adolescence** to describe the critical period of human development when people move through a distinct stage in which they progress, both biologically and emotionally, from being a child to being an adult. His reputation as the leading American child psychologist of the day was cemented in 1904 with the publication of his extensive two-volume book *Adolescence*, which sold over 25,000 copies (Comacchio 2010; Hall 1904). Furthermore, his ideas on adolescence and delinquency had a profound influence on educated Americans, from women who belonged to the National Congress of Mothers (the forerunner of the Parent–Teacher Association), to

adolescence
A term popularized by child development expert G. Stanley Hall to refer to the stage of life during which a person progresses, both biologically and emotionally, from being a child to being an adult.

criminologists, social workers, and advocates of the juvenile court. Hall identified several causes of delinquency, which were mostly environmental, and he argued strongly for a juvenile court system in which juveniles had to be treated separately from adults (Rothman 1980, p. 210). It is a testament to his influence that Hall's ideas on the causes and prevention of delinquency were actively promoted by leading juvenile court advocates at the time (e.g., Richard Tuthill, the first judge appointed to the Chicago Juvenile Court, and Ben Lindsey, the first juvenile court judge in Denver, Colorado). As we will see shortly, Judge Lindsey also had an influence on contemporaneous juvenile justice developments in Canada.

More recently, David Tanenhaus (2004) has published a richly detailed study of the origin and early development of the Chicago Juvenile Court that moves beyond the work of Rothman and other American juvenile justice historians by focusing more attention on "the actual working of juvenile courts in the early twentieth century." In doing so, Tanenhaus (2004, pp. 164–5) shows that rather than being born in an "institutionally intact" or fully complete form, the Chicago Juvenile Court took several decades of "trial and error" innovations to evolve into the model child welfare court that it was, rather inaccurately, reputed to represent from its beginning in 1899. However, like Rothman and other earlier US juvenile justice historians, Tanenhaus (pp. xxiv–xxv) only gives passing attention to developments in other countries. Tanenhaus noted that the Chicago Juvenile Court soon became "a model . . . for policy-makers in European, South American, and Asian nations" and that many of the "child savers" from other countries looked to the US "to learn how to divert children from the criminal justice system and to handle their cases in a less punitive fashion." Nevertheless, Tanenhaus (2004, p. 165) observes that, in general terms, "child savers in the early twentieth century struggled with many of the same issues that twenty-first-century [youth justice] policy-makers must address."

These findings on the long-term continuity in the fundamental issues faced by youth justice policy-makers is consistent with Thomas Bernard's (1992) theory of the cyclical nature of juvenile justice reform. Although Bernard originally proposed his theory to explain the rise of the late-nineteenth-century juvenile court movement in the United States, only recently has it been extended to account for late-twentieth- and early-twenty-first-century reforms in US juvenile justice (Bernard and Kurlychek 2010). According to Bernard's cyclical theory of juvenile justice reform, a movement toward reform "begins at a time when justice officials and the general public are convinced that juvenile crime is at an exceptionally high level, and there are many harsh punishments but few lenient treatments for juvenile offenders." In this circumstance, justice officials often are forced to choose between harshly punishing juvenile offenders and doing nothing at all" and "[a]s a consequence, many minor offenders are let off scot-free because lenient treatments are not available and because justice officials believe that the harsh punishments will make the minor offenders worse (Bernard and Kurlychek 2010, p. 3; see also Figure 1.1)

Bernard illustrates this cyclical reform pattern by comparing the circumstances that led to the creation of the Chicago Juvenile Court in 1899 with earlier reform movements like the creation of "Houses of Refuge" in the 1820s, which were similarly designed to introduce a more lenient and humane approach to dealing with juvenile delinquents and dependent children. Prior to the establishment of "Houses of Refuge," what often occurred was that juries who were disturbed over the harshness of current punishment practices simply

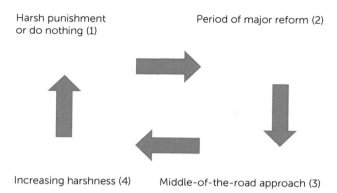

Harsh punishment or do nothing (1)

Period of major reform (2)

Increasing harshness (4)

Middle-of-the-road approach (3)

Figure 1.1 Cycles of Juvenile Justice Reform

1. Juvenile crime is thought to be unusually high. There are many harsh punishments and few lenient punishments. Officials often are forced to choose between harshly punishing juvenile offenders and doing nothing at all.
2. Juvenile crime is thought to be unusually high and is blamed on the "forced choice": that is, both harshly punishing and doing nothing at all are thought to increase juvenile crime.
3. A major reform introduces lenient treatments for juvenile offenders. This creates a middle ground between harshly punishing and doing nothing at all.
4. Juvenile crime is thought to be unusually high and is blamed on the lenient punishments. Harsh punishments gradually expand and lenient treatments gradually contract.

Source: Adapted from Bernard 1992, p. 4, and Bernard and Kurlychek 2010, p. 4.

acquitted youth who were accused of crimes that could have led to their being jailed in an adult penitentiary. Given the choice of continuing to do nothing at all, or working to introduce a more middle-of-the-road approach, supporters of the House of Refuge movement chose this new approach. According to Bernard (1992, p. 99), this was essentially the same pattern repeated in the late nineteenth century, when similar perceptions of "high juvenile crime rates were accompanied by a firm belief that these could be lowered by the proper policy response"—namely, the middle-of-the-road approach promised by the juvenile court.

As we will see in the following sections, Bernard's cyclical theory, alongside Tanenhaus's observation that many of the issues faced by early-twentieth-century juvenile justice reformers are the same as those that policy-makers struggle with today, provides useful insights to keep in mind when examining both historical and contemporary trends in juvenile or youth justice.

Paths of Juvenile Justice Reform in Other Western Countries

The cross-fertilization of ideas on juvenile justice reform pointed to in some of the works of US and Canadian researchers is an important but largely overlooked aspect of juvenile justice history. Among US researchers, it invariably takes the form of noting how the US juvenile court model, rather than being interconnected with and perhaps reciprocally influenced by ideas on juvenile delinquency and juvenile justice reform in other countries, influenced developments in other countries. Part of our interest in this chapter is with learning about the broad range of factors associated with the creation of early delinquency legislation and juvenile courts in the nineteenth and early twentieth centuries. In order to do this, we need to explore briefly what researchers have documented about the origin and outcome of juvenile justice reform movements that emerged in other Western countries during the same period and about how these different paths of juvenile justice reform may have been interconnected.

In an article written in the year of "the centennial of the Chicago Juvenile Court," Jean Trépanier (1999), a leading French-Canadian criminologist and juvenile justice historian, reflected on the operation of juvenile courts in North America and other, mainly European, countries over the century. In doing so, Trépanier recognizes that while the Chicago Juvenile Court undeniably served as the model that was later followed in several other countries, there was also a great deal of "diversity that characterises the history and evolution of juvenile courts in Western societies." Therefore, it is important to examine both the coinciding similar, but also sometimes noticeably different, paths of development that were followed elsewhere (p. 303). One of the commonalities Trépanier points to is the gradual separation of juveniles and adults in court proceedings and institutions of confinement in different countries. In the last half of the nineteenth century, a growing number of young offenders were transferred from adult prisons to variously titled new juvenile "reform prisons," "reform schools," and "industrial schools" (Trépanier 1999, p. 310). This gradual separation of juveniles from adult accused and convicted offenders occurred in many other Western countries during the nineteenth century, as shown in a summary form in Table 1.1.

| Table 1.1 | Juvenile Justice Reforms in Selected Western Countries |

Country or State	Date of Earliest Delinquency Legislation and/or Functioning Juvenile Court	Date of Earliest Separate Juvenile Houses of Refuge, Prisons, Reformatories, and Industrial Schools
Australia (by state)[1]	1895 to 1918	Most states, from 1863 to 1874
Belgium[2]	1912	1847
Canada[3]	1908	1858 (Quebec); 1859 (Ontario)
England and Wales[4]	1908	1838
France[5]	1912	1830
Germany[6]	1923	1833
Netherlands[7]	1922	1857
New Zealand[8]	1906	1867
Sweden[9]	1902	1838
United States[10]	1899	1825

Data Sources:
1. Cunneen and White 2007, pp. 5, 8–9, 14; O'Connor and Cameron 2002, p. 211; Trépanier 1999, p. 310.
2. Shore 2003, p. 117; Trépanier 1999, pp. 304, 312; Trépanier and Tulkens 1993.
3. Minaker and Hogeveen, 2009, p. 48; Trépanier 1999, pp. 307, 310.
4. Corrado and Turnbull 1992, p. 78; Cunneen and White 2007, pp. 8–9; Morgan and Newburn 2007, p. 1024; Shore 2003, pp. 113, 117; Trépanier 1999, pp. 304, 313–14.
5. Blatier 1999, p. 241; Shore 2003, p. 112; Trépanier 1999, pp. 304, 310, 316.
6. Albrecht 2004, p. 443; Crofts 2002, p. 107; Trépanier 1999, pp. 304, 316.
7. Shore 2003, p. 117; Trépanier 1999, pp. 304, 316.
8. Morris 2004, pp. 247–8.
9. Janson 2004, p. 394; Shore 2003, p. 113.
10. Trépanier 1999, pp. 306, 310.

What these comparative historical data shows is that there was an international component to nineteenth-century juvenile justice reform that included an extensive cross-fertilization of reform ideas across various countries. At the same time, however, it is notable that the specific age ranges of young people who came under the jurisdiction of new juvenile justice systems varied across countries and sometimes even between different provinces and states within a country. For example, with the enactment of the **Juvenile Delinquents Act** (JDA) in 1908, individual provinces could set their own maximum age of jurisdiction of the JDA at anywhere between 15 and 17 years old, while different age categories could also be selected for males and females. This was the case in Alberta, where the maximum age of jurisdiction was 15 for boys and 17 for girls (Hackler 1978). In addition, although all Western countries eventually established separate criminal court processes and institutions for dealing with juvenile offenders, the specific nature and timing of these developments varied considerably and, in some jurisdictions, occurred only quite gradually over the course of the first half of the twentieth century (Cunneen and White 2007; Morgan and Newburn 2007; Shore 2003). From examining such cross-national comparative dimensions of juvenile justice reform, we can learn to more adequately appreciate the diversity that characterized the history and evolution of juvenile courts and how the development of the juvenile court in Canada was influenced by ideas and practices that already existed in other countries.

Juvenile Delinquents Act (JDA) Canada's first juvenile delinquency legislation enacted in 1908 and in force until 1984.

Paths to Reform in Canada and the Origins of the JDA of 1908

While the origin of the juvenile court model has not been seriously contested, a few claims have been made that the Chicago Juvenile Court was not the first of its kind. For example, some authors have claimed that the state of South Australia "introduced the first juvenile court in the world" through state legislation enacted in 1895 (O'Connor and Cameron 2002, p. 212; Cunneen and White 2007). It has also been claimed that the state of Colorado established a juvenile court by way of enacting an education law that came into effect earlier in 1899 than the Juvenile Court Act of Illinois, which created the Chicago Juvenile Court (Hagan and Leon 1977, p. 239). In addition, in the Canadian context, it was claimed early on by none other than J.J. Kelso, one of the key lobbyists for the enactment of the Canadian JDA, that it was he who did more than anyone else to create the modern juvenile court. Although Kelso's claim was eventually repudiated by his critics, the fact that he made this claim and created the debate he did with his contemporaries shows a great deal about how Canada's first juvenile justice legislation came into being.

J.J. Kelso was a "young, passionate and crusading Toronto newspaper reporter" who became a key leader in the child-saving movement in Ontario in the 1880s (Davis-Barron 2009, p. 31). He later recalled that as a young reporter in Toronto, he witnessed first-hand the miserable conditions experienced by poor and neglected street children and pledged "to devote his life to 'plead for these little ones' who perished by the wayside 'in a land abounding in Christian activities'" (cited in Sutherland 1976, p. 112). Kelso figured prominently among the "new breed of child-savers" that emerged in Ontario and elsewhere in the 1880s. Along with them, he argued for an expansion of "the definition of needy children to include those who suffered from parental neglect or cruelty" while also promoting "the idea of foster homes as the most efficient, humane, and economical approach to child-welfare" (Bullen 1991, p. 136). In 1887, he "founded the Toronto Humane Society, a voluntary organization dedicated to the protection of women, children, and animals," and by the following year, he had successfully lobbied for the enactment of new Ontario legislation entitled An Act for the Protection and Reformation of Neglected Children. Among other significant changes, this Act empowered local municipalities to appoint commissioners "to conduct trials of juvenile offenders apparently under the age of sixteen" while also providing that all defendants under the age of 21 "be tried apart from other offenders, 'as far as practicable.'" Soon afterward Kelso "founded a charitable society known as the Fresh Air Fund for the purpose of providing poor city children with summer excursions," and in 1891, he created and became the first voluntary president of the Toronto Children's Aid Society.

In 1893, Kelso was recognized for his child welfare and juvenile justice reform efforts by being appointed Ontario's first superintendent of neglected and dependent children, a position created under a new child welfare act (entitled An Act for the Prevention of Cruelty to and Better Protection of Children, commonly called "The Children's Act"), which Kelso himself had lobbied the provincial government to enact. Kelso held the position for the next 41 years and it afforded him the power to oversee the implementation of the Children's Act of 1893 as well as to lobby for additional child-centred social reforms (Bullen 1991, pp. 138–45).

Kelso was in a very a good position to lobby the federal government to enact legislation that would enshrine Ontario's approach to dealing with dependent and delinquent children, and soon did this with the help of the Ottawa lawyer and president of the Ottawa Children's Aid Society W.L. Scott. Kelso and Scott worked together toward the enactment of federal delinquency legislation, and in the course of this effort they took every opportunity they could to strengthen support for their cause from constituencies like the police, judges, and federal politicians in Ottawa. Both Kelso and Scott also travelled to the US to meet with juvenile justice reform experts, and through these initiatives prominent American juvenile court proponents were invited to Ottawa "to address Senators and Members of the House of Commons regarding the benefits of a juvenile justice system for Canada" (Davis-Barron 2009, p. 36).

Among their many cross-border connections, two of the most notable were Judge Harvey B. Hurd, who drafted the Illinois legislation, and Judge Ben Lindsey of Denver, whom Kelso met while travelling to conferences in the US. Significantly, however, historian Neil Sutherland (1976) claims that "Canadians . . . turned neither to Chicago or Denver but to Philadelphia for the model for their first systematic effort to put the notion [of a juvenile court] into practice" (Sutherland 1975, p. 119). This, according to Sutherland, stemmed from an event in May 1906, in which W.L. Scott, as president of the Ottawa Children's Aid Society (CAS), and his paid secretary, John Keane, attended an annual meeting of the National Conference of Charities and Correction in Philadelphia, where they learned about the system of juvenile probation used in that city. The two subsequently returned to Ottawa to persuade the executive committee of the Ottawa CAS to adopt the same system. Later that year, Scott and his influential father, Senator R.W. Scott, invited Mrs Hannah Kent Schoff, chairperson of the Philadelphia Court Committee, to come to Ottawa to "address a special meeting of senators and members of Parliament" on the benefits of creating a juvenile court system like the one in Philadelphia (Sutherland 1976, pp. 119–21). Scott also shortly afterward hosted Judge Ben Lindsey in Ottawa to address members of Parliament on the benefits of enacting legislation for creating a specialized juvenile court (Hogeveen 2001).

Historians commonly recognize that it was W.L. Scott who drafted the JDA and, with his father's help, lobbied most vigorously for the passage of the legislation first through the Canadian Senate and then through the House of Commons. However, in later years Kelso claimed that the juvenile court movement started neither in Chicago nor in Philadelphia but in Ontario, beginning with the effort he undertook in 1888 to lobby for the enactment of An Act for the Protection and Reformation of Neglected Children, which provided for separate trials for juveniles. Moreover, Kelso claimed that he had influenced the creation of the Chicago Juvenile Court by corresponding with "officials in Chicago" and attending three conferences there in 1893, where he advocated his "Children's Court ideas as one of the chief solutions of juvenile crime" (cited in Hagan and Leon 1980, p. 240). However, in response to lingering stories about the role Kelso claimed for himself in the creation of the JDA, in 1933, Scott wrote a letter in which he disputed Kelso's story with his own, more reliable, claim that it was he who had drafted the JDA and played a more important role in its enactment (Hagan and Leon 1980). In the end, however, it would be misleading to give credit for the origin of Canada's modern juvenile justice system solely to the humanitarian conscience and power of the ideas and rhetoric of social reformers like Kelso and Scott. In addition, we must take into account a number of other factors, including earlier precursors to the juvenile court, the changing social and economic climate of the last half of the nineteenth century, the gradual rise of the social welfare state in many countries, and other international influences such as the cross-fertilization of ideas about juvenile justice reform (for a more detailed discussion, see Minaker and Hogeveen 2009).

Regardless of its origins, the JDA represented a fundamental shift in the way juvenile justice was administered in Canada. In addition to making the supervision of juvenile offenders in the community a central feature by way of probation, the Act cast a wide net in defining the types of delinquent and dependent children who would henceforth come under the jurisdiction of the legislation. Specifically, the JDA originally defined a juvenile delinquent as "any child who violates any provision of *The Criminal Code . . .* , or of any Dominion or provincial statute, or of any by-law or ordinance of any municipality, for which violation punishment of a fine or imprisonment may be awarded; or, who is liable by reason of any other act to be committed to an industrial school or juvenile reformatory under the provisions of any Dominion or provincial statute." A 1924 revision to the Act further broadened the definition of *juvenile delinquent* to include any child "who is guilty of sexual immorality or any similar form of vice" (cited in Davis-Barron 2009, p. 41). This broadened definition of delinquent youth led to the creation of what later came to be referred to as **status offences**, or offences that a youth could be found guilty of simply because he or she was underage. These included offences like "the consumption of alcohol, truancy, running away from home, refusal to obey parents, having delinquent friends, and the use of profanity" (Tanner 2015, p. 31). In many provinces, children were committed to industrial or training schools for such offences or for being found guilty of either "unmanageability" or "incorrigibility" (Bala 1997).

The doctrine of *parens patriae* embodied in the JDA also gave juvenile court judges and corrections officials the discretion to sentence children to **indeterminate sentences** of incarceration, which meant that they would not be released until "they were no longer a

status offences
Behaviours that are considered delinquent or criminal only because the person who engages in the behaviour is not yet an adult. Examples include truancy (e.g., skipping school), underage drinking, and promiscuous sexual behaviour.

indeterminate sentences
Sentences of incarceration that have no fixed expiration date, which means that a person can be held in custody until he or she is deemed by correctional officials either to be rehabilitated or to no longer pose a threat to society.

threat to the public . . . or until they reached the age of 21" (Minaker and Hogeveen 2009, p. 59). As a rule, the JDA exerted jurisdiction over children ranging from 7 to 15 years of age. However, the Act also allowed for considerable variation between provinces; each province was allowed to decide the cut-off age, above 15, at which point a trial involving a young person would be held in adult court. In most provinces the age was set at 16 years, while in Manitoba and Quebec it was set at 18 years, and as noted previously, in Alberta these age cut-offs were also made gender specific (Hackler 1978). As in the case of the juvenile courts established in other countries, the child welfare orientation of the JDA was also reflected in the informal nature of proceedings in juvenile courts, where judges (many of whom had no legal training themselves), sought to give hopefully wise advice to "misguided children." Similarly, lawyers were discouraged from appearing in order "that 'unnecessary technicalities' would not interfere with or delay the treatment considered to be in the child's best interests" (Bala 1997, p. 44).

When the JDA came into effect, juvenile courts and probation services, as in other countries, developed unevenly across Canada, and it was well into the twentieth century before many rural and remote areas had a functioning juvenile justice system. In addition, differences in the cut-off age for juvenile offenders contributed to a great deal of inter-provincial and regional variation in the application of the legislation (Sutherland 1976). Even before the JDA became more evenly implemented across the country, its operation began to be criticized on several grounds, and by the 1960 and 1970s the move toward juvenile justice reform in Canada, again noticeably influenced by parallel developments in the United States, was well under way (Minaker and Hogeveen 2009). When the **Young Offenders Act** was finally introduced 1984 to replace the JDA, many criminologists and youth justice policy-makers viewed it as a long-overdue reform that finally brought in needed "due process" rights and safeguards for young offenders, which included most importantly a guaranteed right to obtain and instruct legal counsel (Bala 1997). At the same time, however, critics of the new legislation viewed it as representing an unfortunate shift away from the child welfare–based child-saving approach toward a more justice- and crime-control-based child-blaming approach, in which priority would be given to holding young offenders accountable for their criminal behaviour (Havemann 1986).

The relatively short 19-year life of the YOA was marked with controversy from the outset, and the Act underwent several significant amendments before it was finally replaced with the **Youth Criminal Justice Act** (YCJA) in 2003 (see, generally, Bala 1997; Doob and Sprott 2006; Hogeveen and Smandych 2001; Smandych and Corrado 2018). In the remaining part of this chapter, more attention is given to more recent contemporary trends in youth justice and, in particular, to the question of whether in recent years Canadians have taken a more punitive approach to dealing with young criminals.

Young Offenders Act (YOA)
The federal legislation that replaced the Juvenile Delinquents Act from 1984 to 2003.

Youth Criminal Justice Act (YCJA)
The federal legislation enacted in 2002 to replace the Young Offenders Act and which came into effect on 1 April 2003.

Contemporary Trends in Youth Justice Law and Practice in Canada

With the enactment of the YCJA in 2002 and its formal implementation on 1 April 2003, Canada entered into a new era in the administration of juvenile or youth justice. As in the years following the enactment of the JDA and the YOA, youth justice professionals and criminologists have now taken up the task of attempting to interpret and apply the legal principles underlying the YCJA, while continuing to assess how it has been implemented in practice across the country and what the outcomes of its application have been to date (cf. Alain, Reid, and Corrado 2016; Smandych and Corrado 2018).

The Origins of the YCJA and the Punitive Turn Debate

Like its predecessors, the movement toward the enactment of the YCJA was influenced by both local regional and national concerns with the administration of juvenile/youth justice in Canada along with broader international shifts in juvenile justice legislation and policy that were occurring concomitantly in a number of Western countries starting in the 1980s. One of these was the shift away from child welfare models of juvenile justice toward more legalistic and ostensibly punitive justice and crime-control models. However, in many countries the shift was not solely away from what were perceived as lenient juvenile crime prevention and response strategies and toward harsher ways of punishing wayward youth (Bernard 1992; Muncie 2008). This appears to be particularly the case in Canada. When the YCJA was enacted in 2002, for instance, it contained sections that provided for the harsher, adult-like punishment of violent young offenders while restricting the use of custody sentences for youth convicted of non-violent crimes. The Act also introduced a wide range of formal and informal extrajudicial measures for diverting first-time and less serious young offenders out of the youth justice system. Such measures included police warnings, cautions, and community-based conferences (for details, see Chapter 3 in this volume). In effect, these measures made Canada's new youth criminal justice system, at least formally on paper, a **bifurcated youth justice system**—"wherein petty and non-serious offenders would be handled through community-based and diversionary programs while serious and violent offenders would be subject to more carceral and punitive interventions" (Minaker and Hogeveen 2009, pp. 78–9).

    One of the issues debated by Canadian scholars has been the degree to which the implementation of the YCJA resulted in a shift toward more use of "carceral and punitive interventions" in the youth justice system as opposed to more "community-based and diversionary programs," which are generally perceived to be more lenient (Hogeveen 2005; Doob and Sprott 2006). It is not the purpose of this chapter to try to resolve this still ongoing debate (Smandych and Corrado 2018), but rather to show that a better understanding of the factors that led to the creation of the YCJA and the punitive turn debate itself can be obtained by placing both in their respective historical and comparative contexts.

    Hogeveen and Smandych (2001) locate the immediate origins of the YCJA in the political discourse surrounding the perceived crises in youth crime in Canada in the 1990s. From their study of parliamentary debates and media reports, they found that the dominant view expressed in the speeches of most federal politicians at the time and in newspaper reports on youth justice reform was that the YOA was too lenient on youth offenders and unable to effectively address what was perceived to be a growing crisis of youth crime. While Hogeveen and Smandych did not attempt to predict how young offenders would be dealt with under the YCJA in the future, they did argue, in line with what would later come to be referred to as the "punitive turn thesis," that the wording of the legislation appeared to mark a significant shift away from referring to deviant youth officially as either

bifurcated youth justice system
Literally, a two-pronged justice system, meaning that it provides avenues for diverting first-time and less serious young offenders out of the system while at the same time making possible more punitive forms of punishment for more serious offenders.

"juvenile delinquents" or "young offenders," signifying their reduced responsibility and toward viewing them as "young criminals" and making them "appear much closer to adult criminals" (2001, p. 166).

In two subsequent separately authored studies, Hogeveen (2005) and Smandych (2006) develop arguments that more directly address the issue of the alleged punitive turn in youth justice. Specifically, they offer similar skeptical views of the YCJA's ability to facilitate the promotion of community-based extrajudicial ways of dealing with young offenders, and point to the continuing potential for the YCJA, and its possible perceived failures, to be used to justify more punitive responses to various types of broadly defined "youth violent crime" and "serious violent offenders" (Tanner 2015). Both authors also point out how the growing demand in Canada in the 1990s for tougher legislation to deal with criminal youth paralleled contemporary trends in other countries, such as the United States and Britain, toward "the further dismantling of traditional 'child-welfare' juvenile court procedures" (Smandych 2006, p. 23) and the introduction of new legislation aimed at getting tough on juvenile crime (Hogeveen 2005, p. 77).

In recent years other critics, including criminologists, lawyers, and the leaders of youth-serving and youth advocacy organizations, have added their voices to the growing concern with the **adulteration** of youth justice policy and practice under the YCJA (cf. Smandych, Dyck, La Berge, and Koffman 2016; Smandych and Corrado 2018). A focal issue that prompted some of this criticism was the introduction of the Conservative federal government's omnibus Bill C-10 in the fall of 2012, which, along with "toughing up" on many aspects of the adult criminal justice system in Canada, introduced a number of measures aimed at treating young people accused of crimes more like adult offenders (Government of Canada 2012). One of these measures has been to enable youth justice court judges to consider "specific deterrence" and "denunciation" as valid principles in sentencing convicted youth. While traditionally allowed as principles that judges could consider in sentencing adult offenders, prior to the passage of Bill C-10 neither of these principles could be used in sentencing youth because of provisions of the YCJA. Instead, judicial case precedents embodied the view that the lack of maturity and full legal culpability on the part of most youth made the general use of these sentencing principles in youth cases inappropriate (Tustin and Lutes 2013, pp. 85–7). Another concern raised is the way Bill C-10 substantially broadens the definition of "a violent offence." Prior to Bill C-10, the YCJA and related court decisions reaffirmed that a violent offence in a youth case excluded pure property offences and only referred to "an offence in the commission of which a young person causes, attempts to cause, or threatens to cause bodily harm" (Bala 1997, p. 491). However, since the addition of Bill C-10 amendments to the YCJA, the definition of such an offence now includes any "offence in the commission of which a young person endangers the life or safety of another person by creating a substantial likelihood of causing bodily harm." Critics are concerned that these amendments introduced in Bill C-10 have the potential of opening the door for judges to sentence more young offenders to custody than has previously been the case.

On the other hand, some criminologists have argued that available youth court processing and sentencing data show that there has been no real increase in the punitiveness of the Canadian youth criminal justice system in recent years (Bala, Carrington, and

adulteration
The dismantling of a distinct system of criminal justice for youth and the re-merging with systems of justice for adults.

Roberts 2009; Doob and Sprott 2006). Moreover, Anthony Doob and Jane Sprott (2006) make the contrary claim that the intention of the government of Canada when it introduced the YCJA was not to create tougher legislation but simply to make it appear that it was doing so in order to deflect the criticism from political opposition parties that it was too soft on youth crime. Specifically, they contend that by formally creating a bifurcated youth justice system, federal government legislative drafters had quite astutely "crafted a law" that offered more opportunities than had existed before to "reduce the level of punitiveness" of the youth criminal justice system (p. 224). Whether or not this was the case, it is difficult to predict the direction in which the administration of juvenile justice in Canada will move in the future. One reason for this, as we have begun to learn in this chapter, is that we must consider contemporary trends in Canadian youth justice within the context of comparable adult and juvenile justice developments in other countries (see Bernard and Kurlychek 2010; Feld and Bishop 2013; Muncie 2008).

Criminologists, as well as youth justice policy-makers and professionals across Canada, still have much to learn about how provincial and territorial youth justice systems have adjusted to the implementation of the YCJA (Smandych and Corrado 2018). At present, perhaps the most accurate observation that can be made is the one offered by Julian Tanner (2015, p. 256), who states that "[w]hile the province of Quebec and left-wing academics represent the YCJA as an undesirable swing of the pendulum toward punishment and just deserts, others feel that the pendulum has not swung far enough in that direction." In this respect, Tanner's observation very much complements Bernard's cyclical theory of juvenile justice reform, which, as we have seen, highlights the perennial policy-choice dilemma in youth justice between choosing harsh punishments or doing nothing at all.

Summary

This chapter has emphasized the value of historical and comparative research in understanding contemporary trends in Canadian youth justice. It has shown that Canada's current approach to dealing with young people who come into conflict with the law evolved over many centuries and involved many significant turning points along the way. One of these was the gradual shift that occurred in adult sensibilities about childhood—or what Ariès argued amounted to "the discovery of childhood"; over time, adults changed from viewing young people as little adults from a very early stage in life to viewing and treating them as innocent and vulnerable children who needed to be nurtured and protected for a more extended period of time. By the late nineteenth century this extended period of "growing up," or the transitional years from childhood to adulthood, came to be referred to as adolescence. Social-scientific knowledge about this newly defined stage in life in turn had a noticeable influence on the thinking of social reformers about the causes of juvenile delinquency and the value of having a separate juvenile court for dealing with troubled youth, who now were perceived mainly as either dependent, neglected, or misguided and therefore mostly in need of friendly helpfulness.

Historical research, however, shows that many other factors were in operation that help to account for the enactment of the JDA in 1908. This includes the earlier precursors to the juvenile court, the changing social and economic climate of the last half of the nineteenth century, the gradual rise of the social welfare state in many countries, and the international cross-fertilization of ideas about juvenile justice reform. In its description of the essential research findings on the origins of the YCJA, and the debate over the alleged recent punitive turn in Canadian youth justice, this chapter highlights the value of historical and comparative research to an understanding of more recent, and possibly future, trends in the Canadian youth criminal justice system.

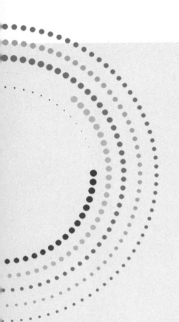

Key Terms

adolescence

adulteration

bifurcated youth justice system

diminished criminal responsibility

doli incapax

indeterminate sentences

juvenile courts

juvenile delinquency

Juvenile Delinquents Act (JDA)

parens patriae

punishable young offender

punitive turn thesis

reformable young offender

status offences

Young Offenders Act (YOA)

Youth Criminal Justice Act (YCJA)

youth criminal justice systems

Review Questions

1. What can we learn from studying the history of childhood that is relevant to understanding the development and operation of modern juvenile justice systems?

2. What were the major factors that contributed to the development of specialized youth justice systems in Western countries, including Canada, in the late nineteenth and early twentieth centuries?

3. How important were humanitarian conscience and the rhetoric of social reformers in the development of early juvenile delinquency legislation and juvenile courts in the US and Canada?

4. What is Bernard's cyclical theory of juvenile justice reform, and how might it be used to explain reforms in Canadian youth justice legislation, such as the introduction of the JDA (in 1908) and the YCJA (in 2002)?

Critical Thinking Questions

1. Is it more difficult to raise children today than in the past? Why?

2. Do we really need a specialized youth justice system in Canada? Why or why not?

3. Has there been a punitive turn in youth justice in Canada? What types of data could you use to try to answer this question?

4. If you were given the power to make changes in the Canadian youth criminal justice system, would you want the system to be more lenient or more punitive? Why?

References

Alain, M., Reid, S., and Corrado, R. (Eds). (2016). *Implementing and working with the Youth Criminal Justice Act across Canada*. Toronto: University of Toronto Press.

Albrecht, H.-J. (2004). Youth justice in Germany. In M. Tonry and A. Doob (Eds), *Youth crime and youth justice: Comparative and cross-national perspectives* (pp. 443–93). Chicago: Chicago University Press.

Ariès, P. (1962). *Centuries of childhood: A social history of family life*. New York: Vintage Books.

Bala, N. (1997). *Young offenders law*. Toronto: Irwin.

Bala, N., Carrington, P., and Roberts, J. (2009). Evaluating the Youth Criminal Justice Act after five years: A qualified success. *Canadian Journal of Criminology and Criminal Justice, 51*(2), 131–67.

Beattie, J. (1986). *Crime and the courts in England 1600–1800*. Princeton: Princeton University Press.

Bernard, T.J. (1992). *The cycle of juvenile justice*. New York: Oxford University Press.

Bernard, T.J., and Kurlychek, M. (2010). *The cycle of juvenile justice* (2nd ed.). New York: Oxford University Press.

Blatier, C. (1999). Juvenile justice in France. *British Journal of Criminology, 39*(2), 240–52.

Bullen, J. (1991). J.J. Kelso and the "new" child-savers: The genesis of the children's aid movement in Ontario. In R. Smandych, G. Dodds, and A. Esau (Eds), *Dimensions of childhood: Essays in the history of children and youth in Canada* (pp. 135–58). Winnipeg: University of Manitoba, Legal Research Institute.

Carrigan, D.O. (1998). *Juvenile delinquency in Canada: A history*. Toronto: Irwin.

Comacchio, C. (2010). Lost in modernity: "Maladjustment" and the "modern youth problem," English Canada, 1920–50. In M. Gleason, T. Myers, L. Paris, and V. Strong-Boag (Eds), *Lost kids: Vulnerable children and youth in twentieth-century Canada and the United States* (pp. 53–71). Vancouver: University of British Columbia Press.

Corrado, R., and Turnbull, S. (1992). A comparative examination of the modified justice model in the United Kingdom and the United States. In R. Corrado, N. Bala, R. Linden, and M. Le Blanc (Eds), *Juvenile justice in Canada: A theoretical and analytical assessment* (pp. 75–136). Toronto: Butterworths.

Crofts, T. (2002). *The criminal responsibility of children and young persons: A comparison of English and German law*. Aldershot, UK: Ashgate.

Cunneen, C., and White, R. (2007). *Juvenile justice: Youth and crime in Australia* (3rd ed.). Melbourne: Oxford University Press.

Davis-Barron, S. (2009). *Canadian youth and the criminal law*. Markham, ON: LexisNexis Canada.

Doob, A.N., and Sprott, J. (2006). Punishing youth crime in Canada: The blind men and the elephant. *Punishment and Society, 8*(2), 223–33.

Empey, L. (1982). *American delinquency: Its meaning and construction*. Chicago: Dorsey Press.

Feld, B.C. (2017). *The evolution of the juvenile court: Race, politics and the criminalizing of juvenile justice*. New York: New York University Press.

Feld, B.C., and Bishop, D. (2013). Juvenile justice. In M. Tonry (Ed), *Oxford handbook of crime and criminal justice* (pp. 627–59). Oxford: Oxford University Press.

Gottlieb, B. (1993). *The family in the Western world from the Black Death to the Industrial Age*. New York: Oxford University Press.

Government of Canada. (2012). *Safe Streets and Communities Act*. Retrieved from https://laws-lois.justice.gc.ca/eng/annualstatutes/2012_1/

Graebner, W. (1994). Juvenile delinquency. In P. Stearns (Ed), *Encyclopedia of social history* (pp. 379–81). New York: Garland.

Griffiths, C., and Verdun-Jones, S. (1994). *Canadian criminal justice*. Toronto: Harcourt Brace.

Hackler, J. (1978). *The prevention of youthful crime: The great stumble forward*. Toronto: Methuen.

Hagan, J., and Leon, J. (1977). Rediscovering delinquency: Social history, political ideology, and the sociology of law. *American Sociological Review, 42*(August), 587–98.

Hagan, J., and Leon, J. (1980). The rehabilitation of law: A social-historical comparison of probation in Canada and the United States. *Canadian Journal of Sociology/Cahiers Canadiens de Sociologie, 5*(3), 235–51.

Hall, G.S. (1904). *Adolescence: Its relation to physiology, anthropology, sociology, sex, crime, religion, and education*. New York: D. Appleton.

Havemann, P. (1986). From child saving to child blaming: The political economy of the Young Offenders Act 1908–1984. In S. Brickery and E. Comack (Eds), *The social basis of law* (p. 225). Toronto: Garamond.

Hogeveen, B. (2001). "Winning deviant youth over by friendly helpfulness": Transformations in the legal governance of deviant children, 1857–1908. In R. Smandych (Ed), *Youth justice: History, legislation, and reform* (pp. 43–63). Toronto: Harcourt.

Hogeveen, B. (2005). "If we are tough on crime, if we punish crime, then people get the message": Constructing and governing the punishable young offender in Canada during the late 1990s. *Punishment and Society, 7*(1), 73–89.

Hogeveen, B., and Smandych, R. (2001). Origins of the newly proposed Canadian Youth Criminal Justice Act: Political discourse and the perceived crisis in youth crime in the 1990s. In R. Smandych (Ed), *Youth justice: History, legislation, and reform* (pp. 144–68). Toronto: Harcourt.

Janson, C.-G. (2004). Youth justice in Sweden. In M. Tonry and A. Doob (Eds), *Youth crime and youth justice: Comparative and cross-national perspectives* (pp. 391–441). Chicago: Chicago University Press.

Minaker, J., and Hogeveen, B. (2009). *Youth, crime, and society: Issues of power and justice.* Toronto: Pearson.

Morgan, R., and Newburn, T. (2007). Youth justice. In R. Reiner (Ed), *Oxford handbook of criminology* (pp. 1024–60). Oxford: Oxford University Press.

Morris, A. (2004). Youth justice in New Zealand. In M. Tonry and A. Doob (Eds), *Youth crime and youth justice: Comparative and cross-national perspectives* (pp. 243–92). Chicago: Chicago University Press.

Muncie, J. (2008). The "punitive turn" in juvenile justice: Cultures of control and rights compliance in Western Europe and the USA. *Youth Justice, 8*(2), 107–21.

Muncie, J., and Goldson, B. (Eds). (2006). *Comparative youth justice: Critical issues.* London: Sage.

O'Connor, I., and Cameron, M. (2002). Juvenile justice in Australia. In A. Graycar and P. Grabosky (Eds), *Cambridge handbook of Australian criminology* (pp. 211–34). Sydney: Cambridge University Press.

Platt, A.M. (1969). *The child savers: The invention of delinquency.* Chicago: University of Chicago Press.

Platt, A.M. (1974). The triumph of benevolence: The origins of the juvenile justice system in the United States. In R. Quinney (Ed), *Criminal justice in America* (pp. 356–89). Boston: Little, Brown.

Pollock, L. (1983). *Forgotten children, parent–child relations from 1500 to 1900.* Cambridge: Cambridge University Press.

Rothman, D.J. (1980). *Conscience and convenience: The asylum and its alternatives in progressive America.* Boston: Little, Brown.

Shore, H. (2003). "Inventing" the juvenile delinquent in nineteenth century Europe. In C. Emsley and G. Dunstall (Eds), *Comparative crime histories* (pp. 110–23). Cullompton, UK: Willan.

Smandych, R. (2001). Accounting for changes in Canadian youth justice: From the invention to the disappearance of childhood. In R. Smandych (Ed), *Youth justice: History, legislation, and reform* (pp. 1–23). Toronto: Harcourt.

Smandych, R. (2006). Canada: Repenalisation and young offenders' rights. In J. Muncie and B. Goldson (Eds), *Comparative youth justice: Critical issues* (pp. 19–33). London: Sage.

Smandych, R., and Corrado, R. (2018). "Too bad, so sad": Observations on key outstanding policy challenges of twenty years of youth justice reform in Canada, 1995–2015. *Manitoba Law Journal, 8*(3), 191–240.

Smandych, R., Dyck, M., La Berge, C., and Koffman, J. (2016). Youth justice in Manitoba: Developments and issues under the YCJA. In M. Alain, S. Reid, and R. Corrado (Eds), *Implementing and working with the Youth Criminal Justice Act across Canada.* Toronto: University of Toronto Press.

Spagnoli, P.G. (1981). Philippe Aries: Historian of the family. *Journal of Family History, 6,* 434–41.

Sutherland, N. (1976). *Children in English-Canadian society: Framing the twentieth-century consensus.* Toronto: University of Toronto Press.

Tanenhaus, D.S. (2004). *Juvenile justice in the making.* New York: Oxford University Press.

Tanenhaus, D.S. (2013). The elusive juvenile court: Its origins, practices and re-invention. In B. Feld and D. Bishop (Eds), *Oxford handbook of juvenile crime and juvenile justice* (pp. 419–41). New York: Oxford University Press.

Tanner, J. (2015). *Teenage troubles: Youth and deviance in Canada (4th ed.).* Toronto: Oxford University Press.

Trépanier, J. (1999). Juvenile courts after 100 years: Past and present orientations. *European Journal on Criminal Policy and Research, 7*(3), 303–27.

Trépanier, J., and Tulkens, F. (1993). Juvenile justice in Belgium and Canada at the beginning of the century: Two models or one? *International Journal of Children's Rights, 1,* 189–211.

Tustin, L., and Lutes, R. (2013). *A guide to the Youth Criminal Justice Act.* Markham, ON: LexisNexis.

Measuring Youth Crime in Canada

An Elusive Challenge[1]

John A. Winterdyk

Overview

This chapter provides an overview of the official and unofficial facts about youth crime in Canada. To provide a contextual framework, a brief historical description of the social and historical influences on youth crime serves to help readers understand both how and why we measure youth crime today. The chapter then reviews the types of data and information that can be gleaned from official data sources, as well as from unofficial data sources (e.g., self-report and victimization surveys). A review of various youth crime characteristics and trends is presented along with an examination of some provincial variations. The findings are discussed within the context of describing some of the key trends and patterns of youth crime.

Key Objectives

After reading this chapter, you should be able to:

- Understand how we define youth crime.
- Understand the importance of social and historical influences on the evolution of youth justice and the measuring of youth crime in Canada.
- Recognize that measuring and recording youth crime is influenced by varying formal social control mechanisms.
- Describe some of the key facts and trends of youth crime over the past several decades.
- Understand the strengths and weaknesses of official statistics in relation to self-report and victimization data.
- Critically reflect on what the three measurement methods both tell us and do not tell us about youth crime.

Introduction

> *Juvenile delinquency is a complex, multi-faceted issue. In order to devise effective prevention and intervention strategies for youth-at-risk, it is important to understand the context in which this behaviour occurs.*
>
> — Public Safety Canada 2012

As a social scientist who has been studying youth crime since the 1970s, I am regularly asked by the media to explain the apparent nature and extent of youth crime locally and at times internationally. Given that some 29 per cent of Canada's population is under the age of 24 (Statistics Canada 2018a), it would seem fair to ask: How serious and how common is it? Is the legislation too lenient? Who is committing these criminal or deviant acts and why do they do it? Unfortunately, researchers are seldom able to provide definitive answers to these questions, and unless the media seek out informed opinions, the presentation of youth crime in the media and through political debate is not always based on empirical reality but on what Schissel (2006, p. 72) describes as "constructed versions that serve political and moral purposes." Nevertheless, Brantingham and Brantingham (1984, p. 41) have pointed out the ongoing motivation for investigating youth crime: "[C]ounting crime seems to satisfy some fundamental urge to know the dimensions of our misery as if knowing by itself makes things better."

To better understand, explain, and ultimately predict youth crime, we need to draw from a variety of measurement sources, each of which has its strengths and weaknesses. In this chapter, we begin by examining the major factors that have contributed to the historical emergence of youth crime and youth justice. Next, we draw on two separate sources of measurement that describe the nature and extent of delinquency and youth crime: (1) official accounts of social control (e.g., police, courts, and corrections) and (2) unofficial sources such as self-report and victimization surveys which allow researchers to determine the nature and extent of unrecorded delinquency, the so-called **dark figure of crime**, and compare the results with official accounts of delinquency. Before we review the various evidence, however, we must first appreciate the complexity of the terms *youth crime* and **"at-risk" youth**.

Although delinquency and youth crime can be and have been defined in several different ways by sociologists (see Siegel and Welsch 2013) and psychologists (see Bartol and Bartol 2016), we will briefly review the legal definitions as they are largely used in the measurement of youth crime.

Defining Youth Crime

Delinquency and *juvenile delinquency* were terms used in the 1908 Juvenile Delinquents Act (JDA) to describe "any child who violates any provision of the Criminal Code or any federal or provincial statute" (s. 2.1). With the passing of the Young Offenders Act (YOA) in 1984, the terms were replaced with the less pejorative phrase *young person* which continues to be used (s. 2.1) under the Youth Criminal Justice Act (YCJA) (2003). A young person who commits an offence is referred to as a "young offender," and when formally acknowledged and counted, the offence becomes a "youth crime" even though it violates the same laws as those that apply to an adult. The shift in terminology, while perhaps appearing subtle, has had an impact on how we measure youth crime today. For example, Bartol and Bartol (2016, p. 29) note that *juvenile delinquency* was "an imprecise, nebulous, social, clinical and legal label for a wide variety of law- and norm-violating behaviour." Meanwhile, the term *young offender* refers only to behaviours against the Criminal Code. Hence, it is important to understand how youth crime is defined and how its meaning has changed.

Legal Definition

Historically, criminologists have tended to focus on the legal rather than on the psychological or sociological definitions of youth crime. The YCJA (s. 2) defines a young person as "a person who is or, in the absence of evidence to the contrary, appears to be twelve years old, or older, but less than eighteen years old and, if the context requires, includes a person who is charged under the Act with having committed an offence while he or she was a young person or who is found guilty of an offence under this Act." Should the young person meet these conditions, their act then constitutes a "youth crime."

Although the JDA definition of *juvenile delinquency* (s. 291) was intended to support the concept of family and to build an informal system of social control (Fetherston 2005), the YCJA places a greater emphasis on a legalistic approach under which young offenders are held legally responsible for their actions (see Chapter 3).

dark figure of crime
Incidents of crime or delinquency that go undetected or unreported by the police.

"at-risk" youth
Young people who are "at risk" of offending or being victimized due to various social, family, and/or personal factors.

Box 2.1 | Youth Justice in Action

Limitations of Using Only a Legal Definition

- *Narrow scope.* Although a contentious concept, some believe that crimes that do not have a "victim" should not be considered criminal offences, while others believe that any behaviour that results in the harm of a human being (even if that harm is to only the perpetrator) should be illegal—in other words, the goal of the law should be to help protect people from themselves as well as others. Certain "victimless" behaviours, such as driving without a seatbelt, loitering, and drug possession, among others, are treated as criminal, while other self-harming and potentially dangerous behaviours (e.g., eating junk food, climbing trees, participating in YouTube challenges, etc.) are not. Similarly, changes in technology create new opportunities for complex crimes to emerge and go undetected (e.g., cyber- and Internet-based crimes). Until a new form of crime is recognized and defined, it is not legally a crime.
- *Policy and administration variation.* At any given time, society's perception of youth crime can affect the legal implementation of the youth justice legislation. Depending on the nature of the deviance, cases of youth crime are often eliminated because they are perceived as lacking enough gravity or are deemed unlikely to result in a conviction owing to insufficient evidence.
- *Reporting rates.* The data used to track youth crime trends, cleared crime, and patterns of youth crime are derived from different administrative sources: police records, judicial records, and correctional records. Although these findings are published annually by Statistics Canada, the resulting statistics can be misleading because Statistics Canada does not enumerate all crimes. Statistics Canada enumerates only those offences both reported to and reported by the police, court, or corrections. The extent to which youth crime is reported often depends on the public's willingness to report youth crime to police, as well as on varying social and economic factors (see Charron 2009). Similarly, local police policies and procedures may affect reporting rates, both in terms of how many crimes they are informed about and how many crimes they deem worth recording. In other words, whoever gathers the data can have an (unintended) agenda that unintentionally skews the published data.

Limitations in Assuming a Purely Legal Definition

Although restrictive from a social science perspective (see Box 2.1), notwithstanding the technical offence of administrative-type transgressions (e.g., breach of conditions), the legal definition of youth crime focuses primarily on predatory (e.g., break-and-enter, robbery) and aggressive (e.g., assault, homicide) behaviour that is deemed punishable by law. These crimes are commonly referred to as "conventional crimes" (Winterdyk 2020). Therefore, the legal definition, although functional, only enables us to describe the problem that is appropriate for this chapter.

As will be discuss later in this chapter, the questions of whether youth crime has increased or decreased and whether public fear is justified are subject to continuous debate. This chapter attempts to shed light on Canadian youth crime trends by examining both official and unofficial sources of data on youthful offending behaviour.

Measuring Delinquency: A Historical Overview

Juvenile delinquency is a social construct and a normative term that has evolved over time and has created certain dilemmas for the youth justice system. Until recently, most interpretations of youth crime have lacked a sense of history (see Chapter 1). Yet, to understand the nature and extent of youth crime today, we need to become familiar with how law-violating young people have become a concern and focus of attention. As philosopher George Santayana (1905) has said, "[T]hose who cannot remember the past are condemned to repeat it."

Our history of youth crime trends can be divided into three periods: pre-Confederation, state intervention, and the twentieth century. The overview will show how and why we created the term *delinquency* and how and why we started to track delinquent acts.

Delinquency Trends: Pre-Confederation to the Nineteenth Century

Given the frontier spirit of the Canadian pioneers during the early seventeenth century, children were afforded considerable freedom, which resulted in crime and hooliganism. Carrigan (1998) notes that children were involved in petty theft, brawling, and vandalism, and young girls in prostitution, as they were swept up in the violence that permeated the fur trade. J.G. Moylan, inspector of penitentiaries in what was then New France, claimed that "immigrant children greatly added to the criminal ranks and that their immigration should be stopped" (cited in Carrigan 1998, pp. 82–3).

Youth crime during the seventeenth century was also most likely caused by the uncontrolled growth of New France. Many young families were enticed to come to the New World with promises of land, prosperity, and opportunity. However, many of these families soon broke up due to extreme economic and physical hardships (Carrigan 1991). This disintegration of families ultimately resulted in numerous young people being abandoned, neglected, and/or abused, and it was this lack of supervision that led to crime and subsequently drew official attention by social service–type agencies (Carrigan 1998).

Until 1876, when the Dominion Bureau of Statistics (now Statistics Canada) began to record official statistics in Canada, accounts of juvenile delinquency were obtainable only through limited newspaper sources that were often based on first-hand observational reports. Consequently, the delinquency problem in pre-Confederation Canada cannot be accurately quantified. Nevertheless, some information is available. Based on the first annual report of the Board of Inspectors of Asylums and Prisons in 1860, Carrigan (1998) concludes that of 11,268 incarcerations, 6 per cent were young offenders under the age of 16, of which only 23.2 per cent were female. Between 1869 and 1889, the rate of juvenile incarceration fluctuated between 23.2 per cent and 31.6 per cent of all offences. And as we will see shortly, the delinquency problem at the end of the nineteenth century in many ways resembles the trends we are experiencing at the beginning of the twenty-first century. Now, as then, boys continue to be disproportionately represented in the youth justice system, most crimes are property related, most delinquencies occur in urban centres (see Table 2.1), and familial problems are often associated with youth crime. Being the product of parental neglect and/or maltreatment is still seen as one of

Table 2.1	Youth Crime Convictions for Indictable Offences by Province, 1885–1889			
	Under 16 Years		**16–20 Years**	
Provinces	**Male**	**Female**	**Male**	**Female**
Ontario	5,687	242	6,550	580
Quebec	2,516	200	3,095	256
Nova Scotia	367	14	446	42
New Brunswick	181	4	218	16
Manitoba	209	7	311	22
British Columbia	174	1	192	19
Prince Edward Island	81	1	57	9
Northwest Territories	21	0	94	4
Totals	9,236	469	10,963	948

Source: Based on Carrigan 1998.

the more common characteristics, or risk factors, among young offenders (see Hoge and Andrews 2010).

Table 2.1 provides an overview of juvenile convictions for indictable (i.e., serious) offences between 1885 and 1889 in the existing provinces and territory. As noted above, significantly more young males than young females were convicted during this period; males accounted for over 90 per cent of all convictions. But what is not clear is to what extent the official data reflect reporting and/or recording bias.

State Intervention: The First Step in Defining and Officially Counting Delinquency

American sociologist Anthony Platt (1977), in the postscript to his acclaimed book *The Child Savers*, suggests that the dramatic increase in youth crime throughout the 1870s can be attributed, in large part, to the deterioration in economic conditions in North America. He notes that, at that time, more than a half-million young persons were neither in school nor employed (see also pp. 10–11 in Chapter 1). By the late nineteenth century, the social support networks that had typically characterized rural or agrarian communities were in a state of deterioration. Urbanization and industrialization were changing the ways in which people lived. Children were less and less supervised, and as a result, they became more criminally active, particularly in the growing cities.

As the nature and extent of delinquency grew, it was believed, especially among the dominant middle and upper social classes, that state intervention could solve the problem. Universal public education was the first step the state took to help alleviate growing delinquency. In 1871, Ontario made school attendance compulsory for 7- to 12-year-olds for four months a year. Several industrial schools (also referred to as residential schools) were also established across the country (Carrigan 1991; for an overview of industrial schools in

Canada, see Milloy 1999). The impetus for this compulsory schooling came primarily from the middle-class "child savers," who believed that the root causes of delinquent behaviour rested in a child's environment, especially that of the family. By keeping count of children's delinquent behaviour, it was then possible to measure the impact of the state's efforts.

The intervention philosophy marked a new era in youth crime, and the need to record and measure delinquent activity was reflected in early twentieth-century law. The JDA was intended to support young offenders within the context of the family as a social unit. It also sought to build an informal system of social control as opposed to a formal system. As discussed in Chapter 1, J.J. Kelso (1864–1935) was instrumental (along with W.L. Scott) in establishing the first Ontario juvenile court system.

Youth Crime Trends: The Twentieth Century

The early twentieth century marked a new era in youth crime due to "the introduction of juvenile courts and a generally more efficient system of responding to juvenile crime." For example, between 1911 and the early 1940s, the rate of conviction for youth between the ages of 10 and 15 rose from 172 to 423 per 100,000. This represents more than a 200 per cent increase as compared to just over 30 per cent growth in the population of youth aged 10 to 15 years (Carrigan 1991, p. 228).

Although a dramatic increase, most of the offences committed during the early twentieth century were petty property-related offences, and the increase reflected the shift in formal attention to young offenders. The fluctuation in property crime (a high of 36 per 100,000 in 1930 to a low of 24 per 100,000 in 1945) coincided with the changing social and demographic climate and to some extent with the increasing desire for the state to exercise social control. DeMause (1988, p. 52) refers to the period circa nineteenth century to mid-twentieth century as the "socialization mode," during which youth were given extra attention by their parents and society. Fathers began to invest more time and effort in training/raising their children.

The youth crime rate slowly dropped from 1940 onward, until 1955 when it was just under 300 per 100,000. DeMause (1988, p. 54) refers to this stage as the "helping mode," during which there was an explosion of faddish techniques for child rearing and discipline. Children were brought up to feel "unconditionally loved." This phase appears to have been short-lived, however, as delinquency rates began to climb again. The increase has been attributed, in part, to improved social and economic conditions as the country emerged from the hardships of World War II. By 1966, the delinquency rate had climbed to 459 per 100,000, as North American society experienced a social and cultural revolution. Families in which both parents worked had become more common, the influence of the mass media was everywhere, and there was a general erosion of values. According to Carrigan (1998), these social changes prompted calls for the revision of the JDA. A special committee report in 1965, entitled "Juvenile Delinquency in Canada," stated that the increase in juvenile crime had become "alarming" and that it could be expected to continue to increase (quoted in Carrigan 1998, p. 159).

Comparing these numbers to those of the 1980s and 1990s is revealing. By 1989, the youth crime rate was 5.5 times that of the 1960s (i.e., 2,568 per 100,000). During the same year, young offenders between the ages of 12 and 17 represented 22 per cent of all persons charged with Criminal Code offences (CCJS 1992a). Then, in 1991, the overall youth crime rate began to decline for the second time in the twentieth century. However, as discussed below, this decline does not pertain to all offences.

Further State Intervention: Solutions for a Changing Society

By the early 1980s, there was a growing sentiment that new laws were needed to address the growing problem of youth crime, even though there was no unanimous agreement that the increase was even due to the JDA (see Tanner 2010). Nevertheless, this socio-politically-motivated need resulted in the introduction of the YOA of 1984. During its 20-year tenure, the YOA underwent numerous reforms and received considerable criticism for not being able to fulfill its objectives of reducing youth crime or providing the appropriate response to the needs of young offenders (see Bala, Carrington, and Roberts 2012) and was eventually replaced with the YCJA in 2003. Since the purpose of this chapter is not to examine the relative impact of the YCJA on youth crime (see instead Chapters 3 and 4), this chapter will focus on presenting some of the facts about youth crime in Canada as obtained through both **official** and **unofficial data** sources.

Characteristics of Today's Young Offenders—The Official Picture

official data
The Canadian Centre for Justice Statistics, a branch of Statistics Canada, collects offender and offence data from the police, courts, and corrections for administrative purposes. The Centre produces regular reports that are readily available to the public.

unofficial data
Refers to data that are collected and usually published by private or independent researchers or research facilities. The primary data-collection techniques are self-report surveys and victimization surveys. Unofficial data are often used to enhance official data.

The chance that an adolescent youth will become involved in some type of anti-social or offending behaviour and/or be a victim of a criminal act varies based on a variety of factors. As we will see throughout this section, those factors can include individual characteristics, family characteristics, peer and school influences, neighbourhood environment, and daily activities. Before we examine some of these more closely, consider the following points that provide some context about today's young offenders.

- While youth make up 7% of the Canadian population, they comprise 13% of persons accused of crime.
- The police-reported youth crime rate has been falling steadily since 2006, continuing a longer-term downward trend since peaking in 1991. Between 2000 and 2014, the youth crime rate declined 42%, a notably larger decline than the drop in overall crime (−34%). This drop in youth crime was primarily driven by a 51% decrease in the rate of youth accused of property crime, particularly in theft of $5,000 and under and break and enter.
- The rate of youth accused of crime in 2014 was lower than the rate for young adults aged 18 to 24 . . . , but over twice the accused rate for adults aged 25 and over. . . . These differences, however, varied by offence. (Allen and Superle 2016)

As was suggested earlier in this chapter, fuelled mostly by the mass media (see Chapter 6), the public has historically had a rather pejorative image of the extent, gravity, and nature of youth crime (see Brooks and Schissel 2015). Although the media is bound by a code of ethical reporting, it is the sensational reporting of negative-related youth crime that triggers cautionary attitudes toward youth and ultimately a *moral panic*. There is little question that youth crime is damaging not only to our youth but also to our communities. Therefore, it is important to know the facts before recommending responses to youth crime.

The term *official data* refers to the records of youth whose illegal activities have come to the attention of, whether reported to or discovered by, the various social control agencies (i.e., police, youth courts, and youth corrections). Agencies in each of the provinces and territories are expected to provide Statistics Canada with their data, which are then compiled and aggregated and made available through standardized publications and/or posted on the Statistics Canada website (see http://www5.statcan.gc.ca/olc-cel/olc.action?objId=85-002-X&objType=2&lang=en&limit=0 to access *Juristat* publications). Not all data received are presented or published; however, if specific data have been collected, they can be purchased from Statistics Canada. Therefore, only youth with a public record are officially counted as young offenders, as opposed to those who commit an infraction but do not become part of the official record because they remain unknown to officials.

While the accuracy of official statistics has been the subject of debate (see Brantingham and Brantingham 1984), these statistics remain the most consistent source of measurement for youth offences and are readily available through the Canadian Centre for Justice Statistics (CCJS) at Statistics Canada in Ottawa. In fact, a recent Statistics Canada evaluation report noted that the CCJS reports have been quite accurate since 2011/12 (Statistics Canada 2018b). In terms of youth crime, CCJS expresses crime data in three ways: (1) the number of youths charged; (2) the rate of youth charged per 100,000 youth ages 12 to 17; and (3) the percentage of change in total youth rate between the reporting year and previous year. Within this context, the offences reported are limited to the Criminal Code offence categories and several drug and trafficking offences. This chapter will provide an overview of some of the information that can be gleaned from various official sources.

Demographic Facts of Young Offenders

Gender

As already mentioned, ever since Canada started collecting official data on young offenders, such statistics have shown that young males tend to commit more reported crimes than females do. According to a 2012/13 Statistics Canada report, based on data from the Integrated Criminal Court Survey, almost 76 per cent of youth court cases involved accused males while 24 per cent involved an accused female (Allen and Superle 2016; Malakieh 2018). This pattern shows a slight shift in the gender balance since the early twenty-first century, when the percentage of young males involved in youth crime was around 80 per cent and of young females around 20 per cent. Additionally, since the introduction of the YCJA, the youth court data reveal that those cases completed tend to be older young persons and that involvement in crime increases with age for both males and females (ages 16–17 as opposed to 14–15 years) (see Malakieh 2018). Males are more likely to be accused of sexual assault (92 per cent), drug possession (85 per cent), attempted murder (82 per cent), and weapons offences (82 per cent), while the highest number of crimes committed by females include prostitution (44 per cent), common assault (36 per cent), and fraud (35 per cent) (Allen and Superle 2016) (see Figure 2.1).

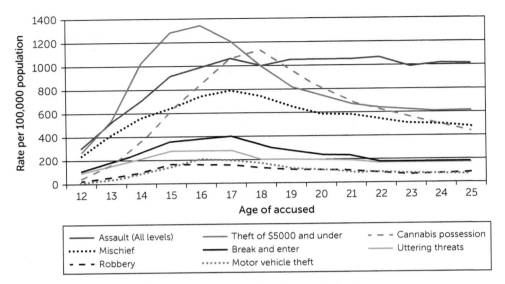

Figure 2.1 Rates of Youth and Young Adults Accused of Crime, by Age, 2014 (Select Offences)

Notes: Rates are calculated on the basis of 100,000 population at each age. Populations are based upon July 1st estimates from Statistics Canada, Demography Division. Assault includes all levels and types of assault (see Table 1), excluding sexual assaults.

Source: Allen and Superle 2016, Chart 5.

It is still unclear as to whether the increase in violent crimes among young persons and the difference in rates and frequency between young males and females can be attributed to a change or set of changes. Such changes could include changes in reporting patterns, media sensationalism, the "crime funnel" effect, the alleged growth of "girl gangs" (see Chapter 7), the use of extrajudicial measures in formal processing, and/or young females becoming more like their male counterparts. For example, some researchers have been paying more attention to crimes committed by both young males and young females and are relying on different sources of data (i.e., police versus court administrative records) to clarify the apparent trends. Nonetheless, the fact remains that males continue to commit most youth crimes. Unfortunately, official measurement of youth crime is unable to tell us what role the various risk and protective factors in society play in helping to explain the gender differences in offending patterns. However, Chapters 7 and 8 offer an overview of different theories that might help to explain such differences.

Age

Next to gender, age is one of the most important determinants on which researchers focus to explain youth crime trends and patterns (see Blumstein 1995). As illustrated in Figure 2.1, the rate of persons accused of crimes steadily increases from age 12, peaking at age 17, and then begins to decline for all offence types. Is this due to social, psychological, and/or biological factors, or a possible interaction of the consequences of formal legislation? Official data are unable to provide any direct answers.

According to various official reports by the CCJS, the age-related pattern of being accused of an offence has remained consistent since the early 1990s, even though the overall youth violent crime rate was 11 per cent higher in 2009 than in 1999 (Sanders 2000 and Dauvergne 2013). Perhaps more revealing are the types of offences in which different age groups engage. For example, those who are younger are more likely to engage in property-related crimes (approximately 45 per cent of their total offences versus about 37 per cent among 17-year-olds). Older youth, on the other hand, are proportionately more likely to commit **administrative offences** (e.g., charges not generally considered to be criminal, such as failure to appear in court and failure to comply with **disposition** [Sanders 2000]), than are 12- or 13-year-olds (i.e., 12 per cent versus 4 per cent, respectively). What is perhaps noteworthy from the official data on the cases completed in youth court by age is that 12- and 13-year-olds are proportionately more frequently charged with "crimes against the person" than are 16- and 17-year-olds (i.e., 41 per cent and 36 per cent versus 24 per cent and 23 per cent, respectively). Again, although the official data do not offer any explanation, Doob and Cesaroni (2004) have suggested that, proportionately, young people engage in more anti-social behaviour because they are less organized and more spontaneous than their older peers. If so, what effect, if any, is the YCJA having on the different age groups?

One of the advantages of using official data is they allow us to examine trends and patterns over time. According to CCJS data, even though 16- to 17-year-olds still commit proportionately more offences than those youth ages 12 to 15 (see Dauvergne 2013, p. 3), since the 1990s young people appear to have been getting involved in delinquent activities at an earlier age than ever before (Allen and Superle 2016). For example, 2001/02 data reveal that, despite the introduction of alternative measures programs, the proportion of youth court caseloads dealing with 12- and 13-year-olds still increased from 10 per cent in 1992/93 to 11 per cent in 2001/02, while for 16- and 17-year-olds, the proportion increased from 52 per cent to 54 per cent during the same years (Thomas 2003). While the increase was perhaps an artefact of the way data were collected as well as police charging practices, there did appear to be a slight increase during the two time periods. For the recording period of 2014/15, the percentage of youth court cases for youth ages 12 to 15 decreased slightly to 39 per cent, while for 16- and 17-year-olds the proportion of cases dropped from 63.4 per cent in 2009 (Miladinovic 2016) to 61.4 per cent in 2016/17 ("Youth Courts" 2019) (see Figure 2.2). The trend may also be explained by one of the objectives of the YCJA—the use of police diversion and extrajudicial measures—as well as by the host of new programs and/or resources made available under the YCJA.

Measuring Youth Violent and Non-violent Crime

Violent Crime

In the mid-1990s there were two opposing viewpoints on whether youth violent crime had been increasing in Canada. Corrado and Markwart (1994) claimed that violent crime among young persons had increased, while Carrington (1995) argued that the violent incident rate among young persons had not increased. In the late 1990s, Gabor (1999) suggested that while youth crime may not have increased dramatically, the level of seriousness had. Several years later, Sally Spencer, then executive director for the group Youth Assisting Youth in Toronto, reinforced Gabor's observation when she stated that "the severity of what is happening is definitely on the rise" ("Violent Crime in Canada" 2008). Consequently, if we take into consideration the youth **Crime Severity Index (CSI)** introduced in 2009, we get a slightly different

administrative offences
Under section 4 of the YCJA, there are provisions under the extrajudicial measures that allow for charges to be laid if the young person fails to comply with his or her disposition or fails to appear before the court. The charge can be initiated by either the police or the Crown.

disposition
For young offenders, this is the equivalent of sentencing for adults. Under the YCJA, a disposition should in theory be more rehabilitative and/or restorative than retributive.

Crime Severity Index (CSI)
Developed and introduced by Statistics Canada, the CSI uses a weighting system to measure (youth) offences according to their seriousness. Although introduced in 2009, CSI data are available back to 1998.

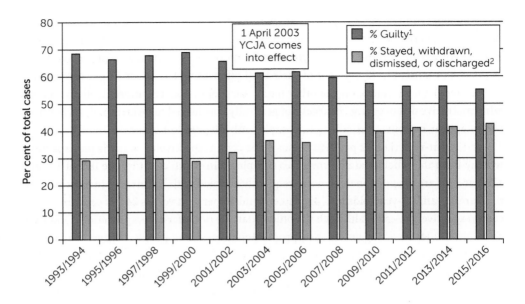

Figure 2.2   Cases Completed in Youth Courts by Gender and Age Group of Accused, Canada, 1993/1994 to 2015/2016

1. Guilty findings include guilty of the offence, of an included offence, of an attempt of the offence, or of an attempt of an included offence. This category also includes cases where an absolute or conditional discharge has been imposed.

2. Includes stays, withdrawals, dismissals, and discharges at preliminary inquiry as well as court referrals to alternative or extrajudicial measures and restorative justice programs.

Note: A case is one or more charges against an accused person or company that were processed by the courts at the same time and received a final decision.

Source: Malakieh 2017.

picture. Instead of simply relying on measures of police-reported crime, the CSI measures the seriousness of crime reported to the police. To calculate the CSI score, each type of offence is assigned a seriousness "weight," which is derived from actual sentences handed down by courts in all provinces and territories. More serious crimes are assigned higher weights; less serious offences, lower weights. Also, to make the Index easier to interpret, it is standardized to "100," using 2006 as a base year. Even though considered an informative measure, it is also having its challenges—primarily the fact that is relies on sentencing data (e.g., recidivism data is not available from the court surveys) (see Statistics Canada 2015a).

The CSI score for all crimes declined steadily from 1998 to 2014, at which point it went up slightly for the first time in over 20 years. Between 2014 and 2016, the CSI rose by around 2 per cent—though it was still over 25 per cent lower than it was in 2006 (Keighley 2017). The same trend holds for youth crime between 2003 and 2013—the index scores dropped from 92 to 65 in 2013. Specifically, the youth violent CSI remained relatively stable at around 95 between 2003 and 2009, when it began to decline, hitting 70.0 in 2013—a 13 per cent drop. However, there was an increase of 5 per cent in 2016 due to increased rates of police-reported crimes including attempted murder (+115 per cent), sexual violations against children (+38 per cent), and robbery (+6 per cent) (Keighley 2017), and in 2017 the CSI for youth crime increased another 2 per cent (Allen 2018). However, the CSI score in 2017 was still 38 per cent lower than 10 years earlier. Meanwhile, the non-violent crime index score has dropped 19 per cent over the past decade, with another large 8 per cent decline in 2016. The report reveals that between 2003 and 2013, the overall CSI score and both the violent and non-violent CSI scores showed a slow but continuous decline (see Allen 2018; Boyce, Cotter, and Perreault 2014). This would appear to bode well for any moral panic that may still be lingering among Canadians; however, the facts may not be that simple. For example, in 2013, University of Toronto criminologist Anthony Doob suggested that "governments and police like to take credit when crime statistics improve, but often, such numbers point to broad long-term trends rather than the effect of specific policies" (Statsna 2013).

While the overall violent crime rate has stabilized in recent years and the CSI has continued to drop since the mid-1990s, if we look at certain types of violent crimes, we see that the characteristics of violent crime suggest a different story. For example, Allen and Superle (2016) observe that youth homicide rates were the highest they had been since the mid-1990s, with the greatest increase and number of incidents occurring in Manitoba. Perhaps what makes these statistics more concerning is the context in which the increases have continued: gang-related homicides are consistently higher for youths than for adults, with 29 per cent of homicides involving a youth being gang related (Allen and Superle 2016). Conversely, between 2010/11 and 2011/12 robbery declined 7.4 per cent and major assaults dropped 14.7 per cent, but homicide rose 2.2 per cent—although this only represented an increase from 45 to 46 homicides (see Figure 2.3 and Dauvergne 2013).

Official sources also reveal that regionally, in 2012/13, British Columbia had the lowest rate of violent youth crimes (i.e., 50.3 per 100,000), while Saskatchewan continued to have the highest CSI (i.e., 169.9 per 100,000) outside of Yukon, Nunavut, and the NWT, whose rates are skewed due to their small population (Boyce, Cotter, and Perreault 2014). In most violent offence cases in 2012, the principal charge was assault (Level 1), with a rate of 481 per 100,000—but this was down from 502 in 2011. Uttering threats was a distant third behind Levels 1 and 2 assaults,

Box 2.2 | Youth Justice in Action

Youth Crime and Risk Assessment Questions to Ponder

Until recently, risk assessment of vulnerable youth was not a common practice. In 2009, a team of Saskatchewan researchers conducted a meta-analysis of three popular forensic instruments of risk assessment (i.e., Level of Service Inventory [YLS/CMI, LSI-SK], Psychopathy Checklist [PCL-YV], and Structured Assessment of Violence Risk for Youth [SAVRY]) for young offenders. They analyzed the predictive accuracy for general, non-violent, violent, and sexual recidivism for the three instruments and found that all three were significant in the prediction of general, non-violent, and violent recidivism (Oliver, Stockdale, and Wormith 2009). In their 2003 study, Catchpole and Gretton found a moderate to strong relationship between using a range of risk assessment instruments and future offending among a sample of 74 violent young offenders in British Columbia. As this is a growing area of interest, further information can be found at the Department of Justice website: https://www.justice.gc.ca/eng/rp-pr/cj-jp/yj-jj/rr03_yj4-rr03_jj4/a1.html.

Critical Thinking Question
To what extent might such instruments serve to enhance clinical service provision to youth clientele?

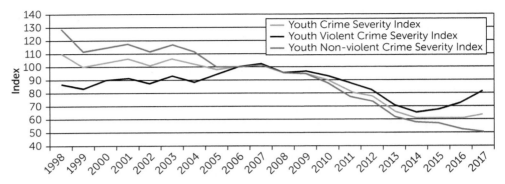

Figure 2.3   Police-Reported Crime Severity Indexes, 1998–2017

Note: Data is based on the number of youth aged 12 to 17 who were either charged (or recommended for charging) by police or diverted from the formal criminal justice system through the use of warnings, cautions, referrals to community programs, etc. The youth Crime Severity Indexes are based on *Criminal Code* incidents, including traffic offences, as well as other federal statute violations. The base index was set at 100 for 2006 for Canada. Populations are based on July 1st estimates from Statistics Canada, Demography Division.

Source: Allen 2018, Chart 17.

at 202, while the rate for attempted murder and murder cases in 2011/12 was 2 per 100,000—accounting for less than 1 per cent of police-reported crimes (see Figure 2.3 and Perreault 2013). What official data cannot tell us is why the regional variations. The regional variations speak to a host of different economic, demographic, cultural, social, and political factors across the country, as well as the availability of supporting resources and potential variations in public fear about youth crime that prompted more reporting. Moreover, while it has been suggested that such variations are reflective of the punitive nature of the official legislation, the trends cannot be explained solely by the introduction of the YOA or the YCJA. As Dauvergne (2013) and Allen (2018) both observe, there is considerable variability between the provincial and territorial jurisdictions in how the YCJA is applied—for example, through variations in police enforcement activity.

Prince Edward Island, for example, had the highest proportion of guilty pleas (21 per cent), while Manitoba had the lowest proportion of guilty pleas (9 per cent) in 2012. The national average was 15 per cent (Dauvergne 2013). Outside of the three territories, Saskatchewan and Manitoba had the highest crime rates among youth in 2014 at 15,958 and 8,992 per 100,000 respectively. Newfoundland had the lowest rate at 3,858, with the national rate being 5,253. The same pattern held true for both violent and property-related crimes (Statistics Canada 2015b).

While official violent crime data are interesting, they do not provide insight into the richer social science interests and issues related to youth crime. For example, to what extent are the rates of different crimes, as well as the seriousness of the crimes, related to the growth of youth gangs (see Chapter 12), an escalation in the use/accessibility of weapons, an apparent increase in female violence (see Chapter 7), or perhaps social and/or cultural diversity in a province/territory, etc.

Non-violent Crime

Non-violent crimes have been declining since the early 1990s, and in 2017 the police-reported crime rate for property crime stood at 1,663 per 100,000—down 57 per cent from 2007 (Allen 2018). Yet, these crimes still account for the greatest proportion of all youth crime. For example, the most frequent criminal offences committed by youth in 2017 were theft of $5000 or

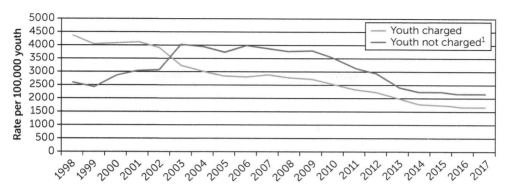

Figure 2.4 Youth Accused of Crime, Canada, 1998 to 2017

Note: Data is based on the number of youth aged 12 to 17 years who were either charged (or recommended for charging) by police or diverted from the formal criminal justice system through the use of warnings, cautions, referrals to community programs, etc. Rates are calculated on the basis of 100,000 youth population. Populations are based on July 1st estimates from Statistics Canada, Demography Division.

Source: Allen 2018, Chart 17.

under (776 accused per 100,000 youth), followed by common assault and then mischief (Allen 2018). However, as shown in Figure 2.4, the CSI for non-violent crime has steady declined since 2007, while for violent crime the CSI has been increasing slightly each year since 2014. As reported by Dauvergne (2013), the drop in property crime can be explained by a notable decline in the rate for frauds and break-ins, as well as a drop in the incident rate of possession of stolen property. As noted above, proportionately, those charged with property crimes tend to fall within the 12- to 13-year-old age spectrum and are mostly young males. Despite the declining rates in youth crime, the federal Conservative government, as indicated in its passage of Bill C-10 in 2012, appeared determined to revamp the YCJA and shift the focus away from rehabilitation toward specific deterrence and retribution (Dauvergne 2013; see also Chapter 3).

Again, as is evidenced by any of the characteristics regarding the nature and extent of youth crime, there is considerable variation across the country as well as among the different crime categories. For example, while property/non-violent crimes have been going down, certain types of illicit drug offences and drug possession have been going up. Between 1996 and 2006, cocaine charges increased 135 per cent, while "other" drug offences went up 156 per cent over the same period. Only heroin-related offences dropped (i.e., 56 per cent) between 1996 and 2006, but they increased 156 per cent from 2005 to 2006 ("Youth Crimes Reported to Police" 2009). However, between 2007 and 2017, the number of cases of drug offences declined 38 per cent (Allen 2018; see also Chapter 10).

In summary, while it is encouraging that the overall youth crime rates declined 44 per cent between 2007 and 2017 (Allen 2018), it is perhaps more disconcerting that violent crime has not followed the same trend. Future researchers should endeavour to better understand and predict such behaviour to more accurately identify relevant risk and protective factors. In addition, we need to be careful when examining crime trends over any period because, for various reasons, some provinces do not report in certain years. In addition, depending on the official source, the numbers are only a valid representation of the youth criminal activity known to the police, the courts, or youth corrections. Hence, such data are a more realistic indicator of youth justice involvement than of youth crime. Yet, we typically rely on such information to construct our "reality" of youth crime.

Youth Court–Related Facts

Court Dispositions

Contrary to public opinion, data from the CCJS show that throughout the 1990s there was a shift toward finding more young offenders guilty and imposing harsher sentencing practices for young offenders. However, since 2004, the trend appears to be moving in a less punitive direction. When examined in more detail (see below) the patterns and trends have not been consistent and are subject to interpretation. For example, the percentage of those youth who were found guilty of a crime and were placed on probation decreased from 68 per cent in 1996/97 to 57 per cent by 2002/03 and was still at 54 per cent in 2016/17 (Miladnovic 2019). And as with other related trends, there remained considerable geographic variation in the use of probation. Keep in mind, however, that official statistics provide no insight into why the variation exists or how the length of probation is determined.

As regularly reflected in the media, Canadians tend to believe we are too lenient when it comes to holding young offenders accountable for their crimes (see Box 2.3). Officially, there would appear to be mixed evidence to support such an opinion. In 1986/87, just over 6 per cent of young offenders were placed in secure custody, while in 1997/98 this portion jumped to 16 per cent and in 2003/04 it peaked at 26.9 per cent (Thomas 2005). However, consistent with the objectives of the YCJA, since 2003/04 fewer youth are being placed in secure custody (see Miladnovic 2019; see also Chapter 3).

Additional evidence would also appear to be reflected in the decline in the number of youth court cases: between 1991/92 and 2002/03, the number of youth court cases declined by 19.8 per cent (CCJS 1992a; Thomas 2005, p. 14). Perhaps what is more telling

---

Box 2.3 | Youth Justice in Action

Can We Learn Something from the Norwegians?

There are at least six different juvenile justice models that can be used to characterize juvenile justice systems around the world (see Winterdyk 2015, p. 6). All the models can be traced back to the welfare paternalistic model of the late 1800s and the justice model that emphasizes ideas of judicial rights and accountability for crimes, but today's models are more complex owing to a variety of factors. Canada has what has been described as a *modified justice model*, and like other countries with a (modified) justice model, it tends to have higher rates of both delinquency and custody (Winterdyk 2015). By contrast, Norway, and to a slightly lesser extent its Scandinavian neighbours, uses a "Nordic" welfare model and has markedly lower offending rates and virtually no juveniles in custody (see Jieru 2013; Winterdyk, Antonopoulos, and Corrado 2016).

Critical Thinking Question
Consider engaging in other cross-cultural comparisons to explore whether there may be other ideas that Canada could consider helping further curb youth offending rates.

is that since the introduction of the YOA and then the YCJA, the incarceration rate has steadily dropped from approximately 110 per 10,000 in 2003/04 to 63 per 10,000 in 2013/14 ("Youth Correctional Statistics" 2013) and declined further to 43 per 10,000 in 2015/16 (Malakieh 2017). This steady decline is largely attributed to the increased use of diversion and other extrajudicial measures, as well as to the fact that, under the YCJA, youth custody sentences have often been followed by a period of probation to ensure some form of supervision on reintegration into the community.

Since the early 1990s and into the "new" millennium, there has been an apparent shift toward greater accountability of young offenders engaged in serious offences. For example, the percentage of youth who received secure custody and supervision orders or sentences of less than one month increased steadily, from 6 per cent in 1986/87 to 30 per cent in 1995/96, and then to 49 per cent in 2003/04 (Thomas 2005). However, after 2008/09, custody and supervision dropped dramatically to around 6 per cent in 2016/17, but these figures again showed considerable variation across the country (Miladinovic 2019). Excluding Nunavut, the percentage of those placed in sentenced custody ranged from a low of around 9.3 per cent in Quebec to a high of 25 per cent in Prince Edward Island. Saskatchewan and Manitoba, which have the highest youth crime rates, had custody rates of 14.1 per cent and 13.5 per cent respectively in 2014/15 (Miladinovic 2016). Even though custody and supervision rates have declined in recent years, between 2015 and 2017 the rates increased in the NWT and in Nunavut (Malakieh 2018). Again, there is no clear evidence as to why the two territories buck the national trend—e.g., –8 per cent from 2015/16 to 2016/17 (see Figure 2.5).

Since 2011/12, the number of youths placed in any type of custody has been the lowest it has been since 1994; although custody sentences decreased steadily following

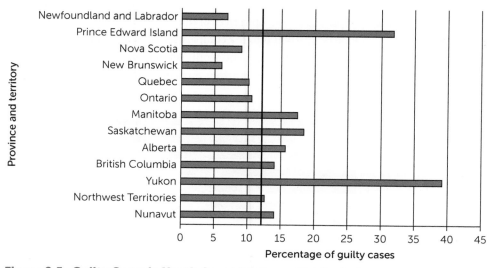

Figure 2.5 Guilty Cases in Youth Court Sentenced to Custody, by Province and Territory, 2016/17

Note: A case is one or more charges against an accused person or company that were processed by the courts at the same time and received a final decision. There are many factors that may influence variations between jurisdictions; therefore, comparisons should be made with caution.

Source: Miladinovic 2019.

the implementation of the YCJA in 2003, rates from 2010 to 2015 have remained stable at around 15 per cent (Miladinovic 2016). In addition to fewer youth being placed in custody, they are also serving shorter sentences. Although some 15 per cent of those case convictions receive secure custody, the median length of sentences in secure custody declined from 94 days in 1992/93 to 40 days in 2014/15 (Miladinovic 2016), but in 2016/17 the median length of sentences increased to 50 days (Miladinovic 2019). In fact, it is perhaps worth noting that the median length of sentence for serious crimes has increased steadily since 2014/15. Although there is no clear explanation for it, the increase is consistent with the intent of section 3(1)(a)(1) of the YCJA.

One of the stated objectives of the YCJA is to ensure that justice is administered more quickly; however, increasingly we hear about delays in our youth justice system. The concern would appear to be somewhat justified. Since the early 1990s, the court case completion time remained steady until the introduction of the YCJA when there was a remarkable spike in the length of time it took to complete a court case.

Again, as with other trends and patterns across the country, there is considerable variation among the provinces and territories in youth crime rates and the proportion of youth charged (see Allen and Superle 2016). In addition, although the provinces and territories are responsible for administering the YCJA, such variations raise concerns about the fairness, efficiency, and effectiveness of youth justice.

After the introduction of the YCJA, the median number of days to complete youth court cases rose steadily, to the point that for 2016/17, the median number was 134 days—almost a month longer than in the year prior to the enactment of the YCJA (see Figure 2.6).

The increase in case processing time that occurred with the introduction of the YCJA may, in part, be because the courts are hearing lengthier cases due to the diversion of less serious cases from the court process (e.g., extrajudicial measures) (Milligan 2010). This, however, is consistent with the principles and objectives of the YCJA (see Chapter 3). Nevertheless, official statistics provide less insight into the complex set of factors that can contribute to case processing delays, including resources and workload, jurisdiction size, case characteristics such as offence type and severity, and various procedural factors (see Chapter 4).

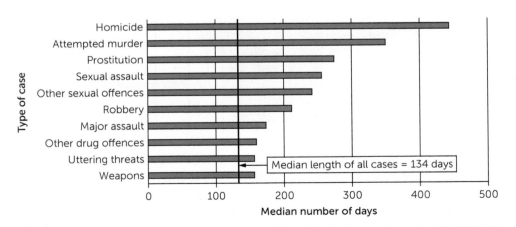

Figure 2.6 Median Number of Days to Complete Youth Court, Canada, 2016/2017
Source: Miladinovic 2019.

Transfers to Adult Court—Adult Sentencing

Under the JDA and during the first few years of the YOA, the respective juvenile justice models have been described as a "tug of war" between *welfare* (i.e., informality, indeterminate sentencing, and a focus on individuals' needs and rehabilitation) and *modified justice* (i.e., due process informality, determinate sentences, and sanctioning of behaviour and provision of treatment) (Winterdyk 2015). As a result, transfers to adult court were relatively infrequent until the early 1990s, when amendments to section 16 of the YOA were introduced to facilitate transfers due to Parliament's concern about the public perception that the YOA was too lenient. The amendments were limited to the most serious offence cases involving youth between the ages of 16 and 17 (unless otherwise ruled by the court).

Between 1986/87 and 1989/90, the number of transfers to adult court dropped from around 80 to approximately 25; however, after the amendments were introduced, the number of transfers increased to a high of 85 cases in 1994. At that point, critics argued that youth incarceration was being overused. In fact, at one time, Canada had the highest youth incarceration rate in the world—even higher than that of the United States. Various scholars began to point out that the transfer process was unfair, too complex, and contributed to lengthy delays (see Thomas 2003).

The current legislation no longer provides for the transfer of youth to adult court, as the focus of the YCJA had shifted toward *rehabilitation* and re-entry into society (i.e., s. 3(1)(a)(ii)). Yet, even though the YCJA no longer includes specific provisions for adult transfer as a measure of denunciation, in 2010, then Conservative Justice Minister Rob Nicholson introduced Bill C-4: dubbed **Sebastien's Law**. The Bill allows young offenders who have committed serious violent acts, or who are serious repeat offenders, to be detained during pre-trial detention. The Bill further allows the courts to consider publishing the names of some young criminals, such as sex offenders, to protect the public from violent young offenders (Perreault 2013). This controversial bill was introduced even though the CSI score for young offenders had been declining since 2001. Nevertheless, one might still want to question the rationale behind Bill C-10, also referred to as the Omnibus Bill, and whether it fulfills or meets its adopted name of the "Safe Streets and Communities Act."

Recidivism

It has been suggested that the success, or failure, of punishment can be measured by **recidivism**, or the rate at which convicted individuals reoffend. However, as reflected in a report by Correctional Service of Canada, the concept is not that straightforward. For example, what is called "recidivism" may also actually refer to return to custody on technical violations and/or new offences (FORUM on Correctional Research 2009). For this section, we will rely on the general definition of recidivism as it relates to instances of individual reoffence.

Recidivism data on young offenders are not regularly recorded. Given the limitations of official information in such cases, official recidivism should perhaps be viewed as "a measure of political success . . . how well (or poorly) our crime control policies are working" (Brantingham and Brantingham 1984, p. 41).

Notwithstanding this cautionary comment, official data show that in the early 1990s about 18.6 per cent of young offenders who appeared in court had five or more prior

Sebastien's Law
The namesake of the law is 19-year-old Sebastien Lacasse, who was beaten and stabbed to death at a 2004 house party in Quebec by a 17-year-old. The incident prompted the courts to consider adult sentences for youth age 14 or older found guilty of serious crimes like murder and aggravated assault. In 2012, the Omnibus Crime Bill was passed, which include an amendment of Section 3(1)(a) of the YCJA to read "protect the public," which encompasses the spirit of Sebastien's Law.

recidivism
Repetition of criminal and/or delinquent behaviour. Recidivism can be measured through official sources or through self-report surveys.

convictions (Moyer 2005). The same report notes that approximately 46 per cent of those charged in youth court had one or more prior convictions since 1984. By the late 1990s, official youth court statistics for 1998/99 showed that nearly 42 per cent of cases with convictions involved repeat offenders (Carriere 2000). The data further reveal that the older a youth gets, the more likely it becomes that he or she has had prior charges. And as with other youth crime facts presented in this chapter, there are also regional variations in recidivism data. For example, if we use data obtained from the Manitoba corrections branch, the reoffending rate for those young offenders who had been incarcerated is a staggering 100 per cent (Morris 2010).

Finally, one of the most comprehensive Canadian studies whose data provides considerable insight into the criminal careers of young persons is the work undertaken by Carrington, Matarazzo, and deSouza (2005). They were involved in the first quasi-national Canadian study of the criminal careers of a birth cohort; it used linked data from the Youth Court Study and Adult Criminal Court Survey for youths born in 1979/80. Their data from six of the provinces paralleled the recidivism results presented above, but in the future, the richness of their data set should provide a deeper understanding of criminal career trends as well as evidence-based insight into how to better address youth crime.

Before we examine the unofficial measures of youth crime, we should reiterate that several real and artificial pitfalls affect the accuracy of official data. Furthermore, official data reflect the action (or inaction) of social control agencies (e.g., police) rather than the real numbers and features of delinquent behaviour. Nevertheless, if we view the data longitudinally, for the most part, the observations remain relatively consistent. If we remain sensitive to some of the pitfalls surrounding the use of official data, these data can provide insight into how official agencies have or have not responded to youth crime over the years.

Measures of Youth Crime: The Unofficial Picture

We will now highlight some of the facts about youth crime based on self-report studies and victimization surveys. These are referred to as *unofficial* sources of data because criminal justice agencies are not required by law to collect this information. Instead, such data are usually compiled by academics and research centres.

Self-Report Surveys

self-report (SR) survey
A social-science questionnaire survey designed to ask respondents to report on their involvement in criminal or delinquent activities.

West (1984, p. 86) suggests that **self-report (SR) surveys** and related scales were developed during the 1940s and 1950s because "police and court statistics were too hopelessly biased." Although self-report studies have become more popular and are proving to be useful in helping to uncover the "dark figure" (i.e., unreported or unrecorded crimes) for certain offences, they are not without their limitations. Some of the more common limitations to conducting SR studies with youth include young people's literacy level and ability to comprehend questions, their short-term versus long-term memory, the extent to which they are willing to give information voluntarily, and the fact that respondents may exaggerate their answers in order to conform—or may even telescope their answers by admitting to something that took place before the actual reference period.

Research methodology textbooks are quick to point out that, despite the problems with SR surveys described above, a great deal of progress has been made in improving the validity and reliability of this method, to the point that SR surveys have gained acceptance as a valid measure of youth crime. Over the years, various studies have repeatedly shown that most youths engage in acts that would have qualified as an offence had these youths been caught. In fact, offending among young persons is far more prevalent than official data or the media report (Le Blanc and Tremblay 1988). Over 80 per cent of youth surveyed admitted to at least one delinquent act, while less than 3 per cent of these acts had been detected by the police. However, one of the first Canadian SR studies to be conducted on young offenders in the 1960s revealed that while offending was common among young people, the nature of offending among middle-class youth was less serious than among lower-class youth (Vaz 1966). Nevertheless, as West (1984) observed in Canada: (1) there is little SR evidence to suggest that youth crime has increased over the years, and (2) the difference between the amount of delinquent activity that males and females engage in is not as dramatic as official data would lead us to believe. For example, West (1984, p. 88) reported the male to female offending ratio to be about 5:1, whereas official statistics indicate that the ratio is between 5:1 and 10:1. In a slightly more recent study, Simourd and Andrews (1996) found the ratio to be 3:1, male to female.

The most recent results from the last National Longitudinal Survey of Children and Youth (NLSCY), which has collected data every two years since 1994, show that about 38 per cent of young persons engaged in a repeated offence in the previous year; of this percentage, almost 70 per cent involved "minor" offences (Department of Justice Canada 2010). However, the NLSCY includes only youth between the ages of 11 and 13 and asks only very general questions about the nature and extent of victimization (see Sprott, Doob, and Jenkins 2001). As of 2019, no further results or updates on the NLSCY have been available.

In addition to examining issues around unreported delinquent behaviour, researchers could also begin to probe specific offence variations, compare demographic relationships, do comparative studies with other countries, and conduct follow-up surveys. Some of these concerns are already being addressed internationally in several ongoing studies involving researchers at the University of Southern California and the Dutch Research and Documentation Centre (see Junger-Tas, Marshall, and Ribeaud 2010; and Junger-Tas 2010). The research involves the largest self-report study of young people in the world: The International Self-Reported Delinquency Survey (ISRD), which started in 2012, marked the beginning of the third international sweep (ISRD 3), involving up to 35 countries and scheduled to be completed in 2019. During the second round of this survey, some 30 countries were included. In 2006, Canada participated for the first time with its International Youth Survey, which was limited to Toronto. Among other findings, the study reported that second-generation immigrant youth remained at higher risk of reporting delinquent acts than their native-born counterparts (Statistics Canada 2009; see also Sprott and Doob 2010).

In summary, while the use of SR surveys has increased, the methodologies and designs used have not been consistent, hence limiting interpretation, comparison, and extrapolation. Nevertheless, SR surveys do serve to provide qualified insight that is not always captured by official statistics.

Victimization and Victimization Surveys

Although society and the media tend to focus on the offences committed by young people, we must remember that young people are also the victims of a great deal of violence, not only from members of their own age group but also from adults. Ironically, compared to adults (see Perreault 2015), there is a dearth of official research of the victimization of young persons. Nevertheless. **victimization survey** data indicate that young people are more likely to be victims of crimes than are adults (Ogrodnik 2010). In fact, several years ago an international report observed that even though 190 countries—including Canada—had signed the United Nations Convention on the Rights of the Child, victimization of children was on the rise (Chin 1998). The report also observed that young people were at greater risk of being victims of assault, sexual assault, and robbery than those over the age of 24 (Perreault 2015).

In the early 1990s, based on information from 13 major police departments across the country, it was determined that nearly one-quarter of all violent crime victims were teenagers (CCJS 1992b). More recent data revealed that most of these victims were males and that children under 12 years of age were most often the victims of common assault or sexual assault, and youth between the ages of 15 and 17 were at the greatest risk of being victims of a violent crime (Ogrodnik 2010).

A review of other Canadian research suggests that victimization rates have continued to increase since 2000. For example, in a 2014 study on the economic impact of just violent crime in Canada, it was estimated that the total cost of victimization of all five crimes was around $12.7 billion, amounting to $376 per Canadian (Hoddenbagh, Zhang, and McDonald 2014). Victimization appears to be common in cases involving bullying and street youth (see Chapter 13) and among Indigenous youth (see Chapter 11). For example, Brzozowski, Taylor-Butts, and Johnson (2006) note that Indigenous youth are three times more likely to be victimized than non-Indigenous youth. Furthermore, results from the 2009 General Social Survey (GSS) indicated that young people (i.e., those ages 15 to 24) were almost 15 times more likely to have been a victim of a violent crime than seniors 65 and older (Perreault and Brennan 2010). Ironically, despite being disproportionately victimized, Scrim (2017, p. 1) points out that "much of the literature on Indigenous [youth] victimization is examined within the framework of family violence given the high prevalence of Indigenous victimization in this context. The victimization of Indigenous children and youth is not often evaluated independently of spousal violence." Furthermore, the GSS only collects data on the victimization of persons 15 years of age or older.

One of the most ambitious Canadian victimization studies, the Canadian Urban Victimization Survey (CUVS), which began in 1983 and was repeated every few years, involved seven major cities and included more than 61,000 interviews. The last cycle was completed in 2004/05 and included 25,000 participants. However, because only youths

---

victimization survey
A social-science questionnaire survey designed to measure the experiences of respondents as victims of crime(s).

15 years of age and older were interviewed for this survey, the results were somewhat limited in terms of adolescents. Using data from the CUVS, Sacco and Johnson (1990) found that

- young persons (composing a 15–24 age group) were the most victimized age group (37 per cent versus 24 per cent for all age groups);
- the age group of 15–24 had the highest incidence of repeat victimization (16 per cent had been victimized two or more times) compared with all other age groups;
- contrary to popular opinion, the difference between males and females in the percentage of victimization was not very large (18 per cent for males and 14 per cent for females, aged 15–24); and
- the group ages 15–24 consistently had higher rates of victimization for personal theft, violent incidents, robbery, sexual assault, and common assault.

In 1999, Paetsch and Bertrand conducted a victimization survey of young persons in Calgary. Their results were generally like those reported by Sacco and Johnson (1990), but they focused more specifically on the relative influence of school. Several of their key findings included the following:

- Overall, males were more likely than females to report they were victimized, but the difference was in type: victimization was greater among those young persons who attended school than those who did not.
- The strongest predictors of victimization were the type of peer group, weak family relations, and socializing more with a youth of similar age than with adults.
- Difficulties in school (e.g., suspension, dropping out, and negative attitude toward school) correlated with the higher likelihood of being victimized.
- Students with psychological challenges were more likely to be victims than those not expressing psychological problems.

Over the years, there have been at least three major *Juristat* reports that have examined children and youth as victims of violent crime. Given the dates of publication, they allow for some general comparisons. When 1996 data (Fitzgerald 1997) is compared to that of 2003 (AuCoin 2005), young females are more often the victims of assault crimes than young males are. More specifically, young females are more likely to be the victims of sexual assault than are young males, and their victimization is more likely to be at the hands of friends and/or acquaintances than at the hands of strangers. Conversely, in terms of physical assault, young males are more likely to be victims than are their female counterparts. However, just as with sexual assault offences, the perpetrators tend to be friends and acquaintances. A more recent *Juristat* report prepared by Ogrodnik (2010) and drawing upon victimization data from the GSS points out that about 80 per cent of "youth aged 15–17 who had been victimized did not report the incident to police" (p. 1). The report indicated that violence against children and youth was highest in Saskatchewan (2136 per 100,000) and lowest in Prince Edward Island (894 per 100,000).

In one of the largest victimization studies of its kind, Tanner and Wortley (2002) found that more than half of the 3400 high school students in Toronto and 400 local street youth surveyed failed to report to an adult that they had been victimized. With the recent concerns surrounding bullying, hazing, and media-profiled cases, the implications of this "code of silence" are alarming; not only is the dark figure for young victims quite large, but there are no clear provisions in the Criminal Code to address the problem. As Tanner and Wortley note, there is no easy solution to the problem of such victimizations. We must educate our youth that it is okay to report such incidents.

Notwithstanding the previous observation, the overall trends of victimization among young persons sharply contrast with what one might be led to believe from most media reports. For example, Mathews (1996) cites research that found that the first time many victimized teens receive attention is when they encounter the legal system because of an offence they have committed. This finding suggests that prior victimization may be a key risk factor for criminal activity, and that we need to look more carefully at the causes underlying youth crime and determine whether accountability and punishment are more important than treatment, counselling, or other forms of support. The underlying assumption is that it is more cost effective and cost efficient to invest and prevent crime from happening than to wait to respond to it (see, for example, "Keeping Communities Safe" 2011).

As we will see in Part III, a notable number of these victimized youth end up turning to a life of drugs, joining gangs, becoming involved in prostitution, and/or following a general path of self-destruction—including suicide (see Navaneelan 2012; Wasserman, Cheng, and Jiang 2005). Consequently, one can ask, do these facts lend support to our need not only to understand the risk factors that lead to victimization but also to learn more about the protective factors that might help to build resiliency among such youth?

Before concluding this section, we should briefly address the relationship between young offenders and young victims of crime. Some academics have argued that these may be artificial categories (see Fagan, Piper, and Cheng 1989), based on the general observation that victims of crime and abused youth are the most likely to become offenders (abusers) themselves. These assertions tend to rely on single disciplinary and theoretical perspectives. For example, why don't all victims become offenders? Why do some non-victims become offenders? Supporters of a victim–offender causality typically subscribe to the influence of the *nurture assumption*, which asserts that anything that goes wrong in our lives can be attributed to our upbringing (see Harris 2006). Thanks in large part to improved research strategies, we can explore the relationship between biological traits and a host of social and psychological factors, as well as how they might more accurately explain the similarities and the differences between young offenders and young victims. As Ezzat Fattah (1991), a Canadian pioneer of victimology, has noted, this will require a new theoretical orientation (see Giannini and Rossi 2009).

Finally, although the quality of victimization and SR studies have improved over the years, they are by no means perfect. The true nature and facts about youth crime will always remain somewhat elusive. After all, youth crime, as something separate from adult crime, has existed ever since the term *delinquency* was coined; and, as reflected above, the trend and patterns have not changed significantly over the years. Nonetheless, as we continue to examine the strengths and weaknesses of data collection, we will better be able to confirm or reject existing theoretical formulations and to develop new ones that have a more practical application in controlling and preventing youth crime. To uncover the dark figure of crime more accurately, researchers can and often do rely on a process that is referred to as **triangulation**. The term refers to the process of using different sources of data to help provide a richer factual accounting of the facts being examined.

triangulation
A research methods technique that involves using more than one source of criminological data to assess the validity of what is being observed. For example, this technique can include combining official crime data with self-report data to obtain a clearer picture of crime or delinquency facts.

Summary

This chapter offers a broad overview of three major sources of information on youth crime in Canada from the pre-Confederation era to the present day. We can make a few observations about these trends. Although there have been periods of increase since 1991 (and based largely on official statistics) there appears to have been a marked decline in official youth crime. However, the true picture of youth crime is not clear because of the nature and quality of our data sources, changes in legislation, shifts in demographics, and so on. The one exception to the declining crime rates among young persons has been violent crimes; this has been particularly evident since the beginning of the new millennium. The overall drop in the severity of youth crime is largely due to declines in property-related crimes. Furthermore, although somewhat controversial, what is perhaps more alarming is the apparent fact that young persons are not only engaging in more serious youth crime but are also becoming active criminals at an earlier age. As well, recidivism rates have steadily risen over the years, the courts have become backlogged, and the public has become increasingly dissatisfied with the judicial system's ability to control the problem. These challenges, in part, explain why we saw several major changes to the former YOA, which was eventually replaced by the YCJA, as well as a move toward alternative solutions, such as restorative justice initiatives, alternative measures programs, and a range of outreach programs (see Chapter 16 for further discussion).

Furthermore, considering that we continue to allocate considerable resources to the attempt to control/manage youth crime with marginal returns, it is even timelier that we refine our crime measurement techniques before we make assumptions about how best to respond to youth crime. Unless we have more reliable and valid data, we risk making poorly informed policy decisions.

Finally, as much as it has become fashionable to focus on identifying and responding to risk factors and on supporting the protective factors and/or helping to build resiliency in our youth (see Rogers, McLachlan, and Roesch 2013; Simich and Andermann 2014), we need to have our facts straight first. While it is relatively easy to identify risk and protective factors associated with youth offending, it is a different matter when it comes to applying and implementing protective factors in intervention. In the meantime, while each measurement method provides useful information, no one technique is better than the other, and until we can improve the quality of how we measure youth crime, the dark figure of crime will remain somewhat elusive for most crimes. Therefore, we are limited to speaking in generalities, and as stated at the beginning of this chapter, there is no clear answer to the question: How serious is youth crime? Hence, as informative and interesting as the data from measuring youth crime might be, the quality of the data remains relatively imprecise and relying on it to predict youth crime trends and patterns remains speculative. Yet, on a positive note, being aware of this fact will hopefully encourage young scholars such as you to embrace and tackle the issue.

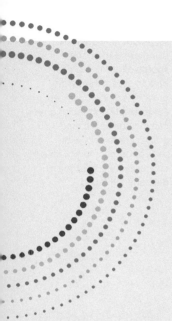

Key Terms

administrative offences

"at-risk" youth

Crime Severity Index (CSI)

dark figure of crime

disposition

official data

recidivism

Sebastien's Law

self-report (SR) survey

triangulation

unofficial data

victimization survey

Review Questions

1. Identify some of the major factors that appear to have led to increased state intervention in the lives of young persons.

2. Identify several advantages and disadvantages of relying on official statistics to provide a picture of youth crime issues.

3. How can self-report studies and victimization surveys be used to better understand youth crime?

4. Review and discuss how violent crime have changed over the years. What explanations can you offer? Try to substantiate your explanations with evidence.

5. What types of youth crime activities appear to be most problematic for Canadians today? Explain your answer and offer a possible creative and constructive solution.

Critical Thinking Questions

1. Why is it considered useful to practice triangulation when describing youth crime trends?

2. Throughout this chapter, we have looked at youth crime trends. Based on the information presented, what do you predict for the future? What, if anything, should society focus on regarding youth crime? Are there particular problem-related areas that might require extra attention?

3. There have been several notable changes in the trends and patterns of youth crime and youth court cases since the enactment of the YCJA. Considering the changes in the trends and patterns since the YCJA came into force, does the Act appear to be

fulfilling its objective in addressing youth crime? What, if any, might be some of the long-term benefits or challenges?

4. This chapter has presented a few cautionary comments about the reliability and validity of youth crime data. Do you agree? If so, how might we begin to improve the collection of such information?

Endnote

1. I would like to acknowledge the assistance of my colleague Dr. Ambrose Leung in updating some of the tables and figures.

References

Allen, M. (2018, July 23). Police-reported crime statistics in Canada, 2017. *Juristat*. Statistics Canada Catalogue No. 85-002-X. Retrieved from https://www150.statcan.gc.ca/n1/pub/85-002-x/2018001/article/54974-eng.htm

Allen, M.K., and Superle, T. (2016). Youth crime in Canada, 2014. *Juristat*. Retrieved from https://www150.statcan.gc.ca/n1/pub/85-002-x/2016001/article/14309-eng.htm

AuCoin, K. (2005). Children and youth as victims of violent crime. *Juristat*, *25*(1). Statistics Canada Catalogue No. 85-002-XIE.

Bala, N., Carrington, P., and Roberts, J. (2012). Implementing youth justice reform: Effects of the Youth Criminal Justice Act. In J. Winterdyk and R. Smandych (Eds), *Youth at risk and youth justice: A Canadian overview* (pp. 80–104). Don Mills, ON: Oxford University Press.

Bartol, C.R., and Bartol, A. (2016). *Criminal behavior: A psychological approach* (11th ed.). Englewood Cliffs, NJ: Prentice-Hall.

Blumstein, A. (1995). Youth violence, guns, and the illicit drug industry. *Journal of Criminal Law and Criminology*, *86*(1), 10.

Boyce, J., Cotter, A., and Perreault, S. (2014). *Police-reported crime statistics in Canada, 2013*. Ottawa: Statistics Canada. Retrieved from http://www.statcan.gc.ca/pub/85-002-x/2014001/article/14040-eng.htm?fpv=2693

Brantingham, P.J., and Brantingham, P.L. (1984). *Patterns in crime*. New York: Macmillan.

Brooks, C., and Schissel, B. (Eds). (2015). *Marginality and condemnation* (3rd ed.). Halifax: Brunswick Books (formerly Fernwood Books).

Brzozowski, J-A., Taylor-Butts, A., and Johnson, S. (2006). Victimization and offending among the Aboriginal population in Canada. *Juristat*, *26*(3). Statistics Canada Catalogue No. 85-002-XIE. Ottawa.

Canadian Centre for Justice Statistics (CCJS). (1992a). Sentencing in youth court, 1986–87 to 1990–91. *Juristat Service Bulletin*, *12*(16).

Canadian Centre for Justice Statistics (CCJS). (1992b). Teenage victims of violent crime. *Juristat Service Bulletin*, *12*(6).

Carriere, D. (2000). Youth court statistics, 1989/90 highlights. *Juristat*, *21*(2). Statistics Canada Catalogue No. 85-002-XIE. Ottawa.

Carrigan, D.O. (1991). *Crime and punishment in Canada: A history*. Toronto: McClelland & Stewart.

Carrigan, D.O. (1998). *Juvenile delinquency in Canada: A history*. Toronto: McClelland & Stewart.

Carrington, P. (1995). Has violent crime increased? Commenting on Corrado and Markwart. *Canadian J. of Criminology*, *37*, 61–73.

Carrington, P.J., Matarazzo, A., and deSouza, P. (2005). *Court careers of a Canadian birth cohort*. Ottawa: Statistics Canada.

Catchpole, R.E.H., and Gretton, H.M. (2003). The predictive validity of risk assessment with violent young offenders. *Criminal Justice and Behavior*, *30*(6), 688–708.

Charron, M. (2009). Neighbourhood characteristics and the distribution of police-reported crime in the city of Toronto. *Crime and Justice Research Series*. Statistics Canada Catalogue No. 85-561-MEI-No. 18. Retrieved from http://www.statcan.gc.ca/pub/85-561-m/85-561-m2009018-eng.htm

Chin, E. (1998, September). Child victimization on the rise. *Crime and Justice International*, p. 13.

Corrado, R., and Markwart, A. (1994). The need to reform the YOA in response to violent young offenders: Confusion, reality or myth? *Canadian Journal of Criminology*, *36*, 343–78.

Dauvergne, M. (2013). Youth court statistics in Canada, 2011/2012. *Juristat*. Ottawa: Statistics Canada. Retrieved from http://www.statcan.gc.ca/pub/85-002-x/2013001/article/11803-eng.htm?fpv=2693

DeMause, L. (Ed). (1988). *The history of childhood*. New York: Peter Bedrick.

Department of Justice Canada. (2010). *The correlates of self-reported delinquency: An analysis of the national longitudinal survey of children and youth.* Retrieved from http://www.justice.gc.ca/eng/rp-pr/fl-lf/famil/rr03_yj2-rr03_jj2/p3.html#sec3_1

Doob, A., and Cesaroni, C. (2004). *Responding to youth crime in Canada.* Toronto: University of Toronto Press.

Fagan, J., Piper, E., and Cheng, Y.T. (1989). Contributions of victimization to delinquency in inner cities. *Journal of Criminal Law and Criminology, 78,* 586–613.

Fattah, E. (1991). *Understanding criminal victimization.* Scarborough, ON: Prentice Hall.

Fetherston, D. (2005). The law and young offenders. In J. Winterdyk (Ed), *Issues and perspectives on young offenders in Canada* (3rd ed.). Toronto: Nelson.

Fitzgerald, R. (1997). Assault against children and youth in the family, 1996. *Juristat, 17*(11). Statistics Canada Catalogue No. 85-002-XIE. Ottawa.

FORUM on Correctional Research. (2009). Retrieved from http://www.csc-scc.gc.ca/research/005008-4000-eng.shtml

Gabor, T. (1999). Trends in youth crime: Some evidence pointing to increases in the severity and volume on the part of young people. *Canadian Journal of Criminology, 41*(3), 385–92.

Giannini, A.M., and Rossi, C. (Eds). (2009). *Victim's care: A handbook.* Milano, Italy: Echo Communications.

Harris, J.R. (2006). *No two alike.* New York: W.W. Norton.

Hoddenbagh, J., Zhang, T, and McDonald, S. (2014). An estimation of economic impact of violent victimization in 2009. Report prepared for Department of Justice Canada. Retrieved from http://www.justice.gc.ca/eng/rp-pr/cj-jp/victim/rr14_01/rr14_01.pdf

Hoge, R.D., and Andrews, D.A. (2010). *Evaluation for risk of violence in juveniles.* New York: Oxford University Press.

Jieru, X. (2013). Learning from the Nordic welfare model: What and how? EU Centre in Singapore. Retrieved from http://aei.pitt.edu/47668/1/WP16-Nordic-welfare-model.pdf

Junger-Tas, J. (2010). The significance of the International Self-report Delinquency Study (ISRD). *European Journal on Criminal Policy and Research, 16*(2), 71–87.

Junger-Tas, J., Marshall, I.H., and Ribeaud, D. (2010). The significance of the International Self-report Delinquency Study. *European Journal of Criminal Policy and Research, 16*(2), 71–87.

Keeping communities safe: Three-year progress report 2008–2011. (2011). Edmonton: Government of Alberta. Retrieved from https://open.alberta.ca/publications/keeping-communities-safe-three-year-progress-report-2008-2011

Keighley, K. (2017). *Police-reported crime statistics in Canada, 2016.* Statistics Canada Catalogue No. 85-002-X. Retrieved from https://www150.statcan.gc.ca/n1/pub/85-002-x/2017001/article/54842-eng.htm

Le Blanc, M., and Tremblay, R.E. (1988). Homeostasis: Social change plus modifications in the basic personality of adolescents' equal stability of hidden delinquency. *International Journal of Adolescence and Youth, 1*(3), 269–91.

Malakieh, J. (2018). Adult and youth correctional statistics in Canada, 2016/2017. *Juristat,* 37 (1). Statistics Canada Catalogue No 85-002-X. Ottawa.

Malakieh, J. (2017). *Youth correctional statistics in Canada, 2015/2016.* Statistics Canada Catalogue No. 85-002-X. Retrieved from https://www150.statcan.gc.ca/n1/pub/85-002-x/2017001/article/14702-eng.htm

Mathews, F. (1996, March). *The invisible boy.* Ottawa: National Clearing House of Family Violence, Health Canada.

Miladnovic, Z. (2019). *Adult criminal and youth court statistics in Canada, 2016–2017.* Ottawa: Statistics Canada. Retrieved from https://www150.statcan.gc.ca/n1/en/pub/85-002-x/2019001/article/00002-eng.pdf?st=lkxudPeY

Miladinovic, Z. (2016). *Youth court statistics in Canada, 2014/2015.* Statistics Canada Catalogue No.85-002-X. Retrieved from https://www150.statcan.gc.ca/n1/pub/85-002-x/2016001/article/14656-eng.htm

Milligan, S. (2010, Summer). *Youth court statistics, 2008/2009.* Statistics Canada Catalogue No. 85-002-XIE. Ottawa. Retrieved from http://www.statcan.gc.ca/pub/85-002-x/2010002/article/11294-eng.htm

Milloy, J.S. (1999). *A national crime: The Canadian government and the residential school system, 1879 to 1986.* Winnipeg: University of Manitoba Press.

Morris, J. (2010, 10 March). *Criminal recidivism rates in Canada.* Retrieved from http://www.employeescreen.com/iqblog/criminal-recidivism-rates-in-canada/

Moyer, S. (2005). *A comparison of case processing under the Young Offenders Act and the first six months of the Youth Criminal Justice Act.* Ottawa: Department of Justice Canada.

Navaneelan, T. (2012). *Suicide rate: An overview.* Ottawa: Statistics Canada. Retrieved from https://www150.statcan.gc.ca/n1/pub/82-624-x/2012001/article/11696-eng.htm

Ogrodnik, L. (2010). Child and youth victims of police-reported violent crime, 2008. *Canadian Centre for Justice Statistics Profile Series,* no. 23. Statistics Canada Catalogue No. 85F0033M.

Oliver, M.E., Stockdale, K.C., and Wormith, J.S. (2009). Risk assessment with young offenders: A meta-analysis of three assessment measures. *Criminal Justice and Behavior, 36:* 329–53.

Paetsch, J.J., and Bertrand, L.D. (1999, Summer). Victimization and delinquency among Canadian youth. *Adolescence, 34*(134), 351–67.

Perreault, S. (2013). *Police-reported crime statistics in Canada, 2012.* Statistics Canada Catalogue No. 85-002-XIE. Ottawa. Retrieved from https://www150.statcan.gc.ca/n1/pub/85-002-x/2013001/article/11854-eng.htm

Perreault, S. (2015). Criminal victimization in Canada, 2014. Statistics Canada, *Juristat*. Retrieved from https://www150.statcan.gc.ca/n1/pub/85-002-x/2015001/article/14241-eng.htm

Perreault, S., and Brennan, S. (2010). *Criminal victimization in Canada, 2009*. Retrieved from https://search.proquest.com/openview/68e2ecf4d17f3eb1670853e09d23b4f1/1?pq-origsite=gscholar&cbl=44168

Platt, A.M. (1977). *The child savers* (2nd ed.). Chicago: University of Chicago Press.

Public Safety Canada. (2012). A statistical snapshot of youth at risk and youth offending in Canada. Retrieved from https://www.publicsafety.gc.ca/cnt/rsrcs/pblctns/ststclsnpsht-yth/index-en.aspx

Rogers, B.J., McLachlan, K., and Roesch, R. (2013). Resilience and enculturation: Strengths among young offenders with Fetal Alcohol Spectrum Disorder. *The First Peoples Child & Family Review*, 8(1). Retrieved from https://fncaringsociety.com/sites/default/files/FPCFRpercent20journalpercent208(1)percent202013_1.pdf#page=62

Sacco, V.F., and Johnson, H. (1990, March). *Patterns of criminal victimization in Canada*. Catalogue No. 11-612E, no. 2. Ottawa: Statistics Canada.

Sanders, T. (2000). Sentencing of young offenders in Canada, 1998/99. *Juristat*, *20*(7). Ottawa: Canadian Centre for Justice Statistics.

Santayana, G. (1905). *The life of reason*. London: Constable.

Schissel, B. (1997). *Blaming children*. Halifax: Fernwood.

Schissel, B. (2006). *Blaming children* (2nd ed.). Halifax: Fernwood.

Scrim, K. (2017). Victims of Crime Research Digest No. 3. Statistics Canada, *Juristat*. Retrieved from http://www.justice.gc.ca/eng/rp-pr/cj-jp/victim/rd3-rr3/p3.html

Siegel, L., and Welsch, B. (2013). *Juvenile delinquency: The core* (5th ed.). Belmont, CA: Wadsworth.

Simich, L., and Andermann, L. (Eds). (2014). *Refuge and resilience*. New York: Springer.

Simourd, L., and Andrews, D. (1996). Correlates of delinquency: A look at gender. In R. Silverman, J. Teevan, and V. Sacco (Eds), *Crime in Canadian society*. Toronto: Harcourt Brace and Co.

Sprott, J.B., and Doob, A.N. (2010). Gender treatment: Girls and treatment order in Bail Court. *Canadian Journal of Criminology and Criminal Justice*, *52*(4), 427–41.

Sprott, J.B., Doob, A.N.M., and Jenkins, J.M. (2001). Problem behaviour and delinquency in children and youth. *Juristat* *21*(4). Statistics Canada Catalogue No. 85-002-XIE. Ottawa.

Statistics Canada. (2009). *Self-report delinquency of immigrant youth: Toronto 2006*. Catalogue No. 81-004-X. Retrieved from http://www.statcan.gc.ca/pub/81-004-x/2008005/article/10799-eng.htm

Statistics Canada. (2015a). Section 1: Crime Severity Index. Retrieved from https://www150.statcan.gc.ca/n1/pub/85-004-x/2009001/part-partie1-eng.htm

Statistics Canada. (2015b). Youth courts, guilty cases by mean and median length of custody. Table 35-10-0044-01. Retrieved from https://www150.statcan.gc.ca/t1/tbl1/en/tv.action?pid=3510004401

Statistics Canada. (2018a). *Canada at a glance 2017: Population*. Retrieved from https://www150.statcan.gc.ca/n1/pub/12-581-x/2017000/pop-eng.htm

Statistics Canada. (2018b). *Evaluation of the Canadian Centre for Justice Statistics Program (2011/2012 to 2015/2016)*. Retrieved from https://www.statcan.gc.ca/eng/about/er/ccjsp

Statsna, K. (2013, 26 July). What's behind Canada's improving crime stats? *CBC News*. Retrieved from http://www.cbc.ca/news/canada/what-s-behind-canada-s-improving-crime-stats-1.1315377

Tanner, J. (2010). *Teenage troubles: Youth and deviance in Canada* (3rd ed.). Toronto: Oxford University Press.

Tanner, J., and Wortley, S. (2002). *Toronto youth crime and victimization survey: Overview report*. Toronto: University of Toronto, Centre of Criminology.

Thomas, J. (2003). Youth court statistics, 2001/02. *Juristat*, *23*(3). Statistics Canada Catalogue No. 85-002-XIE. Ottawa.

Thomas, J. (2005). Youth court statistics, 2003/04. *Juristat*, *25*(4). Statistics Canada Catalogue No. 85-002-XIE. Ottawa.

Vaz, E. (1966). Middle-class adolescents: Self-reported delinquency and youth culture activities. *Canadian Review of Sociology and Anthropology*, *2*: 52–70.

Violent crime in Canada. (2008). Retrieved from http://www.thefreeradical.ca/Violent_crime_in_Canada_fact_sheet.pdf

Wasserman, D., Cheng, Q., and Jiang, G.X. (2005). Global suicide rates among young people aged 15–19. *World Psychiatry*, *4*(2), 114–20.

West, G. (1984). *Young offenders and the state: A Canadian perspective on youth crime*. Toronto: Butterworths.

Winterdyk, J. (Ed.). (2015). *International juvenile justice: Models, trends and patterns*. Boca Raton, FL: CRC Press.

Winterdyk, J. (2020). *Canadian criminology* (4th ed.). Toronto: Oxford University Press.

Winterdyk, J., Antonopoulos, G.A., and Corrado, R. (2016). Reflections on Norway's juvenile justice model: A comparative context. *Crime Prevention and Community Safety*, *18*(2), 105–21.

Youth correctional statistics in Canada, 2013/2014. (2013). *Juristat*. Statistics Canada Catalogue No. 85-002-XIE. Ottawa.

Youth Courts, guilty cases by type of sentence. (2019). Statistics Canada: CANSIM 252-0067.

Youth crimes reported to police for selected Criminal Code offences. (2009). Retrieved from http://www.statcan.gc.ca/daily-quotidien/080516/t080516a-eng.htm

Youth Criminal Justice Act, SC 2002. c. 1.

Understanding the Youth Criminal Justice Act

James Popham and Daniel Antonowicz

3

Overview

This chapter commences with a brief discussion about influential social changes occurring in Canada through the 1990s and their relation to youth crime, precipitating the introduction of the Youth Criminal Justice Act (YCJA) as a replacement to the Young Offenders Act (YOA). Following this discussion, the chapter goes on to describe five major characteristics of the YCJA, linking them to the relevant sections within the Act and describing how they relate to the Canadian Criminal Code or similar pieces of legislation. Finally, the chapter concludes with a retrospective analysis of the YCJA's effectiveness 15 years after its official implementation.

Key Objectives

After reading this chapter, you should be able to:

- Understand the social and political issues that contributed toward the introduction of the YCJA.

- Identify the four declared principles of the YCJA and their interpretation.

- Define core concepts of the YCJA, such as diversion, rehabilitation, and accountability.

- Compare the YCJA to previous forms of youth justice in Canada.

- Identify emerging and future challenges to the application of the YCJA, such as cybercrime.

Introduction

In 1995, a made-for-TV movie called *Little Criminals* (Savath and Surjik 1995) aired on major television networks throughout Canada. The film depicts the story of Des, a troubled 11-year-old boy who often breaks the law while leading a gang of peers, seemingly for the joy of it. The group's adventures include acts of violence, robbery, mischief, and extreme drug use by young children—all occurring without consequence from parents or authorities. As the movie progresses, its message begins to reveal itself through the protagonist's dialogue with others. Specifically, Des is aware that he is immune from criminal sanction in Canada until his twelfth birthday, at which point he will risk custodial punishment for his misdeeds under the Young Offenders Act (YOA).

This film aired at a point in time when significant shifts in the political, social, and technological landscape in Canada (and much of the Western world) had begun to affect public sentiments about crime in general, including that committed by troubled youth (Hartnagel 2004). The rise of the 24-hour news cycle and ubiquitous access to television had altered the way information was conveyed to the public, leading to a hyper-awareness of what one observer called the "lunatic crime rate" (Moynihan 1993). Uncensored imagery of police–public interactions, such as the beating of Rodney King by Los Angeles police and the riots in LA following the exoneration of his attackers, were proof-of-concept for this new manner of reporting. Through the 1990s, the press took on an increasingly sensationalist tone (see Chapter 6 in this textbook), looking for imagery and stories that struck a chord with their viewers—usually one of fear (a tone that largely remains in place today). Unfortunately, the push for winning headlines also had the adverse effect of shaping public opinions, and it ultimately contributed to a culture of fear, helping to inspire a new era of law-and-order responses to crime (Rosenberg and Felman 2008; Simon 2007). For instance, the early to mid-1990s saw the rise of many "tough-on-crime" policies in the United States, such as the infamous three-strike law implemented in California, or the stop-and-frisk policy employed in selected regions of New York City (e.g., Tonry 2011). By 1995, similar legislation had been enacted or updated in 27 other US States.

As discussed by Chris McCormick later in this textbook (Chapter 6), youth crime and delinquency were also subject to this cycle, often called a "moral panic" (Barron and Lacombe 2005; Cohen 1972)—sensationalist headlines garner a disproportionate level of public attention, culminating in heavy-handed, knee-jerk reactions.

Little Criminals articulates how moral panics can affect young people in conflict with the law. Political and media dialogue from the time often called for tougher responses to youth crime in Canada based on assumptions that the youth crime rate was growing and that young people had an easy go of it under the YOA (Alvi 2012; Doob and Cesaroni 2004). Indeed, as Hartnagel (2004) notes, much of the rhetoric about youth crime through the 1990s focused on criticizing the "mollycoddling" (p. 361) of young people by the YOA, with prominent politicians frequently claiming that the Act's inherent protections jeopardized public safety. These claims were further aggravated by a series of high-profile and often sensationalized criminal cases involving youth that distilled into public dialogue about young persons who are predisposed to delinquent and/or anti-social behaviour in Canada (Alvi 2012). This included cases like the murder of 14-year-old Reena Virk in Saanich, BC, at the hands of her teenaged bullies (Jiwani 1999); the playground beating and death of Dmitri (Matti) Barnovski in North York, Ontario (O'Reilly 2002); the murder of Barb Danelesko by three teenage burglars in Edmonton, Alberta (Hogeveen 2007); the murder of an elderly couple, the Toopes, by three youths in Montreal (Faucher 2009); and the random stabbing of Jesse Cadman by a group of youths in Surrey, BC (see Box 3.1). Media-constructed controversies about "out-of-control" youth effectively cast young people as threats to society and provided emotionally charged political talking points. As Royal Roads professor emeritus Bernard Schissel (2006) writes,

> The end result of the condemnation of young people is the continuing scapegoating of youth for political purposes, and, in keeping with the irony of punishment, the alienation of a more uncompromising, more disaffiliated youth population. Increasing punishment, while denying access to civic and political involvement,

Box 3.1 | Youth Justice in Action

Jesse Cadman's Legacy

On October 18, 1992, 16-year-old Jesse Cadman was stabbed during a random encounter with a group of intoxicated youths in Surrey, BC. Jesse and two friends had just exited a bus when they were surrounded by a group of youth and young adults who had recently left a party and who witnesses said were looking for a fight. Eventually, a teenaged boy was tried for Jesse's murder, but the presiding judge did not allow the boy to be tried as an adult. In response to what they felt was a failing youth justice system,

Jesse's parents established an advocacy group called Crime Responsibility and Youth that lobbied for tougher youth criminal legislation in Canada. Chuck Cadman, Jesse's father, eventually ran for public office and was elected as the Reform Party of Canada representative of the Surrey North riding in 1997. During his political career, Cadman championed tougher youth justice strategies, including clauses that could be used to hold parents responsible for the acts of their children.

greatly increases the likelihood of alienation and ultimately of young people's antisocial behaviour. *Despite the political rhetoric to the contrary, we do not collectively consider our children our most valuable resource. In fact, we consider them one of our most dangerous threats* [emphasis added]." (p. 13)

Renewing Youth Justice

By the end of the 1990s, youth crime had been effectively framed as an out-of-control problem that was inadequately curbed by the YOA, requiring a reboot of the youth justice system (Alvi 2012; Doob and Cessaroni 2004). This polemic was codified in a governmental review of its youth justice legislation, communicated through a series of reports and policies. The first of these was a report from the Standing Committee on Justice and Legal Affairs, a task force of members of Parliament who were mandated to review and report on the policies, programs, and expenditure plans of the Department of Justice. In April 1997, the standing committee released a report called *Renewing Youth Justice* to the House of Commons that made 14 recommendations designed to address what they termed "personal and community feelings of insecurity" (Standing Committee on Justice and Legal Affairs 1997, p. 1) stemming from youth crime. Much in line with Schissel's (2003) remarks, the report opened with a statement that reflected popular sentiments about young people in conflict with the law, acknowledging that

> The incidence and impact of youth crime are troubling issues for many Canadians, making them fearful and causing them to take precautions against being victimized. The frequent attempts by those involved in the youth justice system and by knowledgeable observers to reassure Canadians that their communities are among the safest in the world are often of little or no effect. (Standing Committee on Justice and Legal Affairs 1997, p. 1)

While the report's authors would later address the fact that youth criminality was a function of multiple, overlapping causalities, its recommendations nonetheless implied that further changes or even a complete overhaul to the YOA were needed (Hogeveen and Smandych 2001). For example, Recommendation 2 noted that a statement of purpose in future legislative changes should emphasize the fact that "protection of society is the main goal of criminal law and that protection of society, crime prevention and rehabilitation are mutually reinforcing strategies and values that can be effectively applied and realized in dealing with youth offending" (Standing Committee on Justice and Legal Affairs 1997, p. 15). In general, the *Renewing Youth Justice* report reiterated the notion that a separate legal system was needed for young people in conflict with the law, emphasizing the need for a broader range of punitive options beyond imprisonment aimed at improving the rehabilitation of youth in Canada.

Shortly thereafter, in 1998, a response to *Renewing Youth Justice* was issued by Anne McLellan, the then Canadian minister of justice, called *A Strategy for the Renewal of Youth Justice*. This report was predicated on the notion that a Canadian "youth justice system must protect society, reinforce social values and also give youth every opportunity to become productive, responsible citizens" (Department of Justice 1998). Interestingly, it commenced with something of a rebuttal to claims about youth criminality, stating, "Canadians see youth crime as an important issue—even at a time when youth crime rates seem to be falling" (Department of Justice 1998, p. 1). Despite this minor rebuke of contemporary **populism**, the report nonetheless agreed that there was a lack of public confidence in the YOA and promised that "strong and fair" legislation would be created to renew the Canadian youth justice system. The *Strategy* report outlined a series of key directions and specified three main goals: *Prevention and meaningful alternatives*; *meaningful consequences for youth crime*; and *rehabilitation and reintegration* (each goal is further outlined in Box 3.2).

An Act in Respect of Criminal Justice for Young Persons

The first iteration of this legislation appeared in 1999 as federal bill C-68, sponsored by the justice minister. Called "An act in respect of criminal justice for **young persons** and to amend and repeal other Acts" and given the short title Youth Criminal Justice Act (YCJA), it sought to repeal the YOA and implement many of the recommendations that had been set out in the two reports described above. This Act, like the YOA, was intended to define a separate justice system for what the government defined as young people: youths 12 years or older but less than 18. Reflecting public sentiment about "risky children," the bill's opening statement, or preamble, suggested that this new legislation would protect society from youth:

> Whereas society should be protected from youth crime through a youth criminal justice system that commands respect, fosters responsibility and ensures accountability through meaningful consequences and effective rehabilitation and

populism
Appealing to or aiming at what are popular concerns among the public. In the context of criminal justice, this may include tough-on-crime-style legislation, or policy.

young person
The YCJA defines a young person as someone who is at least 12 years old but younger than 18 at the time an offence is committed.

Box 3.2 | Youth Justice in Action

Goals from *A Strategy for the Renewal of Youth Justice*

The report *A Strategy for the Renewal of Youth Justice* provided a set of goals for new youth crime legislation in Canada, focusing on three main points:

1. Prevention and meaningful alternatives: This first goal prioritized the use of community-based crime prevention strategies to address the "root causes" of delinquency, calling for the use of alternative measures in response to non-violent youth crime. The report suggested that these approaches would hold youth accountable for their actions, acknowledge the harm they caused, and instill justice-oriented values.

2. Meaningful consequences for youth crime: The second goal then moved on to explain that youth should be held responsible for their actions, which it rationalized could be accomplished by employing firm measures that aligned with community-based penalties and would foster respect among young people.

3. Rehabilitation and reintegration: The final goal then championed the inclusion of "proper guidance and support" in the administration of justice for young people, which it was argued would help young people return to their communities while also protecting society.

reintegration, and that reserves its most serious intervention for the most serious crimes and reduces the over-reliance on incarceration for non-violent young persons. (Bill C-68, 1999, pmbl.)

The initial draft of the YCJA did not come into effect as it was still under review when the thirty-seventh federal election was called. In the Westminster-style parliamentary system, any legislation is effectively cancelled if it has not received final approval by the state (known as "Royal Assent") when an election is called. However, a revised version of the Act was reintroduced with minor changes in 2001 for the next parliamentary session. Notably, the tone of the preamble had been revised to take a far more holistic approach toward youth justice, reading in part,

> Whereas communities, families, parents and others concerned with the development of young persons should, through multi-disciplinary approaches, take reasonable steps to prevent youth crime by addressing its underlying causes, to respond to the needs of young persons, and to provide guidance and support to those at risk of committing crimes. (Youth Criminal Justice Act 2002, pmbl.)

These changes to the YCJA's preamble denoted a significant departure from earlier language about youth crime. While the changes to Canada's youth justice system had been catalyzed, in part, by populist crime and punishment rhetoric, the Act now indicated that "members of society share a responsibility" for addressing the underlying causes of delinquency. Nonetheless, as Bryan Hogeveen (2005) points out, the YCJA "made [the government's] detestation of youth crime and the harm it causes to victims known in legal form" (p. 75) and formalized punishable young offenders. Shahid Alvi at the University of Ontario Institute of Technology further explains that this legislation symbolized an "astute political compromise" (Alvi 2014, p. 18) as its champions promised that it would simultaneously emphasize preventative measures *and* be tough on youth.

A final version of the YCJA, which included a series of revisions suggested by the House of Commons and the Senate, received Royal Assent in 2002 and came into force for 2003. The Act originally included 164 sections, organized into nine "parts," that set out a detailed set of instructions for dealing with youth in conflict with the law. These sections were oriented around a four-point *declaration of principles* that reinforced the tone of the preamble and the compromise discussed above. Governmental changes over the intervening 15 years have had some impact on the Act's language, but its underlying intention remains one of addressing youth crime through rehabilitative and restorative measures (Smandych and Corrado 2018). In general, the YCJA's declaration of principles sets out that it should (a) establish a youth criminal justice system that promotes protection of the public and prioritizes rehabilitation; (b) administer justice in ways that resonate with the needs of youth; (c) provide for measures that balance restorative justice with accountability; and (d) define special considerations for proceedings against youth (Davis-Barron 2015). (Note: the full version of the declaration is reproduced in Box 3.3).

Box 3.3 | Youth Justice in Action

The Declaration of Principles for the YCJA

Section 3 (1): The following principles apply in this Act:

(a) the youth criminal justice system is intended to protect the public by:

   (i)   holding young persons accountable through measures that are proportionate to the seriousness of the offence and the degree of responsibility of the young person,

   (ii) promoting the rehabilitation and reintegration of young persons who have committed offences, and

   (iii) supporting the prevention of crime by referring young persons to programs or agencies in the community to address the circumstances underlying their offending behaviour;

(b) the criminal justice system for young persons must be separate from that of adults, must be based on the principle of diminished moral blameworthiness or culpability and must emphasize the following:

   (i)   rehabilitation and reintegration,

   (ii) fair and proportionate accountability that is consistent with the greater dependency of young persons and their reduced level of maturity,

   (iii) enhanced procedural protection to ensure that young persons are treated fairly and that their rights, including their right to privacy, are protected,

   (iv) timely intervention that reinforces the link between the offending behaviour and its consequences, and

   (v)   the promptness and speed with which persons responsible for enforcing this Act must act, given young persons' perception of time;

(c) within the limits of fair and proportionate accountability, the measures taken against young persons who commit offences should:

   (i)   reinforce respect for societal values,

   (ii) encourage the repair of harm done to victims and the community,

   (iii) be meaningful for the individual young person given his or her needs and level of development and, where appropriate, involve the parents, the extended family, the community and social or other agencies in the young person's rehabilitation and reintegration, and

   (iv) respect gender, ethnic, cultural and linguistic differences and respond to the needs of aboriginal young persons and of young persons with special requirements; and

(d) special considerations apply in respect of proceedings against young persons and, in particular:

   (i)   young persons have rights and freedoms, such as a right to be heard in the course of and to participate in the processes, other than the decision to prosecute, that lead to decisions that affect them, and young persons have special guarantees of their rights and freedoms,

   (ii) victims should be treated with courtesy, compassion and respect for their dignity and privacy and should suffer the minimum degree of inconvenience as a result of their involvement with the youth criminal justice system,

   (iii) victims should be provided with information about the proceedings and given an opportunity to participate and be heard, and

   (iv) parents should be informed of measures or proceedings involving their children and encouraged to support them in addressing their offending behaviour.

Source: Youth Criminal Justice Act, SC 2002, c 1, http://canlii.ca/t/52hl0

The Youth Criminal Justice Act (YCJA)

While it is difficult to briefly summarize the entirety of the YCJA in a few pages, there are several important points to note. In a practical sense, the YCJA provides a "modified justice model" (Winterdyk 2015, p. 6) that employs due process but encourages informality by prioritizing diversion, sanctioning, and individual-specific needs. As discussed below, the Act establishes a separate set of **youth justice courts** that have exclusive jurisdiction over Canadian youth (defined above) who find themselves in conflict with the law. From a philosophical standpoint, the YCJA was designed to minimize the young person's exposure to the criminal justice system. First, a central component of Canada's approach to youth crime is that of **diversion**, which entails keeping young people out of the criminal justice system through extrajudicial measures. Section 6 of the YCJA instructs police officers to first consider issuing warnings, cautions, or program referrals to youth *before* starting judicial proceedings. While the YOA had a similar section that instructed on *alternative measures*, these alternatives could only be granted after a person was formally arrested and it required that the young person accept responsibility for their actions. As Alvi (2012) explains, this approach was viewed by many scholars and politicians as an example of *net widening*. A second important point to the YCJA is that it was designed to limit the use of incarceration for young people, opting instead for a rehabilitative approach. If the diversionary measures set out above fail to curb criminalized behaviours, judges are instructed to consider proportional responses that reflect seriousness of an offence and the level of responsibility of the accused youth when sentencing them. Again, this contrasts with the YOA, which tended to frame young people as a "special kind of criminal" (Alvi 2012, p. 12) and emphasized individual responsibility. These principles often played out as incarceration, leading to a high number of young people receiving custodial sentences for relatively minor offences (Doob and Sprott 2005).

Finally, amendments made to the law in 2012 also provided an opportunity for the government to re-emphasize the tough-on-crime elements of the Act. For instance, the first declared principle was altered to read as follows:

(a) the youth criminal justice system is intended to protect the public by
   (i) holding young persons accountable through measures that are proportionate to the seriousness of the offence and the degree of responsibility of the young person,
   (ii) promoting the rehabilitation and reintegration of young persons who have committed offences, and
   (iii) supporting the prevention of crime by referring young persons to programs or agencies in the community to address the circumstances underlying their offending behaviour.
(YCJA 2002, s. 3(1)(a))

This change implies greater focus on the individual and emphasizes the YCJA's role in the protection of society. Other changes instructed the police to keep records of extrajudicial measures in order to identify patterns of reoffending, added a new definition of violent offence, and added *specific deterrence* and *denunciation* as principles for sentencing (Alvi 2014).

youth justice court
The court in which young people charged with an offence created by Parliament—usually under the Criminal Code or the Controlled Drugs and Substances Act—appear in order to enter a plea and then to have their trial or be sentenced.

diversion
Responses to transgressions that aim to keep involved parties out of the justice system. Under the YCJA, this includes extrajudicial measures and extrajudicial sanctions.

Despite these changes, the rehabilitative spirit of the YCJA remains. This intentionally contrasted with the YOA, which took an administrative approach to youth justice and established a system that "paid lip service to the possibilities inherent in alternative measures, overemphasized individual responsibilities and traits, and propelled the steady entrenchment of punishment and incarceration" (Alvi 2014, p. 16).

The remainder of this chapter is intended to provide the reader with an overview of the implications and practical realities of the YCJA, broadly organized along the Act's four declared principles. Each of the following sections will begin with a discussion of the relevant principle and its meaning while providing examples of the YCJA in action. The chapter then concludes by introducing contemporary questions about the YCJA that have emerged during the intervening years since its introduction.

Declared Principles of the YCJA

Section 1: Promoting Public Protection through Rehabilitation

Although the first declared principle of the YCJA addresses concepts like public safety and consequences (see discussions above), many researchers have come to interpret it as a confirmation that the Act is designed to emphasize **rehabilitation** (Bala, Carrington, and Roberts 2009; Maurutto and Hannah-Moffat 2007). Indeed, rehabilitation is a longstanding concept within the Canadian approach to youth in conflict with the law, dating back to the late nineteenth century, when humanist social movements paired with the developing field of criminology to champion treatment rather than punishment (Alain and Desrosiers 2016). Bala et al. (2009) explain that the ordering of this statement is intentional, as it implies that rehabilitation *is* a meaningful consequence for harmful actions. They write,

> the long-term protection of the public is seen as the consequence of rehabilitation and accountability, rather than as an independent objective of the youth justice system. This statement directs judges to impose sentences that facilitate the rehabilitation of young offenders, rather than impose custodial sentences that will merely incapacitate them. (p. 136)

Rehabilitation

In a Canadian context, rehabilitation is included as one of the primary goals of our legal and corrections system. For example, section 718(d) of the Criminal Code (1985) explains that one of the primary purposes of sentencing is to assist with rehabilitating offenders, alongside other goals of denouncement, deterrence, separation, reparation, and responsibility. *Rehabilitation* refers to correctional efforts that aim to repair the attitudes and behaviours of an offender. Writing with a little more specificity, Cullen (2007) argues that the rehabilitative ideal focuses on individualized treatment administered at the discretion of experts to achieve meaningful reductions in recidivism. Rehabilitation is mentioned in much the same fashion throughout the YCJA. The most specific mention of it, for instance, is in section 38(1), which sets out the principles for sentencing under the YCJA. This section states that

rehabilitation
An underlying concept in corrections that seeks to repair the harmful attitudes and behaviours of an offender through specialized treatment(s).

The purpose of sentencing under s. 42 (youth sentences) is to hold a young person accountable for an offence through the imposition of just sanctions that have meaningful consequences for the young person and that promote his or her rehabilitation and reintegration into society, thereby contributing to the long-term protection of the public. (YCJA 2002, s. 38(1))

Adding a little more insight, section 38(2)(e)(ii) adds that a sentence imposed upon a young person must "be the one that is most likely to rehabilitate the young person and reintegrate him or her into society." Finally, section 83(1)(b) states that any custodial sentences placed upon youth should have the purpose of "assisting young persons to be rehabilitated and reintegrated into the community as law-abiding citizens, by providing effective programs to young persons in custody and while under supervision in the community."

As mentioned above, the reduction of recidivism (the rate at which individuals reoffend) is a primary goal in rehabilitative approaches to justice. With youth, studies have demonstrated that some of the most effective ways to reduce recidivism is to divert them from the criminal justice system (Wilson and Hoge 2013; Marinos, Innocente, and Goodwin-DeFaria 2017). These diversionary practices help young people avoid the stigma (i.e., labelling theory—see Chapter 5 in this textbook) associated with a criminal record and help them to remain in supportive social situations like their family and school rather than suffering the isolating experiences associated with custodial sentences. Furthermore, research has demonstrated that providing youth with a sense of agency in the diversion process can strengthen their commitment to the prescribed outcomes (Marinos et al. 2017; Hyde, Marinos, and Innocente 2016).

Extrajudicial Measures and Sanctions

Part 1 of the YCJA, which is titled "Extrajudicial Measures" and includes Sections 4 to 12, espouses many of these diversionary concepts and is dedicated toward the rehabilitative principle (see Box 3.4). Broadly defined, *extrajudicial* refers to actions taken outside of the court (Hyde et al. 2016). Thus, in the context of youth justice, extrajudicial measures refer to mechanisms available to authorities that simultaneously reinforce accountability while also largely avoiding entry into the criminal justice system. Sections 4 and 5 of the YJCA identify the principles and objectives for extrajudicial measures, which clearly articulate that they are the preferential form of justice for youth, and section 6 emphatically states that police officers *must* consider extrajudicial measures *before* commencing any other proceedings. Moreover, the YCJA provides an escalating schedule of measures, which include *take no further action*; *warn the young person*; *administer a caution*; and *refer the young person to a program or agency*.

The YCJA also sets out, in section 10, *extrajudicial sanctions*, which are reserved for young people who "cannot be adequately dealt with by a warning, caution, or referral." These are typically more formal applications of the law and can be issued to young people either before or after they have entered the criminal justice system. There are two notable points to this section: First, in order to be granted a sanction, the youth in question must first accept responsibility for their actions. While these conditional admissions cannot

Box 3.4 | Youth Justice in Action

Schedule of Extrajudicial Measures

- **Take no further action**.
- **Warnings**, which are informal warnings given to youth by police officers.
- **Police cautions**, which are more formal warnings given to youth by the police. The YCJA authorizes provinces to establish police cautioning programs. Police cautions may be in the form of a letter from the police to the young person and their parents, or they may involve a process in which the young person and their parents are requested to appear at a police station to talk to a senior police officer.
- **Crown cautions**, which are like police cautions but prosecutors give the caution after the police refer the case to them. Crown cautions are in the form of a letter to the young person and the parents.
- **Referrals**, which are referrals by police officers of young persons to community programs instead of pressing a charge against the youth. The referral may be to a wide range of community resources, including recreation programs and counselling agencies.
- **Extrajudicial sanction**, which is the most formal type of extrajudicial measure, may be issued pre-charge or post-charge. Unlike the other types of extrajudicial measures, they may be used only if the young person admits responsibility for the offending behaviour and consents to be subject to the sanction. The admission of responsibility is not a guilty plea to the alleged offence. In addition, the sanctions must be part of an extrajudicial sanction program designated by the attorney general. If the young person fails to comply with the terms and conditions of the sanction, the case may proceed through the court process. An extrajudicial sanction can be used only if the young person cannot be adequately dealt with by a warning, caution, or referral.

Source: From Kwok, Houwer, HeavyShield, Weatherstone, and Tam 2017, p. 10.

accountability
The YCJA includes provisions intended to ensure meaningful consequences for young people for their actions, with the intent of making clear that they are being held accountable for wrongdoing.

be used as evidence in future trials, they nonetheless force a level of **accountability** onto accused youth. Second, in addition to personal accountability, this section of the YCJA provides a level of agency to youth as well. Specifically, section 10(2)(c) states that a sanction may only be used if "the young person, having been informed of the extrajudicial sanction, fully and freely consents to be subject to it."

Although these sanctions are considered formal applications of the law, they nonetheless afford youth with the opportunity to avoid the traditional court system and the stigma that comes along with it, while being provided with restorative options. In most cases, these sanctions are applied through Youth Justice Committees, which are comprised of community members and tasked by the attorney general of Canada (or their provincial/territorial counterpart) to determine an appropriate sanction for youth in conflict with the law on a case-by-case basis (Marinos and Innocente 2008). The nature and activities of these committees can vary significantly between different jurisdictions within Canada, but their flexible approach to justice generally aligns with the principles of rehabilitation described by Cullen (2007) above, particularly individualized treatment and expert discretion.

As you might expect, this first declared principle provides a great deal of flexibility in terms of interpretation and application of rehabilitation. Maurutto and Hannah-Moffat (2007) warn that the pairing of this level of uncertainty with the YCJA's inclusion of law-and-order language could open the door for excessively punitive risk management–oriented measures under the guise of rehabilitation. Moreover, Hogeveen (2005) explained that the bifurcating line between youths who might be subject to rehabilitation and those who are not remains unclear. These complications are further influenced by the recent incorporation of more tough-on-crime clauses in the YCJA, such as measures related to terrorism, and a broader definition of *violent offence*.

Researchers have suggested that the level of extrajudicial flexibility prescribed in the YCJA may therefore lead to net widening, a situation where overuse of diversionary practices may lead to an increase in the number of interactions between young people and the justice system (Carrington and Schulenberg 2008). Net widening is further explored in Chapter 4 of this textbook, but at this point it's important to understand that well-meaning provisions can have a detrimental effect on justice without adequate and consistent oversight. For instance, the widespread use of pre-sentencing reports (a form of risk assessment tools—see Chapters 2 and 4) may permanently associate a young person with temporary **acute developmental crises**, thus shaping the way justice system members interact with them indefinitely. Nonetheless, as Roach (2003) pointed out, these new measures under the YCJA reflect a growing trend in criminal justice toward community-oriented resolutions to crime. And as noted in Chapter 2, the use of such measures has increased steadily since they were first introduced some 20 years ago.

Section 2: Administer Justice in Ways That Resonate with the Needs of Youth

The second set of declared principles for the YCJA outline the goals of a separate criminal justice system designed specifically for young people. Among these clauses, section 3(1)(b) provides the most direct rationale for a separate system, pointing out that young people have a **diminished moral blameworthiness** or culpability. While these terms are generally (and likely intentionally) vague, they nonetheless imply an underlying assumption that young people are in a developmental stage of their life and thus likely have a different understanding of responsibility, accountability, and consequence than what might otherwise be expected of an adult (Hyde et al. 2016; Soohoo 2016). To this end, the YCJA presumes a standard of "diminished moral blameworthiness or culpability" and proposes that the separate justice system should emphasize proportionate accountability, timely interventions, and procedural protections such as the right to privacy.

This approach extends from the longstanding English common law defence of *doli incapax*, a Latin term that translates to "incapable of crime," which generally held that children under the age of 7 were incapable of differentiating between good and bad. The same principle could be extended to older children (generally 7–13) but was subject to greater scrutiny in the courts and often meant that youths faced adult trials and sentencing (Alain and Desrosiers 2016). For many years *doli incapax* stood as Canada's primary approach to youth crime, a legal tradition inherited from the British Empire, until the

acute developmental crises Rapidly appearing moments of diminished mental health associated with stress of transitioning through stages of life. Youth are particularly prone to these stressors as they attempt to navigate the challenges of young adulthood. While these events are often very distressing, they are generally short-term and they respond well to treatment.

diminished moral blameworthiness Canada's approach to youth justice assumes that young people have not reached the same level of moral and social development as an adult.

doli incapax Literally meaning "incapable of crime," this was a common principle in the English common law tradition that assumed young people (generally younger than 13 years) had the capacity to comprehend the wrongfulness of their actions.

latter half of the nineteenth century, when legal reform began to address more specifically the unique needs of justice-involved youth. To this end, the 1892 consolidation of the Criminal Code included a section specifically dealing with young people under the age of 16, prescribing shorter sentences and lesser fines (Alain and Desrosiers 2016; Brown 1989). Thereafter, a formal and separate system was established for youth in 1908 with the passage of the Juvenile Delinquents Act (JDA), setting in motion a legal tradition that has been carried over through the subsequent YOA and YCJA.

In principle, our modern and separate youth justice system is a continuation of *doli incapax*. As mentioned above, acknowledgement of the diminished cognitive capacity of youths is hardcoded into legislation. This provides an important sheltering effect for what your grandparents might call *youthful indiscretions*: as young people we tend to make poor judgments and engage in risky behaviours with less consideration of our actions. In any case, as Campbell (2015) points out, the Supreme Court of Canada has confirmed that the government and its legislation expects that

> Young people are in a state of "diminished responsibility" and lack a fully developed sense of adult moral judgement. They act without foresight and may lack the intellectual capacity to fully appreciate the consequences of their actions. Diminished blameworthiness and culpability are then related to the degree of a young person's judgement and moral sophistication. (pp. 50–51)

Defining the Youth Criminal Justice System

In terms of application to the law, this principle plays out in several important ways. For instance, Part 2 of the YCJA, called "Organization of Youth Criminal Justice System," outlines a series of instructions for a youth-specific justice system. This includes establishing youth justice courts; the powers of youth justice court judges, clerks, and directors; and the jurisdictions of these courts. Moreover, sections 18 and 19 of the YCJA provide instructions for establishing and operating youth justice committees (described above) and youth justice conferences that can provide advice and expertise to the court when considering a youth in conflict with the law. This second part of the YCJA reflects more than a century of **jurisprudence** on the diminished capacity of young people, and therefore serves to instruct Canada's legal institutions on how to provide a justice system that takes these points into consideration (Campbell 2015; Harris, Weagant, Cole, and Weinper 2004).

Another important point raised under the second declared principle is present in section 3(1)(b)(ii), which explains that "fair and proportionate accountability . . . is consistent with the greater dependency of young persons and their reduced level of maturity." This sentiment is repeated under section 38 of the YCJA, which refers to sentencing. Specifically, section 38(2)(c) states that "the sentence must be proportionate to the seriousness of the offence and the degree of responsibility of the young person for that offence." As Roberts (2004) points out, **proportionality** is a fundamental concept in the Canadian approach to justice. For instance, section 718.1 of the Criminal Code of Canada explains that "a sentence must be proportionate to the gravity of the offence and the degree of responsibility to the offender." In another article, Roberts (1998) explains that this section codifies a retributive *just deserts* penal philosophy that stems from law

jurisprudence
Literally translates to "practical wisdom about the law" and describes the process by which past legal interpretations of policy or law inform present applications.

proportionality
An expectation that the severity of sanctions given for an unlawful act align with the level of harm that the act inflicts. Justice-involved youth in Canada are subject to a qualified version of proportionality that considers their diminished blameworthiness.

and order approaches to justice. While similar language is present in the YCJA, suggesting the similar influence of a **just deserts** philosophy toward youth (Pulis and Sprott 2005), it is tempered by clear explanation that young people should not be committed to custody prior to sentence (s.29[1]), nor as punishment unless specific conditions are met (see Box 3.5 for the specific conditions). The implication here is that when calculating proportionality, the courts must also consider *how* sanctions against young people might best "bring the young person to recognize the wrongfulness of [their] conduct and thereby help to rehabilitate [them] and to reintegrate [them] back into society" (Thornburn 2009, p. 311). In other words, accountability must be incorporated into the formula.

Sanctioning Young People

This second declared principle for the YCJA also clearly denotes that young people should not receive the same sanctions as those faced by adults committing similar acts. This is outlined in section 72 of the Act, which explains that an adult sentence may only be pursued if two conditions are satisfied: (1) that the youth's presumed diminished culpability is rebutted; and (2) that the case can be made that prescribed limitations to youth sentencing (per s. 3[1][b][ii] and s. 38, both described above) are *not* proportional to the misdeeds of the accused (Bala 2015). Interestingly, past versions of the YCJA prescribed a series of so-called *presumptive offences* that necessitated adult sentencing—these included murder, attempted murder, manslaughter, and aggravated sexual assault. However, these presumptions were deemed unconstitutional in a Supreme Court ruling and were repealed from the Act in 2012. Moreover, clauses allowing for the consideration of young people's past encounters with the justice system were also barred from consideration of adult sentencing (Campbell 2015). The implications of these changes made it much more difficult for adult sentencing to be achieved, as the fact that a young person chose to participate in a grievous offence may actually now be construed as evidence of their inability to make mature decisions and thus demonstrative of diminished capacity (Campbell 2015; Bala et al. 2009). As Campbell (2015) notes, the latest version of section 72 now has the impact of making adult sentencing all the rarer among young people in conflict with the law:

> To rebut the presumption that applies to all people under the age of 18, it would seem that there would have to be evidence that this young person was somehow not like others, in terms of his or her maturity of judgment, ability to exercise restraint, and ability to remove himself or herself from an environment that would promote criminal behaviour. (p. 54)

While this approach to youth justice may seem controversial, it nonetheless reinforces the primary rehabilitative mandate of the YCJA, which is presumably better administered through non-custodial sanctioning.

This declared principle also sets out enhanced procedural protections for youth that, in some cases, extend beyond those guaranteed to all Canadians under the Charter of Rights and Freedoms. The most notable of these protections is that of privacy, which is

just deserts
A legal philosophy that gives primacy to retributive punishments over deterrence or rehabilitation.

explicitly set out in section 3(1)(b)(iii) and in Part 6 of the YCJA, titled "Publication, Records and Information." Specifically, under the YCJA personal identifying information about justice-involved youth is protected far beyond what might be expected by an adult: near-absolute prohibitions are placed on the publication of their identities, and specific guidelines restricting the communication of criminal records along official channels are also set out (e.g., when a youth's criminal record can reasonably communicate between investigators, etc.) (Davis-Barron 2015). As Bala (2015) points out, these conditions also play an important role in the reintegrative and rehabilitative principles of the YCJA, sheltering young people from the reach of the press and the potential community-level stigmatization that may come from having their name associated with a crime. This ideal was reinforced by the Supreme Court in *R. v. D.B.*, 2008 SCC 25, which ruled on the presumptive offences described above, as well as measures of privacy. Specifically, the court held that placing the onus on young people to prove why their identity should be protected was deemed unconstitutional, writing that "the stigmatizing and labelling of a young person that can result from publicizing his or her identity sufficiently compromise the psychological security of that young person to engage the security of the person interest protected by section 7 of the *Charter*" (*R. v. D.B.*, 2008, p. 2) (see Box 3.5).

Despite evidence, jurisprudence, and constitutional rights that ascribe the necessity of a justice system that resonates with the needs of youth, these ideals remain ardently contested in public forums. On the one hand, serious criticisms can be levelled against these protections in isolated examples of extreme criminal activity, such as violent murder or sexual assault (Alvi 2014). Conversely, others have argued that these protections do not go far enough, suggesting that the lifting of a publication ban, for instance, is tantamount to making the sentence more severe (*R. v. D.B.* 2008). One of the mechanisms for addressing these concerns rests with the option to impose adult sentences on young people. Should a young person be considered a risk to public security based on the violence of their actions, the Crown Attorney can pursue an adult sentence. Should this option be accepted by the courts, the young person in question will lose their procedural protections,

Box 3.5 | Youth Justice in Action

The case of *R. v. D.B.*

In 2003, a young man (D.B.) engaged in a fight with another youth, Jonathan Romero. D.B. knocked Romero to the ground and punched him, causing Romero to lose consciousness. Romero later died from his injuries and D.B. eventually pleaded guilty to manslaughter. As this charge was originally considered a presumptive offence, D.B. was to be automatically tried as an adult and would subsequently lose his privacy protections.

His trial became a test of the constitutionality of presumptive offences under the YCJA and raised important questions about privacy provisions in the Act. Ultimately, the Supreme Court of Canada ruled in support of D.B.'s case that the reverse-onus nature of the YCJA contravened section 7 of the Canadian Charter of Rights and Freedoms, which protects the right to life, liberty, and security of the person.

including publication bans. Historically, these options have been reserved for the most extreme examples; however, recent amendments to the YCJA passed in 2012 under a Conservative federal government eased the restrictions—for example, young people charged with violent offences may forfeit publication bans on their personal information even if they do not face adult charges (Ontario Federation of Indian Friendship Centres 2011). Despite recent challenges, the substantive body of the YCJA nonetheless remains oriented toward a separate youth system that affords additional, and generally understood to be necessary, protections for justice-involved youth (Davis-Barron 2015).

Section 3: Provide for Measures That Balance Restorative Justice with Accountability

Given the uniquely youth-oriented justice system set out under the YCJA, it should not come as a surprise that it also calls for responses to wrongdoing that align with the circumstances experienced by young people. The previous section of this chapter sets out some of the fundamentals to this principle, such as proportionality, but section 3(1)(c) of the YCJA adds significantly more detail. Specifically, as is discussed above, it clarifies that reinforcing social values and encouraging repair for the harms done must be considered when measures are taken against justice-involved youth; however, it also adds that these measures are meaningful to the individual and respect the diversity of the Canadian population. Davis-Barron (2015) points out that the notion of respect for social values is a new concept under the YCJA, explaining that this new concept is largely undefined, but existing jurisprudence takes into consideration "responsibility, accountability, and respect for people and their property" (p. 167). As Bala (2015) summarizes, the YCJA indicates to legal practitioners that fair and proportionate accountability must be vetted in the recognition that young people often have a diminished understanding of accountability and societal values given their limited life-experiences.

Restorative Justice

Bala (2015) also points out that this clause can also be interpreted as placing emphasis on a restorative approach to justice over other punitive forms. This defined focus represents a dramatic shift in the way young people are sanctioned in Canada. Prior to the YCJA, the provisions of the YOA led to dramatic rise in the number of young people who were incarcerated for relatively minor offences (see Chapter 2 in this textbook). Indeed, as Sprott and Snyder pointed out in 1999, under the YOA Canada had a youth custody rate that was significantly higher than the United States and many other comparable nations. Conversely, the **restorative justice** paradigm holds that the removal of transgressors from the public, or society, to which they belong alienates them from their communities and impedes social healing processes (see Chapter 16 for further discussion). As an alternative approach, then, restorative justice proposes stakeholder inclusion, participatory and deliberative processes, and emphasizing restorative outcomes (Braithwaite and Strang 2017; Crawford and Newburn 2013). This messaging might be familiar to you as it closely aligns with the language set out in section 3(1)(c) of the YCJA. Thus, under the Act, a series of provisions are made that steer the justice system away from incarceration.

restorative justice
A process whereby all the parties with a stake in an offence resolve collectively how to deal with the aftermath of the offence and its implications for the future.

The extent to which this restorative approach should be considered is presented in sections 41 and 42 of the YCJA. Specifically, section 41 instructs the youth court that they should consider convening a conference to seek recommendations on an appropriate sanction (you'll remember from earlier in the chapter that these conferences can be convened to provide advice). Thereafter, section 42(1) explains that

> A youth justice court shall, before imposing a youth sentence, consider any recommendations submitted under s. 41, any pre-sentence report, any representations made by the parties to the proceedings or their counsel or agents and by the parents of the young person, and any other relevant information before the court.

This clause very specifically sets out that "the court consider any recommendations before imposing sentence" and that "the judge, therefore, does not have to order a conference but, if ordered, must consider the outcome" (Hillian, Reitsma-Street, and Hackler 2004, p. 356). From there, section 42(2) sets out a series of 19 sentencing options that follow a continuum of severity, much like the extrajudicial measures described above. These options are outlined in Box 3.4; notably, the sentencing judge must go through 13 options before sentencing a young person to custody (Davis-Barron 2015; Roberts and Bala 2003). Again, reinforcing the notion of restorative justice, many of these sentencing options focus on restitution, whether by fine *or* by providing personal services. Roberts and Bala (2003) point out that these options provide the means by which harms can be redressed, writing,

> As a result of the YCJA, youth justice court judges in Canada now have a wider range of sanctions than most other common law jurisdictions. The increase in the range of available sanctions will, in all likelihood, have two effects: it will help to reduce the number of committals to custody as judges have more options from which to choose, and, at the same time, it may increase the variability of outcome at the sentencing stage. (p. 417)

Interestingly, Doob and Sprott (2004) suggest that the restorative shift under the YCJA is not so much an example of progressive thinking as it is an outcome of the "political youth system" (p. 188). Despite their pessimism, the authors acknowledge that "[Canadian youth justice] legislation has, over time, shifted away from the assumption that the reduction of offending by youths can best be accomplished within the formal youth justice system" (Doob and Sprott 2004, p. 185), and explain that it takes a long-term approach to justice that considers rehabilitation, reintegration, and meaningful consequences as contributors toward protecting the public.

Special Considerations under the YCJA

A second important outcome of this declared principle can be found in its final subsection, which explains that special considerations should be respectful of the diverse makeup of the Canadian population. Legal practitioners are encouraged to consider how a young person's background may, directly or indirectly, have affected their behaviours within the limits of fair and proportionate accountability. Davis-Barron (2015) explains that this subsection is once again an unprecedented addition to Canadian youth justice legislation, and is "designed to raise consciousness, sensitivity, and awareness of decision-makers under the YCJA to the potential relevance in youth cases of gender, ethnicity, culture, language, disability or the young person's [Indigenous] (including Inuit or Métis) heritage" (p. 169). She goes on to explain that this sub-paragraph has influenced several important Supreme Court decisions that have re-emphasized the consideration of justice-involved youths' special needs and has motivated federal and provincial/territorial governments to develop a broader range of programming to address these needs. As with the other principles discussed above, these considerations align with important clauses in the other criminal legislation. For instance, section 718.2(e) of the Criminal Code sets out that the unique circumstances experienced by Indigenous peoples in Canada must be taken into consideration along with all alternatives to custody when sentencing individuals. This section, which was amended in the 1990s, was designed to address the over-representation of Indigenous people in Canada's criminal justice system (Rudin 2012). Subsequent Supreme Court rulings, notably *R v. Gladue*, 1999 1 SCR 688 and *R. v. Ipeelee*, 2012 SCC 13, have significantly strengthened this subsection and codified Indigenous circumstance as a fundamental principle of sentencing (Rudin 2012; see also Chapter 11 in this textbook).

These novel forms of justice present justice-involved youth with an unprecedented number of alternative measures supportive of the YCJA's reintegrative underpinnings and with a greater level of flexibility that reflects the diversity of the Canadian mosaic. For instance, as noted above, young people can be diverted from the justice system beginning with their first encounter with the police. These options carry forward into sentencing options, again set out on the sentencing principles in sections 29 and 38 of the YCJA. Significant challenges remain. For instance, sentencing circles began to gain popularity in contemporary Canadian criminal justice practices beginning in the 1970s, drawing on historic practices of Canada's First Nations, Inuit, and Métis peoples. They have more recently become a part of the spectrum of options available to youth. However, Saskatchewan-based lawyer Charmaine Panko (2005) writes that the use of sentencing circles may result in re-victimization as it calls upon the victim of a crime to recall their experiences in the presence of their aggressor. Similarly, she adds that public engagement in these practices remains a challenge as communities are not always motivated to participate. In a more pragmatic sense, scholars often point out that the holistic principles that underlie alternative practices often conflict with Eurocentric interpretations of justice, leading to public backlash framed in tough-on-crime dialogue (Braithwaite 2002). To a certain extent this raises questions about the employment of alternative measures under the YCJA. If the stated purpose of the Act is to instill social values in youth who come into conflict with the law, should their sanctions be vetted in practices that don't necessarily reflect the ideals of an "industrialized" society? Philosophical questions of morality notwithstanding, numerous studies have demonstrated that restorative justice approaches that balance accountability and reintegration have had positive impact in Canada, particularly for less serious and non-violent offences (Corrado, Markwart, Gronsdahl, and Kimmitt 2016).

Section 4: Providing Additional Special Considerations Unique to Youth

The final declared principle of the YCJA reaffirms the fact that special considerations are required when administering justice to justice-involved youth. Based on what you've read above, this may appear to be common sense, but it bodes well to confirm in writing that a young person should be considered in a similar but different manner from adults in the criminal justice system. Codifying this point provides guidance for future tests of the law and serves to protect young people from inappropriate interpretations such as disproportionate sanctions. The clauses that make up this principle again reiterate the restorative focus of the YCJA by codifying opportunities for participation by stakeholders affected by youth crime, including the accused young person, their parents, and victims of youth crime.

Retaining Youth's Rights as Individuals

The first sub-paragraph provides that young people should be considered as individuals who are protected by the Charter of Rights and Freedoms, giving them the opportunity to participate in many of the functions related to their course through the justice system, and to ultimately shape the decisions that affect them. Thinking back to our earlier discussion of diversion, you should be able to connect the sentiments of sub-paragraph 3(1)(d)(i) with those of 6(1) or 10(2)(d)—specifically, that young people must consent to certain extrajudicial measures. Interestingly, this sub-paragraph does explicitly state one thing: that young people *cannot* be involved in the decision to prosecute. Davis-Barron (2015) clarifies that this clause means there is no legal obligation for the Crown to meet with a young person before deciding to pursue charges; however, she also notes that this clause does not limit the Crown from conferencing with the youth.

Addressing Victims of Crime

The second and third sub-paragraphs then provide allowances for the victims of youth crime. The first of these clauses designates how the youth justice system and its representatives should act toward victims, highlighting dignity, privacy, and minimal inconvenience. The second clause then goes on to impose certain obligations on behalf of the victims, including the provision of information about the proceedings as well as the opportunity to participate. Giles and Jackson (2003) point out that these are new concepts within the domain of Canada's response to youth crime, and moreover, are demonstrative of the conflicting political currents that informed the development of the YCJA. On the one hand, the inclusion of victims in the justice process clearly aligns with the principles of restorative justice provided above as they develop an inclusive, community-oriented approach. Alternatively, Davis-Barron (2015) points out that these clauses can be interpreted as referential to the law-and-order approach to justice of the late 1990s, which often relayed the *destructive* impact of crime on its victims and used this idea to rationalize just-deserts approaches to crime. The lack of clarity in these sub-paragraphs is indicative that section 3(1)(d)(ii) and (iii) might just be lip-service to late-nineties politics, as Davis-Barron (2015) observes:

> These subparagraphs emphasize the respect that should be shown alleged victims during criminal proceedings but they have limited legal significance. They do not

place specific legal obligations on particular criminal justice system participants such as the Crown, for example, to keep victims informed of the status of proceedings, although this is a matter of best practice. (p. 174)

While their roles are somewhat ill-defined, the YCJA nonetheless offers several practical opportunities to engage victims in the youth justice process. Kent Roach (2003) identified both punitive and non-punitive forms of victim involvement under the YCJA, present in both judicial and extrajudicial measures. For instance, he observes that significant inroads to redressing the harms experienced by victims of crime have been made through reconciliation programs in jurisdictions like New Zealand and the United Kingdom, and suggests that "victim–offender reconciliation programs, mediation and restitution programs are particularly well-suited to allowing the harm caused to victims to be acknowledged and repaired" (Roach 2003, p. 976). Returning to Davison-Barron's (2015) critique above, Roach (2003) acknowledges that none of these options are hardcoded into the YCJA as clear rights to participation, but rather as opportunities. For instance, section 157 states that the attorney general of Canada or their provincial/territorial counterparts *may* establish alternative victim-oriented programming such as reconciliation, mediation, or restitution.

Including Parents

The final sub-paragraph of the fourth declared principle then shifts the focus to the parents. Once again, this section is indicative of the YCJA's restorative bent, as it makes clear that parents should be involved in the justice system and be accommodating toward correcting "offending behaviours" (Peterson-Badali and Broeking 2010). The inclusion of parents in the Canadian youth justice system is a notable point when contrasted against historic approaches to youth-involved crime. To contrast, the JDA, which governed youth crime between 1908 and 1984, espoused the doctrine of ***parens patriae*** (parent of the country/fatherland) and assumed that young people who became involved in the justice system had been misguided by their parents. In many cases this led to young people being stripped from their homes and made wards of the state on the assumption that the government's programming would be a suitable replacement to poor parenting (Alain and Desrosiers 2016). While this concept was officially removed from the Canadian justice system with the repeal of the JDA in 1984, vestiges of the "paternal state" principle remained in the YOA, as evidenced by the Act's proneness to incarceration.

On paper, the YCJA brings parents back into the justice processes. The definition of **parent** includes

> ... in respect of a young person, any person who is under a legal duty to provide for the young person or any person who has, in law or in fact, the custody or control of the young person, but does not include a person who has the custody or control of the young person by reason only of proceedings under this Act. (YCJA, 2002, s. 2(1))

Moreover, the Act includes numerous provisions on dealing with parents. For example, a series of sub-paragraphs under section 26 of the YCJA explain that parents are required to be notified in most cases of arrest or detention of a young person. Additionally, the

parens patriae
Literally translates as "parent of the nation;" a historic legal doctrine that the state has a duty to assume the role of a substitute parent in the case of delinquent or dependent children who do not have parents who are able to adequately control or care for them.

parent
The YCJA defines a parent as any person who has a legal duty to provide for a young person, or any person who has custody or control of a young person otherwise.

subsequent paragraph (s. 27) provides a series of instructions that relate to compelling parents to attend a youth court during justice processes, inclusive of the option to issue arrest warrants for parents who fail to attend youth court. Researchers have suggested that this may be more a measure of rhetoric than of practice. In a series of courtroom observations, researchers Michele Peterson-Badali and Julia Broeking (2010) with the Ontario Institute for Studies in Education at the University of Toronto, found that while parents were frequently in attendance at court proceedings, they generally only played passive roles in the court's outcomes.

Looking Forward: The YCJA in the Twenty-First Century

Despite being implemented at the beginning of the twenty-first century, the YCJA is rooted in twentieth-century politics and principles. It was penned at a time when youth crime was perceived to be a rising crisis, a time ignorant of the significant social upheavals that would accompany the post 9/11 North American political climate. The nature of "youth" and "youthfulness" has dramatically shifted in the intervening years since the YCJA's introduction, leaving important questions unanswered and often unaddressed. This final section introduces several of these questions in order to help you develop a critical perspective.

Technology and Youth

When the YCJA took effect in 2004, the Internet was a very different place than what we've grown accustomed to during the intervening 15 years. Social media giants like Facebook and Twitter were still years away from public access, and the smartphone of the day was little more than a pager with email access. The unprecedented social restructuring that has occurred in Canadian society, thanks in large part to the informationalization of culture, could not have been predicted by the YCJA's authors (see Box 3.6). This issue has manifested in several notable ways. First, this new era of broadly accessible personal information has undermined the intent of the privacy clauses within the Act. The near-mandatory requirement of social media participation in youth culture (Marwick and Boyd 2014) ensures that every action and emotion is recorded in a permanent and reproducible manner, accessible across the globe (Lyon 2018). When a young person becomes justice-involved, their personal information, including relationships with their victims, often remains available through these services, allowing the public (and in some cases the press) to access their identifying information (Arvanitidis 2016).

A second issue relates to broader issues in the Canadian criminal justice system. The rapid pace of change occurring online far outpaces legislative processes, meaning that laws governing cyberspace are often ineffective (or wholly absent) (Wadhwa, 2014). This problem is of particular relevance to youth justice as many of the so-called cybercrimes are committed disproportionately by youth, putting the onus on youth courts to develop responses to novel Internet-enabled issues (Holt, Brewer, and Goldsmith 2018; Fric 2014). A third complicating issue arises when the courts *do* implement responses to cyber

Box 3.6 | Youth Justice in Action

Rehtaeh Parsons and the Future of Cybercrime

In 2013, a young Canadian woman named Rehtaeh Parsons attempted suicide. After several days on life support, Rehtaeh's family decided to remove her from the life-sustaining machines, and she passed away on April 7. Rehtaeh had been a student at Cole Harbour District High School in Dartmouth, Nova Scotia. Her suicide was directly connected to a gang rape that occurred in 2011, during which a group of young men sexually assaulted Rehtaeh and took photographs of the incident that were subsequently circulated at her high school. In the aftermath of this tragedy, the Government of Nova Scotia attempted to establish a new law governing cyberspace, with a focus on cyber-bullying. The Cyber Safety Act included provisions that gave school principals and boards more power and responsibility to respond to cyberbullying; established a cyber-investigative civilian unit; and ascribed new anti-cybercrime powers to civil courts such as confiscation of Internet-enabled devices. Despite its positive intentions, the Act was struck down by the Supreme Court of Nova Scotia on the basis that it violated the Charter rights to freedom of expression and liberty.

criminality. Myers and Dhillon (2013) point out that the courts will often provide conditions of release to young people that do not directly connect with their alleged offences, which in some cases include restricting or banning access to the Internet, computers, and cellphones. Considering that access to these technologies is tantamount to a range of essential social services, restricting possession of these devices may contradict the YCJA's stated principle of balanced sanctions. Future applications of justice related to technological deviance will therefore need to take a more granular approach to punishment that avoids considering the Internet and cyber-technologies as zero-sum concepts.

Mental Health

A second unprecedented change in the makeup of Canadian society since the introduction of the YCJA has been public reconsideration of mental health. While these concerns remain subject to significant social stigma, public and private initiatives over the past two decades have worked toward creating greater acknowledgement of the presence of mental health concerns in society (Mackenzie, Erickson, Deane, and Wright 2014). This extends to the youth justice system in Canada, which under the YCJA has drawn attention to the fact that most justice-involved youth meet diagnostic criteria for at least one mental health disorder (Peterson-Badali et al., 2015). Several provisions within the YCJA address mental health needs, providing avenues for assessment as well as remedies such as Intensive Rehabilitative Custody and Supervision (ICRS) and Intensive Support and Supervision Program (ISSP), which is a clinically focused, community-based program. The former program, a form of "therapeutic sentencing," is available for young people convicted of serious violent offences and suffering from mental or emotional disturbances, and entails placing the young person into facilities that provide greater access to rehabilitative resources, such as a mental health facility. The latter is a form of programming administered to young people convicted of less serious offences and entails community-based delivery of support (Bala and Anand 2012).

Despite these provisions, serious questions remain. One of the biggest issues highlighted by researchers is a reluctance among members of the youth criminal justice system to administer these supports. For instance, Peterson-Badali et al. (2015) pointed out that an average of just 117 young people per year receive ISSP, which involves an individualized and comprehensive treatment program. In addition, the young person must be able to function in the community or a living environment with the appropriate supports and supervision. As a result, those who participate in an ISSP represent a small fraction of the number of the youth going through the system. As they note,

> many of the aspects of the YCJA that deal with mental health . . . arise quite infrequently in the day-to-day functioning of the youth justice system. Their rarity stands in contrast to the high prevalence of mental health problems in youth before the courts and suggests that the mental health issues of many young people may not be identified or reflected, at least in a formal way, in their interactions with the youth justice system. (Peterson-Badali et al. 2015, p. 11).

Furthermore, the application of these options may be hindered by the language of the YCJA. As has been explored above in this chapter, the YCJA affords significant protections against incarceration. One such protection is found in section 29(1), which sets out that young people cannot be kept in custody as a substitute for appropriate mental health services—meaning that a judge cannot order a young person to remain in custody for treatment, even when those treatments are not available in the community (Davis-Barron 2015). Peterson-Badali et al. (2015) add that bail or sentencing conditions that include seeking treatment may also present barriers, as requirements such as regular attendance at support meetings may place unreasonable expectations on the youth. As young people become more empowered to voice their mental health concerns, so too will the justice system need to develop a more receptive approach to integrating these considerations into its processes.

Overuse of Pre-trial Custody

A third consideration relates to ongoing issues in the Canadian justice system. While the YCJA has had enormous effects on the reduction of custodial sentencing for justice-involved youth (Bala et al. 2009), scholars have noted that the use of pre-trial custody, or remand, has remained stable since the Act's inception (Sprott 2015). Indeed, Sprott (2015) points out that "there are currently more youths in pretrial detention than there are in sentenced custody—roughly 53% of Canada's incarcerated youth are in custody before they have been legally convicted of anything" (p. 30). This trend is reflective of the so-called remand crisis occurring in the Canadian correctional system, in which an equally high proportion of adults in custody are being held before trial (Mulrooney and Lehmann 2015). This reflects a "modern" and unpredicted change in social perspective that is not adequately addressed by the YCJA, couched in a return to tough-on-crime approaches to justice. Changes made in 2012 by the Conservative federal government, led by Stephen

Harper, re-emphasized the presence of public safety as a priority in the YCJA, which had resonating effects on the interpretation of certain sections. For instance, while section 29(1) (see discussion above) protects young people from pre-trial custody as a form of treatment, 29(2) rationalizes remand if the youth has committed a serious offence or has a pattern of committing similar serious offences; what constitutes a serious offence remains largely undefined (Davis-Barron 2015).

Another viewpoint stems from more "timeless" issues reflective of the formative *parens patriae* approach to youth that has shaped Western notions of justice for centuries. Both Sprott (2015) and Myers and Dhillon (2013) identify consistent patterns in bail conditions, placing requirements on young people with little to no connection with their initial alleged offence—such as the imposition of a curfew when the incident occurred during the day. Again, these conditions tend toward a public safety orientation and have the resulting impact of increasing the rate of charges for "failing to comply with a condition" (Sprott 2015; Sprott and Myers 2011). These approaches to justice pose the risk of net widening, thus undermining the decarceration objectives of the YCJA (Alvi 2012). Moving forward, legal practitioners may need to reconsider how the goals of public safety can be attained while also achieving the YCJA's stated principles.

Summary

This chapter was intended to present the reader with an introductory snapshot of the YCJA and its main principles, contextualized by the historic social environment at the time of the Act's creation. In general, the YCJA presented a renewed emphasis on youth justice designed to steer youth away from the overuse of custody while also addressing public demands for more effective responses and sanctions. To this end, the Act was premised on four distinct principles (promoting public protection through rehabilitation; administering justice in ways that resonate with the needs of youth; providing for measures that balance restorative justice with accountability; and providing additional special considerations unique to youth). These principles established legislation that Alvi (2004) called an "astute compromise," addressing a broad spectrum of political and social perspectives on justice and providing multiple avenues toward rehabilitation. As will be explored throughout the remainder of this book, these compromises have opened major concerns and areas for critique.

Key Terms

accountability
acute developmental crises
diminished moral blameworthiness
diversion
doli incapax
jurisprudence
just deserts
parens patriae

parent
populism
proportionality
rehabilitation
restorative justice
young person
youth justice court

Review Questions

1. What were the social and political issues that contributed to the introduction of the YCJA?

2. What were the goals of the *Strategy for the Renewal of Youth Justice*?

3. What are the four declared principles of the YCJA?

4. What are extrajudicial measures and how does the process work?

5. The YCJA promotes community corrections. Discuss the advantages and disadvantages of "net widening" or increased social control that might result from such programs.

Critical Thinking Questions

1. Should there be a separate justice system in Canada for youth?

2. Analyze the role that citizens and organizations play in Canada's justice system. What are the relative strengths and weaknesses of these roles?

3. Should the privacy rights of young offenders be favoured over the public's right to know the name of the young person charged or convicted under the YCJA?

4. What gaps do you think might become apparent in the YCJA as we progress into the twenty-first century?

5. Can rehabilitative and reintegrative approaches to justice succeed? Why or why not?

6. How should politicians react to public pressure to amend/change the YCJA when they generally feel it does not require change? Try to use examples to develop your argument.

References

Alain, M., and Desrosiers, J. (2016). *A fairly short history of youth criminal justice in Canada*. In M. Alain, R. Corrado, and S. Reid. (Eds), *Implementing and working with the youth criminal justice act across Canada* (pp. 23–40), Toronto: University of Toronto Press.

Alvi, S. (2012). *Youth criminal justice policy in Canada: A critical introduction*. New York: Springer.

Alvi, S. (2014). Recognizing new realities: A left realist perspective on the YCJA. *Canadian Criminal Law Review, 18*(3), 341–58.

Arvanitidis, T. 2016. Publication bans in a Facebook age: How internet vigilantes have challenged the Youth Criminal Justice Act's "secrecy laws" following the 2011 Vancouver Stanley Cup riot. *Canadian Graduate Journal of Sociology and Criminology, 5*(1), 18–32.

Bala, N. (2015). Changing professional culture and reducing use of courts and custody for youth: The Youth Criminal Justice Act and Bill c-10. *Saskatchewan Law Review, 78,* 127–80

Bala, N., and Anand, S. (2012). *Youth criminal justice law* (3rd ed.). Toronto: Irwin Law.

Bala, N., Carrington, P.J., and Roberts, J.V. (2009). Evaluating the Youth Criminal Justice Act after five years: A qualified success. *Canadian Journal of Criminology and Criminal Justice, 51*(2), 131–67.

Barron, C., and Lacombe, D. (2005). Moral panic and the nasty girl. *Canadian Review of Sociology/Revue canadienne de sociologie, 42*(1), 51–69.

Bill C-68. *An act in respect of criminal justice for young persons and to amend and repeal other Acts.* (1999).

Braithwaite, J. (2002). *Restorative justice & responsive regulation*. Oxford, UK: Oxford University Press.

Braithwaite, J., and Strang, H. (2017). *Connecting philosophy and practice*. In H. Strang and J. Braithwaite (Eds), *Restorative Justice* (pp. 203–01). London: Routledge

Brown, D. (1989). *The genesis of the Canadian criminal code of 1892*. Toronto: University of Toronto Press

Campbell, J. (2015). In search of the mature sixteen year old in youth justice court. *Canadian Criminal Law Review, 19*(1), 47–56.

Carrington, P.J., and Schulenberg, J.L. (2008). Structuring police discretion: The effect on referrals to youth court. *Criminal justice policy review, 19*(3), 349–67.

Cohen, S. (1972). *Folk devils and moral panics: The creation of the Mods and Rockers*. London: MacGibbon & Kee.

Corrado, R.R., Markwart, A., Gronsdahl, K., and Kimmitt, A. (2016). The YCJA in British Columbia. In M. Alain, R. Corrado, and S. Reid. (Eds), *Implementing and working with the youth criminal justice act across Canada* (pp. 64–85), Toronto: University of Toronto Press.

Crawford, A., and Newburn, T. (2013). *Youth offending and restorative justice*. London: Willan.

Criminal Code, RSC 1985, c. C-46. Retrieved from http://laws-lois.justice.gc.ca/eng/acts/C-46/

Cullen, F.T. (2007). Make rehabilitation corrections' guiding paradigm. *Criminology & Public Policy, 6*(4), 717–27.

Davis-Barron, S. (2015). *Youth and the criminal law in Canada* (2nd ed.). Toronto: LexisNexis Canada.

Department of Justice. (1998). *A strategy for the renewal of youth justice*. Ottawa: Government of Canada. Retrieved from http://publications.gc.ca/site/eng/9.840078/publication.html

Doob, A.N., and Cesaroni, C. (2004). *Responding to youth crime in Canada*. Toronto: University of Toronto Press.

Doob, A.N., and Sprott, J.B. (2004). Youth justice in Canada. *Crime and Justice, 31*, 185–242.

Doob, A. N., and Sprott, J. B. (2005). *The use of custody under the Youth Criminal Justice Act: A paper prepared for Youth Justice Policy, Department of Justice, Canada*. Ottawa: Department of Justice Canada. Retrieved from http://canada.justice.gc.ca/eng/rp-pr/cj-jp/yj-jj/pdf/doob-sprott.pdf

Faucher, C. (2009). Fear and loathing in the news: a qualitative analysis of Canadian print news coverage of youthful offending in the twentieth century. *Journal of Youth Studies, 12*(4), 439–56.

Fric, A. (2014). Access of evil? Legislating online youth privacy in the information age. *Canadian Journal of Law and Technology, 12*(2), 141–70.

Giles, C., and Jackson, M. (2003). Bill C-7: The new Youth Criminal Justice Act: A darker young offenders act? *International Journal of Comparative and Applied Criminal Justice, 27*(1), 19–38.

Harris, P., Weagant, B., Cole, D., and Weinper, F. (2004). Working "In the Trenches" with the YCJA. *Canadian Journal of Criminology and Criminal Justice, 46*(3), 367–90.

Hartnagel, T.F. (2004). The rhetoric of youth justice in Canada. *Criminal Justice, 4*(4), 355–74.

Hillian, D., Reitsma-Street, M., and Hackler, J. (2004). Conferencing in the Youth Criminal Justice Act of Canada: Policy developments in British Columbia. *Canadian Journal of Criminology and Criminal Justice, 46*(3), 343–66.

Hogeveen, B.R. (2005). Toward "safer" and "better" communities?: Canada's Youth Criminal Justice Act, Aboriginal youth and the processes of exclusion. *Critical Criminology, 13*(3), 287–305.

Hogeveen, B.R. (2007). Youth (and) violence. *Sociology Compass, 1*(2), 463–84.

Hogeveen, B., and Smandych, R. (2001). Origins of the newly proposed Canadian Youth Criminal Justice Act: Political discourse and the perceived crisis in youth crime in the 1990s. In R. Smandych (Ed), *Youth justice: History, legislation and reform* (pp. 144–69), Toronto: Harcourt Canada.

Holt, T.J., Brewer, R., and Goldsmith, A. (2018). Digital drift and the "sense of injustice": Counter-productive policing of youth cybercrime. *Deviant Behavior, 40*(9), 1144–56.

Hyde, C., Marinos, V., and Innocente, N. (2016). What do meaningful consequences and fair and proportionate accountability mean to youth offered extrajudicial sanctions in Ontario? *Canadian Journal of Criminology and Criminal Justice, 58*(2), 194–220.

Jiwani, Y. (1999). Erasing race: The story of Reena Virk. *Canadian Woman Studies, 19*(3), 178.

Kwok, S.M., Houwer, R., HeavyShield, H., Weatherstone, R., and Tam, D. (2017). *Supporting positive outcomes for youth involved with the law*. Toronto, ON: Youth Research and Evaluation eXchange (YouthREX). Retrieved from: https://yorkspace.library.yorku.ca/xmlui/handle/10315/35722

Lyon, D. (2018). *The culture of surveillance*. Cambridge, UK: Polity.

Mackenzie, C., Erickson, J., Deane, F., and Wright, M. (2014). Changes in attitudes toward seeking mental health services: A 40-year cross-temporal meta-analysis. *Clinical Psychology Review 34*(2), 99–106.

Marinos, V., and Innocente, N. (2008). Factors influencing police attitudes towards extrajudicial measures under the youth criminal justice act. *Canadian Journal of Criminology and Criminal Justice, 50*(4), 469–89.

Marinos, V., Innocente, N., and Goodwin-DeFaria, C. (2017). Giving voice: Prioritizing youth agency in criminal justice diversion. In X. Chen, R. Raby, and P. Albanese (Eds), *The sociology of childhood and youth in Canada* (pp. 256–74). Toronto: Canadian Scholars' Press.

Marwick, A.E., and Boyd, D. (2014). Networked privacy: How teenagers negotiate context in social media. *New Media & Society, 16*(7), 1051–67.

Maurutto, P., and Hannah-Moffat, K. (2007). Understanding risk in the context of the Youth Criminal Justice Act. *Canadian Journal of Criminology and Criminal Justice, 49*(4), 465–91.

Moynihan, D.P. (1993). Defining deviancy down. *The American Scholar, 62*(1), 17–30.

Mulrooney, K., and Lehmann, B. (2015). The Pre-cautionary culture: Interpassivity and radical prevention in the making of Canada's remand crisis. *American Society of Criminology Division of Critical Criminology* [Newsletter], *23*(1), 9–11.

Myers, N.M., and Dhillon, S. (2013). The criminal offence of entering any Shoppers Drug Mart in Ontario: Criminalizing ordinary behaviour with youth bail conditions. *Canadian Journal of Criminology and Criminal Justice, 55*(2), 187–214.

O'Reilly, A. (2002). *Mothers and sons: Feminism, masculinity, and the struggle to raise our sons.* London: Routledge.

Ontario Federation of Indian Friendship Centres. (2012). *Submission to the Standing Senate Committee on Legal and Constitutional Affairs in response to bill c-10, Safe Streets and Communities Act.* Toronto: Author.

Panko, C. (2005). *R. v. TDP*: A young offender, his sentencing circle, and the YCJA. *Saskatchewan Law Review, 68*, 455–74.

Peterson-Badali, M., and Broeking, J. (2010). Parents' involvement in the youth justice system: Rhetoric and reality. *Canadian Journal of Criminology and Criminal Justice, 52*(1), 1–27.

Peterson-Badali, M., McCormick, S., Vitopoulos, N., Davis, K., Haqanee, Z., and Skilling, T. (2015). Mental health in the context of Canada's youth justice system. *Canadian Criminal Law Review, 19*(1), 5–20.

Pulis, J., and Sprott, J. (2005). Probation sentences and proportionality under the Young Offenders Act and the Youth Criminal Justice Act. *Canadian Journal of Criminology and Criminal Justice, 47*(4), 709–24.

R. v. D.B., 25 Supreme Court of Canada. (2008).

R. v. Gladue, 1 Supreme Court of Canada 688 (1999).

R. v. Ipeelee, 13 Supreme Court of Canada (2012).

Roach, K. (2003). The role of crime victims under the Youth Criminal Justice Act. *Alberta Law Review 40*(4), 965–89.

Roberts, J. (2004). Harmonizing the sentencing of young and adult offenders: A comparison of the Youth Criminal Justice Act and Part XXIII of the Criminal Code. *Canadian Journal of Criminology and Criminal Justice, 46*(3), 301–26.

Roberts, J.V. (1998). The evolution of penal policy in Canada. *Social Policy & Administration, 32*(4), 420–37.

Roberts, J.V., and Bala, N. (2003). Understanding sentencing under the Youth Criminal Justice Act. *Alberta Law Review, 41*(2), 395–23.

Rosenberg, H., & Feldman, C.S. (2008). *No time to think: The menace of media speed and the 24-hour news cycle.* London: A&C Black.

Rudin, J. (2012). Looking backward, looking forward: The Supreme Court of Canada's decision in *R. v. Ipeelee.* In *The Supreme Court Law Review 57*(2), 375–88.

Savath, P. [producer] and Surjik, S. (1995). *Little criminals* [motion picture]. Canada: Canadian Broadcast Corporation.

Schissel, B. (2006). *Still blaming children: Youth conduct and the politics of child hating.* Winnipeg, MB: Fernwood.

Simon, J. (2007). Rise of the carceral state. *Social Research: An International Quarterly, 74*(2), 471–508.

Smandych, R., and Corrado, R. (2018). "Too bad, so sad": Observations on key outstanding policy challenges of twenty years of youth justice reform in Canada, 1995–2015. *Manitoba Law Journal, 41*(3), 191–240.

Soohoo, C. (2016). You have the right to remain a child: The right to juvenile treatment for youth in conflict with the law. *Columbia Human Rights Law Review, 48*(3), 1–74.

Sprott, J. (2015). How court officials "create" youth crime: The use and consequences of bail conditions. *Canadian Criminal Law Review, 19*(1), 27–39.

Sprott, J.B., and Myers, N.M. (2011). Set up to fail: The unintended consequences of multiple bail conditions. *Canadian Journal of Criminology and Criminal Justice, 53*(4), 404–23.

Sprott, J.B. and Snyder, H.N. (1999). Une comparaison de la délinquance des jeunes au Canada et aux États-Unis. *Criminologie, 32*(2), 55–82.

Standing Committee on Justice and Legal Affairs. (1997). *Renewing youth justice.* 13th report. 35th Parliament, 2nd session.

Thorburn, M. (2009). Accountability and proportionality in youth criminal justice. *Criminal Law Quarterly, 55*, 305–24.

Tonry, M.H. (2011). *Punishing race: A continuing American dilemma.* Oxford: Oxford University Press.

Wadhwa, V. (2014, April 15). "Laws and ethics can't keep pace with technology: Codes we live by, laws, we follow, and computers that move too fast to care." *MIT Technology Review.* Retrieved from http://www.technologyreview.com/view/526401/laws-and-ethics-cant-keep-pace-with-technology

Wilson, H.A., and Hoge, R.D. (2013). Diverting our attention to what works: Evaluating the effectiveness of a youth diversion program. *Youth Violence and Juvenile Justice, 11*(4), 313–31.

Winterdyk, J. (2015). Introduction: Juvenile justice in the international arena. In J. Winterdyk (Ed), *Juvenile justice: International perspectives, models and trends* (pp. 1–24). Boca Raton, FL: CRC Press.

Youth Criminal Justice Act, SC 2002, c. 1.

The Youth Justice System in Action

Adrienne M.F. Peters and Raymond R. Corrado

4

Overview

This chapter provides an overview of how the Canadian youth justice system works in action on a day-to-day basis in different parts of the country. It roughly follows the young offender through various stages of the youth justice process, from the first contact with the police to court appearances, and, in the case of convicted young offenders, into the community and custody-based correctional sanctions. In turn, the chapter also addresses key current challenges and issues faced by professionals working in the youth justice system, including net widening, police racial profiling, the changing scope of the work of probation officers, the challenges of dealing with young offenders with mental disorders, and the increasing and somewhat controversial use of risk assessment and management tools in youth courts and corrections.

Key Objectives

After reading this chapter, you should be able to:

- Understand the different processes undertaken by the police during interactions with young people.
- Outline the overarching procedures followed when a young person becomes formally involved in the youth criminal justice system.
- Identify the roles of key players in the youth justice system, including their relationship to external agency personnel and professionals.
- Comprehend how restorative justice–based principles are integrated into portions of the current Canadian youth justice legislation.
- Explain the more recent approaches utilized across Canada to manage and address the needs of young offenders with mental health issues.
- Discuss the considerations for young offenders once they have completed any imposed disposition(s).
- Outline the larger political and economic systems that have influenced the youth justice system in Canada.

Introduction

As a federal document, the Youth Criminal Justice Act (YCJA) should be applied in a similar way to young offender cases across Canada. Despite its introduction as a progression from the former Young Offenders Act (YOA), the YCJA continues to present challenges in its application owing to the different principles and justice models that were inherent in it, and the diversity that exists in Canada's provinces and territories. Youth, therefore, are processed differently through the Canadian youth criminal justice system at various stages. These differences are not only provincially and territorially based but also municipally based, because of variability in the availability of community-based supports and resources.

Multiple agencies are involved in the processing of young offenders, formally and informally, and in recent years the essential services have been working to enhance their collaborations to provide a fair, meaningful, and holistic response to youth offending. This experience begins with encounters with the police, then moves to community-based services or the courts, the latter of which comprises the involvement of youth defence and Crown lawyers and judges, and possibly goes on to include correctional/custodial or community-based services. Youth justice advocates, youth delegates, community program coordinators, and service providers, Indigenous representatives, and mental health professionals may also be involved at various stages. This chapter outlines each stage of this process and the approaches of different provinces, territories, and municipalities.

Police

In Canada, the entrance of young people into the youth justice system begins with their initial contact with the police. As noted in Chapter 3, children who are under the age of 12 cannot be held criminally responsible for their actions under the YCJA. While the police may be involved in this process at the earliest stages, this terminates quickly given the youth justice system's goal of refraining from stigmatizing and labelling children as delinquent or criminal. If deemed necessary, the police may choose an extralegal response; however, non-criminal community agencies are typically tasked with developing an appropriate response to address the children's behaviour and deter such patterns in the future (see Box 4.1). The goal at this stage is to talk to the young people and explain to them the consequences of their conduct.

The police assume greater discretion and responsibility when responding to youth who are charged with criminal offences than with adults. The options available to the police range from an informal warning to a formal charging of the young person with a criminal offence. British Columbia, Quebec, and New Brunswick, for example, use pre-charge screening during which the police notify the Crown of the interaction and the Crown ensures that an extrajudicial measure or sanction has been considered and deemed inappropriate (Public Prosecution Service of Canada, Government of Canada 2014). The YCJA encourages police to divert young people away from the formal youth justice system

Box 4.1 | Youth Justice in Action

Responding to Children under 12 Years of Age Who Commit Crimes in Canada

An evidence-based program that has been adopted throughout Canada to support children and youth before they become involved in serious delinquency and/or who are not old enough to be charged is Stop Now And Plan (SNAP; Augimeri, Walsh, Levene, and Slater 2015). Established in Ontario in 1985 to support boys under the age of 12 who came into contact with the justice system, SNAP has since expanded and offers support to girls and boys ages 6–11 and their families using a multidisciplinary, gender-based, and culturally sensitive approach that brings together the police, mental health services, child welfare services, Indigenous groups, and community-based programs, and incorporates skills training, cognitive problem solving, self-control and anger management, and family management skills training. SNAP's focus is on early intervention for behavioural problems. There is also a school-based SNAP program for adolescents and a follow-up for youth ages 12–17 to ensure the maintenance of prosocial behaviours instilled through the program. Empirical reviews of SNAP show decreased delinquency (Jiang, Walsh, and Augimeri 2011), and criminal involvement in adulthood (Augimeri, Pepler, Walsh, Jiang, and Dassinger 2010).

Critical Thinking Question
Identify the agencies and stakeholders in your community that could be valuable SNAP partners. What is their role?

by outlining clear objectives related to extrajudicial measures (EJM). Although EJM are applied countrywide, this discretion-based response is exercised the most in the provinces of Quebec and British Columbia (Brennan 2012). Still, for first-time young offenders or youth who have committed minor offences, police are expected to rely on **pre-charge diversion** through EJM, in which the police can decide whether to take no further action and offer the youth an informal caution, make a formal warning to the young person, or make a referral to a community-based agency. Several community programs have been developed and receive funding so the police can develop relationships with these groups and make suitable referrals for young people.

Police officers consider several factors when determining a young person's suitability for extralegal measures. The youth's criminal history and the seriousness of the offence are commonly the most important factors that guide this decision-making (Doob and Chan 1982; McAra and McVie 2007). Police are also more likely to charge male youth and those with higher social disadvantage, while youth who are involved in less serious offences are believed to have the highest probability of completing programming and the lowest probability of reoffending (e.g., Forgays 2008; LeGalbo and Callahan 2001) are the most likely to be diverted.

Across Canada, some police officers have expressed concern regarding the rehabilitative and deterrent effectiveness of diversionary practices. While this issue has been debated in the existing empirical research (see Greene 2011), other officers value the autonomy bestowed through their decision-making powers and ability to rely on their personal experiences in determining the best way to assist youth. In some cases, this decision-making is dictated by broader macro conditions, such as limited financial resources (Ricciardelli, Crichton, Swiss, Spencer, and Adorjan 2017). Although the effectiveness of diversion requires further research, this option has become a bright and successful approach to first-time and minor young offenders. The youth themselves also feel that EJS can be meaningful and hold them accountable, which are each YCJA sentencing principles (Hyde, Marinos, and Innocente 2016).

When the police respond to a call involving a more serious offence and/or repeat young offender, their options become formalized and may include arresting and holding the young person in custody or charging the young person and releasing them into the custody of their parents/legal guardians. Under section 10 of the YCJA, a more formal diversionary measure in the form of a court-ordered extrajudicial sanction (EJS) may be considered during the judicial process. To receive an EJS, the youth must consent to the sanction and accept responsibility for the related offence. One concern associated with this formal regulating of diversionary practices is **net widening**. This may occur because of a rise in the number of EJM/EJSs utilized that surpasses the decline in the number of youths charged or because of the usage of more cautions and community-programming referrals rather than no further action being taken (Carrington and Schulenberg 2005). The 2012 YCJA amendments require that records be kept related to EJM histories so that patterns of police contacts can be observed. Research has yet to determine whether this amendment has been implemented in practice and whether it has had any inadvertent outcomes (e.g., increased police paperwork and net widening).

pre-charge diversion
The diverting of young offenders from the formal youth justice system before they are charged with an offence by the police under the Criminal Code.

net widening
A process whereby, in the attempt to divert individuals away from the criminal justice system, specific policies result instead in a higher number of individuals being formally processed.

On a positive note, police officers today are more educated on youth justice issues than they once were owing to the expansion of criminology and criminal justice programs that are currently offered. Police officers have also developed closer relationships with the courts, thereby improving their knowledge of many procedural aspects of the youth court process and of how they fit into this process (Alain and Hamel 2015; Corrado, Gronsdahl, and Markwart 2015).

Racial and Social Profiling

Despite these promising developments in police education and community partnerships, the police and youth justice system still need to achieve considerable progress in response to Indigenous and minority youth. Many police agencies have been criticized in recent years for practices that involve the social or **racial profiling** of certain groups, particularly youth who are experiencing homelessness, those who are black, or those of Indigenous heritage. This is reflected in the 1990 case of Neil Stonechild, a 17-year-old youth from Saskatoon who was taken into police custody by the Saskatoon Police Service and driven to the outskirts of the city, where he was left outside in −28°C weather; he consequently died of hypothermia. A Commission of Inquiry underscored the problematic relations between the police and Indigenous people in Saskatchewan (Wright 2004). In addition to recommendations to strengthen family supports, community development, and the reliance on alternatives to formal sanctions for youth (Savarese 2015), the police in Saskatchewan expanded training on cultural diversity, modified their complaint process, and initiated ongoing efforts to recruit and hire Indigenous service members (Government of Canada 2006).

Racial profiling is still a contentious issue in police practice discussions. Extending the work of Wortley and Tanner (2003), which revealed that black youth were more likely to be stopped and questioned by the police than were white, Asian, and South Asian youth, Fitzgerald and Carrington's (2011) research corroborated the disproportionate minority police contact results. After controlling for several key "risk factors" for delinquency (e.g., supervision, peers, neighbourhood), they found that the category of "high-risk visible minority youth" was more likely to have police contact compared to other visible minority youth and white youth. Similarly, increased delinquency involvement did not explain the increased police contacts. These studies offer support for the differential treatment hypothesis; still, continued research is needed on racial profiling across Canada.

Some police agencies maintain that racial profiling is not a strategy based on prejudices against certain groups, but that it instead is a technique used to guide police decision-making (Satzewich and Shaffir 2009).

Nevertheless, police services in Ontario have implemented new street-check procedures; one strategy is to provide individuals who have been stopped with a check receipt, which is intended to prevent the repeated over-targeting of certain individuals and/or groups (see Kempa 2013; Rankin 2012). Other important strategies are for police agencies to acknowledge the past relationships and poor treatment from the police (Cao 2014); invest greater resources in developing relationships and trust with members in the community; and recruit/train more officers who reflect the cultural, ethnic, and social diversity of individuals and groups in the communities they service.

racial profiling
The increased surveillance of certain racial groups or culturally distinct neighbourhoods by the police that cannot be explained by such groups' actual increased involvement in criminal activities.

Box 4.2 | Youth Justice in Action

REACH Edmonton—Police and Youth Engagement Program (PYEP)

To reduce negative interactions between young people and the police, community organizations throughout Canada have developed programs to improve police perceptions and interactions. One example is the Police and Youth Engagement Program (PYEP), a two-week, youth-driven program that has been offered through REACH Edmonton since 2014. The PYEP brings together young people, Edmonton Police Service members, and stakeholders to promote positive relationships between youth and the police in ethnocultural communities. The program seeks to enhance young people's trust in the police, particularly for immigrant and refugee youth, through activities such as learning about the law and local crime, joining the police for beat walks, and playing sports. Referrals can be made by community leaders, as well as by young people who have previously completed PYEP; some young people who completed the program have also returned to act as youth leaders and coordinators.

The results of a 2017 outcome evaluation of PYEP including at least 64 PYEP stakeholders (i.e., students, youth leaders, youth coordinators, parents, organizational partners, and community leaders) demonstrated that there was a careful matching of police officers, leaders, and youth that fostered strong relationships and a positive learning environment (Wolbeck, Minke, and Larsson 2018). It found that the program content was well organized and in alignment with the outcome goals of the course, and an attendance policy—by which students received high-school credits upon PYEP completion—was effective. Following program completion, a higher proportion of youth indicated they would feel comfortable asking for help if needed, and as well, their parents' perceptions of and trust in the police improved. The PYEP was also shown to provide youth leaders and coordinators with important skills that were readily transferrable to future leadership opportunities, to offer opportunities for professional network building, and to enhance ethnocultural understanding, both of youths' own and other communities' ethnicities and culture. Two challenges that were highlighted in the evaluative review were the potential for divergent ideas about (1) "at-risk" youth, and (2) PYEP's objectives from community partners. The intention of the overarching REACH council is therefore to bridge the needs and goals of these groups (Wolbeck Minke and Larsson 2018).

Critical Thinking Question
How could PYEP expand its participant inclusion criteria and target other young people in their communities? What would be the potential benefit (direct and indirect) of doing this?

Court

Following the initial contact that young people have with the police, the next step in the formal judicial process is court. Youth reach the court stage if the police formally charge them with a Criminal Code offence. At this point, they may be either charged and released or placed in youth detention. In the first scenario, youth are released on judicial interim release or bail. During this release into the community, youth are required to abide by the court's set conditions or risk being placed in custody. In the latter scenario, a youth can be held in custody awaiting a bail hearing, which is required to occur within 24 hours of this arrest. If the youth is not released at the first appearance before the justice of the peace, there is a second opportunity for him or her to be released during a show-cause hearing. For the continued **pre-trial detention** (also known as **remand custody**) of the youth, the court must show that there is concern related to the young person's presence at the next court appearance and that detention in custody would be necessary to ensure this, or that the youth should be detained to protect the public (see Figure 4.1).

pre-trial detention/ remand custody
The detention of a young person who has been charged with a Criminal Code offence in a youth custody facility as the youth awaits his or her trial/next court date.

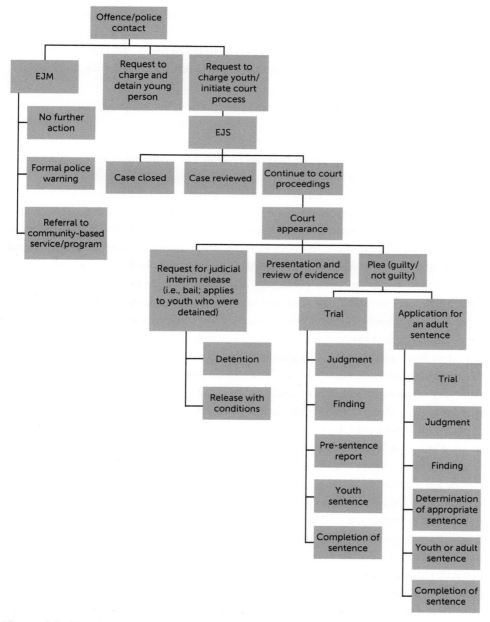

Figure 4.1 The Fundamental Legal/Judicial Process for Young Offenders
Source: Based on Gouvernement du Québec 2009.

There are some restrictions on the use of pre-trial detention. For example, a young person cannot be detained "as a substitute for appropriate child protection, mental health or other social measures" (s. 29(1)) or in cases where the young person could not receive a custodial sentence if found guilty of the offence (s. 29(2)). When youth are released into the community preceding their trial, they are assigned a series of conditions that may prohibit the use of substances and contact with certain individuals, establish a curfew, and/or order the youth to have regular appointments with a youth probation officer (YPO). In some cases, the judge may include an order requiring a money deposit or a **bail surety** to ensure that the youth returns to court on the established date. The youth may also be placed in the care of a responsible person as an alternative to custody and/or if there are potential concerns in returning the young person to his or her home. Finally, the request to be released on bail may be denied, and the youth is returned to custody until the next court appearance.

Since 2012, the YCJA has outlined when pre-trial detention should be used. The new guidelines state that a young person charged with a serious offence (such as a violent offence, or offences that endangered the safety of the public) or who has a history that shows a pattern of outstanding charges or findings of guilt can be detained in a youth custody facility before his or her trial (s.2(1)).

Leading scholars, however, caution about the overuse of pre-trial detention in Canada for youth, a problem that is particularly pronounced in provinces such as Ontario and Manitoba. The YCJA set out to both reduce the use of sentenced custody for youth as well as the use of pre-trial detention; however, it has been unsuccessful in accomplishing the latter. Instead, pre-trial detention's use has increased: in 2003, 35 per cent of incarcerated youth were in pre-trial detention, and in 2015, this percentage had increased to 56 per cent. As suggested by Doob, Sprott, and Webster (2018), "changes in the law do not ensure actual change" (para. 14) and the sections of youth legislation that address pre-trial detention should be strengthened through more explicit instructions on its use. To complement this, increased training and financial resources could improve decision-making and outcomes related to pre-trial detention.

Beyond the determination of bail for a detained youth, the first step in the youth court process is an arraignment, where youth either plead guilty or not guilty to the charges brought against them. If a youth pleads guilty, an appropriate sentence is determined. If a youth pleads not guilty, however, the case will proceed to trial, and a date for this will be set. Under the YCJA, only a youth court judge tries a young person, except in more severe cases in which young offenders have three trial options. When a young person has pled or been found guilty of a crime to which the Crown is seeking an adult sentence, the young person may elect to have either a youth justice court judge without a jury and a **preliminary inquiry**; a trial by judge, without a jury, following a preliminary hearing; or a trial by judge and jury following a preliminary inquiry (s. 67(2)). In some cases, the attorney general may grant permission to override the young person's request and call for a trial by judge and jury for the youth. Preliminary hearings in youth court proceed in the same way they do in adult court.

Before a youth case proceeds to trial or if a young person has pled guilty to an offence, the Crown will determine whether an EJS may be more appropriate than proceeding to trial and a more serious sanction. If this option is not deemed appropriate, a trial will proceed.

bail surety
A promise made by someone connected to the youth to pay the court money if the young person, who was released on bail, fails to return to court on the subsequent court date.

preliminary inquiry
Occurs before the case proceeds to trial and is a hearing in which the judge can determine if there is enough evidence to proceed to trial.

When cases result in a guilty plea or finding, under section 32 of the YCJA youth probation officers are called upon by the courts to assist in the determination of an appropriate sentence through the provision of a **pre-sentence report**. This report details the young person's familial, educational/vocational, social/extracurricular, physical and mental health, and criminal history, as well as additional information on the youth's case, offence, and feelings of remorse. The results of psychological, psychiatric, and educational assessments may also be provided to present a complete and accurate portrayal of the young person (see Chapter 15 for a discussion of how Quebec handles such matters and Figure 4.1).

Under the YCJA, the publication of young offenders' names is prohibited; vulnerable youth victims' names may also be protected from publication. Members of the public can nevertheless attend youth court cases. However, since 2012, judges now have the discretion to lift a publication ban in cases where a young person receives a sentence for a violent offence (i.e., offences that cause, attempt, or threaten to cause bodily harm and endangering the life/safety of another person) or an adult sentence; the objective is to protect the public against any risk the youth poses.

In recent years, most cases that have come before youth courts have been disposed of by way of guilty pleas (see Chapter 2). One explanation for this was that some provinces (i.e., New Brunswick, Quebec, and BC) exercise pre-charge screening. Moyer (2005) also found that guilty verdicts are more common in youth court cases that involve youth who are being charged with multiple offences. The other most common outcomes for youth court cases were the staying, withdrawing, dismissing, or discharging of cases owing to insufficient evidence, referral to extrajudicial measures, or the successful completion of an extrajudicial sanction; this occurred in 41 per cent of youth court cases in 2014/15. In the final two outcomes, 1 per cent of completed youth cases resulted in an acquittal (where the youth was found not guilty), and 1 per cent of cases led to an alternative finding (e.g., the youths were found not criminally responsible or determined unfit to stand trial based on their mental health) (Dauvergne 2013).

In 2014/15, the time needed to complete a youth court case in Canada (i.e., from first court appearance to final court decision) was a median 120 days, which was consistent in comparison to the previous year. The longest court case completion time was found in Newfoundland and Labrador (163 days), and the shortest was in Prince Edward Island (29 days). There are several variables that can affect the speed at which youth court cases are processed. For example, more serious cases require more significant time and resources; thus, as crime trends change, so too does the overall time needed to complete a court case. Also, in provinces such as BC and Newfoundland and Labrodor, youth court judges act as provincial court judges, and the increase in workload because of these cases has negated the impact of the reduction in youth-related cases (Corrado et al. 2015).

The Role of Crown Counsel

Beyond the roles mentioned above that Crown counsel may assume during the youth court process, the Crown may also adopt even greater responsibilities. In some provinces, police officers are not permitted to make determinations on laying formal charges or diverting the young person from the formal system (Corrado et al. 2015); this is the responsibility of Crown counsel, to whom the police file a "Report to Crown Counsel." The prosecutor is

pre-sentence report
Report prepared by a probation officer or youth centre counsellor in Quebec; these written documents present the youth court with detailed information on the young person before his or her sentencing.

tasked with reviewing the report to decide the "likelihood of conviction" (which should be deemed "substantial") and assess the safety of the public and what is "in the public interest." When Crown counsel decides to utilize EJM, the case is referred to a youth probation officer, who conducts an **extrajudicial sanctions** inquiry, or to the identified appropriate community-based program. In cases that are more serious and/or with repeat young offenders, these would typically result in the filing of a formal Crown report in which the Crown makes a final determination.

The Role of Defence Lawyers

The YOA introduced the youth's right to legal representation, which has continued under the YCJA. Legal counsel for a young person can be a representative from Legal Aid, a private lawyer, a duty counsel, or a lawyer who has been appointed by the courts. This last option may be necessary for youth who are not able to obtain their lawyer or who are refused Legal Aid (Doob and Cesaroni 2004). Defence lawyers assist youth in understanding the legal process and, most importantly, their rights. Under the YCJA, defence lawyers have had to familiarize themselves with a series of additional youth-specific sentencing options, including custody and community-based **dispositions**, such as intensive support and supervision program (ISSP) orders, deferred custody and supervision orders (DCSOs), and the intensive rehabilitative custody and supervision (IRCS) program.

The Role of the Youth Court Judge

In most Canadian jurisdictions, youth court judges are provincial court judges who oversee youth cases, in addition to other criminal, family, and civil matters. The definition and role of the youth court judge, as stated in the YCJA (sections 13–14), is set out in the Canadian Criminal Code. The youth court judge assumes a critical role as the leading decision-maker in youth trials and sentencing hearings and as one of the few professionals whose responsibility includes ensuring that the procedures and outcomes are both fair and appropriate. Youth court judges thus make all significant decisions regarding the use of pre-trial detention, the determination of guilt (except in the rare cases youth have a trial by jury), and the final sentence imposed. Some cases also require that the judge request medical and/or psychological assessments (Government of British Columbia n.d.) or youth justice conferences. Additional responsibilities of the judge in youth court are to determine bail conditions and any condition that includes community-based sanctions and to review cases in which young people have violated their conditions.

The Role of Parents/Guardians

Young offenders' parents/guardians also assume responsibilities under the YCJA. These range from their right to be notified that their child has been arrested to supervising their child during any community sentences to supporting their child throughout the court process and assisting them in their rehabilitation (see Chapter 3). Youth also have the right to have their parent(s)/legal guardian present during police questioning. However,

extrajudicial sanctions
Under the YCJA, relatively formal diversion programs that have been authorized by the provincial authorities.

disposition
For young offenders, this is the equivalent of sentencing for adults. Under the YCJA, a disposition should, in theory, be more rehabilitative and/or restorative than retributive.

research has found that parents experience barriers to accessing the youth justice system and court proceedings; because of their single-parent, low-socioeconomic status, many parents are not able to either make it to the police station when their child is arrested or attend any scheduled court hearings (Broeking and Peterson-Badali 2010).

The Role of Youth Probation Officers

Given that most youth who are convicted of an offence will receive some community-based sentence, youth probation officers (YPOs) assume a central role in many justice processes. Probation is the most commonly applied sanction for youth convicted of a Criminal Code offence (Miladinovic 2016; see Chapter 2), and YPOs also supervise youth in the community during their time on bail or while they are serving other community-based sentences (e.g., ISSP orders). Still, youth probation officer caseloads have experienced sizeable reductions in youth cases requiring supervision, falling in some regions in 2011/12 from 30 or more young offenders per youth probation officer to an average of 18 (Corrado et al. 2015).

The maximum possible probation sentence for youth is two years (YCJA 2002); however, the average probation term in 2014/15 was 360 days (Miladinovic 2016). Probation continues to be a favoured sentence because it is viewed as fair and meaningful, can hold the youth accountable, and offers an alternative to the more punitive custodial sentence.

Under the supervision of a youth probation officer/youth delegate, the young person is expected to abide by a series of court-ordered conditions. These conditions always include keeping the peace and being of good behaviour and appearing in court whenever required; they may also include living in a specified location and/or with specified individuals, abiding by a curfew, attending school and/or programs, obtaining employment, abstaining from illicit substances, and regularly reporting to a probation officer. Youth who fail to comply with the probation order assigned to them are often charged with a breach of probation that can eventually result in a custodial sentence (Bala, Carrington, and Roberts 2009).

Youth probation officers play a role in court decision-making, where they act as the communication bridge between judges/lawyers/the courts, corrections, the young person's family, and the young person. They communicate regularly with the court system (e.g., attending court and composing reports) and with corrections (e.g., case management and release planning; Corrado et al. 2015). YPOs balance enforcement and rehabilitative roles by monitoring the youths' compliance with their court order(s), completing screening and risk assessments of the youths, and referring them to appropriate programming and services in the community (Marroney, Quinn, Kinney, and Hufford 2010). Overall YPOs have successfully adapted to the YCJA and have been applying its outlined principles, sanctions, and practices (Kuehn and Corrado 2011).

In some cases, probation conditions are more severe than those received in custody (e.g., some youth have received such restrictive conditions that they are inherently incapable of meeting them). This results in the young person's return to youth court for a reconsideration of a custodial sentence (Alain and Hamel 2015). It is, therefore, the responsibility of the courts to ensure that they balance the goals and principles of the youth sentence.

Other Key Agencies and Stakeholders Involved in the Youth Justice Process

Many young people who have negative contacts with the justice system have also received supports offered through other youth servicing systems. As a result, the critical youth justice professionals presented above are responsible for interacting with professionals and service providers outside the justice system. These external players include those working in child welfare, foster care, social work, and community health/mental health.

"Dually involved" or **crossover youth** have been involved in the protective child welfare system and the youth justice system (Cross-Over Youth Committee 2015), which is attributed to the cumulative exposure to trauma throughout their lifetimes. A large proportion of these young people have encountered challenges in school and received special education services and have also been connected to the mental health system (Wright, Spohn, Chenane, and Juliano 2017). The challenges associated with all these systems present many barriers for these young people and can further exacerbate experiences in the justice system and upon their re-entry into the community.

To mitigate these challenges, youth probation officers, educators, social/justice program administrators, mental health professionals, social workers, and the youth's caregivers participate in ongoing case management meetings to devise collaborative supervision and service plans. The objective is to invite as many relevant agencies to the table as early as possible to collaboratively identify the young person's needs so that the devised care plan is specific to that young person and intersects various environments, including home, school, work, programs/treatment, and the community. Emphasis is placed on incorporating culturally relevant supports, in applicable cases.

Although this is a pervasive difficulty, it is imperative that these professionals and the respective agencies/departments/ministries sustain collaborations during critical developmental and transitional periods, such as during the delicate shift into young adulthood and adult systems. One of the most significant challenges in supporting multi-system youth is the varying age each system has determined to be indicative of "adulthood" or independence, causing an interruption in services offered under the justice system (i.e., 18 years of age) compared to the child welfare system (i.e., 19 years old; BC Representative for Children and Youth 2014; Kovarikova 2017). The main concerns associated with this inconsistency include a breakdown in living accommodations and access to programs and professionals with whom the young person has developed healthy support relationships. There have been cases in Canada in which gaps in or ceasing of services altogether have led to tragic consequences, including victimization/abuse, serious self-harm and substance use, and even death (BC Representative for Children and Youth 2015, 2016).

Many justice and social welfare agencies have made progress working together; however, more formal crossover systems should be implemented, as best as possible, to facilitate effective service provision, enhanced information sharing, coordinated case management, and ongoing support and assistance between professionals (Wright et al. 2017). The Crossover Youth Practice Model in the United States has reduced criminal justice involvement and recidivism among young people (Haight, Bidwell, Seok Choi, and Cho 2016). Some

---

crossover youth
Young people, also referred to as "dually involved" or "multi-system" youth, who become part of the protective child welfare system because of maltreatment, subsequent removal from the home, and placement in foster care, and who later become involved in the youth justice system.

examples of interagency collaborations that exist in Canada are specialized youth courts and probation caseloads, both of which are discussed later in this chapter.

Working with Legislation Beyond the YCJA—Provincial/ Territorial Children/Youth Protection Acts

The YCJA contains several sections related to child welfare and social measures. Section 35 stipulates the conditions under which a youth justice court can make a referral to a child welfare agency to determine whether child welfare services intervention is needed. As discussed throughout this textbook, section 39, subsection 5 is explicit in prohibiting custody as a social measure. Given the previously outlined system crossovers, youth justice personnel also work within the respective child/youth act of their province/territory. Every province and territory has adopted a variation of this type of statute, and several refer to the YCJA, which is especially important regarding section 39, subsection 5. This applies directly to youth court judges, although the police, probation officers, and other justice personnel are also mindful of this in their decision-making. For example, the Child Protection Act (2017) in PEI distinguishes procedures for peace officers when taking a child to a place of safety versus detaining a youth under the YCJA. The Ontario Child and Family Services Act (1990) similarly differentiates what constitutes a residential placement under each act and outlines procedures for committing a child to a secure treatment program. Quebec's Youth Protection Act (1977) includes mention of the use of extrajudicial sanctions. Finally, Alberta's Child, Youth, and Family Enhancement Act (2000) refers to section 35 of the YCJA regarding referral to a child welfare agency.

Sentencing

Although the sentencing principles underlying the YCJA and the variety of sentences handed out by judges have been discussed in Chapter 3, it is essential to devote additional attention to some of the developments and issues surrounding sentencing practices in provincial/territorial youth courts.

At the court stage, youth may receive a reprimand by the youth court judge in which the judge gives a warning to the young person; such a sentence is commonly utilized for minor, first-time offenders and does not include any sanctions. The YCJA offers additional non-sanctioned sentencing options: an absolute discharge or a conditional discharge. In each of these cases, the young person has been found guilty of a minor offence, and it is usually his or her first offence. In the case of an absolute discharge, the judge decides that the offence was not so serious as to warrant the registering of the conviction, and in consideration of the best interests of the young person, as well as the interest of the public, no further actions are taken. Alternatively, in the case of a conditional discharge, the judge assigns a series of conditions to the youth, which he or she must follow in the community. If the young person completes this sentence without breaching the specified conditions in the selected period, the conditional discharge will become an absolute discharge. If the youth does not successfully abide by the conditions set by the court, he or she will be returned to court, where a harsher sentence may be handed down.

Custody-Based Sentences

criminogenic
Situations or environments that cause or exacerbate criminal behaviours. These can even include institutions or programs that have been designed to reduce such behaviours.

A broad body of research literature has shown that custody can be **criminogenic** (e.g., Cullen, Jonson, and Nagin 2011), especially so in the case of low-risk offenders. For this reason, and based on the rehabilitative and reintegrative goals of the YCJA, a custodial sentence is only imposed on a young offender in a select set of circumstances. According to the provisions outlined in section 39 of the Act, custodial sentences can only be imposed for serious violent offences after all other reasonable alternatives have been considered. The expansion of the YCJA's definition of serious offences and violent offences and the Act's inclusion of denunciation and deterrence as youth sentencing principles presented a potential opportunity for the youth justice system to rely on more severe custodial sentences increasingly; however, as of 2019, this appears not to have occurred.

Sentence Lengths

The YCJA establishes the maximum sentence length that a young person can receive, alone or in combination with any of the detailed sentences, as described in section 42, subsections 14, 15, and 16. In addition to the maximum sentences set, there are some rare cases where a young person will reoffend during the time they are serving another sentence. In these situations, the sentence length may be longer than the previously stated maximums. Although it is incredibly uncommon, a young person may be given a life sentence, such as when a youth 16 or 17 years of age has committed murder and has been sentenced as an adult. Parole eligibility is reached after the youth has served 10 years of his or her life sentence.

While the YCJA applies to young people aged 12 to 17, some youth do not reach the sentencing stage of the administrative processing until they have already turned 18 years old. If the young person is age 18 or older during this process and the sentence imposed is less than two years, he or she may be placed in provincial custody. If the sentence imposed is more than two years, however, the youth may be placed in a federal facility. In the case when youth turn 20 years of age while in custody, they are typically moved to an adult facility to serve the remainder of the sentence. If a young person is sentenced as an adult but is under the age of 18, the YCJA stipulates that the young person cannot be placed in an adult prison or penitentiary; this is true as well for youth under 18 years of age who receive a youth sentence.

Adult Sentences

Even though adult sentences are typically reserved for cases involving the most high-risk youth who have committed murder or another severe/violent crime (Corrado et al. 2015), the YCJA sets out that the Crown must consider an adult sentence for a young person if specific criteria are met (see Chapter 3). If it has been determined that an adult sentence would be appropriate but the decision is taken not to make an application, "the Attorney General shall advise the youth justice court before the young person enters a plea or with leave of the court before the commencement of the trial" (YCJA 2002, s. 64(1.1)). In effect, these revisions now direct the Crown to consider a request for an adult sentence for a youth. If the Crown chooses not to pursue this sentence, it is expected to notify the court of this decision. A final comment on the use of adult sentences is that the onus is on the Crown to demonstrate to the court the appropriateness of an adult sentence.

Additional considerations that the youth court must consider in the sentencing of young offenders under the Act are the young person's role in the commission of the offence, the harm done to the victim(s), the reparation (if any) to the victim or the community made by the young person, the time the young person spent in detention (if any) in connection to the offence, the nature and number of previous findings of guilt (if any), and any other relevant aggravating (e.g., gang involvement, lack of remorse, offence planning) and mitigating circumstances (e.g., mental health, lower age) in connection to the youth or the offence (s. 38(3)(a–f); Roberts and Bala 2003).

Youth Corrections: Treatment Regimes in Open- and Closed-Custody Facilities

Youth who are sentenced to serve a custodial sanction in a youth custody centre may be placed in either open or closed custody, which is determined by the youth court during sentencing based on the severity of the offence and the needs of the young person. The safety of other youth in custody may be considered as well, depending on the youth's behaviours in the community and during previous custodial placements. Although recent debates on its use with adults and youth have been raised, youth may also be placed in a secure isolation unit (i.e., solitary confinement or segregation), spending up to 23 hours a day in a cell, if they have been engaging in behaviour that suggests there is a risk of their becoming aggressive and causing serious harm to another person, to themselves, or to the property, and that this behaviour cannot be suppressed by alternative means (Office of the Auditor General of Ontario 2012). Youth in custody also receive daily behavioural ratings from correctional staff that can be used to determine what time they are to be in their cell at night. Since the number of young female offenders who require detention is too small to necessitate a separate facility, there are distinct units for young female offenders in which their accommodations are detached from the male offenders' areas.

During a period of incarceration, youth have access to a range of programming options that can assist in the development of pro-social attitudes and behaviours, such as educational/vocational training, life skills programs, recreational programs, substance abuse programs, individual and group counselling, anger management programming, cultural and religious programs, and culinary activities. There are also more specialized programs offered to youth who have mental health conditions and/or who have committed a sexual and/or violent offence (Corrado et al. 2015). Educational and substance abuse programs—the most commonly delivered programs in youth detention centres— offer promising educational, as well as offending, outcomes once youth are released from custody (Young, Dembo, and Henderson 2007; see also Chapter 10). The most successful substance abuse programs are those that are long in duration rather than high in intensity (Lipsey and Wilson 1998) and that address substance abuse as well as comorbid mental health disorders (Teplin et al. 2006). Research has also highlighted the success of violent offender treatment programming comprising cognitive-behavioural therapy and anger management strategies (see Serin, Gobeil, and Preston 2009). Youth who completed such programs experienced reductions in violent and non-violent recidivism, with lengthier participation having the most significant impact on reducing recidivism (Haerle 2016).

Restorative Justice

Although not explicitly stated in the YCJA, there are practices utilized within the youth justice system that reflect restorative justice ideas (see Chapter 16). These include diversionary measures and youth justice conferences. Like the restorative justice framework, these provisions often require the young person to admit guilt (Wemmers and Cyr 2005), and they can include victims in the related processes. As stated explicitly in the Act's sentencing principles, a youth justice sentence should "promote a sense of responsibility in the young person, and an acknowledgement of the harm done to victims and the community" (YCJA 2002, s. 38(2)(e)(iii)). The Act, therefore, encourages reparation and restorative-based sentences.

As noted in Chapter 16, restorative justice programs exist across Canada and can be especially beneficial to Indigenous young offenders, before or after sentencing. These programs can ensure that the YCJA's proportionality principle is not disregarded. If a young person successfully participates in and completes a restorative-based program or reparation process, the youth court will view this as a **mitigating factor** in his or her case (Roberts 2003).

Youth Justice Committees and Advocates

In relation to EJM, section 18 of the YCJA defines the role of youth justice committees (YJCs). These committees comprise volunteer citizens from the community who are delegated with the task of assisting in administering the Act and/or determining suitable programs for low-risk youth involved in the justice system. YJCs operate in every province and territory (Calgary Youth Justice Society 2014). They collaborate with members of the justice system and community organizations to promote the successful rehabilitation and reintegration of young offenders. In many regions, there is an emphasis on Indigenous youth (Hann and Associates 2003) and restorative justice approaches.

There are regional variations in the role of these advocates. In Manitoba and the Northwest Territories, for example, these committees receive information from Crown counsel for making decisions related to youth programming. In British Columbia and Ontario, YJCs participate in EJM and act as citizen advisors. In Nova Scotia, the police and Crown counsel, rather than youth justice advocates, are relied upon to determine which youth are referred to EJM; however, these advocates then deliver the restorative justice and community service programs (Calgary Youth Justice Society 2014). YJCs may also partake in discussions with the federal and provincial governments, advising them on youth justice policies and procedures (Department of Justice Canada 2013).

mitigating factors
Information presented to the courts concerning the facts of the case and the accused that may result in a lesser charge or sentence if the individual is found guilty. Conversely, aggravating factors are facts presented to the court surrounding the offence or the offender's circumstances that may aggravate or increase the severity of the offence.

Challenges in Dealing with Youth Mental Health Issues in Youth Courts and Corrections

Professionals working in youth justice face immense challenges in attempting to develop more effective ways of dealing with young people suffering from mental health problems. While these challenges are too many and too complicated to cover in detail in a single chapter, in the following sections we attempt to highlight some of the most significant issues being addressed today.

Young Offenders with Mental Health Disorders

A significant proportion of young people in our youth justice system (approximately 50 to 90 per cent) have been diagnosed with or display symptoms of a mental health condition (Gretton and Clift 2011; Penner, Roesch, and Viljoen 2011). This may be explained, at least in part, by the fact that youth with mental health disorders fail to engage in delinquent behaviours discreetly and thus have a greater likelihood of being detected, and/or by youth's inability to understand the detrimental implications—for society and themselves—of their behaviours (Pozzulo, Bennell, and Forth 2009). Young people in the justice system typically present with higher levels of anxiety, depression, and aggression, and lower self-control than young people in the general population (Grisso 2008; Sedlak 2009). As well, youth who have been diagnosed with attention deficit hyperactivity disorder (ADHD), conduct disorder, or attachment disorder are more likely to become involved in delinquency and the justice system (Odgers, Burnette, Chauhan, Moretti, and Reppucci 2005). Many youth involved in the justice system also have comorbid mental health conditions, meeting the criteria for two or more disorders (Gretton and Clift 2011).

Lawyers and judges are required to request mental health assessments if there are reasonable grounds that any mental health disorder(s) appear to be present, if there is a history of repeated convictions for the young person, and/or if the youth "is alleged to have committed a serious violent offence" (YCJA 2002, s. 34(1)(b)(iii)), and the results can be weighed as a mitigating factor in the youth court. After this, the court can impose appropriate programming and treatment recommendations.

The YCJA created the intensive rehabilitative custody and supervision (IRCS) order, which is a specific youth sentencing option offered in cases where young people have committed a serious violent offence and suffer from mental, psychological, or emotional disorders/disturbances. The government has allocated a proportion of youth justice funding to provide specific assistance and resources for these young people during their time in custody and the community to ensure that an individualized case management and treatment plan is developed. Research has shown that this promising sentence has seldom been used (Evaluation Division 2010). This sanction necessitates a special court review process to assess the suitability of the young person for such a sanction and requires the Crown and youth court to support this measure, which may deter the courts from imposing it more often. More recent data shows that the expenditures in some provinces and territories in support of IRCS are more than what is granted from the federal IRCS program, thus requiring the allocation of provincial and territorial funding to cover these additional costs (Department of Justice Canada 2017). This may be another explanation for the under-use of IRCS in areas where youth services may already be limited.

Psychological and psychiatric reports are an essential part of this process. During the completion of such assessments by a youth forensic psychologist or psychiatrist, a young person may be held in remand custody; this cannot continue longer than 30 days and can only be used when the courts and/or a qualified person deem it necessary for the completion of the assessment and with the youth's consent. The completion of court-ordered assessments can take months and wait-lists alone can be over a year. As a result, youth may be tried and sentenced without a comprehensive consideration of their mental and neurocognitive health.

Issues Related to Mental Incapacity and Fitness to Stand Trial

Another challenge related to mental illness in the youth justice system is determining the impact that youth's mental health has on the commission of the offence and youth's ability to participate fully in the court process. The courts must, therefore, assess whether young people's mental illness: (1) prevented their appreciation of their actions, and (2) will prevent them from comprehending and actively participating in the criminal proceedings against them. Comparable to the process with adult offenders, a small number of young offenders may be found **not criminally responsible because of a mental disorder (NCRMD)** or **unfit to stand trial (UST)**. Very few youth court cases result in a finding of NCRMD or UST, as the standards to meet each of these are high and must be determined during a psychiatric assessment.

The Potential for Specialized Youth Mental Health Courts

Specialized services aimed at diverting mentally disordered youth from further court involvement and custodial sentences are effectively working in some jurisdictions. In Ontario, youth mental health courts facilitate a collaborative approach to support youth in the justice system (Campbell 2015). One recognized model is the Ottawa Youth Mental Health Court that assembles monthly to review youth cases that may raise questions related to fitness to stand trial or youth's mental state at the time of the offence (e.g., NCRMD), that would be eligible for and best served by diversion practices, or that involve youth who have diverse needs as a result of their mental health and could benefit from specialized community-based sentencing and case management. Young people may be referred to these courts if they are 12 to 17 years old and "low risk," and have had interactions with the police that may result in formal police charges, have already been charged by the police, or have been found UST or NCRMD. As part of specialized mental health courts, the Crown, a court worker, the defence counsel, a youth team case manager, a psychiatrist, probation officers, addiction workers, and other committed community partners work together to review the youth's related assessments and reports and use this information to guide the young person's treatment plan. The youth's

not criminally responsible because of a mental disorder (NCRMD) Based on the Criminal Code's definition, a mental disorder is viewed as a "disease of the mind." For an individual to be found NCRMD, there must be a mental abnormality (not caused by voluntary intoxication, temporary mental conditions, or uncontrollable urges) causing significant impairment to preclude the individual's understanding of their behaviour.

unfit to stand trial (UST) When an individual is not fully capable of instructing counsel or understanding the nature and consequences of their trial.

parent(s)/guardians are also involved. To participate in this program, the youth must admit guilt and accept his or her responsibility in committing the related activities. Upon determination of the sentence, the Crown remains involved in the monitoring of the young person's progress.

Evidence suggests that these courts in Canada (e.g., the youth mental health court in Toronto) maintain connections with many treatment programs, process cases efficiently (Davis, Peterson-Badali, Weagant, and Skilling 2015), and anecdotally, have moderate impacts on participants' recidivism. Still, work is needed to ensure that youth who access these programs do have a mental illness and that treatments are matched to youth's specific needs. Critiques of these courts have also been raised concerning practices that may criminalize certain populations (i.e., persons who are homeless and "low risk"), the provision of short-term housing rather than investing in long-term sustainable housing options, and the compromising of individuals' privacy rights via enhanced supervision and information sharing (Quirouette, Hannah-Moffat, and Maurutto 2016). More research is needed to explore the impacts of these courts further.

The Use of Risk Assessment Tools in Youth Courts and Corrections

Endorsed as evidence-based tools to assist in youth justice processes, screening and risk assessment instruments are crucial for youth courts, community-based services, and youth centres, where they are relied on to guide case management decision-making and more individualized interventions. **Screening tools** are used to make appropriate service, programming, and treatment referrals, while **risk assessment tools** assess the young person's risk to recidivate based on a set of indicators that typically include, but are not limited to, familial measures, educational/vocational measures, substance use measures, peer measures, and attitudinal measures. These evidence-based tools are an essential part of effectively supporting young people in the justice system.

The foundation for the use of risk assessment lies in Andrews, Bonta, and Hoge's (1990) risk-needs-responsivity (RNR) model. This model outlines three fundamental principles. The first is the *risk principle*, which states that risk assessments should begin by identifying an offender's risk to recidivate. Next, the *needs principle* directs that assessments be used to establish the criminogenic needs, or risk factors, as well as the protective factors that may help the young person's rehabilitation. Finally, the *responsivity principle* includes an assessment of the offender's likely receptivity to any treatment based on their learning style, and strengths and abilities.

Several youth screening and assessment tools have been developed; we present those most commonly used in Canada among youth justice populations. The Youth Assessment and Screening Instrument (YASI) is employed in community and custodial youth justice settings in Ontario and Alberta to assess youth's risk, needs, and protective factors (Andrews et al. 1990). The instrument was designed with no specification based on gender; however, a version has more recently been developed specifically for girls. It collects information on youth's **static risk factors**, such as age, gender, ethnicity, and prior criminal

screening tools
Instruments used to identify youth who have exhibited characteristics associated with delinquency or criminal conduct (including mental health issues) and assist in their referrals to appropriate programs and services.

risk assessment tools
Instruments used to assess the multitude of risk and protective factors that have been and/or are present in young people's lives that can influence the likelihood of recidivism. Youth are rated as low, medium, or high risk, and individualized interventions are developed based on these risk assessment outcomes.

static risk factors
Unchangeable risk factors; they include those traits that may contribute to an individual's offending and recidivism and that cannot be altered through rehabilitation programming.

dynamic risk factors
Changeable risk factors; they are factors that may also contribute to criminal behaviour but that can be modified through targeted interventions and/or treatment.

history, and **dynamic risk factors**, which include substance use, anti-social peers, and gang involvement (Savignac 2010). Preliminary research has found that the YASI is a useful tool to assess young offenders' risk level (Geck 2012).

Another commonly employed screening and risk assessment instrument is the Youth Level of Service/Case Management Inventory (YLS/CMI). Developed in Canada, this tool is used in Nova Scotia, Newfoundland and Labrador, Prince Edward Island, and the Yukon (Savignac 2010) to assess youth's specific set of needs and their risk of recidivism. Youth justice personnel rely on this information to create simple case management plans and interventions. The YLS/CMI has been found to reliably predict future reoffending risk (McGrath and Thompson 2012) for both male and female youth (Andrews et al. 2012); it has also produced improved accuracy in predicting offending and violent offending compared to other risk assessment tools (Viljoen, Elkovitch, Scalora, and Ullman 2009) and in guiding the development of youth interventions (Hoge 2005).

A final standardized risk and needs assessment instrument that is used in British Columbia and the Yukon is the Structured Assessment of Violence Risk in Youth (SAVRY). The SAVRY is intended for youth who have been incarcerated or who require a more in-depth assessment of their risk for violence (Savignac 2010). The tool can successfully predict violent and non-violent recidivism (Vincent, Guy, Gershenson, and McCabe 2012), and has been moderately successful in influencing youth probation outcomes (Catchpole and Gretton 2003; Childs et al. 2013).

Issues with Relying on Risk Assessment Tools

While risk assessment instruments have been widely adopted throughout Canada and other Western countries to supervise and case manage individuals in the justice system, scholars have argued that their popularity has largely been fostered by the focus on risk aversion today (Scott 2000). This emphasis on predicting, identifying, and eliminating risk has naturally permeated the youth justice system, where it is believed numerous young people are evaluated as "high risk" and require prudent management so they do not reoffend. However, greater concerns have been presented, including ambiguity in the interpretation of risk, subjectivity in risk assessment decisions, assessments' impact on pre-sentence reports, and the "framing of rehabilitation within a risk discourse" (Maurutto and Hannah-Moffat 2007, p. 476). Some further issues have been identified and raised by academics and criminal justice professionals related to the suitability of standardized risk assessment tools for specific types of young offenders, such as girls and Indigenous and other ethnic minority youth. The standardization of these instruments is based on comparisons to non-criminal samples and Western, middle-class standards that may not necessarily be representative of the young people involved in our legal system, including these populations (Kempf-Leonard 2007), which are disproportionately overrepresented in the justice system and are growing faster than other populations. Other concerns relate to the problematic conceptualizations of static and dynamic risk (see Hannah-Moffat 2016). These critiques present important considerations of how the justice system has simply adopted these tools as accepted, status quo processes (see also Chapter 7 for more discussion on the challenges and implications of risk assessments).

Issues Related to Youth Records

A young person's involvement in the justice system will result in the creation of different types of records, including police records, youth justice court records, government records, and records classified in an "other" category (e.g., from community agencies during EJM). Furthermore, the imposition of an adult sentence for a young person results in an adult record. Under section 119(2) of the YCJA, youth records have a set **access period**, but based on the rehabilitative principles of the YCJA, after a set period following the completion of the youth sentence, the youth's records are sealed or destroyed; they cannot be used to supplement information collected concerning future adult offending and court involvement or to be held against the young person.

The destruction of youth records occurs at various times following a young person's guilty verdict or the completion of the sentence, and it depends on the type of sanction imposed. These are presented in Table 4.1. Once the access period has passed and a youth's

access period
The designated timeframe during which a young person's youth record is active or disclosable and can be shared among relevant individuals attached to the young person as outlined in the YCJA (e.g., the youth, his or her parents, defence counsel, Crown counsel, or correctional facility director).

Table 4.1	Destruction of Youth Criminal Records
How Offence Is Dealt with/Type of Offence	**How Long before Record Will Be Sealed or Destroyed? (Access Period)**
Youth is acquitted (other than a verdict of not criminally responsible because of mental disorder)	Two (2) months after the time allowed to file an appeal or, if an appeal is filed, three (3) months after all proceedings related to the appeal are completed
The charge is dismissed or withdrawn	After two (2) months
Youth is found guilty and given a reprimand	After two (2) months
Charge is stayed	After one (1) year, if no further court proceedings have been taken
Extrajudicial sanction is imposed	Two (2) years after the young person has consented to the extrajudicial sanction
Youth is found guilty and given an absolute discharge	One (1) year after the young person has been found guilty
Youth is found guilty and given a conditional discharge	Three (3) years after the young person has been found guilty
Youth is found guilty and sentenced for summary conviction offence	Three (3) years after the sentence has been completed (any subsequent offence will result in an extension)
Youth is found guilty and sentenced for an indictable offence	Five (5) years after the sentence has been completed (any subsequent offence will result in an extension)
Murder, manslaughter, attempted murder, or aggravated sexual assault	Record may be retained indefinitely
Certain scheduled offences	A record will be retained for an additional five (5) years
Youth is found guilty and receives an adult sentence	A record is treated as an adult record, and the rules applicable to adult records apply
A person is convicted of an offence committed after they turn 18, while the access period for their youth offence is still open	A record for the youth offence will be treated as an adult record, and the rules applicable to adult records apply

Source: Youth Records factsheet, http://www.justice.gc.ca/eng/cj-jp/yj-jj/tools-outils/sheets-feuillets/pdf/recor-dossi.pdf, Entire table. Department of Justice Canada, 2013. Reproduced with the permission of the Department of Justic, 2019.

record has been closed, police, court, and corrections files, as well as the information contained in them, cannot be disclosed.

The destruction of youth records is essential in protecting the identity and rights of young people; still, these records may remain open after the young person has reached the age of 18. They may also prevent the young person from entering some education programs, accessing specific employment opportunities, or obtaining volunteer positions, and they inhibit the young person's entry into countries outside of Canada.

A Critical Examination of the Changing Youth Justice System

As evidenced throughout this chapter, and others in this textbook, there have been perceptible declines in the number of youth formally charged and sentenced in Canada. While these changes can be explained by the continuing impact of the YCJA's modified justice model, which has included prioritizing diversion and community-based sentencing, they are perhaps more accurately the outcome of shifts in political priorities—i.e., a decreased emphasis on being "tough on crime" and reining in "out-of-control youth," and a shift to neo-liberal cost-cutting agendas. Today, much of the rhetoric around youth delinquency and crime has subsided in Canada. This has facilitated the shift to more community-oriented sanctions, and in effect, the transferring of responsibility for "at-risk" and "high-risk/need" youth to other agencies and organizations. These changes are more likely to occur and be supported in periods of economic shortages and austerity, such as Canada's present situation, not unlike in other countries (see Bateman 2014). This phenomenon was demonstrated earlier in the discussion on external partners and stakeholders in youth justice.

The increased investment in risk measurement and assessment tools has contributed to these changes, including as a component of this the individualization of justice system philosophies and principles. All levels of our (and many Western) youth justice system have embraced evidence-based practices that are rooted in the risk-need-responsivity model of rehabilitation emphasizing the identification of dynamic risk factors that can be modified, and the adoption of intervention strategies that target these risk/need areas. This process has distracted from the attention that was once dedicated to developing strategies to address the broader structural factors (e.g., socio-economic disadvantage, unemployment) that contribute to delinquency and crime (Gray 2009). More problematic is that, although Canada has experienced optically appeasing declines in youth crime, the young people who continue to be charged, tried, and convicted in our justice system are those who are already marginalized and the most disenfranchised. These new systems have resulted in the criminalization of youth and the imposition on these very groups of the responsibility to improve their circumstances and conform to social standards. These contexts are critical to presenting a complete picture of the youth justice system in action and how various players contribute to the functioning of its many parts.

Summary

A young person's movement through the youth justice system can vary depending on the youth's circumstances and offence(s) and in which province/territory he or she is charged. Nevertheless, the standard procedures followed at each stage of the process have been presented in this chapter, beginning with the youth's first contact with the police. This encounter can then lead either to a diversionary response or to a formal charging and continuation into the formal youth justice system. At this stage, the youth will attend court and will receive an extrajudicial sanction or a stern warning from the judge; be found not guilty, not criminally responsible because of mental disorder, or unfit to stand trial; or be sentenced to one or a combination of the more formal options. While a young person's record does not typically remain accessible indefinitely, it can present challenges for future employment and travel.

Key Terms

access period
bail surety
criminogenic
crossover youth
disposition
dynamic risk factors
extrajudicial sanctions
mitigating factor
net widening
not criminally responsible because of
   mental disorder (NCRMD)

pre-charge diversion
preliminary inquiry
pre-sentence report
pre-trial detention/remand custody
racial profiling
risk assessment tools
screening tools
static risk factors
unfit to stand trial (UST)

Review Questions

1. Describe the process that a first-time offender might face when apprehended for a non-violent offence by police.

2. What is one identified limitation of the process utilized by police officers in British Columbia to determine whether a young person should be diverted away from the youth criminal justice system or be formally charged with a criminal offence?

3. How and under what circumstances are young offenders in Canada determined to be unfit to stand trial and NCRMD?

4. What is the longest time that a person's youth record can remain open and under what circumstances? Are youth justice staff allowed to share or rely on any of this information after this time?

5. Identify the central players in the youth justice system as well as the other professionals/ agencies with which they interact. What are the respective roles of each and why? What are the greatest challenges in these collaborations?

Critical Thinking Questions

1. How would a more equably applied approach to responses and sanctions for youth be advantageous and disadvantageous to young offenders?

2. How could specialized probation caseloads help and potentially hinder young offenders' rehabilitation?

3. What could be the potential benefits and hindrances to relying on restorative-based sanctions for young offenders? Should the police and youth courts rely on these approaches more (or less) than they do now?

4. Should the youth justice system avoid the use of custody for first-time/less serious young offenders but continue to impose such a sanction on the most serious/repeat young offenders?

5. What would be the implications to the young person and the justice system of keeping a young person's youth record active indefinitely?

6. Do you share any of the presented concerns associated with the individualization and responsibilization occurring in the youth justice system? What are the possible consequences (positive and negative) to this?

References

Alain, M., and Hamel, S. (2015). The situation in Quebec: "Vive la différence"? In A. Alain, R. Corrado, and S. Reid (Eds), *Implementing and working with the Youth Criminal Justice Act across Canada*. Toronto: University of Toronto Press.

Andrews, D.A., Bonta, J., and Hoge, R.D. (1990). Classification for effective rehabilitation: Rediscovering psychology. *Criminal Justice and Behavior, 17*, 19–52.

Andrews, D.A., Guzzo, L., Raynor, P., Rowe, R.C., Rettinger, L.J., Brews, A., and Wormith, J.S. (2012). Are the major risk/need factors predictive of both female and male reoffending? A test with the eight domains of the Level of Service/Case Management Inventory. *International Journal of Offender Therapy and Comparative Criminology, 56*, 113–33. doi:10.1177/0306624X10395716

Augimeri, L.K., Pepler, D., Walsh, M.M., Jiang, D., and Dassinger, C. (2010). *Aggressive and antisocial young children: Risk prediction, assessment and clinical risk management. Program evaluation report submitted to The Provincial Centre of Excellence for Child and Youth*

Mental Health at cheo. Retrieved from http://www. excellenceforchildandyouth.ca/sites/default/files/gai_ attach/RG-976_Final_Outcomes_Report.pdf

Augimeri, L.K., Walsh, M., Levene, K., and Slater, N. (2015). Scaling deeper: SNAP® model and implementation frameworks. In R. Corrado, A. Leschied, P. Lussier, and J. Whatley (Eds), *Serious and violent young offenders and youth criminal justice: A Canadian perspective*. Burnaby, BC: Simon Fraser University Press.

Bala, N., Carrington, P., and Roberts, J. (2009). Evaluating the Youth Criminal Justice Act after five years: A qualified success. *Canadian Journal of Criminology and Criminal Justice, 51*, 131–67. doi:10.1353/ccj.0.0050

Bateman, T. (2014). Where has all the youth crime gone? Youth justice in an age of austerity. *Children & Society, 28*, 416–424. doi:10.1111/chso.12087

BC Representative for Children and Youth. (2014). *On their own: Examining the needs of BC youth as they leave government care*. Victoria, BC: Office of the Representative for Children and Youth. Retrieved from https://www.rcybc.ca/sites/default/files/documents/pdf/reports_publications/rcy_on_their_own.pdf

BC Representative for Children and Youth. (2015). *Paige's story: Abuse, indifference and a young life discarded*. Victoria, BC: Office of the Representative for Children and Youth. Retrieved from https://www.rcybc.ca/sites/default/files/documents/pdf/reports_publications/rcy-pg-report-final.pdf

BC Representative for Children and Youth. (2016). *Too many victims: Sexualized violence in the lives of children and youth in care*. Victoria, BC: Office of the Representative for Children and Youth. Retrieved from http://rcybc.ca/sites/default/files/documents/pdf/reports_publications/rcy_toomanyvictimsfinal.pdf

Brennan, S. (2012). Youth court statistics in Canada, 2010/2011. *Juristat, 32*(1). Statistics Canada Catalogue No. 85-002-X. Retrieved from http://www.statcan.gc.ca/pub/85-002-x/2012001/article/11645-eng.pdf

Broeking, J., and Peterson-Badali, M. (2010). The extent and nature of parents' involvement in Canadian youth justice proceedings. *Youth Justice, 10*, 40–55. doi:10.1177/1473225409356759

Calgary Youth Justice Society. (2014). *Section 3: Youth justice committees*. Retrieved from http://calgaryyouthjustice.ca/programs/youth-justice-committees/information/for-volunteers/e-learning-course-1/section-3/

Campbell, K.M. (2015). Youth criminal justice law in Ontario. In A. Alain, R.R. Corrado, and S. Reid (Eds), *Implementing and working with the Youth Criminal Justice Act across Canada*. Toronto: University of Toronto Press.

Cao, L. (2014). Aboriginal people and confidence in the police. *Canadian Journal of Criminology and Criminal Justice, 56*, 499–525. doi:10.3138/cjccj. 2013.E05

Carrington, P.J., and Schulenberg, J.L. (2005). *The impact of the Youth Criminal Justice Act on police charging practices with young persons: A preliminary statistical assessment*. Ottawa: Department of Justice Canada. Retrieved from http://www.justice.gc.ca/eng/rp-pr/cj-jp/yj-jj/pdf/prelimin.pdf

Catchpole, R.E.H., and Gretton, H.M. (2003). The predictive validity of risk assessment with violent young offenders: A 1-year examination of criminal outcome. *Criminal Justice and Behavior, 30*, 688–708.

Childs, K.K., Ryals, J., Frick, P.J., Lawing, K., Phillippi, S.W., and Deprato, D.K. (2013). Examining the validity of the Structured Assessment of Violence Risk in Youth (SAVRY) for predicting probation outcomes among adjudicated juvenile offenders. *Behavioral Sciences and the Law, 31*, 256–70.

Corrado, R.R., Gronsdahl, K., and Markwart, A. (2015). Youth justice system and approaches in British Columbia. In A. Alain, R.R. Corrado, and S. Reid (Eds), *Implementing and working with the Youth Criminal Justice Act across Canada*. Toronto: University of Toronto Press.

Criminal Code, RSC 1985, c. C-46.

Cross-Over Youth Committee. (2015). *Cross-over youth: Care to custody*. Toronto, ON: Ryerson University. Retrieved from http://crossoveryouth.ca/wp-content/uploads/2016/03/Cross-Over-Youth_Care-to-Custody_march2015.pdf

Cullen, F.T., Jonson, C.L., and Nagin, D.S. (2011). Prisons do not reduce recidivism: The high cost of ignoring science. *The Prison Journal, 91*, 48S–65S.

Dauvergne, M. (2013). Youth court statistics in Canada, 2011/2012. *Juristat*. Statistics Canada Catalogue No. 85-002-X. Ottawa: Statistics Canada. Retrieved from https://www150.statcan.gc.ca/n1/en/pub/85-002-x/2013001/article/11803-eng.pdf?st=mN2c93b6

Davis, K., Peterson-Badali, M., Weagant, B., and Skilling, T. (2015). A process evaluation of Toronto's first youth mental health court. *Canadian Journal of Criminology and Criminal Justice, 57*, 159–87.

Department of Justice Canada. (2013). *Youth records*. Ottawa: Author. Retrieved from http://www.justice.gc.ca/eng/cj-jp/yj-jj/tools-outils/sheets-feuillets/pdf/recor-dossi.pdf

Department of Justice Canada. (2017). *Youth Justice Initiative evaluation*. Ottawa: Author. Retrieved from https://www.justice.gc.ca/eng/rp-pr/cp-pm/eval/rep-rap/2016/yji-ijj/p5.html

Doob, A., and Cesaroni, C. (2004). *Responding to youth crime in Canada*. Toronto: University of Toronto Press.

Doob, A.N., and Chan, J. (1982). Factors affecting police decisions to take juveniles to court. *Canadian Journal of Criminology, 24*, 25–37.

Doob, A., Sprott, J., and Webster, C. (2018, May 10). Canada's success in reducing youth imprisonment in the last two decades is evidence that reform of the justice system is possible, with the political will. *Policy Options*. Retrieved from http://policyoptions.irpp.org/magazines/may-2018/learning-from-our-success-in-reducing-youth-imprisonment/

Evaluation Division, Office of Strategic Planning and Performance Management. (2010). *The Youth Justice Initiative funding components evaluation: Final report*. Ottawa: Department of Justice Canada. Retrieved from http://www.justice.gc.ca/eng/rp-pr/cp-pm/eval/rep-rap/11/yjifc-vfijj/yjifc-vfijj.pdf

Fazel, S., Doll, H., and Långström, N. (2008). Mental disorders among adolescents in juvenile detention and correctional facilities: A systematic review and metaregression analysis of 25 surveys. *Journal of the American Academy of Child & Adolescent Psychiatry, 47*, 1010–19.

Fitzgerald, R.T., and Carrington, P.J. (2011). Disproportionate minority contact in Canada: Police and visible minority youth. *Canadian Journal of Criminology and Criminal Justice*, 53, 449–86.

Forgays, D.K. (2008). Three years of teen court offender outcomes. *Adolescence, 43*, 473–84.

Geck, C.M.R. (2012). *The Youth Screening Instrument: A psychometric evaluation with Canadian male youthful offenders.* Master's thesis, Carleton University, Ottawa.

Gouvernement du Québec. (2009). *The Youth Criminal Justice Act: The legal procedure.* Justice Québec, Québec City. Retrieved from http://www.justice.gouv.qc.ca/english/publications/generale/ projud-a.htm#sans

Government of British Columbia. (n.d.). *Youth sentences.* Retrieved from https://www2.gov.bc.ca/gov/content/justice/criminal-justice/bcs-criminal-justice-system/youth-justice/youth-justice-in-british-columbia/youth-sentences

Government of Canada. (2006). *International Convention on the Elimination of All Forms of Racial Discrimination, Seventeenth and Eighteenth Reports of Canada.* Gatineau, QC: Human Rights Program, Department of Canadian Heritage. Retrieved from http://publications.gc.ca/collections/Collection/CH37-4-10-2005E.pdf

Gray, P. (2009). The political economy of risk and the new governance of youth crime. *Punishment & Society, 11*, 443–58. doi:10.1177/14624745093341141

Greene, C.T. (2011). *Creating consensus: An exploration of two pre-charge diversion programs in Canada.* Doctoral dissertation. Retrieved from University of Toronto, Open Access Theses and Dissertations.

Gretton, H.M., and Clift, R.J. (2011). The mental health needs of incarcerated youth in British Columbia, Canada. *International Journal of Law and Psychiatry, 34*, 109–15. doi: 10.1016/j.ijlp.2011.02.004

Grisso, T. (2008). Adolescent offenders with mental disorders. *Juvenile Justice, 18*, 143–64.

Haerle, D. R. (2016). Dosage matters: Impact of a violent offender treatment program on juvenile recidivism. *Youth Violence and Juvenile Justice*, 14, 3–25. doi:10.1177/1541204014555436

Haight, W., Bidwell, L., Seok Choi, W., and Cho, M. (2016). An evaluation of the Crossover Youth Practice Model (CYPM): Recidivism outcomes for maltreated youth involved in the juvenile justice system. *Children and Youth Services Review, 65*, 78–85.

Hann & Associates. (2003). *A national survey of youth justice committees in Canada* (RR03YJ-7e). Ottawa: Department of Justice Canada. Retrieved from http://www.justice.gc.ca/eng/rp-pr/cj-jp/yj-jj/rr03_yj7-rr03_jj7/rr03_yj7.pdf

Hannah-Moffat, K. (2016). A conceptual kaleidoscope: Contemplating "dynamic structural risk" and an uncoupling of risk from need. *Psychology, Crime & Law, 22*, 33–46, doi:10.1080/1068316X.2015.1114115

Hoge, R.D. (2005). Youth level of service/Case management inventory. In T. Grisso, G. Vincent, and D. Seagrave (Eds), *Mental health screening and assessment in juvenile justice* (pp. 283–94). New York: Guildford Press.

Hyde, C., Marinos, V., and Innocente, N. (2016). What do meaningful consequences and fair and proportionate accountability mean to youth offered extrajudicial sanctions in Ontario? *Canadian Journal of Criminology and Criminal Justice, 58*, 194–220. doi:10.3138/cjccj.2014.E33

Jiang, D., Walsh, M., and Augimeri, L.K. (2011). The linkage between childhood bullying behaviour and future offending. *Criminal Behaviour and Mental Health, 21*(2), 128–35. doi: 10.1002/cbm.803

Kempa, M. (2013, June 28). Police street checks promote community safety? Prove it. *National Post.* Retrieved from http://fullcomment.nationalpost.com/2013/06/28/michael-kempa-police-street-checkspromote-community-safety-prove-it/

Kempf-Leonard, K. (2007). Disproportionate minority contact after nearly 20 years of reform efforts. *Youth Violence and Juvenile Justice, 5*, 71–87.

Kovarikova, J. (2017). Exploring youth outcomes after ageing-out of care. Toronto: Office of the Provincial Advocate for Children and Youth. Retrieved from https://www.provincialadvocate.on.ca/reports/advocacy-reports/report-exploring-youth-outcomes.pdf

Kuehn, S., and Corrado, R.R. (2011). Youth probation officers' interpretation and implementation of the Youth Criminal Justice Act: A case study of youth justice in Canada. *International Journal of Comparative and Applied Criminal Justice, 35*, 221–41.

LeGalbo, A.P., and Callahan, C.M. (2001). An evaluation of a teen court as a juvenile crime diversion program. *Juvenile and Family Court Journal, 52*(2), 1–11.

Lipsey, M.W., and Wilson, D.B. (1998). Effective intervention for serious juvenile offenders: A synthesis of research. In R. Loeber and D.P. Farrington (Eds), *Serious & violent juvenile offenders: Risk factors and successful interventions* (pp. 313–45). Thousand Oaks, CA: Sage.

McAra, L., and McVie, S. (2007). Youth justice? The impact of system contacts on patterns of desistence from offending. *European Journal of Criminology, 4*, 315–45.

McGrath, A., and Thompson, A.P. (2012). The relative predictive validity of the static and dynamic domain scores in risk-need assessment of juvenile offenders. *Criminal Justice and Behavior, 39*, 250–63. doi:10.1177/0093854811431917

Marroney, G.A., Quinn, T., Kinney, E., and Hufford, S. (2010). *Colorado probation and evidence-based practices: A systemic view of the past, present & future of ebp in Colorado Probation: Progress report.* Denver: Colorado Division of Probation Services.

Maurutto, P., and Hannah-Moffat, K. (2007). Understanding risk in the context of the Youth Criminal Justice Act. *Canadian Journal of Criminology and Criminal Justice, 49,* 465–91.

Miladinovic, M. (2016). Youth court statistics in Canada, 2014/2015. *Juristat.* Statistics Canada Catalogue No. 85-002-X. Retrieved from https://www150.statcan.gc.ca/n1/en/pub/85-002-x/2016001/article/14656-eng.pdf?st=MDhQBMtv

Moyer, S. (2005). *A comparison of case processing under the Young Offenders Act and the first six months of the Youth Criminal Justice Act.* Ottawa: Department of Justice Canada. Retrieved from http://www.justice.gc.ca/eng/rp-pr/cj-jp/yj-jj/pdf/compar.pdf

Munch, C. (2012). Youth correctional statistics in Canada, 2010/2011. *Juristat, 32*(1). Statistics Canada Catalogue No. 85-002-X. Retrieved from http://www.statcan.gc.ca/pub/85-002-x/2012001/article/11716-eng.pdf

Odgers, C.L., Burnette, M.L., Chauhan, P., Moretti, M.M., and Reppucci, D. (2005). Misdiagnosing the problem: Mental health profiles of incarcerated juveniles. *Canadian Child and Adolescent Psychiatry Review, 14,* 26–9.

Office of the Auditor General of Ontario. (2012). *2012 annual report of the Office of the Auditor General of Ontario: Youth justice services program.* Toronto: Author. Retrieved from http://www.auditor.on.ca/en/reports_en/en12/2012ar_en.pdf

Penner, E.K., Roesch, R., and Viljoen, J.L. (2011). Young offenders in custody: An international comparison of mental health services. *International Journal of Forensic Mental Health, 10,* 215–32.

Pepler, D.J., Walsh, M., Yuile, A., Levene K., Vaughan, A., Jiang, D., and Webber, J. A. (2010). Bridging the gender gap: Interventions with aggressive girls and their parents. *Prevention Science, 11,* 229–38. doi:10.1007/s11121-009-0167-4

Pozzulo, J., Bennell, C., and Forth, A. (2009). *Forensic psychology* (2nd ed.). Toronto: Pearson Education.

Public Prosecution Service of Canada, Government of Canada. (2014). Public Prosecution Service of Canada deskbook. Ottawa: Author. Retrieved from http://www.ppsc-sppc.gc.ca/eng/pub/fpsd-sfpg/fps-sfp/tpd/p5/ch04.html

Quirouette, M., Hannah-Moffat, K., and Maurutto, P. (2016). "A precarious place": Housing and clients of specialized courts. *The British Journal of Criminology, 56,* 370–88. doi:10.1093/bjc/azv050

Rankin, J. (2012, March 22). Known to police: No need for review of Toronto police contacts with "racialized" youth, act now, says watchdog group. *The Star.* Retrieved from http://www.thestar.com/news/gta/2012/03/22/known_to_police_no_need_for_review_of_toronto_police_contacts_with_racialized_youth_act_now_says_watchdog_group.html

Ricciardelli, R., Crichton, H., Swiss, L., Spencer, D.C., and Adorjan, M. (2017). From knowledge to action? The Youth Criminal Justice Act and the use of extrajudicial measures in youth policing. *Police Practice and Research, 18,* 599–611. doi:10.1080/15614263.2017.1363971

Roberts, J.V. (2003). Sentencing juvenile offenders in Canada: An analysis of recent reform legislation. *Journal of Contemporary Criminal Justice, 19,* 413–34. doi:10.1177/1043986203259124

Roberts, J.V., and Bala, N. (2003). Understanding sentencing under the Youth Criminal Justice Act. *Alberta Law Review, 41*(2), 395–423.

Satzewich, V., and Shaffir, W. (2009). Racism versus professionalism: Claims and counter-claims about racial profiling. *Canadian Journal of Criminology and Criminal Justice, 51,* 199–226.

Savarese, J.L. (2015). Moving forward & standing still: Assessing restorative based justice in Saskatchewan after the Youth Criminal Justice Act. In A. Alain, R. Corrado, and S. Reid (Eds), *Implementing and working with the Youth Criminal Justice Act across Canada.* Toronto: University of Toronto Press.

Savignac, J. (2010). *Tools to identify and assess the risk of offending among youth.* Ottawa: National Crime Prevention Centre, Public Safety Canada. Retrieved from http://www.publicsafety.gc.ca/cnt/rsrcs/pblctns/tls-dntf-rsk-rprt/tls-dntf-rsk-rprt-eng.pdf

Scott, A. (2000). Risk society or angst society? Two views of risk, consciousness and community. In B. Adam, U. Beck, and J. van Loon (Eds), *The risk society and beyond: Critical issues for social theory* (pp. 33–46). London: Sage.

Sedlak, A.J. (2009). Surveying youths in custody. *Corrections Today, 71,* 92–4.

Serin, R.C., Gobeil, R., and Preston, D.L. (2009). Evaluation of the persistently violent offender treatment program. *International Journal of Offender Therapy and Comparative Criminology, 53,* 57–73.

Teplin, L.A., Abram, K.M., McClelland, G.M., Mericle, A.A., Dulcan, M.K., and Washburn, J.J. (2006). *Psychiatric disorders of youth in detention.* Washington: Office of Juvenile Justice and Delinquency Prevention, Office of Justice Programs, U.S. Department of Justice.

Viljoen, J.L., Elkovitch, N., Scalora, M.J., and Ullman, D. (2009). Assessment of reoffense risk in adolescents who have committed sexual offenses: Predictive validity of the ERASOR, PCL: YV, YLS/CMI, and Static-99. *Criminal Justice and Behavior, 36,* 981–1000. doi:10.1177/0093854809340991

Vincent, G.M., Guy, L.S., Gershenson, B.G., and McCabe, P. (2012). Does risk assessment make a difference? Results of implementing the SAVRY in juvenile probation. *Behavioral Sciences and the Law, 30,* 384–405. doi:10.1002/bsl.2014

Wemmers, J., and Cyr, K. (2005). Can mediation be therapeutic for crime victims? An evaluation of victims' experiences in mediation with young offenders. *Canadian Journal of Criminology and Criminal Justice, 47,* 527–44.

Wolbeck Minke, S., and Larsson, B. (2018). Outcome evaluation of the Police & Youth Engagement Project: 2017 Results. Edmonton: SWM Consulting Services and BIM Larsson & Associates. Retrieved from https://www.albertacrimeprevention.com/wp-content/uploads/2018/05/6-REACH_PYEP_May-9-2018.pdf

Wortley, S., and Tanner, J. (2003). Data, denials, and confusion: The racial profiling debate in Toronto. *Canadian Journal of Criminology and Criminal Justice, 45,* 367–89.

Wortley, S., and Tanner, J. (2005). Inflammatory rhetoric? Baseless accusations? A response to Gabor's critique of racial profiling research in Canada. *Canadian Journal of Criminology and Criminal Justice, 47,* 581–609.

Wright, D.H. (Honourable Justice). (2004). *Report of the Commission of Inquiry into Matters Relating to the Death of Neil Stonechild.* Retrieved from http://www.justice.gov.sk.ca/stonechild/finalreport/ Stonechild.pdf

Wright, E.M., Spohn, R., Chenane, J., and Juliano, N. (2017). The importance of interagency collaboration for crossover youth: A research note. *Youth Violence and Juvenile Justice, 15,* 481–91. doi:10.1177/1541204016686663

Young, D.W., Dembo, R., and Henderson, C.E. (2007). A national survey of substance abuse treatment for juvenile offenders. *Journal of Substance Abuse Treatment, 32,* 255–66.

Youth Criminal Justice Act, SC 2002, c. 1.

Part II

Understanding Contemporary Youth Crime and Justice
Theories and Perspectives

There are many ways one can approach attempting to develop an understanding of youth crime and justice today. What most people believe about youth crime and youth justice is likely based on a variety of sources (e.g., mass media, authority, tradition, personal experience, and common sense) that are not necessarily scientifically based yet serve to inform us about social issues. While these methods might serve us well personally, they risk the problems of overgeneralization and selective observation and, therefore, have been viewed with skepticism by most criminologists, who, depending on their training, prefer instead to rely on a wide range of disciplinary and theoretical perspectives. In this part, we present five chapters that collectively highlight and contrast with the different approaches that have been taken among scholars to try to understand youth crime and justice today.

In Chapter 5, Susan Reid and Sarah Gilliss offer a perspective on the importance of maintaining a separate system of youth justice while at the same time giving youth themselves more of a voice in youth justice policy and practice. Referring to national legislation and the United Nations Convention on the Rights of the Child, the authors present a strong case for why we need to oppose the trend toward treating youth more like adults in the criminal justice system. In addition, they examine the key challenges faced in attempting to address the needs of youth "at risk" and young persons who are already caught up in the criminal justice system. Based on this examination, they argue that there is no one ideal way of trying to address the needs of youth "at risk" and young offenders. This is especially the case, given that many of these youth display different patterns of highly complex emotional, personal, physical, and social needs. In light of this, they conclude that what is needed most is an approach based on principles of effective youth crime prevention and correctional treatment that can be used to direct programs at youth "at risk" and young offenders who can benefit most from crime prevention and correctional interventions. According to Reid and Gilliss, the key to developing such programs is for adults to work as partners with young people in a supportive manner that provides young people with a chance for meaningful participation and a voice in developing youth-focused policy both within and outside the criminal justice system.

Most members of the public have no training in criminology or direct experience with the youth justice system. Instead, they learn what they know about these topics from the media, including both traditional print and electronic media, such as newspapers and television, and more recently, social media. In Chapter 6, Chris McCormick provides a thoughtful analysis of the role of the media in producing knowledge about youth crime and justice. He contrasts this with other ways of learning about reported and unreported youth crime, including official and unofficial statistics—e.g., self-report studies. McCormick critically argues that while most people, including criminologists, tend to privilege "one way of knowing youth crime over the other," it is more useful and valuable to look at a variety of information sources, including the media, statistics, and self-report studies, as complementary but different ways of making sense of youth crime. McCormick's chapter is particularly unique in that it critiques the work of criminologists and media sociologists who tend to either ignore or discount the important role played by the media in contributing to the public debate over crime and justice issues generally and over youth crime and justice more specifically. In essence, McCormick points out that the media provide a crucial public arena in which youth crime and the justice system are debated, and that, as such, the media contribute to a different way of understanding youth crime and justice than that offered through the more narrow study of official crime statistics or self-report studies.

Other ways that criminologists have attempted to learn more about youth crime and justice are, first, through carrying out research with the aim of developing formal, testable theories of juvenile delinquency and youth crime, and, second, through developing critical theoretical insights on the operation of youth justice agencies and practices. In Chapter 7, Lorinda Stoneman, Mandeep Mucina, Thais Amorim, and Sibylle Artz combine these approaches by providing an overview of traditional and contemporary theories of female crime, along with a critical analysis of the differential treatment of girls by the the Canadian youth justice system. They claim there is a failure of the system to adequately address the needs of girls who come into conflict with the law. The authors cover the wide variety of theories that have been used to try to explain female crime and delinquency, ranging from early biological and more recent bio-pyschosocial theories focused on the individual, to more sociologically based strain, control, and gender role theories. The authors also discuss promising directions that are now being taken to more adequately theorize the causes of female crime and delinquency and to more effectively intervene in the lives of girls who are at risk of becoming involved in crime. Particular attention is given to developing an "intersectional" approach for guiding interventions that addresses the unique circumstances faced by girls and their complex and varied pathways toward delinquent behaviour and involvement in the criminal justice system. According to the authors, one of the reasons for the continuing failure of social agencies and the youth justice system to adequately address the needs of "at-risk" and "delinquent" girls has been the lack of sensitivity to the manner in which variables like age, gender, race, class, ethnicity, and sexuality intersect in shaping the life circumstances and behaviour of individuals. In addition, the authors suggest that the failure of even well-intended social agencies and youth justice workers to develop an awareness of these types of complex "demographic intersections" leads to piecemeal and typically overly punitive approaches to dealing with female youth crime.

In Chapter 8, Stephen Baron examines several more recent theoretical perspectives that have been offered to help explain and understand youth crime. Attention is given to recent sociologically based control, strain, and coercion theories that have attempted to improve on the earlier theories discussed by Stoneman et al. in Chapter 7. While some of these new perspectives, like Gottfredson and Hirschi's general theory of crime, build on specific earlier theories, others, like Sampson and Laub's age-graded theory and Tittle's control balance theory, attempt to bring together or integrate several of the previously examined perspectives to create new explanations of criminal behaviour. Other perspectives include Moffit's developmental taxonomy of offenders and interactional theory. Baron provides a systematic examination of the main causal factors identified by each theory, the key research studies that have been carried out to test the amount of empirical support for each theory, and the extent to which these theories complement or conflict with one another. Baron's review of these recent theoretical perspectives on youth crime shows the variety of ways in which positivist-oriented criminologists, who believe in the need for scientifically rigorous theory formulation and testing, have approached the topic. Baron concludes that to successfully understand youth crime, we must identify and include ideas from a range of complementary theoretical perspectives that help to better explain the causal process of youth crime, thus allowing for a more complex and nuanced understanding of how youth crime emerges and evolves.

In the final chapter in this section, Chapter 9, Bryan Hogeveen and Joanne Minaker highlight the framework of critical criminology to understand youth in the risk society. Hogeveen and Minaker argue that while mainstream positivist criminology has tended to focus attention on the "causes, consequences, and control of youth crime," critical criminology attempts to unmask the structural inequalities that marginalize young people and thereby contribute to their behaviours being criminalized and dealt with through various agencies of governmental control, including the youth justice system. For example, critical criminologists have begun to show how social inequalities linked to age, class, race, and gender work to "structure the life chances of the marginalized other—Indigenous youth, the poor, and racial minorities—and translate into overrepresentation in the contemporary youth justice system." Consequently, rather than thinking of youth crime as freely chosen behaviour on the part of youth that can therefore be simply deterred through the threat of punishment, critical criminologists like Hogeveen and Minaker link the criminalization of youth to "systemic conditions of marginalization, exclusion, and social inequality" and advocate forms of "social justice praxis" that are "dedicated to making meaningful changes to improve the life chances of young people." In their chapter, Hogeveen and Minaker offer an engaging introduction to key concepts, theories, and practical experiences that are informing the efforts now being undertaken by critical criminologists in promoting justice for Canadian youth.

Critical Challenges in Hearing the Voice of Youth in the Youth Justice System

Susan A. Reid and Sarah Gilliss

5

Overview

This chapter focuses on the importance of youth participating in decisions that affect them, and recognizes the significance of a young person's developmental differences as a mitigating factor in juvenile justice. The chapter analyzes the ongoing debate about maintaining a separate system of youth justice versus promoting the "adulteration" of youth by treating them as adult criminals. First, it focuses attention on the articles within the United Nations (UN) Convention on the Rights of the Child that point to the importance of giving youth a voice in decisions that affect them. Second, it provides an overview of some innovative youth-led program initiatives inside youth custodial institutions that reflect these principles. The chapter considers the importance of the needs of the young person as well as the relationships that develop between youth and the adults responsible for their care, rehabilitation, and reintegration.

Key Objectives

After reading this chapter, you should be able to:

- Understand the principles behind a separate system of justice for youth.
- Describe the age–crime relationship and the concept of emerging adults as a distinct period of development.
- Understand the challenges faced by youth with complex needs in the youth criminal justice system.
- Understand the importance of recognizing the articles of the UN Convention on the Rights of the Child in hearing the voice of youth in all matters and decisions that affect them.
- Consider how young persons in conflict with the law may contribute to their rehabilitation and reintegration through supportive adult–youth relationships.

Introduction

The chapters that make up this volume draw attention to the myriad issues that are involved in the implementation of youth justice in Canada. This chapter is intended to draw attention to the positive developments in the juvenile justice policy field as well as to some of the challenges that are still ahead as we continue to draw on our research and evidence of the most appropriate means of intervening in the lives of troubled youth. In particular, this chapter focuses on the inclusion of the voice of young people in decisions that affect them and the importance of the relationship between youth and adults in transforming the lives of young people as they transition to young adulthood.

The Legal Regulation of Childhood and Adolescence

The law that regulates criminal conduct for children and youth is based on a binary system, where the state focuses on the protection of children until they cross the threshold, known as the *age of majority*, to adulthood. Before the age of majority, children and youth receive the protection of the state in the form of restrictions on their freedom and investment in their development with the intent that such policies will pay dividends regarding the promotion of competent adults as productive members of society. This is known as the **best interests of the child doctrine.** While there is variation in the upper age of jurisdiction of the youth court throughout the world, the age of majority assumes that the individuals in question have reached a period in their development wherein they can be seen as fully autonomous individuals who are responsible for their actions (Reid 2011). The problem with this binary system, which focuses only on *immature children* and *competent adults*, is that there is no opportunity to include the evolving capacities of children as they mature during their adolescent years. Adolescents' capacity for self-regulation in situations that

best interests of the child doctrine
The approach in which the interests of a young person are paramount in decision-making regarding his or her experience in the criminal justice system.

are emotionally charged is considerably less than that of adults. Similarly, young people's capacity for future-oriented decision-making is also less than that of their adult counterparts. Youth are more sensitive to peer pressure and direct incentives than adults, and this has a dramatic impact on their likelihood of engaging in high-risk behaviours (Skeem, Scott, and Mulvey 2014; Umbach, Berryessa, and Raine 2015).

Where there have been changes to the age of consent, policies have been put in place to allow for changing capacities of young people based on the notion that social welfare and the welfare of the young person can both benefit through such a reclassification. In the case of **youth justice**, however, the rationale for lowering the age is not focused on the promotion of the welfare of youth. Instead, treating youth like an adult for the purposes of criminal responsibility is more a reflection of societal values as reflected in the adage "adult crime equals adult time." Moreover, some juvenile justice statutes undermine the principle of confidentiality in youth justice proceedings by increasing the number of opportunities to share information about the youth defendant with criminal justice, education, and social service agencies, and the media. This punitive stance has been underscored by such repressive policies as zero tolerance, curfews, and naming and shaming rituals (Reid 2011).

The best interests of the child doctrine appears to be in direct opposition to an increasing trend toward the **adulteration** of youth crime throughout the world. Internationally, there are now provisions in juvenile criminal statutes that provide for the transfer of youth who commit criminal offences to the adult system, either for adjudication or punishment. Research evidence is clear, however, that increased criminal justice processing of youth runs counter to the reduction of youth crime.

Petrosino, Turpin-Petrosino, and Guckenburg (2013), in their meta-analysis of 29 studies that assessed the impact of juvenile justice system processing of 7300 juvenile offenders over a 35-year period, concluded that not only does formal processing of juveniles appear not to control crime, it also seems to increase it on all measures studied. A meta-analysis of diversion programs conducted by Wilson and Hoge (2013) found that those programs that were primarily police caution programs were most effective in reducing recidivism for low-risk offenders compared to programs that provided some form of intervention (see Chapter 9 for a discussion of at-risk, low-risk, and high-risk youth). They report that "low risk youth referred to caution programs were 2.44 times less likely to reoffend," while the same low-risk youth who were referred to an intervention program were only "1.49 times less likely to reoffend." Trolio (2018) discusses the academic research on the harms of incarcerating youth generally. Incarceration of young people is much more likely to increase the odds of recidivism and reduce the chances of a young person returning to school. Further, prison slows down the natural process of aging out of crime and exacerbates the likelihood of reoffence. Youth who have spent time in custody and who have existing mental health issues will likely have more problems due to the incarceration. Finally, youth in custody who do not return to school will likely have a diminished success in the labour market as a young adult. Trolio goes on to point out that when youth are incarcerated with adults, the harms are significantly worse. Youth held with adults are 36 times more likely to take their lives by suicide than youth in juvenile facilities.

Imposing adult penalties and including young people in adult prisons have led to severe problems for young people. The case of Ashley Smith, a young person from New Brunswick, who was transferred from youth custody to the federal adult penitentiary system where she

youth justice
A separate and distinct criminal justice system that explicitly meets the unique needs of young people.

adulteration
The dismantling of a distinct system of criminal justice for youth and the re-merging of it with systems of justice for adults.

later took her own life, is one such case. Irwin Elman (2017), child and youth advocate for Ontario, reports that young people are vulnerable and likely to experience bullying, muscling, intimidation, and physical harm when placed in adult penitentiaries. Comments like "no one feels safe here" or "you always have to be on your toes" further elucidate the dangers of placing youth in adult prisons (Elman 2017). The use of adult penalties for children, youth, and young adults has been an ongoing point of controversy throughout the world and has led to some dramatic changes in dealing with young adults in the criminal justice system, particularly in the United Kingdom and Europe. These changes will be discussed further in the sections to follow. First, the importance of maintaining a separate system of youth justice will be examined within Canada's three pieces of youth crime legislation, the Juvenile Delinquents Act, the Young Offenders Act, and the Youth Criminal Justice Act.

Diverting Children from a Life of Crime: Sustaining the Original Purpose of a Separate System of Youth Justice

If we consider the origins of the juvenile justice system in North America, at the turn of the century the "child savers," as they were known, attempted to divert young people from the harshness of the adult system (see Chapter 1). The years that followed the enactment of the Juvenile Delinquents Act (JDA) of 1908 have been replete with arguments for policy changes that centre on the culpability of children as criminals (see Chapters 1 and 3).

The JDA was marked by a singular approach focusing on social welfare concerns with a strong emphasis on the "best interests" doctrine of child welfare and protection hearings. As more attention was drawn to the inequities of justice that were being meted out in the youth court, there was a call for more procedural safeguards. Equally, adults began to question whether the "discipline" of the youth court was sufficient to provide the community with protection from the sometimes heinous acts of young people. This "care" versus "control" argument has been the mainstay of the controversy surrounding the most suitable way to handle youth in conflict with the law since the mid-1960s and the release of a pivotal discussion document, *Juvenile Delinquency in Canada* (Canada 1965).

While the successor of the JDA, the YOA, heralded a change in youth justice with the elimination of social welfare concerns, there were still some provisions within the legislation that recommended that alternatives to the court system—albeit a mitigated accountability court system—were to be preferred for first-time, minor offenders. The implementation of the YOA, with its contrary goals of **rehabilitation** and the protection of society, led to increased use of the youth court and to even greater use of **custodial sanctions** than had been experienced under the former legislation.

Across Canada, the YCJA has had the effect of reducing the number of young people who have been sentenced to custody. The focus is on using alternatives to the formal system while reserving the youth court for the small number of severe and persistent offenders. The YCJA has been able to reduce the number of young people in custody dramatically (see Chapters 3 and 4). The focus on early prevention and intervention through school networks, through communities, and with the assistance of families helps to avoid stigma and labelling and may be the most suitable alternative for the majority of young people who offend. There will always be, however, a small number of young people who are persistent offenders and who require a range of multidisciplinary assistance set within

rehabilitation
A fundamental concept of the Youth Criminal Justice Act that holds that a young person can be reformed or changed as a result of appropriate treatment programs.

custodial sanctions
Under the Youth Criminal Justice Act, the sentencing of a young person to custody.

a clear path over a substantial period. Arguably, we make our biggest mistake when we provide intensive treatments to our low-risk offenders and set them off on a trajectory of net widening and further entrenchment within the system (Bonta and Andrews 2016).

The YCJA is based on research that shows that incarcerating young people can do more harm than good and that our most successful interventions should involve less criminal justice processing for the majority of offenders who present as low-risk, low-need offenders. For these reasons, the YCJA places increased emphasis on extrajudicial measures to respond appropriately to youth while keeping them out of the justice system and on non-custodial sentences for those youth who are formally charged and found guilty. Custodial sentences are seen as a measure of last resort for the highest-need offenders.

Young Adults and the Criminal Justice System

Under the YCJA, youth aged 12 to 17 who are accused of a crime are treated under the law in a manner that takes into account their reduced level of maturity and responsibility. Young people are considered adults under the law once they turn 18. However, if a young person committed an offence while they were 17, the processing of that young person through the system means that some 18-year-olds will still be dealt with in youth court. Further, young people who are serving a sentence who turn 18 during the time of their sentence will not be transferred to the adult system.

Not all laws and policies define youth as under 18 years. There are varying ages for the provinces' age of majority as either 18 or 19 years. The United Nations defines youth as anyone between the age of 12 and 24 years.

The path to adulthood is much more complex and non-linear nowadays than has been the case historically. Many young adults pursue post-secondary education, live with their parents longer, postpone starting their own family, and delay entry into the workforce. Recognizing that the classical pathway to adulthood does not end at the age of majority, but instead includes the need for extended support for young adults, the term *emerging adult* refers to this distinct developmental stage from ages 18 up to 30 (Arnett 2014). Developmental psychologists recently recognized the period from late adolescence to the mid-twenties as a distinct developmental stage which is distinguishable from both adolescence and adulthood (Cesaroni and Peterson-Badali 2017).

Adolescents have been found to be more impulsive, short-sighted, and less able to resist the influence of their peers (Farrington, Loeber, and Howell 2012). Drawing on the literature related to cognitive and behavioural maturation, youth are still likely to be sensation seekers and to act impulsively through their early twenties until full brain development happens around the age of 25 (Steinberg, 2017). In considering literature related to anatomical and functional markers of brain development, Giedd (2008) suggests that the evidence supports a lack of mature decision-making among young adults. Research has shown that given the neurological development of youth well into their twenties, they are not well equipped cognitively to consider the possible adverse consequences of their risky behaviours (Luciana and Collins 2012).

Looking at crime statistics, Allen (2016) points out that youth aged 12 to 17 years and young adults aged 18 to 24 years accounted for over one-third of individuals accused in

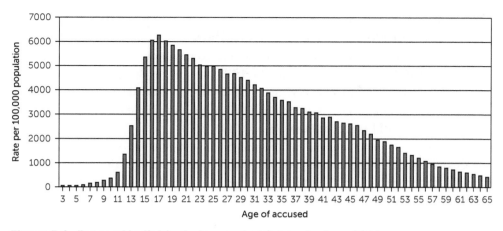

Figure 5.1   Rates of Individuals Accused of Crime, by Age, 2014

Note: Rates for all *Criminal Code* offences (excluding traffic). Rates are calculated on the basis of 100,000 population at each age. Populations are based upon July 1st estimates from Statistics Canada, Demography Division. Accused under age 12 cannot be charged with an offence under the *Criminal Code*.

Source: Allen 2016, Chart 3.

the police-reported crime. Young adults were accused of a crime at higher rates than any other age group (see Figure 5.1).

Farrington et al. (2012) suggest that two indicators of adulthood—lowered offending and lowered impulsivity—are not the norm until a young adult reaches the age of 25 years. They point out that the decrease in offending by age is evidence of this maturation, an assertion supported by the downward slope of the age–crime curve in Figure 5.1. However, Sampson and Laub (2016) argue that while age has a direct effect on offending, there is variability among individual age–crime curves. Research and theorizing on the "aging out" of crime has shown that turning points and life transitions such as employment, marriage, new peer groups, and new residential and social environments affect crime desistance (Nguyen and Loughran 2018). Farrall, Sharpe, Hunter, and Calverley (2011) suggest that while these structural life events are salient, the way in which people view the transitions, as well as their motivation to resist and their confidence in their own ability to stop offending in light of the negative stigma associated with the criminal label are equally important considerations in the desistance from crime in early adulthood. Rocque (2015) suggests that a theoretical perspective on the "aging out" of crime must include a multidisciplinary and integrative notion of maturation rather than focusing on chronological age or isolated processes. Changes that occur during the transition to adulthood include changes in attitudes and identity, changes in views of the self, changes in social relationships, as well as neuropsychological and biological changes.

For young adults who find themselves enmeshed in the criminal justice system, the transition to adulthood is yet more complicated. As one young adult from the United Kingdom noted,

> Outside of prison you have friends, you socialise, you get on with others, you meet new people. It's impossible in prison. You come out at the same stage you go in. Life is on pause. (Howard League for Penal Reform 2015, p. 12)

While other youths are learning things with a peer group and a supportive community, incarcerated youth are not exposed to the same opportunities to learn and grow through adolescence into young adulthood. An incarcerated young adult observes,

> Prison stops the chance of experiencing things that an individual age group are experiencing so we enter adulthood in different places and mature into different things. (Howard League for Penal Reform 2015, p.13)

Cesaroni (2015) suggests that there are key differences between the adult and youth criminal justice systems in Canada. The adult system primarily focuses on the offence while the youth system is more concerned about rehabilitation and the social development of the young person.

secure custody
A form of custody under the YCJA whereby youth are removed from a community and confined to an institution.

The United Nations Convention on the Rights of the Child

In 1985, the UN Standard Minimum Rules for the Administration of Youth Justice, known as the "Beijing Rules," recognized the unique needs of young people and the promotion of diversion from court proceedings. Further, these standards underscored the principle that custody should be used as a last resort for children and that all proceedings against young people should be anonymous in order to protect children from lifelong stigma and **labelling**. The United Nations Convention on the Rights of the Child (UNCRC) expanded on these rules and was proclaimed in 1989.

labelling
The stigmatization of a young person as deviant.

The UNCRC states in Article 3 that "[i]n all actions concerning children and the courts of law, the best interests of the child shall be a primary consideration." Article 40 requires that children who have violated the penal law be treated in a manner consistent with the child's age and the desirability of promoting the child's **reintegration** and his or her taking up a constructive role in society. The UN Convention further underscores socio-educational interventions and diversion from criminal proceedings and extrajudicial solutions. It recommends deprivation of liberty only as a last resort when dealing with young people who offend.

reintegration
The introduction of the young person back into the community after a custodial sentence as a productive member of society.

The UNCRC has laudable objectives in its principles and articles, and it is the most ratified of all human rights instruments, but it is also perhaps the most violated of the human rights treaties. Breaching the provisions of the UNCRC does not lead to any formal sanction. Canada's international obligations to all children who have committed offences support a presumption that young offenders are not to be treated like adults. However, Canada has continually violated the spirit of the UNCRC by insisting on a reservation under Article 34 concerning the rule about housing adults and youth in separate facilities (Winterdyk 2015).

Although Canada has had a formal system of youth justice that has been separate and apart from the adult justice system since the proclamation of the Juvenile Delinquents Act (JDA) in 1908, it was not until the Youth Criminal Justice Act (YCJA) expressly stated in section 3(1)(b) that "the criminal justice system for young persons must be separate from

Box 5.1 | Youth Justice in Action

Ashley Smith

Ashley Smith, a 19-year-old woman from Moncton, New Brunswick, died on 19 October 2007 while in federal custody at Ontario's Grand Valley Institution. Ashley had spent three years in and out of the New Brunswick Youth Centre (NBYC), which is the only **secure custod**y institution in the province. During those three years, Ashley spent two-thirds of her time in segregation. Ashley's trouble with the law began in March 2002, at the age of 14, with offences related to public disturbances, trespass, or violence (harassing telephone calls to unknown persons, assaulting strangers on the streets, and insulting passengers and drivers on public transportation). Ashley was referred for a psychiatric assessment, which concluded that she suffered from learning disorders, ADHD, and borderline personality disorder. While she was at the assessment centre, her behaviour escalated and the police were called twice for her assaults on staff. She was remanded to NBYC for one month where she incurred some institutional charges for not following orders and threatening self-harm. In less than three months, Ashley was in and out of the NBYC five times. She spent approximately three years in the youth jail, and during that time there were hundreds of institutional charges, 50 criminal charges, and over 150 self-harm incidents.

With the promise of more gender-specific programming and therapeutic mental health treatment offered through the Correctional Services of Canada, the provincial director made a successful application under section 92 of the YCJA to transfer Ashley to the adult system. Cesaroni and Peterson-Badali (2017) report that despite Ashley having accrued some institutional offences while in youth custody, her sentences were merged to form a single adult sentence, which amounted to incarceration for well over two years. Ashley was transferred to the Nova Institution for Women, where she was immediately placed in segregation due to her self-harming and acting-out behaviour. During the one year she was housed in the federal system, Ashley spent all of her time in administrative segregation. She was transferred 17 times between three federal penitentiaries, two treatment facilities, two outside hospitals, and one provincial correctional facility in four different provinces. The coroner's report revealed that Ashley died as a result of asphyxiation: she did place a ligature around her neck, but she did not intend to die.

A high-profile coroner's inquest returned a verdict on this case on 19 December 2013, ruling that Ashley's death was a homicide and holding correctional systems accountable for her death. The report provided 104 recommendations detailing the need for a thorough overhaul of the correctional system and its treatment of female young adult offenders, the treatment protocols for inmates presenting with mental health challenges, and more explicit guidelines for administration and training (Reid, Bromwich, and Gilliss 2015).

Critical Thinking Question

This case study has been recommended as a training tool for individuals working in corrections. What impact will this case have on advocacy efforts to have a separate justice system for emerging adults?

that of adults," that Canada was explicit in its law that there were two distinct systems of justice. Before this time, Canada did not expressly adhere to the UNCRC, even though Canada had ratified it in 1991.

The lack of commitment to the UNCRC by Canada has been evidenced in the monitoring reports of the United Nations Committee on the Rights of the Child. In 2012, the committee asked Canada to "bring the juvenile justice system fully in line with the Convention . . . and with other relevant standards . . . including the Standard Minimum Rules for the Administration of Juvenile Justice (the Beijing Rules), the Guidelines for the Prevention of Juvenile Delinquency (the Riyadh Guidelines), the Rules for the Protection of Juveniles Deprived of their Liberty (the Havana Rules) and the Vienna Guidelines for Action on Children in the Criminal Justice System" (p. 3).

The UN Definitions of Child, Youth, and Young Adult: Implications for Criminal Justice

To prepare for the International Youth Year in 1985, the United Nations General Assembly endorsed a definition of youth as those persons between the ages of 15 and 24 years. Under this definition, children are persons under the age of 14 years. However, there are many distinctions made about the definitions of children, youth, and young adults in various treaties, programs, and conventions under the United Nations.

Article 1 of the UNCRC defines a child as "every human being below the age of 18 years unless, under the law applicable to the child, the majority is attained earlier." The UNCRC has been ratified in more than 190 countries and emphasizes that children have a right to be protected from degrading and cruel punishment and to receive special treatment in the justice system. Further, it states that children below a minimum age shall be presumed to lack the capacity to infringe the penal law. For the age of criminal responsibility, the United Nations Standard Minimum Rules for the Administration of Juvenile Justice (the "Beijing Rules"), under Rule 3.3, argues that the principles embodied in the rules for juveniles "shall also be made to extend to young adult offenders."

In 2009, the United Nations Committee on the Rights of the Child issued a General Comment reminding State Parties of this fundamental right of expression and participation (United Nations Committee on the Rights of the Child 2009). The fundamental principles of the UNCRC include non-discrimination, the right to life and development, the best interests of the child, and the right to be heard and taken seriously.

Article 12 of the UN Convention on the Rights of the Child (United Nations General Assembly 1989) provides the following:

1. States Parties shall assure to the child who is capable of forming his or her views the right to express those views freely in all matters affecting the child, the views of the child being given due weight by the age and maturity of the child.
2. For this purpose the child shall in particular be provided with the opportunity to be heard in any judicial and administrative proceedings affecting the child, either directly, or through a representative or an appropriate body, in a manner consistent with the procedural rules of national law.

Brank and Lane (2008) suggest that even though young people have a unique perspective, they are rarely asked for their opinion. The UNCRC outlines, in Articles 12, 13, and 14, the right of children under 18 years of age to fully participate in decisions that affect them, to express their ideas and concerns in any way that is appropriate for them, and to have access to full information about situations that affect them.

Based on the suggestions from the Canadian Coalition on the Rights of the Child (2016) regarding a rights-based approach to being heard and participating, the following list provides ways in which this fundamental principle may be expressed in youth justice:

- The young person is informed about their rights to express their views at all stages of the proceedings, including pre-charge, trial, sentencing, and review. Those who provide information will advocate for youth to ensure that they understand the potential risks and impacts of expressing their views in the youth justice process.
- The context in which the young people are expressing themselves is enabling and encouraging. In the case of youth justice, the right to have additional assistance from parents or other adults is proclaimed in law. Specialized youth courts (e.g., drug courts, mental health courts, healing courts) are designed on the principles of therapeutic jurisprudence so that the environment is structured to be able to hear the input from the accused young person.
- The views of a young person must be given due weight in all decisions according to the age and stage of development and their capacity to express themselves. Advocates and other responsible persons may assist the young person in feeling comfortable to express their views.
- The young person will be informed of the outcome of any process they are involved in and told, in language appropriate to the evolving capacity of the youth, how their views were considered in arriving at the outcome.

Developing Youth Policy with Youth Voice

Bessant (2005, p. 5) argues that the problem with discussions about youth policy is that adult policy-makers try to "imagine what young people want or what they believe they ought to want or need." This, she argues, has produced a history of youth policy-making where "policy makers create knowledge about young people" and act as spokespersons for them and as a "substitute for young people" (p. 5).

Franke (2010) outlines an analytical framework for youth-related policy development and research in Canada, suggesting that it is essential to decompartmentalize how researchers and policy-makers view youth and adopt a holistic approach that builds on the strengths and contributions that youth make to society as opposed to the deficit-based approach that was common in earlier approaches.

In General Comment 12 from the United Nations Committee on the Rights of the Child (2009, p. 24), States Parties are reminded of the role that young people can play in being consulted and participating in the formulation of legislation and policy related to prevention programs and other problem areas and involved in the drafting, development, and implementation of related plans and programs. This would mean that in programs that are developed for young offenders, their input and suggestions must be taken into account.

Box 5.2 | Youth Justice in Action

Youth Voice in Policy and Government

Article 12 of the United Nations Convention on the Rights of the Child declares that "States Parties shall assure to the child who is capable of forming his or her own views the right to express those views freely in all matters affecting the child, the views of the child being given due weight in accordance with the age and maturity of the child" (United Nations General Assembly 1989, p. 5).

This right promises to ensure that youth can have a voice in matters that concern them, mainly when adults are making decisions on their behalf.

The Government of Canada has committed not only to listen to the views of youth but to give them a seat at the table to inform the prime minister, members of Parliament, and other government officials of the views of young people.

Prime Minister Justin Trudeau has a council consisting of 21 youth from all across Canada. Each young person brings their unique perspective and passion to the table to advocate for youth and all Canadians. These young people have also been actively engaged in the creation of Canada's first

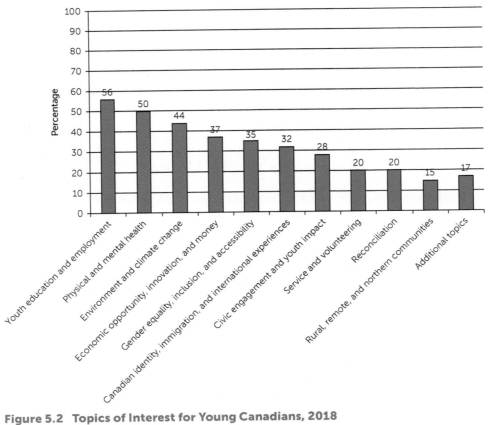

Figure 5.2 Topics of Interest for Young Canadians, 2018

Source: Based on Government of Canada 2019.

youth policy. This policy creation has involved visiting every province and territory, as well as reaching out online, to gather as many youth voices as possible. This youth policy will compile the priorities identified by Canadian youth. Through consultations with other young people in 60 roundtables across Canada and the encouragement of youth to complete online surveys to express their views, the Prime Minister's Youth Council has been actively engaged. In April 2018, the results of this Canada-wide consultation were published, with over 9000 youth voices expressing their top three priorities for youth policy (see Government of Canada, Privy Council Office

2019). Figure 5.2 represents the views of youth on these priorities.

Critical Thinking Questions

Are you surprised about the priorities that the youth have outlined for the government to consider?

The category "youth" is not a homogeneous group. When involving youth in policy conversations, how might you ensure that marginalized young people are included?

Box 5.3 | Youth Justice in Action

Youth Opinion on Cannabis Legalization

On 17 October 2018, cannabis was decriminalized under the Cannabis Act. For young people, this was pertinent because the Act decriminalized possession of up to 5 grams of cannabis by minors under the age of 18 years. All other drug-related offences for youth under the age of 18 will continue to be dealt with under the Youth Criminal Justice Act. Adults over the age of majority set by each province will be allowed to be in possession of legal cannabis purchased through government-approved outlets. This means that youth under the age of 19 in possession of more than 5 grams of cannabis product will be charged criminally with an offence that, for adults, is no longer a crime.

There have been varying opinions about the risks to young people with the legalization of cannabis for adults and the decriminalization of possession under 5 grams for youth under the age of 18. Following the recommendation of the federal Task Force on Cannabis Legalization and Regulation, the age of 18 has been selected as the point of differentiation (Government of Canada, Task Force on Cannabis Legalization and Regulation 2016). The rationale for this

age of access is that it will divert youth access to cannabis from illicit, unregulated markets to a safer and tightly regulated supply. Further, the amount limit will reduce the number of youth charged for possession from entering the criminal justice system.

The Cannabis Act has three main priorities: (1) preventing youth from accessing cannabis, (2) protecting public health and public safety, and (3) eliminating the illegal cannabis market by imposing serious criminal penalties for those operating outside the legal framework. These priorities will be operationalized through the enforcement of laws that prohibit vendors from promoting products that may be appealing to young people, as is the case for tobacco. Further, if an adult is found giving or selling cannabis to a young person, this may result in a maximum penalty of 14 years in prison.

In 2016, 77 young Canadians participated in 20 focus groups across Canada related to their perceptions about cannabis use (McKiernan and Fleming 2017). Many youth indicated that young people smoke cannabis anyway, so it might as well be legalized. One youth reported that if the taboo of the use of cannabis was removed due to decriminalization, then many young people who currently smoke it to be rebellious would stop using:

> I find too that people always say that when you are a teenager drinking is like scandalous, when you turn 19 it's not like a big deal anymore, so that can be part of the appeal [of smoking cannabis] maybe, is that it is illegal and that's why people might be interested in it. (McKiernan and Fleming 2017, p. 32)

The majority of the youth who participated in the focus groups also felt that cannabis was a far less risky substance than alcohol. Youth described alcohol consumption as "destructive" and felt it was more dangerous to be impaired by alcohol than cannabis when driving, and that it caused much more violent physical reactions (such as vomiting and memory loss). One youth even recommended criminalizing alcohol:

> Think about this. Here's another thing. If they were to legalize [cannabis], they could criminalize f'in alcohol and think about [how] much better the world would be. Seeing a bunch of stoners walking around instead of a bunch of drunken alcoholics f'in a bunch of shit? Which one seems like the better of two evils, you know? (McKiernan and Fleming 2017, p. 27)

Not all youth who participated in the study felt that cannabis should be legalized. There were some who worried that drug dealers would shift to pushing a more dangerous substance, such as cocaine, to youth on the streets. Others were indifferent as they recognized that legalization would bring very little change for young people due to the age restrictions that would be imposed. Finally, there were youth who focused their criticisms on the government, arguing that it should not earn the taxes generated from cannabis sales, and some even worried that the government would produce an inferior product by lowering THC levels in cannabis.

Canada has adopted the Lower-Risk Cannabis Use Guidelines (LRCUG) developed by Fischer et al. (2017) (CMHA 2018). These evidence based guidelines are as follows:

- The most effective way to avoid cannabis use–related health risks is abstinence.
- Avoid early age initiation of cannabis use.
- Choose low-potency THC or balanced THC-to-CBD ratio cannabis products.
- Abstain from using synthetic cannabinoids.
- Avoid combusted cannabis inhalation and give preference to non-smoking use methods.
- Avoid deep or other risky inhalation practices.
- Avoid high-frequency (daily or near daily) cannabis use.
- Abstain from cannabis-impaired driving.
- Populations at higher risk for cannabis use-related health problems should avoid the use.
- Avoid combining previously mentioned risk behaviours (e.g., early initiation and high-frequency use).

In response to these guidelines, the consensus from a sample of university students was that youth had not been consulted. If youth had been involved in drafting the policy, they argued, the language would be "less patronizing" and "adult-centred." One young person noted, "The most effective way to avoid sexual health related risks is abstinence, but very few young people would agree with that as a public health education principle." Another pointed to the unlikely success of advising youth to "avoid deep or other risky inhalation practices" given the preponderance in popular culture already of "bongs," "lungs" and other "smoking devices."

Critical Thinking Questions

What are some of the issues that you see related to young people and cannabis use?

How will the LRCUG assist in providing education to young people about cannabis use?

Challenges Faced by Youth with Highly Complex Needs

Statistics from the Canadian Mental Health Association (2018) indicate that only one in five children in Canada who need mental health services receives them, and the majority of young adults living with a mental illness report that their problems began in childhood. Indeed, research has shown that young offenders experience high levels of mental health issues (Kapp, Petr, Robbins, and Choi 2013), and despite these high levels, they do not have their treatment needs met (Whitted, Delavega, and Lennon-Dearing 2013). According to Kempker, Schmidt, and Espinosa (2017), the consensus across studies regarding justice-involved youth is that the vast majority of incarcerated youth (70–100 per cent) meet formal criteria for at least one *DSM*-5 disorder. Of those young people, approximately 20 per cent meet the diagnostic criteria for a severe mental health disorder that results in functional impairment.

A study of 152 youth who were involved with either the youth justice system or the mental health system found that youth who were referred from the mental health sector accessed significantly higher rates of service not only from health care and mental health but also through school support structures than their youth justice counterparts (Liebenberg and Ungar 2014). Further, according to the study, a lack of engagement with treatment service providers has always been problematic for young offenders. This lack of service is particularly disconcerting in that youth who have been diagnosed with multiple mental health disorders are more likely to offend than those without such challenges, and to have a higher likelihood of recidivism (Espinosa, Sorensen, and Lopez 2013).

Programs applying the theory of *therapeutic jurisprudence* (TJ) have been developed that attempt to respond to youth with complex needs (Winick 2003). The primary goal of TJ is to bring together the law with a variety of therapeutic techniques while still allowing other values, such as justice and due process, to be fully respected. One of the central principles of therapeutic jurisprudence is a commitment to dignity, which is required under the UNCRC discussed earlier. Wexler (1992) argues that TJ looks at law as it impacts people's emotional life and psychological well-being. TJ mandates the importance of psychological health and the value of bringing about healing and wellness as a direct outcome of any legal intervention.

Perlin (2017) suggests that TJ is a more relational approach to the practice of law that emphasizes wellness over adversarial triumphalism. Ronner (2002) points out that when individuals feel that the legal system has treated them with fairness, respect, and dignity, it can have a profound therapeutic effect. She goes on to suggest that this type of treatment will not only increase client satisfaction with the legal process but also lead offenders to accept responsibility for their conduct, take charge, and move to reform. In describing TJ, she refers to the three V's: voice, validation, and voluntary participation. Those accused before the court need to have a chance to tell their story to a decision maker. The decision maker must actively listen in order to validate the accused's account and ensure that they feel listened to and taken seriously. When this happens in a court, the accused feels a sense of voluntary participation. In the case of juveniles, Ronner (2002) argues that young people need to feel that their rights as citizens have been heard and they have been validated for voicing their version of the events. When the legal process treats offenders with dignity and respect, there is a greater likelihood that they will feel connected to the process of change necessary to deal with their challenges.

Mental health courts, drug courts, and other "problem-solving" courts have been created in an attempt to combine the goals of justice and the therapeutic needs of the accused (Madell, Thom, and McKenna 2013). Meta-analyses and systematic reviews of the effectiveness of the drug court model have concluded that, overall, drug court participants have lower rates of recidivism than non-participants (Blair, Sullivan, Lux, Thielo, and Gormsen 2016; Sullivan, Blair, Latessa, and Coen Sullivan 2014).

Mental health courts and mental health diversion programs are designed to be treatment-oriented and are based on the assumption that, for certain types of individuals, problem-solving responses are more appropriate than punishment (Madell et al. 2013). Such specialized services intended to improve coordination across justice and social service agencies improve efficiency, increase predictability of the court proceedings, and ultimately improve the quality of justice (Gilbert, Grimm, and Parnham 2001). Skowyra and Powell (2006) argue that many youth with significant mental health issues are in the justice system for relatively minor offences and are placed in jail by default. The provision of diversion for youth with mental health needs not only provides more effective and appropriate treatment but also facilitates the further development of community-based mental health services. Further, reviews of the research on such programs have pointed to the improvement in working relationships of cross-systems groups, an expedited court processing of youth into appropriate services, and a higher likelihood of encouraging family participation in treatment plans (Wiener, Winick, Skovran-Georges, and Castro 2010). Van der Laan and Eichelsheim (2013) suggest that advocates working on juvenile cases should be aware that prison sentences without juvenile-focused therapy will be detrimental to psychological development and that a therapeutic jurisprudence approach to youth cases is the preferred option, particularly for vulnerable youth with mental health challenges.

Youth Engagement, Adult–Youth Partnerships and the Promise of Resiliency

While the research literature is clear that risk can be reduced when the principles of effective intervention are followed, "therapeutic pessimism" abounds for dealing with high-risk youth because the process of treating them is often complicated (Skeem, Scott, and Mulvey 2014, p. 723). Some of the risk factors that contribute to their offending, such as negative attitudes, non-compliance, and disruptive behaviour, often make these youth difficult clients work with. In a meta-analysis of 114 studies of attrition from treatment, those offenders who were most likely to benefit from the treatment intervention, owing to their high-risk and high-needs profile, were the least likely to complete it (Olver, Stockdale, and Wormith 2011).

Box 5.4 | Youth Justice in Action

Youth Voice in Mental Health

The Mental Health Commission of Canada (MHCC), funded by Health Canada, works with all levels of government to create policy, educate, and create programs and tools to promote a better mental health system for all Canadians. Ten to twenty per cent of Canadian youth are affected by a mental illness or disorder, and only a fraction of those who need mental health services receives them (CMHA 2018). The MHCC has recognized how serious the problem is for youth and, in 2008, it decided to invite youth to join the MHCC Youth Council so young people could actively engage with and influence policy creation, work with systems such as criminal justice, and help improve Canada's mental health system. All of the youth who sit on the MHCC Youth Council have experience with mental illness. Members of the Youth Council openly share their own experience dealing with their mental health challenges and the stigma surrounding mental illness. As one young woman noted,

> I always thought being mentally ill made me a bad person, even broken. But when I reached recovery I was able to see everything that my illness taught me: compassion, empathy, appreciation, and resiliency. When I learned to live and thrive with it, I realized it made me a better and stronger person in the end.
> —Nancy (MHCC 2016, p. 5)

Another member of the council emphasized the need for a group response from young Canadians, commenting,

> As a group, youth are too often excluded from providing value or input into the decision-making process. The Youth Council provides a forum for the youth voice to be engaged in mental health advocacy and policy making on a national scale.
> —Amanee (MHCC 2016, p. 29)

Since the MHCC Youth Council formed, it has produced some of Canada's first youth-focused mental health work, including the document *The Mental Health Strategy for Canada: A Youth Perspective*, which adapts the existing adult-oriented strategy to more accurately reflect youth mental health. For youth in the criminal justice system who are living with mental health diagnoses, hearing the voice of their peers living with mental health issues and advocating on their behalf makes a significant positive difference.

Critical Thinking Question

What value is there in involving in this mental health conversation youth who have personal experience with mental illness?

Criminal behaviour in young people cannot merely be tackled as an episode of individual criminality disassociated from the social context or the available child welfare, education and health, social, and recreational provisions (Whyte 2005, p. 9). The social context is just as important as the individual personal and skill development outcomes are because "social circumstances and relationships with others are both the object of the intervention and the medium through which change can be achieved" (Farrall 2002, p. 21).

Box 5.5 | Youth Justice in Action

Youth Matters: Leadership Groups in Closed Custody in New Brunswick

Youth Matters is a youth-led leadership group that brings together—in conferences, youth forums, and discussion groups—traditional and non-traditional leaders from high school and university to discuss issues of importance to young people. Since its inception, Youth Matters has had the mandate of engaging non-traditional leaders, as they are often young people with exceptional abilities and a sense of agency who have just not yet had the chance to exercise them. One provincial conference was held in the same city as the New Brunswick Youth Centre, and two young offenders attended, supported by correctional staff who blended in with Youth Matters facilitators. The youth were so inspired that they asked whether they could develop a similar event for their peers inside the youth jail. The university students worked with these young persons in a series of meetings, and a two-day youth conference was hosted for all young offenders at the institution. The youth explored issues of substance abuse and bullying inside youth custody, and at the end of the event, they requested that a chapter of Youth Matters be established within the youth jail (see Reid 2013). In starting this group, the youth felt that the group should be governed by this set of principles: it should be non-judgmental, inclusive (every voice heard), safe, and meaningful to all involved.

The value of this group to the young people is perhaps best summarized by the following comment made by one of the young persons who worked on the development of the first conference:

> Youth Matters has changed my life. It has made me feel accepted, and helped me have a better sense of belonging. I'm grateful for having Youth Matters find me, it has/will be an amazing experience.

Since 2012, Youth Matters has created a video inside one of the units on institutional bullying so that it can be shown to new young persons when they arrive at the facility. As part of a national grant, a weekly program on gender-based violence was offered to explore the issue of violence in young women's lives, exploring such topics as gendered bullying, sports culture and violence, and youth engagement on the topic.

Further funding opportunities have allowed Youth Matters to explore more topics with young people in custody. These often centred on well-being—youth engaged in a dialogue to understand concepts of what their ideas about well-being were and how they might achieve it. Participants explored indicators of well-being, mental health, Indigenous mental health, self-care practices in custody, and life skills, as well as analyzing their own strengths as they planned for reintegration.

The youth were also given many opportunities to discuss their lived experiences as youth in a custodial environment. The most salient takeaway from speaking with the young people was that many of them had never been asked to share their opinion about the criminal justice system. They welcomed the opportunity to give their opinion and to be active participants in their experience, and many expressed that they would like to work with the criminal justice system to make it better. These youth all expressed a willingness to be understood and to be heard.

Youth described lives filled with risk factors and very few protective factors, and they shared bothersome details of their home life and the pains of imprisonment (Reid 2009). Many of them felt that drugs had a significant role to play in the commission of their offence. One young person commented, "We're all unique," but noted that while incarcerated, they are all treated the same (referring in particular to their grey flannels).

Family factors were essential to the young people, and one youth pointed out that not enough attention was given to those in custody who were also parents. One youth felt that being a father was a "protective factor," helping him to stay away from drugs and crime. Another young person relayed how his incarceration was having an impact on his younger brother; he felt he had lost touch with his brother but also regretted the inappropriate role model that he had become since his incarceration. One youth stated, "If I had a family it would have saved me from this; foster care that's what messed me up." His sense of abandonment was further evidenced not only through the number of placements he had experienced but also through his opinion about his foster parents, to whom he ascribed questionable motives: "I'll take in this troublesome kid so I can get a couple hundred dollars for keeping him."

Youth also commented about reintegration, and it was clear that some of these young people were afraid of breaching their multiple conditions of release: "While we are in here we work on levels, and if you achieve points you get more privileges. When you are released you start back at nothing with a six o'clock curfew, requirements to attend programs, attend school, attend counselling and no opportunity to improve, all the while not being able to talk to your friends because of a non-association order." Another participant said, "We're not robots, we can't go from being in here for six months or a year talking to our friends, to having no friends to talk to. We can't change overnight." There was an acknowledgement from the youth that the probation officers had a job to do concerning reporting to the court, but their complaints stemmed from the perceived inability of officials to "see the positive things" and be able to "cut some slack." One young man noted that he would like to see "less judgement from people in power," and another expanded on this point by adding, "Sometimes people make mistakes. There are too many labels." Another youth remarked, "Understand that everyone has a past and a reason for what they do."

Throughout the conversations, there were participants who felt there was no value in the youth criminal justice system and offered no suggestions as to how they would improve the system for young people. One youth simply said, "I don't like the youth criminal justice system." On the other end of the spectrum, there was a young person who shared positive sentiments about his experience and felt that custody offered him a better life than living on the streets, commenting, "I get better food in jail, I get to shower everyday."

Critical Thinking Question

What are some of the benefits that you see to having young people manage a group such as Youth Matters inside a carceral setting?

Was there anything that surprised you about the comments raised by the young people regarding the youth justice system?

We know from the **resiliency** literature, for example, that not all young people exposed to multiple risk factors become offenders, nor do all young people who offend grow up in low socio-economic classes (Steinberg, Blatt-Eisengart, and Cauffman 2006; Ungar, 2004). Resilience is fostered through the adult–youth relationships present in the milieu in which the young offender is being treated. As Ungar (2013) has argued, resilience might best be defined as the young person's ability to navigate toward resources while the institution provides the necessary resources and possible relationships for the young person. In the

resiliency
The ability of children and youth to develop positive self-esteem and self-efficacy despite facing a crisis, challenges, or adversity.

context of high risk, relationships with supportive adults are crucial in mitigating the toxic effects on youth of incarceration. Unless a youth is empowered to make some choice about engaging with the programs and resources, however, the likelihood of resilience is dramatically weakened.

In a study of 497 high-risk children and youth who were multiple-service users, Ungar (2013) found that it was not the quantity of the services that the youth received, but rather the quality of the relationships between a single service provider and the young person that was predictive of positive outcomes for the youth. Adult–youth relationships that attended to the needs of young people, that engaged their voices through the encouragement of negotiation and choice in decisions that affected them, and that provided for their equal participation whenever it was reasonably available all supported young people becoming resilient (see Box 5.6).

protective factors
Circumstances and experiences that buffer young people's involvement in behaviours that would be damaging to themselves and others.

Positive relationships with adults are essential as a **protective factor** for youth who may be enmeshed in the youth justice system. Throughout the province of Ontario, for example, they have become part of the "relationship custody" framework that guides the work with young persons in secure custody. The relationship custody approach requires staff not only to work from a strengths-based approach that reinforces the skills and talents of the young person but also to engage with young people and develop a rapport that helps them make more positive choices. It requires a balance between the dynamic security approaches (professional, positive relationships between youth and staff) and the static security approaches (physical barriers and surveillance) (Ontario, Provincial Advocate for Children and Youth 2013).

Schubert, Mulvey, Loughran, and Losoya (2012) report that youth who do not feel they can turn to staff for help are more likely to have difficulty in post-release outcomes. Marsh and Evans (2009) found, as well, that when youth in a closed-custody setting were asked to identify the qualities of the staff members they respected, high levels of trust, positive effects on youth, high levels of engagement, and practical problem-solving skills were cited. Those youth who spoke of staff who had these qualities were also more likely to believe they would achieve significant success after their release (see Box 5.6).

youth engagement
The meaningful participation and sustained involvement of a young person in an activity that has a focus outside of him- or herself. Full engagement consists of a behavioural component, an affective component, and a cognitive component.

To actively engage young people (**youth engagement**), adults need to work as partners with them in a supportive manner. Rather than young people working in isolation, away from the individuals and communities whose perceptions and actions they seek to transform, they can be engaged with "adult allies" who support them and act as their advocate every day (Fletcher and Vavrus 2006).

Strong youth–adult partnerships serve a variety of different purposes: they protect youth rights for participation, particularly concerning decision-making; they facilitate positive youth development; and they work to steer youth toward improving their communities and civil society (Stolle and Hooghe 2004; Zeldin, Camino, and Mook 2005).

While these issues only scratch the surface of the myriad issues related to youth in custody and the staff who work with them, the research evidence and the practice evidence is clear that the relationship between adults and youth is essential for young people who are completing their term of custody and their successful reintegration back into their communities.

Box 5.6 | Youth Justice in Action

Adult Ally Training with Correctional Staff in Closed-Custody Facility

In 2013, all of the staff involved with young offenders at the New Brunswick Youth Centre participated in a half-day training seminar led by young people on how to be an adult ally to the youth in the facility (Reid 2013). Wong, Zimmerman, and Parker (2010, p. 100) point out that a great deal of the children and adolescent research has been constructed using an "adult lens" that frequently overlooks the perspectives and real life experiences of young people, and the delivery of a training session by young people shifted the focus so that the staff gained a better appreciation of what the young people might be experiencing. In one of the activities, staff were asked to write down one experience they had with youth at the facility when they were proud to be an adult ally. The responses were then randomly handed out to the participants and read aloud to debrief the exercise (Reid 2013). Here are some examples of the staff's experiences:

- "I had a conversation with an 'at risk/young offender' about him going to [the program]. He told me I was the first person to suggest it, and that he might even consider it."

- "Helped a female youth with low self-esteem learn to be more assertive with her peers."
- "Helped a young person feel better about themselves after they had an upsetting phone call from a family member who told them they were nothing."
- "Once I went through the process of showing a youth sympathy towards another youth. Encouraged youth to see that maybe that youth does not have the same opportunities as him."
- "I gave a youth an idea for a project and then saw him excel in creating a great product."
- "I've encouraged youth to join high school basketball team because of their potential."
- "I have taught different youth how to play the guitar. Taught a youth how to play a new song and made his day better!"

Critical Thinking Question
What kinds of activities can you think of that might fall under the category of an adult ally?

Summary

There is no one ideal way to approach youth with high needs. Youth justice legislation and programing for high-needs youth cannot be developed as a one-size-fits-all model because if this were done, the needs of so many youths would not be met. This chapter presented many of the unique challenges of developing effective policies for youth.

The binary function of the youth justice system, as it is designed today, does not permit the best interests of youth to be addressed. This chapter made the point that, increasingly, youth have been pushed into the adult system through a variety of *practices*. The issue of aging out of crime as well as the psychosocial development of emerging adults was presented to make a case for less adulteration of the criminal justice system, and more attention to the specific needs of this age cohort. As has been pointed out throughout this chapter, a key challenge is to protect public safety while ensuring that the principles of effective correctional intervention are applied to maximize the likelihood that young people will make a healthy developmental transition to non-criminal adulthood.

Throughout the evolution of youth criminal justice, the fundamental belief was that all avenues should be exhausted to prevent youth from embarking on a life of crime. As the research demonstrates, this is best achieved by reserving custodial sentences for the most severe of cases and, instead, imposing meaningful consequences that will promote rehabilitation and reintegration. High numbers of incarcerated youth have been shown to have mental illness or conduct disorders, and their needs cannot be met in a correctional facility. Mental health diversion programs were discussed as one avenue to help these youth.

In order that we might truly understand the needs of youth, youth themselves must be consulted. The UN Convention on the Rights of the Child demands this, and as a signatory to this human rights treaty, Canada must respond. Allowing youth to have a voice in their own experience empowers them and encourages them to take ownership of their path. This chapter described some instances when young people have been consulted and listened to regarding their lived experiences of the youth justice system. This approach was exemplified in the youth-led group Youth Matters, which operates in a closed-custody facility. The value of strong adult–youth partnerships to enhance the voice of young people in closed custody was shown through examples of successful youth-led projects and consultation.

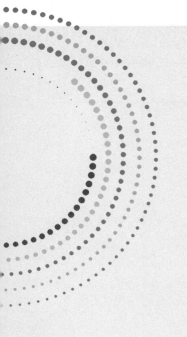

Key Terms

adulteration	reintegration
best interests of the child doctrine	resiliency
custodial sanctions	risk factors
labelling	secure custody
protective factors	youth engagement
rehabilitation	youth justice

Review Questions

1. What is meant by the "best interests of the child"? How does this concept relate to the current legal regulations of young persons?

2. What is meant by "adulteration"?

3. Describe the type of youth justice model that best describes the JDA and YOA. How do these models differ from the youth justice model that characterizes the YCJA?

4. What is the importance of allowing youth a voice in the development of criminal justice policy?

5. Describe three to four of the key characteristics of effective high-needs youth programs. How do they compare to the practical treatment principles for young offenders?

Critical Thinking Questions

1. How important do you think it is to maintain a separate system for young offenders in Canada?

2. To what extent do you feel the UN Convention on the Rights of the Child is, or is not, necessary for empowering and protecting young persons?

3. What are the critical factors that differentiate programs that work from those that don't work? Briefly discuss the implications of these differences (if any).

4. How might we best address the challenges that high-needs youth face today?

5. What are ways to foster positive adult–youth partnerships with high-needs youth?

References

Allen, M. (2016). *Victim services in Canada 2011/12*. Ottawa: Canadian Centre for Justice Statistics.

Arnett, J.J. (2014). *Emerging adulthood: The winding road from the late teens through the twenties*. New York: Oxford University Press

Bessant, J. (2005). Principles for developing youth policy. *Policy Studies, 26*(1), 103–16.

Blair, C., Sullivan, C.C., Lux, J., Thielo, A J., and Gormsen, L. (2016). Measuring drug court adherence to the what works literature: The creation of the evidence-based correctional program checklist–drug court. *International Journal of Offender Therapy and Comparative Criminology, 60*(2), 165–88.

Bonta, J., and Andrews, D.A. (2016). *The psychology of criminal conduct*. New York: Routledge.

Brank, E., and Lane, J. (2008). An experimental juvenile probation program: Effects on parent and peer relationships. *Crime Delinquency, 54*(2), 193–224.

Canada. (1965). *Juvenile delinquency in Canada. The report of the Department of Justice Committee on Juvenile Delinquency*. Ottawa: Department of Justice, Committee on Juvenile Delinquency.

Canadian Coalition on the Rights of the Child. (2016.) *Fact sheet: What is the right to be heard?* Retrieved from http://rightsofchildren.ca/wp-content/uploads/2014/04/Right-to-be-Heard.pdf

Canadian Mental Health Association (CMHA). (2018). *Fast facts about mental illness*. Retrieved from https://cmha.ca/about-cmha/fast-facts-about-mental-illness

Cesaroni, C. (2015). Young adults: An overlooked population in Canadian correctional policy and legislation. *Canadian Criminal Law Review, 19*(1), 115–28.

Cesaroni, C., & Peterson-Badali, M. (2017). Ashley Smith and Incarcerated Young Women: Marginalized at Any Age. *Canadian Journal of Law and Society 32*(2), 249–267. https://www.muse.jhu.edu/article/671579

Elman, I. (2017) *Missed opportunities: The experience of young adults incarcerated in federal penitentiaries*. Ottawa: Correctional Investigator of Canada.

Espinosa, E.M., Sorensen, J.R., and Lopez, M.A. (2013). Youth pathways to placement: The influence of gender, mental health need and trauma on confinement in the juvenile justice system. *Journal of Youth and Adolescence, 42*(12), 1824–36.

Farrall, S. (2002). *Rethinking what works with offenders*. Cullompton, UK: Willan.

Farrall, S., Sharpe, G., Hunter, B., and Calverley, A. (2011). Theorizing structural and individual-level processes in desistance and persistence: Outlining an integrated perspective. *Australia & New Zealand Journal of Criminology, 44*(2), 218–34.

Farrington, D.P., Loeber, R., and Howell, J.C. (2012). Young adult offenders: The need for more effective legislative options and justice processing. *Criminology & Public Policy, 11*(4), 729–50.

Fischer, B., Russell, C., Sabioni, P., van den Brink, W., Le Foll, B., Hall, W., . . . Room, R. (2017). Lower-risk cannabis use guidelines: A comprehensive update of evidence and recommendations. *American Journal of Public Health, 107*(8), e1–e12.

Fletcher, A., and Vavrus, J. (2006). *The guide to social change led by and with young people.* Olympia, WA: CommonAction.

Franke, S. (2010). *Current realities and emerging issues facing youth in Canada: An analytical framework for public policy research.* Ottawa: Government of Canada, Policy Research Institute.

Giedd, J.N. (2008). The teen brain: Insights from neuroimaging. *Journal of Adolescent Health, 42*(4), 335–43.

Gilbert, J., Grimm, R., and Parnham, J. (2001). Applying therapeutic principles to a family- focused juvenile justice model. *Alabama Law Review, 52*(1153), 1196–7.

Government of Canada. (2019). *Canada's Youth Policy.* https://www.canada.ca/en/youth/programs/policy.html

Government of Canada, Privy Council Office. (2019). *Report of the prime minister's youth council.* Retrieved from https://www.canada.ca/content/dam/pco-bcp/documents/pdfs/rpt-eng.pdf

Government of Canada, Task Force on Cannabis Legalization and Regulation. (2016). *Toward the legalization, regulation and restriction of access to marijuana.* Retrieved from https://www.canada.ca/content/dam/hc-sc/healthy-canadians/migration/health-system-systeme-sante/consultations/legalization-marijuana-legalisation/alt/legalization-marijuana-legalisation-eng.pdf

Hoeve, M., McReynolds, L.S., and Wasserman, G.A. (2013). Service referral for juvenile justice youths: Associations with psychiatric disorder and recidivism. *Administration and Policy in Mental Health and Mental Health Services Research, 41*(3), 379–89.

Howard League for Penal Reform. (2015). *Judging maturity: Exploring the role of maturity in the sentencing of young adults.* Retrieved from https://howardleague.org/wpcontent/uploads/2017/07/Judging-maturity.pdf

Kapp, S.A., Petr, C.G., Robbins, M.L., and Choi, J.J. (2013). Collaboration between community mental health and juvenile justice systems: Barriers and facilitators. *Child and Adolescent Social Work Journal, 30*, 505–17.

Kempker, S.M., Schmidt, A.T., and Espinosa, E.M. (2017). Understanding the influence of mental health diagnosis and gender on placement decisions for justice-involved youth. *Journal of Youth and Adolescence, 46*(7), 1562–81.

Liebenberg, L., and Ungar, M. (2014). A comparison of service use among youth involved with juvenile justice and mental health. *Children and Youth Services Review, 39.* 117–22.

Luciana, M., and Collins, P.F. (2012). Incentive motivation, cognitive control, and the adolescent brain: Is it time for a paradigm shift? *Child development perspectives, 6*(4), 392–9.

McKiernan, A., and Fleming, K. (2017). *Canadian youth perceptions on cannabis.* Ottawa: Canadian Centre on Substance Abuse.

Madell, D., Thom, K., and McKenna, B. (2013). A systematic review of literature relating to problem-solving youth courts. *Psychiatry, Psychology and Law, 20*(3), 412–22.

Marsh, S.C., and Evans, W.P. (2009). Youth perspectives on their relationships with staff in juvenile correction settings and perceived likelihood of success on release. *Youth Violence and Juvenile Justice, 7,* 46–67.

Mental Health Commission of Canada. (2016). *Mental Health Commission of Canada - Strategic Plan 2017–2022.* Ottawa.

Nguyen, H., and Loughran, T.A. (2018). On the measurement and identification of turning points in criminology. *Annual Review of Criminology, 1,* 335–58.

Olver, M.E., Stockdale, K.C., and Wormith, J.S. (2011). A meta-analysis of predictors of offender treatment attrition and its relationship to recidivism. *Journal of Consulting and Clinical Psychology, 79*(1), 6–21

Ontario, Provincial Advocate for Children and Youth. (2013). *It depends who's working": The youth reality at the Roy McMurtry Centre.* Toronto: Office of Provincial Advocate for Children and Youth.

Perlin, M.L. (2017). "Have You Seen Dignity?": The story of the development of therapeutic jurisprudence. *New Zealand Universities Law Review,* Westlaw.

Petrosino, A., Turpin-Petrosino, C. and Guckenburg, S. (2013). *Crime Prevention Research Review No. 9: Formal system processing of juveniles: effects on delinquency.* Washington, D.C.: US Department of Justice, Office of Community-Oriented Policing Services. Retrieved from https://ric-zai-inc.com/Publications/cops-p265-pub.pdf

Reid, S.A. (2009). *125 warnings: A review of extrajudicial measures and sanctions in the province of New Brunswick.* Unpublished report for New Brunswick Department of Public Safety.

Reid, S.A. (2011). Age and responsibility. In W. Chambliss and G.J. Golson (Eds), *Juvenile crime and justice.* Key Issues in Crime and Punishment Series. Thousand Oaks, CA: Sage. Retrieved from http://sk.sagepub.com/reference/juvenilecrimejustice/n1.xml

Reid, S.A. (2013, August). *Creating youth–adult partnerships with youth in custody.* Paper presented to the New Brunswick Department of Public Safety.

Reid, S.A., Bromwich, R.J, and Gilliss, S. (2015). *Youth and the law: New approaches to criminal justice and child protection.* Emond.

Rocque, M. (2015). The lost concept: The (re)emerging link between maturation and desistance from crime. *Criminology & Criminal Justice, 15*(3), 340–60.

Ronner, A.D. (2002). Songs of validation, voice, and voluntary participation: Therapeutic jurisprudence, Miranda and juveniles. *University of Cincinnati Law Review, 71,* 89–114.

Sampson, R.J., and Laub, J. H. (2016). Turning points and the future of life-course criminology: Reflections on the 1986

Criminal Careers Report. *Journal of Research in Crime and Delinquency, 53*(3), 321–35.

Schubert C.A., Mulvey, E.P., Loughran, T.A., and Losoya, S.H. (2012). Perceptions of institutional experience and community outcomes for serious adolescent offenders. *Criminal Justice and Behaviour, 39*(1), 71–93.

Skeem, J.L., Scott, E., and Mulvey, E.P. (2014). Justice policy reform for high-risk juveniles: Using science to achieve large-scale crime reduction. *Annual Review of Clinical Psychology, 10,* 709–39.

Skowyra, K., and Powell, S.D. (2006). *Juvenile diversion: Programs for justice-involved youth with mental health disorders.* Washington, DC: National Centre for Mental Health and Juvenile Justice.

Steinberg, L. (2017). Adolescent brain science and juvenile justice policymaking. *Psychology, Public Policy, and Law, 23*(4), 410–20.

Steinberg, L., Blatt-Eisengart, I., and Cauffman, E. (2006). Patterns of competence and adjustment among adolescents from authoritative, authoritarian, indulgent and neglectful homes: Replication in a sample of serious juvenile offenders. *Journal of Research on Adolescence, 16,* 47–58.

Stolle, D., and Hooghe, M. (2004). The roots of social capital: Attitudinal and network mechanisms in the relation between youth and adult indicators of social capital. *Acta Politica, 39,* 422–41.

Sullivan, C.J., Blair, L., Latessa, E., and Coen Sullivan, C. (2014). Juvenile drug courts and recidivism: Results from a multisite outcome and process study. *Justice Quarterly, 33*(2), 291–318.

Trolio, M. (2018, February 27). Locking up youth with adults: An update. *Prison Policy Initiative.* Retrieved from https://www.prisonpolicy.org/blog/2018/02/27/youth

Umbach, R., Berryessa, C.M., and Raine, A. (2015). Brain imaging research on psychopathy: Implications for punishment, prediction, and treatment in youth and adults. *Journal of Criminal Justice, 43*(4), 295–306.

Ungar, M. (2004). Resilience among children in child-welfare, corrections, mental health and educational settings: Recommendations for service. *Child and Youth Care Forum, 34*(6), 445–64.

Ungar, M. (2013). The impact of youth–adult relationships on resilience. *International Journal of Child, Youth and Family Studies, 4*(3), 328–36.

United Nations, Committee on the Rights of the Child. (2009). *General Comment No.12: The right of the children to be heard.* Fifty-first session, Geneva, May 25–June 12, 2009. Retrieved from: http://www.crin.org/en/library/publications/crc-general-comments

United Nations, Committee on the Rights of the Child. (2012). *Concluding observations of the third and fourth periodic report of Canada, adopted by the Committee at its sixty-first session.* Retrieved from https://tbinternet.ohchr.org/_layouts/treatybodyexternal/Download.aspx?symbolno=CRC%2fC%2fCAN%2fCO%2f3-4&Lang=en

United Nations General Assembly. (1989). *Convention on the rights of the child.* United Nations Treaty Series, vol. 1577.

van der Laan, A., and Eichelsheim, V. (2013). Juvenile adaptation to imprisonment: Feelings of safety, autonomy and well-being, and behaviour in prison. *European Journal of Criminology, 10*(4), 424–43.

Wexler, D.B. (1992). Putting mental health into mental health law. *Law and Human Behavior, 16*(1), 27–38.

Whitted, K.S., Delavega, E., and Lennon-Dearing, R. (2013). The youngest victims of violence: Examining the mental health needs of young children who are involved in the child-welfare and juvenile justice systems. *Child and Adolescent Social Work Journal, 30,* 181–95.

Whyte, B. (2005). Effectiveness, research and youth justice. *Youth Justice, 4*(1), 1–21.

Wiener, R.L., Winick, B.J., Skovran-Georges, L., and Castro, A. (2010). A testable theory of problem solving courts: Avoiding past empirical and legal failures. *International Journal of Law and Psychiatry, 33,* 417–27.

Wilson, H.A., and Hoge, R.D. (2013). The effect of youth diversion programs on recidivism: A meta-analytic review. *Criminal Justice and Behavior, 40*(5), 497–518.

Winick, B. (2003). Therapeutic jurisprudence and problem solving courts. *Fordham Urban Law Journal, 30,* 1055–76.

Winterdyk, J. (2015, March 8). Age of criminal responsibility: An illusive dilemma. *LawNow, 39*(4). Retrieved from http://www.lawnow.org/age-of-criminal-responsibility

Wong, N.T., Zimmerman, M.A., and Parker, E.A. (2010). A typology of youth participation and empowerment for child and adolescent health promotion. *American Journal of Community Psychology, 46,* 100–14.

Zeldin, S., Camino, L., and Mook, C. (2005). The adoption of innovation in youth organizations: Creating the conditions for youth–adult partnerships. *Journal of Community Psychology, 33*(1), 121–35.

Youth Deviance and the Media
Mapping Knowledge and the Limits to Certainty

Chris McCormick

6

Overview

The media—including traditional print and electronic media, such as newspapers and television, and more recently social media—are one of society's key sources of knowledge about crime, deviance and control. Despite the media's popularity and influence, however, over the years media scholars have been skeptical of the accuracy and usefulness of media representations of crime and justice, and have instead given more weight to officially produced data (like crime statistics) and data acquired through other data-collection techniques (like self-report and victimization studies). This chapter provides a somewhat different discussion of the media, acknowledging that although the media are often guilty of distorting and sensationalizing crime news stories, they nonetheless create a public arena in which youth crime and criminal justice are debated and understood. Specifically, they create a climate where youth are conceptualized as a problem, a theme which cuts across time and culture.

Key Objectives

After reading this chapter, you should be able to:

- Understand different methods for measuring youth crime.
- Describe criticisms of those methods.
- Explain how new methods of counting youth crime arose from criticisms of official statistics.
- Apply your knowledge of the media to analyzing news stories about youth crime.

Introduction

Narrowly missing being designated a "young offender," an 18-year-old man was charged with attempted murder and various weapons offences. Markel Downey's story, however, started before charges were laid against him in December 2014. He was a promising boxer who won gold at the Canada Winter Games in 2011. On track for the Olympics, he nonetheless lost contact with his coach and the sport he might have used as a ticket out of North Preston, a poor community outside Dartmouth, Nova Scotia. Charged along with two 17-year-old young offenders whose identity was protected under the law, the charges he faced had as much to do with his background as the decisions he made. To the public, however, he is simply the kid who had a great start but for whom things had inexplicably gone wrong (Lau 2014).

This chapter is a reflection on what we know about youth crime and juvenile deviance. Before we can do anything about a social problem, we must lay out the methods for acquiring knowledge about the problem and the limitations of those methods. The premise of this chapter is that what we know about youth crime and juvenile deviance is based on the particular methods we use to map that knowledge. Although there are other methods, this chapter focuses specifically on an analysis of the role of media in the production of knowledge about youth crime and justice, briefly contrasting it with other data-collection techniques, including official statistics, self-report, and victimization studies. (See the discussion of crime measurement in Chapter 2.)

Three different sources of knowledge are official statistics, unofficial data, and the media. These sources are complementary, although they differ both in kind and degree. Official statistics record in detail what is known and reported to the police, while self-report and victimization studies are used to fill out those incidents not reported to the police. The media, however, are the main sources of crime news information for the public (Surette 1998), not statistics, and they highlight emotional and violent extremes of crime (Fishman 1981). Furthermore, the media then create a feedback loop where discussions of youth crime influence public perception and to some extent public policy with calls for more punitive measures (Garofalo 1981). This continues to be an important issue for media studies of youth crime (see Sampert and Froese 2012; Tanner 2001).

Numerous studies by criminologists and media scientists have empirically supported the argument that the media play a significant role in shaping public attitudes toward youth crime (Best 1999; Cohen 1972; Faith and Jiwani 2002; Muncie 2004; Schissel 1997, 2006). One of the earliest and most famous of these is Stanley Cohen's influential book *Folk Devils and Moral Panics: The Creation of the Mods and Rockers* (1972). Cohen's study, which involves field-research interviews and analysis of media reports, shows how rather haphazardly organized groups of youths (or "youth gangs") known as Mods and Rockers came to be famous in England in the 1960s through the sensationalist stories that were written about them in the newspapers of the day. For example, a headline in the *Daily Mirror* on 30 March 1964 read "'Wild Ones' Invade Seaside—97 Arrests." Cohen coined the term **moral panic** to describe the exaggerated fears about youth deviance that were generated by the media, while he used the term **folk devils** to capture the idea that—much like witches in seventeenth-century New England—English youth of the 1960s came to be viewed by adults as a group that posed a potentially serious threat to the traditional values and institutions of English society (Smandych 2001, p. 66).

While the findings of researchers like Cohen (1972) have been influential in evoking skepticism about the accuracy and usefulness of information on youth crime and justice derived from the media, this does not mean that criminologists should entirely discount the value of examining the ways in which the media may contribute a very different knowledge to the public than is available through crime statistics. Overall, in this chapter, we will come to see that the study of youth crime and deviance is more than just counting statistics, since the conditions for creating and knowing meaning are more complex. Knowledge of crime and deviance is both actuarial and interpretive, and it is known by police at the same time as it is socially constructed in the media. The topic of youth crime will be used here as a way to reflect upon our methods for knowing about crime and understanding its occurrence. By grounding the analysis of youth crime within the context of other ways of knowing, we may create a more adequate method of analyzing how our knowledge of youth crime and justice is generated in today's contemporary society, and how to think about the fears around youth and the dangers they pose.

moral panic
Exaggerated fears about social problems, including youth deviance, partly generated by the media.

folk devils
Any group that is perceived to pose a threat to the traditional values and institutions of society.

The Official Version: Statistics on Youth Crime

First, we will briefly look at the official statistics on (youth) crime and consider what they do/do not tell us. (This subject is discussed in more detail in Chapter 2). Overall, these statistics attempt to portray crime as a pattern through uniform descriptions. However, in their doing so, artificial categories are often created that mask important details about events and processes connected with crime, and disguise the fact that official rates are reactive, depending on reports by the public (Haggerty 2001). Consequently, the attempt to know about youth crime from official crime statistics is like trying to dine out by reading restaurant reviews—entertaining but ultimately unfulfilling.

The Canadian Centre for Justice Statistics (CCJS) has collected information on crime every year since 1962 in what is called the Uniform Crime Report (UCR) survey. It provides an aggregate count because it lumps crime into categories based on reports from over 1000 separate police detachments from over 200 different police forces across Canada. The UCR is the official source that represents crimes substantiated through police investigation. The UCR does not reflect the total amount of crime in society, although it might be understood that way. It was originally created as a way to measure police work, and to compare crime across jurisdictions and to justify the use of police resources. And, of course, in order for the UCR to provide meaningful statistics, police have to count crime the same way, consistently and systematically, across jurisdictions.

Any change in the crime rate can be read as a commentary on the effectiveness of the police, courts, and corrections, and the direction of public policy. If the crime rate increases, questions can be raised as to whether the police are doing a good job or whether politicians need to get tough on crime. Similarly, if the crime rate decreases, criticisms can be raised about whether we need to put resources into policing or whether political discourse on "getting tough on crime" is justified. Overall, crime rates have continued to decline. This can be taken to mean that at the aggregate level Canadians have been enjoying an unprecedented level of safety.

The Youth Crime Statistic

In its annual publication on crime, Statistics Canada reports that about 89,000 youth (ages 12 to 17 years) were accused of a criminal offence in 2017. This represents a significant decrease from 2013, when it stood at 104,000. Furthermore, it has gone down significantly from when the Youth Criminal Justice Act (YCJA) was implemented a decade earlier. When viewed in a historical time frame, some general trends can be noted. The youth crime rate peaked in 1991, decreased substantially over the next decade, and then remained relatively stable in the early 2000s until decreasing again by 40 per cent by the mid 20-teens. In contrast to the percentage of youth crime overall, the rate of violent crime steadily increased from the mid-1980s up to about 2007. This rate was double what it had been 20 years earlier and was largely made up of increases in common assault, which accounted for about 6 in 10 violent incidents committed by youth. This increase is accounted for in part by an actual increase in crime, but it also might be due to increased reporting and charging practices. The number of youth accused of homicide rose from 35 in 2012 to 40 in 2013, although the rate was lower than the 10-year average (Statistics Canada 2014). Youth homicide rates can vary considerably from one year to the next because of the relatively small number of offences. This can lead to a misinterpretation, especially if such a change is reported in the media without the underlying absolute change. And, as was seen in the chapter-opening news story about Markel Downey, the aspiring young boxer from Preston, youth homicide can be portrayed as "out of character."

In addition, in 2013, almost 18,000 youth were accused of a drug violation under the Controlled Drugs and Substances Act (CDSA), the majority (81 per cent) of which involved possession of cannabis. While the rates of youth accused of drug offences decreased for most drugs, rates for certain drug violations remained higher than a decade ago. For instance, while possession of cannabis decreased slightly between 2012 and 2013 (−1 per cent), the rate remained 30 per cent higher than in 2003 (600 youth accused per 100,000 youth population versus 462 youth accused per 100,000 youth population) (Statistics Canada 2014). Part of this increase is artificial in that the CDSA, which was introduced in 1997 and which replaced the Narcotic Control Act, strengthened law enforcement.

The CDSA also broadened the range of illegal substances to include amphetamines, LSD, and anabolic steroids (CanLII 1996).

What also deserves mention in terms of the official statistics on youth crime is that many youth who could have been charged with an offence are handled outside the formal justice system. In 2013, 55 per cent of youth accused were dealt with by other means, while the remaining 45 per cent were formally charged by police. The decline in charges against youth accused of a crime coincided with the introduction of the YCJA in 2003. As a general trend, the proportion of accused youth who were cleared by means other than a charge increased for most offences. As discussed in Chapter 3, a primary objective of the YCJA was to divert youth involved in minor, non-violent crimes from the formal justice system, creating procedures for the police use of discretion. Obviously, charges are still the norm for serious offences, such as homicide, but less serious offences, such as minor theft, are more likely to be diverted from the criminal justice system (Barnhorst 2004).

For reasons associated with these legal changes, the youth crime rate and the charge rate can co-vary. Obviously, this means that accused youth are dealt with through means other than the formal system. Since about 2000, the proportion of youth apprehended but not charged has been on the rise, but this trend increased sharply after the introduction of the YCJA (as discussed in Chapter 3).

When it comes to some cases, however, such changes can lead to the charge that the system is now too lenient when it comes to young offenders. For example, in October 2004, 16-year-old Archie Billard ran a red light and crashed into Theresa McEvoy, a teacher's aide and mother of three, killing her instantly. He was speeding, was driving a stolen car, and was being chased by police. He was so high he had no memory of the incident, but he pled guilty to negligence causing death in 2006. The public was outraged because he had a string of convictions and was awaiting trial on other offences ("N.S. Teen Gets Adult Sentence" 2006). The circumstances surrounding the case led to a provincial inquiry (the Nunn Inquiry) that recommended changes to the federal YCJA. After pleading guilty to criminal negligence in McEvoy's death, Billard was sentenced to four years in prison, was released in 2009, and was then readmitted twice for statutory violations in that and the following year. Typical comments at the time were that he was unremorseful, that he was irresponsible, and that he was playing the system. His name appeared in newspapers from Vancouver to Halifax and all points in between, amid criticism that the young-offender law was not tough enough. Social media makes the circulation of these ideas all the more cogent as people share posts with like-minded others, in a process which has been called "crystallization" (Wohn and Bowe 2014). People, and their networks, become their own "agenda-setters" through the looping process of posting, sharing, and liking.

Limits of the Official Version of Youth Crime

Official crime statistics are produced through work—through people reporting crime to police, who then investigate, record, and lay charges that are then prosecuted in court. The machinery of (law and) order, so to speak, creates the product of crime, for until a crime is accepted, defined, and convicted, it is not a tangible thing. Crime is, as noted at the outset of this chapter, a social construct, an actuarial product. However, the quality of the raw material going into the crime machine is affected by five factors because (1) crime is report-sensitive, which means that the willingness of the victim to report the crime determines whether the police know about it; (2) crime is policing-sensitive, which means that the level of police enforcement determines whether the crime gets counted; (3) crime is definition-sensitive, which means that a change in the law affects whether something is called a crime; (4) crime is media-sensitive, which means that if crimes are publicized, a "feedback loop" can change the public's perceptions and their willingness to report; and (5) real trends in the number of crimes in society change over time (McCormick 2008). Let's deal with three of these issues briefly, as they are relevant to the topic of youth deviance: law enforcement, legal definitions, and media practices.

Law Enforcement Practices

The ways in which police departments enforce and record criminal activity affects the UCR statistics. These practices can range from low clearance rates to police discretion (Black 1970; Haggerty 2001). Ironically, increasing police efficiency can increase crime rates, as departments adopt more sophisticated computer technology, hire better-trained employees, and improve record-keeping ability. In addition, discretion affects the way in which police enforce the laws on prostitution, drug crimes, traffic offences, and Internet crimes. For example, cannabis possession went from 2300 cases in 1968 to 44,000 cases in 2006 owing to increased use but also to increased police enforcement. Drug enforcement is higher in jurisdictions where forfeiture laws allow police to retain seized assets, raising drug arrest rates by about 18 per cent (Mast, Benson, and Rasmussen 2000). This enforcement disproportionately affects the young, and in many jurisdictions the law allows for discretion in traffic stops, which can then lead to so-called out-of-sight offences, such as police finding marijuana in the car.

Legal Definitions

Changes to the law affect the crime rate. For example, broadening the Criminal Code's definition of arson 30 years ago to include mischief or suspicious fires resulted in an increase of 17 per cent in the arson rate (McCormick 2008). An even more dramatic example was sexual assault in 1983, 1988, and 1991, when changes were made to remove barriers affecting a victim's willingness to report, thus increasing the rate. Another legislative change worth study is the YCJA, which diverts youths who have committed non-violent crimes from the formal criminal justice system. Early on, the charge rate dropped from 56 per cent to 42 per cent, resulting in an apparent decrease in youth crime, while in fact the number of youth who came into contact with police actually increased (for more recent data see Smandych, Dyck, La Berge, and Koffman 2016).

Media Practices

The media, too, have played a role in the distortion of crime knowledge as measured by what is known by the police. For example, news of crimes committed in public by strangers against innocent victims encourages the perception that crime is random, sensitizing the public to fear crime, perhaps causing changes in police enforcement or legislative changes (Garland 2001; Kappeler 1996). News about crime and deviance can also desensitize the public in the opposite direction. For example, in the 1990s when sex-trade workers started disappearing on the Lower Mainland in Vancouver, media accounts ran stories about "hookers" who police said had simply moved away. This became a predominant version to account for the disappearances even though others insisted that a serial killer was to blame. Years before the name *Robert Pickton* became common knowledge, the message the public got was one that encouraged apathy and disinterest in missing and murdered women (McCormick 2010).

When we extrapolate this theme to youth crime, if there is a disproportionate number of articles on the topic or a disproportionate stress on violent crimes, for example, this is the version the public has knowledge of (see also Adorjan 2011; Pizarro, Chermak, and Gruenewald 2007; Sampert and Froese 2012). Whether it is an accurate version is irrelevant because it becomes the template for reporting and policing youth crime. In the media analysis discussed later in this chapter, the national news almost consistently reports only on homicides committed by youth; thus the reader gets the predominant impression of violent youth, again as in the examples of Downey or Billard discussed earlier in the chapter. This impression has little to do with the conditions that produced the "young offender" in the first place. In the former example, what is left unsaid is that North Preston is the oldest black community in Canada, settled by Loyalists who were not allowed to settle in white communities. The experience of segregation and racism is the background that is left out of the story.

Interestingly, the CCJS *Juristat* series is an important source of data for the media, as it presents complex information in a way that makes it appealing for the media to report. The creation of UCR statistics was as much about providing journalists with information about crime as it was about measuring police workload. Today, the media influence the timing and wording of press releases, the types of statistics used, and the types of information presented. Furthermore, "information officers" provide the media with crime stories, as it is often beyond the scope of a reporter's ability to gather such information otherwise (for example, Schnider 2017).

In conclusion, the official version of crime is the normative version, being the authoritarian representation of crime. Its character as mathematically produced and textually presented contributes to its authenticity. However, its limit is that it represents what the state knows and decides is worthy to count as crime. The official version is a pallid facsimile and aggregated conglomerate of the overall total of youth crime and gives little voice to the practices that produced youth crime or to the violence that is often at its core. Understanding the limits of official statistics, however, does not mean that they are easily rectified, although other attempts to discover the more accurate reality of crime have been tried.

The Unofficial Version: Alternative Methods of Measuring Youth Crime

The various limits of official statistics have led criminologists to seek alternative sources of information to measure deviant behaviour not reported to police and also to measure victimless crimes such as substance abuse. The assumption is that techniques can be devised to catch the dark figure of crime missed in official statistics and thus to supplement and expand official data. As discussed in Chapter 2, unreported crime is measured through victimization surveys, and deviant behaviour can be measured through self-report surveys. Moreover, it is relevant to comment further on these data-collection methods in connection with a discussion of the comparable role of the media in generating knowledge about youth crime.

Self-Report and Victimization Surveys

In brief, self-report surveys ask participants to reveal information about deviance that may have been committed by or against them. Through interviews, telephone surveys, or anonymous questionnaires, self-reports are viewed as a way to get at delinquency in particular, which is often missed by official statistics.

Using self-report studies to collect information on young offenders in school is convenient and practical, and provides a fairly reliable snapshot of a cross-section of the population. Self-reports have also been used to examine the offence histories of prison inmates, drug users, and other groups (e.g., see Cantor and Lynch 2000). They provide a broader picture of the distribution of deviance than do official data, and also provide a check on that data. For example, racial bias may be present if surveys indicate that white and non-white people report unequal levels of police attention, while official data indicate similar rates of whites and non-whites being arrested or stopped by police. Surveys are also a way to see the distribution of criminal behaviour across racial, class, age, and gender lines (e.g., see Smart and Adlaf 1991).

For example, one self-report study surveyed 2001 students ages 12 to 18 in 67 Alberta junior and senior high schools on perceptions of violence and personal safety, their own victimization and delinquent behaviour, and weapons possession (Gomes, Bertrand, Paetsch, and Hornick 2003). A similar study surveyed 3400 high school students and 400 street youth in Toronto about victimization, youth crime, and participation in gangs, and showed how criminality was often chosen as a means of survival (Tanner and Wortley 2002).

In 2010, the Canadian Alcohol and Drug Use Monitoring Survey of 3989 Canadians found the prevalence of cannabis use had decreased significantly; the average age of initiation for cannabis use was approximately 15 years; and 7 per cent reported using at least one of five illicit drugs (cocaine, crack, speed, ecstasy, hallucinogens). The International Youth Survey found that delinquent behaviour was significantly more prevalent among youth who consumed alcohol (35 per cent), took drugs (60 per cent), had delinquent friends (27 per cent), or had little parental supervision (56 per cent) (Health Canada 2010; Savoie 2007).

The Centre for Addiction and Mental Health's national random survey of alcohol and drug use (the Canadian Campus Survey 2004) of over 6000 undergraduate students showed heavy drinking (16 per cent), cannabis use (32 per cent), and other illicit drug use (9 per cent). There is no victim in the traditional sense in such deviance, and so self-report studies are almost the only way to collect such information.

Mentioned above, the International Youth Survey is conducted in over 30 countries, and one cycle of the survey, which studied more than 3200 youth in middle school, revealed that 37 per cent had committed acts of violence, property crime, or drug dealing (Savoie 2007). Over 40 per cent of the students said they had been victimized at least once in the previous year, but many did not report the incidents to the authorities. Overall, about 13 per cent of Toronto youth reported violent behaviour, and about the same number of students reported property-related crime. Carrying a weapon and participating in fights accounted for 88 per cent of violent acts, and vandalism and shoplifting were common property offences. Delinquency was highest in public places where there was less supervision, an obvious risk factor.

Other research has shown that the early onset of delinquency is a significant factor in repeat offences, with youth who began their "court career" at age 12 having an average of about eight incidents. Most of the time, these youth were with other people when they committed delinquent acts, such as arson (92 per cent), vandalism (81 per cent), breaking and entering (80 per cent), threatening someone (70 per cent), and assault (60 per cent). In 58 per cent of the cases, the delinquency was undiscovered, but when it was, it was punished (67 per cent). Youth reported being victimized by theft (28 per cent) or bullying (21 per cent), but reported the incidents in only 14 per cent of the cases. The reasons given for not reporting to the police were that it was "not important enough" (36 per cent) or that it was dealt with another way (20 per cent). Delinquency itself appeared to contribute significantly to victimization, with 56 per cent of delinquent youth reporting being victimized compared to 36 per cent of those who did not (Carrington, Matarazzo, and deSouza 2005).

The risk factors for delinquency studied using data from self-report and victimization surveys (Savoie 2007) include being in step- or single-parent families (35 per cent and 25 per cent, respectively). Not surprisingly, over one-third of youth who reported that they did not get along with their parents had engaged in delinquency, compared to 20 per cent of youth who reported that they did get along well with at least one of their parents. Even less surprisingly, delinquency was relatively rare among youth who said their parents always knew who they were with when they went out (12 per cent), compared to youth (56 per cent) who said their parents never knew. Delinquency was highest among those who used drugs (60 per cent) and alcohol (35 per cent), compared to those who didn't use drugs (16 per cent) or those who didn't drink (9 per cent). Overall, what is significant is the much higher rate of both offending and victimization than the rate reported in official crime statistics. Specifically, the official rate of 7 per cent is far lower than that admitted in the self-report survey population of 37 per cent in both offending and victimization. Also, what we see is that youth commit both violent and property offences relatively equally, quite often undetected, in the company of others with predictable underlying risk factors. And, finally, we also see that most offences are committed by a disproportionally smaller portion of the population.

Overall, official statistics and unofficial data are complementary sources of information. Official statistics reflect those crimes that come to the attention of the police, while self-report and victimization studies reflect a wide range of incidents that might not. In addition, some forms of unofficial data get at a broader range of behaviour, since the deviance under study is quite often soft, such as drug use or truancy. Moreover, these types of studies show the importance of asking people directly about crime, deviance, and victimization.

Youth Crime in the Media

We have looked briefly at youth crime in two ways, discussing both official statistics (represented by police data) and unofficial data (collected through surveys). Official statistics show a steady decline in youth crime, except for a gradual increase in violent crime. Much youth crime has been property related and gender biased, and reflects an interest in diversion since the introduction of the YCJA. On the other hand, unofficial data show that youth commit property and violent crime almost equally and show a much higher rate of offending than is disclosed in official statistics. We also get a more nuanced sense of risk factors in family and friends. The two sources of data are complementary in that they fill out the details of crime not reported to the police and also begin to reveal some of the context in which youth crime occurs. However, the difficulty with both sources of information is that they are not how most people know about youth crime, which is through traditional, and now social, media coverage (see Figure 6.1). Consequently, it is important to see if youth crime in the media is portrayed in a way that is similar to or different from the other two ways of knowing discussed here.

Social scientists have frequently looked at media coverage of crime and deviance (see, generally, classic studies such as Chiricos, Eschholz, and Gertz 1997; Fishman 1981). They have looked at the media more as a source of misinformation than as a source of information, because it often exaggerates the impact of street crime (Fishman 1978) or misconstructs the nature of corporate crime. This helps explain how there is a discrepancy between dropping rates of youth crime and the perception that youth crime is out of

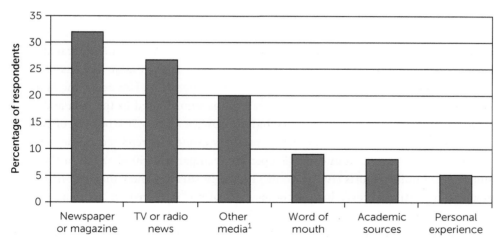

Figure 6.1 Primary Source of Information about the Canadian Youth Criminal Justice System

1. Includes movies, TV shows, and the Internet

Note: Respondents were also asked to identify their primary source of information about the youth criminal justice system in Canada. More than half (59 per cent) relied primarily on newspapers, magazines, or news stories from television or radio. Very few (8 per cent) relied on more academic sources, such as university courses, government reports, or books, and even fewer relied on first-hand experience (5 per cent).

Source: *The 2008 National Justice Survey: The Youth Justice in Canada and the Youth Criminal Justice Act, Figure 1*, https://www.justice.gc.ca/eng/rp-pr/cj-jp/yj-jj/rr08_yj1-rr08_jj1/rr08_yj1.pdf. Department of Justice Canada 2008. Reproduced with the permission of the Department of Justice Canada, 2019

control. It is caused by the fact that media coverage is distorted (Schissel 1997). Whether in the reporting of freeway crashes, shark attacks, serial killers, or youth "super-predators," the media can be blamed for getting it wrong and misinforming the public (again illustrated in the classic constructionist work of Best 1999).

The misrepresentation of crime in the media, for example, can cause fear and anxiety by distorting the frequency or severity of youth crime, thereby creating the impression that youth crime is more of a problem than it really is. However, to rest with the academic criticism that the media simply gets it wrong is inadequate, as it assumes that the media should do as good a job in portraying crime as we do in knowing it as criminologists. What is more important is to understand the consequences of the (distorted) portrayals the public receives.

The Construction of the Research

There is not much research on specifically media coverage of youth crime. Most crime and media research traditionally focuses on more hot-button, social-panic issues, such as child abuse and abduction, diseases, and homicide (Best 1993; Jenkins 1994)—crimes where it is easy to see that the media distort the danger of strangers, the risks to children, and the frequency of serial homicide in society. However, Jane Sprott (1996) gives a good example of how we can begin an analysis using a **context analysis**. Based on the premise that the reality constructed by the news media might not reflect other images of reality, she compared newspaper articles on youth crime in three Toronto papers over a two-month period to the so-called Bala and Lilles Young Offenders Reporting Service over a two-year period.

> **context analysis**
> The analysis of media content for themes such as sensationalism or distortion.

Sprott found that the youth court cases were broken down as follows: charges involving violence (22 per cent), property crime (50 per cent), other Criminal Code offences (18 per cent), Young Offenders Act (YOA) offences (7 per cent), and other federal offences (3 per cent). In comparison, the news media (*Globe and Mail*, *Toronto Star*, and *Toronto Sun*) focused almost exclusively on violent crime (94 per cent). Homicide, for example, constituted 0.02 per cent of youth court cases, was summarized in the Bala and Lilles Report slightly more often (7.8 per cent), and composed a weighty 70.4 per cent of Toronto newspaper coverage. On the other hand, property crime was reported in the news far less often than it appeared in court (5.3 per cent compared to 50 per cent) or than was summarized in the reports (19.7 per cent). We might surmise, then, that property crime is not as interesting to cover, but the consequence of the "if it bleeds, it leads" approach is the over-sensitization of the public to issues of violent youth crime. And this distortion is only apparent when one knows what the statistics are; most of the public will not be in this position.

This type of research methodology is quite simple. Take a sample of media coverage and compare the incidence of its stories to another source of information. In this case, youth court statistics were used, but the source could have been police reports or even self-report survey results. The objective will always be to see if media coverage is distorted in comparison to the more objective information, and if it is, one could conclude that the media exaggerate crimes of violence. The objective will never be to show that court statistics are not entertaining or interesting to read.

As well as a context difference, Sprott also noticed a content difference between the newspaper articles and the sentencing reports: the articles focused more on the impact of the crime, while the sentencing reports focused more on the reasons for judicial disposition. Privileging the latter, she criticized the media for not giving enough information for the public to understand the reasons for sentencing. If the media did that educating, the public would have a better understanding of how the courts work, the reasons for sentencing, and thus the need (sometimes) to be "soft" on youth crime. However, the newspapers focused on the affective dimension by foregrounding the victim, while the sentencing report did not. Which source was doing the better job?

In this vein, because the news media distort the proportion of youth violent crime, it is useful to measure the public perception of youth crime as it probably affects policy changes. Sprott found that those who thought sentences were too lenient were usually thinking specifically of repeat offenders and were slightly more likely to want harsher sentences. Those who believed that sentences were too lenient were also more likely to overestimate the amount of violent youth crime and to think that it had increased. Again, as we will see in the media analysis, this is an easy conclusion to come to when the majority of youth crime stories are about violence. Consequently, the public cannot be blamed for having little knowledge of how youth court works or for thinking violent youth crime is out of control, because the media did such a poor job in reporting cases in comparison to what we know criminologically.

This research dovetails nicely with a survey conducted by Baron and Hartnagel (1996), who found that respondents were quite punitive toward juvenile justice issues. This attitude was not based on experience of victimization but coincided with more conservative social values, which Baron and Hartnagel hypothesize were the result of how the media constructed youth crime. Fully 78 per cent of their respondents felt that youth courts were too lenient, but their own level of victimization was only 22 per cent. Baron and Hartnagel speculate that high-profile coverage surrounding the YOA combined with simplistic coverage of sensational cases brings to awareness "latent public fears," the first step in the spiral of events that can lead to a full public crusade. This is called the "amplification of deviance." While their study was not intended to be a systematic analysis of media coverage, it fits within the "distorted coverage produces public fear" equation proposed by social constructionists.

A more recent study of juvenile homicide in Chicago newspapers (see Boulahanis and Heltsey 2004) between 1992 and 2000 found that juvenile homicide rates declined but the number of cases receiving media coverage increased. There is no good reason for one to reflect the other, but it does mean that the media can overrepresent the amount of violent crime and thus distort public perception. Furthermore, this study found that news articles do a good job of covering youth crime but tend to focus on atypical cases. Most homicides are committed by males (90 per cent), but females made up 30 per cent of media coverage. Additionally, homicides committed against females were covered more than twice as often as cases involving male victims. In Chicago, black youth commit the most murders, but a case got more coverage if it was committed by a white youth. Specifically, more than 59 per cent of cases involving Caucasian offenders received media coverage, compared to those involving African-Americans (21 per cent) and Latinos (17 per cent). The study also found that every one-year increase in offender age corresponded to a 28 per cent reduction in the odds of getting newspaper coverage, and homicides involving victims younger than 14 were 480 per cent more likely to receive coverage than homicides involving victims aged 20 to 29.

cultivation hypothesis
The hypothesis that the media inundate the public with ideas about crime.

After establishing these patterns and using a model called the **cultivation hypothesis** (Gerbner, Gross, Morgan, and Signorielli 1980; Hawkins and Pingree 1980), the researchers felt that distorted media coverage made people more fearful. It was not simply that atypical cases were getting covered and typical cases were not, but rather that there was a mix of coverage with atypical cases getting disproportionately more coverage than the typical cases. The researchers concluded that this mixture made it difficult to see patterns of victimization, just as Sprott (1996) concluded that media coverage makes it difficult for the public to understand sentencing patterns. Boulahanis and Heltsey (2004, p. 155) say that this "uncertainty produces a fear that anyone can be a victim and anyone can be a perpetrator," but go on to state that the resulting distortions include the perception that homicides committed by young persons represent a growing problem, which may or may not be the case but feeds into a deeper subtext that youths are a social danger.

As mentioned before, the rate of youth crime has been steadily dropping. In addition, since the introduction of the YCJA in 2003, the proportion of apprehended youth formally charged with crimes has dropped because the YCJA diverts youth from the court system. However, as this is perhaps not general knowledge, it does not reassure the public when they hear news reports of youth violence.

The Social Constructionist Analysis

social constructionism
An approach that sees social problems as constructed in the media; see *moral panic*.

A large literature on **social constructionism** has developed over the past 40 or so years (see, for example, now classic studies by Altheide 2006; Goode 2009). This approach is more complicated than the context analysis approach mentioned above in that we are not comparing indices, so to speak, or asking how well the media report some objectively constructed reality. Rather, we are looking more closely at the discursive constructions used in media texts. For example, in the analysis of prostitution in the Vancouver news in the 1980s, the word *hooker* desensitized viewers and actually destroyed any empathy the public might have had for the victims of a serial killer (McCormick 2010). This discursive construction contributed to what John Lowman (2000) calls the "discourse of disposal"—that is, how media descriptions of the attempt of politicians, police, and residents' groups to get rid of street prostitution from residential areas actually contributed to a sharp increase in murders of street prostitutes in British Columbia after 1980. A geographic and political marginalization of street prostitution was aided by the symbolic marginalization created in the media, which ultimately led to violence against street prostitutes. (See Chapter 14 for more discussion on the sex trade.)

Social constructionist analysis usually has several main themes. First, there is the suggestion that the media present violence as a growing social problem, much like an epidemic or plague (see Best and Horiuchi 1985; Kupchik and Bracy 2009; Tanner 2001). Second, there are usually innocent victims and guilty predators who prey on those victims (see D'Arcy 2007). Third, there is also usually a link or **convergence** between a new problem and an existing one—for example, stalking and domestic violence, or Internet luring

convergence
When a current issue is framed in terms of its relation to a previous one.

and pedophilia (see Doyle 2000). And fourth, there are claims-makers, such as police, politicians, or advocates, who advance the idea that the described social problem is growing, is out of control, or needs attention (see Dowler 2003; Sampert and Froese 2012). These are all basic elements of a constructionist approach that are easily applied to an analysis of youth crime in the media. By extension, to apply that to social media is to see the virtual democratization of agenda-setting, with every post a potential discussion site for making claims.

In the first example of constructionist research considered here, Spencer (2005) looks at select high-profile coverage of youth violence in 1994. In contrast to accounts that focus simplistically on media distortions that create a sense of (un)certainty in the audience, Spencer adopts the view that the media trades on the ambiguous culpability of youth in that they are both victimizer and victimized. He chose 1994 because it was prior to the Columbine school shooting, youth violence had peaked, and several sensational cases (in the United States and abroad) were the focus of media attention. He chose commentary sections of the news, in venues such as *The New York Times*, *Time* magazine, *Newsweek*, and *US News & World Report*.

Spencer found that youth violence was promoted as though it was at a crisis level, that numerical estimates of its magnitude portrayed it as growing, that it was spreading geographically and could strike anyone and anywhere, and that atrocity tales were used to highlight the sensationalism of the issue. The crisis of youth violence was also linked to existing social problems, such as unemployment, single-parent families (single mom or missing dad), crack cocaine, child abuse, and the increasing use of guns. These are standard elements of a constructionist analysis, and they show how the public can get a distorted perception of youth crime.

Moreover, contextualizing the issue in this way raised issues of how culpable these youth were and how the audience was to relate to them emotionally. The increase in the use of social media over traditional forms heightens this effect even further by creating a "crystallization" of opinion among like-minded others and their networks (see below). In this phenomenon, there are contradictory images: are youth to be feared or sympathized with?; are they responsible or lost?; are they victims or victimizers? Spencer (2005) calls this an **ideological flexibility**, and he suggests that the ambiguity in portrayal might be extended to analysis of other topics, such as mothers who kill their children, female partners who kill their abusive partners, or people who (knowingly) transmit the AIDS virus. This is a stronger version of "uncertainty" in media portrayal than was suggested earlier, and it presents a more complicated reality for the public to digest, as displayed in the opening news story of this chapter. This ideological flexibility also creates confusion when we cannot easily distinguish the victims from the villains.

ideological flexibility
Where the portrayal of persons is ambiguous—for example, a young offender is portrayed as both villain and victim.

Any media analysis in the twenty-first century has to include a nod to social media. And a prominent case makes this all more apparent. In 2011, Rehtaeh Parsons was sexually assaulted at a party, and a photo of the assault was subsequently circulated on social media. Because of the resultant cyberbullying, Rehtaeh attempted suicide in 2013, and died (see Box 3.6 in Chapter 3). (A similar case is that of Amanda Todd.) An independent report found that police and prosecutors failed in their investigation of the matter. Charges were not initially laid against Rehtaeh's attackers (as satirized in an editorial cartoon in the *Halifax Herald* by Michael deAdder, 13 April 2013), just fuelling the social media harassment of Rehtaeh. Police failed to follow proper procedure in interviewing the complainant, and the prosecutor consulted by the police advised against charging, a decision the independent review found critical in the attempt to find justice in the case. The resultant publicity fuelled the public perception that social media was to blame ("Archie Billard Back in Prison" 2015). Other cases anchor this view and increase the perception that youth are to blame for violent acts—but in this instance through a media that is more in their control.

Cyberbullying as a new topic signals a change in both the media and our reaction to it. Whereas in more traditional media analysis, youth are seen as passive subjects of media reports, with social media they are seen as mis/using that technology. They are portrayed as committing negative acts online, and as with traditional bullying, these acts are against some groups more than others. LGBT (lesbian, gay, bisexual, and transgender) students are even more likely to experience online bullying overall, and are more likely to feel unsafe as a result. We already know that victims of bullying are more likely to experience psychological problems that manifest in their interpersonal relations and in school performance, and with online bullying, physical is distance no longer a barrier, so the harm is easier to perpetrate and to experience. Sending harassing emails, posting obscene or slanderous messages to social networking sites, or using websites to disseminate defamatory content are all ways in which bullying has now gone online (Hinduja and Patchin 2006, 2008).

How common is cyberbullying? Surveys of high school students show about 35 per cent having been the victims of online harassment, with girls more likely to experience cyberbullying than boys. In addition, being a victim of cyberbullying is linked to low self-esteem, suicidal ideation, and other school problems. In summary, cyberbullying is a modern variation on an old problem, but with new possibilities to reach into youth's lives.

In general, constructionist analysis would say that the public gets the message that violent youth crime is a significant problem, and that it is more likely to do so because of the media's inordinate focus on victims. This message distorts perception and, in doing so, affects the reported rates of youth crime and the public's willingness to press charges, the eventual result being added pressure on politicians to change the law. Even when elements of youth's background might help portray them in a more sympathetic light, they also help portray youth's fall as all the more tragic.

The Implication of the Patterns in Media Coverage of Youth Crime

As we have seen, there are certain patterns in media coverage of youth crime. Violent youth crime is overrepresented in the media, while youth property crime is underrepresented; atypical cases get disproportionately more coverage than typical cases, emotion gets more foreground than structural background, and the resulting product is a public misperception about youth crimes. None of this really should be surprising. However, simply comparing media coverage to police statistics or court cases and criticizing the former for misrepresentation presumes that the media have an obligation to report faithfully what is known by those other entities; that is, critics often argue that if the media's coverage of crime is distorted and sensationalized in comparison to that of other sources, then the media are inaccurate and responsible for the public's more punitive attitudes and, inevitably, for politicians seeking to cash in on those fears.

This method of characterizing the relationship between media knowledge and crime knowledge makes the mistake of privileging the latter. As we saw earlier, there are problems with both police information and self-report studies, but they are complementary in giving us different images of what is putatively the same universe of behaviours: youth deviance. But they are images only, each with its own benefits and limits. Media knowledge is similarly a window on the world (see McCormick 2010), but there seems to be no ready reason why the media should mirror what is known by the police any more than police statistics should mirror juvenile self-reports. I suggest that instead of being antagonistic bodies of knowledge, these two sources are imbricated scales, ways of measuring behaviour that are slightly overlapping (as shown in Figure 6.2).

Thinking of media knowledge in this way gives it a legitimacy that is often lacking in shallow versions of social constructionism, such as context analysis. Instead of considering how well the media conform to a different way of measuring youth crime, we can use an alternative model such as **frame analysis** to see how the media frame or portray youth crime and how the media allow us to develop deeper cultural understandings of youth, especially when we combine frame analysis with a **critical discourse analysis** (Fairclough 2003; Wodak and Meyer 2000) to see the link between those portrayals and the larger political structure of society.

Using such an approach also opens the door to analyzing in more detail the role of the media in the public sphere. And for there to be a role for the media in the public sphere, the media have to be construed as more than a simple conduit for political opinion or police

frame analysis
Analyzing media content to see how crime and criminals are depicted.

critical discourse analysis
An approach in sociolinguistics that links discourse with political structure.

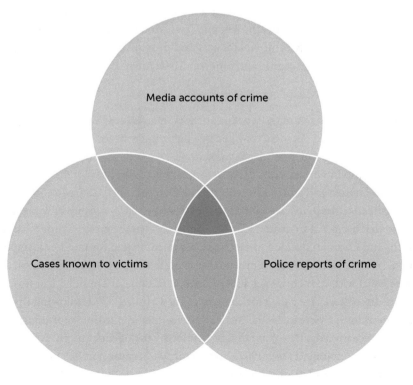

Figure 6.2 Different Ways of Knowing Youth Crime

knowledge. Rather, they have to be seen as a forum for debate, right or wrong, just or unjust. Debates that are divided and difficult do not simply show that hegemony does not exist; instead they show us how hegemony is accomplished through discourse—in the old Marxist phrase, "hegemony is never complete." Making claims about putative conditions and about the persons who it is suggested are responsible for those conditions, especially if we are not quite clear about their responsibility, is a good case study in the building of consensus.

Hogeveen (2005) has looked at this issue of public debate in more detail. Through an analysis of House of Commons debates and some media reports, he explores the construction of the category of "the punishable young offender." According to his analysis, media reports of debates in the House of Commons in the late 1990s created a new discursive category that emphasized protecting the public from risks associated with youth crime. The public concern about young offenders in Parliament and in the media centred on replacing the YOA with a tougher law based on accountability—the YCJA. The shift in how juvenile offenders are characterized is all the more glaring when the YCJA is compared to the Juvenile Delinquents Act of 1908, in which the dominant model was a family-centred, welfare, rehabilitative approach.

The selection of media articles that Hogeveen uses is not systematic, however, but is especially appropriate in showing how there is a valorization of victims in media coverage. For example, former Alliance MP Jay Hill from British Columbia was able to name victims (who would have been in the news) as if everyone knew who they were, as in the following:

> In my home province of British Columbia, the names of Reena Virk, Dawn Shaw, and Trygve Magnusson represent just a few victims who died at the hands of violent youth. Their senseless deaths demand laws from the government that punish and deter those who commit violent acts and provide mandatory rehabilitation programs during incarceration. (*Hansard*, 21 October 1999, cited in Hogeveen 2005, p. 84)

These names would not make sense as anchors in a political argument if they were not well known to the public. As such, they become lightning rods for public indignation and a moralistic discourse about "what needs to be done." As well, the late British Columbia MP Chuck Cadman, an important critic of the YOA, championed victims' rights after his son was a victim of an unprovoked attack in Surrey. In late October 1992, Cadman's 16-year-old son Jesse was stabbed to death in a so-called random street attack by a group of young people. In response to that event, Cadman and his wife, Dona, created the group Crime Responsibility and Youth, and Cadman decided to enter politics to campaign for tougher juvenile justice legislation. In 1997, he introduced a private member's bill, saying, "It's a crapshoot, basically. If I'm successful with it, then we get a lot of good stuff done. If I'm not . . . at least we start to get some discussion." He called for changes to the Criminal Code allowing that there be formal recognition of victims in the justice system, that victims be kept informed of the progress of police investigations, and that restitution by the offender be given for psychological harm done to victims (Fraser 1997). Joe Wambach became another important claims-maker after his son was victimized in Toronto.

These claims-makers are important for their role in the valorization of victims and for laying the groundwork for establishing that juveniles are "getting away with crime." They have used their experiences as media fodder in a way that other victims might not be able to, capitalizing and politicizing those experiences for a public unable to know how normative those experiences might be. They are spokespersons and claims-makers, in both traditional and social media.

Hogeveen argues that the construction of the "punishable young offender" in political and media discourse is based on the perceived inadequacy of current law, on the centrality of victims, on a get-tough discourse, and, of course, on emotionality, as in former MP Mark Crawford's comments: "Where does it end? Local parents and other citizens are calling for vigilante justice. They do not trust our current system of justice that it lets off criminals with a slap upon the wrist while the victims are left in limbo for the rest of their lives" (*Hansard*, 2 May 1994, cited in Hogeveen 2005, p. 79). This comment from 1994 perhaps does not reflect current discourse, but it was uttered in the lead-up to changing juvenile justice legislation. This symbiotic relationship between violent offenders, valorized victims, and calls for tougher legislation is accomplished through debate (in the media). And I argue here that it is through the public arena of the media that this building of consensus happens. It is not as simple as privileging one form of knowledge over another—say, official statistics over media stories. That is too easy a criticism. The media is a site for sensationalism and exaggeration, and at the same time it is a place of debate and correction. For example, in a letter to the editor written in June 1998, Anthony Doob, a leading University of Toronto criminologist, made the following point:

> It is not surprising to see a *Globe and Mail* editorial (March 16) suggesting, once again, that the Young Offenders Act be toughened up. . . . What is surprising, however, is that the *Globe and Mail* editorial board used patently false information . . . to support its editorial position. . . . The manner in which we as a society deal with young offenders is important. We have to decide, for example, whether we are interested in focusing more on ways to make Canada a safer place to live or on making symbolic gestures that make older people feel that they are being tough. These are legitimate choices that should be debated. The debate is not served, however, by dishonest (or incompetent) reporting of what the current law is.

A challenge, indeed.

In the next section, I introduce research findings from an ongoing critical discourse analysis media study of newspaper reporting on young offenders in Canada. This sample of findings from ongoing research supplements the data reported by Hogeveen (2005) and helps us to further appreciate the key role that the media play in producing knowledge about youth crime.

An Example of the Media Analysis of Newspaper Articles on Youth Crimes

The following media analysis research findings are derived from a study carried out by the author that involved searching the *National Post* newspaper from 1995 to 2003 for the term *young offender*. The study is based on Hogeveen's suggestion (2005) that media reports of debates in the House of Commons in the late 1990s created a new discursive category that emphasized protecting the public from risks associated with youth crime—the so-called punishable young offender. The search yielded 121 relevant articles. The results were separated by year and by subject matter, and were analyzed for discursive trends using critical discourse analysis, a qualitative approach that looks for themes in media discourse related to structural issues. The intent was to see what themes, if any, could be found in this national newspaper that would support a tougher approach to juvenile offenders. Five themes were subsequently identified: editorializing, moral outrage, atrocity tales, problem-defining events, and the valorization of victims, as shown in Box 6.1.

Although the *National Post*, being a national newspaper, was found not to have as many stories about young offenders as local papers did, it did contain articles that reflected the national debate over youth crime and the lack of effectiveness of the youth justice system and the disproportionate attention given to youth violent crimes. In this sense, the national paper was both reflecting and reproducing a "national reader." Between 1995 and 1998, there were no stories in the *National Post* directly related to young offenders. However, from 1999 onward stories about young offenders began to appear more frequently.

Description of Findings

The *National Post* ran ten stories about young offenders in 2000; three in 2001; four in 2002; and six in 2003. Stories with little length were put into "briefs"; articles that were really about something else, such as the accidental shooting of an officer by another during pursuit of young offenders, were put into "tangents"; and articles making comments on some aspect of the system were put into "overviews." Some briefs, such as "Ontario: Teen Convicted of Animal Cruelty after Barbecuing Dog" (*National Post*, 29 November 2001, p. A7), are horrifying because of their briefness (see Box 6.1), but in general there was little to comment on. So-called tangential articles were about prison reform, young offender facilities, and politicians inadvertently releasing the names of young offenders, which is against the law.

It was in the category of "overviews" that general comments were often the most measured and the most interesting, such as comments on the law being too soft on young offenders, or Anthony Doob's dispute with Ontario's justice minister over the effectiveness of boot camps in reducing recidivism (Doob and Cesaroni 2004). The government had taken the recidivism statistics from a boot camp facility and had then compared them to those in regular jails and found a significant difference, advocating the success of boot camps. However, the government had taken out those who had dropped out of the program before comparing the two groups statistically, artificially inflating its success. And in 2001, Vic Toews, the then new Canadian Alliance justice critic, voiced his wide-ranging objections to the youth justice reform bill that was to be tabled by Anne McLellan, the justice minister. On 5 February 2001, it was reported in the *National Post* that

> [h]e opposes the new law's emphasis on cautions and out-of-court sanctions and
> its end to the practice of sending the worst offenders to adult court. "If we don't
> bring accountability into our youth justice system, we are breeding criminals in

Box 6.1 | Youth Justice in Action

Media Sample

1. Editorializing

"A Young Killer Gets Kid-Glove Treatment: Special Hearing May Set Murderer Free after Just 29 Months"

"He may be the luckiest young killer in Canada, and if his luck continues to hold, he could end up serving only 29 months for the vicious murder of an elderly Holocaust survivor he stabbed nine times in the throat in broad daylight . . ." (1106 words)

Byline: Christie Blatchford, *National Post*, Feb. 26, 1999, A1.

2. Moral Outrage

"Dead Girl's Dad Says Youth's Sentence a 'Joke': Dangerous Driving: Teenager Gets One Year for Accident that Killed Two"

" . . . he was driving struck and killed two other teens. Court heard that the accused, who can not be named as he is a young offender, drank six beers in two hours before getting behind the wheel. He was originally charged with impaired driving causing . . ." (326 words)

Byline: Kelly Egan (*Ottawa Citizen*), *National Post*, May 11, 1999, A10.

3. Atrocity Tales

"Teen Convicted of Animal Cruelty after Barbecuing Dog"

"A 17-year-old girl was convicted this week of animal cruelty after she beat and then barbecued her family's Pomeranian. The 12-year-old dog, named Peppy, had been a family pet for the past seven years. The young offender could face up to six months in jail, but the horrific case has renewed calls for stiffer penalties." (57 words)

Source: Brief, *National Post*, Nov. 29, 2001, A7.

4. Problem-Defining Event

"'Killer Kelly' Was Toughest Girl in the Gang, Friends Said: Results of Psychiatric Examinations Contradictory"

" . . . At the time of the fatal attack, Ellard was 15 and could have been tried as a young offender. In deciding whether to try her as an adult, the court turned to the evidence of a battery of experts, including . . ." (563 words)

Byline: Mark Hume, *National Post*, Apr. 1, 2000, A8.

5. Valorization of Victims

"Bill to Give Victims of Crime More Rights: Offenders Would Pay into Fund to Help Injured Party"

" . . . Reform MP who has campaigned for increased victims' rights since his 16-year-old son, Jesse, was murdered by a young offender almost seven years ago, welcomed the new legislation. Mr. Cadman noted MPs from all parties supported victims . . . " (461 words)

Byline: Tim Naumetz (*Southam News*), *National Post*, Apr. 16, 1999, A7.

This kind of media-based editorializing has been shown in many research studies to have measurable impacts on public perceptions and legislation affecting youths seen to be "at risk," young offenders in general, and the youth justice system.

youth courts," he said. "Violent, repeat offenders need to be held accountable in adult court." He also wanted broader publication of names of young offenders. "I think it's wrong that people in a community can't be warned about a young offender living among them."

Such reactionary comments from a sitting MP are directly contrary to the spirit of young offender legislation.

Similarly, David Young, the attorney general of Ontario, was quoted as saying on 15 June 2001 that "[n]one of these concerns [about the YCJA] were addressed in the bill. [The] Act is weak-kneed. It fails to protect the public." Unwittingly prescient, such comments presaged the political reaction after the Toronto Boxing Day shooting of 2005. These "overview" articles, with their comments on the system at large, contextualize individual stories that might be published or aired about young offenders committing crimes. The year 2001 confirmed the suspicion that unusual cases are highlighted. There was a story about a Quebec teenager with racist tendencies and psychotic delusions who lured a Cuban-born girl to a gravel pit to kill her, and another about a girl who barbecued the family dog.

Between 2000 and 2003, the *National Post* contained 23 stories on young offenders. Because of this small sample it is difficult to generalize about the overall nature of media coverage. However, the year 2000 saw an article about the murder of a cross-dressing teenager; two articles on the extradition hearing of an Israeli soldier wanted for murder in a park; one on a carjacking in the wealthy Forest Hill neighbourhood of Toronto; one on a first-degree murder case in Newfoundland; two on the trial for the accused in the case of the Chatham, Ontario, boy found hanging from a hook in a school bathroom; two on the swarming death trial of Reena Virk's assailants; and one on the trial of the youth who killed a shop owner by stabbing him 50 times. These cases, mostly murder, are also fairly unusual and highly violent.

Given the number of youth crimes in Canada in 2000 and the number that went to court, the "national reader" is left reading a highly select group of articles. The *Juristat* publication on crimes in Canada that year reported that 22,635 youths were charged with violent crime, of which 16,404 were assaults. Of those charged with homicide, 8 per cent were youths, for a total of 41 cases.

One year, however, stands out in comparison to the rest in the 1995 to 2003 period. In 1999, there were a total of 50 articles, about half of which were primarily about crimes. This represents a remarkable spike in coverage in sheer numbers alone. One article was about a young man who threatened police; the police arrived at his home to arrest him; a scuffle ensued; and people were shot. Another was about the shooting of an 11-year-old boy by a 13-year-old neighbour after a disagreement. Two articles were about a 16-year-old driving a van who struck and killed a police officer who was trying to lay down a nail belt to stop a high-speed chase outside Sudbury. Another concerned an 11-year-old who was set ablaze with kerosene and a lighter. There was an article about a 14-year-old boy who murdered a taxi driver with a baseball bat on a Hobbema reserve while his friends stole the alcohol he was delivering. There were two about the Reena Virk case, two about a young woman who killed her parents on a ranch in Alberta, and one on a young man who severed the hand of another with a machete outside a bar in North York. Again, these articles were almost all about murders, unusual enough events in themselves, and all were told in a sensationalistic style—they were atypical crimes, foregrounding emotion.

In 1999, there were several more general pieces on victims, including one about greater compensation for crime victims; one on a new section of the YCJA, introduced in

1997 by Chuck Cadman, that would punish parents if their children continued to commit crimes while at home (6 March); a comment by Priscilla de Villiers on the need to get tough on the causes of crime (9 March); and several articles on recidivism in youth-care facilities. Chuck Cadman also spoke out on the need to lift publication bans in the cases of young offenders (12 March) and was criticized by then justice minister Anne McLellan for not understanding the youth crime legislation. In addition to these claims-makers, there were also many other general articles on provisions of the YCJA and its implementation, and there were two on the rise in female offenders and overall trends in juvenile offenders.

What sense can we make of this? If we look at the sheer frequency of articles, 1999 is an important turning point. Examined critically, newspaper reporting shows a connection between individual crime stories and the larger political structure. Several features of the 1999 coverage bear this out. There are a lot of overview pieces—more than half of the coverage for 1999—with commentary by experts, by claims-makers who wished to advocate certain points of view about youth crime and its treatment, and by politicians. These articles create a discursive context within which to see youth crime. This is enhanced by primary news articles that also serve as platforms for the valorization of victims and the vilification of young offenders. In one article, "Dead Girl's Dad Says Youth's Sentence a 'Joke': Dangerous Driving: Teenager Gets One Year for Accident that Killed Two" (11 May), for example, a youth is given a sentence of open custody for dangerous driving causing death. The victim's father, who is by extension a secondary victim, uses the occasion of a specific crime to criticize the larger workings of the criminal law. Similarly, the use of headlines to accomplish a quick reading of the cases is easily demonstrated, as in "Daughter Charged in Brutal Slaying of Parents: First-Degree Murder: Two Teens Also Face Charges in Killing of Alberta Couple" (26 May); "15-Year Sentence Given in Home-Invasion Attack: Judge Calls Assault on Elderly Couple Horrific" (1 July); and "Beating Victim Still Comatose: 'Gang-Style Attack'" (10 July), which involved the beating of Jonathan Wamback. There was also the Forest Hill carjacking, "Teen in Forest Hill Carjacking Gets 3 Years: Lawyer and Wife Kidnapped, Beaten and Robbed" (3 September); and "Women Asked to Identify Their Underwear: Teen Charged after Bedroom Search Turns up Booty" (5 November).

The headlines draw in the national reader, who reads about salacious and horrific crimes in the context of a general commentary that is pro-victim and critical of the way youth are treated by the court and under the law. The year 1999 was a year for headlines above articles about highly violent and senseless crimes but also an opportunity for those who wished to make young offenders a social and political issue. In this way, specific crime discourse is tied to a larger political discourse, one that reflects and promotes a view of the world and of young offenders. The media then becomes a forum of debate, a punitive forum that is symbolic and communicative, regardless of youths' actual crimes or their ultimate dispensation. For most, the public forum of the media is the forum of the spectacle, and it is very real.

The key themes identified in this study, as well as examples of specific newspaper articles in which they appear, are highlighted in Box 6.1. These themes arguably frame the claim that the law on young offenders needed to be changed to make it less lenient on youth, and show how the *National Post* served as a venue for giving voice to the claim that youth crime was out of control. Despite the lack of official corroboration by crime statistics, however, it is not simply that the media gets it wrong. The fact is that both sensationalism and correction, outlandish exaggeration and sober caution, are part of the public sphere that is the media. This debate, carried on in the public arena, creates a different way of knowing than is available through official crime statistics and/or self-report and victimization studies. The media constructs the discursive reality that is youth crime, and for most people, that *is* their reality, whether it is grounded in objective information or not. In this case, as Hogeveen says, the media creates the category of "punishable young offender." It is a public criminology.

Summary

It is easy to privilege one way of knowing youth crime over another by using, for example, official statistics to criticize the way in which the media portray youth crime. Doing so would be simple, as the media tend to sensationalize youth crime. Similarly, we could use self-report surveys to criticize police statistics, as if the former were better than the latter. And what we would find is a higher prevalence of "soft crimes" than official statistics indicate. Such approaches as context analysis are useful in using one measure to understand the limits of another. The idea is that one way of "knowing" youth crime is better than another, and now social media gives us new information on youth deviance.

However, instead of privileging one way of knowing youth crime over the other, I suggest here that they are, at best, complementary forms of knowledge and, even better, different ways of knowing the world of youth crime. Yes, the media exaggerate and distort youth crime (from the perspective of official statistics), but perhaps the media are contributing to the public debate in a way that is unaccountable to official statistics and self-report surveys. Perhaps they are speaking to a deeper cultural discourse that is suspicious of youths and their behaviour, and wishes the paternal state to use the law to solve the problem, an idea that stretches back through the course of the twentieth century. Social media just add to this suspicion toward youth, because of their uptake and use within the younger generation.

Some analysts (e.g., see McCormick 2010) have begun to get at some of the reasons this happens by suggesting that the media are part of a public debate at the beginning of the twenty-first century that is not accountable to official ways of knowing. Moving into the age of cybercrime, we have moved to a harsher way of categorizing and conceptualizing youth crime, and the media constitute an important forum for that public debate. They are part of a new age of anxiety, and of incivility.

Key Terms

context analysis
convergence
critical discourse analysis
cultivation hypothesis
folk devils

frame analysis
ideological flexibility
moral panic
social constructionism

Review Questions

1. This chapter describes three ways of knowing youth crime. What are these ways of knowing and how do they overlap?

2. What are the major problems with official statistics on youth crime as outlined in this chapter?

3. This chapter emphasizes the media as an important way for the public to know about youth crime. What do people learn from the media?

4. How do "atrocity tales" and other media patterns create a distorted reality of youth crime for the public?

Critical Thinking Questions

1. The valorization of victims in the media anchors the claim that politicians should get tougher on youth crime. Does this benefit the cause of victims in our society?

2. What would be a way to revise media coverage of youth crime to make it more accurate, less sensationalistic, and more educational for the public?

3. Imagine that you were a journalist who was asked to explain and defend why youth crime is reported in the media in the way that it is. How would you do this? What kinds of arguments would you put forth?

4. If you could work with high school students to design a public education project to highlight youth contributing to the community, what would you suggest? Specific elements would be a topic, such as the environment, venue, or media approach, and creative cultural materials. What would you do?

References

Adorjan, M.C. (2011). Emotions, contests and reflexivity in the news: Examining discourse on youth crime in Canada. *Journal of Contemporary Ethnography, 40*(2), 168–98.

Altheide, D. (2006). Terrorism and the politics of fear. *Cultural Studies, 6*(4), 415–39.

Archie Billard back in prison. (2010, October 25). CBC NEWS. Retrieved from http://www.cbc.ca/news/canada/nova-scotia/story/2010/10/25/ns-archie-billard-release-revoked.html

Barnhorst, R. (2004). The Youth Criminal Justice Act: New directions and implementation issues, *Canadian Journal of Criminology and Criminal Justice, 46*(3), 231–50.

Baron, S., and Hartnagel, T. (1996). "Lock 'em up": Attitudes toward punishing juvenile offenders. *Canadian Journal of Criminology, 28*(2), 191–212.

Best, J. (1993). *Threatened children: Rhetoric and concern about child victims.* Chicago: University of Chicago Press.

Best, J. (1999). *Random violence: How we talk about new crimes and new victims.* Berkeley: University of California Press.

Best, J., and Horiuchi, G. (1985). The razor blade in the apple: The social construction of urban legends. *Social Problems, 32*(5), 488–99.

Black, D. (1970). Production of crime rates. *American Sociological Review, 35*(4), 733–48.

Boulahanis, J., and Heltsey, M. (2004). Perceived fears: The reporting patterns of juvenile homicide in Chicago newspapers. *Criminal Justice Policy Review, 15*(2), 132–60.

Canadian Campus Survey. (2004). Retrieved from http://www.camh.ca/en/research/research_areas/social-epiresearch/Documents/CCS_2004_report.pdf

CanLII. (1996). Controlled Drugs and Substances Act, 1996. Retrieved from http://www.canlii.org

Cantor, D., and Lynch, J. (2000). Self-report surveys as measures of crime and criminal victimization. *Criminal Justice, 4.*

Carrington, P.J., Matarazzo, A., and deSouza, P. (2005). Court careers of a Canadian birth cohort. Crime and Justice Research Paper Series. Statistics Canada Catalogue No. 85-561-MIE, no. 006. Ottawa.

Chiricos, T., Eschholz, S., and Gertz, M. (1997). Crime, news and fear of crime: Toward an identification of audience effects. *Social Problems, 44*(3), 342–57.

Cohen, S. (1972). *Folk devils and moral panics: The creation of the mods and rockers.* London: MacGibbon and Rae.

D'Arcy, S. (2007). The "Jamaican criminal" in Toronto, 1994: A critical ontology. *Canadian Journal of Communication, 32,* 2.

Doob, A. (1998, June 1). Young Offenders Act. *Globe and Mail,* Letter to the editor.

Doob, A., and Cesaroni, C. (2004). *Responding to youth crime in Canada.* Toronto: University of Toronto Press.

Dowler, K. (2003). Media consumption and public attitudes toward crime and justice: The relationship between fear of crime, punitive attitudes, and perceived police effectiveness. *Journal of Criminal Justice and Popular Culture, 10*(2), 109–26.

Doyle, V. (2000). Lead us not into temptation: The London, Ontario, "kiddie-porn ring" and the construction of a moral panic. *International Journal of Canadian Studies, 21.*

Egan, K. (1999, May 11). Dead girl's dad says youth's sentence a "joke": Dangerous driving: Teenager gets one year for accident that killed two. *National Post (Ottawa Citizen),* A10.

Fairclough, N. (2003). *Analyzing discourse: Textual analysis for social research.* London: Routledge.

Faith, K., and Jiwani, Y. (2002). The social construction of "dangerous" girls and women. In B. Schissel and C. Brooks (Eds), *Marginality and condemnation: An introduction to critical criminology* (pp. 83–107). Halifax: Fernwood.

Fishman, M. (1978). Crime waves as ideology. *Social Problems, 25*(5), 531–43.

Fishman, M. (1981). Police news: Constructing an image of crime. *Urban Life, 9*(4), 371–94.

Fraser, K. (1997, December 5). Cadman introduces victims' rights bill. *The Province.*

Garland, D. (2001). *The culture of control: Crime and social order in contemporary society.* University of Chicago Press.

Garofalo, J. (1981). Crime and the mass media: A selective review of research. *Journal of Research in Crime and Delinquency, 18,* 319–50.

Gerbner, G., Gross, L., Morgan, M., and Signorielli, N. (1980). The mainstreaming of America: Violence profile no. 11. *Journal of Communications, 30,* 10–29.

Gomes, J., Bertrand, L., Paetsch, J., and Hornick, J. (2003). Self-reported delinquency among Alberta's youth: Findings from a survey of 2,001 Junior and senior high school students. *Adolescence, 38.*

Goode, E. (2009). *Moral panics: The social construction of deviance.* Oxford, UK: Blackwell.

Haggerty, K. (2001). *Making crime count.* University of Toronto Press. Toronto.

Hawkins, R., and Pingree, S. (1980). Some progress in the cultivation effect. *Communication Research, 7,* 193–226.

Health Canada. (2010). *Canadian alcohol and drug use monitoring survey.* Retrieved from http://www.hc-sc.gc.ca/hc-ps/drugs-drogues/stat/_2010/summary-sommaire-eng.php

Hinduja, S., and Patchin, J. (2006). "Bullies move beyond the schoolyard: A preliminary look at cyberbullying." *Youth Violence and Juvenile Justice, 4,* 148–69

Hinduja, S., and Patchin, J. (2008). "Cyerbullying: An exploratory analysis of factors related to offending and victimization." *Deviant Behavior 29,* 129–56.

Hogeveen, B. (2005). "If we are tough on crime, if we punish crime, then people get the message": Constructing and governing the punishable young offender in Canada during the late 1990s. *Punishment and Society, 7*(1), 73–89.

Hume, M. (2000, April 1). "Killer Kelly" was toughest girl in the gang, friends said: Results of psychiatric examinations contradictory. *National Post,* A8.

Jenkins, P. (1994). *Using murder: The social construction of serial homicide.* New York: Aldine de Gruyter.

Kappeler, V. (1996). *The mythology of crime and criminal justice.* Prospect Heights, US: Waveland Press.

Kupchik, A., and Bracy, N.L. (2009). The news media on school crime and violence: constructing dangerousness and fueling fear. *Youth Violence & Juvenile Justice, 7*(2), 136–55.

Lau, R. (2014, December 2). Former Nova Scotia boxing prodigy charged in Cole Harbour triple shooting. *Global News.* Retrieved from https://globalnews.ca/news/1704501/former-nova-scotia-boxing-prodigy-charged-in-cole-harbour-triple-shooting

Lowman, J. (2000). Violence and the outlaw status of (street) prostitution in Canada. *Violence against Women, 6*(9), 987–1011.

McCormick, C. (2008). *Criminology in Canada: Theories, patterns and typologies.* Toronto: Nelson.

McCormick, C. (2010). *Constructing danger: The mis/representation of crime in the news.* Halifax: Fernwood.

Mast, B., Benson, B., and Rasmussen, D. (2000). Entrepreneurial police and drug enforcement policy. *Public Choice, 104*(3–4), 285–308.

Muncie, J. (2004). *Youth and crime* (2nd ed.). London: Sage.

Naumetz, T. (1999, April 16). Bill to give victims of crime more rights: Offenders would pay into fund to help injured party. *National Post (Southam News),* A7.

N.S. teen gets adult sentence for woman's death. (2006, January11). CTV NEWS. Retrieved from https://www.treatingyourself.org/showthread.php?8935-N-S-teen-gets-adult-sentence/

Pizarro, J.M., Chermak, S.M., and Gruenewald, J.A. (2007). Juvenile "super-predators" in the news: A comparison of adult and juvenile homicides. *Journal of Criminal Justice & Popular Culture, 14*(1), 84–111

Sampert, S., and Froese, R. (2012). Punks, firebugs, and the laughing girl. Youth crime coverage in the *Winnipeg Sun*. In K. Gorkoff, and R. Jochelson (Eds), *Thinking about justice. A book of readings* (pp. 66–82). Halifax: Fernwood.

Savoie, J. (2007). *Youth self-reported delinquency, Toronto, 2006*. Statistics Canada Catalogue No. 85-002-XPE, vol. 27, no. 6.

Schissel, B. (1997). *Blaming children: Youth crime, moral panic and the politics of hate*. Halifax: Fernwood.

Schissel, B. (2006). *Still blaming children: Youth conduct and the politics of child hating*. Halifax: Fernwood.

Schnider, C. (2017). *Policing and social media: Social control in an era of New Media*. Lexington Books.

Smandych, R. (2001). *Youth justice: History, legislation, and reform*. Toronto: Harcourt.

Smandych, R., Dyck, M., La Berge, C., and Koffman, J. (2016). Youth justice in Manitoba: Developments and issues under the YCJA. In M. Alain, R.R. Corrado, and S. Reid (Eds), *Implementing and working with the Youth Criminal Justice Act across Canada* (pp. 86–124). Toronto: Toronto University Press.

Smart, R., and Adlaf, E. (1991). Substance use and problems among Toronto street youth. *British Journal of Addiction, 86*(8), 999–1010.

Spencer, J. (2005). It's not as simple as it seems: Ambiguous culpability and ambivalent affect in news representations of violent youth. *Symbolic Interaction, 28*(1), 47–65.

Sprott, J. (1996). Understanding public views of youth crime and the youth justice system. *Canadian Journal of Criminology, 38*(3), 271–90.

Statistics Canada. (2014). Police-reported crime statistics in Canada, 2013. Retrieved from http://www.statcan.gc.ca/pub/85-002-x/2015001/article/14211-eng.htm

Surette, R. (1998). *Media, crime, and criminal justice: Images and realities*. New York: Wadsworth.

Tanner, J. (2001). *Teenage troubles: Youth and deviance in Canada*. Scarborough, ON: Nelson-Thomson.

Tanner, J., and Wortley, S. (2002). *The Toronto youth crime and victimization survey: Overview report*. Toronto: Centre of Criminology, University of Toronto.

Wodak, R., and Meyer, M. (2000). *Methods of critical discourse analysis*. Thousand Oaks, CA: Sage.

Wohn, D., and Bowe, B. (February 2014). Crystallization: How social media facilitates social construction of reality, Conference paper, Proceedings of the companion publication of the 17th ACM Conference on Computer Supported Cooperative Work & Social Computing.

Canadian Girls and Crime in the Twenty-First Century

7

Lorinda Stoneman, Mandeep Mucina,
Thais Amorim, and Sibylle Artz

Overview

This chapter offers an overview of the ways in which girls who commit criminal offences and encounter the criminal justice system are dealt with in Canada. Readers are presented with material that will help them to understand and critique current Canadian youth justice system responses to female youth crime and to identify promising new directions for dealing with female youth offenders. Readers will also learn that Indigenous girls are vastly overrepresented in Canada's youth justice system. This perpetual overrepresentation, rooted in colonialism, seems to have been exacerbated by the Youth Criminal Justice Act (YCJA; 2003), at least in part because the required funding has not been distributed in ways that make community-based interventions viable, especially in less affluent and remote communities. The connections between mental health and incarceration, particularly for young women, are established in this chapter. The chapter also provides recommendations for instituting policies and practices to reverse systemic and personal abuse and discrimination based on gender and racial inequity.

Key Objectives

After reading this chapter, you should be able to:

- Identify and discuss Canadian female youth offending patterns.
- Understand and critique Canadian justice system responses to female youth crime.
- Outline traditional and contemporary explanations of female crime.
- Identify promising new directions in responding to female youth crime.

Introduction

To understand and respond to girls and crime, it is necessary to examine what we know about female young offenders as well as patterns of crime and trends in youth justice. We begin this chapter by discussing some characteristics of girls in conflict with the law and by examining girls' offending patterns using official statistics and self-report surveys. Next, we present a brief review of the theories that help to explain female crime and delinquency along with a critique of how female youth crime is conceptualized. The chapter ends with a discussion about the challenges of working effectively with delinquent girls in a system that was markedly changed by the last Conservative federal government's Safe Streets and Communities Act. The Act ignored the continual drop in youth crime rates (Handren 2014); toughened responses to youth crime despite evidence that well-funded community-based programs are more successful in deterring crime and curbing recidivism (Cunningham 2014; Webster and Doob 2015); and introduced a "tough on crime" agenda heavily criticized by experts for being wasteful, counterproductive, and ultimately ineffective in dealing with youth crime (Cesaroni and Bala 2008).

Most girls accused of Criminal Code violations have committed minor crimes (Mahony, Jacob, and Hobson 2017). Any apprehension or conviction, however, can have costly implications for them, their families, their friends, and society. Looking critically at the various ways that female crime is understood and responded to in law and practice reveals how social order is established and held in place. This is particularly so in the Canadian context given the history of colonialization and violence against Indigenous and racialized communities. Our critical analysis is therefore informed by intersectionality and anti-colonial theory and shows that crime is not a static phenomenon but one that changes as our ideologies and knowledge about crime and punishment change.

An analysis based on **intersectionality** is used throughout this chapter to reveal how the multiple, changing, and often overlapping and intersecting identities of offenders (e.g., gender, race, class, ethnicity, sexuality, and age) (Berger and Guidroz 2009) impact criminal behaviour. A concept that emerges from black feminist thought (Collins 1990), intersectionality was coined by Crenshaw (1989), who combined critical race theory, antiracism, and feminist theory to talk about the ways in which racism and sexism intersect and interlock to result in a form of oppression that uniquely impacts black women. More recently, Crenshaw's theory has been applied to diverse contexts and groups of people, and

intersectionality
Refers to a movement away from thinking categorically and toward thinking about the connections and crossroads between social facets. Intersectional thinking and theorizing recognize the multiple, changing, and often overlapping dimensions, demographics, roles, and identities of lawbreakers, victims, other individuals, and collectives.

is widely used within feminist criminology (Daly 2010). Intersectionality provides us with a framework that helps us to resist thinking categorically—about girls versus boys—and to move toward thinking about the positions of criminalized girls in society as consisting of connections and crossroads. This approach appreciates that the lives of girls who partake in delinquency are much more complex than the label "delinquent/bad girl" implies.

Intersectionality helps us to make sense of gender as more than merely a simplistic, homogeneous set of uniform sex differences. We accept that those engaged in crime are navigating the world and the systems that construct their race, sexuality, gender, class, and even religion in oppressive ways. We demonstrate that we cannot talk about Indigenous girls' involvement in and overrepresentation in crime and child welfare without recognizing that they come into this world with intergenerational stories of trauma their ancestors have endured since settler occupation of their land disrupting their culture and ways of being. Intersectionality gives us the theory and language to unpack the structures and constructions that frame our systems and the ways in which a person's movement in the world shapes their experiences (Crenshaw 1991).

The Female Young Offender

Girls, like boys, break the law but not often. While girls certainly engage in illegal behaviours, they rarely develop crime specialties (Chesney-Lind and Pasko 2004; Zahn 2009). Self-report data on girls' delinquency gathered in the United States shows that incidence rates have not substantially changed in the past 30 years, and where increases have occurred, they relate to minor and administrative offences, not serious, violent behaviours (Chesney-Lind and Shelden 2014). In the Canadian setting, Silcox (2017) examined official court data over the period 1991/1992 to 2011/2012 to illustrate a downward trend of violent crime for girls (as well as boys). Recent evidence (Silcox 2016) suggests that despite the clear evidence that the rates of female crime have been low and declining—and despite the decrease in the amount of Canadian media coverage of girls' crime since the 1990s—coverage tends to exaggerate the frequency of delinquent acts by young women. Indeed, mainstream media typically frames young female offenders as either "deviously feminine—looking innocent on the surface, but vicious underneath—or increasingly masculine, beginning to outdo boys with their aggression and violence" (p. 159). Chesney-Lind and Shelden (2014) suggest that such false and moral panic–inducing portrayals of young female offenders, which they describe as an anti-feminist backlash, are problematic given how media and public opinion can help shape public policy (e.g., the aforementioned Safe Streets and Communities Act) as well as legal and correctional responses to offending.

Girls commit crime for reasons that are often different from boys (Davidson 2013). Despite this, we should exercise caution when framing girls as distinctive for a number of reasons. For one, "gender differences are often pathologized" (Irwin and Chesney-Lind 2008, p. 842) through locating differences in girls as weaknesses in their biological and psychological chemistry. This approach tends to be translated into gender-responsive correctional programming that focuses on the individual girl rather than examining welfare and institutional cultures and practices that target troubled girls (Sharpe 2016), and it may perpetuate stereotypical, sexist assumptions about young women. Further, if not carefully applied, these interventions conceal within-group differences among girls (e.g., race, class, gender, and sexual identity) (Sharpe 2016). Second, considering young people only in terms of binary male–female sex differences leaves out youth who identify as lesbian, gay, bisexual, trans, queer/questioning, two spirit, intersex, and others (LGBTQ2SI), who may find themselves with intersecting vulnerabilities including homelessness and victimization (e.g., ridicule and physical assault due to homophobia and transphobia) (Abramovich 2012). In order to make visible the experiences of those who are often invisible in the context of criminology, we want to remind the reader that some of the most vulnerable girls who find themselves intersecting with criminalization are victims of interpersonal and structural violence that impacts their everyday lives.

It is clear that there is no typical female young offender. There are, however, some similar hurdles that many female young offenders face that help to describe this population and the pathways girls take into offending. We know that an overwhelming number of youth involved in the criminal justice system face a constellation of adversities, including those related to violence, abuse and trauma, mental and physical health, social and familial dysfunction, and sometimes cognitive difficulties (Chesney-Lind and Jones 2010; Chesney-Lind and Pasko 2013; Chesney-Lind and Shelden 2014; Gretton and Clift 2011; Moretti, Odgers, and Reppucci 2011; Zahn 2009).

Incarcerated adolescents demonstrate exceedingly high rates of mental disorders (100 per cent of incarcerated girls and 91.9 per cent of incarcerated boys in British Columbia show signs of at least one mental disorder) and substance abuse disorders (100 per cent of girls and 85.5 per cent of boys) (Gretton and Clift 2011). As Moretti, Odgers, and Reppucci (2011) found in their longitudinal study, early trauma exposure contributes to developmental challenges, which in turn can lead to mental health issues and substance misuse. Thus, young people confined to custody, as well as youth diverted from the formal system into often under-resourced communities, carry with them the impact of adversity and trauma. As a result, Canadian custody centres mostly house marginalized, under-resourced youth who are often victims of neglect, child abuse, and (especially for females) sexual abuse (Smith, Cox, Poon, Stewart and McCreary Centre Society 2013). Youth justice professionals must therefore find ways to work with youth who have multiple needs and challenges (Mann, Senn, Girard and Ackbar 2007).

In the province of British Columbia, the McCreary Centre Society (MCS) periodically conducts an extensive survey on incarcerated youth in aiming to understand some of the complex factors facing them. The 2012 MCS survey found that virtually all incarcerated girls had suffered physical abuse compared to slightly more than half of incarcerated boys (57 per cent) (Smith et al., 2013). Further, 57 per cent of girls (and 0 per cent of boys) reported physical abuse by an intimate partner, and 75 per cent of incarcerated girls (32 per cent of boys) reported having been sexually abused. Incarcerated girls were also more likely to have reported having mental health concerns (e.g., depression) or emotional issues and were more likely to suffer from multiple conditions than boys. Also, while 18 per cent of both girls and boys reported having engaged in self-harm, girls were four times more likely to report having harmed themselves six or more times. Additionally, the study showed that twice the proportion of girls (50 per cent) than boys (25 per cent) reported having been kicked out of their homes.

This self-reported data show us that female young offenders, particularly those who become incarcerated, face significant mental, emotional, physical, and social challenges, and that, in an overwhelming number of cases, they are victims as well as offenders. The dual victim and offender status experienced by offending girls, and the more numerous and severe needs and risks they must deal with, present significant concerns for intervention and treatment (Chesney-Lind and Shelden 2014). These will be discussed at the close of this chapter.

Patterns of Female Youth Crime and Canadian Justice System Responses

Official Charges

Official police, court, and correctional data provided by Statistics Canada offer key indicators of how the Canadian judicial system responds to some of the illegal behaviours of some girls (see Figure 7.1). It is important to note that official data is an underestimate of youth crimes; it does not include those crimes that do not come to the attention of the criminal justice system (the "dark figure") or those unsolved crimes where the age of the offender is unknown.

As Figure 7.1 suggests, only 2 per cent of all Canadians charged and brought to court in 2016 were girls (Statistics Canada 2017a, 2017f). It is not youth, but adults, especially adult men, who are likely to enter the court system for crimes against persons, property, or the public order. Additionally, although there are nearly equal numbers of girls and boys under the age of 18 in the Canadian population, the vast majority of charges laid by the police and the Crown continue to be against boys. In the early 1980s, one in ten cases involving youth were against girls. Twenty years later, the gender ratio narrowed to one in five, where it remains (Statistics Canada 2017f).

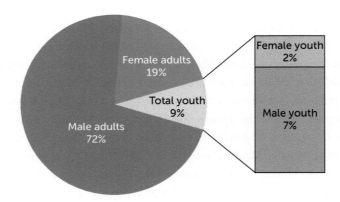

Figure 7.1   Total Canadian Criminal Court Cases 2016

Note: For 7 per cent of adults and 1 per cent of youth, sex was unknown.

Sources: Statistics Canada 2017a, 2017f.

A well-documented increase of youth crime was the subject of public discussion in the late 1980s until the youth crime rate reached its peak in 1991, and scholarly work describing the phenomenon helps us to understand how changes in crime statistics reflect numerous factors apart from or in addition to shifts in criminal behaviour. For example, in 2005, Steffensmeier and his colleagues found that the upward trend of girls' offending could not be replicated using unofficial longitudinal sources. They hypothesized that changes in enforcement, in youth justice policy, and in culture were more likely explanations of the changing charge rates. Because policy had changed in a more expressive and punitive direction (Steffensmeier, Schwartz, Zhong, and Ackerman 2005), actions that previously would not have come to the attention of police were reclassified as criminal matters. These exacerbating and net-widening policies included zero tolerance policies in schools, a lower threshold for what constitutes criminality in domestic arguments, and the inclusion of parent–child and sibling altercations as chargeable domestic offences (Woolford 2009), along with the additional net-widening effect of using criminal charges for minor offences to prevent anticipated criminal risk (Steffensmeier et al. 2005). Such policy changes might also help to explain why there appeared to be an upward trend in female major and minor assault charges from 1991 to 2001 that only began to level off and decrease in 2009.

Following the youth crime peak for both sexes in 1991 (Allen and Superle 2016), the youth crime rate—the rate of youth accused of Criminal Code offences (excluding traffic offences)—has trended downwards, with a 45 per cent reduction in overall youth crime rate from 1998 to 2016 (Statistics Canada 2017h). Over this period, girls have seen a 43 per cent decrease in the rate of charges for property offences and a 25 per cent decrease in the rate of charges for violent offences. Boys have seen a similar decrease in violent offences and a slightly greater decrease in the rate of property offences charges. Like previous trends, the more recent decline in youth accused and charged must also be understood as reflective of a combination of factors, including changes in criminal behaviour, legislative changes, shifts in demographics, and policy changes (Doob and Sprott 2004), like the increased use of informal and pre-charge diversion under the YCJA (Dauvergne 2013; Stoneman 2016).

Coinciding with an overall decline in youth crime, the gap between the number of girls and boys committing criminal offences has been narrowing. Sprott and Doob (2009) suggest that because fewer boys are becoming involved in the justice system as compared to the early 1990s, it is rather the *ratio* as opposed to the frequency of girls' versus boys' crime that is narrowing. These scholars propose that what is really a difference in offending patterns for boys tends to be interpreted as a reason to become alarmed about girls. In fact, delinquent adjudication for girls has remained stable and even dipped slightly, while that for boys has noticeably declined. For these reasons, we need to be cautious when assessing female offending rates as if male offending rates were the accepted benchmark[1] (Sharpe and Gelsthorpe 2009). Caution is also required as we examine girls' delinquency as represented by percentage-based quantitative statistics because the base number of girls involved in crime is so small (Heidensohn and Silvestri, 2012). For example, in 2012, only one girl was accused of homicide. The following year, five girls were accused (Statistics Canada 2017c), accounting for a five-fold jump in these violent offences but representing the involvement of only four more girls.

The rates of females charged started to decline late in the 1990s, and the comparable rate for boys has dropped even more. The number of females charged in 1996 was 2230 per 100,000 Canadian female youth, and the number charged in 2013 was 987 per 100,000. Overall, according to Statistics Canada, between 2004 and 2013, there was a 30 per cent decrease in charges for female youth and a 36 per cent drop in charges for boys (Statistics Canada 2017b, 2017h).

Table 7.1 presents the types of crimes for which girls and boys made court appearances in 2015/16 by principal charge, listed in descending order of seriousness. Most frequently, charges resulting in court appearances for girls focus on **administrative offences**, followed closely by charges for theft and minor assault. Together, these offences amount to 60 per cent of charges for girls in court. For boys, the most frequent charges resulting in court appearances are also for administrative offences (a trend that has held for several years). Next in frequency for boys are charges for minor assaults, followed closely by theft.

administrative offences
Offences against the administration of justice—that is, violations of court-ordered behavioural requirements, such as complying with a curfew, attending mandated programmes, and following through on all manner of bail conditions and probation orders.

Table 7.1	Youth Court Cases, 2015/2016, by Sex	
Youth Court Cases by Principal Charge	**Female % (6411 court cases)**	**Male % (21,650 court cases)**
Homicide and Attempted Murder	0.05	0.20
Robbery	2.0	5.6
Against Person Major*	7.5	6.1
Against Person Minor**	**19.6**	**13.5**
Sexual Offences	0.9	5.8
Theft	**17.3**	**10.3**
Break and Enter	3.4	8.3
Fraud	1.9	1.0
Possess Stolen Goods	6.3	5.7
Drug Trafficking/Possession***	5.9	8.1
Mischief	6.3	6.7
Administrative/Against YCJA****	**23.5**	**18.4**
Other Property Crimes	0.5	1.0
Criminal Code Traffic	1.8	1.8
Other Criminal Code	2.9	7.1
Residual Federal Statutes	0.2	0.5

* Major assault; assault with a weapon (YCJA s. 267), aggravated assault (s. 268), and other assaults (assaulting a police officer and unlawfully causing bodily harm). Excludes murder, attempted murder, and robbery.
** Common assault, criminal harassment, uttering threats, and other crimes against the person.
*** Includes drug trafficking, production, importation, exporting, and possession.
**** Includes failure to comply with disposition, failure to comply with undertaking, assist/interfere/other, contempt against youth court, breach of recognizance, failure to appear, failure to comply with probation order, escape custody, unlawfully at large, and charges against the YCJA.

Source: Statistics Canada 2017f.

Both girls and boys are infrequently charged with major serious violent crimes, including homicide, attempted murder, robbery, and major assault (these charges amount to 9.5 per cent of principal charges resulting in court appearances for girls and 12 per cent for boys).

For over 40 years, 15 or fewer Canadian girls per year have been charged with homicide, and usually far fewer than 10. In 2016, there were only 4 (Statistics Canada 2017c). In 2015/16, female youth were charged and brought to court for 17 per cent of violent youth crime, 15 per cent of property crime involving youth, 21 per cent of administration of justice offences involving youth, and 7 per cent of other Criminal Code offences involving youth (Statistics Canada 2017f). It is, however, worth noting that in the past 25 years, the number of charges relating to Criminal Code violations excluding traffic that has resulted in youth court appearances for girls has decreased by 44 per cent, while the number of such charges for boys has decreased by 61 per cent (Statistics Canada 2017f).

Administrative Offences

Canadian girls are most often brought to court for non-criminal breaches of court orders (i.e., administrative offences). In fact, this has been the case since the enactment of the Juvenile Delinquents Act (JDA) in 1908 (Sprott 2012). The JDA took a paternalistic approach to juvenile delinquency (see Chapter 1), involving the imposition of sanctions, known as status offences, against young people for immoral behaviours, such as "habitual truancy, curfew violations, repeated running away, underage liquor law violations, tobacco offences, and ungovernability or incorrigibility in failing to respond to the reasonable requests of parents" (Thomas 2009, p. 771). It is important to note that "unlike criminal offense cases, court processing decisions in status offense cases [were] less about how much protection to afford the public than how much protection to afford the [young] offender" (Spivak, Wagner, Whitmer, and Charish 2014, p. 229).

Feminist scholars agree that the interpretation and application of such dispositions were embedded in stereotypical and binary notions of masculinity and femininity (Bala and Anand 2009; Chesney-Lind and Pasko 2004; Dean 2005; Spivak et al. 2014). This means that adolescent females who diverged from the dominant ideal of the "naturally fragile, obedient, passive, and chaste" (Artz and Amorim 2013, p. 7) and broke "traditional, patriarchal family values" (Spivak et al. 2014, p. 226) were brought to court and charged for their "reform" and "salvation" (Andrew and Cohn 1974). According to Spivak et al. (2014), "this gender bias . . . manifest[ed itself] into attitudes and discretion biases referred to as judicial paternalism" (Spivak et al. 2014, p. 225). Bala and Anand (2009) add that this kind of enforcement of institutional authority was used mostly against adolescent girls from "socially disadvantaged backgrounds and racial minorities" (p. 9).

The enactment of the Young Offenders Act (YOA) in 1984 decriminalized status offences, making scholars and youth justice professionals hopeful that gender and race biases in sentencing would discontinue (Dean 2005). However, rather than halting the criminal processing of immoral behaviours completely, the YOA instituted the "failure to comply with a disposition" offence, in which youth on bail, probation, or serving other community-based dispositions, who failed to abide by court conditions imposed on them could be charged with a new offence and be sentenced to youth custody

(Latimer 2011; Trepanier 1999). It is critical to note that, under the YOA, court conditions encompassed but were not limited to status offences.

Similarly to what was observed under the JDA, "[failure to comply] cases became a larger part of girls' youth court and custody caseload than of boys" (Sprott 2012, p. 311). The overrepresentation of adolescent females in the justice system between 1983 and 2003 could be explained as a "result of a carry-over of the sexist approach to sentencing young women under the JDA" (Dean 2005, p. 8). The enactment of the YOA allowed authorities to resort to bail and probation for the surveillance and control of girls' behaviours for their own good and safety (Bell 2012). Dean (2005) clarifies that the courts' understanding of safety alluded to "morality rather than physical or emotional well-being" of the teenage girls (p. 7).

The offence of failure to comply with a disposition has contributed significantly to the increase of youth justice convictions and custody sentences (Smandych and Corrado, 2018). For instance, in 1991/92, 7 per cent of charges against girls resulting in court were for breach of probation or failure to comply with administrative orders. Since that time, there has been a sharp increase in the proportion and number of these administrative offences: in 2015/16, for example, 21 per cent of charges for which girls attended court were related to breach of probation or failure to comply (Statistics Canada 2017f). The proportion of breach of probation and failure to comply charges against boys has also risen rapidly though not as dramatically, from 5 per cent in 1991/92 to 15 per cent of all charges resulting in court in 2015/16 (Statistics Canada 2017f).

The striking increase in administrative charges that began in the 1990s and seems to be growing incrementally year-over-year—despite decreases in other charges—is another illustration of how difficult it can be to obtain an accurate picture of girls and crime from statistics. Sprott and Doob (2009) suggest that the continuous rise in administrative charges that started in the 1990s in North America is disproportionately impacting girls, pushing them further into the youth justice system, turning them into recidivists, and leaving them with sizable criminal records that do not accurately reflect their actual engagement in crime (Sprott 2012). This trajectory appears to follow them into early adulthood (Mahony, Jacob and Hobson 2017).

The drafters of the YCJA aimed to reduce both net widening and the practice of crafting bail and probation conditions to achieve paternalistic and child welfare aims; criticisms have, nevertheless, surfaced. Like its predecessors, the YCJA opens the door for gender bias and judicial paternalism in sentencing, impacting girls more harshly (Sprott and Doob 2010; Sprott and Manson 2017; Stoneman 2016).

Court Decisions and Correctional Admissions for Convicted Girls

Not all girls who are charged are convicted and sentenced in youth court. Every year a substantial proportion of girls—51 per cent in 2015/16—have their cases withdrawn, dismissed, or stayed (this category includes referrals by the court to restorative justice programs and extrajudicial measures) (Statistics Canada 2017f). We also know that female youth are admitted to correctional services at a much lower rate than male youth. Research concludes that the trend of admissions to correctional services has been declining for nearly a decade and was hastened by the YCJA. About one in every six adolescents sentenced in 2015/16 was a girl. In 2015/16, female youth made up 17 per cent of all youth sentenced to probation, 13 per cent of those sentenced to custody, 28 per cent of those given conditional sentences, and 17 per cent of those sentenced to intensive support and supervision (Statistics Canada 2017g). While the incarceration rate (including pre-trial detention, remand, and sentenced custody) for female youth in 2015/16 was 18 per 10,000, the rate for male youth was over 2.5 times higher, at 48 per 10,000. Although the total incarceration rates for both boys and girls have been declining since 2000/01, a closer look yields a spike in the rate of girls in pre-trial detention who are either awaiting trial or sentencing from 2004/05 to 2011/12, and this only recently began trending downwards. As expected, a marked decline in the rate of both girls and boys admitted to sentenced to custody is evident following the introduction of the YCJA (−95 per cent for girls and −90 per cent for boys from 2001/02 to 2015/16) (Statistics Canada 2017e, 2017b).

The most common sentence or disposition for girls, like boys, continues to be probation (in 2015/16, 54 per cent of guilty cases involving girls resulted in a sentence of probation) (Statistics Canada 2017g). With the introduction of the YCJA, several new community corrections sanctions became available to rectify the upward trend in youth incarceration rates. In order to allow for reintegration following a custodial sentence, all youth are sentenced to community supervision that commences once they are released from custody (akin to statutory release after serving a third of the sentence in the adult system).

Bail and Probation Orders

A growing body of research reflects on how bail and probation terms under the YCJA contribute to the perpetuation of bias (Myers 2017; Myers and Dhillon 2013; Pulis 2013; Sprott 2015; Toh 2003). The legislation requires decision-makers to be intentional in crafting bail and probation conditions that are meaningful and that bear a causal relationship with the offending act(s) they aim to address (Bala 2003; Myers and Dhillon 2013; Toh 2003). Pulis (2014) clarifies that the disconnect between crime and court order terms is allowed as long as the imposition of unrelated conditions tackles "life circumstances that may increase the likelihood of offending (i.e., poor parenting, school failure, delinquent peers)," (p. 231), to which we may easily add unemployment, substance use, and mental health concerns. This caveat is problematic for two reasons. First, the imposition of lengthy orders filled with broad and unrelated conditions have been observed to "have the unintended consequence of setting youth [particularly girls and racial minorities] up to accumulate further criminal charges of failing to comply" (Sprott 2012, p. 321). Second, just as with the JDA and the YOA, it allows for intense monitoring and criminalization of violations of gender stereotypical non-criminal female behaviours under the current legislation (Pulis 2014).

It is noteworthy that the literature is inconsistent as to whether or not the bail and probation terms imposed on girls differ from those imposed on their male counterparts. Some authors explain that, due to the small female sample in their studies, the comparison between genders was deemed infeasible and, consequently, valid conclusions could not be drawn (Myers and Dhillon 2013; Sprott 2015). Others—for example, Pulis (2014), in an investigation of 6051 youth sentenced to probation in Ontario in 2005 and 2006—found no significant gender discrepancies when it came to the terms of bail and probation orders. A handful of researchers, do, however, show that when compared with males, female young offenders are more likely to get residence orders (reside with parent or other adult; reside where directed by youth worker; and obey the rules/regulations of the home/residence) (Pulis 2013; Sprott and Manson 2017); curfew orders (Pulis 2013; Sprott 2012); attend counselling/treatment or assessment for counselling/treatment orders (Sprott and Doob 2010; Sprott and Manson 2017); and no contact orders "to keep them away from undesirables"—i.e., sexual partners, criminogenic peers, substance-using youth, exploiters and traffickers (Pasko 2017, p. 10). The studies that found that gender was a significant predictor of the aforementioned court order terms emphasized the perpetuation of gender bias across time to explain their findings. Given the disagreements within the literature, more research is needed to clarify whether there is a disproportionate use of certain types of probation and bail terms for girls and whether judicial paternalism and gender bias impacts responses to administrative offences.

On a brighter note, the federal government's proposed Bill C-75 aims to reduce the number of administrative offences by changing sections 29(1) and 38(2)(e.1) of the YCJA and limiting the use of unnecessary and unrelated bail and probation conditions (Department of Justice Canada 2018; Canada, Forty-second Parliament, House of Commons 2018). If this bill becomes law, court order terms will need to "be narrowly drafted and the party requesting the term be able to articulate how it will be necessary (note: not simply desirable or even helpful) to address primary or secondary ground concerns" (Jones 2018). Though the proposed changes do not address the underlying social and structural gender inequalities, they have the potential to curb youth justice professionals' vast discretionary powers and enhance judicial consideration for adolescents' legal and human rights when crafting fair and appropriate bail and probation orders.

Community Supervision

In addition to the YCJA being drafted to address the overuse of probation and bail for social welfare reasons, the legislation was intended to address the growing youth incarceration rate in Canada that surged in the 1990s. The Department of Justice approached the YCJA "with a more inclusive framework, focusing on public awareness, crime prevention, education, child welfare, health, family and the community" (Calverley 2007, p. 2). An important success of the YCJA has been a clearer delineation of serious and minor offences such that the most serious interventions (such as custody) are given to the most serious offenders, while minor offenders have the opportunity to be diverted from the formal system and take part in a community-based program or receive a warning (Sprott 2012). The result—a decrease in charges, guilty findings, and custodial sentences for both boys and girls—has been undeniable (Bala, Carrington, and Roberts 2009), and in British Columbia, it has resulted in the closure of two girls' custody units and later in the complete closure of one youth custody centre (British Columbia 2014). While this reduction in custody spaces is a positive development, resources have not been redirected into the community.

In a qualitative study of the British Columbia context undertaken by Stoneman (2016), less serious offenders were reportedly faced with trying to access non-existent or inappropriate programs in their communities, while more serious offenders were often incarcerated far away from their families and communities. The resulting phenomenon, described by Stoneman as **net narrowing**, occurs when youth who have been diverted struggle to access adequate resources. In her study, youth-serving professionals reported that before they were able to gain access to resources such as clinical assessments, programming, financial assistance, and one-to-one support for their clients, they had to demonstrate that their clients were seriously entrenched in the system. This is perhaps the most pressing disadvantage of diversion since resource allocation only follows after system involvement, and may not be available if clients are diverted. Paradoxically, then, serious criminal behaviour becomes one of the few keys to unlock desperately needed resources.

net narrowing
A phenomenon that occurs when youth who have been diverted from the criminal justice system struggle to access adequate resources.

As the YCJA was moving through the legislative process on its way to becoming law, experts expressed another key concern: that the YCJA's post-custody supervision regulations might increase the number of administrative charges, with new charges laid and a return to custody made possible if supervision conditions were not complied with (Bala et al. 2009). These concerns have in part materialized: though the number of administrative charges for girls has decreased under the YCJA, it is decreasing at a much slower pace than other charges. Although the YCJA has made it tougher to sentence youth to custody (see Chapter 3), incarcerating non-violent youth is still permitted. In fact, some custodial sentences resulting from failure to comply may be lengthier than 93 per cent of custodial sentences (Sprott and Doob 2010). Sprott and Doob (2009) speculate that such occurrences signal the existence of cases where, despite the YCJA's clarity that youth cannot be held in custody for welfare purposes, detention—especially for girls—is still being used for this reason instead of solely for the protection of the public.

Sharpe and Gelsthorpe (2009) discuss community-based alternatives to custody (diversion) but also highlight the concern that girls who fail in community programs will then be "fast-tracked into custody" (p. 202). However, recent research in British Columbia (Artz and Amorim 2013) has found that police, probation officers, and judges share a sense of frustration about the lack of resources and programs to which they can divert or adjudicate young women, and that they invoke administrative charges only as a last resort when "all else fails." Artz and Amorim underline a sense of duty of care rather than a need for control, and suggest that a higher incidence of referrals of girls to programs reflects their greater and more complex needs compared to boys, while their higher rates of administrative charges reflect a dearth of services (see also Box 7.1).

An Overrepresentation of Racialized Girls

One glaring issue that has a long history in Canada is the overrepresentation of Indigenous female youth in custody. In 2012, about 6 per cent of all female youth in this country were Indigenous (Munch 2012). However, in 2015/16, Indigenous female youth represented 43 per cent of girls admitted to total correctional services, 46 per cent of girls admitted to pre-trial detention, 80 per cent of girls admitted to remand, and 49 per cent of all female youth sentenced to custody (Statistics Canada 2017d). Indigenous girls also make up 37 per cent of females admitted to community sentences. In all five categories, Indigenous girls

Box 7.1 | Youth Justice in Action

Resource Deficits under the YCJA—"We've done everything we can"

In her study involving the use of diversion under the YCJA, Stoneman (2016) spoke to professionals in the youth justice field, many of whom recounted numerous cases where they had simply run out of appropriate and meaningful resources with which to treat youth—in particular, young women. One youth worker described a situation where a young woman on her caseload had exhausted all means of treatment available in the community.

I have a youth on my caseload right now. She's been on my caseload for four years. She's very highly addicted to all sorts of drugs, heroin being one of the most pressing ones. She's been in care all through her life, she's gone through, I believe, 25 foster homes. So really, I don't even know how these kids have a chance when they've already suffered through so much. We've

sent her away to programs, given her all sorts of treatment and tried to help her in the community and we're finding that it's just not possible. We just don't have the resources to help her. She said her addictions are too strong. The last thing she said to us was "you guys want me to be normal, I'm just not normal, this is my normal." She is currently in jail and her probation actually expires in February and she's aged out. So, ya. It's bad. It tears on my heartstrings a little bit. . . . We've done everything we can. (n.p.)

Critical Thinking Question
What are the implications of resource deficits for the treatment of girls under the YCJA?

---

are overrepresented at a much greater rate than Indigenous boys. This overrepresentation is exacerbated by the fact that, even as the number of females admitted to sentenced custody has decreased since the introduction of the YCJA, the decline has been much smaller for Indigenous females (Statistics Canada 2017d).

Indigenous girls, many of whom are intergenerational survivors of the residential school system, are the fastest growing population in youth custody (Native Women's Association of Canada for Justice for Girls 2012) and tend to experience very high rates of administrative charges. The overrepresentation of Indigenous girls in the youth justice system reflects a similar trend in the child welfare system (Blackstock 2011) and can be traced to a history of colonialism and genocide directed toward Indigenous communities across Canada, seen most directly in the intergenerational impacts of residential schools. What is now a crisis of Indigenous children and youth in government care—a phenomenon termed the "millennium scoop" and a "humanitarian crisis" (Gilchrist, n.d., as cited in Sinclair 2007, p. 67)—also draws our attention to the care-to-prison pipeline where youth who transition out of care without supports are disproportionately criminalized. For example, a BC study showed that approximately one-third of female youth in the child welfare system are recommended for criminal charges in that province at some point in their youth, compared to 1 in 20 female youth in the general population; this overrepresentation is greater for Indigenous female youth and continues into young adulthood (British Columbia Representative for Children and Youth [RCY] 2009). Accordingly, the overlap among the child welfare and youth justice system populations, particularly among those incarcerated (RCY 2009), is critical to our understanding of the crossroads and connections of race, ethnicity, and gender among female young offenders.

Similar to the overrepresentation of Indigenous children in government care, some studies suggest that black children are disproportionately captured in Ontario's child welfare system, including an overrepresentation among child maltreatment investigations and placement in government care as compared to white children; research is unclear on whether these disparities can be wholly explained by structural factors like poverty, or whether discriminatory bias plays a role (Ontario Human Rights Commission 2018).

Fitzgerald and Carrington (2011) provide us with the first study to systematically examine the overrepresentation of visible minority youth in the Canadian justice system in the light of competing theoretical explanations: differential crime involvement or differential contact. These researchers show that the overrepresentation of Indigenous youth in the Canadian justice system also extends to black, Arab, and West Asian Canadian youth and is significantly linked to differential contact grounded in racially discriminatory police practices. This begs us all to recognize the ways in which racism, sexism, and white supremacy intersect with our current policies (Blackstock 2011; Maynard 2015; Sinclair 2007) and suggests that many of our social service systems are not working or engaging with Indigenous and other racialized young girls (and boys) from a place of equity or justice.

Studies like that of Fitzgerald and Carrington (2011) are rare. We therefore acknowledge that we are still quite limited in our examination of the overrepresentation of Indigenous and racialized girls in the youth justice system because official youth justice system data disaggregated by race and ethnicity, in addition to sex and youth status, is lacking (Owusu-Bempah and Wortley 2015; Reasons et al. 2016). Apart from data on encounters with court and corrections by Indigenous people, Statistics Canada does not collect, or make publicly available, data on ethnicity or race at any level of the criminal justice system (Moscher and Mahon-Haft 2010). There has long been a debate among academics, policy-makers, and criminal justice agencies on whether it is appropriate or feasible to collect sensitive data on race and ethnicity, or if such collection efforts would be undermined by problems of (in)accuracy or, worse, would further perpetuate systemic bias (Owusu-Bempah and Millar 2010). Regardless of one's side in the debate, the lack of data poses significant impediments to research, policy development, and criminological inquiry on race and the criminal justice system. It limits our ability to understand the prevalence of racial discrimination or bias (Hayle, Wortley, and Tanner 2016; Owusu-Bempah and Millar 2010) as well as the intersections between gender, race, and criminal involvement (Wortley and Tanner 2003), especially among female youth, and our ability to increase transparency and accountability in the criminal justice system. Some observers suggest that the status quo amounts to a "de facto ban . . . provid[ing] a convenient shield against allegations of racial bias for justice institutions and Canadian governments" (Owusu-Bempah and Wortley 2015, p. 2).

Theories of Female Crime and Delinquency

Before the 1970s, few theorists concerned themselves with female crime and delinquency. When females *were* considered, the focus was generally on the **gender gap** (the lower crime participation of females in comparison to males), rather than on the conditions or the motivations that move females toward crime and delinquency (Artz 1998; Ryder 2014; Tanner 1996).

The gender gap in crime—still configured in terms of binary sex differences—has been variously explained as located in the biological differences between the two heteronormative sexes, or derived from differences in stereotypically dichotomized gender role socialization. When that gap appeared to close, as it did to some degree when a rise in female crime occurred, this was explained as a failure or double-edged sword of the feminist movement because of the "masculinization" of women brought on by increasing social equity between the sexes (see Adler 1975; Simon 1975). This approach supports the notion that delinquency and crime are ultimately masculine pursuits (Cohen, 1955), but the claims that feminism has perpetrated a rise in delinquency in children as mothers leave their homes to pursue careers have been thoroughly researched and shown to be wrong (Chesney-Lind and Shelden 2014; Miller 1986). It was not until the mid-1980s that theorists shifted away from theories of delinquency that are uncritically grounded in male behaviour (Campbell 1991; Chesney-Lind and Jones 2010; Chesney-Lind and Pasko 2004; Chesney-Lind and Shelden 2014; Reitsma-Street 1998; Zahn 2009). While the gender gap still remains to be explained, the focus among researchers is now on understanding female crime and delinquency as it pertains to females rather than merely as compared to males.

Biological Theories

Early theories of crime were largely informed by the belief that biology was destiny and have explained females' lower involvement in delinquency and crime in terms of their supposed biological inferiority (see Binder, Geis, and Bruce 1988; Cowie, Cowie, and Slater 1968; Pollack 1950; Wilson and Herrnstein 1985). Even Gisela Konopka (1966, 1983), who was one of the first researchers to turn directly to adolescent girls to learn about their involvement in delinquency, assumed that girls and women were largely controlled by biology and sex roles prescribed to them.

Research on biology and crime continues, but in a different vein, with some more recent theories tending to avoid determinism and accepting that individuals have both choice and agency. For example, Tremblay (2003) shows that aggression is innate rather than learned as was widely claimed in the 1980s and 1990s (see Reiss and Roth 1993), and suggests that variability in early aggression is due, in part at least, to some genetic effects (Dionne, Tremblay, Boivin, LaPlante, and Pérusse 2003) such as fetal exposure to testosterone, which can play a role in how easily a child learns to control physical aggression (Rubinow and Schmidt 1996). Additionally, Tremblay suggests that there is good evidence that low levels of serotonin are implicated in impulsive and aggressive behaviour (see Raine 2002). While Tremblay and colleagues point out the need to understand the physiological underpinnings of behaviour that influence the ability to unlearn the use of aggression and violence, they also emphasize the importance of learning to regulate physical aggression in early childhood and highlight the contribution of parental conflict and anti-social behaviour, low income, early childbearing, and maternal smoking to later problematic outcomes for children.

With that in mind, Dodge and Pettit (2003) posit a **biopsychosocial model** and draw attention to the reciprocal influences of biological and socio-cultural contexts on behaviour. They show that biological dispositions like autonomic nervous system hyper-activity, intelligence potential, and temperament can be mediated positively or negatively by prenatal factors such as exposure to toxic substances and by socio-cultural context variables like family income, occupation and education, age of the mother, the absence or presence of parental conflict, divorce, and family violence; and, as the child matures, the mediating effects of positive or negative peer, school, and neighbourhood influences. Dodge and Pettit also note that these dispositions and socio-cultural interactions are not unidirectional but reciprocal, so that a child's sensitivities and temperament can influence parenting behaviour and the behaviour of other family members, which in turn also in-fluence the child's behaviour. In this way, children's early experiences serve to set in place their social knowledge frameworks for how the world works. These frameworks influence how children make sense of what is expected and acceptable, and exert a strong influence on behaviour and personal choice where delinquency is concerned. Thus the development of delinquency is considered interactive.

Further evidence of the interactive dimensions of delinquency is provided by Fishbein, Miller, Winn, and Dakof (2009), who found that although the most salient bio-logical disposition and vulnerability for delinquency for girls appears to be early pubertal maturation, this is not merely a matter of fixed individual biological timing. Early matu-ration also involves heredity, body weight, weight-to-height ratio, stressful life events and associated hormonal and other biopsychological effects, and the quality of a girl's family relations, including the absence or presence of an adult male in the girl's household. The interplay of multiple influences and their effect on mental health plays an enormous role in how any girl becomes involved in delinquency and crime. As Fishbein and colleagues also note, the incidence of mental illness and of co-morbidity—that is, two or more psy-chiatric disorders—is extremely high in offending girls. These disorders are not merely intrinsic to some girls and not others; they have their origins in a complex interplay of personal, relational, social, and cultural factors and can by no means be explained by biological disposition alone. If development involves adverse life conditions, these create dynamic cascading impacts involving multiple interacting effects (Artz et al. 2014) that cannot be reduced to a single biological starting point.

Trauma Theory

The neurobiological and criminogenic impacts of traumatic life experiences and the per-vasiveness of trauma are becoming more well understood as researchers clarify the link between early victimization, later criminal behaviour (Day et al. 2013; Randall and Haskell 2013; Smith, 2017), and recidivism, especially for female youth offenders (Espinoza and Sorensen 2015). Research shows that psychological trauma may result from a single trau-matic episode (acute trauma), or a prolonged traumatic period (complex trauma), during

biopsychosocial model
An approach that addresses interdependent and bidirectional biological, psychological, and social risk factors related to the development of behavioural problems that are implicated in females' involvement with the justice system.

which individuals perceive their emotional well-being or physical safety to be under significant threat (Crosby 2016). As discussed earlier in this chapter, in Canada, an exceptionally high proportion of female young offenders—particularly Indigenous girls—have extensive histories of traumatic exposure (e.g., child abuse, other criminal victimization, exposure to domestic violence, abandonment). In addition to acute and complex trauma, intergenerational trauma as a result of the transmission of profound effects of colonialization on Indigenous peoples across generations and the ongoing racism and social inequality experienced by many Indigenous people also impacts female young offenders (Monchalin 2016).

Complex trauma theory provides us with a framework to understand how prolonged exposure to trauma causes biopsychological alterations to the developing brain as a result of a constantly activated and over-stimulated autonomic nervous system response (the survival instinct involved in a "fight or flight" response), and that complex trauma experienced early in life can have devastating and permanent impacts on the growing brain (Haskell and Randall 2009). When an individual undergoes this type of survival response to threatening events on a regular basis, especially as a young child, the brain becomes highly sensitized to stressful events throughout the person's life (not only those related to the initiating traumatic events). The resulting inability to cope with significant and commonplace stressors in life can be impairing and can lead to consequences including depression, poor emotional self-regulation, impulsivity, difficulty forming pro-social attachments, self-injurious behaviour, addictive behaviour, and exceedingly risky behaviour (Day et al. 2013). Affected individuals may become easily overwhelmed and have a lower capacity to adapt and positively respond to stress throughout their life. Research shows that individuals with early and prolonged trauma exposure may engage in deviance earlier and more frequently (Day et al. 2013).

Like the biopsychosocial model discussed above, the overall context plays a critical role in mediating the effects of traumatic exposure. A person's response to trauma is reliant on individual risk and protective factors (e.g., sex, temperament/personality, parental attachment), event-specific factors (e.g., age of onset, duration, setting, and type of trauma), and socio-cultural factors (e.g., culture, social environment, peers) (Podgurski and Lyons 2014).

Though individual agency and rational decision-making form crucial parts of why individuals engage in delinquent acts, an appropriate response must consider social context (Haskell and Randall 2009). In this vein, Crosby (2016) considers how potentially negative experiences with police and perceptions of police and courts held by a disproportionate number of racialized youth intersect with a young person's traumatic history in ways that make them more vulnerable to engaging in anti-social conduct. Espinosa and Sorensen (2015) examine how gender interacts with traumatic exposure for young women by increasing their risk for re-traumatization in a correctional environment; the interaction between gender and traumatic exposure may lead to an increase in length of time served, probation conditions, and, in some cases, recidivism. Some researchers observe that female survivors of trauma are prone to being misdiagnosed and thus unable to access appropriate resources, causing them to become further entrenched in the criminal justice system. Instead of their symptoms—such as substance use/addiction, poor attachment, depression, and anxiety—being understood as rooted in a history of trauma or abuse, individuals may be incorrectly diagnosed with a wide variety of other psychiatric disorders, and thus treated improperly (Randall and Haskell 2013; Smith 2017).

With this theoretical framework in mind, Randall and Haskell (2013) outline a **trauma-informed approach** as grounded in an awareness of the pervasiveness of trauma among the population served; a recognition of how trauma can impact an individual's well-being in the short and long term; and the identification of advantageous approaches to responding to people with these histories by promoting skills development and resilience in a culturally safe manner that avoids re-traumatizing individuals (Haskell and Randall 2009). The exceptionally high proportion of young female offenders who have traumatic histories requires us to deeply consider and embed into our responses the impacts trauma has had on girls' anti-social behaviour (Podgurski and Lyons 2014) and to view this through a socio-structural lens.

Sociological and Gender Role Theories

Four sociological approaches that fit with a gender role analysis are (1) social learning and differential association theories, (2) social control theories, (3) strain theories, and (4) life course theory (Chesney-Lind and Shelden 2014; Chesney-Lind and Jones 2010; Hagan, Gillis, and Simpson 1985; Zahn 2009). **Gender role theories** explain the differences in male and female crime participation as the outcome of differential gender socialization that imposes higher moral expectations and greater social controls on girls and women. Such theories have largely focused on heteronormativity but are now beginning to shift to a far more fluid understanding of sexual identity that includes those who identify as LGBTQ2SI.

Social Learning and Differential Association Theories

It is well established that the primary source of social learning is the family (Bandura 1965, 1977, 1978, 1986). In an extensive review of the research on family and youth delinquency and crime, Kruttschnitt and Giordano (2009) found that girls and boys both suffer the negative consequences of family conflict, harsh and coercive parenting, and other problematic emotional family dynamics, including exposure to crime by family members, abuse within the family, divorce, and living in stressed lone-parent households. These researchers found few consistent sex differences in the effects of these factors on the socialization of children except in the area of sexual abuse, where girls consistently suffer far higher rates of such abuse and long-term negative effects of this kind of trauma, especially when combined with family criminality. Kruttschnitt and Giordano's analysis calls into question the commonly held belief that girls have stronger connections with their families and are thus more positively socialized and less inclined to become involved in crime and delinquency. They point instead to learned gender performance for dealing with emotional and interpersonal processes as a more promising area for further research in that whatever their social location or exposure to abuse and other difficult circumstances, girls learn early that being "nice" and being "good" have enormous social value and may, therefore, internalize greater constraints on delinquent behaviour.

trauma-informed approach
An approach to practice that incorporates an understanding of how experiences of acute and complex trauma shape the lives, identities, and perspectives of the people we respond to throughout the human services and the legal system. Trauma-informed practice requires us to implement steps that avoid re-traumatizing individuals and support wellness, recovery, and resilience (Randall and Haskell 2013).

gender role theories
Those explanations of delinquent and criminal behaviour that focus on the role that gender socialization plays in the lives of young people who are involved with the criminal justice system.

Peer influence has for some time been known to be significant for delinquency. On the basis of observations that delinquents appear to gather in groups and gangs and have more interaction with those who engage in crime than with those who do not, Sutherland (1939) and others (Sutherland and Cressey 1978) argued that the techniques, motives, and values that facilitate criminal behaviour are transmitted through social and anti-social learning opportunities that arise from close association with others who engage in delinquency and crime. Although Sutherland and his associates studied only males, differential association (or learning theory) holds some promise with regard to explaining female delinquency, and is supported by research that indicates that females who have frequent contact with other deviant youth appear to engage in deviant behaviour to a greater degree than those who do not (Giordano, Cernkovich, and Pugh 1986).

Giordano, Deines, and Cernkovic's (2006) qualitative research shows gendered pathways to crime in which girls' exposure to sexual abuse along with gender non-specific factors such as poverty and association with delinquent peers contribute to offending onset. As well, Peggy Giordano (2009) shows that some socialization practices seem to be involved in protecting girls from greater involvement with delinquent peers: girls generally spend more time in structured social activities than boys and less time simply "hanging out." As well, while the norms of the friendship group they most identify with help to shape the behaviour of both girls and boys, more girls than boys report affiliating with and knowing a greater range of peers, and therefore girls experience a wider range of possible social norms and models than boys do. Girls who are more vulnerable to negative peer influences are those who gravitate toward delinquent friends, especially mixed-gender groups of criminogenic peers, and who become involved with delinquent romantic partners (Giordano 2009). Depending on social context and demographic factors, however, the role of gender may be less important than other aspects of one's identity and life, and Kruttschnitt (2016) suggests that "to make our theories more gender inclusive, we need to reconcile *both* the gender similarities and differences that are related to anti-social behaviour and are contextualized by social class" (p. 9).

Social Control Theories

Social control theories of crime and delinquency focus on the capacity of all human beings to engage in deviance and crime. For social control theorists, self-control, grounded in a positive and socially conventional self-concept, is central to the containment of delinquency and crime (Reckless 1961; Reiss 1951), as are effective family functioning, the existence of a positive social structure (Nye 1958; Toby 1957), and the presence of socially positive attachment, commitment, involvement, and beliefs (Hirschi 1969). Positive bonds with family, friends, peers, school, and neighbourhood are of central importance to social control theorists, as they are to learning theorists.

In applying social control to research with girls, Jensen and Eve (1976), Cernkovich and Giordano (1987) and Ryder (2014) found that attachment to conventional others—especially family members—and a belief in the legitimacy of rules have predictive power for both male and female delinquency. Cernkovich and Giordano and Ryder also found that lower rates of female delinquency could be partly explained by higher levels of parental supervision and more intimate communication and attachment between parents and daughters.

Hagan, Gillis, and Simpson, who developed **power-control theory**, a variant of social control theory, suggest that patriarchal families are structured such that they support, and thus provide greater access for, males' risk-taking and delinquent behaviour, while at the same time, keeping girls' criminal involvement in check via tighter social restrictions and controls (Hagan 1988, 1990; Hagan, Gillis, and Simpson 1985; Hagan, Simpson, and Gillis 1987). These theorists suggest that in egalitarian families with equal thresholds of risky behaviour for both boys and girls, one might expect more similar involvement in delinquency between the sexes. Further, this theory suggests that as families move away from traditional models toward systems where adult women take up more equal power with males or find themselves in the position of being single heads of households, girls will become more like boys and, as a consequence, will also take more risks, including deviant risks, and may experience more victimization.

Nevertheless, based on self-report and official statistics, female delinquency typically declines or remains stable despite the rise in the number of egalitarian and female-headed households (Chesney-Lind and Shelden 2014). Further, power-control theory also falls short in explaining victimization. Despite the consistent finding that boys are more likely than girls to be victims and offenders, patriarchal households do not necessarily protect girls from victimization (Blackwell, Sellers, and Schlaupitz 2002). A substantial body of research shows a consistent and strong relationship between females' sexual and emotional victimization in the context of misogynist and stereotypical gender relations based on hierarchies of power dominated by males (Acoca and Dedel 1998; Artz 1998; Chesney-Lind and Okamoto 2001; Means, 2002). Central to this research is the finding that both males and females use aggression to hold in place males' expectations of female sexual behaviour in that females actively participate in the privileging of males' sexual expectations of their own sex (Artz, Nicholson, and Magnuson 2008). Where dominance and aggression are concerned, both males and females carry what Holland, Ramazanoglu, Sharpe, and Thompson (1998) call "the male in the head" and enact the involuntary and asymmetric institutionalization and regulatory power of males and patriarchy in heterosexual relations (p. 171). As Ryder (2014), following Artz (1998) and Griffiths, Yule, and Gartner (2011) notes, "as a powerless group, girls mimic the oppressor (males) and attack similarly situated females" (p. 34).

Strain Theory

Strain theory builds on the notion that delinquency can be explained as a response to being denied access to socially and conventionally approved opportunities for power and material success (Cloward and Ohlin 1960; Cohen 1955; Miller 1958) (see Chapter 8). While strain theory, in its original form, was criticized for its inability to effectively explain female crime, Agnew's general strain theory (GST) explains the overall differences in female and male rates of crime in terms of the differences in types of strain to which females and males are subjected (Broidy and Agnew 1997). Higher criminal involvement among males is linked to their more often being subject to material- and status-related strains; lower criminal involvement among females is linked to their more often being subjected to oppression via family violence, sexual abuse, and high levels of social controls and restrictions, including restrictions related to criminal opportunity.

power-control theory
Refers to John Hagan and colleagues' integrated (conflict and social control theories) and feminist-informed explanation of the role of gender socialization in crime distributions.

Additionally, Broidy and Agnew (1997) suggest that female and male differences in crime rates can be further explained by socialized gender differences in the processing of the negative emotions associated with strain. Males learn to "act out" with other-directed overt anger, aggression, and violence. Females, in contrast, learn to "act in" with depression, guilt, and shame and inner or relationally directed, more covert aggression. Females also learn to disperse their negative emotions by gaining support from others in their more developed social networks and have been socialized to espouse values and use coping styles that discourage criminal behaviour. Males, on the other hand, are typically rewarded for their displays of aggression and encouraged to use coping styles that support the commission of crime.

Life Course Theory

Developmental and life course theory adds to the study of girls' criminal behaviour by examining how an individual's offending pattern varies over time at different age and role transitions (e.g., gaining/losing employment, marriage, becoming a parent) (Odgers et al. 2008). This theory focuses on a number of facets of criminal behaviour, such as the onset, persistence, and desistance of criminal behavior; the nature and severity of involvement in crime; crime specialization; the protective and risk factors that emerge at different ages; and the impacts these factors may have on offending variations across the lifespan (Farrington, 2005). Known as an "integrative theory," developmental and life course theory bridges sociological theories like strain, control, and differential association.

Similar to the approaches we have discussed, early developmental and life course research has tended to examine offending patterns of boys rather than girls, usually through the use of longitudinal studies as a primary research tool. Unfortunately, these studies suffer from small sample sizes for girls, thus limiting the use of key statistical tests to examine serious offending patterns (Loeber, Jennings, Ahonen, Piquero, and Farrington 2017). In general, longitudinal research that includes females shows that these offenders do not offend as frequently or for as long in duration as males, meaning that they often begin later and/or desist before adulthood (Loeber et al. 2017; Piquero and Piquero 2015).

In their recent work, Schwartz and Steffensmeier (2017) explain the observed within and between sex differences in criminal behaviour over the life course as hinging on individual agency mediated by a combination of gendered risk preferences that are culturally and socially influenced; gender-stratification of crime opportunities and markets; and tangible reproductive and biological differences. Concerning serious and chronic offending, they argue that social positions like age, race, social class, and gender influence individual decision-making by making specific opportunities more or less attractive and more or less available to an individual. They refer to a "glass ceiling" of the underworld where, except in rare circumstances, girls and women are not afforded the opportunity to become involved with criminal associates (e.g., in relation to gang activity and white-collar crime) and thus have fewer opportunities to commit highly profitable property and serious violent crimes. These barriers are not in place where less serious offences are concerned, which may help to explain why we see large variations between the sexes in the commission of serious violent offences, but smaller differences in relation to offences like theft and minor assault.

The limitations on sample size in longitudinal work have made the study of how race, ethnicity, and gender jointly condition developmental processes across the life course even rarer. Broidy et al.'s (2015) Australian longitudinal study is an exception. These researchers had sufficient sample sizes and found that non-Indigenous girls tended to have the least contact with the criminal justice system, while Indigenous girls "offend in ways more similar to non-Indigenous males than females" (p. 118). Their research emphasizes how race/ethnicity intersect with gender and, in particular, illuminates the cultural and structural differences and inequality that is abundant in the Indigenous communities that shape offending patterns across the life course that would have been invisible if not for the intersectional analysis.

Anti-colonial Theory

Throughout this chapter we have drawn attention to the intersections of gender with examples of Indigenous girls, racialized youth, and youth who identity as LGBTQ2SI. We have made the case that it is important to understand how girls from these particular groups encounter oppression and find themselves being overrepresented in the criminal justice system in Canada. Delinquent girls are not a homogeneous group. Neither official crime statistics nor the available theoretical approaches to understanding female crime adequately recognize that Canada's history with Indigenous, racialized, and the queer communities has its roots in racist and gender stereotypical notions of dominance and in colonialism. Anti-colonial theory gives us tools to recognize that colonialism is an ever-present part of our current struggles. As Hogarth and Fletcher (2018) state, "the reality is that colonialism is a modern day, presently occurring phenomenon firmly embedded in our history and even more so present in our everyday. There is nothing post about colonialism" (p. 25).

The report of the Truth and Reconciliation Commission of Canada (2015) was a watershed moment for this country. It called on all of us to see Indigenous peoples' interactions with the systems created by the Canadian government as being a result of the violence of colonialism—including genocide, residential schooling, the Sixties Scoop, and now the "millennium scoop" (Blackstock 2011). Furthermore, researchers and activists, such as Robyn Maynard (2015), El Jones (2016), and George Dei (2006), have worked tirelessly to shed light on the impact of colonialism on racialized youth, showing how oppressive practices in schooling, child welfare, and health care systems have resulted in the criminalization of racialized youth. Very little scholarship focusing on criminality and Indigenous and racialized girls engages with an anti-colonial theory that tries to understand the history and intergenerational impacts of colonization. An exception is Dhillon (2015), an ally, activist, and researcher who argues that any dialogue concerning Indigenous girls must include a conversation about colonial gender violence and what she terms the "war on Indigenous women and girls across Turtle Island" (an Indigenous word for North America) (p. 24). Dhillon's work urges us to decolonize and politicize youth work and programming and to move away from homogenizing the experiences of Indigenous and racialized youth, given that "settler colonialism impacts bodies differently depending on their social markings" (Dhillon 2015, p. 25). This discussion is just the beginning of what we hope inspires readers to seek further knowledge about how colonialism impacts Indigenous and racialized girls, historically and currently; to find ways to decolonize our role as settlers in the ongoing violence of Indigenous communities; and to politicize our work by seeking to understand the realities of vulnerable girls who encounter the criminal justice system.

Promising Directions

Although we have made considerable advancements from the rehabilitative, treatment-focused approaches of the early twentieth century as it concerns boys involved in the justice system, progress for girls has lagged somewhat (Sprott and Doob 2010). We propose that promising directions regarding girls' delinquency must focus both on personal and on social conditions that lead to anti-social behaviour and crime to arrive at interventions that address the strains faced by girls, their complex and varied pathways to social and delinquent behaviours, and the overarching and systemic structural issues that persist. Such a perspective demands attention not only to the individual youth and what can be done to minimize and remove their risks and marginalities (e.g., addictions, gang involvement, and family dysfunction), but also to wider social/structural inequalities and dysfunction (e.g., racism, poverty, and lack of education) (Barron 2011).

Attending to Intersections

There are several directions youth justice professionals must pursue in taking an intersectional approach:

- Discontinue the use of stereotypes and overly simplistic theories.
- Eradicate the use of stereotypical punitive policies and inhumane practices.
- Stop ignoring girls' fundamental requirements for survival, safety, and well-being.

Attending to intersections means not placing Indigenous girls in centres thousands of kilometres from their home and culture. It means radically changing correctional practices to reflect Indigenous respect for spirit and land (Monture-Angus 2000). It means not charging one in three Canadian girls for administrative offences. It means rescinding the ineligibility of youth for welfare or time limits on assistance. It means thinking about preventative measures that can be intersected with child welfare practices to understand the causal connection between children in governmental care and their entry into prisons.

Girls, like boys, are not responsible for the family, race, class, or neighbourhood into which they are born; nor are their families responsible for the poverty, racism, sexism, and queerphobia that impacts their access to resources. Whether they commit major or minor crimes, or none at all, girls are entitled to the requirements for well-being: economic survival, clean air and water, good education, adequate health services and housing, and protection from violence inside and outside their homes. These requirements are necessary so that girls do not trade the dangers and hurt of insecure or violent families for dangerous streets and networks (Joe-Laidler and Hunt 1997; Jones 2010). Moreover, research indicates that quality education, apprenticeship, income assistance, and housing programs that meet the essential requirements of convicted girls are more effective in reducing recidivism and increasing girls' well-being than the general, short-term counselling for primarily emotional, cognitive, or family problems (e.g., Baines and Alder 1996; Chesney-Lind and Pasko 2004).

A straightforward intervention that avoids reducing persons into a select few behaviours that they may exhibit avoids using shorthand phrases such as "violent girl," as the words reinforce inaccurate, hurtful, static stereotypes. The alternative phrase, "a girl who acted violently when . . . " suggests there is an interaction between context and behaviour and that change and growth are possible. Every girl is a complex person, struggling against restrictive stereotypes, including pervasive messages that boys are more important than girls. Every girl lives her life at the nexus of several intersecting factors, including biology, psychology, social dynamics, and the impact of living in a society that contributes to the oppression of particular othered identities. Abolishing simplistic stereotypes and "one-size-fits-all" interventions frees up energy to develop individualized, flexible approaches.

Reconsidering the Application of Gender-Sensitive Responses

Gender-sensitive responses work under the assumption that the pathways to and from crime and the needs of girls—including how incarcerated girls deal with their time—are unique (Chesney-Lind and Pasko 2004; Davidson 2013; Taylor and Blanchette 2009). Feminist criminology demands not only that the varying pathways of female offenders be recognized, but also that risk assessment, treatment, supervision, and other responses taken by the criminal justice system likewise take gender into account (Chesney-Lind and Pasko 2013).

Treatment

Gender-sensitive responses to female offenders should match the needs and learning styles of individual offenders and must be versatile (Blanchette and Brown 2006). One evidence-based example of effective gender-sensitive treatment—particularly useful with girls convicted of an offence who live with serious mental illness, trauma from abuse, and heavy substance use—is dialectical behavioural therapy (DBT), a collaborative, therapeutically based intervention that helps clients to achieve cognitive and emotional self-knowledge and self-regulation and strengthens their ability to deal with stress and trauma (Linehan, 1993a; Linehan, 1993b; Linehan, Heard, and Armstrong 1993; McDonagh, Taylor, and Blanchette 2009; Trupin et al. 1999; Verheul et al. 2003). DBT has been extensively researched and established as a positive intervention, especially because it is based on a strong alliance between client and therapist and on the principle that clients are capable of understanding their processes and participating in the creation of their own well-being.

However, though it is a promising practice where gender-specific youth justice programming is employed, DBT must break away from the implicit and explicit normative, patriarchal assumptions made about stereotypical feminine bodies (Hannah-Moffat 2010) and promote strategies that are responsive to a multitude of femininities (Pasko 2017).

gender-sensitive responses Responses by the criminal justice system that recognize that the pathways to criminal involvement and the needs of female offenders are different from those of male offenders. Such approaches include risk assessments, treatments, and supervision.

To be effective, "[youth] justice professionals [need] to recognize their own stereotypes and assumptions about girls and participate in training that encourages them to critically examine how gender and sexual identity (along with race/ethnicity, age, class, and country of origin) shape life experiences" (Pasko 2017, p. 18).

Canada is recognized as a pioneer in gender-responsive policy and interventions for offending adult women. However, youth justice gender-specific programming is rare—at least partly as a result of the very low number of incarcerated girls. Where it does exist, this type of programming has been criticized as failing to take into account the short trajectory of girls' criminality (Sharpe 2016). Instead, programs tend to focus on offenders' individual and familial criminogenic needs, an approach that legitimates punishing high-needs young women despite their low risk of reoffending (Sharpe 2016).

Risk Assessment

In addition to treatment, a key concern of gender specificity is risk assessment (see Chapter 9). In assessing the complex situations of offenders and making predictions about future criminal and anti-social behaviour, risk assessments can be important tools (see Chapter 4). There is considerable research on the benefits of risk/need assessment tools that have now been widely implemented as part of correctional practices across offender populations in Canada, including young female offenders (Worrall and Gelsthrope 2009). Despite the support and extensive use of the tools, some experts regard them with concern, raising questions ranging from their (non)applicability to female and non-white populations (Hannah-Moffat and Maurutto 2003; Moretti et al. 2011) to their tendency to focus too heavily on individual risk factors rather than on systemic structural inequalities (Barron 2011). Because, as Barron (2011) argues, risk analysis focuses on the present and the future—specifically, what can be done now to affect the future—the risk system necessarily zeroes in on individuals and on whether they are willing to change their identified personal risk factors. There is little to no attention paid to the systemic inequalities that may have laid the groundwork for the emergence of these personal risk factors.

In her research in the province of Saskatchewan, Barron (2011) found that the theory underlying risk assessments was heavily contradicted in correctional practice. For example, incarcerated girls in one institution were scored negatively for a lack of pro-social extracurricular activities (they frequently spent leisure time committing crimes or socializing with delinquent peer groups/gangs). In this instance, the risk assessment tool and the interpretation of it by correctional staff failed to acknowledge the resources required for participation in pro-social activities. So, while the tool was employed in an attempt to measure pro-social connections, it instead illuminated an absence of resources, a clear offshoot of poverty. Worse, within the custody environment, extracurricular activities such as exercise were held as privileges instead of as factors that contribute to individual health. As such, correctional staff held back these privileges as a consequence for non-compliance. Risk assessments used in this way may feed into a correctional culture of control rather than promote a view of the correctional institution as a place where youth's basic needs are met so that they can learn how to care for themselves and leave custody better equipped with the knowledge and skills that will assist them to remain free of crime. As long as risk assessment tools confuse worrisome behavioural symptoms—for example,

the use and misuse of substances—with causes of crime rather than recognize that the same underlying factors are involved in both substance misuse *and* criminal behaviour, these tools may well be contributing to poor risk assessment and treatment choices. Thus, treating an addiction that began as a result of a need to cope with negative circumstances will not address criminal behaviour unless the underlying causes of the addiction and the criminal behaviours are addressed. If we are to see the continued employment of risk/need assessment tools, the copious and overlapping needs faced by "at-risk" girls as discussed throughout this chapter demand that these risk assessments be gender sensitive and focused on actual risk, not just on symptoms that demonstrate the presence of risk (Moretti et al. 2011).

Mobilizing Political Change around Equity, Human Rights, and Social Justice

Throughout this chapter, the importance of addressing the behaviours and marginalities of female young offenders as well as social/structural inequalities resulting from racism and colonialism has been highlighted via an intersectional approach. The approach to girls and crime offers us a number of important ways to change policy (Daly 2008), including the following:

- Institute policies and practices to reverse systemic and personal discrimination.
- Demand gender and racial parity in resources.
- Keep neo-liberal and neo-conservative crime-control policies in check.
- Recognize and confront the colonial underpinnings of our systems that disproportionately oppress Indigenous, racialized, and LGBTQ2SI communities.

Girls who are charged or convicted of crimes have hopes similar to those not charged. They want to stop violence and the destruction of their bodies, health, spirit, and community; they want to get a good education and job; they want to love and care for people and to be loved and cared for; and they want fun and adventure (Nicholson and Artz 2003; Reitsma-Street and Offord 1991). If we take seriously what girls (and boys) say, we then need to ask how particular interests are served by ignoring what girls, their families, and communities tell us. What was the benefit of forcing Indigenous girls to attend residential schools against the wishes of children and parents (see Chapter 11)? Why are services to girls so inadequate and contrary to the best evidence? What privilege makes possible the systematic abuse of girls such as those documented in the inquiry of the Ontario Grandview Training School for Girls (Kershaw and Lasovich 1991)? Unmasking the injustice and the unequal access to decision-making helps to account for what is beneficial or not, and to whom, and clarifies the politically contested nature of policies and practices.

Mobilizing political change around equity and human rights requires dismantling inequitable policies—for example, ceasing to scrutinize and judge the sexual histories of girls but not boys. It means, above all, an insistence that funding and legislative resources for girls in the justice system are proportionate to their numbers and adequate for their well-being (Bloom, Owen, Deschenes, and Rosenbaum 2002; Green and Healy 2003).

Politicizing equity would mean that at least one-fifth of Canadian youth justice funds and resources are explicitly tied to girls and their well-being, with proportionately more allocated to Indigenous girls and aimed at community interventions and other gender-specific supports.

Summary

Girls are involved in all manner of anti-social and criminal behaviours. But their criminal behaviour is infrequent despite fears that youth crime and violence by girls are increasing. Girls commit few serious crimes of violence—a trend that has been remarkably steady for decades. We argue that we need to study crime and our responses to girls and crime as a political project that reveals how social order and gender inequity are established and how they can be changed and also how gender intersects with race and class to exacerbate vulnerability.

Girls' minimal involvement in crime has led to theories about female crime and delinquency that, until the 1970s, largely overlooked girls' experiences or explained girls' criminal behaviour as an aberration of "normal" femininity. More recent gender-neutral explanations decontextualize the complex reality of girls living in a gendered, racist, and unequal world.

Research by Daly (1995), Artz (1998), Katz (2000), Chesney-Lind and Pasko (2004), Reitsma-Street (2004), Zahn (2009), Schissel (2010), and Chesney-Lind and Jones (2010) reminds us that crime is not just a function of interactions within an established order. Illegal and other behaviours are part of active struggles within a changing social order in which power and privilege are unequally distributed and frequently contested. A fully delineated theory of girls' crime invites us to resist applying the male standard to female behaviour and to examine our expectations of girls and our fears and values in relation to them. This means that we must question approaches to constructing knowledge about girls while paying close attention to the impact of different laws and regulations on girls and society. Most of all, we must be willing to attend to what girls themselves say if we are to learn more about girls' crime and to respond positively.

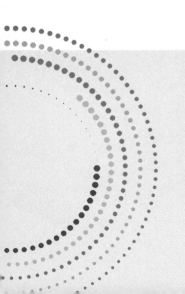

Key Terms

administrative offences

biopsychosocial model

gender gap

gender role theories

gender-sensitive responses

intersectionality

net narrowing

power-control theory

trauma informed approach

Review Questions

1. Do official crime statistics support the claim that female crime is increasing? Can you ever know the "truth" about crime rates?

2. What are administrative offences and why have they increased?

3. What are the prevailing themes about girls in the theories of female crime and delinquency? What do the theories not explain?

4. What is the intersectional approach to intervention and inquiry? What aspects of the intervention apply to boys? What are its strengths and limitations?

Critical Thinking Questions

1. How would you describe and explain the context in which girls commit minor crimes? Serious crimes? How is the context for girls different than for boys?

2. If you are cisgender (your gender identity is consistent with your biological sex) imagine yourself with a gender identity that is LGBTQ2SI. The police have caught you breaking into a neighbour's house late at night and are planning to take you into custody and put you in holding cells until morning when you will see a judge. What are you afraid to tell them about yourself in case this leads to repercussions?

3. What research questions about girls, policies, and crime need to be studied?

4. Should girls who fail to comply with previous non-custodial dispositions under the YCJA be sentenced to custody?

5. You are at a dinner party with family and friends, and someone at the table makes a generalizing statement about black girls being criminals, and they also say they don't understand why Indigenous girls find themselves in jail when they get so many benefits from the government. How do you see yourself confronting these stereotypes?

Endnote

1. We could also ask why females' lower crime rates are not the benchmark against which males' rates are measured and why the overall objective in crime prevention is not to aim to reduce male rates to those much lower rates consistently recorded for females. In other words, why distract ourselves with moral panics about girls instead of asking what continues to work for girls that we can also use with boys?

References

Abramovich, I.A. (2012). No safe place to go: LGBTQ youth homelessness in Canada—reviewing the literature. *Canadian Journal of Family and Youth, 4*(1), 29–51.

Acoca, L., and Dedel, K. (1998). *No place to hide: Understanding and meeting the needs of girls in the California juvenile justice system.* San Francisco: National Council on Crime and Delinquency.

Adler, F. (1975). *Sisters in crime.* New York: McGraw-Hill.

Allen, M.K., and Superle, T. (2016). *Youth crime in Canada, 2014.* Ottawa: Canadian Centre for Justice Statistics.

Andrew, R.H., and Cohn, A.H. (1974). Ungovernability: The unjustifiable jurisdiction. *Yale Law Journal, 83,* 1383–409.

Artz, S. (1998). *Sex, power and the violent school girl.* Toronto: Trifolium.

Artz, S., and Amorim, T. (2013, January 31). *Girls in custody, a final report prepared for the Law Foundation of BC Legal Research Fund*. Vancouver: Law Foundation of British Columbia.

Artz, S., Jackson, M., Rossiter, K., Nijdam-Jones, A., Géczy, I., and Porteous, S. (2014). A comprehensive review of the literature on the impact of exposure to intimate partner violence on children and youth. *International Journal of Child, Youth and Family Studies, 5*(4), 493–87.

Artz, S., Nicholson, D., and Magnuson, D. (2008). Examining sex differences in the use of direct and indirect aggression. *Gender Issues, 25*(4), 267–88.

Baines, M., and Alder, C. (1996). Are girls more difficult to work with? Youth workers' perspectives in juvenile justice and related areas. *Crime and Delinquency, 42*(3), 467–85.

Bala, N. (2003). Diversion, conferencing, and extrajudicial measures for adolescent offenders. *Alberta Law Review, 40*, 991–1027.

Bala, N., and Anand, S. (2009). *Youth criminal justice law*. Toronto: Irwin Law Inc.

Bala, N., Carrington, P.J., and Roberts, J.V. (2009). Evaluating the Youth Criminal Justice Act after five years: A qualified success. *Canadian Journal of Criminology and Criminal Justice, 51*(2), 131–67.

Bandura, A. (1965). Influence of models' reinforcement contingencies on the acquisition of imitative responses. *Journal of Personality and Social Psychology, 1*(6), 589.

Bandura, A. (1977). Self-efficacy: Toward a unifying theory of behavioural change. *Psychological Review, 84*(2), 191.

Bandura, A. (1978). Reflections on self-efficacy. *Advances in Behaviour Research and Therapy, 1*(4), 237–69.

Bandura, A. (1986). *Social foundations of thought and action*. Upper Saddle River, NJ: Prentice Hall.

Barron, C. (2011). *Governing girls: Rehabilitation in the age of risk*. Winnipeg: Fernwood.

Bell, S. (2012). *Young offenders and youth justice: A century after the fact*. Toronto: Nelson.

Berger, M.T., and Guidroz, K. (2009). Introduction. In M.T. Berger and K. Guidroz (Eds), *The intersectional approach: Transforming the academy through race, class and gender* (pp. 1–22). Chapel Hill: North Carolina Press.

Binder, A., Geis, G., and Bruce, D. (1988). *Juvenile delinquency: Historical, cultural, legal perspectives*. New York: Macmillan.

Blackstock, C. (2011). The Canadian Human Rights Tribunal on First Nations Child Welfare: Why if Canada wins, equality and justice lose. *Children and Youth Services Review, 33*(1), 187–9.

Blackwell, B., Sellers, C., and Schlaupitz, S. (2002). A power-control theory of vulnerability to crime and adolescent role exits—revisited. *Canadian Review of Sociology and Anthropology, 39*(2), 199–218.

Blanchette, K., and Brown, S.L. (2006). *The assessment and treatment of women offenders: An integrative perspective*. New York: Wiley.

Bloom, B., Owen, B., Deschenes, E.P., and Rosenbaum, J. (2002). Improving juvenile justice for females: A statewide assessment in California. *Crime and Delinquency, 48*(4), 526–52.

British Columbia. (2014). Information bulletin. Retrieved from http://www2.news.gov.bc.ca/news_releases_2013-2017/2014CFD0018-000771.htm

British Columbia Representative for Children and Youth (RCY). (2009). *Kids, crime and care: Health and well-being of children in care: Youth justice experiences and outcomes*. Retrieved from https://www.rcybc.ca/sites/default/files/documents/pdf/reports_publications/kids_crime_and_care.pdf

Broidy, L., and Agnew, R. (1997). Gender and crime: A general strain theory perspective. *Journal of Research in Crime and Delinquency, 34*(3), 275–306.

Broidy, L.M., Stewart, A., Thompson, C.M, Chrzanowski, A., Allard, T., and Dennison, S.M. (2015). Life course offending pathways across gender and race/ethnicity. *Journal of Developmental Life Course Criminology, 1*, 118–49.

Calverley, D. (2007). Youth custody and community services in Canada, 2004/2005. *Juristat, 27*(2). Statistics Canada Catalogue No. 85-002.

Campbell, A. (1991). *The girls in the gang* (2nd ed.). New York: Basil Blackwell.

Canada, Forty-second Parliament, House of Commons. (2018, March 28). Bill C-75 - First reading. Retrieved from http://www.parl.ca/DocumentViewer/en/42-1/bill/C-75/first-reading

Cernkovich, S., and Giordano, P. (1987). Family relationships and delinquency. *Criminology, 25*, 295–321.

Cesaroni, C., and Bala, N. (2008). Deterrence as principle of youth sentencing: No effect on youth, but significant effect on judges. *Queen's Law Journal, 34*, 447.

Chesney-Lind, M., and Jones, N. (2010). *Fighting for girls: New perspectives on gender and violence*. New York: SUNY Press.

Chesney-Lind, M., and Okamoto, S. (2001). Gender matters: Patterns in girl's delinquency and gender responsive programming. *Journal of Forensic Psychology Practice, 1*(3), 1–28.

Chesney-Lind, M., and Pasko, L. (Eds). (2004). *Girls, women and crime: Selected readings*. Thousand Oaks, CA: Sage.

Chesney-Lind, M., and Pasko, L. (2013). *The female offender: Girls, women and crime*. Thousand Oaks, CA: Sage.

Chesney-Lind, M., and Shelden, R. (2014). *Girls, delinquency and juvenile justice* (4th ed.). Belmont, CA: West/Wadsworth.

Cloward, R., and Ohlin, L. (1960). *Delinquency and opportunity*. New York: Free Press.

Cohen, A. (1955). *Delinquent boys: The culture of the gang*. New York: Free Press.

Collins, P.H. (1990). *Black feminist thought: Knowledge, consciousness, and the politics of empowerment.* New York: Routledge.

Cowie, J., Cowie, V., and Slater, E. (1968). *Delinquency in girls.* London: Heinemann.

Crenshaw, C. (1991). Mapping the margins: Intersectionality, identity politics, and violence against women of color. *Stanford Law Review, 43,* 1241–99.

Crosby, S. (2016). Trauma-informed approaches to juvenile justice: A critical race perspective. *Juvenile and Family Court, 67*(1), 5–18.

Cunninghan, S.C. (2014). Sentencing and recidivism: The probable lack of success of the Safe Streets and Communities Act (Bill C-10). *Western Undergraduate Psychology Journal, 2*(1), Article 6.

Daly, K. (1997). Different ways of conceptualizing sex/gender in feminist theory and their implications for criminology. *Theoretical Criminology, 1*(1), 25–51.

Daly, K. (2008). Seeking justice in the 21st century. In H. Ventura Miller (Ed), *Restorative justice: From theory to practice.* Bingley, UK: Emerald Group.

Daly, K. (2010). Feminist perspectives in criminology: A review with Gen Y in mind. In E. McLaughlin and T. Newburn (Eds), *The Sage handbook of criminological theory* (pp. 225–46). Thousand Oaks, CA: Sage.

Dauvergne, M. (2013). Youth court statistics, 2010/2011. *Juristat, 33*(1). Statistics Canada Catalogue No. 85-002.

Davidson, J.T. (2013). Female offenders, community supervision, and evidence-based practices. In M. Chesney-Lind and L. Pasko (Eds), *The female offender: Girls, women and crime* (pp. 153–87). Thousand Oaks, CA: Sage.

Day, D.M., Hart, T.A., Wanklyn, S.G., McCay, E., Macpherson, A., and Burnier, N. (2013). Potential mediators between child abuse and both violence and victimization in juvenile offenders. *Psychological Services, 10*(1), 1–11.

Dean, A.R. (2005). Locking them up to keep them "safe": Criminalized girls in British Columbia: A systemic advocacy project conducted for Justice for Girls. Vancouver: Justice for Girls. Retrieved from http://www.justiceforgirls.org/publications/pdfs/jfg_complete_report.pdf

Dei, G. (2006). Introduction: Mapping the terrain—Towards a new politics of resistance. In G. Dei and A. Kempf (Eds), *Anti-colonialism and education: The politics of resistance.* Rotterdam: Sense Publication.

Department of Justice Canada. (2018, March 29). *Charter statement—Bill C-75: An Act to amend the Criminal Code, Youth Criminal Justice Act and other Acts and to make consequential amendments to other Acts.* Retrieved from Department of Justice Canada: http://www.justice.gc.ca/eng/csj-sjc/pl/charter-charte/c75.html

Dionne, G., Tremblay, R., Boivin, M., Laplante, D., and Pérusse, D. (2003). Physical aggression and expressive vocabulary in 19-month-old twins. *Developmental Psychology, 39*(2), 261–73.

Dhillon, J. (2015). Indigenous girls and the violence of settler colonial policing. *Decolonization: Indigeneity, Education and Society, 4*(2), 1–31.

Dodge, K.A., and Pettit, G.S. (2003). A biopsychosocial model of the development of chronic conduct problems in adolescence. *Developmental Psychology, 29*(2), 349–71.

Doob, A., and Sprott, J. (2004). Youth justice in Canada. In M. Tonry and A. Doob (Eds), *Crime and justice: A review of the research*, vol. 31 (pp. 185–242). Chicago: University of Chicago Press.

Espinoza, E.M. and Sorensen, J.R. (2015). The influence of gender and traumatic experiences in juvenile justice settings. *Criminal Justice & Behavior, 43*(2), 187–203.

Farrington, D. (2005). Introduction to integrated developmental and life-course theories of offending. In D.P. Farrington (Ed.), *Integrated developmental and life-course theories of offending* (pp. 1–14). New York: Routledge.

Fishbein, D., Miller, S., Winn, D.M., and Dakof, G. (2009). Biopsychological factors, gender and delinquency. In M. Zahn (Ed.), *The delinquent girl* (pp. 84–106). Philadelphia: Temple University Press.

Fitzgerald, R.T. and Carrington, P.J. (2011). Disproportionate minority contact in Canada: Police and visible minority youth. *Canadian Journal of Criminology and Criminal Justice, 53*(4), 449–86.

Giordano, P. (2009). Peer influences on girls' delinquency. In M. Zahn (Ed.), *The delinquent girl* (pp. 127–45). Philadelphia: Temple University Press.

Giordano, P., Cernkovich, S., and Pugh, M. (1986). Friendships and delinquency. *American Journal of Sociology, 91,* 1170–202.

Giordano, P.C., Deines, J.A., and Cernkovic, S.A. (2006). In and out of crime: A life course perspective on girls' delinquency. In K. Heimer and C. Kruttschnitt (Eds). *Gender and crime: Patterns in victimization and offending* (pp. 17–40). New York: NYU Press.

Green, R., and Healy, K. (2003). *Tough on kids: Rethinking approaches to youth justice.* Saskatoon: Purich.

Gretton, H.M., and Clift, R.J. (2011). The mental health needs of incarcerated youth in British Columbia, Canada. *International Journal of Law and Psychiatry, 34,* 109–15.

Griffiths, E., Yule, C., and Gartner, R. (2011). Fighting over trivial things: Explaining the issue of contention in violent altercations. *Criminology, 49*(1), 61–94.

Hagan, J. (1988). *Structural criminology.* Saint John, NB: Polity Press.

Hagan, J. (1990). The structure of gender and deviance: A power-control theory of vulnerability to crime and the search for deviant role exits. *Canadian Review of Sociology and Anthropology, 27*(2), 137–56.

Hagan, J., Gillis, A., and Simpson, J. (1985). The class structure of delinquency: Toward a power-control theory of common delinquent behaviour. *American Journal of Sociology, 90,* 1151–78.

Hagan, J., Simpson, J., and Gillis, A. (1987). Class in the household: A power-control theory of gender and delinquency. *American Journal of Sociology, 92,* 788–816.

Handren, L. (2014). Political expediency and the Youth Criminal Justice Act. *The Public Policy & Governance Review.* Retrieved from https://ppgreview.ca/2014/10/06/political-expediency-and-the-youth-criminal-justice-act/

Hannah-Moffat, K. (2010). Sacrosanct or flawed: Risk, accountability and gender-responsive penal politics. *Current Issues in Criminal Jusice, 22*(2), 193–215.

Hannah-Moffat, K., and Maurutto, P. (2003). *Youth risk/need assessment: An overview of issues and practices.* Ottawa: Department of Justice Canada. Retrieved from http://www.justice.gc.ca/eng/rp-pr/cj-jp/yj-jj/rr03_yj4-rr03_jj4/rr03_yj4.pdf

Haskell, L., and Randall, M. (2009). Disrupted attachments: A social context complex trauma framework and the lives of Aboriginal peoples in Canada. *Journal of Aboriginal Health, 5*(3), 48–99.

Hayle, S., Wortlety, S., and Tanner, J. (2016). Race, street life, and policing: Implications for racial profiling. *Canadian Journal of Criminology & Criminal Justice,* 322–53.

Heidensohn, F., and Silvestri, M. (2012). Gender and crime. In R. Morgan and R. Reiner (Eds), *The Oxford Handbook of Criminology* (5th ed., pp. 336–69). Oxford: Oxford University Press.

Hirschi, T. (1969). *Causes of delinquency.* Berkeley: University of California Press.

Hogarth, K., and Fletcher, W. (2018). *A space for race: Decoding racism, multiculturalism, and post-colonialism in Canada and beyond.* New York: Oxford University Press.

Holland, J., Ramazanoglu, C., Sharpe, S., and Thomson, R. (1998). *The male in the head: Young people, heterosexuality and power.* London: Tufnell Press.

Irwin, K., and Chesney-Lind, M. (2008). Girls' violence: Beyond dangerous masculinity. *Sociology Compass, 2*(3), 837–55.

Jensen, G., and Eve, R. (1976). Sex differences in delinquency. *Criminology, 13,* 427–48.

Joe-Laidler, K., and Hunt, G. (1997). Violence and social organization in female gangs. *Social Justice, 24,* 148–69.

Jones, B. (2018, April 1). Bill C-75 and the YCJA—Post 2: Making bail and sentencing conditions reasonable. *Youth Criminal Justice: A blog about recent developments in youth justice law in Canada.* Retrieved from https://youthcriminaljustice.ca/2018/04/01/bill-c-75-and-the-ycja-post-2-making-bail-and-sentencing-conditions-reasonable/

Jones, E. (May 21, 2016). New residential schools and slavery's afterlife. *Halifax Examiner.* Retrieved from www.halifaxexaminer.ca/featured/new-residential-schools-and-slaverys-afterlif/#->.

Jones, N. (2010). "It's about being a survivor . . .": African American girls, gender, and the context of inner-city violence. In M. Chesney-Lind and N. Jones (Eds), *Fighting for girls: New perspectives on gender and violence* (pp. 203–18). New York: SUNY.

Katz, R. (2000). Explaining girl's and women's crime and desistance in the context of their victimization experiences. *Violence against Women, 6*(6), 633–60. Reprinted with permission in M. Chesney-Lind and L. Pasko (Eds) (2004), *Girls, women and crime* (pp. 24–41). Thousand Oaks, CA: Sage.

Kershaw, A., and Lasovich, M. (1991). *Rock-a-bye baby: A death behind bars.* Toronto: McClelland & Stewart.

Konopka, G. (1966). *The adolescent girl in conflict.* Englewood Cliffs, NJ: Prentice-Hall.

Konopka, G. (1983). *Young girls: A portrait of adolescence.* New York: Hayworth Press.

Kruttshnitt, C. (2016). The politics, and place, of gender in research on crime. *Criminology, 54*(1), 8–29.

Kruttschnitt, C., and Giordano, P. (2009). Family influences on girls' delinquency. In M. Zahn (Ed), *The delinquent girl* (pp. 146–63). Philadelphia: Temple University Press.

Latimer, J. (2011). *Criminalizing adolescence? Understanding probation and probation violation in the Canadian youth criminal justice system* (Doctoral dissertation). Retrieved from ProQuest Dissertations and Theses: http://search.proquest.com.ezproxy.library.uvic.ca/docview/882873964?accountid=14846.(882873964)

Linehan, M.M. (1993a). *Cognitive behavioural treatment of borderline personality disorder.* New York and London: Guilford Press.

Linehan, M.M. (1993b). *Skills training manual for treating borderline personality disorder.* New York and London: Guilford Press.

Linehan, M.M., Heard, H.L., and Armstrong, H.E. (1993). Naturalistic follow-up of a behavioral treatment for chronically parasuicidal borderline patients. *Archives of General Psychiatry, 50,* 971–4.

Loeber, R., Jennings, W.G., Ahonen, L., Piquero, A.R., and Farrington, D.P. (2017). *Female delinquency from childhood to young adulthood: Recent results from the Pittsburgh Girls Study.* New York: Springer.

McDonagh, D., Taylor, K., and Blanchette, K. (2009). Correctional adaptation of dialectical behaviour therapy (DBT) for federally sentenced women. Correctional Services of Canada Forum on Corrections Research. Retrieved from http://www.csc-scc.gc.ca/text/pblct/forum/e142/e142i-eng.shtml

Mahony, T.H., Jacob, J. and Hobson, H. (2017). Women in Canada: A gender-based statistical report—Women and the criminal justice system. *Juristat*. Statistics Canada Catalogue No. 89-503-X.

Mann, R.M., Senn, C.Y., Girard, A., and Ackbar, S. (2007). Community-based interventions for at-risk youth in Ontario under Canada's Youth Criminal Justice Act: A case study of a "runaway" girl. *Canadian Journal of Criminology and Criminal Justice, 49*(1), 37–74.

Maynard, R. (2015). Policing black lives: State violence in Canada from slavery to the present. Halifax: Fernwood.

Means, R. (2002). *Decreasing the raise in female delinquency through gender specific program and proactive police involvement.* Unpublished report, Department of Interdisciplinary Technology as part of School of Police Staff and Command Program Eastern, Michigan University.

Miller, E. (1986). *Street women: The illegal work of underclass women*. Philadelphia: Temple University Press.

Miller, W. (1958). Lower-class culture as a generating milieu of gang delinquency. *Journal of Social Issues, 14*, 5–19.

Monchalin, L. (2016). *The colonial problem: An Indigenous perspective on crime and injustice in Canada*. North York, ON: University of Toronto Press.

Monture-Angus, P. (2000). Aboriginal women and correctional practice. In K. Hannah-Moffat and M. Shaw (Eds), *An ideal prison?: Critical essays on women's imprisonment in Canada* (pp. 52–60). Halifax: Fernwood.

Moretti, M.M., Odgers, C., and Reppucci, N.D. (2011). Serious conduct problems among girls at risk: Translating research into intervention. *International Journal of Child, Youth and Family Studies, 1* and *2*, 142–61.

Moscher, C., and Mahon-Haft, T. (2010). Race, crime and criminal justice in Canada. In A. Kalunta-Crumpton (Ed), *Race, crime and criminal justice* (pp. 242–69). London: Palgrave.

Munch, C. (2012) Youth correctional statistics in Canada, 2010/2011. *Juristat, 32*(1). Statistics Canada Catalogue No. 85-002-X.

Myers, N.M. (2017). Eroding the presumption of innocence: Pre-trial detention and the use of conditional release on bail. *British Journal of Criminology, 57*, 664–83.

Myers, N.M., and Dhillon, S. (2013). The criminal offence of entering any Shoppers Drug Mart in Ontario: Criminalizing ordinary behaviour with youth bail conditions. *Canadian Journal of Criminology and Criminal Justice, 55*(2), 187–214.

Native Women's Association of Canada and Justice for Girls. (2012). *Gender matters: Building strength in reconciliation.* Retrieved from http://www.nwac.ca/gender-matters/

Nicholson, D., and Artz, S. (2003). Preventing youthful offending: Where do we go from here? *Relational Child and Youth Care Practice, 16*(4), 32–46.

Nye, F. (1958). *Family relationships and delinquent behaviour.* New York: Wiley.

Odgers, C.L. Moffitt, T.E., Broadbent, J.M., Dickson, N., Hancox, R.J., Harrington, H., . . . Capsi, A. (2008). *Female and male antisocial trajectories: From childhood origins to adult outcomes. Developmental and Psychopathology, 20,* 673–716.

Ontario Human Rights Commission (2018). *Interrupted childhoods: Over-representation of Black children in Ontario child welfare.* Retrieved from http://www.ohrc.on.ca/en/interrupted-childhoods#4.Research%20on%20racial%20disproportionality%20in%20child%20welfare

Owusu-Bempah, A., and Millar, P. (2010). Research note: Revisiting the collection of "justice statistics by race" in Canada. *Canadian Journal of Law & Society, 25*(1), 97–104.

Owusu-Bempah, A., and Wortley, S. (2015). Race, crime, and criminal justice in Canada. In S. Bucerius and M. Tonry (Eds)., *Race, crime, and criminal justice in Canada. The Oxford Handbook of Ethnicity, Crime, and Immigration.* New York: Oxford University Press. Retrieved from *Oxford Handbooks Online*: https://www.oxfordhandbooks.com/view/10.1093/oxfordhb/9780199859016.001.0001/oxfordhb-9780199859016

Pasko, L. (2017). Beyond the confinement: The regulation of girl offenders' bodies, sexual choices, and behavior. *Women & Criminal Justice*, 4–20.

Piquero, N.L. and Piquero, A.R. (2015). Life-course persistent offending. In F.T. Cullen, P. Wilcox, J.L. Lux, and C.L. Jonson (Eds)., *Bringing gender into criminology* (pp. 67–82). New York: Oxford University Press.

Podgurski, I., and Lyons, J.S. (2014). Understanding bad girls: The role of trauma in antisocial behavior among female youth. *Residential Treatment for Children & Youth, 31*(1), 80–8

Pollack, O. (1950). *The criminality of women*. New York: Barnes.

Pulis, J.E. (2013). Understanding failure to comply convictions with young offenders: A snapshot of one Canadian courthouse. *Community Focused Research*, 28–31.

Pulis, J.E. (2014). *Set up for failure? Understanding probation orders and breaches of probation for youth in conflict with the law* (Doctoral dissertation). Retrieved from UWSpace: https://uwspace.uwaterloo.ca/handle/10012/8475

Raine, A. (2002). Annotation: The role of prefrontal deficits, low autonomic arousal, and early health factors in the development of antisocial and aggressive behavior in children. *Journal of Child Psychology and Psychiatry, 43*, 417–34.

Randall, M., and Haskell, L. (2013). Trauma-informed approaches to law: Why restorative justice must understand trauma and psychological coping. *Dalhousie Law Journal, 36*, 501.

Reasons, C., Hassan, S., Ma, M., Monchalin, L., Bige, M., Paras, C., and Arora, S. (2016). Race and criminal justice in Canada. *International Journal of Criminal Justice Sciences, 11*(2), 75–99.

Reckless, W. (1961). *The crime problem* (3rd ed.). New York: Barnes.

Reiss, A. (1951). Delinquency as the failure of personal social controls. *American Sociological Review, 16,* 196–207.

Reiss, A., and Roth, J. (Eds). (1993). *Understanding and preventing violence.* Washington: National Academy Press.

Reitsma-Street, M. (1998). Still girls learn to care; girls policed to care. In C. Baines, P. Evans, and S. Neysmith (Eds), *Women's caring: Social policy in Canada* (rev. ed., pp. 87–113). Toronto: Oxford University Press.

Reitsma-Street, M. (2004). Connecting policies, girls, and violence. In M. Moretti, C. Odgers, and M. Jackson (Eds), *Girls and aggression: Contributing factors and intervention principles* (pp. 115–30). Boston: Kluwer.

Reitsma-Street, M., and Offord, D.R. (1991). Girl delinquents and their sisters: A challenge for practice. *Canadian Social Work Review, 8*(1), 11–27.

Rubinow, D., and Schmidt, P. (1996). Androgens, brain, and behavior. *American Journal of Psychiatry, 153*(8), 974–84.

Ryder, J.A. (2014). *Girls & violence: Tracing the roots of criminal behavior.* London: Lynne Rienner.

Schissel, B. (2010). Ill health and discrimination: The double jeopardy for youth in punitive justice systems. *International Journal of Child, Youth and Family Studies, 1*(2), 157–78.

Schwartz, J., and Steffensmeir, D. (2017). Gendered opportunities and risk preferences for offending across the life course. *Journal of Developmental Life Course Criminology, 3,* 126–50.

Sharpe, G. (2016). Re-imagining justice for girls: A new agenda for research. *Youth Justice, 16*(1), 3–17.

Sharpe, G., and Gelsthorpe, L. (2009). Engendering the agenda: Girls, young women and youth justice. *Youth Justice, 9*(3), 195–208.

Silcox, J. (2016). *Representations of youth crime in Canada: A feminist criminological analysis of statistical trends, national Canadian newspapers, and moral panics* (Doctoral dissertation). Retrieved from Western Libraries: https://ir.lib.uwo.ca/etd/3800

Silcox, J. (2017). Are Canadian girls becoming more violent? An examination of Integrated Criminal Courts Survey statistics. *Criminal Justice Policy Review,* 1–26.

Simon, R. (1975). *Women and crime.* Lexington, MA: Lexington Books.

Sinclair, R. (2007). Identity lost and found: Lessons from the sixties scoop. *First Peoples Child And Family Review, 3*(1), 65–82.

Smandych, R., and Corrado, R. (2018). Too bad so sad: Observations on key outstanding policy challenges of twenty years of youth justice reform in Canada 1995 to 2015. *Alberta Law Journal, 41*(3), 191–240.

Smith, P. (2017). A qualitative examination of the self-medicating hypothesis among female juvenile offenders. *Women & Criminal Justice, 29*(1), 14–31.

Smith, A., Cox, K., Poon, C., Stewart, D., and McCreary Centre Society. (2013). Time out III: A profile of BC youth in custody. Vancouver: McCreary Centre Society. Retrieved from http://www.mcs.bc.ca/pdf/Time_Out_III.pdf

Spivak, A.L., Wagner, B.M., Whitmer, J.M., and Charish, C.L. (2014). Gender and status offending: Judicial paternalism in juvenile justice processing. *Feminist Criminology, 9*(3), 224–48.

Sprott, J.B. (2012). The persistence of status offences in the youth justice system. *Canadian Journal of Criminology and Criminal Justice, 54*(3), 309–32.

Sprott, J.B. (2015). How court officials 'create' youth crime: The use and consequences of bail conditions. *Canadian Criminal Law Review,* 27–39.

Sprott, J.B., and Doob, A.N. (2009). *Justice for girls? Stability and change in the youth justice systems of the United States and Canada.* Chicago: University of Chicago Press.

Sprott, J.B., and Doob, A.N. (2010). Gendered treatment: Girls and treatment orders in bail court. *Canadian Journal of Criminology and Criminal Justice, 52*(4), 427–41.

Sprott, J.B., and Manson, A. (2017). YCJA bail conditions: "Treating" girls and boys differently. *Canadian Criminal Law Review, 22,* 77–94.

Statistics Canada. (2017a). Adult criminal courts, number of cases and charges by type of decision. CANSIM Table 35100027.

Statistics Canada. (2017b). Estimate of population, by age group and sex for July 1, Canada, provinces and territories. CANSIM Table 17100005.

Statistics Canada. (2017c). Homicide victims and persons accused of homicide by age group and sex. CANSIM Table 3510007001.

Statistics Canada. (2017d). Youth custody and community services (YCCS), admissions to correctional services, by sex and Aboriginal identity, 1997/1998 to 2011/2012. CANSIM Table 35100007.

Statistics Canada. (2017e). Youth custody and community services (YCCS), admissions to correctional services, by sex and age at time of admission, 1997/1998 to 2011/2012. CANSIM Table 35100006.

Statistics Canada. (2017f). Youth courts, number of cases and charges by type of decision 1997/1998 to 2011/2012. CANSIM Table 35100038.

Statistics Canada. (2017g). Youth courts, guilty cases by type of sentence 1997/1998 to 2011/2012. CANSIM Table 35100041.

Statistics Canada. (2017h). Incident-based crime statistics, by detailed violations. CANSIM Table 35100177.

Steffensmeier, D., Schwartz, J., Zhong, H., and Ackerman, J. (2005). An assessment of recent trends in girls' violence using diverse longitudinal sources: Is the gender gap closing? *Criminology, 43*(2), 355–406.

Stoneman, L. (2016). *Community-based responses to youth offending: Politics, policy and practice under the Youth Criminal Justice Act* (Unpublished doctoral dissertation). University of Victoria, Victoria, BC.

Sutherland, E. (1939). *Principles of criminology*. Philadelphia: Lippincott.

Sutherland, E., and Cressey, D. (1978). *Criminology* (10th ed.). Philadelphia: Lippincott.

Tanner, J. (1996). *Teenage troubles: Youth and deviance in Canada*. Toronto: Nelson.

Taylor, K.N., and Blanchette, K. (2009). The women are not wrong: It is the approach that is debatable. *Criminology and Public Policy, 8*(1), 221–9.

Thomas, S.S. (2009). Status offenses. In H.T. Greene and S.L. Gabbidon, *Encyclopaedia of race and crime*. Thousand Oaks, CA: Sage.

Toby, J. (1957). Social disorganization and stake in conformity: Complementary factors in predatory behaviour in hoodlums. *Journal of Criminal Law, Criminology and Police Service, 48*, 12–17.

Toh, K. (2003). *Annotated Youth Criminal Justice Act*. Markham, ON: Lexis Nexis Canada Inc.

Tremblay, R. (2003). Why socialization fails: The case of chronic physical aggression. In B. Lahey, T. Moffitt, and A. Caspi (Eds), *Causes of conduct disorder and juvenile delinquency* (pp. 182–224). New York: Guilford.

Trepanier, J. (1999). Juvenile delinquency and youth protection: The historical foundations of the Canadian Juvenile Delinquents Act of 1908. *European Journal of Crime, 7*(1), 41–62.

Trupin, E., Stewart, D., Boesky, L., McClurg, B., Beach, B., Hormann, S., and Baltrusis, R. (1999, February). Evaluation of a dialectical behavior therapy with incarcerate female juvenile offenders. Paper presented at the 11th annual research conference: A System of Care for Children's Mental Health: Expanding the Research Base, University of South Florida, Tampa, FL.

Truth and Reconciliation Commission of Canada. (2015). Honouring the truth, reconciling for the future. Ottawa: Author. Retrieved from http://www.trc.ca/assets/pdf/Honouring_the_Truth_Reconciling_for_the_Future_July_23_2015.pdf

Verheul, R., van den Bosch, L.M.C., Koeter, M.W.J., de Ridder, M.A.J., Stijnen, T., and Van den Brink, W. (2003). Dialectical behaviour therapy for women with borderline personality disorder: 12-month, randomised clinical trial in the Netherlands. *British Journal of Psychiatry, 182*, 135–40.

Webster, C.M., and Doob, A.N. (2015). US punitiveness "Canadian style"? Cultural values and Canadian punishment policy. *Punishment & Society, 17*(3), 299–321.

Wilson, J., and Herrnstein, R. (1985). *Crime and human nature*. New York: Simon & Schuster.

Woolford, A. (2009). *The politics of restorative justice: A critical introduction*. Halifax: Fernwood.

Worrall, A., and Gelsthrope, L. (2009). "What works" with women offenders: The past 30 years. *Probation Journal, 56*(4), 329.

Wortley, S., and Tanner, J. (2003). Data, denials and confusions: The racial profiling debate in Toronto. *Canadian Journal of Criminology and Criminal Justice, 45*(3), 367—90.

Zahn, M.A. (Ed.). (2009). *The delinquent girl*. Philadelphia: Temple University Press.

Theoretical Perspectives on Youth Crime

Stephen W. Baron

8

Overview

This chapter reviews a number of theoretical perspectives that have emerged in the past three decades to explain youth crime. It outlines the main theoretical premises of each perspective, scrutinizing the way each attempts to understand how youth become involved in offending. In addition, attention is given to the empirical status of each theory with a focus on research undertaken to date. This overview helps determine whether each theory provides valuable insights into young people's offending, where future research is needed to clarify aspects of a particular perspective, and whether theoretical revisions are required to better understand youth involvement in crime.

Key Objectives

After reading this chapter, you should be able to:

- Identify and distinguish the theoretical perspectives developed to explain youth crime.
- Better understand the way different theoretical concepts can be integrated to improve our understanding of youth crime.
- Appreciate the complexity required to understand youth crime.
- Recognize some of the empirical weaknesses of theoretical approaches offered to explain youth crime.

Introduction

In this chapter, we examine the most recent theoretical perspectives developed to explain youth crime. Until quite recently, explanations of youth crime were dominated by theories developed prior to the 1970s (e.g., strain, social control, social learning/differential association; see Chapter 7 for a review). Researchers exploring these perspectives, however, discovered that these explanations provided only a limited account of why young people offend. In response, scholars began critically reviewing these theories and identifying of number of weaknesses that needed to be addressed. They observed that there was an isolationist approach to examining explanations for crime, and a failure to recognize the potential complementary connections between perspectives. Further, it became apparent that the traditional theories limited their focus to explaining the onset of offending, paying little attention to why people continue, or cease, offending. In addition, research began to uncover multiple patterns of offending that traditional perspectives could not adequately address. Finally, many scholars argued that the scope for understanding youth crime was too restricted and needed broadening to include how environmental factors and the criminal justice system might impact offending (see Chapter 16, for example).

In reviewing scholars' attempts to address these weaknesses, we will see some of these new perspectives build on existing perspectives, while others integrate previously developed perspectives with innovative causal concepts. Both of these strategies have created novel explanations for criminal behaviour. We will also review theories that focus on the development of offending and on explanations of different offender types. These theories concentrate on why youth begin offending at different ages, engage in different types of crime, and how their offending patterns change as they age. Finally, we explore perspectives that explain how environments and daily activities, as well as the criminal justice system, influence youth crime. As our agenda suggests, these recent theoretical developments reflect the evolution of the understanding of crime.

The General Theory of Crime: Self-Control

The general theory of crime, as outlined by Gottfredson and Hirschi (1990), focuses on the key concept of self-control. *Self-control* refers to the ability to restrain oneself from momentary temptations. The failure to develop self-control leaves one more likely to engage in crime.

Low self-control is made up of six different features. First, those who lack self-control are impulsive. They are unable to defer gratification and are more inclined to focus on rewards in the here and now, and are less likely to consider the future ramifications of their behaviour. For those who are impulsive, criminal activities satisfy personal desires immediately. Second, those without self-control are short-sighted. People who are short-sighted will choose the quickest and easiest path, including crime, to satisfy their desires. Third, people with low self-control are risk-takers, enjoying activities that provide adventure, thrills, and excitement. Criminal acts are attractive to such people because they often involve these elements. Fourth, those with low self-control are physical and do not value cognitive skills. Crime is attractive because most illegal acts are not cognitively challenging, and many involve physical activity. Fifth, those with low self-control are self-centred and insensitive. They do not consider the physical and emotional harm their criminal acts cause to others. Finally, those with low self-control have low frustration tolerance. Slights from people can lead to assaults, frustrating tasks can lead to property damage, and difficult interpersonal interactions can lead to violent resolutions. These six traits are argued to come together in the same people, to operate in tandem, and to persist over the lifespan (see Figure 8.1).

Beyond its connection to crime, low self-control has negative social consequences. It shapes people's ability to succeed in social institutions and to form **social bonds**. Those lacking self-control will be more likely to leave school, be unemployed, fail in romantic relationships, and associate with others short on self-control. The negative impact of low self-control, therefore, is broad.

Causes of Variation in Self-Control

How does an individual end up with low self-control? It is the result of ineffective socialization. Teaching self-control requires that caregivers (1) monitor a child's behaviour; (2) recognize the characteristics of low self-control when exhibited; and (3) correct those behaviours. This child-rearing process, however, can be undermined. First, the caregiver

low self-control
A trait made up of impulsivity, short-sightedness, risk-taking, physicality, insensitivity, and low frustration tolerance, which leaves individuals less able to refrain from activities that provide short-term pleasure or gain.

social bonds
The degree to which individuals, through socialization, have connections to people and institutions in a society and believe in the rules of the society. These connections serve as restraints against criminal opportunities and behaviour.

Poor socialization ⟶ Development of low self-control traits ⟶ Crime

Failure to supervise person
Failure to recognize indicators of low self-control
Failure to correct or sanction behaviour

Impulsivity
Lack of diligence
Risk-taking
Physicality
Insensitivity
Low frustration tolerance

X
Opportunity

Figure 8.1 The General Theory of Crime

may not care about the child. Second, there might be a lack of time or resources for proper supervision of the child's activities and conduct. Finally, caregivers may not recognize the characteristics of low self-control as problematic. Without proper socialization, low self-control becomes stable and difficult to alter.

Current Empirical Research into the General Theory of Crime

A broad review of the findings suggests that those with low self-control are more likely to engage in crime and deviance (Vazsonyi, Mikuska, and Kelley 2017). Low self-control is also predictive of negative social consequences, including unemployment, homelessness, accidents, criminal associates, and criminal victimization (Baron 2003; Pratt, Turanovic, Fox, and Wright 2014). Research, however, has tended to find less support for the stability of low self-control. The condition is malleable and can be influenced by programming (Piquero, Jennings, and Farrington 2010), levels of social control (Na and Paternoster 2012; Ray, Jones, Loughran, and Jennings 2013), peer influence, and victimization experiences (Meldrum, Young, and Weerman 2012; Ray et al. 2013). Further, research shows that low self-control is not the only cause of crime, and other causal factors argued to disappear once self-control has been accounted for remain important (Baron 2003). In sum, while there is general support for the idea of a link between low self-control and crime, the theory itself has shown to have less clear support and current research continues to uncover nuances and to challenge some of its key arguments. It has nevertheless emerged as broadly influential. We will see that the concept has been integrated into a number of the other recent theoretical perspectives to be reviewed, suggesting its potential usefulness in understanding offending.

General Strain Theory (GST)

Robert Agnew's (1992, 2001) general strain theory (GST) focuses on how negative situations, or **strains**, can lead to crime. He explores emotional reactions to strain and details how other factors influence people to respond to strain with crime. In the theory, three broad areas of strain are outlined (see Figure 8.2).

strains
Experiences or situations that individuals perceive as being negative, creating a negative emotional reaction that provides the possible incentive for using crime as a coping mechanism.

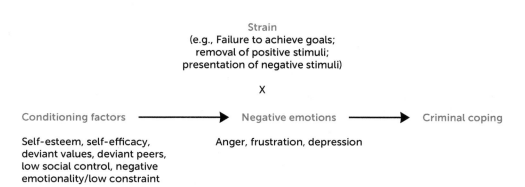

Strain
(e.g., Failure to achieve goals;
removal of positive stimuli;
presentation of negative stimuli)

X

Conditioning factors ⟶ Negative emotions ⟶ Criminal coping

Self-esteem, self-efficacy,   Anger, frustration, depression
deviant values, deviant peers,
low social control, negative
emotionality/low constraint

Figure 8.2 General Strain Theory

Types of Strains

Failure to Achieve Goals

The first broad area of strain detailed in GST is the failure to achieve positively valued goals. This form of strain, however, can be further divided into three sub-areas. The first sub-form, similar to the classic strain theory argument (see Chapter 7), encompasses the disjunction between achievement aspirations and achievement expectations. Here, a gap between what people desire and what they expect to achieve leads to unpleasant feelings that pressure them into crime to meet those aspirations.

The second sub-area focuses on the disjunction between expected achievements and actual achievements. This moves away from aspirations that are often unrealistic. A gap between more realistic achievement expectations and what is actually achieved motivates individuals to utilize crime to address the gap. The third sub-area centres on the disjunction between just or fair outcomes and actual outcomes. When people experience outcomes that are different from what they believe to be fair or just, they may use crime to alter the outcomes.

Removal of Positive Stimuli

The second broad source of strain is the anticipated or actual removal of positively valued stimuli. These stimuli might include property or relationships (e.g., losing a romantic partner; having something stolen). Potential deviant responses to losses may include trying to prevent the loss (e.g., fight for the property), seeking revenge against those who removed the stimuli, or attempting to recover or replace the lost stimuli (e.g., theft). Drug and alcohol use may also address the negative emotions that losing positively valued stimuli generate.

Presentation of Negative Stimuli

The third broad source of strain is the anticipated or actual presentation of negative stimuli. Examples of negative stimuli include criminal victimization, child abuse, and adverse school environments. Deviant responses to negative stimuli may include attempting to avoid or escape the stimuli (e.g., truancy), or seeking revenge against the source. Individuals may also attempt to bring an end to the stimuli through direct confrontation. Finally, the negative emotions generated by the negative stimuli can be addressed with drug and/or alcohol use.

Strains Most Likely to Cause Crime

The impact of strain may vary depending upon its severity, duration, recency, and centrality. Strains that are severe, long term, frequent, and recent can all generate a greater likelihood of offending. Certain older forms of strain, including severe child abuse, however, can have longer-term effects. Extreme events that jeopardize an individual's central values, goals, needs, and identity are also more criminogenic. Strains associated with, or caused by, low social control (a lack of conventional commitments, attachments, and supervision; see Chapter 7) also increase illegal coping probabilities. All of these variations in strain increase the likelihood of criminal coping because they reduce the perceived costs of crime. Finally, certain strains (e.g., criminal victimization and physical abuse) provide access to the values, beliefs, and models that support and reinforce criminal coping strategies (see Chapter 7, social learning/differential association theory).

Negative Emotions

Strain can lead to a range of negative emotions. The critical emotion, however, is anger. Anger amplifies feelings of injury and generates a need for revenge, retaliation, or corrective action. It also lowers inhibitions and reduces fear of punishment. For all of these reasons, those who respond to strain with anger are more likely to engage in crime.

Conditioning Factors

GST details a number of factors that can increase the criminogenic effect of strain. First, strain will be more likely to lead to crime when a person also lacks self-efficacy and self-esteem. Those lacking these qualities will be more sensitive to negative events and will believe they lack the ability to alter events through non-criminal means. Second, those who associate with criminal peers and hold values supportive of criminal behaviour will be more likely to react to strain with crime. Criminal peers supply support by modelling illegal behaviour, defining certain illegal activities as appropriate responses to strain, and serving as instigators of criminal behaviour. Third, those lacking social support (financial assistance, guidance, and emotional backing) are more likely to respond to strain with crime. Criminal responses to strain are also more likely when the potential rewards from illegal behaviour are greater than the potential costs.

Finally, negative emotionality and low constraint will influence responses to strain. Individuals with negative emotionality are easily upset and angered and tend to have aggressive interaction styles. Those with low constraint tend to be impulsive risk-takers, with little empathy for others. These characteristics increase the likelihood people will respond to strain with crime. Box 8.1 provides an example of recent research that applies the GST to explaining crime.

Current Empirical Research into General Strain Theory

General strain theory has generated a great deal of research. There is much support for linkages between various negative experiences and criminal coping, particularly for those forms of strain outlined to be the most criminogenic (Agnew 2006, 2013). Baron (2004, 2019), for example, shows that factors such as homelessness, unemployment, parental rejection, physical neglect, emotional, physical, and sexual abuse, property and violent victimization, witnessing violent victimization, perceptions of relative deprivation, and monetary dissatisfaction, can all lead to crime. Thaxton and Agnew (2018) have found that adverse school environments and negative interactions with the police increase the likelihood of offending, while Simons Chen, Stewart, and Brody (2003) outline the link between racial discrimination and criminal coping.

There is also evidence for the link between negative experiences and emotions (such as anger) and crime, particularly for aggressive offending forms (Moon and Morash 2017).

Box 8.1 | Youth Justice in Action

Agnew's General Strain Theory

Thaxton and Agnew (2018) set out to examine whether Agnew's GST could help to explain why some young people with certain negative experiences engage in crime while others do not. The researchers were interested in whether the presence of an amalgamation of factors, or what they referred to as a propensity, escalated the likelihood that a negative experience would lead to a criminal response. The researchers used information on the negative experiences of over 5000 grade eight students who reported on how often they had been victimized (e.g., hit, robbed, attacked with a weapon), experienced negative interactions with the police (e.g., officers were rude, unfriendly), and been exposed to negative events at school (e.g., violence between other students; students assaulting teachers). The students also provided information on factors that might increase their propensity to crime, answering questions that tapped into the lack of attachment to their mother, absent monitoring from parents, their dislike of school, and indications that they were impulsive and liked to take risks. The researchers also used evidence on the students' moral acceptance of

crime, lack of guilt for offending, and association with delinquent peers. All of these factors were added together to create the concept of criminal propensity. Finally, the research used information on 16 different forms of offending that participants might possibly have engaged in.

Thaxton and Agnew (2018) found that each negative experience (victimization, negative police contact, and negative school environment) increased the likelihood of offending. Further, high criminal propensity also increased the likelihood of offending. Lastly, the researchers discovered that each type of negative experience was more likely to lead to offending when the young person also had a greater propensity for crime. For those who had a low propensity for offending, the negative experiences were less likely to translate into criminal behaviour.

Critical Thinking Question
What other factors might influence whether strain leads to offending?

There are now calls for work to explore other emotions—depression, for example—to determine which strains might generate alternative emotions and coping forms (e.g., suicide, eating disorders, substance use) (Agnew 2013). Limited work on this issue has produced uneven results so far (Moon and Morash 2017). Recent work has also established that strain can increase other criminogenic factors, including low self-control and associations with criminal peers, which increase offending (Baron 2015). Research exploring the conditioning factors has also generated mixed findings (Agnew 2006, 2013). Agnew (2013) has recently suggested that it is the combination of the moderators that creates the strong propensity for offending rather than each factor in isolation. While limited, work has begun to show that an aggregate moderator that includes a range of factors is likely to influence the relationship between a range of strains and crime (Baron 2019; and Thaxton and Agnew 2018 for support and reviews). Overall, while there is much support for the basic strain–crime relationships, additional work is still required to help clarify how the conditioning factors and emotions work to explain crime.

Control Balance Theory

Charles Tittle's (1995, 2004) **control balance** theory focuses on how control—either having it or not having it—can be criminogenic. The idea of *being controlled* keys on how an individual's behavioural choices are restricted by others who have the power or resources to impede or assist in goal achievement. Being controlled also includes physical or social-structural arrangements that block goal attainment. *Exercising control*, in contrast, focuses on how people escape the behavioural restrictions imposed by others. It also refers to a person's capacity to overcome structural or physical obstacles to realize goals. It might also include the ability to help or impede others in their goal quests.

control balance
The degree of control that an individual perceives they have over their environment relative to the degree of control they perceive their environment has over them.

Control Balance Ratios and the Process Leading to Crime

The amount of control a person experiences relative to the amount of control they exercise is referred to as a *control ratio*. This ratio influences the likelihood of deviance. People have specific control ratios associated with each of their roles, statuses, and environments as well as a general control ratio reflecting their overall situation.

When the amount of control that an individual exercises is equal to the amount they experience, their control ratio is balanced. This does not lead to deviance. In contrast, control ratio imbalances leave individuals to consider deviance to alter the imbalance. These control ratio imbalances can take two forms. Individuals will have a *control surplus* when the amount of control they exercise is greater than the amount of control they experience. Perceiving having more control over your friends than they over you is a control surplus. *Control deficits* arise where the amount of control a person experiences exceeds the amount of control they exercise. If you felt school had greater control over you than you over it, this is a control deficit.

The two types of control imbalance predispose a person to undertake deviance. This predisposition, however, only transforms into a motivation for deviance under certain circumstances. In particular, people need to experience a provocation that reminds them, or makes them aware, that they have control imbalance for this transformation to take place. Motivation, conversely, will only lead to crime if there is opportunity. People need human or property targets, for example, for assault or theft. Given motivation and opportunity, individuals review a range of possible deviant acts. The actual act chosen is influenced by *constraint*. Constraint includes the seriousness of the act being considered and situational risk. Seriousness focuses on the amount of punishment the act might elicit. Situational risk keys on concern about getting caught for the act and actually experiencing the punishment. Individuals, therefore, will be more likely to choose acts where detection probabilities are lower and penalties less severe.

Also important will be an individual's level of self-control. Low self-control makes people more vulnerable to provocation, more easily motivated for crime, more likely to react instantly, less likely to consider act-associated punishment, and less likely to consider gains. In contrast, those high in self-control can restrain themselves from instantaneous action, leaving them more likely to consider different types of acts than those selected by individuals with low self-control.

Contingencies

The process leading to deviance may also be influenced by a person's moral beliefs, self-efficacy, prior deviant experience, and subcultural involvement. For example, viewing certain illegal activities as morally acceptable increases the likelihood a control imbalance will be addressed through crime. A person with higher self-efficacy is more likely to confront controls and/or take advantage of deviant opportunities when faced with control imbalance. Prior success with deviance provides personal historical evidence that crime can successfully alter control imbalances. Finally, subcultural involvement exposes people to forms, excuses, rationalizations, and expectations of deviance that increase criminal responses to control imbalance.

Types of Deviance

Control imbalances (surpluses or deficits) are argued to explain all forms of deviance (Tittle 2004). Different deviant acts are distinguished by their *control balance desirability*. Control balance desirability has two components. The first surrounds the potential long-term change in the control ratio that may result from the act. The second focuses on the degree to which the offender needs to be personally or directly involved with the victim. Acts with little direct contact with victims that allow for long-term changes in control balance ratios have the greatest control balance desirability. Acts that involve direct contact and shorter-term impact on control balance ratios have less control balance desirability.

Actors with substantial control surpluses, high self-control, and opportunities with few constraints will undertake behaviours high in control balance desirability (e.g., commit sophisticated white-collar crime or lead an organized crime syndicate). In contrast, people who have small-to-medium control deficits, low self-control, and opportunities for low-desirability acts (e.g., assaulting a boss or robbing a convenience store) with few constraints, will commit acts of low control balance desirability. Acts around the middle of the desirability continuum point toward various levels and amalgamations of the causal variables. Those with extreme deficits will, however, resort to *submission*, a passive rather than active response, which excludes it from the continuum (see Figure 8.3).

Current Empirical Research into Control Balance Theory

Most empirical work on the control balance perspective has found that both control balance deficits and control balance surpluses are related to deviant behaviours, including assault, theft, drug and alcohol use, deviant sexual practices, eating disorders, stalking,

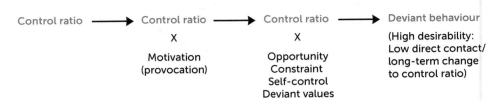

Figure 8.3 Control Balance Theory

cheating, and criminal victimization (Baron and Forde 2007; Nobles and Fox 2013). To date, there has been little focus on the link between different types of control ratio imbalances and behaviours that might have different control balance desirability (Baron 2010; Hughes, Antonaccio, and Botchkovar 2015; Nobles and Fox 2013). Research on the contingency variables shows mixed support for self-control and constraint, but some evidence of peer association increasing the criminogenic impact of control imbalances (Baron and Forde 2007). Work on the other contingencies is absent to date. Overall, research suggests that while the basic, direct causal process appears to be related to deviance, support for the more nuanced causal process has either yet to be determined or investigated, leaving room for future work to fill in the blanks.

Differential Coercion Theory

Mark Colvin (2000) outlines a theory that integrates social control, social learning, general strain, control balance, and the general theory perspectives with a Marxist approach to explain offending. Central to this perspective are two dimensions of control. The first is **coercion**, which ranges from extremely coercive to completely non-coercive. Coercion is punitive, causing emotional and/or physical pain as well as taking away vital sources of instrumental and social support. The second dimension is the consistency with which coercion is delivered. Consistency can range from highly erratic to extremely consistent (see Figure 8.4).

coercion
A personal or an impersonal force that compels or frightens individuals to behave in a certain way.

Direct and Indirect Coercion

Coercion can be direct or indirect. Control from an interpersonal relationship (e.g., the family) would be direct coercion. Control emerging from forces beyond an individual's control is indirect coercion (e.g., economic conditions). Both direct and indirect coercion can be consistent or erratic. Parental punishment for every single infraction by a child would be consistent direct coercion. Irregular parental sanctions are inconsistent direct coercion. Broad labour market conditions that move an individual in and out of employment are erratic and indirect. Those that exclude someone from the labour market long-term are consistent and indirect.

Coercion has numerous sources—including family, peers, criminal justice and social service agencies, and the broader economy. In these settings, individuals will differ in

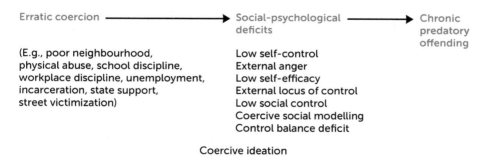

Figure 8.4 **Erratic Coercion and Chronic Predatory Offending**

the degree to which they experience coercion. In families where force, intimidation, and threats are used frequently to gain compliance, children experience coercion. Individuals in peer groups where they continually encounter violent victimization and verbal degradation suffer coercion. Impoverished individuals under the formal supervision of state agencies that remove financial support, or threaten or impose sanctions, are exposed to coercion. Incarceration, or being held by force against one's wishes, is coercive. Finally, poverty and economic necessity, and the stress and desperation they produce, are coercive.

Types of Control Structures

Four types of control structures can be identified based on the degree of coercion (coercive/non-coercive) and the consistency (consistent/erratic) with which coercion is delivered. The different types of control structures influence the development of a number of social-psychological mechanisms. Each control structure will impact levels of anger, social bonds, self-efficacy, locus of control, self-control, social learning of behaviour, and control balance ratios in different ways. In turn, the type of control experienced, and the psychological mechanisms that develop, will influence participation in crime.

A Consistent, Non-coercive Environment

The first type of control structure is a consistent, non-coercive environment. Control is applied firmly and fairly and accompanied by explanations and reasoning for application. Instrumental means, like offers of money or gifts, to gain compliance are avoided. This type of environment limits the generation of anger and control imbalance and promotes greater social control, self-control, self-efficacy, and an internalized sense of control. As a result, people show little inclination toward criminal activities.

An Erratic, Non-coercive Environment

The second type of control structure is erratic and non-coercive. This control form is lenient, negligent, and weak. There is often an indifference or detached involvement between individuals in the environment and application of control is faint and inconsistent. Instrumental tactics of control surrounding money or other incentives are often used, but these still occur only erratically. This environment does not generate anger. The lack of emotional attachment and inconsistent control, however, generate low self-control, low social control, control balance surpluses, high self-efficacy, and an internal sense of control. People with these histories are most likely to engage in pleasurable forms of deviance (e.g., drinking, drug use, and illicit sex). Further, because these individuals have historically exchanged compliance for instrumental rewards, they also tend to lie to, and manipulate, authority figures. According to the theory, this type of control structure, and the forms of deviance it produces, accounts for the majority of offenders.

A Consistent, Coercive Environment

The third type of control structure is consistent, coercive control. Here control is regularly and repeatedly delivered but in a highly coercive form. This creates a highly punitive relationship between the controller and the object of control. These relationships usually lack instrumental and emotional support. This environment incites a control ratio deficit, a low sense of self-efficacy, and an external locus of control. Further, since external reactions to control are punished, the consistent coercion incites internal anger and high self-control. Finally, since social supports are weak, and constantly under threat of removal, more calculative forms of social bonds tend to develop.

Consistent, coercive control limits the probability of both criminal and pro-social behaviour. The highly restrictive environment does not allow for deviance, and fear of consequences for compliance failure leads to highly self-monitored behaviour. Highly self-monitored behaviour inhibits the initiative and creativity necessary for success in education and other pursuits. Instead, this control structure leads to an increased likelihood of mental health problems (e.g., chronic depression).

An Erratic, Coercive Environment

The final control structure is the erratic, coercive form. In this type, control takes the shape of irregular punitive responses to transgressions. Sometimes serious misbehaviour is overlooked, while other times minor misconduct is severely punished, or in yet other circumstances punishment is meted out when no violation has occurred. The erratic and arbitrary punishment practices lead to externally directed anger, low self-efficacy, low social control, and low self-control. They also create an external locus of control, control balance deficits, and the learning of coercive behaviour. The coercion, along with the social-psychological mechanisms, generate *coercive ideation* (see Figure 8.4). Coercive ideation emerges when individuals come to interpret their world as enveloped in coercion that requires coercive responses.

The ramifications of erratic coercion are an increased likelihood of chronic involvement in predatory street crime, intimidation and coercion of others, as well as hostility and defiance toward authority. Offenders begin offending at an early age and are more likely to be violent due to exposure to violent models and coercive ideation.

Current Empirical Research into Differential Coercion Theory

Most research on differential coercion theory has focused on the crime-causing impact of erratic coercive control. This research shows that different forms of coercion, including parental coercion, coercive school environments, coercive neighbourhoods, incarceration, state support, and street victimization, are related to crime generally and to violent offending specifically (Baron 2009; Unnever, Colvin, and Cullen 2004). Limited work also reveals that erratic coercion is related to the development of low self-control, anger, coercive modelling, and coercive ideation. The social-psychological deficits of social control, low self-control, anger, control imbalances, coercive social models, and coercive ideation have also been shown to be related to crime (Baron 2009; Unnever, Colvin, and Cullen 2004). The only research to look at consistent coercion and mental health outcomes shows that oppressive coercion is associated with depression (Brauer, Tittle, and Antonoccio 2019).

Recent theoretical extensions have stressed the importance of consistent versus erratic social supports (Antonaccio, Tittle, Brauer, and Islam 2015; Baron 2015; Colvin,

Cullen, and Vander Ven 2002). Evidence shows that levels of erratic conventional social support decrease social control and self-control, and increase anger and participation in illegitimate social support networks. These factors in turn all affect criminal participation (Baron 2015). Future empirical work will need to more fully explore the roles of all control structure types, clarify issues surrounding the degrees and consistency in coercion, and investigate the links between specific control structures and broader forms of deviance. Box 8.2 provides an example of research examining the recent extension to the theory.

Box 8.2 | Youth Justice in Action

Differential Coercion Theory

Kurtz and Zavala (2017) set out to explore how positive and negative experiences might be linked to the development of social-psychological mechanisms that increase offending. Drawing on the recent extension to differential coercion theory, they were interested in whether supportive experiences with others decreased the likelihood of developing impulsivity. At the same time, they wanted to establish whether coercive experiences increased the development of impulsivity. Kurtz and Zavala then hypothesized that social support and low impulsivity would be associated with less violence, while greater coercion and high impulsivity would increase the likelihood of violent behaviour.

To investigate this, Kurtz and Zavala drew on data gathered from students in 11 US cites designed to explore involvement in gangs. The participants provided information on their experiences of coercion through questions tapping into how often they had ever been intentionally physically injured, had a weapon used on them, or been subject to force to surrender their property. The students also offered information about the racial conflict in their school, fights between students, and pressure to join gangs. To investigate social support, the participants responded to questions focusing on about how often their mother/father talked to them, gave them advice, and praised them, as well as how much supervision they received from parents. In light of the potential importance of peers, the respondents also gave information regarding their friends' offending. A series of questions on the youths' tendency to take risks, act on the spur of the moment, act without thinking, and engage in dangerous acts for excitement afforded insights on impulsivity. Finally, the researchers were able to determine how much violence these young people were involved in by the frequency of assaults, robberies, gang fights, and encouragement of gun use they reported.

Kurtz and Zavala discovered that greater social support was associated with a decreased tendency to develop impulsivity, while experiences with coercion and friendships with criminal peers increased the likelihood of developing impulsivity. Further, consistent with their hypotheses, they discovered that greater social support and low impulsivity were associated with less violence, while coercion, high impulsivity, and criminal peers were linked to greater amounts of violent behaviour.

Critical Thinking Question
What other factors might develop as a result of coercive experiences? Could social support buffer the development of these factors?

Situational Action Theory

Wikström's (2006, 2012) situational action theory (SAT) strives to understand how personal and environmental factors influence people's decision to engage in crime. SAT outlines that crimes are best understood as **moral actions**, or behaviours shepherded by moral rules. Moral rules outline behavioural acceptability in specific situations and crimes are violations of moral rules outlined by laws.

moral actions
Actions steered by moral rules that outline what behaviours are allowed or disallowed in particular circumstances.

Action Alternatives

SAT asserts that people's actions are the result of perceptions of "action alternatives," which set the boundaries for behavioural choices. Individuals will differ in these perceived action alternatives. For some, the perception–choice process may take the form of habitual action, where the individual perceives only one applicable action alternative and automatically selects this act. Habitual reactions develop through repeated experiences in specific situations, leading actions to become automated in these and comparable situations. In contrast, some perception–choice cases will involve deliberation where there is no perceived prominent action alternative. The choice of actions in these situations, therefore, is the result of calculating the positives and negatives of the range of perceived alternatives.

The central characteristic guiding perceptions of action alternatives is an individual's morality. This is made up of moral rules and the emotions attached to these rules. Some individuals will hold moral beliefs against breaking the law and will feel shame or guilt if they violate the law. Others may hold moral beliefs allowing law breaking and display no negative emotional responses when they commit crime. Morality can create moral habits where the individual acts in accordance with moral rules automatically without deliberation. This is due to the familiarity of circumstances or previously established favoured action alternatives.

When an individual's morality has not developed into a habit, however, it permits the consideration of action alternatives when there is a motivation for crime. Motivation might result from provocation or a presented temptation. Here, individuals with weaker levels of law-relevant morality may engage in crime, depending on other factors.

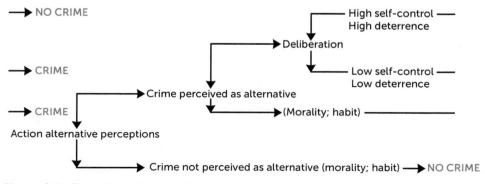

Figure 8.5 Situational Action Theory

Self-Control and Fear of Sanctions

The first of these factors is self-control. Self-control influences whether those whose morality allows deliberation of action alternatives will engage in crime. Those with lower self-control will be the most likely to engage in crime in this situation. Self-control does not influence choices between action alternatives for those with strong moral habits, since they do not consider action alternatives.

The second factor is deterrence. The fear of sanctions will influence individuals under conditions where they deliberate over action alternatives. For individuals who act out of habit and do not see crime as an action alternative, potential sanctions are irrelevant. When the individual engages in deviance out of moral habit, there is little consideration of action alternatives, again leaving the evaluation of consequences immaterial. The action alternatives considered by those with lower morality, however, may be influenced by potential sanctions. When sanctions are low, those with lower morality will be more likely to engage in crime. In contrast, when perceived sanctions are high, it is those with lower morality who will be the most likely to be deterred from offending.

Environments and Moral Habits

According to SAT, settings vary in their moral norms that promote or deter rule breaking. Further, settings vary in the degree to which they monitor for, and sanction, moral rule violations. These are the "deterrent qualities" of the setting. Settings perceived to be highly monitored for rule violations, and where moral violations will be severely sanctioned, leave action alternatives more likely to be deliberated.

When moral habits and personal morality are strong and in line with the moral rules of the setting, then the action alternatives that emerge for the individual will be consistent with moral rules of the setting. Therefore, in situations where moral habits and the moral rules of the setting discourage law breaking, illegal action is unlikely. Similarly, in circumstances where morality, moral habits, and the moral rules of the setting encourage law breaking, criminal acts are likely.

However, in situations where individuals have weak moral habits, or habits in conflict with the setting's moral rules, illegal action alternatives will emerge. It is here that self-control and deterrence become important. In situations where personal morality discourages deviance but setting moral rules encourage this action alternative, self-control influences choice. Those with greater self-control will be less likely to choose the illegal action alternative, while those with lower self-control will be more likely to select the illegal option. In circumstances where the individual's morality supports illegal action but the setting moral rules discourage it, perceived risk of apprehension and sanction severity will influence decisions. Sanctions seen as certain and severe reduce the likelihood of an illegal action being selected. Perceptions of uncertain sanctions or minimal costs increase the likelihood of illegal action alternatives being selected.

Current Empirical Research into Situational Action Theory

Much of the research on SAT has been supportive of the perspective. Research shows those with weaker morality are more likely to commit offences (Wikström and Svensson 2008, 2010). Research has also established that self-control tends to have a direct impact on the undertaking of criminal action alternatives. Further, it reveals that low self-control does not influence the behaviour of those with strong morality. In contrast, the criminal choices of those with weaker morality are influenced by the (in)ability of the individual to execute self-control (Pauwels, Svennson, and Hirtenlehner 2018; Wikström and Svensson 2010). Scholarship on the role of deterrence indicates that levels of monitoring and detection have a direct effect on behaviour (Gallupe and Baron 2014; Haar and Wikström 2010). Further, those with low self-control and with criminal moral propensities are the most influenced by deterrence (Pauwels, Svennson, and Hirtenlehner 2018; Wikström, Tseloni, and Karlis 2011). Initial evidence also suggests that environments are important. Here research indicates that those with morality-based criminal propensities and low abilities to exert self-control, those who frequent locations that lack guardianship, and those who attract other offenders are more likely to offend (Wikström and Svensson 2008).

Research has yet to establish, however, if individuals act out of habit, or if there is deliberation in their responses (Pauwels, Svennson, and Hirtenlehner 2018). Further, there is still the need to disentangle the general ability to exercise self-control from a more situational self-control ability in settings that encourage offending. This is also applicable to the need to empirically distinguish general morality from situational morality (Pauwels, Svennson, and Hirtenlehner 2018). Therefore, all the research puzzles within the perspective have yet to be fully solved.

Age-Graded Theory of Social Control

Sampson and Laub (1993; Laub and Sampson 2003) outline an age-graded theory of **informal social control**. At the framework's core is a focus on the continuity of behaviour as one moves from childhood through to adulthood, while also focusing on experiences and events that alter the behavioural patterns. The emphasis is on how informal social controls at different stages of a person's life influence continuity and change in offending behaviour as they move from childhood to adolescence to young adulthood and beyond (see Figure 8.6).

informal social control The control over people's behaviour that develops as a result of relationships and attachments to significant others and investments in conventional activities that could be damaged by engagement in illegal activities.

Mechanisms of Adolescent Informal Social Control

The theory begins by identifying three informal social control mechanisms within the family context: attachment, monitoring, and consistent discipline. Those without strong emotional bonds, direct supervision of behaviour, and dependable discipline will be more likely to engage in crime. Second, the theory identifies school as an additional source of socialization. Here the degree of attachment to the people within the institution, as well as academic performance, can influence participation in delinquency.

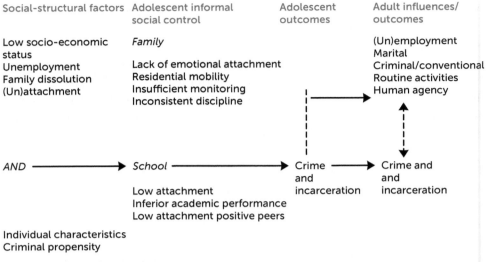

Figure 8.6 Age-Graded Theory of Social Control

Social-structural factors are argued to influence the quality and levels of these social bonds. Socio-economic status, unemployment, family dissolution, and residential mobility can all undermine the bonds. For example, socio-economic disadvantage may increase the likelihood of parental coping difficulties and impede parental ability to offer proper social control. The stress of poverty and dense households may undermine parent–child attachment, reduce emotional social control, and interrupt monitoring. This **disrupted social control** within the family destroys attachments to school. In addition to a lack of explicit support for education, the absence of monitoring and supervision for school attendance and homework increases educational deficits.

Social bonds can also be undermined by individual differences in criminal propensity. This propensity can be characterized by a difficult temperament and early conduct disorder. A child's anti-social behaviour can be challenging for parents and disrupt positive approaches to parenting. Anti-social conduct can provoke angry and hostile reactions from parents that inhibit or destroy social bonds. This absence of bonding in turn creates additional negative behaviour from the child. Similarly, in school, teachers may react negatively to difficult and disruptive children, damaging student–teacher relationships. This decreases school attachment, potentially undermines the child's academic performance, and increases the potential for criminal activities. A child's anti-social characteristics can also lead to a rejection by conventional peers, destroying another source for positive socialization. This makes those with negative traits more likely to move into groups of youths displaying similar anti-social characteristics, again increasing the likelihood of offending.

Adult Influences/Outcomes

Sampson and Laub (1993) suggest that adult crime can be understood in terms of **cumulative continuity**, where behaviour is sustained by the process of its consequences. Early negative behaviours, such as crime, are associated with negative adult behaviours,

disrupted social control
Events or life circumstances that weaken or destroy the relationships, attachments, and activities that provide barriers to engaging in criminal activities.

cumulative continuity
A developmental model that outlines how crime in adolescence has negative consequences for future life chances in areas such as education, relationships, and employment, and increases the likelihood that criminal behaviour will continue into adulthood. These in turn undermine further life chances, escalating the probability of continued, persistent criminal behaviour.

including continued participation in crime. Further, criminal behaviour persists into adulthood because it undermines prospective life chances and adult social control. Negative life experiences associated with earlier criminal participation, arrest, conviction, and incarceration may lead to school failure and unemployment, thereby decreasing future opportunities. Moreover, previous criminal involvement can jeopardize informal social bonds with family, friends, and school, making vulnerable the creation and progress of adult social bonds. Thus, childhood criminal behaviour leads indirectly to adult criminal behaviour by undermining adult social bonds.

While there is continuity in criminal behaviour, socialization experiences and significant life events in adulthood can offset or neutralize the sway of earlier life events. **Life-course turning points**, such as employment and marriage, can modify and shift life **trajectories**. In particular, transitions that contain social ties, monitoring, and social support that supply social control can alter a person's trajectory away from offending. Alternatively, transitions that destroy sources of social control can move a person from non-offender to offender. In either case, pathways to both crime and conformity, independent of prior criminal propensity, can be modified by key social control institutions.

The type of routine activities the individual engages in also influences trajectories. Different routines influence the behavioural choices available to individuals. For example, spending time out on the street at night with other offenders increases the likelihood of involvement in crime. In contrast, spending time with extended family or at work decreases criminal choices. Further, individuals whose social controls become damaged or undermined in adulthood are likely to change their routine activities, increasing the likelihood of anti-social behaviour.

Human agency is the last factor that shapes offending trajectories. Individuals are seen to be actively involved in actions to transform their situations. This is the idea of **situated choice**. People make choices to get involved in certain relationships, be they work or personal, but these choices are situated under certain structural and historical conditions. These choices, in turn, will influence behaviour.

Current Empirical Research into the Age-Graded Theory of Social Control

The age-graded theory of social control has been the target of a range of research. The work on childhood and adolescence provides a great deal of support for the associations of weak family and school bonds with youth crime (Laub, Sampson, and Sweeten 2006; Sampson and Laub 1993). Further, research outlines the negative impact social-structural factors have on social bonds (see Laub et al. 2006). There is also considerable evidence that criminal behaviour continues from adolescence into young adulthood and beyond. Part of this persistence is explained by the continuing effect of the anti-social propensity, such as low self-control. But research also details the effects that this propensity and adolescent offending have on undermining adult opportunities and social bonds.

There is also corroboration for behavioural change. For example, research indicates that creating a social bond through education, associations with conventional others

life-course turning points
Events such as marriage/divorce or employment/unemployment that serve to direct an individual's developmental criminal career path toward either desistance or onset.

trajectories
Paths or avenues of development throughout the lifespan. These are long-term patterns of behaviour that often consist of marriage, parenthood, employment, and involvement in criminal activities.

situated choice
The choices individuals make to become involved in certain relationships, be they work or personal, that are situated under certain structural and historical conditions and that can influence future behaviour.

(Blomberg, Bales, Mann, Piquero, and Berk 2011; Melde and Esbensen 2014; Pyrooz 2014; Pyrooz, Decker, and Webb 2014; Sweeten, Pyrooz, and Piquero 2013), marriage (where an attachment bond is formed with a conventional partner), or getting a stable job (that establishes a social bond) leads to desistance, even where there are poor criminal justice histories and criminal propensity (Berg and Heubner 2011; Laub et al. 2006; Sampson and Laub 1993). In addition, social control relationships that change routine activities and reduce offending opportunities decrease offending. Finally, work on agency suggests that people do make decisions to desist or persist in offending (Laub and Sampson 2003; Laub et al. 2006). At the same time, it appears that these changes often begin prior to the turning points (e.g., employment). This indicates that people prepare and make an effort to seek change and these changes in social bonds serve to reinforce and facilitate the change (Skardhamar and Savolainen 2014).

Moffitt's Developmental Taxonomy of Offenders

Terrie Moffitt's (1993) developmental taxonomy sets out to identify the different types of offenders that exist. Moffitt argues there are two key types of offending paths. The first is the *adolescence-limited* path. For Moffitt, offending in adolescence is common and "near normative," and the adolescence-limited path includes the majority of young people who participate in crime. **Adolescence-limited offenders** (ALs) restrict their offending to their adolescent years. Their criminal behaviour is linked to two key factors: the maturity gap and deviant peers. The *maturity gap* refers to the situation where adolescents start to resemble adults biologically. At the same time, these young people are not yet socially and legally recognized as adults, depriving them of adult privileges and obligations. For some young people, the incongruity between their biological maturity and their social maturity leads to perceptions of strain. This creates deviant responses to close the biological/social position gap. Offending usually takes the form of behaviours that reflect adult status, including alcohol use, smoking, sexual activities, and property crimes to fund these activities. The second key factor, deviant peers, is important because such peers are the source from which the deviant activities are learned.

Moffitt argues that ALs will discontinue their offending as they move from adolescence into adulthood and the maturity gap closes. As adults, they are legally able to engage in their preferred activities. Further, since these youth were pro-social prior to their offending onset, they have a catalogue of pro-social behaviour to draw from that allows for an easy transition back into conventional life. However, for a small number of ALs this transition is difficult because of the poor education, criminal record, and/or addiction acquired during their offending. This may snare them in an anti-social environment that can delay movement back into a conventional lifestyle.

The second group that Moffitt identifies are **life-course persistent offenders** (LCPs). These offenders have early onset of anti-social behaviour and continue to engage in crime over much of their lives. They comprise a small proportion of the offenders (5 to 10 per cent) but account for the bulk of offending (research suggests 50 per cent). The root cause

adolescence-limited offenders
Individuals who begin their offending in, and restrict their offending to, adolescence.

life-course persistent offenders
Individuals who begin their offending in early childhood and continue to engage in offending throughout adolescence and adulthood.

of LCP behaviour stems from neuro-psychological deficits developed prior to birth or soon thereafter, leaving the child in a long-term position of disadvantage. These deficiencies can be either obtained or inherited. Maternal substandard prenatal nutrition and drug and alcohol abuse, exposure to toxins, brain trauma during delivery, and heritable conditions can be linked to neuro-psychological deficiencies. Poor nutrition, a lack of affection and stimulation, as well as harsh, abusive, and erratic parenting can lead to the postnatal development of neuro-psychological deficits. These deficits leave individuals more likely to have difficult temperaments and to be hyperactive and limited or delayed in their verbal and intellectual skills.

The link between these deficits and offending is influenced by an individual's environment. Those with deficits growing up in negative environments are more likely to have negative outcomes. Disadvantaged environments are less likely to have the required social and economic resources to buffer the negative impact of deficits and redirect behaviour towards a pro-social path. Given a lack of resources, these neuro-psychological deficiencies can lead to poor family bonding, school failure, substance abuse, unstable interpersonal relationships, violent offending, and negative reactions from authorities. These outcomes, in turn, lead to the creation of barriers and the destruction of opportunities to move from anti-social behaviour, leaving LCPs more likely to offend into adulthood.

Since adolescence-limited delinquency is viewed as a normative behaviour in teens, an explanation to understand those who do not offend is required. The final group identified in the theory are the **abstainers**, or those youth who never offend. These comprise the minority of all teenage youth (approximately 10 per cent). These youth may have little interest in social activities, as well as possess certain negative personal characteristics that leave them isolated from other youth. This eliminates exposure to deviant peers as sources of learning anti-social behaviour. Further, some youth do not experience a maturity gap, therefore eliminating the basis for strain that might cause crime.

abstainers
Youth who do not offend because of negative personality characteristics, social and biological maturation consistent with each other, and a lack of exposure to criminal peers.

Current Empirical Research into the Developmental Taxonomy of Offenders

Research has tended to provide strong support for the theory of the two key offender types (see Moffitt 2006, 2018 for a review). Work shows that life-course persistent offenders can be predicted by both individual neuro-psychological deficits and negative environmental factors. Further, LCPs tend to continue offending past their teenage years into early adulthood, specializing in serious offences. In contrast, adolescence-limited offenders tend to be drawn from "normative backgrounds," to engage in less serious offense types, and to decrease their offending upon reaching adulthood. Some work suggests that the recent societal extension of adolescence can leave some AL offenders to desist later than anticipated. Research also indicates that AL offenders can suffer from maturity gaps, be heavily influenced by their peers, and offend as a form of rebellion or exertion of greater autonomy.

Work on abstainers is more mixed. While findings indicate they are rare, making up between 5 and 13 per cent in the samples examined, some research shows that these youth are better adjusted than portrayed in the theory. They have good relationships with parents and teachers, and associations with other pro-social peers. In contrast, other work shows them to be socially isolated, to have few social skills, and to be overcontrolled by adults. Scholarship has also identified an additional group labelled *low-level chronic offenders*. The age of onset for this group can be either childhood or adolescence, and their offending appears to continue into adulthood. These offenders are similar to LCP offenders in childhood, but in adulthood they tend to exhibit different characteristics, including mental health problems (anxiety, depression, neuroticism) and social isolation. In sum, research on the taxonomy to date provides a great deal of support, with future work needed to focus on fine tuning the perspective (Moffitt 2018).

Integrated Cognitive Antisocial Potential Theory

Farrington's Integrated Cognitive Antisocial Potential Theory (Farrington 2005, 2006) is another perspective that tackles different patterns of offending. It is designed to specifically explain the criminal behaviour of lower-class males. Its central concept is **anti-social potential** (AP), the individual's probability of undertaking criminal and other anti-social behaviours. Whether this potential is translated into criminal behaviour is contingent on the individual's thinking, resulting decisions, and crime opportunities. In the theory, there is a focus on (a) between-individual differences in long-term anti-social potential and (b) short-term within-individual differences in anti-social potential.

A person's **long-term anti-social potential** is influenced by life events, socialization, strain, observational learning, and impulsiveness. Negative life events can include family poverty, poor child rearing, disrupted families, and school failure. Socialization is associated with low attachment to parents, parental rejection, and inconsistent parental sanctions. Strain includes quests for peer group status, material goods, and excitement. Anti-social potential is also more likely to develop when individuals are constantly exposed to anti-social models, including criminal parents, siblings, and peers. Finally, impulsiveness—partly a result of poor socialization and partly perhaps inherited from high AP parents—increases long-term AP and failure in other environments (e.g., school) that influence long-term AP. Positive life events, effective parenting, and isolation from criminal models all decrease the likelihood of developing long-term AP. Once developed, both high and low long-term anti-social potential are argued to be stable. Those with high long-term AP have a greater probability of early onset anti-social behaviour, versatility in forms of offending and anti-social behaviour, very high offending rates, and persistence in offending for long periods of time.

Whereas long-term AP differs between individuals, **short-term anti-social potential** varies within the individual. Short-term AP is influenced by motivational factors that are time limited. Time-limited factors might include intoxication, negative emotions, boredom, peer influences, or enticing offending opportunities that lead to short-term increases in a person's AP.

Whether individuals commit a crime will depend on their long-term AP level, the availability of opportunities and victims, and their short-term AP. The likelihood of offending is influenced by cost/reward assessments of the behaviour, expected outcomes,

anti-social potential
An individual's probability of undertaking criminal and other anti-social behaviours.

long-term anti-social potential
The probability of a person engaging in a criminal or anti-social act that develops as a result of life events, socialization, strain, anti-social models, and impulsiveness.

short-term anti-social potential
The probability of engaging in offending that is influenced by factors limited in time, including intoxication, peers, and negative emotions.

and offending histories. Individuals with low long-term AP are unlikely to commit offences even under conditions of high rewards and few risks. However, those with low long-term AP can offend when they experience high levels of short-term AP (e.g., offences associated with intoxication or anger).

The outcomes of offending lead to a learning process that alters long-term AP levels and influences future behaviour. Success and approval can increase levels of long-term AP. Failure, including sanctions or social disapproval from family and friends, might decrease long-term AP. However, sanction forms that include stigmatization or labelling can escalate levels of long-term AP. Therefore, while there is stability in long-term AP, learning and labelling can lead to within-person changes in anti-social potential.

Empirical Research into the Integrated Cognitive Antisocial Potential Theory

Much of the empirical support for the perspective comes from Farrington's own work and its influence on the theory's development. As director of the Cambridge Youth Study for over 50 years, Farrington first empirically established a list of risk factors. He then investigated how these risk factors were independently linked to crime, exploring specific causal relationships. This allowed him to parcel out the factors outlined above and pay specific attention to the importance of each. From this vast established knowledge, Farrington (2003 for a review) developed the perspective, drawing on those factors found to be linked to crime. Since the perspective evolved from Farrington's own empirical work, little independent research has emerged. This likely also reflects the theory's complexity and the lack of extensive longitudinal data, including all the theoretical nuances required to properly assess the perspective. The limited arms-length work that does exist (e.g., Van der Laan, Blom, and Kleemans 2009), however, is supportive. This work shows the greater the number of long-term risk factors—including those related to the individual, family, and school—the greater the involvement in serious forms of crime. Further, contextual and short-term factors, such as drug and alcohol use, increase offending even after long-term factors are accounted for. Farrington and colleagues continue to fine tune the perspective as they move to extend their examinations further into the life course (see Farrington, Piquero, and Jennings 2013; Kazemian and Farrington 2018).

Interactional Theory

Terrance Thornberry's interactional theory (1987; Thornberry and Krohn 2001, 2005) draws on core arguments from social control and social learning theories to explain variations in offenders, and offending, across the life course. Beginning with social control assumptions, the theory outlines how weak social bonds (a lack of attachment to parents, commitment to school, and beliefs in conventional values) increase the behavioural and moral freedoms that lead to crime onset. Unlike the social control model, however, these factors do not necessarily lead to crime. Instead, a learning environment is important to help route low social control to crime. Key are criminal peer associations and the adoption of values supportive of crime. Peers provide the models and social reinforcement for engaging in crime, and values accepting of illegal conduct also increase offending.

Unique to the interactional approach is its premise that this developmental process is reciprocal, or bi-directional across time. First, this can happen within the social control concepts. For example, poor parental attachment can lead to school failure and detachment. Over time, in turn, school disengagement can lead to further reduced attachment to parents. Second, this can also take place in the links between social control and social learning factors. Low social control can lead to entry into deviant peer groups and to the adoption of non-conventional values, but these in turn can further damage relationships with parents and undermine school commitment. Third, there is a **reciprocal relationship** between social learning concepts and crime. While deviant peers and deviant values can increase the likelihood of crime, criminal participation can also lead individuals to select into deviant peer groups and can strengthen acceptability of offending. Finally, crime itself can influence social control. While a lack of parental attachment and school failure might lead to crime, crime may also lead to decreased attachment to parents and school.

The reciprocal relationships outlined above generate distinctive offending trajectories, highlighting different behaviours. Those youth with strong family and school bonds, and an isolation from deviant peers, are unlikely to offend. In contrast, serious and chronic offenders emerge from families with problems that undermine home and school bonds and provide access to criminal peers. In between these two ideal types are trajectories reflecting differing levels of the causal factors. Initial values on the factors producing the trajectories are influenced by structural elements including social class and neighbourhood. Young people in poor families living in areas of extreme poverty will be more likely to experience the pressures leading to weak bonds and criminal peer access.

The theory is also concerned with timing of offending onset. Childhood onset is explained by three influences: social disadvantage, individual factors, and ineffectual parenting. Early initiators will tend to exhibit a range of undesirable developmental traits and neuro-psychological deficits including risk-seeking, negative emotionality, and impulsivity. These children are often immersed in extremely disadvantaged homes in communities of severe poverty. They are more likely to experience minimal parental monitoring and affection, and greater maltreatment risk. The stresses of disadvantage leave parents with few support and coping resources to properly respond to negative childhood temperamental factors, contributing to the further development of traits and deficits.

Late childhood/early adolescence onset of offending is more strongly linked to environment. These are the processes in the general model where diminished bonds, deviant peers and values, and their reciprocal consequences influence crime participation. Finally, late adolescence/early adult onset is influenced by other individual deficits. These individuals may have lower human capital (e.g., academic competence) as well as suffer from anxiety, depression, and other complications. At early ages, these human capital and individual deficits are often compensated for by family, school, and community support. However, as the individual moves toward independence and away from institutional protection, these individual deficits begin to manifest anti-social conduct.

reciprocal relationship
The process where two causal factors influence each other.

Continuity and Change

While there is some expected relationship between early onset and continuity in offending, persistence in offending is possible regardless of onset timing. Persistence in offending will depend on two factors. The first, the stability of factors contributing to initial onset, is most applicable to early childhood onset offenders. The stability of poverty, negative personality factors, and poor parenting styles will continue to negatively influence behaviour and they partially explain continuity. The second process is more general and applies to all offenders regardless of onset age. The reciprocal relationships between the crime-causing factors continue to intensify their criminogenic influence, leading to continued offending.

Most offenders, however, are expected to desist from offending. The transition from adolescence to adulthood offers prospects for new social bond forms that can alter offending paths. These may be employment, romantic relationships, and/or parenthood. The relationships and role expectations create new attachments and values, reduce negative associations with peers, and disrupt offending. The result is reciprocal relationships that begin to work in reverse. Pro-social attachments, commitments, and beliefs lead to pro-social behaviours, which in turn increase pro-social attachments, commitments, and beliefs. Individuals who fail to find conventional roles will persist in offending. Those most seriously embedded in the criminal trajectory find transition difficult since they are less attractive as workers, romantic partners, and peers.

Empirical Research on Interactional Theory

There has been a large amount of empirical support for interactional theory. A review of research exploring the reciprocal effects shows that weak bonding leads to offending, which then feeds back and further decreases bonding. Further, peer associations and criminal moral values increase offending, which then solidifies peer relationships and beliefs (see Thornberry, 1996; Thornberry, Lizotte, Krohn, Smith, and Porter 2003 for reviews of research). There is also support indicating that involvement in crime disrupts adolescent development and creates long-term consequences for transitions into adulthood. Thornberry (2005, 2009) has also begun theoretical extensions, examining the importance of intergenerational transmission in the process. This research has uncovered that children of parents who themselves have anti-social histories are more likely to become involved in crime. This is a result of parents having gone through the developmental path described above. The parents tend to have histories of drop-out and failure, unstable romantic formations, and patterns of under-/unemployment and crime that complicate transitions into adulthood, increasing the likelihood of personal poverty and residence in disadvantaged neighbourhoods. These backgrounds increase the likelihood of additional adverse experiences, including financial difficulties, mental health issues, and family conflict, which undermine parenting. Further, there are often continued deviant peer association and anti-social activities but little bonding to conventional activities and institutions. The inconsistent monitoring, absence of affective relationships, and inconsistent and often extreme disciplinary strategies that emerge combine to support the child's anti-social behaviour.

Coercion Theory

Gerald Patterson (Patterson, DeBaryshe, and Ramsey 1989) offers a developmental model in which coercion is the vital factor. The model argues that the developmental process begins with child socialization in the home. Anti-social children will tend to be drawn from homes where there is poor monitoring and supervision; few rewards for pro-social conduct; minimal parent–child involvement; and inconsistent, harsh disciplinary techniques. These conditions lead to regular parent–child interactions that reward coercive behaviour. The process begins with children using "aversive" behaviours in response to parental interventions. An example of a typical cycle might be the child responding coercively (complaining) to parent requests for obedience. Continued parental demands for compliance are met with escalated coercive responses from the child (temper tantrum). Frustrated with the coercive responses and lack of compliance, parents capitulate, permitting compliance avoidance. This rewards the child's defiant behaviour and increases the likelihood of further coercive responses to future compliance requests. Further, the respite from the coercive displays (temper tantrums) received by withdrawing compliance expectations leaves parents more likely to withdraw from future coercive interactions with the child. Over time, both child and parent progressively increase the severity of their actions, often to the point of physical assaults by the child. These exchanges replicated over time provide the groundwork for early childhood aggression. Individuals learn to be aggressive from parental tolerance for coercion and from observations of parental use of violence to control family members. These environments, however, fail to provide pro-social skills and problem-solving strategies.

Aggressive behaviour and deficient social skills disadvantage these children when they begin school, initiating a process that further entrenches anti-social tendencies and outcomes. The lack of pro-social problem-solving skills and coercive behaviour patterns leads to academic failure. The child's unco-operative tendencies undermine learning. They are less likely to attend school regularly, follow classroom protocol, respond to requests from authority, and complete required tasks. At the same time, their aggressive behaviour leads to peer rejection. Their underdeveloped social skills leave them disadvantaged in understanding group entry processes, group expectations, and proper pro-social responses to interactions within groups. Coercive interaction styles and conventional peer rejection lead anti-social youth to select into anti-social peer groups. Weak parental supervision serves to exacerbate this process. In these anti-social groups, peers provide the opportunities, motivations, and rationalizations that increase the likelihood of offending. Anti-social peers become vital in maintaining and producing crime and other negative life outcomes, including unemployment, marital problems, and incarceration.

Patterson distinguishes between early and late starters. People who start offending in late childhood are at an increased risk of developing into chronic offenders. These **early starters** tend to follow the pattern described above. These types of people exhibit high levels of anti-social behaviour in early childhood and move to more aggressive behaviours in middle childhood. As they progress, they develop histories of early criminal justice system contact, chronic participation in crime as teenagers, early adulthood arrest, and chronic offending in adulthood.

early starters
Youth who exhibit anti-social behaviour in preschool years, have early arrest and chronic offending in adolescence, and become adult career offenders.

People who commit their first offence in middle to late adolescence are **late starters**. They do not experience peer rejection or school failure and their offending behaviour tends to be transient. Further, they tend to have developed social skills that allow them to identify and interpret social cues from others. Unlike early starters, for whom deviant peer groups are key in maintaining already strongly established anti-social inclinations, for late starters, peers are more firmly linked to the development of deviant behaviour. Overall, because late starters lack the training of early starters, they are unlikely to continue their anti-social activities into adulthood.

late starters
Youth who begin offending in adolescence with patterns of criminal behaviour that are transient rather than chronic and that dissipate upon entry into adulthood.

Empirical Support for Coercion Theory

Patterson provides a great deal of evidence in support of the perspective, and work continues to provide more nuanced and sophisticated models to understand the process (for review, see Granic and Patterson 2006). For example, research shows that parental attributions for children's initial misbehaviour (e.g., argues, disobeys, has tantrums) is linked to parental hostility and ineffective discipline, which increases child misbehaviour at both home and school (Snyder, Cramer, Afrank, and Patterson 2005). Other work details that as teacher social support, academic support, and conventional peer social support decline, there is an increase in deviant peer affiliation. The lack of social support from all three sources, as well as deviant peer affiliation, lead to increased offending over time (Wang and Dishion 2011). Granic and Patterson (2006) have begun to broaden the theory, taking into account how heritable factors, negative prenatal experiences (e.g., exposure to lead, alcohol, and drugs), and birth complications might influence initial propensity. Further, parental constraints influencing parenting styles, including depression and negative socio-economic contexts, are also now being suggested for exploration. Therefore, the theory has provided a range a positive results but continues to evolve in response to theoretical development and empirical research.

Peacemaking Criminology

Peacemaking criminology (see Pepinksy and Quinney 1991) outlines how philosophies and doctrines of peace can be utilized in achieving justice. Peacemaking theorists argue that the current criminal justice system approach of attempting to deter people from offending through threats and the application of force is violent and likely to lead to additional violence. To address this issue, a social justice approach is advocated as a method of correcting wrongs or improving problems.

The key premise of the theory is that various forms of suffering, including inequality, poverty, alienation, racism, and sexism, foster criminogenic responses and must be alleviated or mitigated. Addressing these problems requires micro- and macro-level societal transformation. Therefore, economic factors, environmental features, social components, cognitive and spiritual development, and political ideologies/agendas all must be dealt with to achieve a more peaceful society. Further, peacemaking criminology offers a philosophy of non-violent punishment that stresses alternative criminal justice approaches, including restoring the offender to the community, rather than policies focusing on deterrence, retribution, or punishment.

peacemaking criminology
A theoretical approach that emphasizes non-violent punishment and stresses alternative criminal justice approaches, including restoring the offender to the community, rather than deterrence and retribution.

Fuller and Wozniack (2006) outline six key themes central to a peacemaking approach. The first is *non-violence*. This applies both to offenders, who peacemaking theorists argue should not engage in violence, and to the criminal justice system, which they say should not perpetuate violence through responses to offending. Next, *social justice* stresses opposition to any form of classism, sexism, or racism, in the criminal justice system. Peacemaking criminologists outline that "only by promoting the welfare of all, including those without power, can society develop a long-term atmosphere of cooperation and commitment" (Fuller and Wozniack 2006, p. 261). The principle of *inclusion* in the criminal justice system is also essential. All victims, offenders, family members, and interested community members should have a voice in the criminal justice process. Inclusion promotes conciliation, encourages forgiveness, and helps restoration. The process should also avoid coercion and utilize *correct means*. This stresses the need for the system to derive an outcome in a moral and ethical manner. The process should also include *ascertainable criteria*. There should be a transparency in the process. Further, to ensure that participants understand the criminal justice process, all should be educated in the procedures of the proceedings. The final theme, *categorical imperative* emphasizes that responses should be similar for all participants regardless of gender, class or race, and that all individuals should be considered with value and propriety. At the same time, the theory recognizes that individualized justice may be appropriate to restore relationships and assist in healing and rehabilitation.

Empirical Research on Peacemaking Theory

The theory has been criticized as abstract, untestable, and limited by unrealistic ambitions (see Akers and Sellers 2009; Fuller and Wozniack 2006; Klenowski 2009), but peacemaking criminology has been at the heart of many policies and programs within the criminal justice system (see Chapter 16). Many of these have their heritage in ideas of restorative justice, a form of justice that looks to address both the wrongs and harms of offenders while also taking into account the victim's and broader community's perspectives and insights about appropriate responses. Some examples of restorative justice programs include victim–offender mediation, community policing, programs focusing on conflict resolution, diversion and informal punishment approaches, offender reintegration, and programs stressing treatment or rehabilitation over retributive forms of punishment (Braswell, Fuller, and Lozoff 2001). While these programs may not have developed or been evaluated explicitly within the peacemaking theoretical approach, they do provide indirect evidence of its usefulness. However, Fuller and Wozniak (2006, p. 271) warn that it will take "another generation of criminologists before peacemaking criminology develops into a testable theory that can concretely guide criminal justice policy."

Crime Pattern Theory

Paul and Patricia Brantingham's (1991, 2008) crime pattern theory outlines the interweaving among an offender's motivation for crime, the attractiveness of potential targets for crime, and the environmental backdrop within which this takes place. Based on past empirical research and theoretical advances, the theory provides rules to help understand patterns in crime.

The theory outlines that people's daily routines (both legitimate and illegitimate) require them to make decisions. Regularized activities can lead to regularized decisions, or scripts, that guide future decisions. For those involved in crime, these are referred to as "crime scripts," and with more knowledge of the activities, they can become **crime templates** (2008, p. 80). Contained within these templates are often assessments of rewards and risks that shift the individual toward specific offence forms (e.g., violent versus property crime).

Second, social networks are very important because they provide access to others' templates, which individuals can also draw upon in making their decisions. If these collective templates are pulled from those who support criminal activities, then they become an important part of the causal process. Individuals or groups of individuals will engage in an offence when an offending opportunity fits with information within the individual or group crime template. Success or failure in the offence then leads to an alteration in the crime template for future reference.

Third, crime pattern theory outlines that there are "activity nodes" and pathways among nodes where people undertake their daily routine activities (home, school, employment, leisure, shopping). These activity nodes, and the routes among them, are referred to as **activity spaces**. Since individuals develop familiarity with these pathways and their environments, the areas become "awareness space." In the theory, crime will take place near activity and awareness spaces. The activity spaces of potential offenders and potential victims and targets will tend to overlap since these are part of, or within, normal activity spaces. Potential human or property targets will become actual targets if they set off perceptions within an offender's crime template. Offences will often occur simply through offenders encountering opportunities in their daily routine activities. Alternatively, offenders may seek opportunities at activity nodes within their awareness spaces.

Activity nodes where crime is more likely tend to have large flows of human traffic. These include entertainment, shopping, and leisure sites, or nodes with reputations for offending opportunities, including drug markets, nightclubs or bars, and areas associated with sex trade activities. Victimization increases when a large number of targets are available for those with motivation for offending at these sites.

Empirical Research into Crime Pattern Theory

Empirical support for the theory has been extensive. Work shows that offending does tend to take place in certain activity spaces. Research indicates that offenders do draw on their prior experiences, and on assessments of opportunities, rewards, and risks, in developing offending templates. These prior offences provide information on locational accessibility, guardianship, and escape routes. Scholarship also shows that prior offending locations have a strong impact on choosing future offending locations (Bernasco, Johnson, and Ruiter 2015; Lammers, Menting, Ruiter, and Bernasco 2015). The literature on repeat victimization details that victims are often targeted again within a short period. In an extension to the perspective, scholars have discovered that beyond current activity spaces, an offenders' prior activity space (former residential locations) can also influence offending (Bernasco 2010). Further, research shows that the timing of previous offences (e.g., the time of day and week when the offence takes place) in certain locations is also important

crime templates
Guidelines for behavioural decisions regarding crime that people derive from their regular activities, offending experiences, and knowledge.

activity spaces
The broad areas that encompass the locations where individuals conduct their daily regular activities, and the routes among these locations.

because of the specific information it provides that does not necessarily transfer to other times and offences (Van Sleeuwen, Ruiter, and Menting 2018). Support for the perspective grows as researchers continue to explore the puzzles associated with different locations and offences, and with the timing of offences.

Summary

Our review of emerging theoretical perspectives on youth crime has provided a breadth of possible explanations for youth offending. These theories have all attempted to go beyond the limited explanatory power of the traditional arguments on the subject. Recognizing both the strengths and weaknesses in past perspectives, these theories bring together aspects of social learning, social control, and strain theories to deliver more comprehensive explanations for offending. But the theories also build on these past perspectives with unique and novel ideas, ranging from the importance of control imbalances and self-control to issues of coercion and emotions. We have also reviewed a number of perspectives that have tried to understand the different offending patterns of youth and why people enter, continue, and leave offending. These perspectives are important in that they identify both continuity and change within individuals. Further, they integrate aspects of the traditional explanations, as well as ideas from the other newly developed perspectives, including self-control and coercion, to extend explanations of offending. They also point us to the importance of recognizing how broader negative environments can shape individual-level responses that have implications for socialization and behaviour. We have also examined how these types of broader issues might shape criminal justice responses that are criminogenic and offer insights into changes that might offer ways to influence future behaviour in a more humane, just, and successful fashion. Finally, we see how the environment itself, and how we conduct our daily activities and create views and approaches towards acting in various spaces, is influential in offending.

Our review of the recent theoretical developments in youth crime shows the variety of ways in which scholars have approached the topic. Further, our empirical reviews show that all of the approaches have some merit in understanding crime. Some, such as the general theory of crime, have focused on a mono-causal approach. Others have outlined perspectives that incorporate a broader range of factors that attempt to more clearly specify how the central factor will lead to crime and under what conditions. Further, some of these approaches have adopted a strategy for theoretical development whereby they attempt to bring in useful pieces of other theoretical perspectives. Rather than viewing different theoretical perspectives as competitors, we would do well to recognize that, to successfully understand youth crime, we must recognize and include ideas not normally viewed as complementary. These ideas need to be gathered up and incorporated in the causal process, allowing for a more complex and nuanced understanding of how youth crime emerges and evolves. This strategy enables researchers to posit various possible entry points for youth to explore crime; it also establishes that there may be more than one possible causal path to crime. As we think about youth crime, we must provide a number of possible answers to the many questions we might pose. Then, theories provide a number of insights into how we might answer such questions.

Key Terms

abstainers

activity spaces

adolescence-limited offenders

anti-social potential

coercion

control balance

crime templates

cumulative continuity

disrupted social control

early starters

informal social control

late starters

life-course persistent offenders

life-course turning points

long-term anti-social potential

low self-control

moral actions

peacemaking criminology

reciprocal relationship

short-term anti-social potential

situated choice

social bonds

strains

trajectories

Review Questions

1. Gottfredson and Hirschi's argument suggests that low self-control leads not only to crime but also to negative social outcomes. Why would this be the case?

2. Using general strain theory, outline the type of young person who would most likely turn to criminal activities in an attempt to cope with his or her strain.

3. Outline the key differences among adolescence-limited offenders, life-course persistent offenders, and those who never engage in crime.

4. Outline the main causal process that could lead a youth to desist from crime, according to the age-graded theory of social control.

5. Summarize Colvin's four types of controls, and discuss which of the four types is most likely to lead to serious offending and for what reasons.

6. Outline the conditions under which a person, upon entering an activity space, might engage in offending.

Critical Thinking Questions

1. In Colvin's theory of crime and coercion, a number of social-psychological mechanisms are identified. How do these mechanisms relate to some of the other perspectives that we have read about or discussed in class? Do we benefit from including various perspectives together?

2. Gottfredson and Hirschi's general theory of crime sees self-control as a trait that is relatively stable and unchangeable, leading to a life of participation in crime and other negative activities. Compare this with how Sampson and Laub might view this issue.

3. Explore the ways in which different types of contingency variables (e.g., peers, values, self-efficacy), either together, or individually, may be more important in moderating the impacts of certain forms of strain on crime than others.

4.   Thornberry details reciprocal relationships between social control, learning factors, and crime. Are there other factors that might be introduced into this model from some of the other theories examined in this chapter that could strengthen this perspective?

References

Agnew, R. (1992). Foundation for a general strain theory of crime and delinquency. *Criminology, 30*(1), 47–87.

Agnew, R. (2001). Building on the foundation of general strain theory: Specifying the types of strain that most likely lead to crime and delinquency. *Journal of Research in Crime and Delinquency, 38*(4), 319–61.

Agnew, R. (2006). *Pressured into crime: An overview of general strain theory.* Los Angeles: Roxbury.

Agnew, R. (2013). When criminal coping is likely: An extension of general strain theory. *Deviant Behavior, 24(8),* 653–70.

Akers, R.L., and Sellers, C.S. (2009). *Criminological theories: Introduction, evaluation, and application* (5th ed.). New York: Oxford University Press.

Antonaccio, O., Tittle, C.R., Brauer, J.R., and Islam, M.Z. (2015). Supported or coerced? A cross-site investigation of the effects of social support and coercion on criminal probability. *Journal of Quantitative Criminology, 31*(1), 49–92.

Baron, S.W. (2003). Self-control, social consequences, and criminal behavior: Street youth and the general theory of crime. *Journal of Research in Crime and Delinquency, 40*(4), 403–25.

Baron, S.W. (2004). General strain, street youth, and crime: Testing Agnew's revised theory. *Criminology, 42*(2), 457–83.

Baron, S.W. (2009). Differential coercion, street youth, and violent crime. *Criminology, 47*(1), 239–68.

Baron, S.W. (2010). Street youths' control imbalance and soft and hard drug use. *Journal of Criminal Justice, 38*(5), 903–12.

Baron, S.W. (2015). Differential social support, differential coercion, and organized criminal activities. *Justice Quarterly, 32*(6), 1089–117

Baron, S.W. (2019). Strain, criminal propensity, and violence: Examining the role of the composite moderator in Agnew's extension to GST. *Crime & Delinquency, 65*(6), 801–21.

Baron, S.W., and Forde, D.R. (2007). Street youth crime: A test of control balance theory. *Justice Quarterly, 24*(2), 335–55.

Berg, M.T., and Huebner, B.M. (2011). Reentry and the ties that bind: An examination of social ties, employment, and recidivism. *Justice Quarterly, 28*(2), 382–410.

Bernasco, W. (2010). A sentimental journey to crime: Effects of residential history on crime location choice. *Criminology, 48*(2), 389–416.

Bernasco W., Johnson S.D., and Ruiter S. (2015). Learning where to offend: Effects of past on future burglary locations. *Applied Geography, 60*, 120–9.

Blomberg, T.G., Bales, W.D., Mann, K., Piquero, A.R., and Berk, R.A. (2011). Incarceration, education, and transition from delinquency. *Journal of Criminal Justice, 39*(4), 355–65.

Brantingham, P.L., and Brantingham, P.J. (1991). *Environmental criminology* (2nd ed.). Prospect Heights, IL: Waveland Press.

Brantingham, P.L., and Brantingham, P.J. (2008). Crime pattern theory. In R. Wortly and L. Mazerolle (Eds), *Environmental criminology and crime analysis* (pp. 78–93). Portland, OR: Willan.

Braswell, M., Fuller, J., and Lozoff, B. (2001). *Corrections, peacemaking, and restorative justice: Transforming individuals and institutions.* Cincinnati, OH: Anderson.

Brauer, J.R., Tittle, C.R., and Antonaccio, O. (2019). The costs of coercive control: Assessing behavioral and mental health correlates of erratic and oppressive coercion. *Justice Quarterly, 36*(2), 255–86.

Colvin, M. (2000). *Crime and coercion: An integrated theory of chronic criminality.* New York: St Martin's Press.

Colvin, M., Cullen, F.T., and Vander Ven, T. (2002). Coercion, social support, and crime: An emerging theoretical consensus. *Criminology, 40*(1), 9–42.

Farrington, D.P. (2003). Key results from the first forty years of the Cambridge Study of Delinquent Development. In T.P. Thornberry and M.D. Krohn (Eds), *Taking stock of delinquency: An overview of findings from contemporary longitudinal studies* (pp. 133–83). New York: Kluwer/Plenum.

Farrington, D.P. (2005). The integrated cognitive antisocial potential (ICAP) theory: In D.P. Farrington (Ed.), *Integrated developmental and life-course theories of offending* (pp. 73–92). New Brunswick, NJ: Transaction.

Farrington, D.P. (2006). Building developmental and life-course theories of offending. In F.T. Cullen, J.P. Wright, and K.R. Blevins (Eds), *Taking stock: The status of criminological theory. Advances in criminological theory,* vol. 15 (pp. 335–64). New Brunswick, NJ: Transaction.

Farrington, D.P., Piquero, A.R., and Jennings W.G. (2013). *Offending from childhood to late middle age: Recent results from the Cambridge study in delinquent development.* New York: Springer.

Fuller, J.R. and Wozniack, J.F. (2006). Peacemaking criminology: Past, present and future. In F.T. Cullen, J.P. Wright, and K.R. Blevins (Eds), *Taking stock: The status of criminological* theory. *Advances in criminological theory*, vol. 15 (pp. 251–73). New Brunswick, NJ: Transaction.

Gallupe, O., and Baron, S.W. (2014). SAT and street youths' drug use. *Crime and Delinquency*, 60(2), 284–305.

Gottfredson, M.R., and Hirschi, T. (1990). *A general theory of crime*. Stanford: Stanford University Press.

Granic, I., and Patterson, G.R. (2006). Toward a comprehensive model of antisocial development: A dynamic systems approach. *Psychological Review, 113*(1), 101–31.

Haar, D.H., and Wikström, P.H. (2010). Crime propensity, criminogenic exposure and violent scenario responses: Testing situational action theory in regression and Rasch models. *European Journal of Applied Mathematics, 21*(4–5), 307–23.

Hughes, L.A., Antonaccio, O., and Botchkovar, E.V. (2015). How general is control balance theory? Evidence from Ukraine. *Justice Quarterly, 32*(6), 950–75.

Kazemian, L., and Farrington, D.P. (2018). Advancing knowledge about residual criminal careers: A follow-up to age 56 from the Cambridge study in delinquent development. *Journal of Criminal Justice, 57*, 1–10.

Klenowski, P.M. (2009). Peacemaking criminology. Etiology of crime or philosophy of life? *Contemporary Justice Review, 12*(2), 207–22.

Kurtz, D.L., and Zavala, E. (2017). The importance of social support and coercion in the development of impulsivity and juvenile offending. *Crime & Delinquency, 63*(14), 1838–60.

Lammers, M., Menting, B., Ruiter, S., and Bernasco, W. (2015). Biting once twice: The influence of prior on subsequent crime location choice. *Criminology, 53*(13), 309–29.

Laub, J.H., and Sampson, R.J. (2003). *Shared beginnings, divergent lives: Delinquent boys to age 70*. Cambridge: Harvard University Press.

Laub, J.H., Sampson, R.J., and Sweeten, G.A. (2006). Assessing Sampson and Laub's life-course theory. In F.T. Cullen, J.P. Wright, and K.R. Blevins (Eds), *Taking stock: The status of criminological theory: Advances in criminological theory*, vol. 15 (pp. 313–33). New Brunswick, NJ: Transaction.

Melde, C., and Esbensen, F.A. (2014). The relative impact of gang status transitions: Identifying the mechanisms of change in delinquency. *Journal of Research in Crime and Delinquency, 51*(3), 349–76.

Meldrum, R.C., Young, J.T.N., and Weerman, F.M. (2012). Changes in self-control during adolescence: Investigating the influence of the adolescent peer network. *Journal of Criminal Justice, 40*(6), 452–62.

Moffitt, T.E. (1993). Adolescence-limited and life-course-persistent antisocial behavior: A developmental taxonomy. *Psychological Review, 100*(4), 674–701.

Moffitt, T.E. (2006). A review of research on the taxonomy of life-course persistent versus adolescence-limited antisocial behavior. In F.T. Cullen, J.P. Wright, and K.R. Blevins (Eds), *Taking stock: The status of criminological theory. Advances in criminological theory*, vol. 15, (pp. 277–311). New Brunswick, NJ. Transaction.

Moffitt, T.E. (2018). Male antisocial behavior in adolescence and beyond. *Nature Human Behaviour, 2*, 177–86.

Moon, B., and Morash, M. (2017). A test of general strain theory in South Korea: A focus on objective/subjective strain, negative emotions, and composite conditioning factors. *Crime & Delinquency, 63*(6), 731–56.

Na, C., and Paternoster, R. (2012). Can self-control change substantially over time? Rethinking the relationship between self- and social control. *Criminology, 50*(2), 427–62.

Nobles, M.R., and Fox, K.A. (2013). Assessing stalking behaviors in a control balance theory framework. *Criminal Justice and Behavior, 40*(7), 737–62.

Patterson, G.R., DeBaryshe, B.D., and Ramsey, E. (1989). A developmental perspective on antisocial behavior. *American Psychologist, 44*(2), 329–35.

Pauwels, L.R., Svensson, R., and Hirtenlehner, H. (2018). Testing situational action theory: A narrative review of studies published between 2006 and 2015. *European Journal of Criminology, 15*(1), 32–55.

Pepinsky, H.E., and Quinney, R. (Eds). (1991). *Criminology as peacemaking*. Bloomington: Indiana University Press.

Piquero, A.R., Jennings, W.G., and Farrington, D.P. (2010). On the malleability of self-control: Theoretical and policy implications regarding a general theory of crime. *Justice Quarterly, 27*(6), 803–4.

Pratt, T.C., Turanovic, J.J., Fox, K.A., and Wright, K.A. (2014). Self-control and victimization: A meta-analysis. *Criminology, 52*(1), 87–116.

Pyrooz, D.C. (2014). From colors and guns to caps and gowns? The effects of gang membership on educational achievement. *Journal of Research in Crime and Delinquency, 51*(1), 56–87.

Pyrooz, D.C., Decker, S.H., and Webb, V.J. (2014). The ties that bind: Desistance from gangs. *Crime & Delinquency, 60*(4), 491–516.

Ray, J.V., Jones, S., Loughran, T.A., and Jennings W.G. (2013). Testing the stability of self-control. *Criminal Justice and Behavior, 40*(6), 588–607.

Sampson, R.J., and Laub, J.H. (1993). *Crime in the making: Pathways and turning points through life*. Cambridge: Harvard University Press.

Simons, R.L., Chen, Yi-Fu, Stewart, E.A., and Brody, G.H. (2003). Incidents of discrimination and risk for delinquency: A longitudinal test of strain theory with an African-American sample. *Justice Quarterly, 20*(4), 827–54.

Skardhamar, T., and Savolainen, J. (2014), Changes in criminal offending around the time of job entry: A study of employment and desistance. *Criminology, 52*(2), 263–91.

Snyder, J., Cramer, A., Afrank, J., and Patterson, G.R. (2005). The contributions of ineffective discipline and parental hostile attributions of child misbehavior to the development of conduct problems at home and school. *Developmental Psychology, 41*(1), 30–41.

Sweeten, G., Pyrooz, D.C., and Piquero, A.R. (2013). Disengaging from gangs and desistance. *Justice Quarterly, 30*(3), 469–500.

Thaxton, S., and Agnew, R. (2018). When criminal coping is likely: An examination of conditioning effects in general strain theory. *Journal of Quantitative Criminology, 34*(4), 887–920.

Thornberry, T.P. (1987). Toward an interactional theory of delinquency. *Criminology, 25*(4), 863–91.

Thornberry, T.P. (1996). Empirical support for interactional theory: A review of the literature. In J.D. Hawkins (Ed), *Delinquency and crime: Current theories* (pp. 198–235). New York: Cambridge University Press.

Thornberry, T.P. (2005). Explaining multiple patterns of offending across the life course and across generations. *Annals of the American Academy of Political and Social Sciences, 602*(1), 156–95.

Thornberry, T.P. (2009). The apple doesn't fall far from the tree (or does it?): Intergenerational patterns of antisocial behavior. *Criminology, 47*(2), 297–325.

Thornberry, T.P., and Krohn, M.D. (2001). The development of delinquency: An interactional perspective. In S.O. White (Ed), *Handbook of youth and justice* (pp. 289–305). New York: Plenum.

Thornberry, T.P., and Krohn, M.D. (2005). Applying interactional theory to the explanation of continuity and change in antisocial behavior. In D.P. Farrington (Ed), *Integrated development and life course theories of offending: Advances in criminological theory*, vol. 14 (pp. 183–210). Pisctaway: Transaction.

Thornberry, T.P., Lizotte, A.J., Krohn, M.D., Smith, C., and Porter, P.K. (2003). Causes and consequences of delinquency: Findings from the Rochester Youth Development Study. In T.P. Thornberry and M.D. Krohn (Eds), *Taking stock of delinquency: An overview of findings from contemporary longitudinal studies* (pp. 11–46). New York: Kluwer Academic/Plenum.

Tittle, C.R. (1995). *Control balance: Toward a general theory of deviance*. Boulder, CO: Westview.

Tittle, C.R. (2004). Refining control balance theory. *Theoretical Criminology, 8*(4), 395–428.

Unnever, J.D., Colvin, M., and Cullen, F.T. (2004). Crime and coercion: A test of core theoretical propositions. *Journal of Research in Crime and Delinquency, 41*(3), 244–68.

Van Der Lann, A., Blom, M., and Kleemans E.R. (2009). Exploring long-term and short-term risk factors for serious delinquency. *European Journal of Criminology, 6*(5), 419–38.

Van Sleeuwen, S.E.M., Ruiter, S., and Menting, B. (2018). A time for crime: Temporal aspects of repeat offenders' crime locations. *Journal of Research in Crime and Delinquency, 55*(4), 538–68.

Vazsonyi, A.T., Mikuska, J. and Kelley, E.L. (2017). It's time: A meta-analysis on the self-control deviance link. *Journal of Criminal Justice, 48*, 48–63.

Wang, M., and Dishion, T.J. (2011). The trajectories of adolescents' perceptions of school climate, deviant peer affiliation, and behavioral problems during middle school years. *Journal of Research on Adolescence, 22*(1), 40–53.

Wikström, P.H. (2006). Individuals, settings, and acts of crime: Situational mechanisms and the explanation of crime. In P.H. Wikström and R.J. Sampson (Eds), *The explanation of crime: Context, mechanism, and development* (pp. 61–107). New York: Cambridge University.

Wikström, P.H. (2012). Does everything matter? In C.J. Sullivan, J.M. McGloin, and L.W. Kennedy (Eds), *When crime appears: The role of emergence* (pp. 53–72). New York: Routledge.

Wikström, P.H., and Svensson, R. (2008). Why are English youths more violent than Swedish youths? A comparative study of the role of crime propensity, lifestyles and their interactions in two cities. *European Journal of Criminology, 5*(3), 309–30.

Wikström, P.H., and Svensson, R. (2010). When does self-control matter? The interaction between morality and self-control in crime causation. *European Journal of Criminology, 7*(5), 395–410.

Wikström, P.H., Tseloni, A., and Karlis, D. (2011). Do people comply with the law because they fear getting caught? *European Journal of Criminology, 8*(5), 401–20.

Critical Criminology and Youth Justice in the "Risk Society"
Issues of Power and Justice

Bryan Hogeveen and Joanne Minaker

9

Overview

This chapter highlights the importance of a critical criminology perspective for the study of youth justice and draws attention to questions concerning social (in)justice, choice, and power. Critical scholarship attends to the systemic inequality, marginalization, uncaring practices, and social exclusion that underpin, and are often at the centre of, young people's encounters with the law. We encourage readers to think critically about youth justice issues and engage in what Minaker and Hogeveen (2009, p. 5) call "social justice praxis." To explore how justice for young people may become possible and what meaningful societal changes may look like, the chapter draws heavily on the theoretical work of scholars like Jacques Derrida and Michel Foucault. At the same time, we encourage students to theorize and ask some practical questions—such as, *What is to be done? What is my responsibility to this end?* Critical criminology offers a unique lens from which to consider what a humane, hospitable, and just Canadian society might entail.

Key Objectives

After reading this chapter, you should be able to:

- Explain what it means to be critical.
- Explore how young people, especially youth who are female and/or Indigenous, are marginalized in Canada.
- Highlight the political dimensions of space and their implications.
- Describe Jacques Derrida's understanding of deconstruction and hospitality as it relates to critical criminology.
- Highlight Foucault's unique understanding of power.
- Describe the "risk society," and the critical criminological critique of it.
- Discuss the place of young people in risk discourse and alternative ways to frame young people's experiences.
- Illustrate cultural criminology and its contribution to critical scholarship.
- Identify new questions about care, community, and young people that will enable you to see and think differently about youth justice.

Introduction

> *We are not content to teach our students about the social world—to pass on knowledge claims about what is—without also encouraging a process of critical reflection and social engagement about what could be.*
>
> —Minaker and Hogeveen 2009, p. 5

Conceptions of what youth, crime, and justice entail are contentious. Society lacks definitive answers to pressing concerns about young people and social harm. Nevertheless, newspaper headlines and nightly news stories caution about "troubling kids" and tend to advocate punishment as the primary solution. Lost among sensational headlines about the disobedience of young people today or efforts by the federal government to "get tough" on youth crime by overhauling legislation is the number of young people who are suffering. Media representations taint our understanding of youth crime and young criminals. Obscured from this picture are the inequalities, discrimination, abuse, trauma, and neglect that characterize the life histories of many of the young people who make their way into the youth justice system. Rarely do we see headlines like "Injustice Is a Way of Indigenous life, Say Advocates Dismayed at Verdict in Tina Fontaine Murder Trial" (Marley, Penman, and Dufresne 2018). Instead, series like *Riverdale* and *Criminal Minds*, as well as the 24-hour social media news feeds, would have us believe that young people are not being victimized but are victimizers. The average young offender in popular discourse is a gun-toting violent monster who preys on the unwitting. Many people in Western society would be surprised to hear that the majority of reported crime is property related and non-violent in nature. But this misperception is not surprising given that for the vast majority of Canadians the media are their primary sources of crime information (see Chapter 6 and Scotti 2017). When the conception of youth crime and young offenders is stockpiled with violent images, intrusive and carceral solutions are most often proposed as the only viable alternatives to the violent young offender (see, e.g., Harper 2008; see also Box 9.1). For example, the news articles "More Youth, Charged with Violent Crime, Filling Juvenile Jails" (Lepola and McGrew 2018) and "RCMP's Open Letter to Alberta Communities Addresses 'Youth Wreaking Havoc'" ("RCMP's Open Letter" 2014), along with the discussion in Chapter 6 of this book, provide empirical support for the way media narratives impact public discourse on youth and crime.

This chapter is on critical theories, not mainstream criminology. Chapter 8 outlines the major elements of the discipline of criminology. While mainstream criminology does its part to examine the causes, consequences, and control of youth crime, **critical criminology** begins from a very different starting point. A critical criminology perspective on youth justice would examine questions about social (in)justice, choice, care, and power. We are still asking, *Is there justice for youth?* (Hogeveen 2007). Critical scholarship on youth justice takes contemporary criminal justice processes to task for their part in contributing to the structural inequalities that marginalize youth. Others presume that Canadian society is organized by hierarchies of age, gender, race, ethnicity, class, sexuality, and ability. Recognizing the effects of difference and disadvantage under law has been the passion of feminist writers like Carol Smart (1989). Since the 1960s, feminist scholars have clearly articulated the disadvantaged social position of women and girls in the justice system and in society. Feminist criminology examines how criminology as a "decidedly male-centred enterprise" considers girls and women involved in crime as "monsters, misfits and manipulators" (Balfour and Comack 2014, p. 16). Female offenders are often stigmatized multiple times, as breaking socio-cultural gendered conventions, as a criminal, and especially if marginalized in other ways. In more recent decades, feminist analyses have extended beyond a singular emphasis on gender to examine intersectional inequities. For instance, Indigenous and feminist scholars have revealed the race/class/gender implications of the overrepresentation of female Indigenous young people in the youth justice system, and how these youth experience greater overrepresentation than their male counterparts (Chartrand and McKay, 2006; Scrim 2013).

Like feminist scholarship, critical criminology begins from the perspective that the lives of the most marginalized in contemporary society are lived out in circumstances not of their own choosing. They are thrown into a world that is discriminatory, racist, and sexist. These conditions structure the life chances of the marginalized other—Indigenous youth, the poor, and racial minorities—and translate into overrepresentation in the contemporary youth justice system. This chapter will explore the unique insights of such scholars as Henri Lefebvre, Jacques Derrida, Michel Foucault, and of cultural criminologists, and will discuss our own work of grappling with youth injustice. In our work, drawing on the theoretical tools of these critical scholars, we focus on systemic inequality, marginalization, uncaring practices, and social exclusion that conditions and contours the lives of the young people who find their way into the youth criminal justice system (YCJS). A critical criminology for youth justice is concerned

critical criminology Scholarship on crime and justice that seeks to examine and alter inequalities, marginalization, and social exclusion.

with the social positioning of youth and the impact that systemic oppression has on their process of becoming.

We encourage you to think critically about the issues presented in this chapter. Minaker and Hogeveen (2009, p. 5) suggest that critical inquiry is a first step toward "social justice praxis," which is aimed at "addressing the systemic conditions of **marginalization**, exclusion and social inequality that lead to the involvement of youth in crime in the first place." Critical criminology is dedicated to making meaningful changes to improve the life chances of young people. It asks, *What is to be done?* and *What is my responsibility to this end?* As you will see, critical criminology offers unique opportunities to envision a more just, humane, hospitable, and inclusive society.

marginalization
The exclusion of certain groups from mainstream society who routinely suffer as the result of gross inequalities.

What Does It Mean to Be Critical?
Why Is Critique Important?

> To say all this is deconstructable does not amount to disqualifying, negating, dis-avowing, or surpassing it, of doing the critique of critique (the way people wrote critiques of the Kantian critique as soon as it appeared), but of thinking its possi-bility from another border, from the genealogy of judgment, will, consciousness or activity, the binary structure, and so forth. (Derrida 1995, p. 357)

What does it mean to be critical? Criticism routinely appears as negative judgment. From this broad perspective, in one way or another, all of us are critical. One area often the subject of scorn among Canadians is the school system; a recent case in point is outcries about "sex ed" or the provincial health and human sexuality curriculum. Others direct their contempt toward the massive destruction of land and water by excavation in the Alberta oil sands. We need look no further than our own daily lives for critiques—some statements are benign, while others are wholly inappropriate: "This traffic light takes far too long to change colour"; "The dress she is wearing is far too short"; "This professor gives far too much homework." Criticism, it seems, is all around us. One group never far from criticism is young people, particularly criminalized youth. Think right now of a slight or a demeaning remark aimed at youth today. Most likely, you can recall times when people criticized, even shamed, you during your adolescence.

If offering judgments or assessments is something we all do, what sets critical scholars apart? Put another way, how are critical criminologists distinct in their critiques? Some strands of criminology and criminal justice studies are concerned with criticizing gov-ernment policy and suggest alternative approaches that might better respond to youth crime, to offenders, or to victims. In recent years, for example, restorative justice advo-cates have successfully argued that traditional youth justice processing fails victims of crime and alienates communities from the process (Minaker and Hogeveen 2009; see also Chapter 16 in this book). Restorative justice scholarship calls traditional and existing gov-ernmental process into question and proposes alternatives (e.g., circle sentencing). At a more practical level is the Edmonton-based Youth Restorative Justice Project (YRAP). A diverse group of young people (ages 14 to 24) grew concerned that young people were silent in youth justice matters and were otherwise alienated from the process. In response, YRAP was initiated and now administers the world's first restorative justice committee for and by youth, and challenges the Western status quo whereby adults alone are responsible for delivering and administering justice (Hogeveen 2006).

YRAP and other restorative justice groups who oppose traditional criminal justice orthodoxy are certainly critical in the conventional sense of casting judgment upon existing programs and suggesting that the object of criticism falls somewhat short of an established ideal. Nevertheless, youth justice officials can comfortably incorporate this flavour of critique (as mere modification) within existing processes without much concern that the established infrastructure and foundations of the criminal justice system would crumble to the ground. Indeed, without fear of significantly altering contemporary mandates and with the goal of streamlining existing practices, many youth justice systems actively encourage this form of intervention—that is, small modification to existing system parts.

In contemporary times, critique is most closely associated with individual judgment. Such judgmental criticism derives its meaning and its efficacy from an established mean or aesthetic. Consider, for example, current entertainment programming, such as *The Voice*, *America's Got Talent*, and *So You Think You Can Dance*, among others. Each program is premised upon supposed experts offering sage banter in the wake of a competitor's performance. Much to the delight of the viewing audience, the experts stand before this group conferring witty and (often) shaming critique upon the performer. The program would be rather dull without the experts' judgments, which make the show a success. How many regular viewers can remember the winner of each season of *American Idol*? By contrast, how many people, whether viewers or not, would recognize Jennifer Lopez as one of the show's judges? We speculate that many more would answer the latter question correctly. What does it say about our society that the judges who often heap appalling criticism on unwitting contestants are the "real" stars?

Criteria provide the benchmark for judgment and suggest that we make an assessment of something (e.g., a performance, beauty, or youth justice programming) against a normative standard—that is, the ultimate comparison by which those things should be measured. For example, the *Mona Lisa*, Sidney Crosby, and Luciano Pavarotti are considered the ideal criterion against which all else in their particular field (i.e., art, hockey, opera singing) is measured. Youth justice officials, too, employ normative standards to judge the behaviour of criminalized youth and assess youth justice programming. Recidivism rates are *seemingly* objective measures of a program's success. Whether or not a subject who has been adjudicated by YRAP, for example, has reoffended is typically the "appropriate" means through which to determine this youth justice committee's (YJC) effectiveness.

Two problems become immediately evident with this approach. On the one hand, other favourable outcomes may not be readily observable in re-arrest rates. Indeed, a young person may acquire a skill set in the adjudication process that will keep him or her off the streets. On the other hand, police administrative policies and severity of the offence of record for entry into the program tend to affect recidivism rates. As a result, the recidivism rates for this program are artificially higher than for more traditional YJCs. Employing standardized criteria often leads to overlooking practical differences that may qualitatively and positively affect the young person. Consider, for instance, a street-entrenched youth who finds secure housing and a stable job through the assistance that YRAP provides but misses a court appearance because her employer insists she work a shift. The young person may be charged with "failure to appear." In this instance, the case would be logged as a failure because it resulted in a new charge. Such an approach to determining the success of a program misses how the young person was unquestionably affected by her or his involvement with YRAP or another intervention program.

Critical criminology stands in stark contrast to those forms of critique that seek to improve the functioning and efficacy of the existing youth justice system. Instead of chasing down programming that will work effectively within contemporary justice processes, critical criminology seeks "to take the system to task rather than tinker with its parts" (Ratner 1971). But, what does it mean to "take the system to task?" Since Ratner's keen insight, which differentiated a critical brand of Canadian criminology some 40-odd years ago, much debate has emerged concerning what counts as pushing the system *hard* enough or *long* enough, or what kind of critique qualifies as doing *more* than merely criticizing the system for reinforcing race, class, gender, age, and other hierarchies. Within critical criminological scholarship, there are many positions regarding the extent to which meaningful change can be found in increments, institutional policy, and community practice, or if it only "counts" when expressed as radical transformation. For our purposes, the point is not to judge it as "just enough." Rather, a critical approach is one that emphasizes and examines systemic issues of power and justice vis-à-vis youth, crime, and society with an orientation toward social transformation. Critical scholars reject traditional assumptions of mainstream criminological theory (i.e., emphasis on crime control and law and order) and direct their gaze at structural inequities both within and outside the criminal justice system (CJS) and at the implications of unequal social arrangements.

As we hope you will come to see, critical scholars are concerned with more than exposing systemic conditions of marginalization. They are dedicated to opening up more ethical and caring ways of being with others, imagining more just and caring systems, and working to see beyond the social world as it is. This involves critical and serious reflection about how things could be otherwise. Critical criminology engages "with the challenges and contradictions involved in making ameliorative changes in our social world that offer hope instead of despair, compassion instead of intolerance, and justice instead of marginalization, exclusion, and suffering" (Minaker and Hogeveen 2009, p. xiii).

Take economic marginalization and the exclusion that accompanies lack of access to material resources and economic power. Empirical data in criminology has long confirmed the correlation between economic disadvantage and engaging in conventional crimes, such as property offences and minor violent crime. The critical criminologist doesn't focus squarely on law violation or the social fact of poverty, but rather grapples with the complex ways in which choices are constrained by social forces that all too often close down possibilities for safe, healthy, and productive lives. In practical terms, then, for critical criminology, the lens shifts away from the criminal justice system itself and toward the other systems in which a young person's life is embedded. Rather than offering responses located in the criminal justice language of "offender," "victim," "recidivism," or even "crime prevention," critical scholars engage in an unsettling of social arrangements of care and look toward other considerations like sense of belonging and community connectedness, social support systems, and other personal and cultural resources that build resiliency.

Critical criminology works to avoid the trap of collusion with criminal justice processes that serve only to further marginalize the least powerful in society. Hogeveen and Woolford (2006) encourage scholars to become intensely creative in their approaches and to conjure up alternatives that will push beyond established limits of youth justice orthodoxy. It is this disinclination toward, and/or attempt to avoid being complicit with contemporary systems of governance—no matter how favourable they appear—that also sets critical criminology apart. Drawing on the scholarship of Derrida, Foucault, and Lefebvre, among others, and on cultural criminology, critical criminology emphasizes the desirability of interventions that push beyond established hegemony. Instead of well-worn strategies, these scholars and those inspired by their claims promise an art of critique that *unsettles*, *disrupts*, or otherwise *challenges* contemporary unjust relations (both inside and outside the CJS) in the name of justice to come and amelioration of suffering. In a world bent on sexism, racism, classism, and various practices of exclusion of the marginalized young other, critical scholars work to imagine more just ways of being together and of becoming for youth. It is in imagining more just alternatives that hope for personal transformation and social change can be found.

"Risk" and the "Risk Society": The Social Construction of "Risk"

Risk is seemingly omnipresent today. To illustrate this point, consider how, like many contemporary Canadian post-secondary institutions, the University of Alberta boasts a department of risk management services (RMS). Take a moment to search your own post-secondary institution's website for risk management services. Campus security, emergency management, and insurance and risk management all fall under the RMS rubric. The very existence of such a unit on campus implies there are numerous risks at the university and that these require some form of regulation. According to the University of Alberta's RMS website, the department's "vision is to make risk management an integral part of all decision making, at all levels, across the University." It seems that managing risk is such a fundamental part of the contemporary ethos at the university that all decisions require an assessment of risk levels.

It is not only at universities that discourses concerning risk have become pervasive. It seems that almost everything we do can be understood in risk terms. A quick Google search returns countless websites dedicated to providing information on all manner of diseases. Not only do such sites provide knowledge about the medical problem, but they also act as instruments for you to ascertain your own individual level of risk for such calamities as heart disease, sexually transmitted infections, stroke, cancers, and, but certainly not limited to, diabetes. There is nothing inherently risky about having sexual relations or eating a diet rich in fat. Rather, it is only when these problems are translated into statistics via actuarial techniques for determining probability that they become socially constructed as risky. That is, only when we are able to accumulate sufficient data on a problem

risk
The calculated probability of an event, action, or circumstance occurring. Risks are calculated and managed through class, gender, age, and race categories.

and then assemble that data into a form amenable to calculation do seemingly random events become constituted into the language of risk. Patterns of probability emerge when incidents are tabulated across time and space. Without this ability to translate events and actions into probabilities, events would only be as they are or as we encounter them. As you will see, risk rhetoric can be incredibly powerful in shaping our sense of safety and place in the world.

Risk has come to order our social world to such a significant degree that social theorist Ulrich Beck (1992) deemed our contemporary ethos the **risk society**. Whether through advertising, television programming, or word of mouth, citizens in the West are increasingly made aware of their risks for all manner of calamity and are taking steps to remedy these seemingly inevitable ends. For Beck (1992) and others (Ferrell and Hayward 2011), this practice is very much characteristic of a reflexive modern society that is consistently reflecting back upon itself with a wary eye toward the future. Whereas previous societies were constantly looking backward and were reactive, the risk society is preoccupied with predicting "future" risk and allaying future harms. Because contemporary citizens are very much aware of looming risks, they trim their hedges, install burglar alarms, remove all of the valuables from their vehicles, avoid the "wrong" part of town, and eat a diet free of harmful pesticides and hormones. However, Beck (1992) does not argue that contemporary society is any more at risk than society at any other point in history. Rather, insurential technologies have organized our lives according to risks that are seemingly ubiquitous.

Awareness of predictable crime patterns often shapes our decision-making processes. How many readers, or parents of readers, of this chapter have purchased a burglar alarm for their homes? Or have engaged campus security measures and services like Safe Walk to reduce perceived risk of danger? What prompted these decisions? Or, how many have altered their diet because of the latest research tying disease or being unwell to this or that food category? Did you consider why you made this decision? Ewald (1991, p. 199) maintains that there is nothing in our world that is in and of itself a risk; rather, "it all depends on how one analyses the danger, considers the event." Thus, the invention of instruments that calculate risk orders our social world through technologies that render risk knowable and thus governable. In other words, if we *know* that having a burglar alarm, trimming the hedges around our homes, purchasing strong locks, and turning on lights at night will reduce our risk of victimization, we can take action, following the steps to lower the probability that we will become targets.

Risk is the probability of an event or an action occurring (Ewald 1991). Insurance agents ask a number of probing questions (e.g., in questionnaires) that are intended to determine a person's level of risk and that are used to provide a quotation for their services: *How old are you? What gender? Have you ever had an "at fault" accident? How many traffic tickets?* By comparing your answers to data aggregated across time (i.e., accident reports and police statistics), insurance companies determine your level of risk and the probability that they will be called upon to pay a claim on your behalf. Young, unemployed, and undereducated males with several traffic tickets are likely to pay much more for their coverage than married women with no blemishes on their driving record. Calculating risk in this way orders seemingly random occurrence in a form that can be used to definite ends (Dean 1999). These actuarial techniques have real implications: A person in Edmonton,

risk society
This refers to a break with modernity into an emerging societal form characterized by the production of risks and of tools for their management. In contrast to the view that social problems are to be solved, issues in the risk society (i.e., crime) are risks to be managed.

Alberta, in 2018 officially changed the gender of "his" driver's licence from male to female in order to save on insurance rates, by his own admission.

"Risk" and Youth Justice

Contemporary calculations of risk are not the exclusive domain of the insurance industry. Risk has become central to the administration of Canadian youth justice. The perceived ability of these technologies to efficiently and accurately match disciplinary practice to offender characteristics has meant that risk governance strategies have become boundless (O'Malley 1996). Youth, it seems, are "at risk" for more predicaments and misadventures than any other segment of the Canadian population (Health Canada 1998). Studies of young people have revealed a series of risk factors that may increase their probability of being victimized or of developing behavioural problems that may lead to crime and other anti-social behaviour (Hawkins and Pollard 1999; Howell 2005; Shader 2003; Wyrick and Howell 2004). Canada's National Crime Prevention Centre (NCPC 2007) identifies a variety of risk factors that may lead to gang involvement. Based on accumulated knowledge and data, the NCPC argues that the following are predictive of gang involvement: over-reliance on anti-social peers, poor parental supervision, prior delinquency, aggression, and, but not limited to, early or precocious sexual activity. Risk factors such as these do not stand alone but are often combined toward a variety of ends. For example, Hoge and Andrews (2010) have aggregated risk factors into the latest incarnation of the Youth Level of Service/Case Management Inventory (YLS/CMI), which, they maintain, now takes into account gender and cultural factors. Hoge and Andrews (2010, para. 1) argue that the "YLS/CMI helps probation officers, youth workers, psychologists, and social workers identify the youth's major needs, strengths, barriers, and incentives; select the most appropriate goals for him or her; and produce an effective case management plan."

The discussion so far has demonstrated how risk has become increasingly pervasive in contemporary society. Risk discourse has also become a growing subject of study for critical scholars, including youth justice researchers (Hannah-Moffat 2001). While risk orders our contemporary manner of being in the world, critical criminologists recognize that there are inherent problems with applying risk management thinking in the youth justice system. In particular, when risk structures our thinking about social problems (i.e., poverty, drug use, violence, youthful offending, and punishment), these unfortunate conditions cease to be viewed as obstacles to a more just ordering of the social world. Instead, such issues become constituted as risks that require management, not signs that radical social change is necessary (Hogeveen and Woolford 2009). For example, a 10-year-old Indigenous boy living in poverty is determined to be at risk for joining a gang because of his family history of crime, his low birth weight, and, since he lives in poverty, his poor performance in school. When risk is calculated independently without consideration for structural conditions that buoy marginality, poverty (for example) is constituted as a risk factor rather than as an intolerable condition that demands redress and amelioration (Minaker and Hogeveen 2009). In other words, poverty, racism, and violence are issues to be managed rather than social problems to be addressed. This, for the critical criminologist examining issues of youth, crime, and society, is troubling.

Problematizing the "Risk Society": Seeing Suffering and Attending with Care

> There is no doubt that the loss of Indigenous women and girls to all forms of violence is a national tragedy. It has traumatized generations of families, and it will continue to traumatize communities if we do not commit to action and change. (Buller, Audette, Evolfson, and Robinson 2017, p. 7)

In the risk society, paradoxically, risks like the risk of violent victimization are too often viewed as individualized rather than understood in social context. Take, for instance, devastating statistics on violence against Indigenous women (Aboriginal Healing Foundation 2003). According to the Interim Report of the National Inquiry into Missing and Murdered Indigenous Women and Girls, Indigenous girls and women are 12 times more likely to be missing or murdered than any other women in Canada, and 16 times more likely in comparison to Caucasian women (Buller, Audette, Evolfson, and Robinson 2017, p. 7). Indeed, we may say that Indigenous females are "at risk" of violent victimization (Royal Canadian Mounted Police 2014; Royal Commission on Aboriginal People 1996). The critical criminologist asks, *Is it simply being a certain gender, age, or from a cultural group that makes one more or less at risk, or is something more complex going on?* According to a recent Statistics Canada report, youth are dramatically overrepresented as victims of violent crimes. The rates of violent victimization including sexual assault, robbery, and physical assault were highest among those aged 15 to 24 (Malakieh, 2018). Critical criminology aims to complicate our understanding of the problems we see associated with youth, gender, race, class, age, etc. Critical criminology is not only concerned with data—like the fact that in 2014, more than a quarter of Indigenous people over 15 reported in the last 12 months that they or someone in their household were a victim of at least one offence measured by the General Social Survey (Statistics Canada 2014). Critical criminology aims at changing the social conditions underlying the fact that the overall rate of violent victimization was more than double that of non-Indigenous people (p. 5). (Chapter 11 in this book provides a more thorough analysis of Indigenous young people's experiences with crime, suffering, and violence.) What these statistics reveal is that in risk terms, some youth have a heightened vulnerability. Yet, when we problematize the risk society and look more closely and critically at lived experiences we see remarkably blurred boundaries between victimization and offending histories for youth, especially for Indigenous girls and young women and street-involved youth who are criminalized.

Proponents of risk assessment instruments claim that these tools are designed to assess and treat risk, relying on what Andrews and Bonta (2007) call the risk-need-responsivity (RNR) model. (See Chapter 7, which explores this area in more detail than can be covered here.) For Andrews and Bonta, the "risk principle" is about matching level of service to an offender's risk to reoffend (i.e., the higher the risk, the higher the security and treatment needs). The "need principle" refers to criminogenic needs, which Andrews and Bonta (2007) define as dynamic risk factors directly linked to criminal behaviour (such as community functioning, work, substance abuse). Finally, the "responsivity principle" relies on cognitive, behavioural learning, taking into account bio-social factors like gender, race, learning style, and personality. In their analysis, *Mental Health in the Context of Canada's Youth Justice System*, Peterson-Badali et al. (2015, p. 9) explain,

> Within the RNR framework, mental health problems are generally construed as weak predictors of offending and are therefore not considered criminogenic needs (i.e. risk factors) in assessment and treatment planning. The corollary is that mental health issues should *not* be the primary target of rehabilitative interventions; rather, interventions should focus on strong, direct predictors of recidivism such as antisocial attitudes, peers, and personality features. Mental health issues *are* captured under the construct of specific responsivity, however.

Peterson-Badali et al. go on to argue that disorders like depression and anxiety are responsivity considerations, not strongly related to offending, yet they should be attended to "alongside primary criminogenic needs targets" (p. 13). This all matters for rehabilitative services and case management practice. From a critical lens, we may ask, *What are the implications of the RNR model for youth probation services?*

Risk management programming for youth is part of a "responsibilization model" of crime control (O'Malley 1992). Youth involved in crime are made responsible (or responsibilized) for the decisions they make. Their choices are understood in the language of risk as *risks* to be *managed*. For example, perhaps a 14-year-old youth cuts school, loiters at the mall, steals clothing, is aggressive with a security guard, etc. Consider now how systems engage in attempts to "manage" risk in our hypothetical case. Teachers and school officials, mall security staff, and potentially police and judges are all involved in making sense of the young person in an individualized and decontextualized manner around the category of risk. Risk language and discourse offers only one account of a young person's wrongdoing and troubles—one that does little to appreciate how young people are vulnerable, socially situated beings in a process of becoming.

Given that critical criminology frames risk critically, next we briefly identify some areas for concern with the proliferation of risk discourse and practice. One critique points to the different cultural meanings embedded in notions of risk (O'Malley 1996). Patricia Monture-Angus (1999, p. 27) points out that when criminogenic needs categories in the risk-need-responsivity model are applied to Indigenous youth, the impact is particularly troubling. "What is being measured," she argues, "is not 'risk' but one's experiences as part of an oppressed group." What's more, risk constructions are racialized and gendered. Risk assessment categories can mask the complex and contradictory ways in which gender and other dimensions of power shape identity, opportunities, and experiences. A risk lens is one framing, albeit an individualized construction. There are other more sociological, more critical, and more empathetic ways to make sense of youth, their behaviours, their lives, and the processes of marginalization and criminalization that they confront as they navigate adolescence in their process of becoming.

One such alternative is a trauma-informed lens, which recognizes *both* the psychological impact (i.e., personal level) and the social and structural underpinnings and effects (i.e., context). Even if we look at trauma as a mental health issue, it does not preclude us from understanding the social situatedness of traumatic experiences.

Next, we turn our attention to dilemmas associated with the YCJS responding to a young person's law violation and/or getting involved to address the individual's particular struggles, especially when psychological problems are a factor.

Intersections between Mental Health and Youth Justice

If youth is a process of becoming, then a key question is—becoming what? Who? Implicit within risk discourse is that some young people are "at risk" of failing to achieve desirable futures—of losing the opportunity to become a responsible, self-reliant, conforming neo-liberal citizen. Elizabeth Comack (2018) suggests that to counter the tendency to reduce the systemic impact of colonialism, gendered violence, and poverty to the psychological level, "we need to understand trauma not as 'response' but as 'lived experience.' We need to see it as being located within particular historical and social conditions in which individuals live their lives" (p. 33). Young people's lives are embedded in multiple systems, including family, school, and community—and for criminalized youth, their experiences and struggles with youth justice, child welfare, and other systems are far too commonplace. The YCJA contains provisions for assessment of youth in cases where there are mental health concerns. This may be done by psychologists, mental health workers, and psychiatrists, though some screening is done by people without training. On the one hand, identifying youth with unmet care needs may lead to positive transformative intervention; but on the other hand, screening may lead to more intrusive measures that may further entrench and marginalize young people within systems of control. This is a dilemma that critical criminology confronts. Little research currently exists on how and why youth are referred or on the impact of these assessments on a young person's life (Peterson-Badali et al. 2017). Clearly, this is an area for further critical scholarship and more research.

The youth criminal justice system, through the Youth Criminal Justice Act (YCJA), provides for customized sentencing for youth who suffer from mental illness; however, in practice, there are gaps in mental health services and, for some youth, inaccessible or inappropriate treatment. Mental health courts have operated in Canada since 2008, yet still little is known about how they work and what effect they are having. Some groups are disproportionately affected by both systemic challenges and personal struggles with wellness—among them are girls and non-binary people, persons with (dis)abilities, and Indigenous youth. When mental health is framed as a "risk" to be managed, rather than a care need to be tended to, youth are more likely to experience depersonalized, overly restrictive, and detached encounters with health care providers and/or front-line workers in the youth justice system. Framing mental health as risk also raises questions about fundamental fairness: behaviours associated with mental illness are being criminalized, and criminal justice processing may exacerbate mental health issues. From a psychological perspective, mental health is a risk factor for offending, yet acknowledging the association between mental health and criminalization need not imply a decontextualized analysis of young people's choices and opportunities for meaningful engagement in healthy and/or healing activities.

Youth, especially those situated at the social margins, have unique needs and vulnerabilities. In recent years, mental health courts, delivery of mental health services and a more health focused style of therapeutic jurisprudence have impacted how criminalized youth who also present with complex mental health needs are processed. The YCJA, in part, takes a community safety perspective, viewing mental illness as something posing a "risk" to community safety. Custody, in principle, should be a last resort, not used as a proxy for mental health resources. Judges have access to therapeutic sentencing options like intensive rehabilitative custody and supervision (IRCS) and intensive support and supervision programs (ISSP). However, structural issues, such as system organization and jurisdiction, shape the law in practice. In British Columbia, for example, adolescent health, youth justice, and child welfare are all integrated, so coordinating services are administered through the Ministry of Children and Family Development (Kasper 2017). In contrast, in Alberta, the Ministry of Justice and Solicitor General and the Ministry of Children's Services are divided, resulting in more fragmented service delivery for young people (Kaspar 2017). To be eligible for such interventions, youth must undergo more screening and testing, which inevitably results in *over-* and *under-*serving—that is, some youth who could really benefit from supportive treatment are left out, and others are subjected to more systemic involvement than necessary. This all begs the question, what support and care resources are available for young people in their own communities if, and when, they are struggling, hurting, and/or harming others? Sadly, more support services for young people and increased funding for youth secure mental health treatment facilities and community resources across the country, especially in rural and remote areas, if available, would unlikely keep pace with growing demand. One estimate puts the portion of youth in the justice system who suffer from some form of mental illness at 90 per cent (Kasper 2017).

Trauma is a mental health issue that is historical and contextual, not solely personal, although the harm associated with traumatic experiences is felt very personally. The lens of critical criminology directs our attention to structure and experience within social systems. We could interrogate what support and care looks like from the perspective of the youth. What *could* support look like that offers young people the tools, time, and space they need to meet their mental health needs? Unlike traditional criminal justice approaches directed *to* or *at* youth, critical criminology aims in practice to stand and work *with* youth. In short, a critical criminology perspective, directs inquiries toward envisioning and bringing about the transformations that would address young people's mental health needs in a way that shifts their experience from social exclusion to inclusion, from managing their risks in order to "prevent crime" toward relieving their suffering and truly attending to their concerns. What we would call a "critical criminology for youth justice" ponders to what extent any intervention is intrusive or responsive, fear-based or based in care and community building. Extending beyond the criminal justice system, a critical criminology for youth justice looks to communities as sites of personal transformation and social change for young people.

Outcast Spaces, Caring Places

Over a decade ago, when we wrote the book *Youth, Crime and Society: Issues of Power and Justice*, we devoted one full chapter to the topic of street-involved youth (Minaker and Hogeveen 2009). Since that time, research in Canada in this subject area, as well as policy and practice dealing with youth homelessness, has blossomed. Yet, still, young people continue to lack support and to experience little sense of belonging, finding themselves in what can best be described as "**outcast spaces**." They have been called runaways, street kids, high-risk individuals, and disconnected youth. Street-involved youth are a heterogenous group between the ages of 15 and 25 who are underhoused or who lack housing, and are living on or about the streets. One key characteristic we found that they tend to share is chronic instability (Minaker and Hogeveen 2009). This instability shows itself in unstable support, unstable accommodation, and unstable relationships. They also often find themselves experiencing unstable income, unstable work, and lack of social supports. Being impoverished, homeless, and anchored in undesirable and outcast spaces (Mallea 2010) does not lend itself to a quality of life amenable to thriving in these young people's process of becoming adults. Hogeveen and Freistadt (2013) refer these undesirable and outcast spaces as "outcast stretches of the inner city that are far removed from the consumer spaces and homes of the affluent" in their article "Hospitality and the Homeless: Jacques Derrida in the Neoliberal City." A critical criminologist might ask: to what extent can such a context provide a caring place for youth?

Although Karl Marx was relatively silent on the question of space, Marx-inspired authors like Edward Soja, Henri Lefebvre, and David Harvey have drawn critical attention to the importance of space in class relations. Marx's relative silence on this issue may have been due to the fact that cities were just beginning to take on their current configuration during his lifetime (Elden 2007). Lefebvre (1996) famously took up this gap in Marx's work and argues that space is political. He maintains that city spaces become divided up in very definite ways that betray their ethos. Space is socially constructed rather than being naturally constituted. This condition has a dramatic impact on the actors living out their lives in particular areas. Social space, Lefebvre suggests, is allocated along class lines such that city planning reproduces and maintains the existing class structure. It follows that the quality of space allotted provides obvious clues as to its owners (Elden 2007).

The inner-city spaces and core areas of town, such as Winnipeg's North End, are older, crowded, and often abandoned, yet are also over-policed. By contrast, sprawling suburbs complete with white picket fences and open "green" spaces are reserved for the more affluent. Whereas children growing up in suburbia enjoy new schools and growing recreational centres, the "playground" for poor children and their families looks more like a grey concrete mass and is shared with the mentally ill, the criminal, and the drug user. Harvey (1989) maintains that the history of capitalism is the history of a struggle for the command of space, noting, "[T]he whole history of territorial organization, colonialism and imperialism, of uneven development, of urban and rural contradictions, as well as of geopolitical conflict testifies to the importance of such struggles within the history of capitalism" (p. 237).

All people are contained in their space so as to better facilitate rule and control of the recalcitrant and marginalized other. Consider how space is allocated and lived in

outcast spaces
More than geographical locations at the social margins, outcast spaces are contexts characterized by exclusion, vulnerability, precarious resources, and barriers to belonging and community where youth are more likely to experience harm than healing, disregard than care.

Edmonton, Alberta. Rather than providing open spaces where strangers may intersect and interact, Edmonton's city planners have seemed to sweep away and confine the poor within spaces of disorder. For some, Edmonton *feels like*, and indeed *is*, a cold city (see Box 9.1). As "blots" on the otherwise serene and tranquil city, the street-involved youth roam the streets routinely shooed and shunted into the least coveted and most dangerous places.

Box 9.1 | Youth Justice in Action

When Space Becomes Place: Creating Warm Places in Cold Cities for Youth

Daena Crosby's (2018) Ph.D. dissertation research is a critical ethnography of four youth-serving agencies in two Prairie cities. Her work demonstrates what a critical criminology of care could look like. The project blends research, theory, and practice by focusing on the complex and multifaceted needs of Indigenous youth living on and off the streets in Edmonton and Winnipeg. Crosby writes of her ability "to move in between community and academic worlds [and] build meaningful relationships with youth" and notes that her "reputation as researcher and community worker" situates her within the community and in the research project (p. 49). As a research methodology, Crosby (2018) engaged in peace-making circles with marginalized and vulnerable youth. She gave each young person a puzzle piece, instructing them "to produce a visual representation of what inclusion means to them." She notes this "was a creative way for youth to generate their initial ideas about their definitions and experiences of inclusion at the organizations and to become more comfortable in the circle with their peers" (p. 68). Warm places, Crosby argues, come from a sense of welcome and belonging, which can provide some Indigenous youth with temporary reprieve from the cold of the cities (p. 5). A relational ethic of care in youth work practice transforms organizations into warm places. Crosby identified four relational, interconnected elements that could be explored in other sites and contexts, including

- understanding and attention to youths' Indigeneity and youthfulness;

- physical spaces that become meaningful places for Indigenous youth;
- opportunities, programs, and resources to meet youth's needs; and
- respectful, optimistic, and trusting interpersonal relationships among Indigenous youth and frontline staff.

Warm places dramatically contrast with outcast spaces because a warm place is a "caring environment" that encourages youth to feel welcome and fosters a sense of belonging. Crosby (2018, p. 41) explains, "Spaces are transformed as places of care through interpersonal connections and art" (p. 41). For her research participants, "caring interpersonal, mutual and reciprocal relationship building" was key to youth work practice (p. 42). Crosby's analysis illustrates how young people need respectful places and relationships, as well as real opportunities where they can share who they are and who they are becoming.

Critical Thinking Question

Explore your own community for supports, resources, or services that most closely resemble the approach Crosby recommends for youth work practice. Suppose you were given the task of writing an entry in the chapter's glossary for "critical criminology of care." What would you create for a definition?

This includes johns' cars, drug houses, river valleys, and (for some) jail. Most people never see where the truly marginal live, as they are tucked away in spaces long forgotten and out of the way of those in the business classes, who can scurry back to the suburbs hopeful that the disorder will not touch their lives.

In their study "Youth Geographies of Urban Estrangement in the Canadian City: Risk Management, Race Relations and the 'Sacrificial Stranger,'" Jo-Anne Dillabough and Ee-Seul Yoon (2018) interviewed street-involved youth to explore the ways that urban social divisions change race relations and impact disadvantaged youth living on the periphery of Vancouver and Toronto. They argue, "Borders, enclaves and varied states of legitimacy, recognition, and abjection do indeed exist—as expressed by young people on the urban scene—but they are more or less visible and highly uneven across the spatial urban land-scapes of Canadian cities (pp. 140–1). Dillabough and Yoon (2018, p. 132) argue that the interviewees' responses demonstrated othering through exclusionary language such as "'them,' 'they,' the 'Native,' the potentially diseased, the drug user on the street." Other young interviewees saw the presence of homelessness as stigmatization.

Even when the capitalist state seeks to ameliorate the marginalized other's suffering, its programs are carried out not in the centres of affluence but in the most downtrodden and overburdened areas of the city. Since 2009, following the lead of Calgary and Seattle, Edmonton has been engaged in a "Housing First" initiative. Under this plan, the chronically homeless are allotted housing for a one-year period, during which they are provided with a residence and a limited amount of support to help manage and deal with their addictions and other social problems (see Edmonton Committee to End Homelessness 2009). What will happen to these residents after the program time limits run out remains to be seen. However, units to house the marginalized—including but not limited to street-involved youth who have left home to escape abuse, former inmates who have left prison and who have no family or work to go to, and drug-addicted clients who are no longer welcome in de-toxification centres—are not evenly spread throughout the city. Indeed, there are no group homes for the homeless and drug addicted in affluent neighbourhoods. Instead, the city has placed these units in the city's most economically depressed spaces. What's more, even before the Housing First initiatives, these outcast spaces were already saturated with social services, as well as crime, disorder, drug addiction, and homelessness (Kleiss 2010). It seems the city is willing to help only so far as doing so does not upset the tranquility of suburban space. The critical criminological approach encourages thoughtful consideration of what more just and hospitable social spaces could look like, which is where we will now turn.

Jacques Derrida (1930–2004) and Justice

Our discussion so far has contemplated the (in)justices facing young people today, espe-cially those marginalized by class, race, gender, and other forms of inequity and social privilege/oppression. Clearly, marginalized populations are excluded from full and mean-ingful participation in contemporary Canadian society. Quite simply, racial divisions are reflected spatially and assist in underwriting patterns of exclusion (Herbert and Brown 2006). What is to be done about the heinous social injustices that marginalized youth face? Can we envision alternative practices that challenge the existing social conditions that exclude, punish, and "other" young people? Instead of shunting the marginalized other into cities' least desirable spaces, what if the approach was one of welcome? Consider how this paradigm shift could impact how these young people view themselves and affect their sense of feeling cared for and cared about? Toward this end, we suggest the deconstructive work of Derrida (1999, 2002, 2005; Derrida and Dufourmantelle 2000). Derrida's understanding of **hospitality** and **justice** has much conceptual and practical applicability for questions of justice for youth.

Although Derrida has become widely known as the philosopher of **deconstruction**, he was rather reticent when it came to spelling out what exactly he meant by the term. In fact, the word *deconstruction* rarely appears in his many works. Deconstruction is not synonymous with destruction. Derrida was concerned with opening up taken-for-granted words and works and subjecting them to intense scrutiny. He argued that "deconstruction, if such a thing exists, should open up" (Derrida 1987, p. 261). Thus, if there is such a thing as deconstruction, it is intended to "re-construct, re-constitute or re-affirm" a given word structure (Bradley 2008). Deconstruction works to unbolt language and reveal its silent, hidden, or repressed elements that provide them with their meaning. On the rare occasion where Derrida (1985) did articulate a meaning for deconstruction, he maintained that it represented the undoing of language to disclose "how an 'ensemble' was constituted." We extend this notion of an "ensemble" to include ways of speaking and thinking about, and being with, young people.

Language dramatically affects what happens at the level of society. How things are named holds significance for how they are understood and acted upon. Derrida maintains that to understand what is going on at the heart of language, we must comprehend the **trace**, which refers to the silent components of our language that assign meaning. However, this quiet element is tremendously slippery and difficult to grab hold of. Trace is present in all flows of conversation and in all language, but it is constantly deferred and silent. Each sign (word) must always already contain *traces* of other signs through which the original sign derives meaning. For example, marginalization has traces in words like *social order*, *power*, and *freedom*.

For Derrida, everything that is present before us contains traces of other elements that are ostensibly absent or not readily apparent (Bradley 2008). For instance, contemporary discussions of the overrepresentation of Indigenous youth in the YCJS and/or in the child welfare system may not overtly recognize colonization (the historical and ongoing processes that began with the arrival of Europeans to Canada and various attempts to dominate and assimilate Indigenous peoples). The trace remains hidden, but it is still there. Derrida claims that all things oscillate between being present and absent without ever being wholly at hand or wholly silent.

Deconstructing "Hospitality"

Let us consider deconstruction at work, or what happens when we examine our everyday language more closely. Consider, for example, the term *hospitality*. It might conjure images of welcome mats, dinner parties, or a weekend guest who is visiting from out of town. In the Western world, it is customary to invite people into our places of residence

---

hospitality
An unrestrained welcome to a stranger. It calls for open spaces that welcome the other as he or she arrives.

justice (Derrida)
For Derrida, justice is a messianic promise of a more just future "to come."

deconstruction
Process that involves opening up words to their hidden or closed-off possibilities in an attempt to reveal what is going on behind language.

trace
The silent elements that provide words with their essential meaning (Spivak 1976) and that underlie all language.

with the greeting "Make yourself at home." We do not, for the most part, mean this in the literal sense. Not immediately evident in this seemingly gracious term is an inalienable tension—between a welcome to a stranger and an uncertain hostility concealed within that welcome. Quite simply, the welcome itself already assumes a stranger in its very utterance. Fashioning the other as "other" in the instance of the welcome sets in motion and entrenches relations of dominion over space. Anyone who has hosted particularly odious houseguests can begin to understand the duality endemic to hospitality. A guest who has overstayed his or her welcome becomes a source of stress for the host (e.g., their children, pets, household schedule). Welcoming a guest into one's home is conditional upon the guest's accepting and attending to established rules of decorum. When I say "Welcome, please make yourself at home," I am actually commanding my guest to be comfortable in a space that belongs to me and over which I am sovereign.

Derrida observes that hospitality, as we know and practice it in the West, contains a trace of restraint and hostility that "preserves the distance between one's own and the stranger, between owning one's own property and inviting the other into one's home. So, there is always a little hostility in all hosting and hospitality" (Derrida and Caputo 1997, p. 110). Opening language to its silent but essential elements is at deconstruction's core. Let's shift our attention now to the practical level.

Over the summer months of 2010, the Edmonton Police Service (EPS) increased its **surveillance** and presence in Churchill Square, which is situated firmly within the city's downtown core and is also the site of countless festivals that attempt to attract the affluent and their dollars. Marginalized young people, as you might imagine, were not similarly welcomed into this site. Instead, police officers stationed around the square were instructed to stop, question, and search any "suspicious-looking" young people (read: an Indigenous person). With their rather unkempt appearance and lack of surplus income, these youths were unwelcome in Churchill Square and were constituted as "other" to the affluent suburbanites that city officials were attempting to attract (Hogeveen and Freistadt 2012). State responses to marginalized young people are often similarly hostile.

What would a politics of hospitality for youth look like here? Hospitality without the trace of hostility and exclusion would stretch established limits and work toward welcoming all without any imposed limitations. It would, at the same time, encourage "others" to be as they are and as they arrive (Derrida 2005, p. 66). Hospitality demands acts of *extreme generosity* and an opening of space to an unknown and unknowable other: "It is a politics that does not accept limits imposed upon itself, but always asks 'what's next?' and in response relentlessly pushes against established exclusionary boundaries of being" (Carroll 2006, p. 825). Such a way of being in the world is founded upon a reverence for the other who appears at a person's threshold whether or not he or she may even be perceived as unpredictable or dangerous.

surveillance
The direct or indirect observation of conduct, which is intended to produce a desired outcome (i.e., conformity).

Searching for "Justice"

The discussion in this chapter all leads to the question, *What kinds of transformative changes does a critical criminological approach to youth justice suggest?* Searching for justice means moving from the abstract to the practical level. Opening up new ways of being, and understanding what lies beyond them, encourages adherents of deconstruction to think outside of contemporary mentalities that imprison and exclude others in favour of more just practices and social relations. If that is what we are after, should we now deconstruct or open up "justice"? It might be extremely rewarding and intellectually expedient if this were indeed possible. Unfortunately, Derrida insists that justice is *impossible*. It does not exist because it must forever remain in the future (Derrida 2002). If justice does not and cannot exist here and now, then why does Canada have a youth justice system, justices of the peace, and the Youth Criminal Justice Act (YCJA)? Surely, these are all instances of justice. Derrida and others maintain that these are merely instruments of vengeance that imprison and confine and do little to ameliorate suffering (see Hogeveen and Woolford 2009). That is, the youth justice system is authorized under the YCJA to deliver pain to juvenile offenders as payment for this or that harm they caused. Jails and penitentiaries are run based on this misdirected understanding of justice. Justice that finds its end in retribution is not just—it is a form of revenge and is fully at odds with the logic and spirit of justice that Derrida encourages. Further, it is the marginalized other who is typically on the receiving end of this brand of vengeance, masquerading as justice. What we have, then, is a so-called justice system predicated on punishing the poor and the marginalized, the silenced and the vulnerable.

Derrida has something much different (more transformative) in mind. He understands justice to be a "promise" that is "beyond law, and is itself incalculable, infinite and undeconstructable" (Pavlich 2007, p. 989). Understood from Derrida's perspective, justice becomes an ideal much different from the benchmark criterion referred to earlier in the chapter. Derrida's just ideal exists beyond current ontological limits and must be doggedly pursued. To maintain that our system of punishment is just would be to claim that all of the hard work is done. Suggesting that the youth criminal justice system is just because it administers the laws of Canada would be to deny the suffering of "the Indigenous other" who is overrepresented at all stages of the "justice" system or "the othered female" who is subject to different standards of care that masquerades as justice for girls.

Justice does not exist and does not lend itself to the infinite play of signifiers in the fashion of hospitality, community, or violence. Caputo (Derrida and Caputo 1997, p. 139) argues that it "would be the height of injustice to think that justice exists [or] existed." Justice is not and cannot be a "thing." The potency of this manner of thinking lies in how it stimulates us to fight for the other. Caputo asserts, "Justice haunts us, disturbs our sleep, stalks us like the specter of old Marx whom we can't quite bury, keeps us up pacing the floors well into the night, has us seeing ghosts" (p. 139). Derrida was involved in a variety of justice struggles that seemed to trouble his slumber. As one of the world's best-known philosophers, he levied his celebrity to rally against racism, apartheid, and practices of discrimination that plagued French immigration policy. Thus, to say that justice is impossible or messianic (i.e., always "to come") is not to inspire nihilism. Rather, the spectre of justice aims at provoking restlessness. The critical criminologist aims to push the normative narrative that youth are obstacles to be removed, or risks to be managed. Justice for youth calls us to be infinitely responsible, without calculation or vengeance, to all others. In the name of those for whom justice was denied, we may ask, *What is justice "to come"?*

Michel Foucault (1926–1984) and Power

Like Derrida, Michel Foucault was a highly influential French philosopher. His many books include *The History of Sexuality* (three volumes), *Power/Knowledge*, and *The Archaeology of Knowledge*. Given his disdain for the discipline of criminology, it may seem odd to include a section on Foucault in a book on youth crime and criminology. Foucault thought criminology to be replete with "garrulous discourse" and "endless repetition" and was convinced that the discipline's primary and perhaps only function was to relieve criminal justice officials of their guilt for delivering pain and suffering upon the other (Foucault 1980, p. 47). That is, he was certain that criminology only served to make judges, for example, feel better about sending young people away from their families and communities because doing so was for "their own good" and a protection for society. Nevertheless, and despite Foucault's distaste for criminology, scholars interested in the subject have successfully drawn on his voluminous work to render contemporary systems of governance intelligible. Foucault's book *Discipline and Punish* and his series of articles on governmentality have been particularly influential.

Foucault's work has been prominent in several studies that attend to how young people are governed and disciplined. As we have seen already, youth, and particularly those deemed to be disobedient and marginalized, are increasingly the targets of surveillance. Ericson and Haggerty (1999) have examined this phenomenon through a governmentality lens. Through this perspective, they argue that "governance is organized in terms of risk management technologies that identify dangers" and maintain that police collaborate with other agencies to provide knowledge about youth (i.e., using street-stop recording systems and missing persons registries) (p. 163). The authors maintain that police function as "the fulcrum of risk communication systems for governing the young" (p. 164). Predictably, marginalized youth and those identified as having the highest levels of risk are subjected to the most intensive surveillance.

Foucault's Understanding of Power

power (Foucault)
Rather than as a quantity held or possessed by the state, Foucault understood power to be relational, positive, and exercised.

Scholars have been particularly drawn to Foucault's unique understanding of **power**. Prior to Foucault's interdiction, many writers were convinced that power was concentrated in the hands of a few. By contrast, Foucault maintains that power extends beyond a particular class or state and is evidenced only when it is exercised. From this view, power is not something that can be held, accumulated, or stored up for later use. It is only ever evident when it is being put to use. Think about this for a minute. Can you show me power? Can you hold it in your hands and bring it to me?

Money as power is a common theme in contemporary music. From Fergie's song "Glamorous" to "Billionaire" by Bruno Mars, artists make clear to the listener that becoming powerful and successful is dependent on first acquiring money. Foucault would challenge this assertion. For him, money becomes power only when it is spent; it has no power in and of itself.

Foucault (1977, 1980, 1991) was deeply interested in how power shaped the conduct and lives of those subjected to its disciplinary effects. In his classic work on the rise of the prison and punishment system, Foucault (1977) traces the emergence of a new economy of discipline that continues to dominate our thinking about how best to govern and train human beings. He was convinced that discipline was characterized by micro-powers that shaped human subjects in preferred ways. These micro-powers, Foucault argues, operate at the minutiae of our existence but are nevertheless momentous in their effects. Every bit of our being is shaped through the exercise of this kind of micro-power. All things, from holding a pencil, to martial arts, to riding a bike, are taught to us through an exacting discipline. Instead of punishing the body via capital punishment or the stock and pillory for that matter, discipline takes hold of the soul and shapes it in ways that are functional and desirable. Thus, rather than seeing power as being repressive or negative, Foucault suggests that power is creative and positive: not in terms of being good or exceptional but in terms of producing some desirable behaviour or outcome. He argues that "we must cease once and for all to describe the effects of power in negative terms. . . . In fact, power produces; it produces reality; it produces domains of object and rituals of truth" (Foucault 1979, p. 194). In this way, Foucault urges scholars to avoid the trap of examining how power dismantles social relations and instead consider what is created through power's exercise.

Foucault was convinced that these micro-powers are not confined to the prison but have been diffused into the larger social world. Following Foucault (as well as David Garland 1985), Chunn (1992) has demonstrated how disciplinary powers were disseminated throughout early twentieth-century Canadian society to create a dense and interlocking web of surveillance intended to discipline the working classes. We encourage you to think about your everyday lives. What forms of discipline are acting upon you? What forms of surveillance are encouraging you to act appropriately? Consider your social media accounts and questions of privacy. What about other monitoring on your campus? Are there closed-circuit television cameras at your college or university? If you drive, will you pass a photo radar vehicle on your way to or from school? How does your behaviour change as a result of this surveillance?

Foucault's work has been routinely challenged for conceptualizing human subjects as "docile" bodies who are the subject of discipline without at the same time resisting incursion into their lives. Foucault addresses this criticism in a 1982 essay entitled "The Subject and Power," where he argues that power operates on individuals so long as they are free. For Foucault (1982), power operates on the actions and behaviour of others, which implies that power can only ever work on a subject who is capable of action and who is (relatively) free. Power seeks to structure subjects' choices in ways that bring their behaviour in line with the needs and desires of governors. For example, during their trip to Disney World, Clifford Shearing and Phillip Stenning (1984) noticed that, despite the hordes of people and without overt signs of discipline and control, the amusement park seemed to function like clockwork. They found that "designed-in" features, like carefully marked roadways and smiling employees, control and shape behaviour in ways conducive to good order at the park. One does not have to travel to Florida to witness similar effects. One of the authors of this chapter recently visited IKEA to purchase an item for his home. When he arrived, he knew exactly what he wanted and where he could find it (in the warehouse). Despite this knowledge, the configuration of the store shaped his actions such that he was "encouraged" by the partition separating the entrance (on one side) from the warehouse (on the opposite side) to venture through the entire store. Those familiar with the massive size of IKEA can imagine his frustration.

Today, micro-powers abound and assist in ordering contemporary life. Policing has been bolstered by the promulgation and circulation of micro-power. Consider how you adjust your driving after noticing a police car in your vicinity. Whether or not the officers are directly observing your behaviour is secondary to how their presence alters your conduct. Our earlier example of surveillance in Edmonton's Churchill Square further reveals the contemporary distribution of micro-powers. In 2010, the City of Edmonton released its blueprint for the future of the square and the larger downtown area (City of Edmonton 2010). Edmonton city planners call this a "bold vision for Edmonton's downtown" that enhances the "overall aesthetic quality of Sir Winston Churchill Square" (City of Edmonton 2010, p. 162). Mention of spaces for marginalized young people is conspicuously absent. Instead, the report spotlights several strategies to address crime and disorder. Among the plans is a call for all major downtown streets to be open, to be designed with continuous store-front retail, and to have wide sidewalks. You might be wondering how this relates to crime control. Such tactics expand "natural surveillance" through having more "eyes on the street" and creating unobstructed lines of site throughout the space (City of Edmonton 2010, pp. 82, 102). City planners are convinced that this will have the intended effect of improving "safety and security in the Downtown" (p. 26).

As you can now see, Foucault's work helps crime scholars understand modern configurations of power by alerting them to how the behaviour of active subjects is shaped and contoured in ways often hidden from view, but that have very real effects.

While the works of Derrida and Foucault are useful to describe the central goals of critical criminology, they are often abstract. We need to ask, *What could a critical criminological approach look like in practice?* Reconsidering how we define youth crime and youth justice in terms of marginalization and suffering allows us to imagine what kinds of changes a critical criminological approach would create or advocate. In her article provocatively titled "Against Youth Justice and Youth Governance, for Youth Penalty," Jo Phoenix (2016, p. 124) writes about youth justice and governance in the United Kingdom, provoking a debate about what she calls "a critical politics of youth justice broadly based on the assumption that, as currently constituted, youth justice is *unjust*." To make it more just, she asserts, "it would be necessary to revive and re-institutionalize the relationship between higher ethical principles of intervening in young lawbreakers' lives and what we then do to them (i.e. intentions and deeds)" (p. 124). Phoenix notes further, "the issue is one of conceptualizing 'change.' The question: what framework would enable us to delineate the necessary and sufficient conditions of possibility for a more just or even a non-penal response to youthful lawbreaking. At the political level, the issue is of *imagining* what such a response would be" (p. 124). Take a moment now to reflect on what, in the Canadian context, in your local community, such a critical criminology framework could look like. Toward this end, instead of youth justice, Phoenix offers the concept of "critical youth penology" (p. 132) and encourages scholars of youth justice to ask practical questions like "Is it more just to respond to youthful lawbreaking through out of court diversion schemes?" (p. 133).

Cultural Criminology

Beck's (1992) and Ferrell and Hayward's (2011) works, among others, alert us to the growing importance and seeming omnipotence of risk in contemporary societies. However, this scholarship does little to help criminologists understand and conceptualize how young people on the ground experience and understand this phenomenon. Evidence suggests that young people today are engaging in and enjoying more risky behaviour simply because they are constituted to do so (Hunt, Evans, Moloney, and Bailey 2009; Sanders 2005). Sean Morrissey (2008), in his examination of voluntary risk-taking behaviour among a Scottish dance education company, suggests that young people find risk-taking to be particularly alluring. He argues that transgressive conduct is particularly tempting in societies of caution, where young people are heavily surveilled and policed (Morrissey 2008). Indeed, risk-taking behaviour among young people is evident in a several divergent and diverse domains of youth culture, from BASE jumping (using a parachute to jump from buildings, antennas, spans, and earth) to ecstasy use in the rave scene.

Contemporary criminological theories have difficulty accounting for these seemingly absurd and baseless choices. Rational choice theory, for example, is among the most prominent perspectives in criminology for understanding youthful offending. It posits that young people are rational actors who make informed and rational decisions about rule-breaking. While criminologists have widely applied this theory in the context of crime, other scholars have attended to how almost all behaviour (e.g., purchasing a television) can be understood in relation to how we understand perceived costs and benefits. Nevertheless, such a perspective does little to account for the emotional and visceral elements of crime and deviance. Cultural criminology, by contrast, is attentive to what renders "transgression and the consumption of transgression so seductive" (Hayward 2002). Scholars working in this tradition direct academic attention to crime as a lived experience that can best be understood through **ethnography**.

Transgressive Elements of Youth Deviance

Cultural criminologists also engage in critical criminological critique but are less concerned with state definitions of crime and the pragmatism of crime control than they are with the adrenaline surge and emotion that accompany the commission of crime. Fenwick and Hayward (2000) suggest that this insight challenges one of the most widely held and central assumptions of criminology: that crime is "routinized" and rather "banal." They maintain that this "is undoubtedly the case if one adopts the perspective of the police. . . . however, it is not necessarily true for those participating in criminal activity, for whom the most innocuous transgression may well represent an exhilarating form of experience" (p. 36). Thus, while home invasion may not make rational sense to the average crime scholar, cultural criminologists may argue that this crime is more often the result of the adrenaline rush emerging from the commission of the crime than of reasoned forethought.

Cultural criminology enjoys considerable intellectual momentum at present (Ferrell and Hayward 2011; Ferrell and Young 2004). This group of scholars, all of whom are critical of the methods and orthodox criminology and its inability to conceptualize the

ethnography
A form of participatory research that involves immersion in the field of study. Because it allows for rich and descriptive findings on areas that are often hidden from view, ethnographic research is fundamental to cultural criminology.

adrenaline and emotions intrinsic to offending, interweave a number of intellectual threads. These include cultural studies, postmodern theory, critical theory, textual/media analysis, and ethnographic methodologies (Ferrell 1999). Considered more broadly, the very notion of cultural criminology indexes the increasing attention crime scholars lend to popular culture constructions of crime and its control (Ferrell 1999; McCormick 2010). Through innovative theoretical and methodological precepts, cultural criminologists aim to expand and enliven the discipline (Ferrell and Sanders 1995, p. 17).

Innovative methodologies provide cultural criminologists with unique insight into the visceral nature of crime and deviance. According to Kane (2004, p. 303), "participant observation remains the methodological touchstone for the culture-worker." Ethnographic research is particularly appropriate for the subject of cultural criminology. This method attends to the "nuances of meaning within particular cultural milieu" (Ferrell 1999, p. 399). Deep immersion in criminal or deviant fields encourages researchers to formulate richly textured descriptions of these worlds, which are often hidden from view. However, cultural criminologists do not only employ participant observation to their academic ends. Maggie O'Neill (2004), for instance, uses a method she calls "ethno-mimesis" to capture the complexity of lived reality. For example, she had sex workers use art and prose to detail not only their life experiences but their ideas for social change (O'Neil 2004). Consider what an ethnographic study not of, but with, street-involved youth, might look like. Which aspect of the human experience—subsistence, intimacy, care, or perhaps well-being might you as a student of critical criminology want to explore deeper.

Cultural criminology possesses much potential for transgression. Like the other critical projects discussed in this chapter, cultural criminology unflaggingly challenges taken-for-granted assumptions about crime and its study so as to expose how these are "culturally constructed and delimited by a particular world view" (Hogeveen and Woolford 2009, p. 354; Morrison 2004). Jock Young (2004, p. 1) maintains that because we are "confronted at this moment with an orthodox criminology which is denatured and desiccated," the need for a cultural criminology that captures the phenomenology of crime, its adrenaline, its pleasure and panic, its excitement, and its anger, rage and humiliation"— has never been more pressing. In these ways, scholarly investigation of the lived realities of young people's lives may be at once about knowledge creation and social transformation.

Summary

Critical criminology directs attention to the structural inequalities both within and outside the criminal justice system and looks critically at the circumstances of, and suffering within, young people's lives. Critical criminologists advocate social engagement in ways that would transform marginalization and bring about justice for youth. Critical criminology recognizes that young people are marginalized through power relations along, but not limited to, age, class, gender, and racial lines, and acknowledges our responsibility to the marginalized young other. In Canada, while marginalization is widespread, the situation that Indigenous youth—especially girls—are facing is particularly egregious; this is evident in incarceration rates and homelessness, and in the tragic history and impact of colonialism that continues unabated, despite calls for truth and reconciliation in contemporary society. In the era of the #MeToo and Time's Up movements, gendered violence and othering toward girls and young women persists.

Deconstruction, as understood by Derrida, opens language to its hidden and its silent elements. While almost all language can be deconstructed, justice resists our attempts, as it is forever "to come." Considered in this way, justice encourages tireless ameliorative efforts on behalf of marginalized others, *with* the communities touched by suffering.

Foucault's impact on critical scholarship is particularly significant. He attuned scholars to new ways of thinking about and understanding power. Instead of seeing power as solely repressive, he thought it was creative and productive. Foucault argued that rather than being housed in some place or entity (i.e., the state), power is evident only in its exercise. Through discipline, surveillance, and governmentality, Foucault maintained that power shapes individuals in ways that render them more amenable to governance.

Critical criminologists have also made use of, and critiqued, the concepts of risk, actuarialism, and the risk society to critically examine contemporary society's preoccupation with insurance-like predictions of potential harm. Because of their age, level of maturity, and propensity for precarious behaviour, young people are particularly prone to be subjects of such forms of calculation and risk management techniques. Critical scholarship attends to the social contexts that produce the risk society and encourages academics to draw attention to how marginalization is camouflaged in risk management approaches to youth justice. Similarly, cultural criminology is critical of contemporary scholars who reject crime as a visceral phenomenon. Critical scholarship on youth justice is aimed at both critical reflection and social engagement toward a more just and caring social order (Minaker and Hogeveen 2009). The question remains, *How is youth for youth possible?* Meaningful change is materialized as just and human moments when young people—not youth as they are constructed in youth discourse, but youth as they *are*—matter, belong, are acknowledged, and are seen and understood as worthy, valued and valuable members of the human community.

Key Terms

critical criminology	outcast space
deconstruction	power (Foucault)
ethnography	risk
hospitality	risk society
justice (Derrida)	surveillance
marginalization	trace

Review Questions

1. Explain how critical criminologists understand and operationalize critique.

2. Highlight and provide examples of how systemic oppression contributes to social suffering and to the marginalization of youth.

3. Describe and provide examples of how cultural criminology is critical.

4. How would critical criminology problematize "youth at risk" discourse?

5. Explain and provide an example of deconstruction (pay particular attention to the trace).

6. Explore why Derrida claims justice is not deconstructable.

7. Imagine ways to bring about transformative change that would challenge and change the suffering of youth, especially those at the social margins.

Critical Thinking Questions

1. Explain what being critical means to you. Discuss the differences and similarities between your own understanding of being critical and that of critical criminology.

2. Marginalization of the other is found in every Canadian city. Discuss what responsibility, if any, you might have to ameliorate the suffering experienced and lived by the other in your local community.

3. How might the insights of the various scholars outlined in this chapter be practically implemented in the real world?

4. Recall Foucault's understanding of power. How does this conception differ from more widely held beliefs about power in Western society? Explore how your everyday behaviour is disciplined and made the subject of surveillance or governed. To what ends is this governance exercised?

5. How would *you* define justice for youth?

References

Aboriginal Healing Foundation. (2003). *Aboriginal domestic violence in Canada*. Ottawa: Anishinabe Press.

Andrews, D.A., and Bonta, J. (2007). The risk-need-responsivity model of assessment and human service in prevention and corrections: Crime-prevention jurisprudence. *Canadian Journal of Criminology and Criminal Justice, 49*, 439–64.

Balfour, G., and Comack, E. (2014). *Criminalizing women: Gender and (in)justice in neoliberal times* (2nd ed.). Halifax: Fernwood.

Beck, U. (1992). *Risk society: Towards a new modernity*. London: Sage.

Bradley, A. (2008). *Derrida's of grammatology*. Bloomington: Indiana University Press.

Buller, M., Audette, M., Evolfson, B., and Robinson, Q. (2017). National Inquiry into Missing and Murdered Indigenous Women and Girls: Our women and girls are sacred. Interim report. http://www.mmiwg-ffada.ca/wp-content/uploads/2018/03/ni-mmiwg-interim-report.pdf

Carroll, D. (2006). "Remains" of Algeria: Justice, hospitality, politics. *Modern Language Notes, 121*(4), 808–27.

Chartrand, L., and McKay, C. (2006). *A review of research on criminal victimization and First Nations, Métis and Inuit People, 1990 to 2001*. Ottawa: Department of Justice.

Chunn, D. (1992). *From punishment to doing good: Family courts and socialized justice in Ontario, 1880–1940*. Toronto: University of Toronto Press.

City of Edmonton. (2010). *Capital City downtown plan*. Retrieved from https://www.edmonton.ca/projects_plans/downtown/capital-city-downtown-plan.aspx

Comack, E. (2018). *Coming back to jail*. Halifax: Fernwood.

Crosby, D. (2018). *Creating warm places in cold cities: A relational youth work practice with Indigenous youth* (Unpublished doctoral dissertation). University of Alberta, Edmonton.

Dean, M. (1999). *Governmentality: Power and rule in modern society*. London: Sage.

Derrida, J. (1985). Letter to a Japanese friend. In D. Wood, and R. Bernasconi (Eds), *Derrida and différance* (pp. 1–6). Warwick: Parousia.

Derrida, J. (1987). Some questions and responses. In N. Fabb, D. Attridge, and C. MacCabe (Eds), *The linguistics of writing: Arguments between language and literature* (pp. 252–64). Manchester: Manchester University Press.

Derrida, J. (1995). *Points—interviews, 1974–1994*. E. Weber (Ed.). (P. Kamuf, Trans.). Stanford: Stanford University Press.

Derrida, J. (1999). Hospitality, justice and responsibility: A dialogue with Jacques Derrida. In R. Kearney and M. Dooley (Eds), *Questioning ethics: Contemporary debates in philosophy* (pp. 65–83). New York: Routledge.

Derrida, J. (2002). Force of law: The "mystical foundation of authority." In G. Anidjar (Ed.), *Jacques Derrida: Acts of religion* (pp. 229–98). London: Routledge.

Derrida, J. (2005). *The principle of hospitality. Paper machine* (R. Bowbly, Trans.) (pp. 66–9). Stanford: Stanford University Press.

Derrida, J., and Caputo, J.D. (1997). *Deconstruction in a nutshell: A conversation with Jacques Derrida*. New York: Fordham University Press.

Derrida, J., and Dufourmantelle, A. (2000). *Of hospitality*. Stanford, CA: Stanford University Press.

Dillabough, J., and Yoon, E. (2018). Youth geographies or urban estrangement in the Canadian city: Risk management, race relations and the "sacrificial stranger." *Children's Geographies, 16*(2), 128–42.

Edmonton Committee to End Homelessness. (2009, January 29). *Edmonton Committee to End Homelessness releases 10-year plan* [News release]. Retrieved from http://www.endedmontonhomelessness.com/docs/mediapackagewithgoals.pdf

Elden, S. (2007). There is a politics of space because space is political: Henri Lefebvre and the production of space. *Radical Philosophy Review, 10*(2), 101–16.

Ericson, R., and Haggerty, K. (1999). Governing the young. In R. Smandych (Ed.), *Governable places: Readings on governmentality and crime control* (pp. 163–90). Aldershot, UK: Ashgate.

Ewald, F. (1991). Insurance and risk. In G. Burchell, C. Gordon, and P. Miller (Eds), *The Foucault effect: Studies in governmentality* (pp. 197–210). Chicago: University of Chicago Press.

Fenwick, M., and Hayward, K. (2000). Youth crime, excitement and consumer culture: The reconstruction of aetiology in contemporary theoretical criminology. In J. Pickford (Ed.), *Youth justice: Theory and practice* (pp. 31–50). London: Glasshouse.

Ferrell, J. (1999). Cultural criminology. *Annual Review of Sociology, 25*(1), 395–418.

Ferrell, J., and Hayward, K. (2011). *Cultural criminology*. Surrey, UK: Ashgate.

Ferrell, J., and Sanders, C. (1995). *Cultural criminology*. Boston: Northeastern University Press.

Ferrell, J., and Young, J. (2004). Cultural criminology: Some notes on the script. *Theoretical Criminology, 8*(3), 259–73.

Foucault, M. (1977). *Discipline and punish*. New York: Vintage.

Foucault, M. (1979). *The history of sexuality*. New York: Vintage.

Foucault, M. (1980). *Power/knowledge: Selected interviews and other writings*. New York: Pantheon.

Foucault, M. (1982). The subject and power. In H. Dreyfus and P. Rabinow (Eds), *Michel Foucault: Beyond structuralism and hermeneutics* (pp. 208–26). Chicago: University of Chicago Press.

Foucault, M. (1991). Governmentality. In G. Burchell, C. Gordon, and P. Miller (Eds), *The Foucault effect: Studies in governmentality* (pp. 87–104). Chicago: University of Chicago Press.

Fournier, S., and Crey, E. (1997). *Stolen from our embrace: The abduction of First Nations children and the restoration of Aboriginal communities*. Vancouver: Douglas and McIntyre.

Garland, D. (1985). *Punishment and welfare: A history of penal strategies*. London: Gower.

Gorkoff, K. (2011). Othering or protecting? The discursive practice of saving youth prostitutes. *Annual Review of Interdisciplinary Justice Research, 2*(Fall), 5–34.

Hannah-Moffat, K. (2001). *Punishment in disguise: Penal governance and federal imprisonment*. Toronto: University of Toronto Press.

Harper, S. (2008). Prime Minister Stephen Harper delivers remarks at the 6th Annual Gala and Fundraiser for the Canadian Crime Victims Foundation. Retrieved from http://pm.gc.ca/eng/media.asp?id=2145

Harvey, D. (1989). *The condition of postmodernity: An inquiry into the origins of cultural change*. London: Blackwell.

Hawkins, D., and Pollard, J. (1999). Risk and protective factors: Are both necessary to understand diverse behavioural outcomes in adolescence? *Social Work Research, 23*(3), 145–58.

Hayward, K. (2002). The vilification and pleasures of youthful transgression. In J. Muncie, G. Hughes, and E. McLaughlin (Eds), *Youth justice: Critical readings* (pp. 80–93). London: Sage.

Health Canada. (1998). *Meeting the needs of youth-at-risk in Canada: A summary of the learnings*. Ottawa: Health Canada.

Herbert, S., and Brown, E. (2006). Conceptions of space and crime in the punitive neoliberal city. *Antipode, 38*(4), 755–77.

Hoge, R.D., and Andrews, D.A. (2010). YLS/CMI: Youth level of service/case management inventory 2.0. *mhs Assessments*.

Retrieved from http://www.mhs.com/product.aspx?gr=safandprod=yls-cmiandid=overview

Hogeveen, B. (2006). Unsettling youth justice and cultural norms: The Youth Restorative Action Project. *Journal of Youth Studies, 9*(1), 47–66.

Hogeveen, B. (2007). Is there justice for youth? In G. Pavlich and M. Hird (Eds), *Questioning sociology: Canadian perspectives* (pp. 210–25). Don Mills, ON: Oxford University Press.

Hogeveen, B., and Freistadt, J. (2012). Youth justice and hospitality: Overcoming "scarecrow policing." In R. Jochelson and K. Gorkoff (Eds), *Thinking about justice: A book of readings.* Halifax: Fernwood.

Hogeveen, B., and Freistadt, J. (2013). Hospitality and the homeless: Jacques Derrida in the neoliberal city. *Journal of Theoretical and Philosophical Criminology 5*(1), 39–63

Hogeveen, B., and Woolford, A. (2006). Critical criminology and possibility in the neoliberal ethos. *Canadian Journal of Criminology and Criminal Justice, 48*(5), 681–702.

Hogeveen, B., and Woolford, A. (2009). Contemporary critical criminology. In R. Linden (Ed.), *Criminology: A Canadian perspective* (6th ed.) (pp. 339–70). Toronto: Pearson Education.

Howell, J. (2005). Moving risk factors into developmental theories of gang membership. *Youth Violence and Juvenile Justice, 3*(5), 334–54.

Hunt, G., Evans, K., Moloney, M., and Bailey, N. (2009). Combining different substances in the dance scene: Enhancing pleasure, managing risk and timing effects. *Journal of Drug Issues, 39*(3), 495–522.

Kane, S. (2004). The unconventional methods of cultural criminology. *Theoretical Criminology, 8*(3), 303–21.

Kasper, L. (2017, December 12). The state of mental health treatment for youth in the justice system. *Law Now.* Retrieved from https://www.lawnow.org/the-state-of-mental-health-treatment-for-youth-in-the-justice-system

Kleiss, K. (2010, October 11). Housing dollars fuel social chaos: Residents. *Edmonton Journal.* Retrieved from http://www.edmontonjournal.com/business/Housing%20+dollars+fuel+social+chaos+residents/3653120/story.html

Lefebvre, H. (1996). *Writing on cities.* London: Blackwell.

Lepola, J., and McGrew, P. (2017, May 31). More youth, charged with violent crime, filling juvenile jails. *Fox 45 News* (Baltimore). Retrieved from https://foxbaltimore.com/features/operation-crime-justice/a-trend-of-young-violent-criminals

McCormick, C. (2010). *Constructing danger: Mis/Representation of crime in the news.* Halifax: Fernwood.

Malakieh, J. (2018). Adult and youth correctional statistics, 2016/2017. Statistics Canada Catalogue No. 85-002-X.

Retrieved from https://www150.statcan.gc.ca/n1/pub/85-002-x/2018001/article/54972-eng.pdf

Mallea, P. (2010). *The fear factor: Stephen Harper's "tough on crime" agenda.* Ottawa: Canadian Centre for Policy Alternatives.

Marley, K., Penman, A., and Dufresne, S. (2018, February 23). Injustice is a way of Indigenous life, say advocates dismayed at verdict in Tina Fontaine murder trial. CBC Radio: *The Current.* Retrieved from https://www.cbc.ca/radio/thecurrent/the-current-for-february-23-2018-1.4547552/injustice-is-a-way-of-indigenous-life-say-advocates-dismayed-at-verdict-in-tina-fontaine-murder-trial-1.4548471

Minaker, J., and Hogeveen, B. (2009). *Youth, crime, and society: Issues of power and justice.* Toronto: Pearson Prentice Hall.

Monture-Angus, P. (1999). Women and risk: Aboriginal women, colonialism, and correctional practice. *Canadian Woman Studies, 19*(1–2). Retrieved from https://cws.journals.yorku.ca/index.php/cws/article/view/8068

Morrison, W. (2004). "Reflections with memories": Everyday photography capturing genocide. *Theoretical Criminology, 8*(3), 341–58.

Morrissey, S.A. (2008). Performing risks: Catharsis, carnival and capital in the risk society. *Journal of Youth Studies, 11*(4), 413–27.

National Crime Prevention Centre. (2007). *Youth gang involvement: What are the risk factors?* Ottawa: National Crime Prevention Centre of Public Safety Canada.

O'Malley, P. (1992). Risk, power and crime prevention, *Economy and Society 21*(3), 252–75.

O'Malley, P. (1996). Risk and responsibility. In A. Barry, T. Osborne, and N. Rose (Eds), *Foucault and political reason: Liberalism, neoliberalism and rationalities of government* (pp. 189–208). Chicago: University of Chicago Press.

O'Neill, M. (2004). Crime, culture, and visual methodologies: Ethno-mimesis as performative praxis. In J. Ferrell, K. Hayward, W. Morrison, and M. Presdee (Eds), *Cultural criminology unleashed* (pp. 219–29). London: Glasshouse.

Pavlich, G. (2007). Deconstruction. In G. Ritzer (Ed.), *Blackwell encyclopedia of sociology* (pp. 986–9). Malden: Blackwell.

Peterson-Badali, M., McCormick, S., Vitopoulos, N., Davis, K., & Haqanee, Z., & Skilling, T. (2015). Mental health in the context of Canada's youth justice system. *Canadian Criminal Law Review, 19*, 1–20.

Phoenix, J. (2016). Against youth justice and youth governance, for youth penality. *British Journal of Criminology, 56*, 123–40.

Ratner, R. (1971). Criminology in Canada: Conflicting objectives. Unpublished manuscript.

RCMP's open letter to Alberta communities addresses youth wreaking havoc. (2014, July 15). *Global News.* Retrieved from https://globalnews.ca/news/1452669/rcmps-open-letter-to-alberta-communities-addresses-youth-wreaking-havoc/

Royal Canadian Mounted Police. (2014, July 10). *Missing and murdered Aboriginal women: A national operational overview.* Retrieved from http://www.rcmp-grc.gc.ca/pubs/mmaw-faapd-eng.pdf

Royal Commission on Aboriginal Peoples. (1996). *Report of the Royal Commission on Aboriginal Peoples.* Ottawa: Indian and Northern Affairs Canada.

Sanders, B. (2005). In the club: Ecstasy use and supply in a London nightclub. *Sociology, 39*(2), 241–58.

Scotti, M. (2017). Canadians still wildly overestimating the level of violent crime. *Global News.* Retrieved from https://globalnews.ca/news/3645766/canadians-still-wildly-overestimating-the-level-of-violent-crime/

Scrim, K. (2013). *Aboriginal victimization in Canada: A summary of the literature.* Ottawa: Department of Justice.

Shader, M. (2003). *Risk factors for delinquency: An overview.* Washington, DC: Office of Juvenile Justice and Delinquency.

Shearing, C., and Stenning, P. (1984). From the panopticon to Disney World: The development of discipline. In A. Doob and E. Greenspan (Eds), *Perspectives in criminal law* (pp. 335–49). Toronto: Aurora.

Smart, C. (1989). *Feminism and the power of law.* London: Routledge.

Spivak, G. (1976). Translator's preface. In J. Derrida, *Of grammatology* (G. Spivak, Trans.) (pp. ix–lxxxvii). Baltimore: Johns Hopkins University Press.

Statistics Canada. (2014). *Admissions to Youth Correctional Services in Canada, 2011/2012.* Retrieved from http://www.statcan.gc.ca/pub/85-002-x/2014001/article/11917-eng.htm

Wyrick, P., and Howell, J. (2004). Strategic risk based response to youth gangs. *Juvenile Justice Journal, 9*(1), 20–9.

Young, J. (2004). Voodoo criminology and the numbers game. In J. Ferrell, K. Hayward, W. Morrison, and M. Presdee (Eds), *Cultural criminology unleashed* (pp. 13–27). London: Glasshouse.

Part III

Criminalized Youth in Canada
Selected Types and Problems

When discussing the subject of delinquency or criminalized youth, some conversations inevitably shift toward specific subject areas such as substance use, Indigenous youth, ethnic minority youth, street-involved youth, and youth involved in sex work. Any discussion about the different expressions of criminalized youth may include a variety of different perspectives that generally reflect the complexity of delinquency and the interdisciplinary and/or multidisciplinary nature of the study of youth crime. Practical constraints do not allow us to cover all the topics that we might aspire to address in a book of this nature. Therefore, in this section, we focus on four different types of delinquent behaviour and/or phenomena. Collectively, the chapters serve to illustrate not only that young persons' conduct is complicated but that any efforts to prevent, control, treat, or otherwise respond to young persons are both challenging and fraught with varying degrees of controversy. The topics covered in this section also serve to illustrate that we cannot rely on comprehensive solutions, programs, or treatment techniques to (re)solve youth crime.

Most of the subject areas included in Part III tend to reflect themes and topics that have dominated the youth justice literature for some years now. Entire scholarly books have been devoted to some of the issues presented. Therefore, we do not profess to provide a comparable level of depth of analysis. Nevertheless, each of the chapters offers a concise and yet informative overview of the subject matter being addressed.

Chapter 10, by Jordon Diplock, Nick Pauls, and Gwendolyn Geuze, examines the topic of substance use and related crime in adolescence. The authors provide a contextual framework as to why young people experiment with and/or use drugs, and they discuss a range of risks (e.g., physical health and psychological health). Diplock, Pauls, and Geuze then describe how substance use is related to various youth crimes as a result of such risk factors as impaired judgment, social pressure, and so on. In recognizing the multiple harms of substance use, the authors then examine a range of formal and informal intervention and prevention strategies (most of which are school-based) that have been successfully used to prevent youth from ever experimenting and to "just say no." Although substance use among Canadian adolescents has stabilized after previous years of decreasing consumption, the authors indicate that alcohol, cannabis, electronic cigarettes, and tobacco use are common among adolescents today. Usage rates for marijuana and illicit substances are higher for adolescents than those of adults. Therefore, the authors assert that it is critical that further efforts be undertaken to avoid the negative consequences of substance use.

Chapter 11, by Hirsch Greenberg and Jana Grekul, focuses on Indigenous youth, who, like other minority groups around the world, are overrepresented in the youth justice system. After providing some disheartening statistics on the nature and type of this overrepresentation, the authors move on to provide a comprehensive historical context by which to understand how and why Indigenous youth have become so closely aligned with youth crime. Through a series of examples, the authors show how specific past policies have contributed to intergenerational experiences of trauma and the overrepresentation of Indigenous youth in the criminal justice system. Then, by drawing on the Indigenous perspective, they show how using Indigenous-based approaches to justice may better fit the needs and values of these youth. Greenberg and Grekul present a critically compelling argument for a significant reform of how we have traditionally dealt with young Indigenous offenders.

A new contribution to this edition of the book is presented in Chapter 12. Harpreet Aulakh and Julius Haag focus on ethnic minority youth's involvement with the justice system. The authors highlight the lack of available data related to race, ethnicity, and the youth criminal justice system. The chapter also examines ethnic minority youths' involvement in youth gangs, the potential risk factors for engagement, and theoretical models linking immigration and crime. Aulakh and Haag also review how police policies and practices have impacted ethnic minorities and discuss the outcomes of current (aggressive) policing arrangements. They conclude the chapter by presenting some promising examples of culturally sensitive intervention programs that have been developed to address the risk factors of ethnic minority youth.

In Chapter 13, Bruce MacLaurin and Catherine Worthington focus on street-involved youth in Canada. Although the topic is regularly overlooked or given only passing attention in most books on young offenders, the authors offer insight into the relationship between street-involved youth and youth crime. Through their review of the different typologies of street involvement, they identify the various risk factors (i.e., pathways) that may result in street youth turning to delinquent behaviour. In addition to discussing the impact of street involvement on the education system and child welfare, MacLaurin and Worthington include an examination of the effect of street involvement on the criminal justice system. Then, as with all the chapters in this section, they discuss intervention and prevention strategies but point out that such services are underutilized. However, drawing on their related work, they offer some examples that have proven promising. The authors conclude their chapter by reiterating that not only are street youth a marginalized group, but they are also a diverse and complex group of young people who, despite their resilience, have their unique challenges that deserve careful attention.

In the final chapter of this section (Chapter 14), Kelly Gorkoff, Anne Miller, Chloe Shepherd, and Courtenay Bolton examine young people involved in systems of sexual exploitation and sex work. The chapter explores the stigmatized nature of the SET (sexual exploitation trade), suggesting this as a significant roadblock in assisting those involved. After reviewing the conflicting and diverse definitions, terminology, and conceptualizations of young people's involvement, the authors examine legislative initiatives across the country and discuss the social structural factors that shape the SET for young people. The chapter reviews research focused on the experiences of life in the SET, including health, wellness, homelessness, identity, and violence. The chapter concludes with a discussion of the different regulatory paradigms through which young people are both punished and protected via state intervention in their lives.

Issues of Substance Use and Related Crime in Adolescence

Jordan Diplock, Nick Pauls, and Gwendolyn Geuze[1]

10

Overview

This chapter provides an overview of some of the major issues surrounding substance use among youth in Canada and the link to involvement in criminal behaviour. To provide background for these issues, the first half of the chapter presents information on the nature and extent of adolescent substance use, the reasons young people use drugs and alcohol, and the potential harms of substance use for adolescents. The chapter then discusses how adolescent substance use relates to crime in this age group. The sections focus specifically on the evidence suggesting a link between substance use and crime and the nature and extent of adolescent participation in drug-specific crimes. Finally, the chapter discusses the most promising practices for substance use prevention and treatment for adolescents and youth offenders. This chapter allows students to critically assess the current situation surrounding substance use among youth in Canada to inform their opinions about the future steps that policy-makers, researchers, law-enforcement officials, and those tasked with implementing substance use prevention and intervention activities should take to deal with these many issues.

Key Objectives

After reading this chapter, you should be able to:

- Identify which substances are most commonly used by adolescents in Canada and discuss trends in substance use.
- Recognize some of the reasons youth become involved with drugs and have an understanding of the issues surrounding this topic.
- Identify the potential harms to adolescents from substance use.
- Discuss the link between adolescent drug use, criminal behaviour, and victimization.
- Discuss best and promising practices for substance use prevention and treatment and harm reduction with youth in general and youth involved in the justice system specifically.

Introduction

As is the case in most parts of the world, the use of licit and illicit substances has become a part of the social landscape in Canada. For example, although smoking across Canada has reached its lowest rate ever recorded, nearly four million (13 per cent of) Canadians over the age of 15 currently smoke (Health Canada 2017b). Alcohol consumption represents a major component of leisure-time culture, with Canadians ranking among the world's top 50 in per capita alcohol consumption (World Health Organization 2014). In addition to legal substance use, illegal drugs have become a serious concern in Canada. Canada's opioid crisis, the rapid rise in opioid-related overdose deaths in recent years, has received international attention (United Nations Office on Drugs and Crime [UNODC] 2018). The country is also home to more than 100,000 intravenous drug users, many living in urban areas such as Vancouver's infamous Downtown Eastside (Urban Health Research Initiative 2009). This current reality inevitably exposes young Canadians to these substances and contributes to the ongoing concern that Canadian youth may face serious life problems related to substance use.

The most recent Canadian Drugs and Substance Strategy from the Government of Canada (Health Canada 2017a) places a strong focus on the prevention and treatment of problematic substance use by youth. The prevention strategy emphasizes the use of evidence-based approaches to present prevention messages to youth, and give parents the tools to speak with their adolescent children about substance use. The strategy also intends to increase justice system capacity to target illegal drug production and distribution, particularly focusing on interrupting the profits from illegal drug markets going to organized criminals. The pillar of harm reduction was reintroduced into the strategy in 2016 after its removal by the previous government. Additionally, addressing the growing opioid crisis in Canada is a prominent theme throughout the proposed actions within the strategy.

Are the hundreds of millions of dollars spent annually across the country on prevention initiatives, research, policing, courts, corrections, and treatment programs in the hope of discouraging youth from starting or continuing drug and alcohol use warranted? Or, conversely, is more emphasis needed on youth substance use issues, with increased enforcement powers, more and better treatment options, and more pervasive educational programs? This chapter will provide the reader with some of the information needed to begin to answer these and other related questions.

Substance Use among Canadian Youth

The majority of Canadian adolescents do not report using illicit drugs, and the use of alcohol and tobacco by youth remains stable after years of decline (Health Canada 2017b). However, a significant percentage of adolescents are still using substances and that is concerning, as youth are more likely than adults to engage in risky alcohol and drug use behaviour and experience greater harms associated with that use (Adlaf, Begin, and Sawka 2005). On the contrary, for every year an adolescent delays drug use, the risk of developing a serious problem with substance use is reduced by 5 per cent (Behrendt, Wittchen, Holfer, Lieb, and Beesdo 2009).

Drug Use Trends

In general, after years of decline, substance use rates among adolescents have stabilized and even shown an increase for some substance use activities, such as the use of e-cigarettes (Health Canada 2018). Usage trends for several common substances are discussed in detail below.

Alcohol Use

Alcohol is the most common substance used by youth. While alcohol is a legal substance, there are age restrictions and other regulations to control its use in Canada. The legal minimum age to purchase and consume alcohol is 19 in all provinces other than Alberta, Manitoba, and Quebec, where the legal minimum age is 18. In a 2016–2017 survey of students in Grades 7 to 12, 44 per cent reported using alcohol at least once in the previous year, and 24 per cent reported consuming five or more drinks on a single occasion in the past year (Health Canada 2018). Overall, 59 per cent of youth between the ages of 15 and 19 reported past year use of alcohol (Health Canada 2017b).

Tobacco Use

Although much less common than drinking alcohol, tobacco smoking is one of the most common substance use activities engaged in by youth. As with alcohol, each province has a minimum age of 18 or 19 to purchase tobacco products. Tobacco use has greatly declined over recent years, considering that a small minority of youth (10 per cent) between the ages of 15 and 19 reported current engagement in cigarette smoking, and only 4 per cent reported being daily cigarette smokers (Health Canada 2017b). Although tobacco use among youth appears to be declining (Health Canada 2017b), the addictive

Box 10.1 | Youth Justice in Action

The Impact of Cannabis Legalization on Adolescents

The Government of Canada has legalized the recreational use of cannabis by adults. Following years of a gradual shift in public opinion away from the prohibition of cannabis, adults are no longer prohibited from possessing and purchasing 30 grams or less of dried cannabis from authorized sources or from growing four or fewer cannabis plants within their residence. This change has caused provincial governments across the country to establish legitimate distribution systems for cannabis and to introduce additional regulations to accompany those outlined federally (Government of Canada 2018).

Opponents of legalization argue that, among other issues, it could increase the use of cannabis by Canadian adolescents. This question has been explored by research on youth consumption in the US states that have legalized the use of medical cannabis and those few that have already legalized recreational cannabis for adults. Generally, the research has found no evidence that the legalization of medical cannabis increased the rates of adolescent cannabis use, although many of these states were found to already have high rates of use among this age group (Chadi, Weitzman, and Levy 2018; Hasin et al. 2015). Washington State experienced a small increase in adolescents' rates of use following legalization of recreational use, although Colorado did not (Cerdá et al. 2017). Oregon did not experience an increase in adolescent consumption rates, but those adolescents who did use increased the amount they consumed (Rusby, Westling, Crowley, and Light 2018).

While existing evidence does not yet suggest that Canada's change to legalization will dramatically affect trends in adolescent cannabis use, there is evidence to suggest that the law change may have some effects on adolescents. In Washington State, the perception that cannabis use is harmful dropped significantly among youth relative to states without legalization (Cerdá et al. 2017). This effect was also found in states that legalized medical cannabis use (Chadi et al. 2015). Canadian youth may experience a similar change in perception with the increased attention to cannabis brought on by the legalization of recreational use. Additionally, the presence of legal dispensaries and home cultivation could lead some adolescents to experiment with vaping, consuming cannabis edibles, and initiating use earlier, as was found in some US states that legalized recreational use for adults (Borodosvky et al. 2017).

Critical Thinking Question

In what ways could legalization of cannabis change how adolescents perceive the harms of cannabis and other substance use?

quality of nicotine, the stimulant drug within tobacco, and the numerous negative health consequences associated with long-term cigarette smoking make its use among youth a continued major concern in Canada.

Cannabis Use

Cannabis is also a commonly used drug among adolescents in Canada, second behind only alcohol. Importantly, the most recent Canadian Tobacco Alcohol and Drugs Survey (CTADS) reports that cannabis use is most common among youth between the ages of 15 and 19 and young adults between the ages of 20 and 24. Twenty-one per cent of youth and 30 per cent of young adults reported having used cannabis in the past year, compared to a reporting rate of only 10 per cent for adults aged 25 and older (Health Canada 2017b). Across Canada, 17 per cent of students in grades 7 to 12 reported past year use (Health Canada 2018).

Other Drug Use

With the exception of cannabis use, rates of illicit drug use in the general Canadian youth population are relatively low; however, some youth do report worrisome substance use behaviours, and these behaviours differ across geographic boundaries. For example, inhalant use among youth, and particularly Indigenous youth, continues to be a prominent issue in Canada's more isolated communities (Coleman, Charles, and Collins 2001). However, across Canada as a whole, the next highest rates of use of substances are for synthetic cannabinoids (3.3 per cent) and hallucinogens (3.0 per cent) (Health Canada 2018). Although the use of substances other than alcohol, cannabis, and tobacco is relatively rare, the decline in the use of these substances observed in previous years may have hit a plateau, matching the trends observed for the more common substances (see Table 10.1).

Inherent Challenges of Measuring Adolescent Substance Use

Drug and alcohol surveys are inherently unable to procure information from the entire youth population. The information obtained through these types of surveys typically comes from the youth who attend public schools or from youth who can be contacted through telephone surveys and who agree to participate in the surveys. In addition to an array of potential methodological problems with these types of self-report surveys—such as **social desirability effects**, errors in memory, exaggeration, and deception (Palys

social desirability effects Biases in research caused by respondents' desire to provide what they feel is the socially acceptable response or "what the researcher wants to hear."

Table 10.1	Changes in Substance Use among Canadian Youth,* 2013–2015			
Substance	**% of Youth Who Used (2013)**	**% of Youth Who Used (2015)**	**% Change**	
Alcohol (past year)	60.0	59.0	−1.0	↓**
Cannabis (past year)	22.0	21.0	−1.0	↓**
Tobacco (current users)	11.0	10.0	−1.0	↓**
Electronic cigarettes (ever used)	20.0	26.0	+6.0	↑
Any of five drugs (past year—cocaine/crack, speed/methamphetamines, ecstasy, hallucinogens, heroin)	5.0	5.0	0.0	—

* Youth aged 15–19
** Not a statistically significant change from previous survey.

Source: Health Canada 2017b.

and Atchinson 2014)—the selection biases necessarily exclude the drug use of those youth who do not attend or rarely attend school, and those youth who are homeless or otherwise marginalized. In Canada, estimates of the number of **street-involved youth** have been cited at 150,000 (Public Health Agency of Canada 2006). While these adolescents do not compose a substantial portion of the age group, researchers who have studied these populations have found that they are at greater risk than mainstream youth to use both non-injection and injection drugs and to suffer from various physical and mental health problems (Werb, Kerr, Li, Montaner, and Wood 2008). Without information obtained from these marginalized youth, the official rates of national drug use likely underestimate to some degree the true extent of adolescent usage.

street-involved youth
People 25 years of age or younger who do not have a safe home or are underhoused; who have been forced to leave their family of origin; who have run away from their home without the consent of their parents or guardian or who left foster- or group-care placements; or who are not living on the street but who experiment and engage in street-involved activities and identify with street culture and street peer groupings.

Reasons Youth Use Alcohol and Other Drugs

Most adolescents experiment with different attitudes and behaviours as part of the process of developing a sense of self separate from their family and other authority figures (Newcomb and Bentlar 1989). Neuroscience researchers suggest that the differing maturation patterns of the areas of the brain responsible for emotions and reasoning may significantly contribute to risk-taking and novelty-seeking behaviour by youth (Steinberg 2004). Although this willingness to take risks and try new things is normative and functionally adaptive, it can lead to substance use that can be problematic with the developing brain (Winters and Arria 2011). Although many youth indicate that their original use was provoked by curiosity, and the majority will not continue to use these substances, a significant percentage will. The question becomes, "What motivates adolescents to continue to use substances?"

For Pleasure

One key rationale that adolescents offer for substance use in self-report surveys is "enjoyment" (Terry-McElrath, O'Malley, and Johnston 2009). Such enjoyment is equated with increasing positive experiences while at parties or other social events. While there may be other underlying reasons, such as a lack of enjoyable pro-social alternatives, many young people are drawn to the promise of leisure offered by drugs. They may also have an overly positive expectation of the effects of drugs, as researchers have found that users may downplay the negative aspects of their drug use experiences (Hayaki et al. 2010). Since adolescents may perceive substance use as a normative method of enjoyment, the role of pleasure should not be overlooked by the assumption that all substance use necessarily stems from an underlying pathology (Hunt, Moloney, and Evans 2009).

As a Result of Peer Pressure

Researchers generally accept that young people are influenced by their peers as they seek to establish their identity and that much socialization occurs within these groups (Harris 1995). Feeling pressure from peers is often emphasized as a reason for adolescent substance use. This is exacerbated by the tendency for youth to regularly overestimate the prevalence and regularity of alcohol and drug use among their peer group (Martens et al. 2006). If drug and alcohol use is perceived as normative, young people may view the social consequences of not partaking as more detrimental than the consequences prescribed by the law or others in authority.

Social factors may, however, be less important to continuation than the perceived psychological and physical effects of the drug (Cooper, May, Soderstrom, and Jarjoura 2009), as those youth who do not enjoy their first experience are likely to make the choice to discontinue. While it is common that youth with friends who use alcohol and drugs also tend to be involved with these substances, it is also true that youth who abstain tend to associate with peers who also abstain (Bauman and Ennett 1996). Therefore, while peer pressure may influence a young person's decision to try alcohol and other drugs, the interplay between social factors and personal choices becomes more complex as youth decide whether to continue.

As a Means of Coping

Adolescence is a time of transition and development that often includes many challenges. During this time, some adolescents use substances to cope with the struggles they face (Terry-McElrath et al. 2009). In addition to experimenting with substances for recreational purposes, difficulty coping with life stressors is also related to initiation into substance use for many youth. For example, youth experiencing a difficult home life, bullying at school, or self-esteem issues may use drugs and alcohol to escape the difficult emotions or experiences they are facing. The risk of using substances in adolescence is also increased when youth experience trauma or maltreatment during childhood (Tonmyr, Thornton, Draca, and Wekerle 2010). This risk factor is particularly prevalent for youth in the foster care system (Stevens, Brice, Ale, and Morris 2011), as these youth experience disproportionate levels of trauma and strain across the life course. Given that childhood maltreatment and trauma are linked to long-term emotional, psychological, and physical health problems (see Danese et al. 2009), coping is also a potential reason for the continuation of substance use across the life course, particularly when alternate coping methods and external supports are absent (Stockburger, Parasa-Pajouh, Leeuw, and Greenwood 2005). Even youth who begin using substances for achieving excitement or as a result of peer pressure may eventually equate the positive feelings associated with substance use as a method of coping with life stressors.

Potential Negative Effects of Adolescent Substance Use

Consequences of Impairment

Substance use places youth at risk of serious negative consequences because of impairment and intoxication. The effects of intoxication produce acute changes in cognition, perception, and psychomotor functioning that can increase the risk of injury. This is particularly true for alcohol (Cherpitel et al. 2017). Although less common, unintentional injuries also occur because of the use of cannabis and other substances (Rao et al. 2018).

In addition to injuries, young people often experience other potentially negative consequences of substance use. Substance use may result in unplanned or unprotected sexual activity; a drive in a car driven by an intoxicated driver; an inability to remember events; an argument with family; and criminal acts (Centre for Addictions Research of BC 2009). Even if the intention of consuming drugs and alcohol is to have fun, youth run the risk of engaging in behaviours that can have immediate and long-term negative repercussions.

General Health Risks

method of administration
The path by which a drug or other substance is brought into contact with the body. Common methods include smoking, ingestion, injection, and intranasal inhalation.

Both the type of substance used and the **method of administration** can have serious adverse effects on the health of users young and old. The most serious potential harm of drugs and alcohol use is death, which occurred in 4258 cases related to alcohol, in 1695 cases related to illegal drugs, and in 37,209 cases related to tobacco use in Canada in 2002 (Rehm et al. 2007). Health-related alcohol-related deaths were most commonly linked to cirrhosis of the liver (1246), esophageal cancer (501), and cardiac arrhythmias (449). Tobacco-related deaths were typically caused by lung cancer (13,401), ischemic heart disease (5343), and respiratory diseases such as chronic obstructive pulmonary disease (7533). More than half of all deaths related to illegal drug use were as a result of overdose (958), while hepatitis C (165) or HIV (87) was also a major cause of death (Rehm et al. 2007).

Other negative health conditions linked to substance use can range from debilitation to inconvenience. For example, the nicotine in tobacco can cause the narrowing of arteries, reducing the blood supply to the heart and making it work harder (Benowitz 2009). Cocaine and other stimulants produce a similar effect on the cardiovascular system and can lead to increased respiration, rapid and irregular heartbeat, increased blood pressure, and hyperthermia (National Institute on Drug Abuse [NIDA] 2018). These symptoms increase the risk of heart attack and stroke (Treadwell and Robinson 2007). Heroin and other opioids (e.g., codeine, morphine, oxycodone, and fentanyl) can slow respiration to dangerous levels (NIDA 2018). In addition, heavy alcohol use, or **binge drinking**, has also been linked to liver and kidney diseases, various cancers, heart disease, and malnutrition (Rehm et al. 2006).

binge drinking
Heavy alcohol consumption over a short period for the purpose of becoming intoxicated. Generally, the concept is operationalized as the consumption of five or more drinks on one occasion (four or more for females).

The method of administration of the drug can also be a factor in the negative health consequences of consumption. For substances administered through smoking combusted plant matter, such as tobacco or cannabis, the majority of the harm stems from the introduction of chemicals into the lungs (see Diplock and Plecas 2009). Intravenous injection of drugs such as heroin, cocaine, and methamphetamine not only can be damaging to the veins but can also put the user at a greatly increased risk of contracting illnesses such as hepatitis B and C, HIV, and other infections (Thorpe et al. 2002). Intranasal administration, or snorting, can cause irritation to the nasal lining, chronic running or bleeding nose, loss of ability to smell, and difficulty swallowing (NIDA 2018). Therefore, while it is important to stress the negative health consequences of the drugs themselves to discourage use among adolescents, it is equally important to disseminate information about the harms associated with particular methods of consuming those drugs and to offer alternatives that will reduce the potential for harm caused by the method of administration (see Table 10.2).

Table 10.2	Commonly Used Drugs and Their Effects
Category and Street Names	**Acute Effects and Health Risks**
Alcohol (ethyl alcohol) Booze, drinks, liquor, sauce	Low doses: euphoria, mild stimulation, relaxation, lower inhibitions. High doses: drowsiness, slurred speech, nausea, emotional volatility, loss of coordination, visual distortions, impaired memory, sexual dysfunction, loss of consciousness, increased risk of injuries, violence, fetal damage (in pregnant women), depression, neurologic deficits, hypertension, liver disease, and fatal overdose.
Cannabis Marijuana, blunt, roach, dope, ganja, grass, gas, herb, joint, bud, Mary Jane, J, pot, reefer, green, trees, smoke, sinsemilla, skunk, weed, hash, hash oil, hemp, flower, kush	Euphoria, relaxation, slowed reaction times, distorted sensory perception, impaired balance and coordination, increased heart rate and appetite, impaired learning and memory, anxiety, panic attacks, psychosis, respiratory problems, possible mental health decline.
Tobacco Found in cigarettes, cigars, and smokeless tobacco (snuff, spit tobacco, and chew)	Increased blood pressure and heart rate, chronic lung disease, cardiovascular disease, stroke, cancers of the mouth, pharynx, larynx, esophagus, stomach, pancreas, cervix, kidney, bladder, and acute myeloid leukemia, adverse pregnancy outcomes.
Cocaine Cocaine hydrochloride, blow, bump, C, candy, nose drinks, Charlie, coke, crack, flake, rock, snow, white, toot	Increased heart rate, blood pressure, body temperature, metabolism, feelings of exhilaration, increased energy, mental alertness, tremors, reduced appetite, irritability, anxiety, panic, paranoia, violent behaviour, psychosis, weight loss, insomnia, cardiac or cardiovascular complications, strokes, seizures, nasal damage from snorting.
Methamphetamine Desoxyn, meth, ice, crank, chalk, crystal, fire, glass, go fast, speed, gak, tweak	Increased heart rate, blood pressure, body temperature, metabolism, feelings of exhilaration, increased energy, mental alertness, tremors, reduced appetite, irritability, anxiety, panic, paranoia, violent behaviour, psychosis, weight loss, insomnia, cardiac or cardiovascular complications, strokes, seizures, severe dental problems.
Amphetamine Biphetamine, Dexedrine, berries, black beauties, crosses, hearts, LA turnaround, speed, truck drivers, uppers	Increased heart rate, blood pressure, body temperature, metabolism, feelings of exhilaration, increased energy, mental alertness, tremors, reduced appetite, irritability, anxiety, panic, paranoia, violent behaviour, psychosis, weight loss, insomnia, cardiac or cardiovascular complications, strokes, seizures.
MDMA Methylenedioxymethamphetamine, Ecstasy, Molly, M, Lover's Speed, Peace, uppers	Mild hallucinogenic effects, increased tactile sensitivity, empathic feelings, lowered inhibitions, anxiety, chills, sweating, teeth clenching, muscle cramping/sleep disturbances, depression, impaired memory, hyperthermia.
Anabolic Steroids Anadrol, Oxandrin, Durabolin, Depo-Testosterone, Equipoise, roids, juice, gym candy, pumpers	No intoxication effects, hypertension, blood clotting and cholesterol changes, liver cysts, hostility and aggression, acne, in adolescents—stoppage of growth, in males—prostate cancer, reduced sperm production, shrunken testicles, breast enlargement, in females—menstrual irregularities, development of beard and other masculine characteristics.

continued

Table 10.2	Continued
Category and Street Names	**Acute Effects and Health Risks**
Inhalants Solvents (paint thinners, gasoline, glue), gases (butane, protane, aerosol, propellants, nitrous oxide), nitrates (isoamyl, isobutyl, cyclohexyl), laughing gas, poppers, snappers, whippets	(Varies by chemical)—stimulation, loss of inhibition, headache, nausea or vomiting, slurred speech, loss of motor coordination, wheezing/cramps, muscle weakness, depression, memory impairment, damage to cardiovascular and nervous systems, unconsciousness, fatal overdose.
(Prescription) Opioids Codeine, fentanyl, carfentanil, methadone, morphine, oxycodone, oxymorphone	Slow breathing, pain relief, drowsiness, nausea, constipation, euphoria, miscarriage or infants with low birth weight in females, death, high risk of accidental misuse, fatal overdose.

Source: Excerpted from NIDA 2018.

Effects on the Developing Brain

Consuming alcohol and other drugs may result in serious negative effects on the adolescent, as the developing brain may be more vulnerable to the effects of these substances (Vaccarino 2007). Recent research has suggested that substance use in adolescents can lead to abnormalities in brain functioning (Squeglia, Jacobus, and Tapert 2009). However, because few adolescent drug users do not also use alcohol, challenges arise in separating the effects of various substances on adolescent brain development (Squeglia, Jacobus, and Tapert 2009). Thoma et al. (2010) found that heavy alcohol and cannabis use in adolescents leads to reduced attention and executive functions and to memory detriments, respectively. While further research is necessary, these changes to the structure and processes in young developing brains may put early-onset substance users at greater risk of acquiring long-term cognitive impairment, mental illness, and addiction.

Psychological Risks

Substance use can lead to serious negative consequences for a person's mental health. There is some evidence that the use of stimulants—such as cocaine, amphetamines, and methamphetamine—can cause **psychosis** (Dore and Sweeting 2006). Furthermore, cannabis use might also trigger the onset of psychosis in those people with an existing predisposition (Degenhardt and Hall 2006). In other cases, prolonged or heavy substance use can result in drug-induced psychosis, a condition where the user exhibits psychotic symptoms, such as hallucinations, delusions, memory loss, and confusion, for a temporary period (Centre for Addiction and Mental Health [CAMH] n.d.). Drug use, particularly exposure at an earlier age, may put users at a greater risk of developing psychosis resulting from or triggered by substance use (Smith, Thirthalli, Ben Abdallah, Murray, and Cottler 2009).

As is the case with psychosis, studies have found high levels of **co-morbidity** of substance use and mental health problems among adolescents similar to levels among adults (Chan, Dennis, and Funk 2008). Other mental health problems co-occurring with substance use include depression and anxiety (O'Leary-Barret 2014). However, trying to

psychosis
A symptom of mental illness involving a substantial alteration to an individual's personality and a loss of contact with objective reality.

co-morbidity
Two or more independent and coexisting medical conditions.

determine whether substance use is a causal factor in mental illness presents researchers with a considerable challenge. Studies are often limited because it is difficult to determine if substance use caused a change to brain functioning that in turn led to mental illness, or if the onset of mental illness was a factor in the initiation of drug use (Degenhardt, Hall, and Lynskey 2002). While the sequence of events that explain the link between substance use and mental illness requires continued study, the evidence suggests that some substances may trigger mental illness in those already predisposed and may exacerbate symptoms in those already experiencing mental illness (O'Leary-Barret 2014).

Addiction

Some researchers believe that substance use during the adolescent stage of brain development may put the user at a greater risk of changes to brain structure and functioning that could lead to addiction (Squeglia et al. 2009). Addiction typically refers to the condition of repeatedly engaging in a behaviour because of the rewarding effects that behaviour brings. Accordingly, addiction is not specific to substance use (see Alexander and Schweighofer 1988). Individuals may be addicted to any number of behaviours, including those that may be physically, emotionally, or psychologically beneficial to the individual. With respect to substance use, addiction differs from **dependence**, which typically refers to the level of physical or psychological reliance an individual has on a substance. According to the Centre for Addiction and Mental Health (CAMH 2012), psychological dependence exists when a substance becomes so central to an individual's life that he or she needs to continue using the drug in order to function or feel normal. Physical dependence occurs when an individual's body develops a tolerance to a substance and requires a higher dosage of the substance to achieve the desired effect. Dependency symptoms can range from tolerance, to withdrawal, to taking the drug for longer periods or in larger doses than intended, to an increase in the time spent obtaining the drug and recovering from its effects, to ignoring other important activities, or to continuing use despite undesirable consequences (Looby and Earleywine 2007).

According to Statistics Canada, in 2012 approximately 21.6 per cent of Canadians met the criteria for a substance use disorder in their lifetime (Pearson, Janz, and Ali 2013). This included not only people who met the criteria for dependency but also those who met the criteria for **substance abuse**. Youth aged 15 to 24 years had the highest rate of substance use disorders among all the age groups, at 11.9 per cent.

Despite the low rates of dependence in Canada, addiction is a serious concern. The psychological dependence that accompanies addiction often compels the addicted substance user to take greater risks to obtain the substance, to use more, and to continue to use despite negative experiences (Friedman 2009). Continued drug use puts the user at greater risk of developing the health and mental health afflictions discussed earlier. These consequences are exacerbated by the social **stigma** surrounding drug use—a stigma fuelled by the self-destructive, burdensome, and victimizing behaviour that can result from addiction (Room 2005). Therefore, the consequences of drug addiction are dire because it is a condition where individuals often require a great deal of support and yet are separated or marginalized from the mainstream sources of that support (Mooney 2005).

dependence
When use of a substance is needed to achieve normal daily functioning, or when substance use leads to tolerance. Abruptly stopping use may lead to symptoms of withdrawal.

substance abuse
Characterized by a pattern of recurrent use of a substance where at least one of the following occurs: failure to fulfill roles in major life areas, use in physically dangerous situations, recurrent alcohol- or drug-related problems and continued use despite this use contributing to social or interpersonal problems.

stigma
An attitude of disapproval, discredit, or shame directed towards an individual, or group of individuals, based on a particular behaviour or attribute.

Adolescent Substance Use and the Link to Criminal Behaviour

The connection between substance use, delinquent activity, and criminality in adolescents has been well documented (Dowden 2003). Adolescents involved in the justice system tend to initiate substance use at earlier ages (Murray and Belenko 2005), use a greater variety of substances, and use more frequently and at higher doses than their peers the same age (Erickson and Butters 2005). Youth who continue to use substances across adolescence are more likely to have longer criminal careers and increased contact with the criminal justice system (Hussong, Curran, Moffitt, Caspi, and Carrig 2004). In general, research has found a strong relationship between adolescent substance use and crime, although other underlying factors likely contribute to both (Harrison, Erickson, Adlaf, and Freeman 2001).

Adolescent Crime Caused by Impairment

Crimes such as property damage, public disorder, violent offences, shoplifting and other thefts, and driving offences are some of the most common offences committed by adolescents and adults under age 25 (Diplock and Plecas 2010). These offences are also commonly linked to alcohol and drug use (Felson, Savolainen, Aaltonen, and Moustgaard 2008). In his research on adolescent male offenders in Toronto and Montreal, Brochu (2013) found that intoxication was the main factor that led to their violence and offending, although often the youths indicated that they used intoxication to make it possible for them to commit crimes that they would find difficult to do sober.

There are also offences that involve drug impairment as a major component of the offence. The most obvious example is impaired driving, which necessitates the consumption of alcohol or drugs. A recent change to Canada's impaired driving laws has set new blood concentration limits for cannabis, other substances, and cannabis in combination with alcohol. It has also established new penalties for impaired driving offences. Police have the power to demand that a driver complies with a standard field sobriety test or provide an oral fluid sample if they suspect a driver is impaired by drugs. If those tests produce reasonable grounds to believe an offence has occurred, an officer may demand a blood sample or a **drug recognition expert (DRE) evaluation**.

Drug and alcohol impairment may also lead youth to become easier targets of violence, thefts, and sexual assaults. It is well known that alcohol intoxication contributes substantially to the vulnerability of adolescents to victimization (Shepherd, Sutherland, and Newcombe 2006). Research has indicated that heavy drinking puts young males at a greater risk of victimization than young females, while illicit drug use puts young females at greater risk of victimization than their young male counterparts (Wells and Thompson 2009).

Research on female university students in Canada and the United States indicates that approximately 25 per cent of young college women are victims of sexual assault or attempted sexual assault, and the comparatively higher rates of substance use among college-aged men and women contributes to this increased level of risk (Status of Women

drug recognition expert (DRE) evaluation
A standardized procedure performed by a trained drug recognition expert—involving visual cues, vital signs, questioning, and the provision of bodily fluids by the potentially impaired driver—that is used for determining impairment by drugs or by a drug in combination with alcohol.

Canada 2016). Indeed, 54 per cent of sexual assault victims believe alcohol use played a role in the incident (Conroy and Cotter 2017).

Additionally, the Canadian criminal justice system has long been struggling with significantly high underreporting rates of sexual assault, and substance use among young persons may contribute to this. Self-report victimization data suggest that only 5 per cent of sexual assaults committed on individuals aged 15 or older are reported to police (Rotenberg 2017). While there are a number of identified barriers to the reporting of sexual assaults (such as lack of confidence in the criminal justice system, shame, guilt, self-blame, stigma, and the normalization of unwanted sexual behaviour) the role that substance use plays in the facilitation of sexual assaults may contribute to the high underreporting rates in Canada (Conroy and Cotter 2017). Where substance use plays a role in the occurrence of sexual assaults, victims may feel guilt or self-blame, or be unable to recall crucial details in relation to the offence, and therefore may refrain from reporting to police.

Adolescent Crime Resulting from the Search for Drugs

Some individuals who use substances resort to crime to obtain money for drugs. These crimes may include theft or other illegal money making activities such as prostitution or selling drugs (Bennet and Holloway 2009). Youth have fewer opportunities to make money through work, employment insurance, social welfare, or selling possessions and, therefore, may be more likely to resort to crime to acquire money. However, Brochu (2013) found that the youth in his samples were least likely to explain their offending as having been caused by the need to obtain drugs because of their dependency. This explanation may be more likely for those youth already comfortable with delinquent behaviour or for those who are addicted or in withdrawal (Bennet and Holloway 2009).

Youth Involvement in Drug Crimes

Many of the activities involved in the use of drugs are illegal, as outlined in Canada's Controlled Drugs and Substances Act (Controlled Drugs and Substances Act [CDSA] 1996). The possession, production, distribution, importation, and exportation of specifically scheduled substances are prohibited, each having its own criminal sanctions that vary by the type (or schedule) of the substance. Depending on the schedule of the substance, some offences such as trafficking, importation or exportation, and production carry a maximum penalty of life imprisonment (CDSA 1996).

Approximately 109,000 incidents of drug crimes were reported by police in Canada in 2013, fewer than in 2012, but still much higher than a decade ago. As an age group, youth (12–17) offenders had the second-highest offending rates for drug offences, lower than only those aged 18–24, although the vast majority of youth drug offences were related to cannabis, mainly resulting from possession (Cotter, Greenland, and Karam 2015). Many drug offences go undetected, with most reported offences resulting from **proactive police work**. Therefore, the statistics largely reflect the direction of police focus on drug crimes (Cotter, Greenland, and Karam 2015).

proactive police work Enforcement activities that are police initiated rather than in response to a call for service.

Possessing Drugs and Alcohol

Possession offences are the most common drug offences (Cotter et al. 2015), and official rates of possession offences represent only a fraction of the offences committed. Based on the rates of self-reported substance use, adolescents are regularly in possession of prohibited substances. Therefore, substance use itself necessarily implicates the youth in criminal or delinquent behaviour. While possession alone may seem like a minor offence, it can be accompanied by other related deviant behaviours such as using fake identification, stealing from family or friends, hiring bootleggers, or buying from people involved in the criminal lifestyle. In addition, since possession is likely to lead to use and intoxication, possession offences can be seen as linked to the crimes that may result.

Selling Drugs

The fact that adolescents have a higher likelihood of using cannabis and illicit drugs than adults do (Health Canada 2017b) has provided an opportunity for some youth to get involved in the distribution of these drugs to other youth. While most adolescents access illicit drugs through social sources and very few exclusively buy their own drugs, a majority of youths who use drugs have bought them from people they know, often their friends (Harrison, Fulkerson, and Park 2000). This creates opportunities for youths to sell drugs to their peers.

For those mainstream youth who sell drugs, doing so appears to be dependent on close peer connections and is largely limited to cannabis (Harrison et al. 2000). Dealing in "harder" drugs or dealing outside the close peer group is more common among youths who are more entrenched in drug cultures and already involved in criminal activity. In fact, selling drugs is common among chronic youth offenders (MacRae, Bertrand, Paetsch, and Hornick 2008) and street-involved youth (Werb et al. 2008). The economic instability that accompanies homelessness, addiction, and criminal justice system involvement was found to lead to the initiation of selling drugs by street-involved youth in Vancouver (Hepburn et al. 2016).

Organized Crime Affiliation through the Illicit Drug Industry

Participation in gangs or organized criminal groups may also lead youth to sell drugs to those outside of their peer groups. Youth involvement in gangs continues to be a concern in Canada (Dunbar 2017). Similar to what is observed among chronic youth offenders and street-involved youth, dealing drugs is common among the adolescent males who make up the street gangs and criminal groups in Toronto's housing projects. The violent geographic territoriality of these gangs around their criminal and other behaviours within their neighbourhoods makes this type of drug dealing very dangerous (Urbanik and Haggerty 2018). Drug dealing is also a key activity of street-involved, gang-affiliated youth in Vancouver (Fast, Shoveller, and Kerr 2017).

While many Canadian youth who participate in the drug industry through gangs and organized crime come from disadvantaged backgrounds and may engage in drug use themselves, economic survival is often not the primary motivation for their activities. Drug dealers who started as adolescents getting connected to older gang-affiliated drug dealers report that they saw involvement in the drug trade as a means to have success and access a social status they could otherwise not achieve (Fast et al. 2017). Police in British Columbia (Combined Forces Special Enforcement Unit [CFSEU] BC 2015) have also reported that many youth who appear to come from affluent and mainstream family backgrounds are being recruited into organized drug trafficking as **dial-a-dopers**, drawn in by the perception of the status surrounding criminal gangs and the promise of easy money.

dial-a-dopers
Individuals, often youth or young adults, who are given one or more cellphones by a criminal organization and deliver drugs to specific locations when customers wanting drugs call the phone to place an order.

Organized crime groups are highly active in the illegal drug production and trafficking industry in Canada. Recent data suggested that organized crime groups were benefitting from 57 per cent of drug trafficking and 15 per cent of drug production incidents uncovered by police (Munch and Silver 2017). Because drug markets are typically controlled by adult offenders, adolescent participation in drug distribution markets is largely dependent on whether young people are needed to access niche markets, such as schools, to meet market demand, or to insulate adult offenders from law enforcement and other risks (Bouchard, Alain, and Nguyen 2009). Those under 18 make up only a small proportion of those accused of drug offences for the benefit of organized crime groups, but they make up an equal proportion of victims of organized crime-related homicide incidents and an even larger portion of those accused of organized crime-related homicide incidents. Those between the ages of 18 and 25 made up higher portions in all three of those categories (Munch and Silver 2017). Although getting drawn in by the promise of an exciting life and easy money, for those who do get involved in the illicit drug industry as youth through affiliations with organized criminals, many later report feeling manipulated by their criminal employers and find themselves isolated from both legal and illegal avenues of success due to addiction, mental illness, destitution, and the lack of employable skills or education (Fast et al. 2017).

A number of factors influence adolescent initiation into illegal drug market activities. These include economic disadvantage, boredom, early childhood adversity, criminal involvement, homelessness, addiction, and manipulation by older associates involved in the drug market. Given the various forces that come together to influence the decision of youth to participate in these illegal activities, it is likely that prevention efforts will require a combination of improved employment and recreational opportunities for youth, consistent messaging about not just the negative effects of drug use but also the societal impact of the entire drug industry, and effective substance use and addictions treatment.

Adolescent Substance Use Prevention

The significant harm to individuals and to society as a whole warrants considerable effort on preventing adolescent substance use. Research on effective prevention programs has shown a cost saving of $15 to $18 on every dollar spent on substance use prevention (Canadian Centre On Substance Abuse and Addiction [CCSA] 2013). To get the most benefit possible from prevention efforts, it is imperative that these efforts be focused on strategies that incorporate evidence-informed practices.

What Works?

Considerable time and effort have been spent in researching key factors in effective prevention programs. According to the CCSA's Compendium of Best Practices (Roberts et al. 2001), keys to effective substance use prevention programs include building a strong framework, striving for accountability, and actively listening to and involving young people in the shaping of the program. These components emphasize the need for the message to be credible and based on accurate information that recognizes adolescent development and perceptions. Such standards also promote opportunities for youth to become active participants in their own relationship with substances, rather than remain passive audiences to anti-drug campaigns. Furthermore, since many programs rely on teachers, student leaders, law-enforcement officers, and other professionals to take part as facilitators, those who lead or facilitate the programs must be competent, credible, empathetic, and able to interact well with youth (Roberts et al. 2001).

The Canadian Standards Task Force, in partnership with the CCSA, has developed the Canadian Standards for Youth Substance Abuse Prevention. The key principles expressed in these standards are as follows:

1. Prevention is most successful when schools, families, and organizations throughout the community are involved.
2. School-based prevention is most successful when it's integrated into the school's core mission and links to community initiatives.
3. Family skills training should be included in prevention initiatives (CCSA 2014).

The United Nations Office on Drugs and Crime (UNODC 2014) reviewed prevention programs for all age groups and identified programs and policies that were found to have positive prevention outcomes. Its review concluded that substance use prevention should ideally be delivered continuously over a lifetime with programs matched for the developmental and situational needs of the individual and group (UNODC 2014). These effective prevention programs included a variety of approaches—universal, selective, and indicated programs. *Universal* prevention programs include initiatives that are appropriate for the population at large. *Selective* prevention programs include strategies appropriate for groups that are particularly at risk. *Indicated* prevention programs include strategies appropriate for individuals at risk.

School-Based Initiatives

Since most eventual drug users and those with substance use problems started their substance use before adulthood, and because early initiation is a risk factor for later problems (Lubman, Hides, Yucel, and Toumbourou 2007), adolescence is an appropriate time to implement substance use prevention. Schools present an ideal setting for the delivery of all types of prevention programming—universal, selective, and indicated. Some types of universal prevention that were broadly delivered, such as Drug Abuse Resistance Education (DARE), have had disappointing results (Pan and Bai 2009), although the newer DARE Keepin' It Real curriculum may hold more promise than past iterations of the program (see DARE BC Society 2019). Other programs, such as Life Skills Training and Project ALERT, have been found to be effective at reducing the levels of substance use, although not necessarily at preventing initiation (National Crime Prevention Centre 2009). The most effective type of universal school-based substance use prevention programs are skill-based—youth are taught resistance skills and learn about the social influences of substance use while receiving other life skills training (UNODC 2014).

A combination of universal and selective prevention in schools results in school policies and culture that support prevention goals. Reviews of the effects of school policies and culture on adolescent substance use have found that ideal policies are created in consultation with all key stakeholders (e.g., students, parents, and staff). These policies include the mandate that substances will not be used on school property or at school events by anyone and include selective components such as cessation support and referral to promote healthy behavioural change rather than a focus on punishment (UNODC 2014). There are also prevention benefits to addressing the school environment; these entail increased commitment to school, student participation, and positive relationships, all of which show a positive effect in reducing substance use and other risk behaviours (UNODC 2014).

Indicated prevention can include programs to support individual adolescents who have specific psychological vulnerabilities to substance use. Certain internalizing problems, such as mood and anxiety disorders, and externalizing disorders, such as ADHD and conduct disorders, can greatly increase the likelihood of a person's developing substance use disorders (Abu-Shakra and Cox 2014). These prevention programs are based on identifying youths at greater risk for substance use and training them to cope positively with difficult emotions. There is mounting evidence that these personality-centred interventions are effective in delaying the onset of alcohol and drug use (Conrod, Castellanos-Ryan, and Mackie 2011).

Although one of the benefits of school-based interventions is that these programs will reach the majority of adolescents, some of the high-risk adolescents who could most benefit from prevention programming may not be attending school and therefore do not have access to these programs (Saewyc 2007). These youths are often in greater need of prevention services (e.g., Bodnarchuk, Patton, and Rieck 2006). Therefore, to reach this population, it is important that other prevention initiatives are in place, such as multi-faceted community-based interventions and family-based interventions.

Community-Based Multi-component Initiatives

Opportunities to prevent problematic substance use and increase positive developmental outcomes for adolescents occur in many different settings and contexts. Positive prevention outcomes are most likely when prevention initiatives take a comprehensive approach that links school and families with other settings and organizations in the community (CCSA 2014). These community-based initiatives can be universal or selective in their targeting for the prevention initiative. Key components of successful community initiatives include supporting the enforcement of tobacco and alcohol policies; working in a range of community settings (families and schools, workplace, entertainment venues, etc.); and involving universities in the implementation of evidenced-based programs and their monitoring and evaluation (UNODC 2014).

Family-Based Initiatives

Brotnow and Sinha (2014, p. 75) point out that "stable and supportive family structures buffer the impact of stress and promote resilience in the child. Without that stability and support, the impact of other risk factors can be intensified." Family-based initiatives can be universal or selective prevention. Characteristics of an effective family-based initiative include enhancing family bonding; supporting parents in taking a more active role in their children's lives; supporting parents on how to provide positive and developmentally appropriate discipline; supporting parents in how to be role models for their children; and, making it easier for parents to participate (out of office hours, meals, child care, etc.). The Strengthening Families Program (SFP) is an example of a well-established family intervention program that focuses on family communication and parenting skills to reduce a variety of negative outcomes, including substance use. This program has been found to reduce children's problematic internalizing and externalizing behaviours, reduce parent and child substance use, and improve family communication and interaction styles (Trudeau, Spoth, Randall, Mason, and Shin 2012). The success of SFP also demonstrates that not all successful drug prevention programs predominantly rely on drug education or refusal skill training. Instead, focusing on fulfilling the basic needs of individuals by promoting pro-social bonds and interpersonal relationships and fostering a sense of belonging can in turn reduce the need for substance use at the individual level.

Anti-drug Media Campaigns

The message of substance use prevention is often spread through mass media campaigns, as they are highly visible and can carry a universal or selective prevention message. These media campaigns are intended to reach a wide audience and present messages that will resonate with youth as well as with adults. Media campaigns have traditionally involved television and print ads but have since expanded to online platforms such as social media websites. While there may be potential for media campaigns to effectively change the beliefs and behaviours of youth, improperly guided campaigns could simply be wasting resources (Palmgreen and Donohew 2003). Based on an understanding of the characteristics of youth who are most likely to use illicit drugs, anti-drug media campaigns may be more effective if they appeal to sensation-seeking youth by having novelty and a high level of visual stimulation (Palmgreen and Donohew 2003). The UNODC (2014) indicates that, among other things, effective media campaigns are those that precisely identify target groups; target parents as well as children; aim to change cultural norms and/or educate about the consequences of substance use; have messages based on strong research; connect to existing drug prevention programs in the home, school, and community; achieve adequate exposure to the target group; and suggest strategies to reduce substance use.

Alternatives to Fear-Based Communication

fear-based communication
Messages used to frighten youth away from experimentation with substances by emphasizing the potential negative effects of use.

Researchers generally agree that **fear-based communication** is an ineffective approach to dissuading youth from using substances such as alcohol, tobacco, and cannabis (National Crime Prevention Centre 2009). The fear-based approach, although not untruthful in presenting information, overemphasizes the potential harms, highlighting worst-case scenarios and intentionally increasing the perceptions of the likelihood of harm. These messages contradict what the majority of youth will later or already know about the effects of substance use, potentially causing the messenger to lose credibility (Tupper 2008). Perhaps, rather than emphasizing what youth should not do, messages should instead focus on promoting healthy living in general. The challenge is in finding ways to dissuade problematic substance use among adolescents without resorting to strategies that rely on fear and on the condemnation of the substances and substance users.

Tupper (2008) suggests that drug education should adopt the discourse of drugs as "tools," which, when used properly and for the right reasons, may be very beneficial, but when misused, can be socially harmful. Ideally, messaging would change the perception that unhealthy behaviours are "just part of growing up," perhaps by emphasizing that substance use is actually less normative than many youth perceive (Martens et al. 2006). Other prevention approaches might include increased taxation of unhealthy substances, regulation to ensure appropriate use and deter unsafe use, and **harm-reduction strategies** to address factors that contribute to the negative consequences associated with substance use (Toumbourou et al. 2009). These efforts could promote healthy lifestyles while providing the support necessary for those who are struggling with substance use issues. Consistency in the social messages across the lifespan is also important to consider, since the portrayal of substance use as normative for adults through advertising, entertainment, and actual consumption will influence adolescents (American Academy of Pediatrics 2010).

harm-reduction strategies Any policy or program that is designed to reduce the level of harm associated with substance use without requiring the cessation of use.

Harm Reduction

Harm reduction differs from traditional prevention approaches in that its primary goal is to reduce the adverse health, social, and economic harms that accompany substance use rather than to prevent substance use altogether. In other words, the philosophy of harm reduction is not concerned with "fixing individuals" (Pauly 2008, p. 6) but is instead interested in reducing the preventable risks associated with substance use. Although first gaining traction during the 1980s AIDS epidemic (Fischer 2005), harm reduction programs and policies have garnered much attention and support in recent years because of the growing opioid epidemic in Canada and the United States. Examples of harm reduction strategies enacted in Canada include supervised consumption sites (e.g., Insite) and drug-checking stations (see Kerr and Tupper 2017), opioid substitution therapy programs (e.g., suboxone, methadone), needle exchange programs, and the availability of over-the-counter Naloxone (a low-risk opioid antagonist). Despite the wealth of empirical evidence demonstrating that harm-reduction strategies are effective in reducing crime and other harms associated with substance use (e.g. Wood, Tyndall, Montaner, and Kerr 2006), critics continue to scrutinize harm-reduction approaches, arguing that they enable and further contribute to substance use, crime, and addiction. Although this critique has limited empirical credibility, most would agree (including proponents of the harm-reduction approach) that harm reduction is only one avenue of treatment, and that effective policies should draw from a range of interventions along a full continuum of care.

Box 10.2 | Youth Justice in Action

Canada's Opioid Crisis

Canada is in the midst of a major public health crisis. Sparked largely by the widespread distribution of fentanyl, a drug 100 times more powerful than morphine, opioid overdoses have increased dramatically across the country over the last several years. According to the most recent national report, 72 per cent (2104) of the 2923 opioid-related deaths in Canada in 2017 were related to fentanyl or fentanyl analogues (Public Health Agency of Canada 2018), a rate more than three times higher than the 655 fentanyl-related deaths between 2009 and 2014 (CCSA 2015).

Provincial health authorities have attempted to decrease overdose death rates by implementing numerous programs and interventions, most of which fall under the scope of harm reduction. These strategies have included supervised injection sites, drug-checking stations, and take-home Naloxone kits. Although these strategies have been successful in preventing and reversing overdose deaths, they have been largely targeted towards high-risk injection drug users and have neglected what has now become the one of the riskiest drug-user populations: recreational or first-time drug users who use in the home.

Unlike previous drug crises (e.g., the 1980s crack-cocaine epidemic), which disproportionately affected high-risk lifetime drug users, the current opioid crisis has affected all drug-user demographics, including first-time users. According to a recent report from the BC Coroners Service (2018), 90 per cent of the province's overdose deaths in 2018 occurred indoors, and approximately 50 per cent of those who overdosed were under the age of 39. These statistics likely relate to the limited access to harm-reduction services for young casual users and the commonplace idea that only "addicts" experience overdoses.

A recent article from the *Vancouver Sun* (Culbert 2018) provides an unfortunate example of this trend: "Dylan was a 21-year-old art student at Capilano University. Battling anxiety, he bought some Oxy-Contin that he did not know was laced with fentanyl. He fell asleep in his father's North Vancouver condo and never woke up" (para. 4). Stories like this, about young adults and teenagers overdosing from contaminated substances, are now common in the media. These cases demonstrate that overdoses do not discriminate and that any individual who uses substances is at risk of experiencing overdose. Such cases also suggest that service providers, policy-makers, and citizens alike may need to reshape their understanding of what a "typical" drug user looks like to ensure that all individuals receive equal access to services and programs.

Critical Thinking Question

Given what we now know about adolescent substance use prevention and treatment practices, what strategies would be most effective in targeting young recreational drug users who are at a high risk of opioid overdose?

Substance Use Treatment for Young Offenders

Research has demonstrated the need for substance use treatment for young people involved in the justice system. Although substance use creates many life challenges, both male and female young offenders show positive outcomes from participating in treatment programs (Dowden 2003). Unfortunately, even though many justice programs for adolescents contain in-house substance use treatment programs or link to community-based treatment programs provided by non-profit organizations funded through provincial health regions or health authorities, there has been very little focus on the effectiveness of the strategies used in the programs (Chassin 2008). As there are limited resources, it is important to ensure that the programs that are implemented are based on evidenced-based best practices.

Adolescent Substance Use Treatment Best Practices

No single treatment has been shown to be effective for all individuals who use substances. This should be no surprise, as all individuals (including those who use substances) have different goals, needs, and life experiences. When these factors are taken into consideration and matched by appropriate treatment programs, the likelihood of successful program completion has been proven to increase (Peters and Wexler 2005). What is troubling, however, is that programs originally designed for adults are often delivered to youth. This problem is particularly common in smaller isolated communities where funding for youth-specific resources is limited. Accordingly, it is important to identify best practices for adolescent treatment. Health Canada (2008) has suggested such practices based on a review of relevant research, interviews with key experts, and focus groups with youth.

The following were identified as strategies for strengthening service delivery orientations:

- Use a readiness-to-change model. A widely accepted model for understanding and assessing treatment readiness was developed by Prochaska and DiClimente (1986) and outlines the stages that people go through when making major life changes. The stages include pre-contemplation, contemplation, preparation, action, maintenance, and relapse. Understanding the stage that a youth is in allows the program to match the youth appropriately to a treatment strategy most likely to increase his or her chance of succeeding in the behaviour change. This model is usually paired with brief interventions that incorporate cognitive-behavioural approaches, motivational interviewing, and a focus on the youth's strengths (Levy, Vaughn, and Knight 2002).
- Strength-based programs that are designed to promote positive change by recognizing and engaging the strengths of youths, their families, and their communities.
- Youth perspectives should be pursued and youth leadership encouraged when organizing and delivering community-based, youth-focused services and programs. This includes the perspectives of non-users as well as those at risk of substance use issues.
- Youth-specific services should be offered rather than adult-oriented services that youths can also attend. These services should be developmentally appropriate, easily accessible, and available, with quick response times when youths express a desire to change their behaviour.
- Inclusive versus exclusive policies should be formulated that foster relationship development with positive adults and peers to encourage a sense of belonging and attachment to school and community.

Treatment Best Practices with Young Offenders

Young offenders have also been identified as the group most likely to resist substance use treatment programs (Health Canada 2001). This high level of treatment resistance is largely attributed to the unique barriers that young offenders face. Some of these barriers include a lack of suitable correctional treatment programs available to incarcerated youth, a lack of substance use knowledge by correctional staff members, difficulty accessing community-based treatment programs, and the "closed culture" of substance use among young offenders that promotes secrecy and group loyalty (Health Canada 2001). For this reason, it is important to consider the unique needs and experiences of criminally involved youth when implementing treatment programs for young offenders. Dowden (2003) identified the importance of considering client characteristics, in-treatment factors, and post-treatment factors.

Key Client Characteristics

Key client characteristics to take into consideration when implementing a substance use treatment program for young offenders include age, gender, race/ethnicity, psychopathology, and overall risk (Dowden 2003). With respect to age, there is widespread consensus among scholars and practitioners that early intervention is one of the most important factors in reducing substance use problems and offending outcomes (Carney and Mayers 2012). Ultimately, experts agree that the earlier an individual receives treatment, the better the chances of their recovery. With respect to gender, research has clearly demonstrated that treatment programs directed towards female young offenders should be equitable, strength-based, and actively aware of the unique and complex challenges that female youth face, particularly the high rates of sexual abuse and sexual abuse related disorders (Molidor, Nissen, and Watkins 2002). However, despite the fact that female youth tend to experience dependency problems more quickly than male youth (Poole and Dell 2005), substantially less research has been focused on female juvenile offenders with substance use problems than on their male counterparts. Research on the impact of race/ethnicity and treatment outcomes for young offenders is also lacking, but the existing research suggests that treatment that is culturally appropriate has improved outcomes over generic programs (Dowden 2003).

As noted earlier in this chapter, psychopathology plays a role in the development of substance use problems and research supports the need to address co-occurring disorders within treatment programming. Level of risk is another important client characteristic to take into consideration when planning substance use treatment strategies. Treatment effectiveness is enhanced by matching the youths' needs with the appropriate treatment approach, and in the case of young offenders, this includes matching the young offender's level of involvement in substance use and criminal offending with the intensity of treatment programming (Chassin 2008).

In-Treatment Factors

In-treatment factors to be considered in planning effective substance use treatment programs for adolescents include program content, delivery, and the organizational environment in which the program was delivered. Dowden (2003) found that, to increase program effectiveness, content should target multiple areas for young offenders, including family, academic, and peer problems, and incorporate elements of relapse prevention and cognitive-behavioural therapy. For program delivery, key factors for improving program effectiveness include program staff training, monitoring, and minimizing turnover (Chassin 2008). Organizational environment includes the setting and context of program delivery. Research into the ideal setting for substance use treatment for young offenders has found little difference in outcomes for in-patient versus out-patient substance use treatment (Annis 1990). This lends credence to the value of treatment matching—where the needs of the individual client are matched with the appropriate treatment program. It is important to have a number of treatment options available to assist in the matching of each individual adolescent with the appropriate program. Some adolescents would find treatment in a residential wilderness setting helpful as an opportunity to be removed from drug-using peers and/or family members and be exposed to experiential learning opportunities, while other youths, unfamiliar and uncomfortable with being in a wilderness setting, may see the location as a barrier to treatment. Similarly, attending a treatment group on-site in a justice setting may be a positive connection point for some adolescents, giving them the opportunity to deal with some difficult issues in a controlled setting, while other adolescents would feel unsafe sharing information about trauma and abuse with their peers in custody.

Post-treatment Factors

Two post-treatment factors that correlated with reductions in offending are aftercare services and initiatives that enhance protective factors (Dowden 2003). Aftercare services include activities and supports designed to help adolescents maintain their behaviour change following treatment. The substantial relapse rates associated with substance use have prompted some researchers to suggest that substance use should be managed as a chronic disorder characterized by relapse and remission (Chassin 2008). Therefore, researchers have argued that enhancing protective factors, or inherent strengths of youths, their families, and communities, should be an important goal of post-treatment interventions (Dowden 2003).

Summary

Recent figures demonstrate that substance use among Canadian adolescents has remained steady after previous years of decreasing trends (Health Canada 2017b). When considering these relatively low rates, we must not allow them to overshadow the fact that alcohol, cannabis, electronic cigarettes, and, to a lesser but still notable degree, tobacco use is common among adolescents and that usage rates for cannabis and illicit substances are higher than those of adults (Health Canada 2017b). In fact, when considering adolescent populations outside the mainstream population, even the use of so-called hard drugs is common (Public Health Agency of Canada 2006). While experimenting, coping with the struggles of adolescence, and generally fitting in all contribute to a substantial proportion of youth trying and using substances, it is also important to remember that Canadian adolescent substance use generally reflects how the use of substances in modelled by Canadian adults. What will be critical to observe in subsequent years is whether the parallels in substance use patterns across youth and adult populations remain constant once cannabis is legalized in Canada. One of the major questions posed by scholars is whether the legalization of cannabis will spark an increase in substance use initiation, frequency, and sustained use in both adolescent and adult populations.

Adolescent substance use, its consequences on the future of Canada's young people, and its potential to create problems associated with crime and criminality are ongoing concerns in this country. There are many government strategies as well as prevention, harm reduction, and treatment activities in place across the country that show promise for helping youth to avoid the negative consequences of substance use, but further efforts are likely needed to address some of the remaining gaps. Students in the field of crime control, policing, and criminology must critically assess the direction of drug policies, other prevention strategies, and treatment programs; work toward improving these programs where needed; and forge new directions when existing ones prove inadequate, inappropriate, or counterproductive.

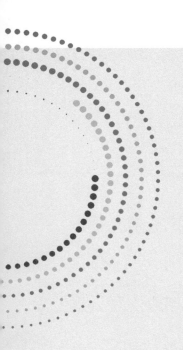

Key Terms

abuse	method of administration
binge drinking	proactive police work
co-morbidity	psychosis
dependence	social desirability effects
dial-a-dopers	stigma
drug recognition expert (DRE) evaluation	street-involved youth
fear-based communication	substance abuse
harm-reduction strategies	

Review Questions

1. Although it is recognized that cannabis is not a "gateway drug" leading directly to the use of other drugs, are there ways that cannabis use might contribute to other drug use?

2. What are the potential physical and psychological harms that adolescents may experience with substance use?

3. In what ways can the use of substances by youth contribute or lead to criminal offending?

4. As was discussed in this chapter, some Canadian youth become involved in drug crime beyond "simple" possession (drug dealing, working in cannabis growing operations, joining gangs who traffic in drugs, etc.). What factors might lead young Canadians to engage in this type of criminal behaviour?

5. What are the differences between universal, selective, and indicated prevention?

6. What are the key components of a substance use treatment program for adolescents?

Critical Thinking Questions

1. In your opinion, what are the reasons that adolescents use drugs and what causes experimentation to lead to substance use?

2. Many schools and law-enforcement agencies in Canada work in concert to provide drug prevention information to children and adolescents, with police officers taking on the role of drug prevention educators. What might be some advantages and disadvantages of police officers taking on this role in substance use prevention?

3. If you were responsible for designing a program in your community to dissuade youth from impaired driving, what would you focus on?

4. In your opinion, how well do your province's alcohol, tobacco, electronic cigarette, and cannabis regulations (minimum-age limits, rules surrounding advertising, licensing of drinking establishments, anti-smoking regulations, etc.) reduce adolescent substance use or make it less harmful? In what ways do you feel these regulations inadvertently contribute to adolescent substance use or make it more harmful?

5. As a result of the association between substance use and crime, substance use issues become of concern to health-care and criminal justice systems, among others. What do you think would be the ideal balance between the health-care and criminal justice systems to reduce and prevent the harms associated with substance use?

Endnote

1. The authors would like to acknowledge the contributions of Darryl Plecas and Ronda Trumper as authors on previous editions of this chapter.

References

Abu-Shakra, M., and Cox, S. (2014). The externalizing developmental pathway to substance use disorders. In M. Leyton and S. Stewart (Eds), *Substance abuse in Canada: Childhood and adolescent pathways to substance use disorders* (pp. 27–47). Ottawa: Canadian Centre on Substance Abuse.

Adlaf, E.M., Begin, P., and Sawka, E. (Eds). (2005). *Canadian Addictions Survey (CAS): A national survey of Canadians'* *use of alcohol and other drugs: Prevalence of use and related harms: Detailed report*. Ottawa: Canadian Centre on Substance Abuse.

Alexander, B.K., and Schweighofer, A.R.F. (1988). Defining "addiction." *Canadian Psychology, 29*(2), 151–62.

American Academy of Pediatrics. (2010). Policy statement—Children, adolescents, substance abuse, and the media. *Pediatrics, 126*(4), 791–9.

Annis, H.M. (1990). Effective treatment for drug and alcohol problems: What do we know? *Forum on Corrections Research, 2*(4), 18–23.

Bauman, K.E., and Ennett, S.T. (1996). On the importance of peer influence for adolescent drug use: Commonly neglected considerations. *Addiction, 91*(2), 185–98.

BC Coroners Service. (2018). *Illicit drug overdose deaths in BC: January 1, 2008 to January 31, 2018*. Retrieved from https://www2.gov.bc.ca/assets/gov/public-safety-and-emergency-services/death-investigation/statistical/illicit-drug.pdf

Behrendt, S., Wittchen, H.U., Holfer, M., Lieb, R., and Beesdo, K. (2009). Transitions from first substance use to substance use disorders in adolescence: Is early onset associated with a rapid escalation? *Drug and Alcohol Dependence, 99*(1–3), 68–78.

Bennet, T., and Holloway, K. (2009). Causal connection between drug misuse and crime. *British Journal of Criminology, 49*(4), 513–31.

Benowitz, N.L. (2009). Pharmacology of nicotine: Addiction, smoking-induced disease, and therapeutics. *Annual Review of Pharmacology and Toxicology, 49*, 57–71.

Bodnarchuk, J., Patton, D., and Rieck, T. (2006). *Adolescence without shelter: A comprehensive description of issues faced by street youth in Winnipeg*. Winnipeg: Addiction Foundation of Manitoba.

Borodovsky, J.T., Lee, D.C., Crosier, B.S., Gabrielli, J.L., Sargent, J.D., and Budney, A.J. (2017). US cannabis legalization and use of vaping and edible products among youth. *Drug and Alcohol Dependency, 177*, 299–306.

Bouchard, M., Alain, M., and Nguyen, H. (2009). Convenient labour: The prevalence and nature of youth involvement in the cannabis cultivation industry. *International Journal of Drug Policy, 20*(6), 467–74.

Brochu, S. (2013). When youth combine drugs and violence: An explosive cocktail. *Istanbul Universitesi Huku Fakultesi Mecmuasi, 71*(1), 177–93.

Brotnow, L., and Sinha, R. (2014). *A developmental approach to prevention and intervention*. Ottawa: Canadian Centre on Substance Abuse.

Canadian Centre on Substance Abuse and Addiction (CCSA). (2013). *A case for investing in youth substance abuse prevention*. Retrieved from http://www.ccsa.ca/Resource%20Library/2012-ccsa-Investing-in-youth-substance-abuse-prevention-en.pdf

Canadian Centre on Substance Abuse and Addiction (CCSA). (2014). *Drug prevention standards*. Retrieved from http://www.ccsa.ca/Eng/topics/Children-and-Youth/Drug-Prevention-Standards/Pages/default.aspx

Canadian Centre on Substance Abuse and Addiction (CCSA). (2015). *Deaths involving fentanyl in Canada, 2009–2014*. Retrieved from http://www.ccsa.ca/Resource%20Library/CCSA-CCENDU-Fentanyl-Deaths-Canada-Bulletin-2015-en.pdf

Carney, T., and Myers, B. (2012). Effectiveness of early interventions for substance-using adolescents: Findings from a systematic review and meta-analysis. *Substance Abuse Treatment, Prevention, and Policy, 7*(1), 1–15.

Centre for Addiction and Mental Health (CAMH). (2012). *Opioid addiction*. Retrieved from https://www.camh.ca/en/hospital/health_information/a_z_mental_health_and_addiction_information/Opioid-Dependence/Pages/default.aspx

Centre for Addiction and Mental Health (CAMH). (n.d.). *Psychosis*. Retrieved from http://www.camh.ca/en/hospital/health_information/a_z_mental_health_and_addiction_information/psychosis/Pages/Psychosis.aspx

Centre for Addictions Research of BC. (2009). *Adolescent substance use and related harms in British Columbia*. Victoria, BC: Author.

Cerdá, M., Wall, M., Feng, T., Keyes, K.M., Sarvet, A., Schulenberg, J., . . . Hasin, D.S. (2017). Association of state recreational marijuana laws with adolescent marijuana use. *JAMA Pediatrics, 171*(2),142–9.

Chadi, N., Weitzman, E.R., and Levy, S. (2018). Understanding the impact of national and state medical marijuana policies on adolescents. *Current Addictions Report, 5*(2), 93–101.

Chan, Y., Dennis, M.L., and Funk, R.R. (2008). Prevalence and co-morbidity of major internalizing and externalizing problems among adolescents and adults presenting to substance abuse treatment. *Journal of Substance Abuse Treatment, 34*(1), 14–24.

Chassin, L. (2008). Juvenile justice and substance use. *Future of Children, 18*(2), 165–83.

Cherpitel, C.J., Ye, Y., Andreuccetti, G., Stockwell, T., Vallance, K., Chow, C., and Brubacher, J.R. (2017). Risk of injury from alcohol, marijuana and other drug use among emergency department patients. *Drug and Alcohol Dependence, 174*(1), 121–7.

Coleman, H., Charles, G., and Collins, J. (2001). Inhalant use by Canadian aboriginal youth. *Journal of Child & Adolescent Substance Abuse, 10*(3), 1–20.

Combined Forces Special Enforcement Unit (CFSEU) BC. (2015). *Understanding youth and gangs: A parent resource*. Retrieved from http://www.cfseu.bc.ca/wp-content/uploads/2015/06/Gang_Prevention_Booklet_English-Arabic_compressed.pdf

Conrod, P.J., Castellanos-Ryan, N., and Mackie, C. (2011). Long-term effects of personality-targeted intervention to reduce alcohol use in adolescents. *Journal of Consulting and Clinical Psychology, 79*(3), 296–306.

Conroy, S., and Cotter, A. (2017). Self-reported sexual assault in Canada, 2014. *Juristat, 37*(1). Statistics Canada Catalogue

No. 85-002-X. Retrieved from http://www.statcan.gc.ca/pub/85-002-x/2017001/article/14842-eng.pdf

Controlled Drugs and Substances Act (CDSA), S.C., c.19. (1996). Retrieved from http://laws-lois.justice.gc.ca/eng/acts/C-38.8/FullText.html

Cooper, K., May, D., Soderstrom, I., and Jarjoura, G.R. (2009). Examining theoretical predictors of substance use among a sample of incarcerated youth. *Journal of Offender Rehabilitation, 48*(8), 669–95.

Cotter, A., Greenland, J., and Karam, M. (2015). Drug-related offences in Canada, 2013. *Juristat, 35*(1). Statistics Canada Catalogue No. 85-002-X. Retrieved from https://www150.statcan.gc.ca/n1/pub/85-002-x/2015001/article/14201-eng.pdf

Culbert, L. (2018, January 15). Four people per day fatally overdose in BC: What politicians are saying (or not saying) about the crisis. *Vancouver Sun*. Retrieved from https://vancouversun.com/news/politics/four-people-per-day-fatally-overdose-in-b-c-what-politicians-are-saying-or-not-saying-about-the-crisis

Danese, A., Moffitt, T.E., Harrington, H., Milne, B.J., Polanczyk, G., Pariante, C.M., . . . Caspi, A. (2009). Adverse childhood experiences and adult risk factors for age-related disease. *Archives of Pediatrics & Adolescent Medicine, 163*(12), 1135–43.

DARE BC Society. (2019). *D.A.R.E. keepin' it REAL Program*. Retrieved from http://darebc.com/d-a-r-e-keepin-it-real-program/

Degenhardt, L., and Hall, W. (2006). Is cannabis use a contributory cause of psychosis? *Canadian Journal of Psychiatry, 51*, 556–65.

Degenhardt, L., Hall, W., and Lynskey, M. (2002). Testing hypotheses about the relationship between cannabis and psychosis. *Drug and Alcohol Dependence, 71*, 37–48.

Diplock, J., and Plecas, D. (2009). *Clearing the smoke on cannabis: Respiratory effects of cannabis smoking*. Ottawa: Canadian Centre on Substance Abuse.

Diplock, J., and Plecas, D. (2010). Revisiting age and crime. *Journal of Criminal Justice Research, 1*(2), 1–12.

Dore, G., and Sweeting, M. (2006). Drug-induced psychosis associated with crystalline methamphetamine. *Australasian Psychiatry, 14*(1), 86–9.

Dowden, C. (2003). *The effectiveness of substance abuse treatment with young offenders*. Ottawa: Department of Justice Canada.

Dunbar, L.K. (2017). *Youth gangs in Canada: A review of current topics and issues*. Ottawa: Public Safety Canada.

Erickson, P.G., and Butters, J.E. (2005). How does the Canadian juvenile justice system respond to detained youth with substance associated problems? *Substance Use and Misuse, 40*(7), 953–73.

Fast, D.B., Shoveller, J.C., and Kerr, T.B. (2017). The material, moral, and affective worlds of dealing and crime among young men entrenched in an inner city drug scene. *International Journal of Drug Policy 44*, 1–11.

Felson, R., Savolainen, J., Aaltonen, M., and Moustgaard, H. (2008). Is the association between alcohol use and delinquency causal or spurious? *Criminology, 46*(3), 785–808.

Fischer, B. (2005). Harm reduction. In *Substance use in Canada: Current challenges and choices* (pp. 11–16). Retrieved from http://www.ccsa.ca/Resource%20Library/ccsa-004032-2005.pdf

Friedman, D.P. (2009). Drug addiction: A chronically relapsing brain disease. *North Carolina Medical Journal, 70*(1), 35–7.

Government of Canada. (2018, March 9). *Introduction of the Cannabis Act: Questions and answers*. Retrieved from https://www.canada.ca/en/services/health/campaigns/introduction-cannabis-act-questions-answers.html#a4

Harris, J.R. (1995). Where is the child's environment? A group socialization theory of development. *Psychological Review, 102*(3), 458–89.

Harrison, L.D., Erickson, P.G., Adlaf, E., and Freeman, C. (2001). The drugs–violence nexus among American and Canadian youth. *Substance Use and Misuse, 36*(14), 2065–86.

Harrison, P.A., Fulkerson, J.A., and Park, E. (2000). The relative importance of social versus commercial sources in youth access to tobacco, alcohol, and other drugs. *Preventive Medicine, 31*, 39–48.

Hasin, D.S., Wall, M., Keyes, K.M., Cerda, M., Schulenberg, J., O'Malley, P.M., . . . Feng, T. (2015). Medical marijuana laws and adolescent marijuana use in the USA from 1991 to 2014: Results from annual, repeated cross-sectional surveys. *The Lancet, 2*(7), 601–8.

Hayaki, J., Hagerty, C.E., Herman, D.S., de Dois, M.A., Anderson, B.J., and Stein, M.D. (2010). Expectancies and marijuana use frequency and severity among young females. *Addictive Behaviours, 35*, 995–1000.

Health Canada. (2001). *Treatment and rehabilitation for youth with substance use problems*. Retrieved from https://www.canada.ca/en/health-canada/services/health-concerns/reports-publications/alcohol-drug-prevention/best-practices-treatment-rehabilitation-youth-substance-use-problems.html#f_5

Health Canada. (2008). *Best practices: Early intervention, outreach and community linkages of youth with substance abuse problems*. Retrieved from http://www.hc-sc.gc.ca/hc-ps/alt_formats/pacrb-dgapcr/pdf/pubs/adp-apd/bp-mp-intervention/Youth_Outreach.pdf

Health Canada. (2017a). *Canadian drugs and substances strategy*. Retrieved from https://www.canada.ca/en/health-canada/services/substance-abuse/canadian-drugs-substances-strategy.html

Health Canada. (2017b). *Canadian tobacco alcohol and drugs (CTADS)*: 2015 summary. Retrieved from https://www.canada.ca/en/health-canada/services/canadian-tobacco-alcohol-drugs-survey/2015-summary.html

Health Canada. (2018). *Canadian student tobacco, alcohol and drugs survey 2016–17.* Retrieved from https://www.canada.ca/en/health-canada/services/canadian-student-tobacco-alcohol-drugs-survey/2016-2017-summary.html

Hepburn, K., Barker, B., Nguyen, P., Dong, H., Wood, E., Kerr, T., and DeBeck, K. (2016). Initiation of drug dealing among a prospective cohort of street-involved youth. *American Journal of Drug and Alcohol Abuse, 42*(5), 507–15.

Hunt, G., Moloney, M., and Evans, K. (2009). Epidemiology meets cultural studies: Studying and understanding youth cultures, clubs and drugs. *Addiction Research and Theory, 17*(6), 601–21.

Hussong, A.M., Curran, P.J., Moffitt, T., Caspi, A., and Carrig, M.M. (2004). Substance abuse hinders desistance in young adults' antisocial behavior. *Development and Psychopathology, 16*(4), 1029–46.

Kerr, T., and Tupper, K. (2017, December). *Drug checking as a harm reduction intervention: Evidence review report.* Retrieved from https://www.bccsu.ca/wp-content/uploads/2017/12/Drug-Checking-Evidence-Review-Report.pdf

Levy, S., Vaughn, B.L., and Knight, J.R. (2002). Office-based interventions for adolescent substance abuse. *Pediatric Clinics of North America, 49*, 329–43.

Looby, A., and Earleywine, M. (2007). Negative consequences associated with dependence in daily cannabis users. *Substance Abuse: Treatment, Prevention, and Policy, 2*, 3.

Lubman, D.I., Hides, L., Yucel, M., and Toumbourou, J.W. (2007). Intervening early to reduce developmentally harmful substance use among youth populations. *Medical Journal of Australia, 187*, S22–S25.

MacRae, L.D., Bertrand, L.D, Paetsch, J.J., and Hornick, P. (2008). *A profile of youth offenders in Calgary: An interim report.* Prepared for the City of Calgary and the Alberta Law Foundation. Calgary: Canadian Research Institute for Law and the Family.

Martens, M.P., Page, J.C., Mowry, E.S., Damann, K.M., Taylor, K.K., and Cimini, M.D. (2006). Differences between actual and perceived student norms: An examination of alcohol use, drug use, and sexual behaviour. *Journal of American College Health, 54*(5), 295–300.

Molidor, C.E., Nissen, L.B., and Watkins, T.R. (2002). The development of theory and treatment with substance abusing female juvenile offenders. *Child and Adolescent Social Work Journal, 19*(3), 209–25.

Mooney, G.H. (2005). Addictions and social compassion. *Drug and Alcohol Review, 24*, 137–41.

Munch, C., and Silver, W. (2017). Measuring organized crime in Canada: Results of a pilot project. *Juristat, 37*(1). Statistics Canada Catalogue No. 85-002-X. Retrieved from https://www150.statcan.gc.ca/n1/en/pub/85-002-x/2017001/article/14689-eng.pdf?st=oyuLI492

Murray, L.F., and Belenko, S. (2005). CASASTART: A community-based school-centered intervention for high-risk youth. *Substance Use and Misuse, 40*(7), 913–33.

National Crime Prevention Centre. (2009). *School-based drug abuse prevention: Promising and successful programs.* Ottawa: Author.

National Institute on Drug Abuse (NIDA). (2018). Commonly abused drugs charts. Retrieved from https://www.drugabuse.gov/drugs-abuse/commonly-abused-drugs-charts

Newcomb, M.D., and Bentlar, P.M. (1989). Substance use and abuse among children and teenagers. *American Psychologist, 44*(2), 242–8.

O'Leary-Barrett, M. (2014). The internalizing developmental pathway to substance use disorders. In M. Leyton and S. Stewart (Eds), *Substance abuse in Canada: Childhood and adolescent pathways to substance use disorders* (pp. 1–82). Ottawa: Canadian Centre on Substance Abuse.

Palmgreen, P., and Donohew, L. (2003). Effective mass media strategies for drug abuse prevention campaigns. In Z. Sloboda and W.J. Bukoski (Eds), *Handbook of drug abuse prevention: Theory, science, and practice* (pp. 27–43). New York: Kluwer Academic/Plenum.

Palys, T.S., and Atchinson, C. (2014). *Research decisions: Quantitative and qualitative perspectives* (5th ed.). Toronto: Harcourt Brace & Company.

Pan, W., and Bai, H. (2009). A multivariate approach to a meta-analytic review of the effectiveness of the DARE program. *International Journal of Environmental Research and Public Health, 6*, 267–77.

Pauly, B. (2008). Harm reduction through a social justice lens. *International Journal of Drug Policy, 19*(1), 4–10.

Pearson, C., Janz, T., and Ali, J. (2013). Mental and substance use disorders in Canada. *Health at a Glance* (September). Statistics Canada Catalogue No. 82-624-X. Retrieved from https://www150.statcan.gc.ca/n1/pub/82-624-x/2013001/article/11855-eng.htm

Peters, R.H., and Wexler, H.K. (2005). *Substance abuse treatment for adults in the criminal justice system.* Treatment Improvement Protocol (TIP) Series, No. 44. Substance Abuse and Mental Health Services Administration/Center for Substance Abuse Treatment (US). Retrieved from https://www.ncbi.nlm.nih.gov/books/NBK64137/pdf/Bookshelf_NBK64137.pdf

Poole, N., and Dell, C.A. (2005). *Girls, women and substance use.* Ottawa: Canadian Centre on Substance Abuse.

Prochaska, J., and DiClimente, C. (1986). Towards a comprehensive model of change. In W.R. Millet and N. Heather (Eds), *Treating addictive behaviours: Process of change* (pp. 3–27). New York: Plenum.

Public Health Agency of Canada. (2006). *Street youth in Canada: Findings from enhanced surveillance of Canadian street youth, 1999–2003*. Ottawa: Author.

Public Health Agency of Canada. (2018). *National report: Apparent opioid-related deaths in Canada*. Retrieved from https://www.canada.ca/en/public-health/services/publications/healthy-living/national-report-apparent-opioid-related-deaths-released-march-2018.html#a2.1

Rao, D.P., Abramovici, H., Crain, J., Do, M.T., McFaull, S., and Thompson, W. (2018). The lows of getting high: Sentinel surveillance of injuries associated with cannabis and other substance use. *Canadian Journal of Public Health, 109*(2), 155–63.

Rehm, J., Geisbrecht, N., Popova, S., Patra, J., Adlaf, E., and Mann, R. (2006). *Overview of positive and negative effects of alcohol consumption-implications for preventive policies in Canada*. Toronto: Centre for Addiction and Mental Health.

Rehm, J., Gnam, W., Popova, S., Baliunas, D., Brochu, B., Fischer, B.,. . . Taylor, B. (2007). The costs of alcohol, illegal drugs, and tobacco in Canada, 2002. *Journal of Studies on Alcohol and Drugs 68*, 886–95.

Roberts, G., McCall, D., Stevens-Leavigne, A., Anderson, J., Paglia, A., Bollenbach, S., . . . Gliksman, L. (2001). *Preventing substance use problems among young people: A compendium of best practices*. Ottawa: Canadian Centre on Substance Abuse/Health Canada.

Room, R. (2005). Stigma, social inequality and alcohol and drug use. *Drug and Alcohol Review, 24*, 143–55.

Rotenberg, C. (2017). Police-reported sexual assaults in Canada, 2009 to 2014: A statistical profile. *Juristat, 32*(1). Statistics Canada Catalogue No. 85-002-X. Retrieved from https://www150.statcan.gc.ca/n1/en/pub/85-002-x/2017001/article/54866-eng.pdf?st=ev-L-WQe

Rusby, J.C., Westling, E., Crowley, R., and Light, J.M. (2018). Legalization of recreational marijuana and community sales policy in Oregon: Impact on adolescent willingness and intent to use, parent use, and adolescent use. *Psychology of Addictive Behaviors, 32*(1), 84–92.

Saewyc, E.M. (2007). Substance use among non-mainstream youth. In *Substance abuse in Canada: Youth in focus* (pp. 14–21). Ottawa: Canadian Centre on Substance Abuse.

Shepherd, J.P., Sutherland, I., and Newcombe, R.G. (2006). Relations between alcohol, violence and victimization in adolescence. *Journal of Adolescence, 29*, 539–53.

Smith, M.J., Thirthalli, J., Abdallah, A.B., Murray, R.M., and Cottler, L.B. (2009). Prevalence of psychotic symptoms in substance users: A comparison across substances. *Comprehensive Psychiatry, 50*(3), 245–50.

Squeglia, L.M., Jacobus, J., and Tapert, S.F. (2009). The influence of substance use on adolescent brain development. *Clinical eeg and Neuroscience, 40*(1), 31–8.

Status of Women Canada. (2016). *Issue brief: Sexual violence against women in Canada*. Retrieved from http://www.swc-cfc.gc.ca/svawc-vcsfc/index-en.html

Steinberg, L. (2004). Risk taking in adolescence: What changes and why? In R.E. Dahl and L.P. Spear (Eds), *Adolescent brain development and opportunities,* vol. 1021 (pp. 51–8). New York: Annals of New York Academy of Sciences.

Stevens, S.B., Brice, C.S., Ale, C.M., and Morris, T.L. (2011). Examining depression, anxiety, and foster care placement as predictors of substance use and sexual activity in adolescents. *Journal of Social Service Research, 37*(5), 539–54.

Stockburger, J., Parasa-Pajouh, B., Leeuw, S., and Greenwood, M. (2005). Youth voices on the prevention and intervention of youth substance abuse. *Centre of Excellence for Children & Adolescents with Special Needs*. Retrieved from https://www.unbc.ca/assets/centreca/ english/piysa.pdf

Terry-McElrath, Y.M., O'Malley, P.M., and Johnston, L.D. (2009). Reasons for drug use among American youth by consumption level, gender, and race/ethnicity: 1976–2005. *Journal of Drug Issues, 39*(3), 677–714.

Thoma, R.J., Monnig, M.A., Lysne, P.A., Ruhl, D.A., Pommy, J.A., Bogenschutz, M.,. . . Yeo, R.A. (2010). Adolescent substance abuse: The effects of alcohol and marijuana on neuropsychological performance. *Alcoholism: Clinical and Experimental Research, 35*(1), 39–46.

Thorpe, L.E., Ouellet, L.J., Hershow, R., Bailey, S.L., Williams, I.T., Williamson, J., . . . Garfein, R.S. (2002). Risk of hepatitis C virus infection among young adult injection drug users who share injection equipment. *American Journal of Epidemiology, 155*(7), 645–53.

Tonmyr, L., Thornton, T., Draca, J., and Wekerle, C. (2010). A review of childhood maltreatment and adolescent substance use relationship. *Current Psychiatry Reviews, 6*(3), 223–34.

Toumbourou, J.W., Stockwell, T., Neighbors, C., Marlatt, G.A., Sturge, J., and Rehm, J. (2009). Interventions to reduce harm associated with adolescent substance use. *Lancet, 369*, 1391–401.

Treadwell, S.D., and Robinson, T.G. (2007). Cocaine use and stroke. *Postgraduate Medical Journal, 83*, 389–94.

Trudeau, L., Spoth, R., Randall, G.K., Mason, A., and Shin, C. (2012). Internalizing symptoms: Effects of a prevention intervention on developmental pathways from early adolescence to young adulthood. *Journal of Clinical Child and Adolescent Psychology, 42*(3), 287–301.

Tupper, K.W. (2008). Drugs, discourses and education: A critical discourse analysis of a high school drug education text. *Discourse: Studies in the Cultural Politics of Education, 29*(2), 223–38.

United Nations Office on Drugs and Crime (UNODC). (2014). *International standard on drug prevention.* Retrieved from https://www.unodc .org/unodc/en/prevention/prevention-standards.html

United Nations Office on Drugs and Crime (UNODC). (2018). *World drug report 2018.* Retrieved from https://www. unodc.org/wdr2018/en/booklets.html

Urban Health Research Initiative. (2009). *Drug situation in Vancouver.* Vancouver: British Columbia Centre for Excellence in HIV/AIDS.

Urbanik, M., and Haggerty, K.D. (2018). "#It's dangerous": The online world of drug dealers, rappers and the street code. *British Journal of Criminology, 58*(6), 1343–60.

Vaccarino, F. (2007). Drug abuse, addiction and youth: A neuroscience perspective. In *Substance abuse in Canada: Youth in focus* (pp. 30–7). Ottawa: Canadian Centre on Substance Abuse.

Wells, S.L., and Thompson, J.M. (2009). Alcohol-related victimization among young adult Canadian drinkers: The explanatory roles of hazardous drinking and illicit drug use. *Canadian Journal of Public Health, 100*(1), 55–9.

Werb, D., Kerr, T., Li, K., Montaner, J., and Wood, E. (2008). Risks surrounding drug trade involvement among street-involved youth. *American Journal of Drug and Alcohol Abuse, 34,* 810–20.

Winters, K.C., and Arria, A. (2011). Adolescent brain development and drugs. *Prevention Researcher, 18*(2), 21–4.

Wood, E., Tyndall, M.W., Montaner, J.S., and Kerr, T. (2006). Summary of findings from the evaluation of a pilot medically supervised safer injecting facility. *Canadian Medical Association Journal, 175*(11), 1399–404.

World Health Organization. (2014). *Global status report on alcohol and health 2014.* Geneva: Author.

Indigenous Youth Crime in Canada

Hirsch Greenberg and Jana Grekul

11

Overview

This chapter explores historical policies that influence Indigenous youth crime and youth justice in Canada, outlining the historical relationship between Indigenous and non-Indigenous peoples and the intergenerational effects of this relationship on Indigenous youth. It is founded on an understanding of Indigenous youth crime, outlining specific historical policies and processes contributing to the intergenerational trauma of lived experiences expressed as a loss of identity, family dysfunction, substance abuse, violence, lack of education, unemployment, poverty, experiences of racism and discrimination, gang involvement, and overrepresentation in the criminal justice system. Furthermore, the chapter draws on Indigenous authors and representations to explore the possibility and value of Indigenous-based approaches to justice that more appropriately fit with, and address, the traumas that lead to criminal behaviours in the first place.

Matt Smith/The Canadian Press

Key Objectives

After reading this chapter, you should be able to:

- Understand the complexities of youth and crime in an Indigenous context.
- Contextualize Indigenous youth crime with respect to individual risk factors, protective factors, and social environmental factors.
- Understand complex Indigenous youth crime behaviours from individual, community, and historical perspectives.
- Review Canadian judicial responses to Indigenous youth crime.
- Compare mainstream responses with alternative justice approaches.
- Identify future interventions that are culturally sensitive and socially responsible, hold individuals accountable, and can positively affect Indigenous youth.

Introduction

Crime, committed by a youth or an adult, is often reported by mainstream media as ubiquitous. Criminals are painted as faceless strangers invading our communities. Media reports neglect to mention that criminals are members of our communities, are a creation of our communities, and that the solution to crime resides in these same communities (see Box 11.1). This outlook drives a wedge between "law-abiding citizens" and those who "choose" to commit unlawful acts. A "get tough" approach is considered by some to be the definitive answer to crime.

Yet, while we recognize and acknowledge the suffering of victims, the suffering and victimization of many offenders passes unnoticed. For example, many offenders feel they do not or cannot meet the social and economic ideals of society, and consequently, these individuals can be identified by their disengagement and detachment from acceptable social connection. Punishment in the form of incarceration confirms their world view that social acceptance is biased and unjust, that they are outsiders and unworthy of belonging. While "getting tough" on offenders is a popular crime intervention in some circles, Dietrich Bonhoeffer (1906–1945), a Lutheran minister and anti-Nazi dissident whose experiences emerged from the concentration camps of World War II, suggests a different response: "We must learn to respond to people less in the light of what they do or omit to do, and more in the light of what they suffer" (in Braswell 2005, p. 447).

If we are to recognize the suffering caused by crime and compassionately respond to victims and offenders, we must acknowledge all those who suffer.

The approach taken in this chapter is to understand **Indigenous** youth crime as an outcome of historical policies and practices resulting in severe and entrenched trauma among generations of Indigenous peoples in Canada. The underlying contributing factors in Indigenous youth crime are varied and reflect a complex web of historical and existing conditions that in some ways set their actions apart from other criminal events. Car theft

Indigenous
Includes individuals who identify as First Nations, Métis, or Inuit.

Box 11.1 | Youth Justice in Action

Gang Rates Dropping in Maskwacis Leading to New Hope

APTN National News, 25 September 2015 by Brandi Morin

For almost two decades, Sherman Louis lived the hard-core life as a gangster.

"I found it was hard being a father, husband and a gangster. I told them I was done," said Louis.

He used his will power and reconnected to his culture to get out of gangs.

Now, he reaches out to kids in his home community of Maskwacis, Alta., to encourage them to walk the straight road through the Maskwacis Youth Initiative, a program aimed at helping youth who may be vulnerable to becoming involved with gangs.

"I just let them (youth) know that it's really not a good life. It may sound cool, but it's really not after you really open your eyes and notice what you're doing is bad," said Louis.

The program started a year ago and is thriving, according to Leslie Montour, an outreach worker.

"It was definitely needed with our youth. With our program we talk to them about better choices, education, what they're showing their younger siblings . . . it's done so well for the ones that really needed us the most. To hear them, to take charge," said Montour. "This has been so great because the majority of them we've gotten to look for jobs, stay in school, they've really come a long, long way from when we started."

Source: Retrieved 13 May 2018 from http://aptnnews.ca/2015/09/25/gang-rates-dropping-in-maskwacis-say-police-and-band-officials

by a 13-year-old Indigenous youth whose home and other socio-economic environments are unhealthy is not perceived as equivalent to the same criminal offence committed by a 56-year-old white male who is a middle-class income earner.

As we explore the issues, we will observe that for some Canadians crime is not about an act committed against the Queen or about a law broken (see Chapter 2); rather, it is about harm and harmed relationships. Often these harms as criminal offences are heavily influenced by relationships between individuals, families, and communities and intersect with broader societal institutions such as education. They are manifestations of anomie, strain, or normlessness—in other words, of feelings of being lost, hopeless, and desperate. **Values** from Indigenous knowledge and experience inform us that expressions of anomie are essentially about broken relationships, a consistent theme throughout Indigenous justice perspectives. If we take this approach to understanding youth misbehaviour, it becomes more difficult to "get tough" and becomes more relevant to explore responsive alternatives to crime. Understanding the offender and the context within which he or she has "chosen" to commit an offence leads us to consider the value of a healing perspective that focuses on redressing the harms done instead of exacerbating already damaged relationships.

Who is an offender? Is it someone who shows little regard for the law or who disregards right relationships, demonstrating little respect for others? Navajos say of such a person, "He acts as if he has no relatives." So, what do you do when someone acts as if they have no relatives? You bring in the relatives (Chief Justice Robert Yazzie, Navajo First Nation, in McCaslin 2005, p. 85).

values
A collective conception of what is considered proper, desirable, and good—or improper, undesirable, and bad—in a culture.

How we define crime—by a law or by a relationship harmed—decides the path we take toward understanding, explaining, intervening, and resourcing solutions. We are reminded of an Indigenous youth who shared his story with the first author when he was apprehended with a weapon while attending school: "Why do you have a weapon?" I asked. "For protection!" the youth responded. "Protection from what?" I responded quizzically. "Someone wants to beat me up," stated the youth. "Why?" I asked. "Because my brother beat him up!" Pursuing his logic, I explored the story further: "Why did your brother beat him up?" "Because," said the youth, "he stole my brother's bike!" Pausing, I thought about the youth's responses. "So, why is the boy going after you, and not your brother?" (I thought there was a hole in his story.) "Because my brother is bigger than he is!" he argued. Ah . . . retribution, I thought. I asked, "Who do you think is winning this fight, you, the boy who is after you, or your brother?" "My brother! Because he beat up the boy who stole his bike." "Yes, I can see that," I said, "but your brother doesn't have a bike!" The youth was silent.

In this anecdote, the three Indigenous youths did not turn to any legal or school authority, or even to an adult with their problem of a relationship harmed. They simply took matters into their own hands. We can speculate as to how many times this story plays out among Indigenous youth. Cousins reflects that before the "Great Law" was introduced, the Haudenosaunee[1] lived pretty much like these three youths: engaged in blood feuds and revenge and repeating the cycle of vengeance. In response to this internal violence and strife, the Creator sent the Peacemaker to convince the Haudenosaunee to accept the Great Law of Peace and to establish one of the most powerful political alliances on the North American continent (as cited in McCaslin 2005, p. 145).

Injustices in the lives of Indigenous youth beckon redress, but with nowhere to turn, retribution, either against each other or against those with more social privilege, seems the only answer. This is an outcome of policies set in motion centuries ago and is reflective of the destruction of social, cultural, and economic well-being since contact with Europeans (Monchalin 2016). What happened to this once flourishing and rich social fabric comprising "a variety of languages, cultures and social traditions" (Royal Commission on Aboriginal Peoples 1996, p. 6), existing in social cohesion and characterized by group conformity, reverence for nature and community, and awareness of the Creator (Dumont 1996)?

Understanding the Complexities of Indigenous Youth Crime

This report is for Lawrence Wegner, Rodney Naistus, Pamela George, Leo La Chance, and the many unnamed Aboriginal men and women who have paid the ultimate price for ignorance and neglect. . . . While these men, and women, who were sons, daughters, fathers and mothers, are gone . . . they are not forgotten.

—Commission on First Nations and Métis Peoples and Justice Reform (2003–04, s. 1, p. 1)

The complexities of Indigenous youth crime interlace two main features. First is the shared experience of Indigenous peoples—historically, culturally, socially, and economically—as defined by their relations with the settlers; relations marked by racism, broken treaties, assimilation attempts, and domination. A second feature is intergenerational trauma and the repercussions felt in daily lived experiences of Indigenous youth. Effects include poverty, underemployment, dropping out of school, family violence, high rates of substance abuse, poor health, overrepresentation in the criminal justice system, and experiences of racism and discrimination.

The *common experience* and resulting individualized traumatic experiences are so tightly woven together in the life stories of Indigenous communities and individuals that they should be observed as one. This has been a failing of intervention strategies, which are, in the main, "programming fixes" for the problem of crime, all the while ignoring root causes for such behaviours. Margaret Wheatley writes, "When we start a conversation by asking, 'What's wrong and how can we fix it?' we spark criticism, and not necessarily of the healthy sort. . . . When we ask questions like, 'Who cares and what is possible?' we immediately open ourselves to one another" (as cited in Borne 2008, p. 49). Shared community and individual healing must occur concurrently (as we will discuss later in the chapter). First, however, we briefly discuss the historical context critical to understanding the **criminalization** of Indigenous youth.

criminalization
The process whereby individuals are assigned the label of "criminal."

Historical Context

Broken Relations and Promises

The historical context illustrates the link between Indigenous youth's common experience—traumatization and victimization—and criminalization. Relationships between Indigenous and non-Indigenous (settler) peoples have been marred by broken relations and promises. After some 500 years of a relationship that has swung from partnership to domination, from mutual respect and co-operation to paternalism and attempted assimilation, Canada must not only work out fair and lasting terms of coexistence with its Indigenous peoples (Royal Commission on Aboriginal Peoples 1996, p. 4), but must also work to "redress the legacy of residential schools and advance the process of Canadian reconciliation (Truth and Reconciliation Commission of Canada 2015, p. 1) (see Figure 11.1).

There is little doubt that a relationship problem exists between Canadians of European ancestry and the first peoples of North America. Figure 11.1 provides a brief chronology of attempts to redress this relationship. These broken relations and promises included policies of domination and assimilation. The establishment of reserves isolated and impoverished Indigenous peoples. "[The Indian Act] has . . . deprived of us of our independence, our dignity, our self-respect and our responsibility," stated Katherine June Delisle of Kanien'kehaka First Nation, Kahnawake, Quebec, to the Royal Commission on Aboriginal Peoples (1996, p. 10). Ceremonies such as the potlatch—giveaways or gifting—were outlawed; a pass system for reserves was instituted, forbidding outsiders from doing business with Indigenous peoples without permission of the Indian agent; and in 1849 residential schools were created to deal with Indigenous independence and "savagery" (Royal Commission on Aboriginal Peoples 1996, p. 11). Along with imposed poverty and economic, social, cultural, and linguistic marginalization, non-compliant behaviours were defined as illegitimate. For example, Indigenous students in residential schools were

Provincial/Regional	Title
1989	The Royal Commission on the Donald Marshall Inquiry
1990	The Osanburgh/Windigo Tribal Council Justice Review (Northern Ontario)
1991	Report of the Aboriginal Justice Inquiry of Manitoba
1991	The Task Force on the Criminal Justice System and Its Impact on the Indian and Métis People of Alberta
1991	Policing in Relation to the Blood Tribe (Southern Alberta)
1992	Indian Justice Review Committee and Métis Justice Review Committee (Saskatchewan)
1993	The Caribou Chicoltin Justice Report (Interior British Columbia)
1995	Report and Recommendations of the Advisory Committee in the Administration of Justice in Aboriginal Communities (Quebec)
2001	Aboriginal Justice Implementation Commision, Manitoba
2018	Premier Notley apologizes to Sixties Scoop survivors on behalf of the Alberta government in the legislative assembly
Federal	
1969	Statement of the Government of Canada on Indian Policy (The White Paper)
1990	Indian and Northern Affairs Canada: Indian Policing Policy Review
1991	Correctional Services Canada: Task Force on Federally Sentenced Women
1991	Law Reform Commission of Canada: Aboriginal Peoples and Criminal Justice
1996	Royal Commission on Aboriginal Peoples: Bridging the Cultural Divide
2009	Truth and Reconciliation Commission of Canada
2015	A National Inquiry into Missing and Murdered Aboriginal Women (Phase 1)
2015	Truth and Reconcilliation Commission of Canada: Calls to Action
2019	National Inquiry into Missing and Murdered Indigenous Women and Girls Report

Figure 11.1 Justice Inquiries and Commissions

Source: Adapted from *A Review of Research on Criminal Victimization and First Nations, Métis and Inuit Peoples 1990 to 2001* (2006). Appendix A: List of Justice Inquiries and Commissions, 106. Retrieved from http://www.justice.gc.ca/eng/rp-pr/aj-ja/rr06_vic1/rr06_vic1.pdf. Department of Justice Canada, January 2006. Reproduced with the permission of the Department of Justice Canada, 2015.

forbidden to speak their own language or allowed to grow their hair long (an important element of self-identity for Indigenous males).

Indeed, from a historical analysis of Indigenous peoples and the criminal justice system, the Canadian Criminal Justice Association (Canadian Criminal Justice Association [CCJA] 2000) summarizes its findings:

[T]he historical problems of many Aboriginal peoples stem directly from assimilation, which fundamentally changed the economic, political, and social life—indeed the very culture—of First Nations people. Assimilation policies were based partly on the European belief that Aboriginal people were uncivilized and incapable of governing themselves. Because of the devaluation of their language, traditions, and customs after this experience, Aboriginal people began to suffer cultural uncertainties. This cultural crisis can be linked to specific internal problems that currently plague Aboriginal communities, including disproportionate levels of Aboriginal incarceration, poverty, unemployment, alcohol abuse, domestic violence, and an absence of economic self-sufficiency and business infrastructure. (p. 3)

For Indigenous youth, the intergenerational effects of **colonization** are felt to this day. Robert Yazzie, a chief justice emeritus of the Navajo Supreme Court, writes, "In time of legend, Navajos slew monsters. Today, Navajos [youth] face new monsters . . . domestic violence, child abuse, and neglect . . . alcoholism. . . . These problems are today's monsters . . . which get in the way of success (Yazzie, in Boyes-Watson 2008, p. 23).

Historical policies aimed at "civilizing" and "assimilating" Indigenous peoples have created a legacy wherein Indigenous youth are confronted with "violence, fear, abandonment, neglect, economic hardship, discrimination and displacement" (Boyes-Watson 2008, p. 23). As Youngblood (2008) notes, these disadvantages create self-identity issues and frustration for Indigenous youth.

Traumatization

Lack of freedom to gain independence; powerlessness to engage in healthy choices because of a lack of decent housing, safety, clothing, and diet; and the absence of a sense of belonging (intergenerational violence and substance abuse, lack of family cohesion) create an overwhelming sense of oppression. Herman (1997) explains:

> Traumatic events call in question basic human relationships. They shatter the construction of the self that is formed and sustained in relation to others [crime behaviour, for example]. They undermine the belief systems that give meaning to human experience. They violate the victim's faith in natural or divine order and cast the victim into a state of existential crisis. (p. 51)

Five and a half centuries after the Europeans arrived in the Americas, "Indigenous populations [today] are characterized by poverty, subsistence holdings [reserves]" (Youngblood 2008, p. 28). Such conditions have undermined Indigenous culture, languages, self-governance, and relations (e.g., residential schools), the result being a profound sense of loss about how the Indigenous world should work. Positive self-identity has been diminished by colonialism, and racism makes acceptance within the larger social and cultural space socially incongruent. This has an impact "not only on individual psychological structures of the self (e.g., Indigenous youth who commit crime) but also on the systems of attachment and meaning that link individual and community" (Herman 1997, p. 51). Policies, programs, and activities that the government implemented over the history of colonization have undermined Indigenous traditions, identity, and social cohesion (Monchalin 2016).

colonization
Refers to historical and ongoing processes that began with the arrival of Europeans to the country and that include attempts to dominate and assimilate Indigenous peoples.

Lane, Bopp, Bopp, and Norris (2002) state,

> It becomes clear when considering these various sources of trauma, that the eventual impact of trauma originating from outside Aboriginal communities was to generate a wide range of dysfunctional and hurtful behaviours (such as physical and sexual abuse) which then began to be recycled generation after generation inside communities. (p. 3)

There is a long history of deliberate disenfranchisement of a great proportion of Indigenous peoples in Canada, resulting in not only barriers to prosperity but post-colonial stress expressed through addiction, depression, health problems, suicide, and violence (Monchalin 2016). As Episkenew (2009, p. 25) observes, "Because those steeped in imperial ideology believed without question in their superiority over the Indigenous people, neither the regime nor colonial society in general was willing to welcome the Indigenous peoples into its midst. To do so would have required tolerance of difference, and the colonizers interpreted difference as evidence of inferiority."

Educational and Socio-economic Implications of Crime

For youth and young adults who are of First Nations heritage, historical and current societal power structures have predisposed them to pervasive disadvantage and to a suppression and repression of personal value that are apparent across many contexts, one of which is the experience of "schooling."

Individuals' experience of school varies greatly. Personal characteristics, including gender, social class, religious creed, and ethnicity, not only affect students' objective chances of academic success but also have an impact on the subjective experience of school, including attitudes toward the institution. In addition, educational systems differ according to the context and culture in which they are located (Raveaud 2005, p. 460). Essentially, educational institutions based on academic or vocational streams that reflect Judeo-Christian values demonstrate a vacuum of perspectives, processes, and supports that can address the personal characteristics and subjective experiences of Indigenous children and youth (e.g., the impoverishment and racism that can affect learning).

The Indigenous population is younger on average than other groups in Canada, and Indigenous people have higher unemployment rates than other ethnic groups in Canada. They are more likely to live in crowded conditions and have higher residential mobility, and their children are more likely to be members of a lone-parent family. In addition, they have lower levels of education (Statistics Canada 2015). A 2016 Canadian Centre for Policy Alternatives (CCPA) study provides insight into the troubling socio-economic state of many Indigenous communities and peoples in Canada. Sixty per cent of children living on reserves in Canada live in poverty; Indigenous children in Canada (on and off reserve) are more than twice as likely to live in poverty as their non-Indigenous counterparts (Macdonald and Wilson 2016). There is regional variation to degrees of poverty, with Indigenous children living on reserve experiencing the highest rates of poverty in Manitoba (76 per cent) and Saskatchewan (68 per cent). Poverty is one very serious characteristic of many Indigenous communities in Canada, leading many to liken these communities, particularly reserves, to developing nations, a situation that is shocking and disheartening in a country as rich as Canada. As one of the authors of the CCPA report stated in an interview, "The shameful reality in Canada is that devastatingly high child poverty on reserves is getting worse, not better . . . we are risking a new lost generation of Indigenous youth who are growing up in unconscionable poverty" (CCPA 2016, para. 3). The CCPA study reports that "First Nations children living on reserve in Manitoba have a poverty rate fifteen times that affecting children in Denmark, Finland, Norway, and Sweden . . ." (2016, p. 6). High rates of poverty, along with crowded housing, underfunded schools and child welfare services, and undrinkable water, have been linked to mental health issues, addiction problems, high rates of suicide, and other social problems, including crime.

For policy-makers, focusing on crime (managing the symptom) may be more practical than addressing the underlying social problems, including the **marginalization** of people on economic and racial grounds (the causes), from which crime emerges. Band-Aid solutions (i.e., "getting tough on crime") are quick fixes diverting attention from the broader issues, like poverty, that require more sustained attention, more critical analysis, more resources, and more comprehensive social change.

marginalization
The partial exclusion of certain groups from mainstream society who routinely suffer as the result of gross inequalities.

Contemporary Context

Victimization: A Statistical Profile

Trauma and **victimization** characterize Indigenous populations, yet observers point to a noticeable lack of information on Indigenous victimization. Research shows that the link between victimization and future criminalization is a significant one (Minaker and Hogeveen 2009). Although a person can be a victim one day and an offender the next, most reports focus on the role of Indigenous youth as offenders rather than as victims (Chartrand and MacKay 2006, p. 20) (see Figure 11.2).

trauma
Experience that is psychologically painful, distressful, or shocking (such as suffering sexual abuse or witnessing serious violence) and often results in long-term mental or physical problems (such as depression, anxiety, or insomnia). Also, the community-level and individual-level damage, pain, and suffering of Indigenous peoples—physically, spiritually, emotionally, and psychically—is a result of the historical and current processes of colonization.

victimization
The experience of being a victim, which can be linked to future criminalization.

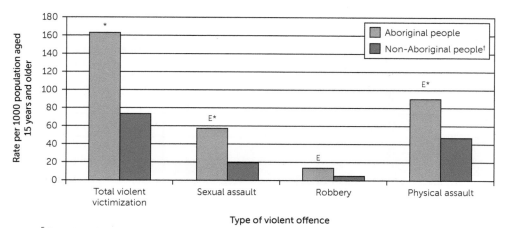

E Use with caution
* Significantly different from reference category (P < 0.05)
† Reference category

Figure 11.2 Indigenous People More Likely to Be Victims of Violent Crime, 2014

Source: Statistics Canada, General Social Survey, 2014.

Chartrand and McKay (2006, pp. 25–32), for example, report the lack of comprehensive data on Indigenous youth victimization. Further, Kingsley and Mark (2000, p. 42) and Elliot (1997) caution "that historical, cultural and economic factors experienced by Aboriginal children and youth are different and unique and that 'these factors limit application of the non-Aboriginal research, programs and policy to Aboriginal youth-at-risk'" (in Chartrand and McKay 2006, p. 31). As Chartrand and McKay (2006, p. 32) explain, "while Aboriginal youth often become engaged in criminality [gangs, sex-trade, etc. . . .], their involvement is often a component of their continued victimization."

Figure 11.2 illustrates the relative victimization of Indigenous peoples compared to non-Indigenous peoples. While there are no specific studies we are aware of that focus on comparative Indigenous youth victimization, it is clear from Figure 11.2 that Indigenous youth victimization is likely similar to that of their families. According to one Statistics Canada study, in 2014, 28 per cent of Indigenous people aged 15 and older reported that they or their household had been victimized in the past year (compared to 18 per cent for non-Indigenous people) (Boyce 2016). Indigenous peoples' violent victimization is affected to some extent by the fact that the Indigenous population in Canada is younger on average than the non-Indigenous population and the fact that victimization in general is associated with being young. This, however, does not entirely explain the significant difference in violent victimizations between Indigenous and non-Indigenous populations (Boyce 2016). As the Statistics Canada study reports, the overall rate of violent victimization among Indigenous people was more than double that of non-Indigenous people (163 violent incidents per 1000 people compared to 74 per 1000) (Boyce 2016). While the study does not separate youth from adults, it is likely safe to assume that the patterns are similar for young people and adults in these populations.

Risk of victimization is not the same for everyone and it is higher for the Indigenous population. Risk of victimization is also gendered, especially for Indigenous girls and women. As Figure 11.3 shows, Indigenous females between the ages of 15 and 24 have

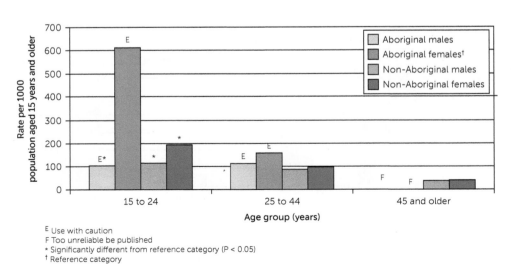

Figure 11.3 Indigenous Girls and Women Are at Greater Risk of Violent Victimization

Source: Statistics Canada, General Social Survey, 2014.

a violent victimization rate that is more than triple that of non-Indigenous females of the same age (Boyce 2016). It is important to note that when Statistics Canada researchers conducted their study on victimization, they found that the higher rates of victimization among Indigenous people could be explained largely by the presence of numerous risk factors within this population (e.g., childhood maltreatment, poor mental health, substance abuse); Indigenous identity on its own was not linked to higher rates of victimization. However, for Indigenous females, Indigenous identity did emerge as a risk factor for victimization (Boyce 2016). In other words, there is something about being an Indigenous female (other risk factors aside), that puts Indigenous girls and women at risk of violent victimization (see Box 11.2).

Box 11.2 | Youth Justice in Action

Tina Fontaine

Slipping through the cracks? Or Systemic Issues? Tina Fontaine was a 15-year-old girl from Sagkeeng First Nation who was loved by many. Her family describes her as a loving girl with a big heart. She lived with her great aunt and uncle, Thelma and Joseph Favel, for over a decade as her father had been ill from cancer and then was beaten to death. Her aunt and uncle reported that Tina did well in school and loved to play with other children. The family reports that she did not start having any problems until she visited the city of Winnipeg to be with her birth mother. They could not get Tina back from the city and worried about her circumstances. She was in foster care under the protection of Manitoba's Child and Family Services (CFS) to protect her. Her aunt and uncle had no idea that they would never see Tina alive again. (Palmater 2016, pp. 260–1)

The tragic story of Tina Fontaine, unfortunately, is not uncommon within the experience of Indigenous girls and women in this country. For decades, Indigenous women have been disappearing from their communities. Finally, in 2015, the Liberal government created the National Inquiry into Missing and Murdered Indigenous Women and Girls, long overdue in the eyes of many. Researchers, front-line workers,

community groups, and families of victims have long acknowledged the critical role of colonialism, sexualized violence, male and state violence, and institutionalized racism and sexism in this crisis. To put it bluntly, there is a perception, played out daily by individuals and agencies, that the bodies of Indigenous girls and women are disposable and not worthy of the same care and attention afforded other, non-Indigenous, girls and women.

As Palmater succinctly states, "Canada has had a long-standing problem with both societal and institutional racism against Indigenous peoples, especially within the justice system" (2016, p. 253). This problem has been well-documented over the years through numerous studies, inquiries, commissions, and investigations, all of which conclude that "every level of the justice system has failed Indigenous peoples" (Palmater 2016, p. 253). The problem is systemic at an institutional and individual level. As Razack (2016) points out, the fact that people in Winnipeg have organized "Drag the Red," a recurring event at which volunteers "dredge the [Red] river that runs through the city of Winnipeg looking for bodies of Indigenous girls and women who have disappeared" (p. i) is a testament to the "commonplace" nature of this situation.

Every level of the justice system fails Indigenous people. In this sense, Tina Fontaine is one example

continued

representing thousands of similar cases. Despite what many consider overwhelming evidence of his guilt, Raymond Cormier, the alleged killer of Tina Fontaine, was found not guilty of the crime on 22 February 2018. In the hours leading up to Tina's death, Winnipeg police officers found her in a vehicle with an intoxicated older man, ran her name through the system, and then sent her out into the night at 3 a.m., alone (Palmater 2016, p. 261). Later, her unconscious body was found by paramedics and she was treated and released into the care of Manitoba's Child and Family Services (CFS). She was placed in a hotel where foster children are housed, and she then disappeared. Given this unfolding of events, Palmater (2016) makes the poignant point that Tina did not "slip through the cracks," a claim often made when tragedies like this occur. Rather, "Tina was left unprotected by an entire system that is indifferent to the well-being of Indigenous women and girls. She was made vulnerable to well-known predators because

those legally bound to protect her did not fulfil their responsibilities" (p. 261). Despite their apparent complicity in the tragedy and an internal investigation into their actions, the police officers who found and released Tina that night were not charged.

The National Inquiry into Missing and Murdered Indigenous Women and Girls is, in the minds of many, a step in the right direction, but much more needs to be done on an individual and institutional level to address the systemic racism and sexism that continues to take the lives of Indigenous girls and women daily in this country.

Critical Thinking Question
Reflecting on the tragic circumstances surrounding the life and death of Tina Fontaine, identify three points at which a different response could have potentially changed the outcome of her life path.

Victimization, Criminalization, and Justice System Involvement

Victimization in the form of family violence and abuse, bullying, and other types of assault is far too common in the lives of far too many Indigenous youth. And the link between victimization and criminalization means that many of these victimized youth are at risk of adopting criminal behaviours.

While youth 12 to 17 years old who self-identify as Indigenous represent about 7 per cent of youth in Canada, in 2015/16 they made up about 39 per cent of youth admitted to custody (Malakieh 2017). Female Indigenous youth are overrepresented in the system compared to non-Indigenous female youth, and they experience greater overrepresentation than their male counterparts. As Malakieh (2017) reports, "the proportion of Indigenous youth in provincial/territorial custody relative to their proportion in the population is about five times higher for Indigenous male youth and seven times higher for Indigenous female youth" (p. 2). Figure 11.4 illustrates the relative proportion of Indigenous youth in the correctional system, compared to non-Indigenous youth.

There are also geographical patterns indicating the overrepresentation of Indigenous youth in the correctional system. While Indigenous youth are overrepresented in most jurisdictions in Canada, the overrepresentation is most pronounced in British Columbia, Manitoba, and Ontario (Government of Canada, Department of Justice 2017). The disturbing number of Indigenous youth coming into conflict with the law occurs even

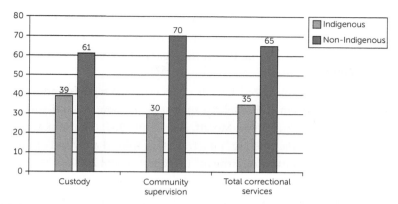

Figure 11.4 Indigenous and Non-Indigenous Youth in the Correctional System
Source: Malakieh 2017.

though certain "rights" are constitutionally guaranteed in the Canadian Charter of Rights and Freedoms (1982): "every individual is equal before and under the law . . . without discrimination and, in particular, *without discrimination based on race* [author's emphasis], national or ethnic origin, colour, religion, gender, age, or mental or physical disability" (s 15(1)). Indeed, the problem is systemic. Indigenous people, both adults and youth, are disproportionately represented as offenders and as victims of crime in our country (Department of Justice Canada 2017).

Understanding the Causes/Influences of Crime

There is resistance to considering offenders as victims, yet the link between victimization and criminalization is well established (Minaker and Hogeveen 2009). This link can be understood more clearly if we consider the following question: How much suffering does one individual have to undergo before he or she retaliates against another human being (Gilligan 1996, p. 50)? Gilligan (1996), an experienced psychiatrist, reports that he has not encountered an individual who has harmed another who was not first him- or herself a victim of harm: "Children who fail to receive sufficient love from others fail to build those reserves of self-love and mostly feel numb, empty, and dead" (p. 50). Feelings of low self-worth often lead to a sense of shame. This shame, according to Brown (2007), is a sense of not fitting in. Since marginalization and disenfranchisement mean there are limited options for finding self-worth, some Indigenous youth turn to criminal behaviours and gang involvement to provide such an option.

Identity, Self-Esteem, and Risk-Protective Factors

Part of the attraction of gangs is the sense of belonging, protection, and identity they promise to provide their members. Identity is a life story or a set of stories that adults have internalized to make sense of their life to themselves and others. Youth are expected to develop a core identity that is reasonably stable and sustainable while living within a society that is characterized by change. This is an enormous task. Indigenous youth today inherit the legacy of the residential school experiences of previous generations, as well as the intergenerational trauma that is the legacy of colonization (see, for example, Wesley-Esquimaux and Smolewski 2004).

Identity issues have implications for self-esteem. Recent reports find strong connections between low self-esteem and problems such as aggression and anti-social behaviour (see Donnellan, Trzesniewski, Robins, Moffitt, and Caspi 2005). The term *at risk* has come to be a code for young people who are "on a trajectory toward a myriad of problems that threaten their present and future adjustment" (Schonert-Reichl 2000, p. 3). The term itself is problematic: neo-liberal ideologies and risk discourses turn social structural issues like poverty, disadvantage, and oppression into individual pathologies, essentially responsibilizing individuals to deal with problems that are structural and systemic (Goddard and Myers 2017). This places significant (and unfair) pressure on "at risk" youth to take responsibility for their lives in a context that has set them up for almost inevitable failure. Even though the very conception of the term *at risk* rests on the premise of deficit, various interpretations of what composes that deficit do exist. Yessine and Bonta (2009), for example, found that chronic high-offending Indigenous offenders shared common background characteristics, including an impoverished background, an unstable family environment, substance use, and negative peer associations. But "risk protective" factors are not solely about risk. Protective factors refer to those elements in a young person's life that offer insulation against negative influences: a healthy family situation, a positive role model, pro-social friends, involvement in positive activities, and positive educational experiences (Totten 2012). For many Indigenous youth, the situation is such that risk factors tend to outweigh the protective factors. One particularly salient risk factor that Indigenous youth face is the trauma referred to throughout this chapter, which is seldom measured or spoken to.

Much is acknowledged about the trauma of Indigenous youth because of their common experience. Joe Solanto, a faculty member of the Justice Institute of British Columbia, lectures widely on intergenerational trauma and healing. In his presentation to the Public Business and Law Institute Aboriginal Justice Forum (Solanto 2008), he outlined how the trauma of residential schools is experienced not only by those who attended them, but also by family and community who never attended, as the experience is passed on from parents to children and grandchildren. Substance abuse becomes an attempt to dull the pain of the residential school experience and is a learned behaviour to cope with poverty, violence, and family breakdown (see also Chapter 10).

This intergenerational experience has a role in producing symptoms that contribute to higher rates of risk among Indigenous youth. "When some parents feel their lives are spiraling out of control, that parent is more likely to direct a form of violence, verbal, emotionally, physical, sexual, neglect or abandonment towards their child. This form of adult bullying can transfer down to sibling abuse and parental attack" (Commission on First Nations and Métis Peoples and Justice Reform 2004, p. 2).

Kelly and Totten (2002) make clear the numerous dimensions and layers to issues of crime and criminalization. Up to this point, we have emphasized the role of history and social processes in the marginalization of Indigenous youth and have attempted to show how the line between victimization and criminalization is a porous one. We have discussed the importance of the discriminatory policies and practices that have created a context within which criminal behaviour becomes a viable option for some youth, as well as how the criminal justice system is more apt to label Indigenous youth as offenders and to treat them more harshly than their non-Indigenous counterparts:

> Through an exploration of a portion of the ample literature base as human beings, we are far more complicated than simply our biology, our environment or our psychology. It is the complex interaction of factors within us and outside of us mixed with the intangible of human agency that makes accurate predictions of human behaviour difficult. (Nelson 2011, p. 5)

Several different perspectives consider other influences on behaviour. We will touch on some of these next and then discuss the ways in which they might affect Indigenous youth specifically.

Biological/Genetic Influences

A wide assortment of behavioural problems and personality and mood disorders have been determined to be influenced by genes, many of which are related to criminal behaviour. Intellectual functioning, personality characteristics (e.g., negativity), and temperamental factors (e.g., impulsivity) all have genetic roots. Behavioural precursors to delinquency and crime (e.g., attention deficit hyperactivity disorder [ADHD]) have also been traced in the behavioural genetics research (Wright, Tibbetts, and Daigle 2008). While substantial importance is attached to what is inherited, genes do not operate in isolation. The environment into which a child is born holds considerable sway.

Psychological Influences

From a psychological perspective, it is critical how people perceive themselves, how they understand what they experience and the meaning they place on that experience within the context of their life, and how valued they feel as a person (Harms and Pierce 2011). We seek to understand why some people do terrible things to other people and what makes violent people different from "us." Classifications have been created to distinguish one type of offender from another and to make sense of the statistics that show that crime is more often located in one group than in another. These classifications may be based on characteristics that lead to stereotypical depictions of who is, and who is not, a criminal (Hollin 2007).

Socio-cultural Influences

Explanations for criminal behaviour that rest on social control look outside the individual to the social systems that surround her or him. From this perspective, delinquent behaviour results from the failure of personal and social controls to produce behaviour that conforms to the norms of the social system. Delinquency occurs when those norms have not been internalized (e.g., due to marginalization, anomie). The common thread among the socio-cultural explanations for criminal behaviour is the critical importance of the interaction between an individual and others in her or his immediate and extended social world. Children with peer relationship difficulties are at an increased risk for aggression, academic problems, anxiety, depression, and loneliness, all of which can contribute to delinquent or criminal behaviour (Ooi, Ang, Fung, Wong, and Cai 2006) and can lead to membership in gangs owing to a desire for social belonging and social identity (White 2008; see also Chapter 9 in this volume).

Demographic Influences

The influence of the interrelationship between demographic variables, such as poverty, race, and neighbourhood, has been explored (Spano, Rivera, Vazsonyi, and Bolland 2008). The sense of physical and social disorder that can be characteristic of neighbourhoods that house large numbers of poor, marginalized people has been shown to exert damaging influences on an individual's social, physical, and psychological health (Farrington 2007; Weyers et al. 2008). With poverty restricting people's access to supports, their present is compromised, and their future is uncertain. Such absence of resources has been implicated in the likelihood of criminalization (Reiman 2013).

The Influence of Fetal Alcohol Spectrum Disorder

fetal alcohol spectrum disorder (FASD) Refers to a medical diagnosis of fetal alcohol syndrome (FAS), partial fetal alcohol syndrome (pFAS), alcohol neurodevelopmental disorder (ARND), and alcohol-related birth defects (ARBD), all of which refer to some degree of permanent central nervous system damage to a fetus because of maternal alcohol consumption during pregnancy.

One group of individuals that is at a higher risk of criminalization includes individuals diagnosed as having **fetal alcohol spectrum disorder (FASD),** the result of maternal alcohol consumption during pregnancy. The degree to which prenatal exposure to alcohol affects the fetus is dependent on several factors, including genetics, maternal characteristics, nutrition, duration and exposure to alcohol, as well as a few other factors. FASD can affect an individual's physical, cognitive, behavioural, and social functioning. This disorder provides a poignant example of the ways in which biological, psychological, and social influences coalesce in such a manner as to heighten the risk of both victimization and criminalization. For Indigenous youth, histories marred by neglect, abuse, and violence exemplify the victimization–criminalization connection. FASD serves to complicate the situation and increase the risk of both.

As estimating the incidence and prevalence of FASD is difficult, largely because of difficulties in diagnosis, it is likely that the disorder is highly under-diagnosed. There is, however, some indication that rates of FASD are higher in Indigenous populations but there is no consensus. Given the prevalence of family violence in Indigenous communities, diagnosis in these communities is further complicated by the overlap of FASD symptoms with post-traumatic stress disorder symptoms (see Table 11.1). According to one estimate, the incidence of FASD within the Canadian Indigenous population ranges from 25 to 200 per 1000 births compared to the estimated incidence rate of 1 to 10 per 1000 births in the general Canadian population (Adler, Mueller, Laufer, and Grekul 2012). What appears to be clearer is the link between FASD and criminalization. Studies in Saskatchewan and

Table 11.1	Examples of How the Cognitive and Behavioural Characteristics of FASD Apply to Offenders, Victims, and Witnesses in Court

Category	Characteristic	Difficulty in Court
Intellect	Do not learn from previous experiences	Difficulty understanding legal terms
	Difficulty generalizing from one event to another	Confused by sarcasm or abstract examples used by lawyers
Attention	Restless	Distracted by others entering and leaving courtroom
		Unable to focus on questions being asked
		Easily frustrated or overwhelmed in court setting
Memory	Impaired short- and long-term memory	Forgetful of time of day
		Difficulty recollecting events
		Unsure of time frames or duration of events
		Unknowingly adding false statements when trying to remember events
Language	Speech difficulties	Unable to articulate thoughts effectively
Social communication	Social cues	Going along with whatever argument the Crown, police, or lawyer is saying in order to please them
	Shy	Easily agreeing to leading questions

Source: Adapted from Fraser 2015.

Manitoba report that at least 50 per cent of young offenders were born with FASD. Another in British Columbia found that of 415 individuals with FASD, 60 per cent ages 12 and over had been in trouble with the law (Adler et al. 2012). It must be noted that FASD largely comes to the attention of police and the courts rather than the health system. Thus, Indigenous youth with FASD become criminalized, when the reality of this condition demands a health intervention.

FASD, however, also appears to increase the risk of victimization. Because of the nature of the disorder and the problems associated with it, individuals with FASD are particularly vulnerable to being taken advantage of, especially by family members and friends. Complicating matters is the fact that some victims with FASD may not realize that certain behaviours are wrong (e.g., sexual advances and inappropriate touching), may not fully understand what it means to be a victim of crime, and may have difficulty navigating through the court process as a victim or witness (see Table 11.1). Researchers, professionals, and communities alike emphasize the need for more research on FASD and its impact on individuals, as well as more support for prevention programming and diagnostic assessment. An emerging concern is that gangs have begun to target youth with FASD because these young people are vulnerable, eager to please, and easily influenced.

Colonization and Intergenerational Trauma: A Compounding of Factors Related to Marginalization and Criminalization

In this section, we provide a look at how the various influences on crime discussed earlier might interact in a unique way in the lives of some Indigenous youth. This discussion is not meant to be exhaustive or definitive; the objective is to begin thinking critically about how the influences of colonization, intergenerational trauma, the legacy of residential schools, and the situations of many Indigenous communities today might contribute to an understanding of criminalization of Indigenous youth. Any discussion of Indigenous peoples in Canada must start with reference to the importance of the land (see Monchalin 2016 for more on this). Colonization is first and foremost about the taking of the land of the First Nations peoples; assimilation efforts in the form of residential schools and attempts at genocide have implications for loss of culture, family structure, parenting, identity, domestic violence, and substance abuse. In turn, education and employment are affected, as is mental health. Without healthy family structures in place, role modelling is impacted in negative ways; Indigenous youth are overrepresented in the child welfare system. One study on offenders (Chalas and Grekul 2017), most of whom were Indigenous, found that over half of the participants had been in the care of social services (foster care or group home) at some point in their lives. About 37 per cent had three to six foster placements and 21 per cent had *11 or more* such placements. We see then, how the various influences—biological, psychological, and socio-cultural—conflate in unique ways to affect the vulnerability of Indigenous youth when it comes to criminalization. Also critical to this discussion are the demographic factors mentioned earlier: Canada's Indigenous population is significantly younger than the non-Indigenous population (Statistics Canada 2017). Youthfulness is associated with both criminal offending and victimization, so this demographic pattern increases the chances that Indigenous youth will become an offender or victim. Many Indigenous people in Canada also experience mobility: migration between reserves and urban areas occurs frequently (Statistics Canada 2017). The implications of this are that a large proportion of young Indigenous people experience transiency, which is linked to lack of belonging, poverty, and homelessness. The case of Tina Fontaine (see Box 11.2) illustrates the ways that movement from reserve to city can result in isolation, anonymity, and loss of connection to family. Add to the mix important structural factors such as systemic discrimination and racism, and it is perhaps not surprising that Indigenous overrepresentation in the criminal justice system is an enduring problem in this country. It is a crisis that has observers referring to the child welfare system and criminal justice system as the "new" residential schools in Canada. Many of these factors that contribute to criminalization of Indigenous youth also help to explain the attractiveness of gangs to some Indigenous youth.

The complexity of factors that influence youth crime, and Indigenous youth crime specifically, is increasingly reflected in the types of approaches communities and front-line workers use to help prevent and intervene in youthful misbehaviour. For example, WrapEd is an approach used for identifying the needs of individual youths—both Indigenous and non-Indigenous—and of tailoring the type of support they require to their specific needs. In this approach, the personalized care team of professionals and community members (e.g., social worker, police officer, Elder, etc.), led by a youth facilitator, collectively "wrap" the young person with supports to help address their needs. WrapEd focuses on the prevention of violent crime and gang involvement, which we discuss next.

Investigating Indigenous Youth Gangs

Many gang members started selling illegal drugs when they were quite young. Jerry said to us: "I grew up on this corner here [near the Merchants Hotel] selling drugs." He was about twelve years old when he started. He got some drugs from his older brother, and "We sold that shit in ten minutes." Soon Jerry was selling while in school: "An hour of selling drugs at lunchtime, you know, put a hundred dollars in your pocket."

— Comack, Deane, Morrissette, and Silver 2013, p. 103

In *"Indians Wear Red": Colonialism, Resistance, and Aboriginal Street Gangs* (2013), Elizabeth Comack and her co-authors provide an in-depth look at the links between colonization, racism, poverty, trauma, and masculinity and their complex connections to the emergence and perpetuation of Indigenous street gangs.

The attraction to gangs felt by young people from all ethnic groups is based in part on the media sensationalization of these groups. Movies, music, and Internet representations present a glamorous "gangsta" identity and lifestyle that appear to provide an endless supply of money, drugs, women, sex, and status to its members. Arguably this search for identity is one of the main underlying causes of gang association for Indigenous youth who have, as we saw earlier, lost an important part of their identity—their culture—because of historical and current discriminatory processes. Several risk factors can lead to gang involvement among youth. The gang promises to serve as a substitute family for its members. It promises to provide money and excitement, and it serves as a source of identity, prestige, and status for members. For young Indigenous youth, many of whom experience violence inside and outside the home, gangs promise protection and loyalty. Protection as a reason for joining a gang becomes more significant for incarcerated youth. Some research suggests that many Indigenous youth first join a gang inside prison as a means of protection (Grekul and LaBoucane-Benson 2008). Over-incarceration of Indigenous youth, then, becomes additionally problematic in that it ostensibly contributes to growth in gangs.

Also related to the unique configuration of social-structural and individually based factors that contribute to gang involvement among Indigenous youth is recruitment by family members (Grekul and LaBoucane-Benson 2008). Indigenous gangs were first identified as a growing concern in the early 1990s in Manitoba. Now, 30 years later and because of official government and correctional policies that led to the flourishing of these groups across the Prairie provinces, Indigenous communities are witnessing intergenerational gang involvement.

In some cases, youth are even expected to follow in the footsteps of gang-involved parents, uncles, or family members by becoming members. In one case, a gang-member father involved his two teenage sons in a conspiracy to commit murder. The sons ended up going to jail (as young offenders) for the offence, but the father did not. Out of jail now, the two boys have Facebook pages proudly stating their gang affiliation. In other cases, reports exist of babies being welcomed into their father's gang. Nimmo (2001), in her study on the role of females in Winnipeg's Indigenous gangs, found that "blessing-in ceremonies" were an important ritual in some groups. Totten (2012) reports that some of his participants had "multiple family members in different, rival gangs—cousins, uncles, stepbrothers" (p. 145). While most of these participants reported 10 or more gang-involved family members, a minority claimed that over 20 of their family members were gang involved (p. 145). At the same time, research in Alberta based on interviews with 207 (ex) gang members, the majority of whom were Indigenous, found that 98 per cent of participants would not want their child to become involved with a gang (Chalas and Grekul 2017).

The intergenerational element is perhaps a sign of the entrenchment of gangs in some Indigenous communities and in the lives of some Indigenous families. As one of the men in Comack et al.'s study (2013, p. 93) explains,

> When I was younger, all I looked up to was gang members, right, 'cause of my family and my older cousins and uncles. And I just wanted to be something, you know. But I didn't only want to be part of it. I wanted to be someone . . . so I thought that if I went there [the penitentiary] that it would help me, help my record of, you know, gangsters, you know what I mean?

Social-structural problems of the type discussed earlier have led to social-structural responses that have become long-term and enduring. A gang unit detective (whose father and brother are also police officers) who works closely with these groups explains,

> You have a guy like [name] of the Redd Alert sitting there with his kid in a red bandana showing the gang sign in pictures . . . I have pictures of me and my brother wearing police hats when we were 10 and 8, or 5 and 3 and it's the same thing. We've allowed this thing to get to the level of where you have generational gang membership. (personal communication 14 April 2010)

The gang unit detective goes on to explain the significance of this, not only as a commentary or reflection on the entrenched nature of social-structural factors but in terms of ways of addressing the gang issue: "Intervention strategies on generational gang membership aren't going to work . . . you're not going to get to those youth before anyone else gets to them because they're being taught from a young age: police are bad, gangs are good, this is what you're in." The implication is that Band-Aid solutions—programs or policies that target individual-level issues and risk factors—cannot operate successfully without efforts to address the structural level or broader factors that contribute to the general social-structural disadvantage faced by Indigenous communities and that manifest themselves in gang involvement.

Many, if not all, of these social-structural issues arise out of colonization. It follows that an effective response to dealing with the issues should be rooted in decolonization (Comack et al. 2013)—undoing the impact of forced assimilation and all that has come with it. Comack and her co-authors show how gangs are a manifestation of colonization and in fact are a form of collective resistance, albeit a negative one, on the part of some Indigenous peoples. In speaking with Elders from Indigenous communities, the authors show how social programming alone is not enough to prevent and intervene in gang involvement. Rather, a broader approach to dealing with gangs effectively involves, for example, challenging stereotypes about Indigenous peoples and gangs, drawing on Indigenous ways of knowing, teaching young Indigenous men about a kind of "masculinity" that is not rooted in the gang version of what it means to be a man, teaching Indigenous peoples about who they are and where they have come from, and reconnecting them with their culture (Comack et al. 2013). Importantly,

> Aboriginal people need to be at the centre of a process of building communities in which they can safely live and work as Aboriginal people, aware of and proud of their identity, while making a living in ways consistent with their traditional values. (p. 146)

Members of Indigenous communities and researchers are increasingly turning to an understanding of intergenerational trauma as a framework for contextualizing the social-structural and individual-level risk factors we have been discussing. The suggestion is that a root contributing factor to youth crime and gangs in Indigenous communities can be found in the generational "piling up" of trauma and grief that originated centuries ago with the arrival of the colonizers. Yet this kind of thinking is somewhat at odds with the approach to justice currently informing our criminal justice system.

Attribution of Responsibility: The Youth Justice System

We live in a society whose members must take personal responsibility for criminal action according to the law: "You do the crime, you do the time." However, this personal responsibility is not only for the criminal action itself but also for the conditions and the response to the conditions that gave rise to the criminal behaviour in the first place: "Criminal law rests on the notion of attributing personal responsibility for the crime . . . consequently the social, political and cultural context in which the problem occurred disappears into the background" (Law Commission of Canada 2003, p. 13).

Healing: A More Appropriate Alternative to Indigenous Youth Crime?

There has been a focus in the literature on causality of crime, on the characteristics of those who get involved in criminality, on the success or failure of interventions, and on the identification of the educational needs of youth involved in criminal activity. Some studies look at the problems of youths coming out of custody from the perspective of those youths

(Mazzotta 2004) or consider the societal perceptions of race, class, and gender that engender inadvertent bias toward youth who are at risk (Crenshaw 2005). What appears to be under-explored is how a sense of "self as learner" could potentially be enhanced through recognition of past experiences and the learning that has resulted. It is within that gap that we now turn our attention to some Indigenous perspectives and explanations.

Indigenous Perspectives

The destruction of Indigenous peoples' way of life changed their relationships with one another and with the larger society. We have presented how the lives of Indigenous youth are affected by both historical conditions and contemporary insights. From Indigenous perspectives—especially those of Indigenous youth—to take a vibrant and meaningful step toward healing, the dominant culture must break down the barriers it has created.

The most unfruitful response, from a healing perspective, would be for non-Indigenous readers to dismiss, or refuse to deal with, what Indigenous youth have expressed. It has been this sense of white privilege that has contributed to such a gap in awareness in the first place. The fact that Indigenous people often "speak the truth" in these ways and that non-Indigenous people often are unfamiliar with this level of truth-telling suggests where the healing process might start—namely, with listening to voices and views that are often not heard (Breton, in McCaslin 2005, p. 19). In this sense, the Royal Commission on Aboriginal Peoples (1996) strikes a chord for the future: "The starting point is recognition that Aboriginal people are not as some Canadians think, an inconsequential minority group with problems that need fixing and outmoded attitudes that need modernizing. They are unique political entities, whose place in Canada is unlike that of any other people" (p. 67). The Truth and Reconciliation Commission's recommendations (2015) are a call to all Canadians to be more inclusive and understanding of the history and treatment of Indigenous peoples in Canada, and work toward reconciliation.

The number of Indigenous perspectives, values, and beliefs is far too great and rich to discuss in this chapter (please see Monchalin [2016] for more on this). However, some shared beliefs and values include the following:

- Having a connection to nature and to each other
- Knowing the importance of circles and ceremonies
- Resisting justice as force
- Healing broken relations with mainstream society
- Peacemaking and respecting community

Rupert Ross, Canadian Crown prosecutor and author of *Dancing with a Ghost: Exploring Aboriginal Reality*, learned that he was routinely misinterpreting the behaviour of Indigenous victims, witnesses, and offenders, both in and out of court. He discovered that he regularly drew incorrect conclusions when he encountered witnesses who would not make eye contact, victims who would not testify in the presence of the accused, and parents who showed great reluctance to interfere in their children's offending behaviour.

With the assistance of Indigenous teachers, he began to see that behind such behaviour lay a complex web of coherent cultural commandments that he had never suspected, much less understood (Ross 2006).

What Ross learned—as discussed in this chapter—was that trauma is a fundamental experience of Indigenous peoples and, importantly, of Indigenous youth. For example, Ross reports a traditional Indigenous ethic is to not burden others, especially when talking about feelings or self. A possible manifestation of this is that Indigenous witnesses often describe traumatic events in a flat, emotionless manner. The resulting perception is that Indigenous youth are unresponsive, do not care, and are cavalier about the criminal justice process. Former deputy minister of justice and attorney general of Saskatchewan Robert Mitchell mentioned, after attending the Royal Commission on Aboriginal Issues in the early 1990s, that Indigenous peoples are less concerned with who committed the crime (guilt) and more concerned with how to repair the harm. The concern is not really with punishment (personal communication).

Summary

When it comes to moving health-care practices forward efficiently, Canada is a country of perpetual pilot projects. We seldom move proven projects into stable, funded programs, and we rarely transfer the outcomes of pilot projects across jurisdictions. This approach is not serving our health-care system well. (Bégin, Eggertson, and Macdonald 2009, p. 1185)

Esteemed Norwegian criminologist Nils Christie writes, "My suspicion is that criminology to some extent has amplified a process where conflicts [criminal offences] have been taken away from the parties directly involved and thereby have either disappeared or become other people's property [professionals, researchers]. In both cases a deplorable outcome" (1977, p. 1). The sentiment of these scholars, Bégin et al. and Christie, informs us of two problems with "programs": (1) programs come and go as ideas wax and wane in popularity; and (2) programs are not owned by the participants but, rather, are owned by the professionals. In the case of the latter, an Indigenous youth stated to the Commission on First Nations and Métis Peoples and Justice Reform (2004), "In many instances I think we would have experiences of bureaucracies who want to maintain control and power over programs that are under various departments" (p. 2–1). Another youth addressing the commission speaks to the former point:

And we did a bit of play with words here and thought that maybe we could use, instead of saying crime prevention all the time, we could maybe start talking about community promotion and create a sense of that among our youth, and from an early age—whether we're talking about the far North, in a small community, or a large city, or your part of the city, that we could be promoting our part of the communities to our children, our youth, so that sense of pride and self esteem is attached to that. (s. 2, p. 1)

Many programs can be identified across the country. If we draw on Hester and Miller's (1995, p. 1) idea that there is no "one true light" explanation or effective response for substance abuse and we extrapolate this observation to the broader set of issues, the implication is that successful interventions into the human condition require considerate and "multivariate" explanations and responses. Dr. Rod McCormick, an Indigenous psychologist and mental health consultant, speaks to this understanding: "Not all strategies will work for everyone as each community is different. That is why it is necessary to explore different strategies and adapt and modify them so that it fits the needs of your [our] youth" (McCormick, in White and Jodoin 2007, p. ii).

One approach that is particularly impressive and that confirms the belief that change is about ownership, resilience, self-esteem, community, and then individuals, is found in the *First Nations Community Justice Guidebook*, developed and published by the Restorative Justice Unit (2010) of the File Hills Qu'Appelle Tribal Council (a member of Treaty 4). The book states that a "program" is a "facilitated learning process [that] allows for the full and active involvement of all participants and so enriches learning, promotes community development and enables change" (p. 9) and is "[t]he art of leading people through processes towards agreed-upon objectives in a manner that encourages participants, ownership and creativity by all those involved" (p. 10). The guidebook is an important document, as many of the Treaty 4 (Southern Saskatchewan and Western Manitoba) languages are incorporated, as is important First Nation artwork by Lawrence (Henry) Shepherd. In the guidebook, 12 elements are presented in a circle and are equally represented at each hour of the clock (p. iii):

- The Youth Criminal Justice Act (12:00)
- Policing and Peacekeeping (1:00)
- Community Justice Committees (2:00)
- First Nations Law (3:00)
- Nurturing Leadership (4:00)
- Wellness and Balance (5:00)
- Inherent Authority and Treaty Relationships (6:00)
- Lands and Resources (7:00)
- Ancestral Laws (8:00)
- Restoring Balance (9:00)
- Justice and Healing (10:00)
- The Legal System and Legislation (11:00)

Surrounding the clock are the nations of their community, written in English, and the language representing each nation. What the guidebook has successfully accomplished is the integration of history, mainstream thinking, expertise, and practices with a strong sense of community, harmony, the land, and their own knowledge, experience, and expertise. Punishment is not a response: "In the Commission on First Nations and Métis Peoples and Justice Reform report, Willie Littlechild spoke of people who are 'Champions of Change' in our communities who are true leaders" (Restorative Justice Unit 2010, p. 3). It is not about a single successful program or one that failed; it is instead about developing the culture for change, working collaboratively across "broken promises and relationships" to reduce effectively the social-structural and individual-level challenges faced by Indigenous youth that contribute to their victimization and criminalization in this country.

We have briefly discussed and made a case for the importance of understanding the complexities of Indigenous youth crime. The historical context illuminates the policies of domination and assimilation, phrases we equate with broken relationships and promises. We suggest that to address Indigenous youth crime, any intervention must incorporate elements that address poverty, racism, and self-determination. Further, interventions must include family and community as part of the process.

We have also discussed several approaches to understanding the factors that contribute to criminal behaviour and criminalization, including those based in biology, sociology, and psychology. We suggest that the criminalization of "deviant" Indigenous youth behaviours is largely a result of victimization at the individual and social-structural levels. Finally, our conclusion is that any effort to deal effectively with the issues facing Indigenous youth and Indigenous offenders must be based on an understanding of Indigenous culture, values, and justice and must involve Indigenous communities. Ultimately, any approach to reducing the criminalization of Indigenous youth must be situated against a backdrop against which social-structural issues are also addressed.

Key Terms

colonization

criminalization

fetal alcohol spectrum disorder (FASD)

Indigenous

marginalization

trauma

values

victimization

Review Questions

1. What happened to once flourishing First Nations societies that contributed to Indigenous youth crime?

2. Indigenous youth experience victimization in greater numbers than their non-Indigenous counterparts. Explain.

3. Indigenous youth experience criminalization in greater numbers than their non-Indigenous counterparts. Discuss.

4. What are the arrays of influences or explanations that contribute to Indigenous youth crime?

5. What types of programs or approaches hold the most hope for effectively preventing the criminalization of Indigenous youth?

Critical Thinking Questions

1. If Indigenous youth are to succeed in Canada, partake as full citizens in the economy and educational system, and reduce their undesirable position in the criminal justice system, what critical changes would you make to policies? To legislation? To public education?

2. There have been numerous federal and provincial inquiries and reports on the historical relationships between First Nation and Métis peoples and European settlers. Yet Indigenous children and youth today remain disadvantaged in many ways. Can the damaged relationships between First Nation and Métis peoples and European settlers ever be healed? Is the criminal justice system the vehicle for such change?

3. Carol LaPrairie is one of Canada's most prolific authors on Indigenous justice. She was a committed advocate for Indigenous justice reform. She applied sound empirical evidence and research practices to evoke change (Murphy and Stenning 2014). Here is a question LaPrairie might challenge us to think about: "What are the community-based reforms that would address the policies and practices needed for Indigenous youth who are involved in the criminal justice system?"

Endnote

1. "Called the Iroquois Confederacy by the French, and the League of Five Nations by the English, the confederacy is properly called the Haudenosaunee Confederacy, meaning People of the long house" (Haudenosaunee Confederacy 2018).

References

Adler, F., Mueller, G.O.W., Laufer, W.S., and Grekul, J. (2012). *Criminology* (2nd Canadian ed.). Toronto: McGraw-Hill Ryerson.

Bégin, M., Eggertson, L., and Macdonald, N. (2009). A country of perpetual pilot projects. *Canadian Medical Association Journal, 180*(12), 1185.

Borne, P. (2008). *Community conversations.* Toronto: BPS.

Boyce, J. (2016). Victimization of Aboriginal people in Canada, 2014. *Juristat.* Statistics Canada Catalogue No. 85-002-X.

Boyes-Watson, C. (2008). *Peacemaking circles and urban youth: Bringing justice home.* St Paul, MN: Living Justice.

Braswell, M.C. (2005). Criminal justice: An ethic for the future. In M.C. Braswell, B.R. McCarthy, and B.J. McCarthy (Eds), *Justice, crime, and ethics.* Conklin, NY: Matthew Bender & Company.

Brown, B. (2007). *Shame resilience theory.* In S.P. Robbins, P. Chatterjee, and E.R. Canda (Eds), *Contemporary human behavior theory: A critical perspective for social work* (rev. ed.). Boston: Allyn and Bacon.

Canadian Centre for Policy Alternatives (CCPA). (2016, May 17). *Study reveals Canada's shameful Indigenous child poverty rates* [News release]. Retrieved from https://www.policyalternatives.ca/newsroom/news-releases/study-reveals-canada%E2%80%99s-shameful-indigenous-child-poverty-rates

Canadian Charter of Rights and Freedoms, s 15, Part I of the Constitution Act, 1982, being Schedule B to the Canada Act 1982 (UK), 1982, c11.

Canadian Criminal Justice Association (CCJA). (2000). *Aboriginal Peoples and the criminal justice system.* Retrieved from http://caid.ca/CCJA.APCJS2000.pdf

Chalas, D., and Grekul, J. (2017). I've had enough: Exploring gang life from the perspective of (ex) members in Alberta. *Prison Journal, 97*(3), 364–86.

Chartrand, L., and McKay, C. (2006). *A review of research on criminal victimization and First Nations, Métis and Inuit peoples 1990–2001.* Ottawa: Policy Centre for Victim Services, Department of Justice Canada.

Christie, N. (1977). Conflict as property. *British Journal of Criminology, 17*(1), 1–15.

Comack, E., Deane, L., Morrissette, L., and Silver, J. (2013). *"Indians wear red": Colonialism, resistance, and Aboriginal street gangs.* Winnipeg: Fernwood.

Commission on First Nations and Métis Peoples and Justice Reform. (2004). *Legacy of hope: An agenda for change,* Final Report, vol. I. Saskatchewan.

Commission on First Nations and Métis Peoples and Justice Reform. (2003–04). *Submissions to the commission,* vol. II. Saskatchewan.

Crenshaw, S.J.N. (2005). *The role of systemic public education in the retention and attrition of students placed at risk: Closing or creating the achievement gap* (Doctoral dissertation). Retrieved from Dissertation Abstracts International. (66/04, 1220).

Department of Justice Canada. (2017). Indigenous overre-presentation in the criminal justice system. *JustFacts* (January). Retrieved from http://www.justice.gc.ca/eng/rp-pr/jr/jf-pf/2017/jan02.html

Donnellan, M.B., Trzesniewski, K.H., Robins, R.W., Moffitt, T.E., and Caspi, A. (2005). Low self-esteem is related to aggression, anti-social behaviour and delinquency. *Psychological Science, 16*(4), 328–35.

Dumont, J. (1996). Justice and Aboriginal people. In Royal Commission on Aboriginal Peoples (Ed.), *Bridging the cultural divide. A report on Aboriginal peoples and the criminal justice system in Canada* (p. 69). Ottawa: Queen's Printer.

Elliot, D. (1997). Social and health-care pilot project for sex trade workers: Interim report. In L. Chartrand and C. McKay (Eds), *A review of research on criminal victimization and First Nations, Métis and Inuit peoples 1990–2001.* Ottawa: Policy Centre for Victim Services, Department of Justice Canada.

Episkenew, J. (2009). *Taking back our spirits: Indigenous literature, public policy and healing.* Winnipeg: University of Manitoba Press.

Farrington, D.P. (2007). Advancing knowledge about desistance. *Journal of Contemporary Criminal Justice, 23*(1), 125–34.

Fraser, F. (2015). Victims and fetal alcohol spectrum disorder (FASD): A review of the issues. *Victims of Crime Research Digest.* Ottawa: Department of Justice Canada. https://www.justice.gc.ca/eng/rp-pr/cj-jp/victim/rr07_vic4/p4.html

Gilligan, J. (1996). *Violence: Our deadly epidemic and its causes.* New York: Putnam.

Goddard, T., and Myers, R. (2017). Against evidence-based oppression: Marginalized youth and the politics of risk-based assessment and intervention. *Theoretical Criminology 21*(2), 151–67.

Grekul, J., and LaBoucane-Benson, P. (2008). Aboriginal gangs and their (dis)placement: Contextualizing recruitment, membership and status. *Canadian Journal of Criminology and Criminal Justice, 50,* 31–57.

Harms, L., and Pierce, J. (2011). *Working with people: Communication skills for reflective practice.* Don Mills, ON: Oxford University Press.

Haudenosaunee Confederacy. (2018). About the Haudenosaunee Confederacy. Retrieved from https://www.haudenosauneeconfederacy.com/who-we-are/

Herman, J. (1997). *Trauma and recovery.* New York: Basic Books.

Hester, R.K., and Miller, W.R. (1995). *Handbook of alcoholism treatment approaches: Effective alternatives* (2nd ed.). Needham Heights, MA: Allyn and Bacon.

Hollin, C.R. (2007). Criminological psychology. In M. Maguire, R. Morgan, and R. Reiner (Eds), *The Oxford handbook of criminology* (4th ed., pp. 43–77). New York: Oxford University Press.

Kelly, K.D., and Totten, M. (2002). *When children kill: A social psychological study of youth homicide.* Peterborough, ON: Broadview Press.

Kingsley, C., and Mark, M. (2000). Sacred lives: Canadian Aboriginal children & youth speak out about sexual exploitation. In S. McKay, D. Fuchs, and I. Brown (Eds), *Passion for action in child and family services: Voices from the Prairies.* Regina, SK: Canadian Plains Research Centre.

Lane Jr., P., Bopp, M., Bopp, J., and Norris, J. (2002). *Mapping the healing journey: The final report of a First Nation research project on healing in Canadian Aboriginal communities.* Ottawa: Solicitor General of Canada and the Aboriginal Healing Foundation.

Law Commission of Canada. (2003). *What is a crime? Challenges and alternatives.* Retrieved from http://www.lcc.gc.ca

McCaslin, W. (2005). *Justice as healing: Indigenous ways.* St Paul, MN: Living Justice Press.

Macdonald, D., and Wilson, D. (2016). *Shameful neglect: Indigenous child poverty in Canada.* Ottawa: Canadian Centre for Policy Alternatives.

Malakieh, J. (2017, June 19). Youth correctional statistics in Canada, 2015/2016. *Juristat.* Statistics Canada Catalogue No. 85-002-X.

Mazzotta, M.A. (2004). *Perceptions about schooling and substance abuse treatment success from court mandated adolescent males* (Doctoral dissertation). Retrieved from Dissertation Abstracts International. (65/02, 412).

Minaker, J.C., and Hogeveen, B. (2009). *Youth, crime, and society: Issues of power and justice.* Toronto: Pearson Prentice Hall.

Monchalin, L. (2016). *The colonial problem: An Indigenous perspective on crime and injustice in Canada.* Toronto: University of Toronto Press.

Murphy, C., and Stenning, P. (2014). Introduction. In *Essays to honour the life and work of Dr. Carol LaPrairie*. Toronto: University of Toronto Press. Special issue of *Canadian Journal of Criminology and Criminal Justice, 56*(4).

Nelson, R. (2011). *Reconstruction of a learner self: A phenomenological study with youth and young adults' post-incarceration*. (Unpublished doctoral dissertation). University of Regina, Regina, Saskatchewan.

Nimmo, M. (2001, June). *The "invisible" gang members: A report on female gang association in Winnipeg*. Ottawa: Canadian Centre for Policy Alternatives. Retrieved from https://www.policyalternatives.ca/publications/reports/invisible-gang-members

Ooi, Y.P., Ang, R.P., Fung, D.S.S., Wong, G., and Cai, Y. (2006). The impact of parent–child attachment on aggression, social stress and self-esteem. *School Psychology International, 27*, 552–66.

Palmater, P. (2016). Shining light on the dark places: Addressing police racism and sexualized violence against Indigenous women and girls in the national inquiry. *Canadian Journal of Women and the Law, 28*, 253–84.

Raveaud, M. (2005). Hares, tortoises and the social construction of the pupil: Differentiated learning in French and English primary schools. *British Educational Research Journal, 31*(4), 459–79.

Razack, S. (2016). Sexualized violence and colonialism: Reflections on the inquiry into missing and murdered Indigenous women. *Canadian Journal of Women and the Law, 28*, i–iv.

Reiman, J. (2013). *The rich get richer and the poor go to prison* (10th ed.). New York: Pearson.

Restorative Justice Unit, File Hills Qu'Appelle Tribal Council. (2010). *First Nations community justice handbook*. Saskatchewan: File Hills Qu'Appelle Tribal Council.

Roberts, J., and Doob, A.N. (1997). Race, ethnicity, and criminal justice in Canada. In M. Tonry (Ed.), *Ethnicity, crime and immigration: Comparative and cross-national perspectives*, vol. 21 (pp. 469–522). Chicago: University of Chicago Press.

Ross, R. (2006). *Dancing with a ghost: Exploring Aboriginal reality*. Toronto: Penguin.

Royal Commission on Aboriginal Peoples. (1996). Highlights from the report *People to people, nation to nation*. Ottawa: Indian and Northern Affairs Canada.

Schonert-Reichl, K. (2000, April). *Children and youth at risk: Some conceptual considerations*. Paper presented at the Pan-Canadian Educational Research Agenda (PCERA) Symposium "Children and Youth at Risk," Ottawa.

Retrieved from http://www.educ.ubc.ca/research/ksr/docs/schonert-reichl_childrenatrisk2000.pdf

Solanto, J. (2008). Aboriginal Justice Forum presentation: *Intergenerational trauma and healing. Found on the National Day of Healing and Reconciliation, January 28, 2010*. Forum organized by Pacific Business and Law Institute with support from the Aboriginal Directorate, Justice Canada. Retrieved from https://vimeo.com/ondemand/intergenerationaltrauma

Spano, R., Rivera, C., Vazsonyi, A.T., and Bolland, J.M. (2008). The impact of exposure to violence on a trajectory of (declining) parental monitoring: A partial test of the ecological-transactional model of community violence. *Criminal Justice and Behavior, 35*(11), 1411–28.

Statistics Canada. (2015). *Aboriginal Statistics at a Glance* (2nd ed.). Catalogue No. 89-645-x2015001.

Statistics Canada. (2017, October 25). Aboriginal peoples in Canada: Key results from the 2016 Census. *The Daily*. Statistics Canada Catalogue No. 11-001-X.

Totten, M. (2012). *Nasty, brutish, and short: The lives of gang members in Canada*. Toronto: James Lorimer.

Truth and Reconciliation Commission of Canada. (2015). *Truth and Reconciliation Commission of Canada: Calls to action*. Winnipeg: Author.

Wesley-Esquimaux, C.C., and Smolewski, M. (2004). *Historic trauma and Aboriginal healing*. Ottawa: Report prepared for the Aboriginal Healing Foundation.

Weyers, S., Dragano, N., Mobus, S., Beck, E., Stang, A., Möhlenkamp, S., . . . Siegrist, J. (2008). Low socio-economic position in association with poor social networks and social support: Results from the Heinz Nixdorf Recall Study. *International Journal for Equity in Health, 7*(13), 1–13.

White, J., and Jodoin, N. (2007). *Aboriginal youth: A manual of promising suicide prevention strategies*. Edmonton: Centre for Suicide Prevention, Canadian Mental Health Association, Alberta Division.

White, R. (2008). Disputed definitions and fluid identities: The limitations of social profiling in relation to ethnic youth gangs. *Youth Justice, 8*, 149–61.

Wright, J.P., Tibbetts, S.G., and Daigle, L.E. (2008). *Criminals in the making: Criminality across the life course*. Thousand Oaks, CA: Sage.

Yessine, A.K., and Bonta, J. (2009). The offending trajectories of youthful Aboriginal offenders. *Canadian Journal of Criminology and Criminal Justice, 51*(4), 435–72.

Youngblood, H.J. (Sa'ke'j). (2008). *Indigenous diplomacy and the rights of peoples: Achieving un recognition*. Saskatoon: Purich.

Racialized Youth Crime and Justice in Canada

Harpreet Aulakh and Julius Haag

12

Overview

This chapter explores the perceptions and reality of racialized youth's involvement with the justice system. The chapter begins by providing a discussion of racialized youth as a social category in Canada by highlighting their social, demographic, and economic profile in an attempt to understand their interaction with the criminal justice system. In the absence of official public crime statistics related to race and ethnicity, the media representations of racialized youth as violent and dangerous are discussed, as such representations lead to misinformed policy and interventions. This is followed by an examination of racialized youth's involvement in youth gangs, the potential risk factors, and theoretical models linking immigration and crime. The issue of disproportionate contact of ethnic minority youth with law enforcement—especially harassment, discrimination, and racial profiling by the police as a contributing factor for their overrepresentation in the criminal justice system—is examined. The need for prevention and intervention measures that are sensitive and responsive to the specific needs of contemporary ethnic minority youth is highlighted.

Key Objectives

After reading this chapter, you should be able to:

- Understand the role of media and politics in generating moral panic about racialized youth.
- Appreciate the complexity of understanding racialized youth involvement in crime and gangs.
- Understand the connection between immigration, ethnic minority, and crime.
- Understand the role of proactive policing strategies on the policing of youth from ethnic minority backgrounds.
- Analyze the role that racial profiling and racialization play in police decision-making as it relates to racialized youth.
- Analyze the policing of ethnic minority youth as it relates to domestic radicalization and terrorism.
- Understand the impact of negative police–citizen encounters on youth from ethnic minority backgrounds and their communities.

Introduction

In the wake of the increasing migration of an ethnic minority population to Canada in the recent decades, it is projected that by 2036, the ethnic and visible minority groups will represent roughly one-third of Canada's total population (Press 2017). As a consequence, the size of diverse racialized youth populations has grown significantly in the Canadian cities. This development warrants more understanding of the experiences of different ethnic groups and cultures within our criminal justice system.

In our contemporary Western society, where the populist view has often linked immigrants to the crime that has captured media headlines and shaped political debates, there is much public speculation as to the extent to which racialized youth have been involved in various crimes (Sohoni and Sohoni 2014). In the absence of official crime statistics on immigration, race, and ethnicity in Canada (Millar and Owusu-Bempah 2011), the media representations of racialized youth as violent and dangerous is discussed by politicians and policy-makers, as such representations lead to misinformed policy and intervention. Wortley and Tanner (2006) note that the public not only perceives that racialized youth gang activity is increasing but also implies that gangs themselves are foreign to Canada and that the country's immigration policies are to be blamed for importing "gangsters" from other countries. Recently, the immigration debate is also targeting specific ethnic and religious groups for their involvement in radicalized terrorist activities. These political contexts lead to the conflicts between police and youth from certain ethnic minority groups and bring into question the racialized policing practices of harassment, profiling, and use of force. Biased policing practices contribute to the overrepresentation of racialized youth in the criminal justice system (Millar and Owusu-Bempah 2011).

This chapter begins by exploring the social, economic, and demographic profile of the ethnic minority population in Canada in order to situate the marginalized position of youth and their interaction with the criminal justice system.

Racialized Youth in Canada

For the purpose of this chapter, the terms *racialized* and *ethnic minority* refer to non-white people who are also non-Indigenous. Canada's demographic composition is ethnically heterogeneous as it is open to settlement by people from different countries of origin and cultural backgrounds, and who speak different languages. This multicultural demographic makeup of Canada is largely driven by the immigration policies that have been in place in the country since the 1960s. The new immigration system of 1967 removed race restrictions for entry to Canada and introduced a merit-based point system. The points accorded for various qualifications—education, job skills, knowledge of official languages (Albanese 2009)—allowed skilled immigrants and families of diverse ethnic and racial backgrounds from around the world to enter Canada. This policy shift has drastically changed the current demographic landscape of the country, which has no longer continued to be of European descent.

In 1986, the Canadian government officially introduced the term **visible minority** to refer to people with origins in Africa, China, India, Pakistan, Japan, Korea, Southeast Asia, the Philippines, the Pacific Islands, the Arabic countries, and Latin America (Statistics Canada 2017). As shown in Figure 12.1, the population of visible minorities in Canada is gradually increasing and is projected to comprise more than one-third of the Canadian population by 2036.

visible minority
An official term for persons, other than Indigenous peoples, who are non-white.

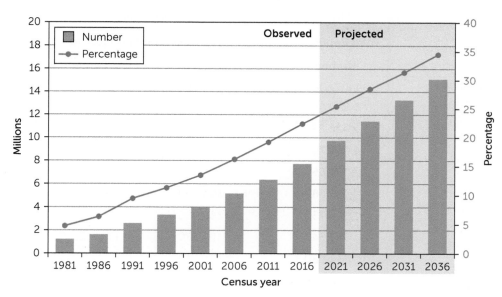

Figure 12.1   Number and Proportion of Visible Minority Population in Canada, 1981 to 2036

Source: Statistics Canada 2017.

The 2016 census recorded the largest proportion of the visible minority group in Canada as South Asian, followed by Chinese and then black people (Statistics Canada 2017). The fourth and fifth largest visible minority groups are Filipino and Arab people, respectively (Statistics Canada 2017). As the racial and ethnic composition of Canada is drastically changing, this has important implications for the criminal justice system. Evidence indicates that the justice system, which is inherently based on a European system, values, and traditions, does not reflect the shifted demographics of the general public, which leads to discrimination and marginalization of racialized groups.

Like other immigrants, visible minority immigrants also have a propensity to live in highly populated urban areas—seven out of ten lived in Toronto, Vancouver, and Montreal (see Table 12.1 for the proportion of the ethnic/visible minority population in metropolitan cities of Canada).

Life in big cities is not without its challenges; visible minority immigrants face language barriers, an absence of Canadian work experience, and a lack of recognition of foreign education and work experience (Madibbo 2005), resulting in their accepting low-paying jobs and often living in social housing projects.

On average, people in visible minority groups are younger than other Canadians. In 2016, the majority (more than 75 per cent) of immigrant children and youth under the age of 25 belonged to visible minority groups; among them, South Asians, Chinese, and black people are the prevalent ethnic groups. In 2016, about 2.2 million children, which is about 37 per cent of all Canadian children under the age of 15, were either foreign-born (i.e., first-generation immigrants) or had at least one foreign-born parent (i.e., second-generation immigrants) (Statistics Canada 2017). Immigrant children and youth face pressure from parents and schools to quickly integrate into new institutions and do well.

Table 12.1	Visible Minority Population in Metropolitan Areas in Canada, 2016		
	Total Population	**Visible Minority Population**	
	Number	**Number**	**Percentage**
Canada	34,460,060	7,674,580	22.3
Toronto	5,862,850	3,011,905	51.4
Vancouver	2,426,235	1,185,680	48.9
Montreal	4,009,790	904,840	22.6
Calgary	1,374,650	463,450	33.7
Edmonton	1,297,280	363,990	28.1
Ottawa-Gatineau	1,300,730	280,985	21.6
Winnipeg	761,540	195,370	25.7
Hamilton	734,880	130,310	17.7
Kitchener-Cambridge-Waterloo	516,085	99,735	19.3
London	486,500	78,325	16.1

Source: Adapted from Statistics Canada 2016.

However, difficulties arise when young people are torn between these expectations and the peer pressure to "fit in" with the Canadian youth culture (Tyyska 2008). In addition, visible minority immigrant children and youth face negative racial stereotypes. A young research participant in a project conducted by the Social Planning Council of Ottawa (2010, p. 15) reported, "because we are Black some people are somehow afraid of us. They have the perception we can harm them somehow. Hence we are seen by the police as a threat." Such negative perceptions about visible minority youth and crime increase these young people's interactions with the justice system.

Public Perceptions of Racialized Youth Criminality

Criminologists have established very well the ways in which news media promote panic and fear of immigrants and "ethnic" crime (Cohen 2002; Goode and Ben-Yehuda 2009; Schissel 2006). Ethnic youth crimes are portrayed as worse than other crimes, and racialized youth's images are exaggerated to reinforce the ethnic character of criminality in a way that stigmatizes the whole community, thereby creating moral panic among the public (Hall, Critcher, Jefferson, Clarke, and Roberts 2013).

It has been argued that media play an important role in shaping general public attitudes of receptivity or opposition to immigrants and ethnic minorities (Chan and Chunn 2014). Through their discourses—whether aural, visual, or written—media construct negative images and stereotypes. Social scientists have recognized that media are often key players in a process of racialization that may negatively impact the interactions of minority groups with the institutions and values of the majority groups (Chan and Chunn 2014). Grekul and LaBoucane-Benson (2006) assert that "the ways in which the gang threat is portrayed and constructed in the media and by agents of social control affects gangs, their members, and members of the public" (p. 24). In popular media, youth crime and violence are largely depicted in racial terms—for example, labels such as "black," "Asian," "Vietnamese," "Indo-Canadian," or "Indigenous" are used to categorize different gangs. As Schissel (2006) notes, the labels serve as tools to "paint the entire racial category with the same brush" (p. 61). Part of the "construction" of gangs by the media and by politicians is the use of stereotyping by ethnic group; various constructions dominate at particular periods in history and they vary by region. Most recently, we have been confronted by the "Asian" gang problem, the problem of black gangs in the east, "Aboriginal gangs" in the Prairies, and Indo-Canadian gang wars in the West. Seldom do we hear of "white" gangs. On the contrary, "white" male criminal groups are referred to as "biker gangs," a discourse that avoids the use of race as an identifier. This racist undertone of the media coverage (whether unconscious or conscious) strengthens the public's belief that the issue of gangs in Canada is an "imported" phenomenon.

These racial and ethnic "scripts" used in describing gangs "lump different groups together and refer to them as . . . pieces of 'one big gang problem'" (Grekul and LaBoucane-Benson 2006, p. 25) or a racialized problem. This results in a sensationalization of the gang problem and creates the dichotomy of "us" and "them" (Grekul and LaBoucane-Benson

2006, p. 26; Schissel 2006). This process only makes differences more visible, thereby creating "mistrust and hostility between groups" (Grekul and LaBoucane-Benson 2006, p. 25). Media constructions and exaggerations of the "otherness" of gang members, coupled with the invoking of racial and ethnic stereotypes, encourage an authoritative response to the situation, spurring lawmakers and law enforcers to publicize stricter, harsher, and lengthier prison sentences for young offenders—which Grekul and LaBoucane-Benson (2006) refer to as "Easy. Simple. Quick fix." solutions (p. 24). O'Grady, Parnaby, and Schikschneit (2010) point to the media coverage of the murder of Jordan Manners, a black teen student who was shot dead in a public school in Toronto's Jane and Finch community. The media created a folk devil of black teens by referring to black culture, the social underclass, racialized neighbourhoods, poverty, guns, and gangs. The reaction to Manners's murder included installing metal detectors and constant video-surveillance cameras, using sniffer dogs to detect guns in schools, and hiring "more school police" (Silcox 2016, p. 123).

Racialized Youth, Crime, and Gangs

Media studies has demonstrated the ways in which Western media creates public perceptions and racialized images of immigrants that result in public fear of immigrants because people perceive that certain ethnic minority immigrants engage in criminal behaviours, such as gangs, violence, and terrorist activities (Chan 2013; Jiwani 2009; Sohoni and Sohoni 2014). However, the available research has consistently shown that the foreign-born are *less* likely to engage in crime (Bersani, Loughran, and Piquero 2014; Ferraro 2016; Ghandnoosh and Rovner 2017; Katz, Fox, and White 2011; Sohoni and Sohoni 2014; Vaughn, Salas-Wright, DeLisi, and Maynard 2014). In a study of self-reported survey data from youth in Toronto, Bersani (2014) reported that foreign-born youth reported a significantly lower rate of engagement in criminal activities compared to Canadian-born youth of immigrant parents. The reported crime rates of Canadian-born youth of immigrant parents were not much different from the rates of children whose parents were native-born. The findings of Wortley and Tanner's (2006) study on 3393 high school students in Toronto also reported that foreign-born youth were less likely to report involvement in delinquent activities and gang membership compared to Canadian-born youth. However, the survey findings also indicated that as foreign-born youths spent more time in Canada, their reported involvement with gangs increased. In addition, their findings revealed that gang membership among respondents was strongly related to their racial/ethnic background. Black, Hispanic, and Indigenous youth were more likely to report gang involvement compared to youth from other ethnic backgrounds; however, the majority of gang members in the study were white youth born in Canada.

At the national level, the information on the ethnic composition of gangs relies on the findings of the 2002 Police Survey on Youth Gangs (Chettleburgh 2004). The information collected from police officers regarding the demographic profile of youth gang members in their jurisdictions highlighted that black Canadians formed the largest proportion of youth gang members in Canada, followed by youth who were First Nations, white, East Indian/Pakistani, Asian, Latino/Hispanic, and Middle Eastern/Arabic. The limitation of this dated survey is that it is based on police officers' perception of the ethnic origins of youth gang members rather than the gang members' self-identification with others based on their culture, origins, and ancestry.

The scant academic research on youth gangs indicates that the ethnic composition of gangs in Canada corresponds with the country's multicultural mosaic. Almost all predominant ethnicities are represented in the gangs—white, Indigenous, Asian, Indo-Canadian, Hispanic, and black (De Iaco 2006; Fast 2013; Gordon 1995; Joe and Robinson 1980). The distribution of ethnic gang members echoes regional population variations in Canada. Indigenous gangs have a presence in the urban centres throughout the country; however, they are most dominant in the Prairie Provinces. Black gang members are primarily found in Central Ontario, Quebec, and Nova Scotia (Totten and Totten 2012). The youth most often associated with gangs in British Columbia are Asian, Indo-Canadian, and Pakistani, and white youth gang members are broadly distributed across the country (Chettleburgh 2004).

Understanding Ethnic Youth Gang Involvement

Conventional research on gangs has put forward numerous traditional risk factors for youth gang involvement, such as poverty, substance abuse, school failure, dysfunctional families, childhood abuse, and poor parenting. In the absence of nationwide data on gang membership, Canadian research on gangs is characterized by small-scale case studies (e.g., Wortley and Tanner 2006) on specific ethnic youth groups that provide an understanding of the reasons of their gang involvement.

In one of the earliest studies on Chinatown's immigrant gangs in Vancouver (Joe and Robinson 1980), members of all Chinese youth gangs in the study were male and recent immigrants. Young gang members suffered from language barriers and behavioural problems, which impacted their academic success in school. This led to strained and blocked opportunities to achieve success by acquiring wealth and material possessions. Similarly, ethnic minority gang members in Gordon's research study (1995), the majority of whom were born in Canada, stated the desire for material goods—such as cars, clothes, and sound systems—as reasons for gang involvement.

De Iaco (2006) studied gang-involved racialized youth (Haitian, Jamaican, and Latino) in Montreal who identified racism and discrimination as a significant issue in their lives and chose to be in gangs of their own ethnicity because they wanted to bond with others who resembled their life patterns and cultural/racial experiences. Former gang members in Winnipeg, who came to Canada as child refugees, outlined the lack of positive support mechanisms in their lives—lives marked with experiences of marginality and economic/opportunity deprivation (Fast 2013). Ngo (2010) studied current and former gang members from immigrant families in Calgary. He summarized the entrance of youth into gangs as a gradual process marked by the disintegration of the youth's relationships with families, schools, and communities, and by the formation of relationships with other youth with similar experiences. These social cliques progressed towards gang membership.

The few studies stated above are inconclusive in generalizing the phenomenon of ethnic youth gangs in Canada because their study objectives have a limited scope in terms of their consideration of different ethnic groups, their regionalization, and their different definitions of a gang. However, the studies uniformly conclude that racialized youth who are involved in gangs experience economic disadvantage, marginalization, and discrimination. They face language barriers and subsequent academic struggles in school, which block legitimate means of achieving success.

Cultural and Migration Differences

To better understand the position of racialized youth and their involvement in gangs, we need to appreciate the cultural differences between ethnic groups and their migration experiences. Though the research on gangs identifies some commonalities among young people involved with gangs, migration studies stress the importance of appreciating the life circumstances, experiences, and reasons for migration of different groups (White, Perrone, Guerra, and Lampugnani 1999). The lived experiences of a skilled economic immigrant in Canada are drastically different from those of a refugee (Canadian Council for Refugees 2008). Economic-class immigrants make a conscious decision to come to Canada for a better life; they study the language, explore employment opportunities, and can visit their country of origin when they need to (International Rescue Committee 2018, "Who is an immigrant?"). Refugees, on the other hand, are forced to leave their country with no prior preparations. Many flee wars in which they may have lost family members or friends (British Columbia Ministry of Education 2015). They come with trauma rather than with any preparation for a better life in Canada, and they are significantly more likely than economic-class immigrants to face language, employment, and economic difficulties (Canadian Council for Refugees 2008). These different contexts of migration are important for comprehending the racialized youth's experiences and reasons for involvement in deviant behaviour and gangs. An understanding and appreciation of different contexts is crucial to the success of prevention and intervention programs developed for youth from different ethnic groups (Gordon and Foley 1998, pp. 127–8).

In the following sections, we will review information on two racialized youth groups for whom a growing public concern has been expressed in the last couple of decades: Somali youth and Indo-Canadian/South Asian youth. The discussion of social and migration contexts of these two ethnic groups in Canada is presented in an effort to understand the conditions under which racialized youth become involved with gangs.

Somali Youth

In 2018, the Canadian government faced criticism for trying to deport Abdoul Abdi to Somalia, a country he has never been to. Abdoul was born in Saudi Arabia and had lived in a Djibouti refugee camp for four years after his parents fled war-torn Somalia. After his mother's death, Abdoul, along with his sister and two aunts, arrived in Nova Scotia as a child refugee. Shortly after his arrival in Canada, Abdoul and his sister faced racialized bullying at school (Boseveld 2018), which led their aunt to take them out of school. The province's child welfare services intervened and put the siblings into the foster care system until Abdoul aged out of the system. Abdoul lived in 31 different forms of "care arrangements: permanent and temporary foster homes, halfway houses, hospitals, wards and so on" (Silverman and Nethery 2018, para 4). He became a permanent ward of the state at age nine. During his teenage years, Abdoul started getting into trouble with the law, and when he was 18 years old, he was convicted on charges of aggravated assault and served more than four years in prison. At the age of 24, he was facing deportation because of his criminal offences. The federal court judge set aside the government's decision to deport and, after immense pressure from activists and the public, the federal government finally dropped the deportation case against Abdoul.

Abdoul Abdi's story is no different from those of many other Somali youths who get into trouble with the law. More than 35 Somali male youth either born or raised in Ontario have died violently in Toronto, Calgary, and Fort McMurray in northern Alberta over the past 15 years (Fortney 2015). Drawing on little factual evidence, media reports have labelled these murders as gang- and drug-related (Jibril 2011). Media coverage of this violence presents an image of an immigrant problem rather than a Canadian one since most of these young men are either child refugees like Abdoul Abdi or were born in Canada to refugee parents.

To understand the state of Somali male youth violence and their involvement in gangs, it is important to understand their context of migration from Somalia to Ontario and then to Alberta, which is marked by conflicts, civil war, and racial and socio-economic adversities. Between 1988 and 1996, it is estimated that anywhere from 55,000 to 70,000 Somalis who escaped war and civil war came to Canada as refugees (Abdule 2000; Spitzer 2006). The majority of them settled in Toronto and Ottawa.

The Somali refugees who came to Canada during this period are reported to have suffered from mental health issues and post-traumatic stress (Ontario Council of Agencies Serving Immigrants 2016) due to the violence they experienced in Somalia and years of life in refugee camps. As a result of language barriers and gaps in schooling, both parents and children faced numerous challenges. Statistics from the Toronto District School Board demonstrate that Somali students have high dropout and suspension rates and lower achievements in standardized tests (Brown 2010; Ontario Council of Agencies Serving Immigrants 2016). Most Somalis live in public and affordable housing, with high concentrations living in low-income and high-poverty neighbourhoods. The family unit in the Somali community is comparatively large, with an average of six or seven members. Like other black ethnic groups, nearly half of Somalis live in single-parent households often headed by mothers (Ornstein 2000). The civil war and consequent dislocation resulted in more Somali women being single mothers who were left to take responsibility for the household and raising children on their arrival in Canada (Jibril 2011; Ontario Council of Agencies Serving Immigrants 2016). The challenges faced by Somali parents created a slippery slope for their children's successful integration into the mainstream society. Low educational achievements and minimal skills put immense pressure on young Somali men who, in their culture, are expected to take on the responsibility for the household. Unlike their parents, second-generation youth have no language barriers; however, their challenges are no different from their parents' when it comes to employment and discrimination due to their ethnicity, religion (the majority of Somalis are Sunni Muslims)

(Berns-McGown 2013), and skin colour (Jibril 2011). These systemic barriers pushed youth to migrate from Toronto to Alberta in mid-2000 with the hope of finding a job in the booming oil industry. In Alberta, their hopes of finding employment were met with the same socio-economic circumstances and structural barriers that had pushed them from Toronto. Lack of skills and education resulted in unemployment and underemployment, ultimately leading many of the young men to engage in criminal activities.

The Somali Canadian Association of Etobicoke (2003) reports that Somali-Canadian youth's deviance begins on school grounds with name-calling, racial slurs, and fist fights, which later evolve into both inter-ethnic and intra-ethnic group fights. Friendship networks are strong, and a fight between two individuals can quickly turn into a fight between groups, resulting in a "cycle of vendettas as each group takes every opportunity to avenge a previous encounter" (Somali Canadian Association of Etobicoke 2003, p. 20). Most Somali youth are involved in gangs that are neighbourhood- and turf-based. An example is the Dixon Bloods, a notorious Etobicoke gang of mostly Somali youth members that controls a cluster of high-rise apartment buildings on Dixon Road that house a high density of the Somali population (Cotroneo 2013).

Indo-Canadian/South Asian Youth Gangs in British Columbia

The terms *Indo-Canadian* and *South Asian* are used interchangeably in the media, and official reports use them refer to the youth of immigrant families from the northern Indian region of Punjab. The settlement history of this ethnocultural group in the Lower Mainland area of British Columbia dates back to the 1900s and is marked by the racist discriminatory immigration laws of the nineteenth and twentieth centuries (for example, the Continuous Journey Regulation of 1907 and the well-known incident of Komagata Maru in 1914). Over time, this ethnic group has established itself through South Asians assuming roles as prominent members of Canadian society (Basran and Bolaria 2003). Since the mid-1990s, the **Indo-Canadian/South Asian** community in British Columbia has often been depicted as one plagued by violence and gangs because this community's young men are overrepresented as victims of gang-related homicides (Combined Forces Special Enforcement Unit of British Columbia [CFSEU-BC] 2014). Between January 2006 and March 2014, more than one in five victims of gang-related homicides in the province were South Asians/Indo-Canadians (CFSEU-BC 2014). The majority of these incidents (80 per cent) occurred in public places, and more than 70 per cent of them involved a firearm (Jingfors, Lazzano, and McConnel 2015). This deadly public display of gang warfare is reported to be unique to Indo-Canadian gangs in Vancouver and that city's surrounding areas (Hemmati 2006, p. 17).

Singh (2006) conducted a comprehensive study on Indo-Canadian gang members that expanded the understanding of the reasons that youth from this community are attracted to gangs. He found three types of mutually exclusive gang members: newcomers, first-generation, and the wealthy. Newcomers are youth who were born in India and immigrated to Canada with high aspirations during their pre-teen or teen years. They described feeling the constant pressure from the family and the community to be successful, despite having had little help and guidance. With English as their second language, they faced challenges and difficulties in school, ultimately resulting in a lack of the skills necessary to

Indo-Canadian/South Asian

The term *Indo-Canadian* refers to people of Indian heritage who are living in Canada as first- or second-generation immigrants. *South Asian* is an official term for a visible minority group that includes people whose country of origin is India or other South Asian countries. The terms are used interchangeably in the media and official reports to describe gang members of this ethnic origin.

access higher status jobs. Newcomers experienced the most difficulty assimilating into the dominant society and faced discrimination from both the dominant society and their own community, who labelled them as "dippers" or "FOB" ("fresh off the boat," a slur used to refer to new immigrants who are unable to speak English and assimilate). This shunning led to resentment, and youth in this group used gang life as a way to achieve respect and status. The second group in Singh's study, the first-generation immigrants, "have spent the majority of their formative years" in Canada (Singh 2006, p. 26) and were able to successfully assimilate to the dominant culture. They came from middle-class families and had access to good education. As Singh points out, the young men in this group were raised in an environment designed to make life easier for them; they enjoyed the privileges of being a male child in the family and escaped parental supervision and associated with friends who had criminal and gang associations. Their gang involvement has also been linked to the patriarchal culture of this ethnic group, in which boys in the family are given privilege over the girls, and adolescent boys enjoy the freedom to associate and hang out with friends without much parental monitoring and knowledge about their whereabouts. The youth in Singh's study were expected to be successful in school and move into a good career; however, the easy life they had experienced as children gave them a sense of entitlement and an unwillingness to be patient and work toward a goal. The third category of gang members in Singh's research were somewhat similar to first-generation immigrants, the distinction being that they came from wealthy families that were well respected in the community. This group displayed no push factors to join gangs and seemingly lacked the traditional risk factors of needing to prove worth and gain respect and money. However, they still became core gang members who provided resources to other gang members, although staying away from the everyday gang activities themselves. In essence, the profile of Indo-Canadian gang members varies across socio-economic status, education levels, immigrant or Canadian-born status, but the need for wealth, power, and status remains common (McConnell 2015). Most of these gangs are opportunistic and loosely knit. Their violence typically erupts as a result of personal rivalries and issues of pride, jealousy, revenge, lack of respect, or insult.

Risk Factors for Gang Involvement among Racialized Youth

Youth who are involved in gang violence come from multiple backgrounds—from young people who would be considered "traditionally" at risk due to their poor socio-economic backgrounds, substance abuse, and unstable families to those who display "non-traditional" risk factors, with intact families and multiple life opportunities, as described above in the case of Indo-Canadian youth. (Though widely criticized for labelling and criminalizing marginalized youth in society, the concept "at risk" is a central part of Western youth justice systems. Refer to Chapter 9 for a detailed discussion of this concept). The non-traditional at-risk youth are part of well-functioning families and have sufficient resources and connections to their cultural identity (Singh 2006). These ethnic youth pose challenges to the professionals who use standardized tools and programs to address the criminal behaviour of youth. These risk assessment tools do not adequately assess the non-traditional risk factors for criminal and gang involvement that are prevalent among

Table 12.2	Traditional and Non-traditional "At-Risk" Factors for Gang Involvement among Racialized Youth	
Traditional "At-Risk" Youth	**Non-traditional "At-Risk" Youth**
	First-born son; only son
Single-parent home	Intact families—both biological parents in home
Nuclear families	Extended families
Issues of addiction and abuse in the family	Extended family criminality
Need for physical safety and protection	Higher income neighbourhoods based on postal codes
Lower-income neighbourhoods based on postal codes	Uni-ethnic neighbourhoods
Poverty	Parents own/operate business
Limited life opportunities	Underachiever; not mastering a skill
Looking to belong	Presence of siblings with post-secondary education
Earlier police contacts	Gang aspirations
	Later police contacts
Higher unexcused absences	Poor use of time
First disciplinary incident in high school	
Higher changes in addresses and schools attended	Fewer unexcused absences
	First disciplinary incident in elementary school
	Fewer changes in addresses and schools attended

Source: Adapted from British Columbia Crime Prevention Association 2014.

the culturally diverse youth. Table 12.2 describes the differences between traditional and non-traditional risk factors for youth in Surrey, BC, where most of the ethnic gang members are from the Indo-Canadian community.

Indo-Canadian/South Asian gangs are considered non-traditional in that members in these gangs come from a mix of affluent and middle-class families with both parents in the home and good income, which is not a stereotypical gang profile. A youth worker from Surrey describes the gang involvement among Indo-Canadian youth as a "choice to pursue the gang lifestyle instead of necessity due to lack of opportunities" (as cited in Ference and Company Consulting 2018, p. 7).

The widespread popularity of the gangster image among young Indo-Canadian youth has led to the acceptance of "gangsterism" as a means to attain quick money and enjoy the pleasure of power and respect that comes with it.

Linkage between Immigration, Ethnicity, and Crime

The four sociological models used in the literature to explain the relation between immigration and crime (Wortley 2009) are the importation model, the strain model, the cultural conflict model, and the bias model. According to Wortley (2009), the *importation model* presents the direct relationship between crime and immigration. It states that the youth who come to Canada from countries where crime is a common occurrence are more likely to commit crimes in Canada. The development of criminal gangs, organized crime groups, and terrorist organizations is often explained using this model. A direct outcome of this model is the intensification of the moral panic toward certain ethnic groups and an increase in more right-wing approaches to deal with the criminal behaviour of immigrants, such as restrictions on immigration from "crime-prone" nations and the "swift deportation of immigrants" convicted of criminal offences (Wortley 2009, p. 352). The case of Abdoul Abdi, described earlier, highlights the widespread use of unjust methods in Canada against immigrants. The *strain model* recognizes that the criminal behaviour and gang involvement of youth from immigrant families is a result of their marginalized and disadvantaged position in the host country. The social and economic experiences of immigrants are marked by difficulties in seeking employment; low household incomes; and discrimination in housing, education, and politics (Wortley 2009). This **multiple marginality** pushes youth toward street socialization, which often leads to criminal and gang involvement. In contrast to the importation model, the strain model puts the blame for youth criminal behaviour on the negative experiences of immigrants in the new country and therefore proposes that instead of law enforcement options, the focus should be on resolving social (in)justice by eliminating discrimination and reducing the economic disadvantages of immigrants (Wortley 2009, p. 353).

The *cultural conflict model* proposes that the intersection of immigration and culture are at the root of criminal behaviour. According to this model, the vast majority of immigrants do not intend to commit crime in their host country. However, racialized youth from certain cultures "maintain cultural or religious practices" that condone actions that conflict with the laws of their host country, such as violence, prostitution, and drug use/trafficking (Wortley 2009, p. 354). But although this model may be able to explain some of the crime of new immigrants, it fails to do so for the criminality and gang involvement of youth who are born in Canada. Lastly, the *bias model* argues that the overrepresentation of certain racialized groups in the criminal justice system is a result of racial discrimination and bias within the criminal justice system. Youth from certain ethnic and racial backgrounds face systemic discrimination at the hands of criminal justice professionals that results in their being "more likely to come under intense police surveillance (racial profiling), more likely to be arrested by the police, and more likely to be convicted and given tough sentences by the criminal courts" (Wortley 2009, p. 355).

Disproportionate Minority Contact

The treatment of racialized youth by the police has been a topic of considerable concern for the public, the media, and the government (Commission on Systemic Racism in the Ontario Criminal Justice System 1995; McMurtry and Curling 2008). In particular, long-standing allegations of abuse, harassment, discrimination, and racism on the part of the police against youth from ethnic minority and **racialized** backgrounds have come to characterize this issue (Brunson and Miller 2005). Research has suggested that youth from specific ethnic minority backgrounds are more likely to experience involuntary contact

multiple marginality
The combined disadvantages, marginalization, and powerlessness that racialized youth face, which often result in street socialization and gang involvement.

racialized
A term that denotes that race is not biological but a social construct ascribed to persons on the basis of differential power relations in society.

with the police. The overrepresentation of minority youth in the criminal justice system has been widely framed in relation to **disproportionate minority contact (DMC)**, which occurs "at all stages of the juvenile justice process" (Piquero 2008, p. 60), and **systemic racism**. In particular, youth from black, Indigenous, South-Asian, and Latino communities have publicly complained about differential treatment by the police, including harassment, illegal searches, and **street interrogations**, excessive use of force, and unjustified arrests and laying of charges.

While research has consistently shown that racialized youths are overrepresented in police–citizen contacts, searches, and arrests, the causes of this disparity remain disputed. For some, variations in police–citizen contacts are caused by "differential involvement," or differences in offending between minority youth and whites. Conversely, some attribute this to "differential selection," whereby the police treat youth from minority backgrounds differently than white youth. Further, a combination of these factors is also posited as the cause of the observed disparities, a perspective known as the "mixed-model hypothesis" (Piquero 2008, p. 59). According to the differential involvement hypothesis, minority youth are overrepresented in police encounters because they commit more crime, for longer periods in their life, and they commit more serious crimes (Piquero 2008, p. 64). In contrast, the differential selection hypothesis contends that minority youth are overrepresented in police encounters because the actions of the police, including aggressive policing of high-crime neighbourhoods that also have large minority populations, and the targeting of certain crimes contributes to excessive police–citizen contacts, especially for blacks (Bishop 2005, p. 24). The mixed-model hypothesis contends that it is both differential involvement and differential treatment that produce racial disparities in criminal justice outcomes, with involvement potentially being more important at the earlier stages of the criminal justice process and selection impacting later processing (Piquero 2008, p. 67).

Several studies have examined the issue of DMC in the US context, using either the differential involvement or differential selection hypothesis or a combination of the two (Fitzgerald and Carrington 2011). Research has found that controlling for self-reported offending behaviour largely accounts for observed disparities in police–citizen contacts between minority youth and whites (Bishop 2005; Piquero 2008). Lauritsen (2005) notes that data sources provide a conflicting account of racial differences in youth offending and that an overreliance on any one source can contribute to biased outcomes. However, a review of the available data reveals that, for more common types of criminal offences, there are few differences in commission rates between racial groups, while more serious forms of offending tended to involve more black and Latino youth (2005, p. 25).

In their examination of DMC within the Canadian context, Fitzgerald and Carrington (2011) examine a representative, national-level sample of youth ages 12 to 17, finding that youth from "high-risk" visible minority categories (Indigenous, black, and West Asian) were three times more likely to report police contacts in the past year than other youth (p. 473) (see Figure 12.2). When controlling for relevant risk factors, including self-reported delinquency, household income, peer associations, and parental supports, the authors found no support for the differential involvement hypothesis. As such, the reported DMC was attributed to racially discriminatory policing. In particular, DMC was evidenced among non-violent youth who should be least likely to come to the attention of the police.

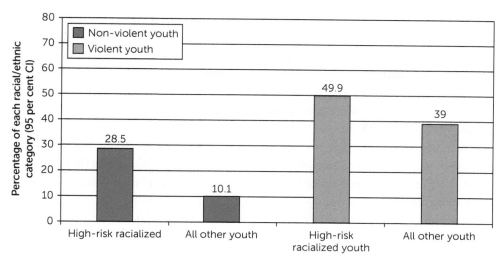

Figure 12.2 Police Contact among Non-violent and Violent Youth, Ages 12–17 (2000 and 2001)

*Statistically significant from "All Other Youth" category, (P < 0.01).

Source: Fitzgerald and Carrington 2011, p. 470. Reprinted with permission of the publisher.

Harassment and Racial Profiling

By the very nature of their mandate, police officers in a pluralistic, democratic society are expected to act in a lawful, professional, and equitable manner to all citizens (Remington 1965). However, a growing body of scholarship suggests that for young men and boys from specific minority backgrounds living in inner-city communities, disrespectful treatment by the police including harassment has become a "frequent and disagreeable part of everyday life" (Jones 2014, p. 34). Harassment by the police has also been reported by black and brown LGBTQ youth (Mallory, Hasenbush, and Sears 2015), ethnic minority youth in Canada (Eid, Magloire, and Turenne 2011; Wortley and Owusu-Bemaph, 2011), and homeless/street-involved youth (O'Grady, Gaetz, and Buccieri 2013). In particular, it has been widely argued that the over-policing of youth from certain racialized minority backgrounds can be attributed to racial stereotyping by police—a practice that has widely become known as **racial profiling** (Ontario Human Rights Commission 2003; Wortley and Owusu-Bempah 2011).

Why are racialized youth disproportionately subject to police attention? Why are the activities of the police likely to result in behaviours that are considered by these youth to be antagonistic or harassing? As discussed above, the police are deployed disproportionately to communities with sizeable ethnic minority populations (Brunson and Miller 2005). Policing practices in these neighbourhoods have come to be characterized by aggressive **order-maintenance strategies** that emphasize intensive police surveillance, especially over youth. Prior research has found that there is a social ecological dimension to police–citizen contacts, with the race of suspects and the characteristics of the neighbourhood they reside in contributing to officers' perceptions of suspiciousness (Meehan and

racial profiling
The use of the perceived "race" or ethnicity of a person as a factor in determining police suspicion, rather than that person's involvement in a specific criminal incident. Victims of racial profiling are often subject to excessive police–citizen contacts, detentions, interrogations, searches, and police brutality.

order-maintenance strategies
Policing tactics designed to regulate the use of public spaces and to address signs of "disorder." Order-maintenance objectives have been associated with aggressive policing strategies that target high-crime areas through proactive arrests for minor crimes.

social ecology of crime
The impact of human interactions with the lived environment on crime causation and victimization. Crime has been found to be concentrated in areas with high levels of socio-economic disadvantage and disorder. These areas are therefore also prone to high levels of police supervision.

"hot spots" policing
A strategy of identifying the specific areas, usually in urban settings, where crime has been shown to be concentrated. Through "hot spots" policing, the police are able to focus their resources on areas most likely to experience criminal activity.

Ponder 2002). The impact of the **social ecology of crime** has been well documented as it relates to racialized youth and the police, with race and place remaining key predictors of negative experiences with the police, in particular for black youth (Brunson and Miller 2005; Fitzgerald and Carrington 2008).

The growing concern over racial bias in policing misconduct toward racialized youth can be linked to the advent of **"hot spots" policing**, an approach that considers the relationship between crime and place, with the neighbourhood as the unit of analysis. This approach contends that crime is localized in "hot spot" communities within a city that generate a disproportionate amount of criminal activity, and even within those communities there are areas where crime is more concentrated (Sherman, Gartin, and Buerger 1989; Braga 2005).

The use of "hot spots" tactics has been found to be popular among US and Canadian police departments (Braga 2005; Owusu-Bempah 2014; Rankin and Winsa 2012a). In Canada, the Government of Ontario has spent upwards of $5 million a year on "hot spots" policing through the Toronto Anti-Violence Intervention Strategy (TAVIS) initiative (see Box 12.1) and the Provincial Anti-Violence Intervention Strategy (PAVIS) (Gillis 2016; Ministry of Community Safety and Correctional Services 2011).

Despite the widespread adoption of the practice, a review of the available evidence suggests that the implementation of "hot spots" strategies has contributed only to short-term reductions in crime (Braga 2008); however, it has yet to be determined whether it

Box 12.1 | Youth Justice in Action

"Hot Spots" Policing: The Toronto Anti-Violence Intervention Strategy (TAVIS)

In 2005, Toronto experienced a spike in gun-related homicides, with 52 people being murdered by gunfire. Many of the deaths occurred during the summer months, leading observers to dub that season the "Summer of the Gun" (Ross, Chowdhry, and White 2016). In response, the Toronto Police Service's (TPS) Toronto Anti-Violence Intervention Strategy (TAVIS) was launched (Winsa and Rankin 2013). TAVIS was billed as a multi-prong strategy that included community engagement and the use of "hot spots," tactics with teams of high-visibility officers deployed to high-crime areas in an effort to deter gun- and gang-related crimes (Gillis 2016). However, the unit proved controversial, garnering complaints of aggressive tactics (Winsa and Rankin 2015) and illegal stops and searches (Gillis 2015b). TAVIS officers also stopped, questioned,

and documented black persons at the highest rate of any Toronto Police unit (Gillis 2015b). Dedicated funding for TAVIS was cut in 2015 as officials announced they would be moving away from enforcement-based policing tactics toward a focus on crime prevention efforts (Gillis 2015a). It would later be announced that the unit would be restructured as a component of efforts to modernize the TPS (Gillis 2016).

Critical Thinking Question
How can police use "hot spots" tactics in a way that both responds to and prevents crime while also maintaining trust and confidence in the police?

will lead to long-term crime reductions (Rosenbaum 2006). Several qualitative studies have evidenced the collateral consequences of these approaches, including diminished police–community relations and a diminished perception of **police legitimacy** (Weisburd, Hinkle, Famega, and Ready 2011). In particular, the impact of these strategies has been felt acutely by racialized youth, who are disproportionately the target of aggressive policing tactics (Brunson and Miller 2005; Wortley and Owusu-Bempah 2011).

In a study by Wortley and colleagues (2012), data collected as a component of a youth-gang prevention and intervention initiative for high-risk youth in the Greater Toronto Area (GTA) found high levels of police–citizen contacts among young black male program participants (as cited in Owusu-Bempah 2014). Almost all youth in the study (87.5 per cent) reported being stopped by the police in the past six months, with many noting they had been stopped on multiple occasions. Participants also reported a high frequency of physical searches by the police, with 75 per cent indicating they had been searched in the past six months and 25.4 per cent indicating they had been searched more than ten times. Further, negative police–citizen contacts were a frequent occurrence, with 74.1 per cent of respondents reporting activities including the use of excessive force, frequent police-initiated stops and searches, verbal abuse, harassment, the use of disrespectful language, false arrests, and evidence planting. Conversely, only 31.1 per cent reported having a positive experience.

Racial disparities in rates of "carding" or "street checks" (see Box 12.2) have been evidenced in various Canadian jurisdictions, including Toronto, Hamilton, Edmonton, Calgary, Peel Region Vancouver, and Ottawa. According to Toronto Police data, between 2008 and mid-2011 the number of young black men aged 15 to 24 who were carded was 3.4 times their representation in the city's population (Rankin and Winsa 2012a). The data also showed that the disproportionality in carding encounters was maintained across all of the Toronto Police's 72 "patrol zones," with black persons being up to 5 to 10 times more likely to be carded than whites in areas that are predominantly white and more affluent ("Known to Police" 2013).

Data from Lethbridge, Alberta, found that black and Indigenous peoples were disproportionately represented in street check data, comprising nearly a quarter of all street checks involving young people aged 18 to 25 (Labby 2017). An analysis of data from the Edmonton Police Service found that, between 2012 and 2016, Indigenous Edmontonian males were four times more likely to be documented than white people, while Indigenous women were carded at 6.5 times the rate of white women. Black Edmontonians were found to be documented at 3.6 times the rate of white people (Heidenreich 2017). Data obtained by the Union of British Columbia Indian Chiefs and the BC Civil Liberties Association shows that Indigenous persons represented 15 per cent of all carding encounters between 2008 and 2017 while only representing 2 per cent of the population (Canadian Press 2018).

Other studies have examined the policing of racialized and marginalized ethnic youth and found higher rates of police contacts and searches. In a study of Toronto youth, Hayle, Wortley, and Tanner (2016) found that, when controlling for factors such as social class, frequency of engaging in public activities such as hanging out on the street or in a park, and self-reported criminality, black youth were 5.8 times more likely to be stopped than white youth and 6.5 times more likely to be searched. By comparison, non-black ethnic

police legitimacy
The extent to which individuals find the police to be legitimate has been linked to number of law-related behaviours, including compliance with the police and obeying the law. Legitimacy has been found to be predicated on the extent to which the police are seen to be acting in a fair or just manner consistent with the tenets of procedural justice.

Box 12.2 | Youth Justice in Action

Regulating Police "Street Checks" in Ontario

In 2016, Ontario moved to regulate the controversial practice of **"street checks" or "carding."** Carding allowed police officers to stop, question, and document persons in non-arrest situations. Carding activities have been found to disproportionately target young people, and in particular black and brown males. In Toronto, between 2008 and 2011, the carding incidence rate for black and brown males aged 15 to 24 was higher than their total population in the city. Carding interactions were widely cited as having a negative impact on youth, with many feeling harassed

when questioned by police (Rankin and Winsa 2012b). The new policy, which came into effect on 1 January 2017, seeks to eliminate the collection of "arbitrary" or "race-based" information. The new regulations include the following: persons being carded must be informed of their right not to provide identifying information; the reason for the stop cannot be based on race or on residence in a high-crime location; and a receipt must be provided indicating the name of the officer and their badge number (Government of Ontario 2016).

"street checks" or "carding"
A common policing tactic involving police-initiated stops against persons in situations that typically do not involve an arrest. During these encounters, the police collect personal information from those stopped, which is later entered into a police database.

radicalization
The process whereby persons holding moderate beliefs are converted to extreme social, political, and religious beliefs that justify and compel violence. This has been a primary concern of the post-9/11 security discourse, the focus of which has been young black and brown men from Arab and Muslim backgrounds living in Western nations.

minority high school students were no more likely to be stopped and searched than their white counterparts. Further, the authors found that good behaviour did not protect black youth from being targeted by the police to the same extent as white youth, with 26.6 per cent of black youth who self-reported "no deviance" indicating that they had been stopped on two or more occasions in the past year, compared to 4.1 per cent of white youth. As the authors note, "black race serves as a master status that increases the probability of being stopped and searched by the police" (p. 340).

Policing Domestic Radicalization and Terrorism

Recently, the issue of domestic terrorism against various Western countries has come to factor prominently in academic, policing, and policy discourses (Crone and Harrow 2011; Public Safety Canada 2013, 2014). An increasingly featured issue has been Islamic-inspired terror groups and so-called domestic **radicalization,** whereby persons living in Western nations are converted to extreme social, political, and religious beliefs that justify and compel violence. The focus of concern has been young men from Arab and Muslim backgrounds, a concern exacerbated by high-profile domestic terrorism cases in Canada, including the so-called Toronto 18, a group of young Muslim men from the Greater Toronto Area who conspired to launch a series of coordinated attacks against popular locations in downtown Toronto. In Canada, a significant focus of the official policy response to the threat posed by radicalization and domestic terrorism has been identifying youth considered to be "at risk" for radicalization and the strategies for de-radicalizing youth who already hold extreme beliefs (Public Safety Canada 2014, 2017).

The policy response to domestic terrorism may be broadly conceived as containing both "harder" and "softer" approaches (Spalek and Imtoual 2007, p. 189). Harder approaches can include intelligence gathering and expanded police powers. Traditionally, these efforts have been focused at the neighbourhood level, targeting entire communities considered to be "at risk" (Spalek and Imtoual 2007). Conversely, softer policy strategies are seen to emphasize community engagement and dialogue as a means of engendering trust and information sharing that may aid in identifying potential threats and developing individuals and communities who are resilient to terror attacks and radicalization efforts (Weine and Ahmed 2012). Critics have alleged that hard approaches, in particular, have been overly broad in their application and disproportionately targeted toward young Muslim males and their communities and that they can contribute to the criminalization and alienation of Muslims, especially young males, and aid in the appeal of radical ideologies (Choudhury and Fenwick 2011).

However, while there is substantial evidence that racial profiling of Arabs and Muslims has increased since 9/11, there is relatively little in the way of broad-ranging data documenting how the Canadian Arab and Muslim communities have been affected. Muslim youth respondents in a study by Bullock and Nesbitt-Larking (2013) indicated that they were negatively impacted by the construction of Muslims as security risks in Canadian society, with one youth reporting that the RCMP had visited the Muslim Students Association at his university under the guise of "outreach" and "prevention" work, which he perceived as insulting and alienating (2013, p. 199). Another youth spoke to the wide-spread "culture of fear" that has been generated by the post-9/11 Canadian security apparatus and how this culture had resulted in their feeling unsafe when engaging in certain lawful activities in Canada, due to their concern that it may result in their being flagged as a security risk.

An emerging body of scholarship has documented the experiences of young Canadian Muslims when travelling abroad. These experiences included being stopped, detained, questioned, and harassed by security personnel, all of which respondents attributed to their Muslim identities (Nagra and Maurutto 2016). These experiences were linked to feelings of diminished citizenship, including negatively impacted perceptions of "belonging and recognition as a Canadian" (2016, p. 181). In another study of Canadian Arab youth's experiences crossing the border, respondents noted experiences of racial discrimination by law enforcement, including feelings that "flying while Arab" exposed them undue scrutiny and that they were forced to "minimize their Arab identity" to avoid unwanted scrutiny (Finn, Hennebry, and Momani 2018, p. 680). These findings are consistent with studies in the United States and Western Europe, and they speak to the salience of racial profiling in the post-9/11 security state.

Impacts of Racial Profiling

A growing body of scholarship has evidenced that black and brown youth are consistently overrepresented in police–citizen contacts, and this disparity cannot be adequately explained by differences in self-reported deviance, criminal activity, or other relevant factors (Bowling and Phillips 2002; Brusnon and Miller 2005; Rosenbaum 2006; Wortley and Owusu-Bempah 2011). In other words, these situations are consistent with claims of racial profiling, whereby the perceived race of a person and not suspected involvement in illegal activity becomes the determining factor for police suspicion (Wortley and Owusu-Bempah 2011). Racial profiling has a profoundly negative effect on the individuals and communities involved, including emotional, psychological, and social impacts (Ontario Human Rights Commission 2003).

Racial profiling contributes to excessive police surveillance of persons considered to be at a higher risk for involvement in crime. Those profiled therefore become more likely to be apprehended by the police for committing the same types of criminal offences as persons from other racial backgrounds (Wortley and Owusu-Bempah 2011). These practices contribute to the overrepresentation of racialized minority groups in the criminal justice system while also contributing to the alienation of those targeted and the diminished legitimacy of the police and the criminal justice system.

Research has shown that persons subjected to repeated involuntary police–citizen contacts are more likely to hold negative views of the police than those who are not (Wortley and Owusu-Bempah 2009). Furthermore, negative experiences have been shown to have a stronger impact on perceptions of police legitimacy. Conversely, positive experiences are less frequent and often have a small or negligible effect on perceptions of police legitimacy (Skogan 2006).

Fair treatment by the police that is consistent with the tenets of **procedural justice** is the most influential factor in determining youth's perceptions of police legitimacy. Research has shown that youth who have been stopped and treated disrespectfully by the police are more likely to hold negative views of the police and that these views can contribute to hostile attitudes toward police during police–citizen encounters (Hinds 2007). This cycle of disrespectful behaviour on both sides can engender youth's negative views of police and contribute to an unwillingness on their part to comply with police directives or to assist the police with their investigations, thus furthering high rates of crime (Gau and Brunson 2015).

Policing strategies that are consistent with the tenets of procedural justice, such as the use of fair procedures, have the potential to play an essential role in shaping the character of police–youth relations. According to Murphy (2013), the police "by virtue of their role as social regulators in society, must often take unpopular actions as punishing rule breakers or asking people to 'move on'" (pp. 70–1), and it is these interactions over contested urban space and signs of disorder that have come to characterize much of the contact between the police and racialized and marginalized youth (Gau and Brunson 2015; Jones 2014; Wortley and Owusu-Bempah 2011). To address issues of procedural injustice and diminished police legitimacy among youth, police must develop specific practices designed to repair these damaged relationships in a procedurally fair manner. These strategies must be specifically tailored to the needs of youth and also be sensitive to the specific needs of those from different racial and ethnic backgrounds (Hinds 2007).

Police Use of Force

Recent high-profile incidents of police violence against persons from ethnic minority backgrounds have served to refocus the attention of the public and media on police misconduct and use of force. In the United States, the killing of black youth by police, including the shootings of Tamir Rice, Michael Brown, and Antwon Rose, have sparked public outrage and protests against the racial disparities in police violence and have contributed to the formation of the Black Lives Matter movement (Chernega 2016). Indeed, experiences of physical abuse, assault, and aggressive police searches are common among racialized youth (Brunson and Miller 2005; Fine et al. 2003; Jones 2014). Canada has also

procedural justice
A process-based approach to legitimacy whereby judgments are made about the quality of treatment received by the police and the fairness of the process by which the police make decisions (see Tyler 1990). For young men residing in disadvantaged neighbourhoods, a heightened police presence can represent a further source of danger rather than protection against criminal activity (Gau and Brunson 2015). Furthermore, low levels of police legitimacy can also contribute to the use of self-protective behaviours among youth as a means of ensuring their personal safety. This can include a willingness to engage in violence rather than rely on the police, thus furthering the cycle of high crime rates (Gau and Brunson 2015, p. 144).

experienced police killings of black and brown youth, with the names of victims such as Sammy Yatim and Jermaine Carby factoring prominently in calls for greater transparency and police accountability (Gillis 2016). While Canada does not collect systematic, disaggregated race-crime statistics, a number of studies have found evidence of racial disparities in police use of force.

In his examination of Ontario's Special Investigations Unit (SIU), which investigates cases of serious injury or death of civilians involving police in Ontario, Wortley (2006) found that "both Aboriginal [i.e., Indigenous] Canadians and African Canadians are highly over-represented in SIU data" (2006, p. 37), with blacks being 3.3 times more likely to be involved in an SIU investigation than their representation in the population, and Indigenous people being 4.2 times more. Members of the black community also expressed concern that police were more likely to use lethal force against them than against white people, and that police sought to harass and verbally abuse black youth to elicit a reaction that would justify the use of force (Wortley 2006).

When looking more closely at serious cases of violence, including shootings, the over-representation of blacks in SIU data becomes more pronounced. While black Canadians represented only 3.6 per cent of Ontario's population during the study period, they comprised "12.0% of all SIU cases, 15.8% of investigations into police use of force and 27.4% of investigations into police shootings" (Wortley 2006, p. 41). Indigenous people were also found to be overrepresented in police shooting investigations, comprising 1.7 per cent of Ontario's population but 6.8 per cent of civilians in SIU case files. Further, the data found that young black males, aged 29 or younger, were more likely to be victims of police use of force than whites or Indigenous people. According to Wortley (2006), "This finding is consistent with allegations from the Black community that the police frequently target young Black males. However, this finding is also consistent with the argument that young Black males are involved in more criminal activity" (p. 47).

Wortley's argument here supports the differential involvement hypothesis. However, his consideration of the criminal records of persons involved in SIU cases showed that black civilians were less likely (45 per cent) to have a criminal record than whites (72 per cent) and Indigenous people (80 per cent). Furthermore, blacks were found to be less likely to be intoxicated, less likely to be presenting mental health issues, and less likely to have allegedly assaulted or threatened a police officer or civilian bystander than whites or Indigenous people. However, blacks were found to be more likely to be armed and more likely to be armed with a firearm than whites or Indigenous people (Wortley 2006).

In his analysis of the experiences of young black men involved in a gang intervention-prevention project in Toronto, Owusu-Bempah (2014) found that 83 per cent of those surveyed believed that police often used violent or unfair methods to obtain information (p. 123). Furthermore, 36 per cent of those surveyed reported being physically assaulted by the police, including experiences of brutality or excessive use of force (p. 132). However, youth also reported having an "an uncooperative or disrespectful demeanour" when dealing with police, consistent with the mutual hostility framework, or having illegal drugs or a weapon on their person (p. 136). Despite these factors, "many if not most" of the stops and searches experienced by the young men did not result in an arrest or charge (p. 137). Owusu-Bempah argues that these assaults on individuals solely for their demeanour are tantamount to "street justice" or extra-legal sanctions administered directly by the police (p. 138).

Procedural Justice and Youth

Contact with police can have a significant impact on the public's perceptions of police legitimacy and the legitimacy of the wider criminal justice system (Skogan 2006). As discussed earlier in this chapter, research has shown that perceptions of police legitimacy are linked to a number of important law-related behaviours, including compliance with the police and willingness to assist with police investigations (Tyler and Fagan 2008). A growing number of police departments throughout the world have adopted programs and policies designed to engender police legitimacy and increase citizen satisfaction with the police (Mazerolle, Bennett, Davis, Sargeant, and Manning 2013). In Canada, the Toronto Police Service has recently sought to adopt policies consistent with the tenets of procedural justice as a means of increasing legitimacy (Toronto Police Service 2017). Procedural justice is a process-based approach to legitimacy, whereby judgments are made about the quality of treatment received by the police and the fairness of the process by which the police make decisions (Tyler and Fagan 2008). The consideration of procedural justice is of particular importance in relation to youth, as experiences with the police in childhood can condition adult judgments of police (Hinds 2007). However, research has found that youth from ethnic minority backgrounds have particularly low levels of public confidence and trust in the police and poor evaluations of police legitimacy (Brunson and Miller 2005; Wortley and Owusu-Bempah 2011; Gau and Brunson 2015).

Research on perceptions of and experiences with the police in Canada has also found that black Canadians are significantly more likely to perceive police–citizen contacts as unfair and as motivated by racial bias (Cao 2011; Wortley and Owusu-Bempah 2011). In their examination of police stop and search practices, Wortley and Owusu-Bempah (2011) found that black respondents were significantly more likely than white or Chinese respondents to interpret the behaviour of the police during their most recent police stop as disrespectful, unfair, racially motivated, and very upsetting (p. 400). Black Canadians were also found to be significantly more likely to report indirect or vicarious experiences of racial profiling, meaning that a friend or family member had been the victim of racial profiling by the police (p. 401). Repeated negative experiences with the police, whether experienced directly or vicariously, have been shown to erode trust and confidence in the police (Rosenbaum et al. 2005).

Experiences consistent with racial profiling have been found to contribute to broader feelings of marginalization and exclusion from society on the part of those targeted, including reduced participation in civic life, reduced integration, and unwillingness to access public institutions or use public spaces (Ontario Human Rights Commission 2003). Moreover, aggressive police surveillance and harassment can also lead to increased levels of anxiety and trauma among those targeted, including the development of post-traumatic stress disorder (PTSD) (Geller, Fagan, Tyler, and Link 2014). It is clear that aggressive policing strategies have an adverse effect not only on the victims of this behaviour but also on the wider community, and that this impact has the potential to influence perceptions of the police, the larger CJS, and society at large. However, in Canada there is a lack of evaluation activities related to aggressive policing strategies, thus making it difficult to assess their effectiveness in reducing crime, or their impact on the individuals and communities targeted by these strategies.

As police forces continue to try and achieve better policing through procedural justice, recent research examining the effects of training officers in the tenets of procedural justice has proven promising. Officers who have received this training were found to have improved attitudes toward citizens and support for granting them voice and treating them with dignity, respect, and neutrality (Skogan, Craen, and Hennessy 2015) while also reducing reliance on use of force (Owens, Weisburd, Amendola, and Alpert 2018).

Culturally Responsive Approaches

Efforts to address the diverse needs of racialized youth require shared vision and collaboration among the different stakeholders—families, schools, communities, and law enforcement (Ngo 2010). A lack of understanding of the lived experiences of ethnic minority groups can lead to strained relationships and hinder crime prevention and community safety efforts. An example of this provided earlier in the chapter is the unsolved murders of Somali-Canadian youth. The police in this instance blame the community for an apparent lack of co-operation in police investigations, whereas the community believes that this concept of "no snitching" is used by the police as a scapegoat for the justice system's failure and reflects the racism that ethnic minority groups experience in Canadian society. Initiatives by the Edmonton and Toronto police forces to assign community liaison officers are much-needed first steps to build community relationships. The establishment of culturally sensitive intervention programs to address the risk factors of Indo-Canadian youth (Surrey Wraparound Program) and Somali-Canadian youth (RAJO Somali Youth Empowerment Project, see Box 12.3) have made positive contributions.

Box 12.3 | Youth Justice in Action

The RAJO Somali Youth Empowerment Project

The RAJO Somali Youth Empowerment Project is a therapeutic crime prevention and intervention program for high-risk Somali-Canadian youth 12 to 18 years of age and their families. It is a multi-agency program offered in both Ottawa and Edmonton with the aim of reducing youth violence, gang involvement, and drug-related activities (Department of Public Safety Canada 2018). The project is based on the trauma systems therapy for refugees (TST-R) model, which serves as a culturally appropriate intervention for Somali youth in North America. The RAJO project takes a multifaceted approach to address refugee trauma, poverty, and cultural isolation, which increase the vulnerability of youth to mental health issues, substance abuse, and related criminal activities (Department of Public Safety Canada 2018). RAJO is a Somali word for "hope."

Critical Thinking Question
What challenges could law enforcement, school, and child and family care officials face while working with ethnic communities on culturally responsive programs such as RAJO?

Summary

This chapter explored the position of racialized youth in Canada and within the criminal justice system. We analyzed the interaction of these young people with the justice system through the use of available Canadian scholarship, while also highlighting the relative lack of available data related to race, ethnicity, and the criminal justice system. In the absence of official crime statistics, media portrayals of racialized youths in gangs and radicalized groups generate negative public and political perceptions. In the chapter, we briefly outlined some of the available information on racialized youth gang involvement and highlighted the cultural differences in understanding and responding to their criminal behaviour. We also examined how police policies and practices have impacted ethnic minorities and the effects of current aggressive policing arrangements, including experiences of excessive police–citizen contacts, harassment, discrimination, police use of force, and the policing of domestic radicalization and terrorism. Finally, the chapter considered the ways in which negative experiences with the police can contribute to a decrease in perceptions of police legitimacy and an increase in negative views of the wider criminal justice system.

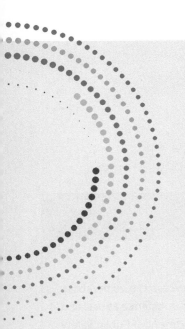

Key Terms

"carding" or "street checks"	racialized
disproportionate minority contact	racial profiling
"hot spots" policing	radicalization
Indo-Canadian/South Asian	social ecology of crime
multiple marginality	street interrogations
order-maintenance strategies	systemic racism
police legitimacy	visible minority
procedural justice	

Review Questions

1. Discuss how the media generates moral panic about racialized youth, their criminality, and gang involvement.

2. Which of the four models connecting immigrants, ethnicity, and crime best explains ethnic youth criminality and gang involvement? Provide reasons to support your answer.

3. Compare and contrast the reasons for gang involvement of Somali-Canadian and Indo-Canadian/South Asian youth.

4. How do negative experiences with the police contribute to the criminalization and alienation of youth from racialized minority backgrounds?

5. The police have been widely criticized for engaging in practices considered consistent with racial profiling. Discuss.

Critical Thinking Questions

1. Find news media articles on a specific ethnic minority group and discuss how that ethnic group's youth gang problem is portrayed in the media stories.

2. Negative experiences with the police have been found to be detrimental to youth from racialized and marginalized backgrounds and their communities. What changes could be made to legislation and policies, as well as policing practices, to address these negative impacts?

3. How can we compare the experiences of youth considered to be "at risk" for involvement with gun and gang activity and youth considered to be "at risk" for domestic radicalization and terrorism?

4. The relationship between the police and youth from racialized and marginalized backgrounds has been characterized by animosity and mutual suspicion. What can the police do to improve relations and engagement with these groups while balancing this goal with concerns over community safety and the need to respond to serious crimes?

References

Abdule, M. (2000). *Somali immigrants in Ottawa: The causes of their migration and the challenges of resettling in Canada* (Unpublished master's thesis). University of Ottawa, Ottawa.

Albanese, P. (2009). Ethnicity, immigration and family life. In Maureen Baker (Ed) *Families: Changing trends in Canada* (pp. 130–53). Toronto: McGraw-Hill Ryerson.

Basran, G.S., and Bolaria, B.S. (2003). *The Sikhs in Canada: Migration, race, class and gender*. New Delhi: Oxford University Press.

Berns-McGown, R. (2013). "I am Canadian": Challenging stereotypes about young Somali Canadians. *IRPP Study, 38*. Retrieved from http://irpp.org/wp-content/uploads/assets/research/diversity-immigration-and-integration/i-am-canadian/IRPP-Study-no38.pdf

Bersani, B. (2014). An examination of first and second generation of immigrant offending trajectories. *Justice Quarterly, 31*(2), 315–43. Retrieved from https://www.tandfonline.com/doi/abs/10.1080/07418825.2012.659200

Bersani, B., Loughran, T., and Piquero, A. (2014). Comparing patterns and predictors of immigrant offending among a sample of adjudicated youth. *Journal of Youth Adolescence, 43*, 1914–33. Retrieved from https://link.springer.com/article/10.1007%2Fs10964-013-0045-z

Bishop, D.M. (2005). The role of race and ethnicity in juvenile justice processing. In D.F. Hawkins and K. Kempf-Leonard (Eds), *Our children, their children: Confronting racial and ethnic difference in American juvenile justice* (pp. 23–82). Chicago, IL: University of Chicago Press.

Boseveld, S. (2018, March 7). Canada is trying to deport a former child refugee. Did the system fail him? *Chatelaine*. Retrieved from https://www.chatelaine.com/news/abdoul-abdi-deportation

Bowling, B., and Philips, C. (2002). *Racism, crime and justice*. Harrow: Longman.

Braga, A. (2005). Hot spots policing and crime prevention: A systematic review of randomized control trials. *Journal of Experimental Criminology, 1*(3), 317–42. Retrieved from https://link.springer.com/article/10.1007%2Fs11292-005-8133-z

Braga, A. (2008). *Crime prevention research review No. 2: Police enforcement strategies to prevent crime in hot spot areas*. Washington, DC: US Department of Justice Office of Community-Oriented Policing Services. Retrieved from https://ric-zai-inc.com/Publications/cops-p140-pub.pdf

British Columbia Crime Prevention Association. (2014). *Surrey WRAP Program: Evidence based strategies for addressing youth gang involvement and delinquency. A gang intervention and reduction program funded by Public Safety Canada*. Retrieved from http://bccpa.org/wp-content/uploads/2014/11/Strategies-for-Addressing-Youth-Involvement-in-Gangs-Surrey-WRAP-Program.pdf

British Columbia Ministry of Education. (2015). *Students from refugee backgrounds: A guide for teachers and schools*. Retrieved from https://www2.gov.bc.ca/assets/gov/education/administration/kindergarten-to-grade-12/diverse-student-needs/students-from-refugee-backgrounds-guide.pdf

Brown, R. (2010). The grade 9 cohort of fall 2004 (Research Report No. 09/10-15). Toronto: Toronto District School Board.

Brunson, R.K., and Miller, J. (2005). Young black men and urban policing in the United States. *British Journal of Criminology, 46*(4), 613–40. Retrieved from https://academic.oup.com/bjc/article-abstract/46/4/613/457918?redirectedFrom=fulltext

Bullock, K., and Nesbitt-Larking, P.W. (2013). Becoming "holistically indigenous": Young muslims and political participation in Canada. *Journal of Muslim Affairs, 33*(2), 185–207. Retrieved from https://www.tandfonline.com/doi/abs/10.1080/13602004.2013.810116

Canadian Council for Refugees. (2008). *Facing facts: Myths and misconceptions about refugees and immigrants in Canada.* Retrieved from https://ccrweb.ca/en/facing-facts-myths-and-misconceptions-about-refugees-and-immigrants-canada

Canadian Press. (2018, June 14). Racial profiling cited as groups demand probe into Vancouver police carding. *Vancouver Sun.* Retrieved from https://vancouversun.com/news/local-news/racial-profiling-cited-as-groups-demand-probe-into-vancouver-police-carding

Cao, L. (2011). Visible minorities and confidence in the police. *Canadian Journal of Criminology and Criminal Justice, 53*(1), 1–26. Retrieved from https://muse.jhu.edu/article/414621

Chan, W. (2013). *News media representations of immigrants in the Canadian criminal justice system.* Working Paper Series. Metropolis British Columbia, Centre of Excellence for Research on Immigration and Diversity. Retrieved from http://mbc.metropolis.net/assets/uploads/files/wp/2013/WP13-03.pdf

Chan, W., and Chunn, D. (2014). *Racialization, crime and criminal justice in Canada.* Toronto: University of Toronto Press.

Chernega, J. (2016). Black Lives Matter: Racialised policing in the United States. *Comparative American Studies an International Journal, 14*(3–4), 234–45, Retrieved from https://www.tandfonline.com/doi/full/10.1080/14775700.2016.1267322

Chettleburgh, M. (2004). *Results of the 2002 Canadian police survey on youth gangs.* Toronto: Astwood Strategy Corporation.

Choudhury, T., and Fenwick, H. (2011). The impact of counter-terrorism measures on Muslim communities. *International Review of Law, Computers & Technology, 25*(3), 151–81, Retrieved from https://www.tandfonline.com/doi/abs/10.1080/13600869.2011.617491

Cohen, S. (2002). *Folk devils and moral panics: The creation of the Mods and Rockers* (3rd ed). London: Routledge Taylor and Francis Group.

Combined Forces Special Enforcement Unit of British Columbia. (2014). BC's anti-gang police 2014 community report: Prevention and public engagement. Retrieved from http://www.cfseu.bc.ca/media/cfseu-bc-community-report-2014/

Commission on Systemic Racism in the Ontario Criminal Justice System. (1995). *Report of the Commission on Systemic Racism in the Ontario Criminal Justice System.* Toronto: Queen's Printer for Ontario.

Cotroneo, C. (2013, November 8). Dixon Bloods, AKA Dixon Goonies: The gang behind the Rob Ford crack video. *Huffington Post Canada.* Retrieved from https://www.huffingtonpost.ca/2013/11/08/dixon-city-bloods-goonies-rob-ford_n_4226753.html

Crone, M., and Harrow, M. (2011). Homegrown terrorism in the West. *Terrorism and Political Violence, 23*(4), 521–36 Retrieved from https://www.tandfonline.com/doi/abs/10.1080/09546553.2011.571556

De Iaco, G. (2006). *Juvenile street gang members and ethnic identity in Montreal, Canada* (Unpublished doctoral dissertation). McGill University, Montreal.

Department of Public Safety Canada. (2018). *RAJO Somali youth empowerment project: Program snapshot.* Retrieved from https://www.publicsafety.gc.ca/cnt/cntrng-crm/crm-prvntn/nvntr/dtls-en.aspx?i=10193

Eid, P., Magloire, J., and Turenne, M. (2011). *Racial profiling and systemic discrimination of racialized youth. Report of the consultation on racial profiling.* Montreal: Commission des droits de la personne et des droits de la jeunesse.

Fast, M. (2013). *Making a way when there is no way: The experiences of gang affected young adult refugees in Winnipeg* (Unpublished master's thesis). University of Manitoba, Winnipeg.

Ference and Company Consulting. (2018). *Mayor's task force on gang violence prevention: Findings and action steps.* Surrey, BC: City of Surrey.

Ferraro, V. (2016). Immigration and crime in the new destinations, 2000–2007: A test of the disorganizing effect of migration. *Journal of Quantitative Criminology, 32*, 23–45.

Fine, M., Freudenberg, N., Payne, Y., Perkins, T., Smith, K., and Wanzer, K. (2003). "Anything can happen with police around": Urban youth evaluate strategies of surveillance in public places. *Journal of Social Issues, 59*(1), 141–58.

Finn, M., Hennebry, J., and Momani, B. (2018). Canadian Arab youth at the border: Cultural dissociation, fear management, and disciplining practices in securitized spaces. *Journal of International Migration and Integration, 19*(3), 667–82. Retrieved from https://link.springer.com/article/10.1007%2Fs12134-018-0559-z

Fitzgerald, R.T., and Carrington, P. J. (2008). The neighbourhood context of urban Aboriginal crime. *Canadian Journal of Criminology and Criminal Justice, 50*(5), 523–57. Retrieved from https://muse.jhu.edu/article/253963

Fitzgerald, R.T. and Carrington, P.J. (2011). Disproportionate minority contact in Canada: Police and visible minority youth. *Canadian Journal of Criminology and Criminal Justice, 53*(4), 449–86. Retrieved from https://muse.jhu.edu/article/461414.

Fortney, V. (2015, January 11). Success stories are possible, but Somali-Canadians are faced with overcoming trauma, racism first. *Calgary Herald*. Retrieved from https://calgaryherald.com/news/national/success-stories-are-possible-but-somali-canadians-are-faced-with-overcoming-trauma-racism-first

Gau, J.M., and Brunson, R.K. (2015). Procedural injustice, lost legitimacy, and self-help: Young males' adaptations to perceived unfairness in urban policing tactics. *Journal of Contemporary Justice, 31*(2), 132–50. Retrieved from https://doi.org/10.1177%2F1043986214568841

Geller, A., Fagan, J., Tyler, T., and Link, B.G. (2014). Aggressive policing and the mental health of young urban men. *American Journal of Public Health, 104*(12), 2321–7. Retrieved from https://ajph.aphapublications.org/doi/10.2105/AJPH.2014.302046

Ghandnoosh, N., and Rovner, J. (2017). *Immigration and public safety*. Washington, DC: The Sentencing Project. Retrieved from https://www.sentencingproject.org/wp-content/uploads/2017/03/Immigration-and-Public-Safety.pdf

Gillis, W. (2015a, September 9). Ontario dramatically cuts funding for TAVIS police unit. *Toronto Star*. Retrieved from https://www.thestar.com/news/crime/2015/09/09/ontario-dramatically-cuts-funding-for-tavis-police-unit.html

Gillis, W. (2015b, May 12). Sudanese man wins $27,000 in carding lawsuit against police. *Toronto Star*. Retrieved from https://www.thestar.com/news/crime/2015/05/12/sudanese-man-wins-27000-in-carding-lawsuit-against-police.html

Gillis, W. (2016, June 14). Toronto police anti-violence unit to be restructured. *Toronto Star*. Retrieved from https://www.thestar.com/news/crime/2016/06/14/toronto-police-anti-violence-unit-to-be-restructured.html

Goode, E., and Ben-Yehuda, N. (2009). *Moral panics: The social construction of deviance* (2nd ed.). Oxford, UK: Wiley-Blackwell.

Gordon, R. (1995). Street gangs in Vancouver. In James H. Creechan and Robert A. Silverman (Eds), *Canadian Delinquency*. Scarborough, ON: Prentice Hall.

Gordon, R., and Foley, S. (1998). *Criminal business organizations, street gangs and related groups in Vancouver: The report of the greater Vancouver gang study*. Vancouver: BC Ministry of Attorney General.

Government of Ontario (2016). Final Regulation Regarding Police Street Checks. Ottawa: Ministry of Community Safety and Correctional Services. Retrieved from https://news.ontario.ca/mcscs/en/2016/03/final-regulations-regarding-police-street-checks.html

Grekul, J., and LaBoucane-Benson, P. (2006). *An investigation into the formation and recruitment processes of Aboriginal gangs in western Canada*. Ottawa: Aboriginal Corrections Policy Unit, Public Safety Canada.

Hall, S., Critcher, C., Jefferson, T., Clarke, J., and Roberts, B. (2013). *Policing the crisis: Mugging, the state and law and order* (2nd ed.). Basingstoke: Palgrave Macmillan.

Hayle, S., Wortley, S., and Tanner, J. (2016). Race, street life, and policing: Implications for racial profiling. *Canadian Journal of Criminology and Criminal Justice, 58*(3), 322–53. Retrieved from https://www.utpjournals.press/doi/abs/10.3138/cjccj.2014.E32

Heidenreich, P. (2017, June 12). Edmonton police's controversial street check practice to undergo third-party review. *Global News*. Retrieved from https://globalnews.ca/news/3594386/edmonton-polices-controversial-street-check-practice-to-undergo-third-party-review/

Hemmati, T. (2006). *The nature of Canadian urban gangs and their use of firearms: A review of the literature and police survey*. Department of Justice Canada. Retrieved from http://www.justice.gc.ca/eng/rp-pr/csj-sjc/crime/rr07_1/rr07_1.pdf

Hinds, L. (2007). Building police youth relationships: The importance of procedural justice. *Youth Justice, 7*(3), 195–209. Retrieved from https://journals.sagepub.com/doi/10.1177/1473225407082510

International Rescue Committee. (2018). *Migrants, asylum seekers, refugees and immigrants: What's the difference?* Retrieved from https://www.rescue.org/article/migrants-asylum-seekers-refugees-and-immigrants-whats-difference

Jibril, S. (2011). "Cashberta": Migration experiences of Somali-Canadian second generation youth in Canada. *Master of Environmental Studies (MES) Major Research Paper, 17*(1). Faculty of Environmental Studies, York University. Retrieved from https://yorkspace.library.yorku.ca/xmlui/handle/10315/13776

Jingfors, S., Lazzano, G., and McConnell, K. (2015). A media analysis of gang-related homicides in British Columbia from 2003 to 2013. *Journal of Gang Research, 22*(2), 1–17. Retrieved from http://kora.kpu.ca/facultypub/44

Jiwani, Y. (2009). Race and the media: A retrospective and prospective gaze. *Canadian Journal of Communication, 34*, 735–40.

Joe, D., and Robinson, N. (1980). Chinatown's immigrant gangs: the new young warrior class. *Criminology, 18*(3), 337–45. Retrieved from https://onlinelibrary.wiley.com/doi/abs/10.1111/j.1745-9125.1980.tb01369.x

Jones, N. (2014). "The regular routine": Proactive policing and adolescent development among young, poor Black men. *New Directions for Child and Adolescent Development, 2014*(143), 33–54. Retrieved from https://onlinelibrary.wiley.com/doi/abs/10.1002/cad.20053

Katz, C., Fox, A., and White, M. (2011). Assessing the relationship between immigration status and drug use. *Justice Quarterly, 28,* 541–75.

Known to police: Chances of being carded. (2013, November 12). *Toronto Star.* Retrieved from https://www.thestar.com/news/gta/knowntopolice2013/2013/09/27/chancesofbeingcarded.html

Labby, B. (2017, June 20). Lethbridge police accused of "racist" carding practices. *CBC News.* Retrieved from http://www.cbc.ca/news/canada/calgary/lethbridge-police-racist-carding-blood-tribe-1.4169754

Lauritsen, J.L. (2005). Racial and ethnic differences in juvenile offending. In D.F. Hawkins and K. Kempf-Leonard (Eds), *Our children, their children: confronting racial and ethnic difference in American juvenile justice* (pp. 83–104). Chicago: University of Chicago Press.

McConnell, K. (2015). *The construction of the gang in British Columbia: Mafioso, gangster, or thug? An examination of the uniqueness of the BC gangster phenomenon* (Unpublished doctoral dissertation). London Metropolitan University, London, United Kingdom.

McMurtry, R., and Curling, A. (2008). *The review of the roots of youth violence: Executive summary.* Toronto: Queen's Printer for Ontario. Retrieved from http://www.children.gov.on.ca/htdocs/english/documents/youthandthelaw/rootsofyouthviolence-summary.pdf

Madibbo, A. (2005). *Immigration, race, and language: Black francophones of Ontario and the challenges of integration, racism, and language discrimination.* Toronto: CERIS, The Ontario Metropolis Centre.

Mallory, C., Hasenbush, A., and Sears, B. (2015). *Discrimination and harassment by law enforcement officers in the lgbt community.* Los Angeles: Williams Institute, UCLA School of Law.

Mazerolle, L., Bennett, S., Davis, J., Sargeant, E., and Manning, M. (2013). Procedural justice and police legitimacy: A systematic review of the research evidence. *Journal of Experimental Criminology, 9*(3), 245–74. Retrieved from https://link.springer.com/article/10.1007/s11292-013-9175-2

Meehan, A.J., and Ponder, M.C. (2002). Race and place: The ecology of racial profiling African American motorists. *Justice Quarterly, 19,* 399–430. Retrieved from https://www.tandfonline.com/doi/abs/10.1080/07418820200095291

Millar, P., and Owusu-Bempah. A. (2011). Whitewashing criminal justice in Canada: Preventing research through data suppression. *Canadian Journal of Law and Society, 26* (3), 653–61. Retrieved from https://muse.jhu.edu/article/466839

Ministry of Community Safety and Correctional Services. (2011). *Results-based plan briefing book 2011-12.* Toronto: Queen's Printer for Ontario. Retrieved from https://www.mcscs.jus.gov.on.ca/english/publications/RbP201112.html

Murphy, K. (2013). Does procedural justice matter to youth? Comparing adults' and youths' willingness to collaborate

with the police. *Policing and Society, 25*(1), 53–76. Retrieved from https://www.tandfonline.com/doi/abs/10.1080/10439463.2013.802786

Nagra, B., and Maurutto, P. (2016). Crossing borders and managing racialized identities: Experiences of security and surveillance among young Canadian Muslims. *Canadian Journal of Sociology, 41*(2). Retrieved from https://journals.library.ualberta.ca/cjs/index.php/cjs/article/view/23031

Ngo, H. (2010). *Unravelling identities and belonging: criminal gang involvement of youth from immigrant families.* Calgary: Centre for Newcomers.

O'Grady, W., Parnaby, P., and Schilschneit, J. (2010). Guns, gangs, and the underclass: A constructionist analysis of gun violence in a Toronto high school. *Canadian Journal of Criminology and Criminal Justice, 52*(1), 55–77. Retrieved from https://muse.jhu.edu/article/371515

O'Grady, B., Gaetz, S., and Buccieri, K. (2013). *Policing street youth in Toronto. In youth homelessness in Canada: Implications for policy and practice.* Toronto: Canadian Homelessness Research Network Press.

Ontario Council of Agencies Serving Immigrants. (2016). *Somali refugee resettlement in Canada.* Paper presented at the 18th National Metropolis Conference in Toronto on Getting Results: Migration, Opportunities and Good Governance. Retrieved from http://ocasi.org/sites/default/files/OCASI_Presentation_Somali_Resettlement_Metropolis_2016.pdf

Ontario Human Rights Commission. (2003). *Paying the price: The human cost of racial profiling.* Retrieved from http://www.ohrc.on.ca/en/paying-price-human-cost-racial-profiling

Ornstein, M. (2000). *Ethno-racial inequality in the City of Toronto: An analysis of the 1996 Census.* Institute for Social Research, York University. Retrieved from https://povertyandhumanrights.org/docs/ornstein_fullreport.pdf

Owens, E., Weisburd, D., Amendola, K.L., and Alpert, G.P. (2018). Can you build a better cop? Experimental evidence on supervision, training, and policing in the community. *Criminology & Public Policy, 31,* 199–214. Retrieved from https://onlinelibrary.wiley.com/toc/17459133

Owusu-Bempah, A. (2014). *Black males' perceptions of and experiences with the police in Toronto* (Doctoral dissertation). Retrieved from https://tspace.library.utoronto.ca/bitstream/1807/68227/1/Owusu-Bempah_Akwasi_201411_PhD_thesis.pdf

Piquero, A.R. (2008). Disproportionate minority contact. *Future of Children, 18*(2), 59–79. Retrieved from https://muse.jhu.edu/article/254202/pdf

Press, J. (2017, October 25). Visible minorities may comprise one-third of Canadians by 2036. *Canadian Press.* Retrieved from https://www.macleans.ca/news/visible-minorities-may-comprise-one-third-of-canadians-by-2036/

Public Safety Canada. (2013). *Building resilience against terrorism*. Retrieved from https://www.publicsafety.gc.ca/cnt/rsrcs/pblctns/rslnc-gnst-trrrsm/index-en.aspx

Public Safety Canada. (2014). *2014 Public report on the terrorist threat to Canada*. Retrieved from https://www.publicsafety.gc.ca/cnt/rsrcs/pblctns/2014-pblc-rpr-trrrst-thrt/2014-pblc-rpr-trrrst-thrt-eng.pdf

Public Safety Canada. (2017). *2017 Public report on the terrorist threat to Canada*. Retrieved from https://www.publicsafety.gc.ca/cnt/rsrcs/pblctns/pblc-rprt-trrrst-thrt-cnd-2017/pblc-rprt-trrrst-thrt-cnd-2017-en.pdf

Rankin, J., and Winsa, P. (2012a, March 16). Known to police: Chief Bill Blair releases crime hot spot maps used to focus Toronto policing efforts. *Toronto Star*. Retrieved from https://www.thestar.com/news/gta/2012/03/16/known_to_police_chief_bill_blair_releases_crime_hot_spot_maps_used_to_focus_toronto_policing_efforts.html

Rankin, J., and Winsa, P. (2012b, March 9). Known to police: Toronto police stop and document black and brown people far more than whites. *Toronto Star*. Retrieved from https://www.thestar.com/news/insight/2012/03/09/known_to_police_toronto_police_stop_and_document_black_and_brown_people_far_more_than_whites.html

Remington, F.J. (1965). The role of police in a democratic society. *Journal of Criminal Law, Criminology, and Police Science*, *56*(3), 361–5.

Rosenbaum, D.P. (2006). The limits of hot spot policing. In D. Weisburd and A.A. Braga (Eds), *Policing innovation: Contrasting perspectives* (pp. 245–63). New York: Cambridge University Press.

Rosenbaum, D.P., Schuck, A.M., Costello, S.K., Hawkins, D.F., and Ring, M.K. (2005). Attitudes toward the police: The effects of direct and vicarious experience. *Police Quarterly*, *8*(3), 343–65. Retrieved from https://journals.sagepub.com/doi/10.1177/1098611104271085

Ross, S., Chowdhry, A., and White, P. (2016, May 20). Three theories that may explain Toronto's gun violence spike. *Globe and Mail*. Retrieved from https://www.theglobeandmail.com/news/toronto/three-theories-for-the-cause-of-torontos-gun-homicide-spike/article30114135

Schissel, B. (2006). *Still blaming children: Youth conduct and the politics of child hating* (2nd ed.). Black Point, NS: Fernwood.

Sherman, L.W., Gartin, P.R., and Buerger, M.E. (1989). Hot spots of predatory crime: Routine activities and the criminology of place. *Criminology*, *27*, 27–55. Retrieved from https://onlinelibrary.wiley.com/doi/abs/10.1111/j.1745-9125.1989.tb00862.x

Silcox, J. (2016). *Representations of youth crime in Canada: A feminist criminological analysis of statistical trends, national Canadian newspapers, and moral panics* (Doctoral dissertation). Electronic Thesis and Dissertation Repository, 3800. Retrieved from https://ir.lib.uwo.ca/etd/3800

Silverman, S., and Nethery, A. (2018, March 13). The shameful attempt to deport a man who's been in Canada since childhood. *The Conversation*. Retrieved from http://theconversation.com/the-shameful-attempt-to-deport-a-man-whos-been-in-canada-since-childhood-93262

Singh, H. (2006). *Violence & silence: Exploring the development of South Asian street gangs in the Lower Mainland of British Columbia*. Abbotsford, BC: University College of the Fraser Valley.

Skogan, W.G. (2006). Asymmetry in the impact of encounters with police. *Policing & Society*, *16*(2), 99–126. Retrieved from https://www.tandfonline.com/doi/abs/10.1080/10439460600662098

Skogan, W. Craen, M., and Hennessy, C. (2015). Training police for procedural justice. *Journal of Experimental Criminology*, *11*(3), 319–34. Retrieved from https://link.springer.com/article/10.1007/s11292-014-9223-6

Social Planning Council of Ottawa. (2010). *Immigrant children, youth and families: A qualitative analysis of the challenges of integration*. Retrieved from https://www.spcottawa.on.ca/sites/all/files/pdf/2010/Publications/Immigrant-Family-Report-English.pdf

Sohoni, D., and Sohoni, T.W.P. (2014). Perceptions of immigrant criminality: Crime and social boundaries. *Sociological Quarterly*, *55*, 49–71. Retrieved from https://www.tandfonline.com/doi/full/10.1111/tsq.12039

Somali Canadian Association of Etobicoke. (2003). *Getting to the root: Understanding and addressing inter-group youth conflict between Somali and other ethnic minority youth in Etobicoke*. Etobicoke, ON: Somali Canadian Association of Etobicoke in partnership with Centre for Research and Education in Human Services. Retrieved from http://www.communitybasedresearch.ca/resources/394/FINAL%20Somali%20Report.pdf

Spalek, B., and Imtoual, A. (2007). Muslim communities and counter-terror responses: "Hard" approaches to community engagement in the UK and Australia. *Journal of Muslim Minority Affairs*, *27*(2), 185–202. Retrieved from https://www.tandfonline.com/doi/abs/10.1080/13602000701536117

Spitzer, D. (2006). The impact of policy on Somali refugee women in Canada. *Refugee*, *23*(2), 47–54. Retrieved from https://refuge.journals.yorku.ca/index.php/refuge/article/view/21354

Statistics Canada. (2016). Number and percentage of the visible minority population by Census Metropolitan Area, Canada, 2016. *Focus on Geography Series, 2016 Census*. Retrieved from https://www12.statcan.gc.ca/census-recensement/2016/as-sa/fogs-spg/Facts-can-eng.cfm?Lang=Eng&GK=CAN&GC=01&TOPIC=7

Statistics Canada. (2017). *Immigration and ethnocultural diversity: Key results from the 2016 census*. Retrieved from https://www150.statcan.gc.ca/n1/daily-quotidien/171025/dq171025b-eng.htm

Toronto Police Service. (2017). Action plan: The way forward. Retrieved from http://www.torontopolice.on.ca/TheWay Forward/files/action-plan.pdf

Totten, M., and Totten, D. (2012). *Nasty, brutish, and short: The lives of gang members in Canada.* Toronto: James Lorimer & Company.

Tyler, T. (1990). *Why people obey the law.* New Haven: Yale University Press.

Tyler, T. and Fagan, J. (2008). Legitimacy and cooperation: Why do people help the police fight crime in their communities? *Ohio State Journal of Criminal Law, 6,* 231–75. Retrieved from https://digitalcommons.law.yale.edu/cgi/viewcontent.cgi?referer=https://duckduckgo.com/&httpsredir=1&article=4027&context=fss_papers

Tyyska, V. (2008). Parents and teens in immigrant families: Cultural influences and material pressures. *Canadian Diversity, 6*(2), 79–83. Retrieved from http://canada.metropolis.net/pdfs/Pgs_can_diversity_parents_spring08_e.pdf

Vaughn, M., Salas-Wright, C., DeLisi, M. and Maynard, B. (2014). The immigrant paradox: immigrants are less antisocial than native-born Americans. *Social Psychiatry and Psychiatric Epidemiology, 49*(7), 1129–37.

Weine, S., and Ahmed, O. (2012). *Building resilience to violent extremism among Somali Americans in Minneapolis St. Paul.* College Park, MD: National Consortium for the Study of Terrorism and Responses to Terrorism.

Weisburd, D., Hinkle, J.C., Famega, C., and Ready, J. (2011). The possible "backfire" effects of hot spots policing: An experimental assessment of impacts on legitimacy, fear and collective efficacy. *Journal of Experimental Criminology, 7*(4), 297–320. Retrieved from https://link.springer.com/article/10.1007%2Fs11292-011-9130-z

White, R., Perrone, S., Guerra, C., and Lampugnani, R. (1999). *Ethnic youth gangs in Australia—do they exist?: Overview report.* Victoria: Australian Multicultural Foundation.

Winsa, P. and Rankin, J. (2013, September 27). TAVIS police unit in the eye of the storm. *Toronto Star.* Retrieved from https://www.thestar.com/news/gta/knowntopolice2013/2013/09/27/tavis_police_unit_in_eye_of_the_storm.html

Winsa, P., and Rankin, J. (2015, October 27). Video captures aggressive tactics used by TAVIS officers. *Toronto Star.* Retrieved from https://www.thestar.com/news/insight/2015/10/27/video-captures-aggressive-tactics-used-by-tavis-officers.html

Wortley, S. (2006). *Police use of force in Ontario: An examination of data from the special investigations unit—final report.* Toronto: Attorney General of Ontario (Ipperwash Inquiry).

Wortley, S. (2009). Introduction. The immigration-crime connection: Competing theoretical perspectives. *Journal of International Migration and Integration, 10,* 349–58. Retrieved from https://link.springer.com/article/10.1007%2Fs12134-009-0117-9

Wortley, S., and Owusu-Bempah, A. (2009). Unequal before the law: Immigrant and racial minority perceptions of the Canadian criminal justice system. *Journal of International Migration and Integration, 10*(4), 447–73. Retrieved from https://link.springer.com/article/10.1007%2Fs12134-009-0108-x

Wortley, S., and Owusu-Bempah, A. (2011). The usual suspects: Police stop and search practices in Canada. *Policing and Society, 21*(4), 395–407. Retrieved from https://www.tandfonline.com/doi/abs/10.1080/10439463.2011.610198

Wortley, S., and Tanner, J. (2006). Immigration, social disadvantage and urban youth gangs: Results of a Toronto-area survey. *Canadian Journal of Urban Research, 15*(2), 18–37. Retrieved from http://hdl.handle.net/10680/383

Wortley, S., Tanner, J., Brooks, M., and Somerton, S. (2012). *Prevention Intervention Toronto program final report.* Toronto: University of Toronto.

Street-Involved Youth in Canada

Bruce MacLaurin and Catherine Worthington

13

Overview

This chapter provides an overview of street-involved youth in Canada. It focuses specifically on definitions and typologies of street involvement; pathways to the street from home or alternative care; key risk and protective factors associated with street involvement; institutional experiences with the education, child welfare, and juvenile justice systems; and street services and strategies for effective intervention.

Key Objectives

After reading this chapter, you should be able to:

- Discuss why there is such a significant number of street-involved youth in Canadian cities.
- Identify key risks and concerns for youths living on the streets.
- Describe why youth may become involved in street life.
- Outline types of services required by street youth.

Introduction

Street-involved youth are visible living on the streets of most major Canadian urban centres. This is not a recent phenomenon; nineteenth-century literature popularized Huckleberry Finn and Oliver Twist in stories of street children existing and surviving on their own. Street-involved youth may be more visible today, however, as newspapers during the past decade have consistently highlighted the lives of young street teens, describing them as runaways, throwaways, panhandlers, squeegee kids, or teen parents (Abate 2001; Anonymous 2010a, 2010b; Cuthbertson 2012; Derworiz 2010; Goar 2009; McCarter 2010). Despite this increase in recognition and awareness, the plight of street-involved youth arguably continues to deteriorate in Canada.

Street-involved youth are generally defined as individuals who are 25 years of age or younger, who are either runaways, homeless, or **underhoused** (i.e., living in temporary or unreliable housing). A variety of typologies, or classifications, of street-involved youth has been developed to describe this population. This chapter will describe some of the typologies documented in current North American research to provide a comprehensive overview of street-involved youth. These typologies are based on the intent, or purpose, of the street involvement, the time spent on the street, the factors associated with street involvement, and whether there is a choice of returning home. In spite of some limitations, such as being too simple or vague, typologies can assist us in understanding this population and the specific risks that street-involved youth face on the street.

Street-involved youth experience a decrease in rights, opportunities, and social supports (Grover 2007; Worthington et al. 2008), and this may exacerbate the risks associated with living on the streets. Street-involved youth are also at higher risk of developing mental health problems, some of which can lead to suicide (Boivin, Roy, Hayel, and Galbaud du Fort 2005); becoming involved in survival or obligatory sex (Haley, Roy, Leclerc, Boudreau, and Boivin 2004b); developing physical health concerns, including contracting sexually transmitted diseases (Public Health Agency of Canada 2006a); getting involved in criminal and delinquent activity (Baron and Hartnagel 2006); using and abusing drugs (Roy, Haley, Leclerc, Cedras, and Boivin 2002); and simply not meeting their basic physical needs for food, clothing, and shelter (Dachner and Tarasuk 2002). A review of the literature will illustrate how these risk factors have a significant impact on youth when on the streets.

underhoused
Youth who are underhoused live in housing that is temporary in nature and inadequate for space, that does not meet safety or health thresholds or has high risk for eviction.

Insufficient attention has been given to the service needs of street-involved youth. Services are needed that will support these youth while they are on the streets and when they try to leave the street life. As well, we need to focus more on prevention if we are to understand the factors that provide the earliest indications of risk of street involvement. While much literature has described street youth populations over the past decades, more attention is required to develop rigorous intervention research to determine what services are best for what groups. This chapter describes effective forms of intervention available to street-involved youth in Canada as well as barriers to service utilization.

Defining Street-Involved Youth versus Homeless Adults

As mentioned, the literature generally defines **street-involved youth** as being young people 25 years of age or younger who do not have a safe home or are underhoused; have been forced to leave their family of origin (**throwaway**); who have run away from their home without the consent of their parents or guardian; or who left foster- or group-care placements (runaway) (Hammer, Finkelhor, and Sedlak 2002). These youth may be described as the most street entrenched; however, recent evidence indicates that additional youth are becoming involved in street life who are less recognized or understood, who have significant and specific risks, and who would benefit from prevention and support services. Recent definitions of street-involved youth have expanded on the runaway and homeless definition to include youth who are not living on the street but who experiment and engage in street-involved activities and identify with street culture and street peer groupings (Worthington et al. 2008). In this chapter, the term *street-involved youth* will be used to describe this entire population.

Youth living on the streets present as a unique service population distinct from the adult homeless population. Homelessness for adults is described first and foremost as a housing and poverty issue, which establishes the context in which individual risk factors can trigger a homeless episode (Burt 2001, as cited by Tutty et al. 2010). Four specific structural issues contribute to adult homelessness: (1) an increasing number of people are being priced out of the affordable housing market; (2) employment opportunities for those individuals with secondary education are dwindling; (3) institutional supports have been reduced for those people with severe mental health and addiction concerns; and (4) people are excluded from affordable housing owing to racial, ethnic, and/or class discrimination (Burt 2001). Street-involved youth have experienced many of the same individual risk factors associated with the adult homeless population, including high rates of childhood maltreatment, child welfare involvement, mental health concerns, incomplete education, and drug use; however, the factors that trigger their street involvement are different (Tutty et al. 2010). Gaetz, O'Grady, Bucieri, Karabanow and Marsolais (2013) summarize three key domains seen to drive youth homelessness in Canada, including (a) individual and relationship factors of the youth and family; (b) structural factors related to poverty, housing, and discrimination against "at-risk" communities; and (c) institutional and systems failures related to child welfare, health, juvenile justice, education, and mental health.

street-involved youth
Youths 25 years of age or younger who do not have a safe home or are underhoused; who have been forced to leave their family of origin; who have run away from their home without the consent of their parents or guardian or who left foster- or group-care placements; or who are not living on the street but who experiment and engage in street-involved activities and identify with street culture and street peer groupings.

throwaways
Youths who are asked, or encouraged, to leave home by their parents/guardians, with the purpose of ending parental responsibility for the well-being of the youths.

Many of these youth have experienced adverse trajectories as they move to increased levels of street involvement.

Typologies of Street-Involved Youth

A number of typologies have been developed in Canada and the United States over the past 30 years to help researchers and practitioners better understand the unique characteristics of youth who are involved in the street and to develop services designed to meet their current needs (Adlaf and Zdanowicz 1999; Auerswald and Eyre 2002; Kufeldt and Nimmo 1987; Toro, Lesperance, and Braciszewski 2011). Typologies generally include, but are not limited to, youth who experiment with street life by occasionally running away or practising truancy, children who run away from home to escape maltreatment and harm, and those young people who have spent years living on the streets and are firmly entrenched in the street lifestyle. Some models highlight the recurring nature of street involvement and homelessness (Auerswald and Eyre 2002; National Alliance to End Homelessness [NAEH] 2012).

Gaetz (2014) expands on a typology developed by the National Alliance to End Homelessness (2012) that distinguishes these youth based on the frequency, duration, and recurrence of homelessness. This typology includes (a) temporarily disconnected, (b) unstably connected, and (c) chronically disconnected (Gaetz 2014, p. 25). Temporarily disconnected youth are generally younger, have better chances to maintain connections with family and school, and make up the majority of the homeless youth population (Gaetz 2014; NAEH 2012). Unstably housed youth present with a more complex history and trajectory of homelessness and are frequently disengaged from school or employment but have potential for family intervention. The third group, chronically disconnected youth, represent the smallest sector of homeless youth but are seen to have critical needs related to mental health concerns or addictions. Their involvement is longer term, more repetitive, and requires more comprehensive interventions and follow-up (Gaetz 2014; NAEH 2012).

These typologies assist practitioners and researchers in understanding the Canadian street youth population and the specific risks that are associated with the street lifestyle. These classification systems consider pathways to the street, the frequency and duration of street involvement, the level of individual choice for being on the street, and options for leaving the street. While these classifications provide an understanding of the range of street-involved youth, further work is required to test and validate these typologies (see Figure 13.1).

Numbers of Street-Involved Youth

To date, there are no accurate estimates of the Canadian street-involved youth population. It is difficult to estimate these numbers because of the challenges in defining street-involved youth, the unique differences within this population, and differential service use by subgroups of street-involved youth. Recent estimates based on the national incidence studies of missing youth in the United States suggest that more than 1.6 million youths

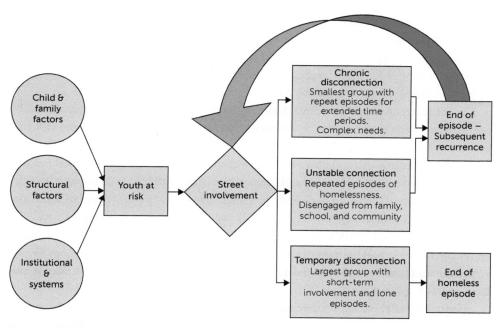

Figure 13.1 Risk of Street Involvement

Source: Adapted from and based upon Gaetz 2014 and National Alliance to End Homelessness 2012.

in the US can be described as street involved (i.e., those who left home or were asked by a parent or guardian to leave the home) (Hammer et al. 2002). The number of street-involved youth in Canada—those who are homeless or living in shelters on any given day—is frequently suggested to be approximately 150,000 (Public Health Agency of Canada 2006b). The 150,000 estimate is attributed to DeMatteo et al. (1999), but this number was generated in 1988 for an earlier study (Radford, King, and Warren 1989) and was based upon an approximate percentage of US street youth. It is clear that the number of street-involved youth as well as the factors that lead to youth homelessness have changed dramatically over the past 30 years, and there is no accurate estimate for the total number of street-involved youth in Canada.

Gaetz, O'Grady, and Vaillancourt (1999) report that the Toronto Hostel Division estimated that an average of 325 to 340 youths between the ages of 16 and 24 were living in shelters on any given night in Toronto in 1999; however, Toronto street surveys indicate that this figure was less than one-quarter of the total street-involved youth population in that city (Gaetz et al. 1999). This is supported by a recent US study that found that approximately 7 per cent of the street youth population used shelters (Carlson, Sugano, Millstein, and Auerswald 2006).

Other cities in Canada face similar challenges when estimating the number of youth who are street involved. For example, **homeless youth** currently represent approximately 18.5 per cent of the total 2627 individuals reported as homeless in Calgary in 2018, using administrative data. As well, homeless youth were 19.4 per cent of the 4432 homeless individuals in Alberta for that same reporting period (Seven Cities on Housing and

homeless youth
Youth who either have left or have been urged to leave home with the full knowledge or approval of legal guardians. They have no alternative home in which to live.

Homelessness 2018). Homeless count methodologies have improved over the past decade; however, these figures remain a conservative estimate of the total youth population in jurisdictions, as uncounted street-youth may include those who sleep in public areas, those who rely on friends for short-term accommodation (couch surfing), or those who engage in the street lifestyle only during the day.

In Halifax, the numbers of homeless adults and youths have increased dramatically over the past decade (Community Action on Homelessness 2009; Nova Scotia Housing and Homelessness Network 2012). Youth ages 16 to 19 made up 9.8 per cent of the 1973 homeless individuals using shelters in 2011, while those under age 16 composed roughly 4.5 per cent (Nova Scotia Housing and Homelessness Network 2012). These numbers describe only a part of the youth homeless population, as a higher percentage of children and youth do not access shelter services. A study by the Halifax Regional Municipality (2005) reported that in 2004 youth under age 18 made up 12 per cent of homeless respondents and those aged 19 to 24 composed 22 per cent. Seven per cent of youth under age 18 and 12 per cent of youth aged 19 to 24 lived in shelters, while 20 per cent of youth under 18 and 43 per cent of youth aged 19 to 24 lived on the streets.

Cross-sectional counts of those on the streets, in shelters, or in other service agencies do not capture the fluidity or diversity of the street-involved youth population, and the majority of street-involved youth report moving to large Canadian cities and spending time in different cities (Gaetz et al. 1999). Counts of the actual street-involved youth population in Canada will continue to be conservative estimates of this at-risk population. The range in the estimates of street-involved youth in Canada and the United States raises several questions about the accuracy of estimates. These variations can definitely be attributed to the methodological challenges of developing an accurate count and estimate (Peressini, McDonald, and Hulchanski 1995). The following are several critical issues to consider when planning an estimate or count of the number of street-involved youth:

- What criteria determine street involvement? Definitions of who should be counted need to be established. For example, if runaway youth are included in the street-involved youth counts, should those who have run away but are staying with friends and not on the streets be included?
- How should street-involved youth be contacted? Some estimates of street-involved youth have used street counts at random periods over the course of a year, while other estimates have been based upon counts submitted by service providers. Different methods of contact will run the risk of missing different types of street-involved youth.
- Should shelter numbers be used as a basis for predictions of the uncounted street-involved population who do not use shelters or services? Estimates may be generated to include youths who do not use traditional street resources; however, the accuracy of these estimates remains unknown. This group would typically include youths involved in the formal sex trade, youths who access adult services, or highly transient youths who do not use any services.

Box 13.1 | Youth Justice in Action

Growing Up on Streets Trumps Dysfunctional Home Life; Family Dynamics—Not Drugs or Alcohol—Is the Main Reason Why Thousands of Teens Choose to Run Away from Home

By Bronwyn McCarter

Christopher Brown, a 19-year-old homeless man, stood barefoot in a damp black hoodie, shivering, one bleak afternoon on Granville Street. His hard-luck story began, he said, when he was kicked out of his home at a young age. He spent days sitting on the steps of the Vancouver Art Gallery until the police found him and put him in foster care, he recalled in an interview. As he grew older, Brown said he tired of being shuffled from foster home to foster home, feeling that no one truly cared for him. At the age of 18, he turned to the streets. "It's a hard life out here," he said. Unfortunately, Brown isn't unique in feeling like the streets are the only place left to go. He is one of 65,000 homeless teenagers in Canada who struggle to find a safe, dry place to sleep each night. "You don't know if you're gonna wake up in a car with a bag over your head, or with a knife to your throat," said Brown, who mostly sleeps with a group of friends in various locations on Vancouver's side-walks. On the streets, Brown said, teens make their own families. It is often hard to find someone to trust, but when that connection is made on the streets, he said, the relationships are strong and more meaning-ful than those he made at school.

Brown has been trying to get a job for more than three years. He began his search while in foster care, but now that he is homeless he said it [is] impossible to find employment. "No one wants to hire someone like me," Brown said. Employers don't want to hire a person who looks dirty, or doesn't have an address. They worry such an employee would turn away customers, and potentially hurt their businesses. That traps teens in a vicious cycle: They have nowhere to go except the streets, but they can't get jobs because they don't have stable families to live with, or easy access to showers and clean clothes. Money is by far the hardest thing to come by for homeless teens. While food, used clothing, showers and laundry fa-cilities can be found in downtown Vancouver, young people often start trying to collect money through pan handling—until desperation forces them to con-sider more drastic measures, such as prostitution and drug dealing.

For many people, dropping a couple of quar-ters into someone's hat is a difficult decision. They are unsure where the money will be spent: Will it go toward a new pair of shoes, an umbrella, or some-one's next high? Directions Youth Services offers a job program that is Brown's personal favourite. The program is called Street Youth Job Action (SYJA), and allows young people to clean up the streets, do needle sweeps and leave at the end of the day with some cash in their pockets. Brown and other teens who sleep on Vancouver's streets applaud the SYJA program because they get a chance to give back to the community. Many people believe it is drugs or alcohol that bring young people to the streets. While that may be true for some, experts say it is often family dynamics that drive teens to the wet streets of Vancouver. Some are runaways from home; others are kicked out. Drugs often become the problem after they reach the streets.

Many homeless young people also have mental health problems and turn to drugs as a way of self-medicating, said Michelle Clausius, associate director of development and communications at Covenant House, a facility for youth on Drake Street. Jennifer Hanrahan, a manager at Directions Youth Services Centre, said crystal meth is one of the lead-ing drugs causing addiction among young people. It

continued

is the cheapest drug on the market, and easily available. However, not all teens on the street are involved with drugs. A group of homeless teenagers on Granville recently told The Vancouver Sun they would never smoke anything more harmful than marijuana because becoming addicted to a stronger drug often means "the drugs start doing you, you don't do the drugs." Some of Brown's friends said their biggest dream is one day to get off the streets, and they believe that doing hard drugs could make it harder to get a roof over their heads.

Brown's two biggest goals, he said, are to find a home and go to college to study culinary arts. When asked what he thought would get him off the streets, he said that if he was given $125 more a month on his welfare cheque, he would be able to find a place to live. Then, he said, he could shower every day, feel safe sleeping, and try to pull himself together to get a job. Brown now gets the standard welfare rental rate of $375 a month for housing, but in Vancouver it is getting increasingly hard to find a place in which to live for that price. According to a recent report by the Carnegie Community Action Project, single-room occupancy hotel rooms in the Downtown Eastside rented at welfare-friendly rates have gone down from 29 per cent of available rooms in 2009, to 12 per cent this year.

Helping homeless teens may seem like a hopeless task. How does society know where to start? Is it housing, food, and employment? Or just someone to believe in them and to encourage them along the way? People who work with homeless teens say the solutions vary. Hanrahan believes young people need the help of people who are non-judgmental and who will convey they are worth caring for, because sometimes they feel they have little self-worth. Every teen has potential, if given the chance. If a community can help one teen follow his or her dream, advocates say, it can become a win-win situation for society and, most importantly, for the young person on the street.

Bronwyn McCarter is a Grade 11 student at West Vancouver Secondary School.

Source: Bronwyn McCarter, *Vancouver Sun*, Vancouver, BC: Nov. 18, 2010. p. A17. Reprinted with permission of Bronwyn McCarter.

Perspectives on Street-Involved Youth

The lens, or perspective, with which we view street-involved youth in Canada has a great impact on the way we respond to the needs of this population. The lens has shifted constantly over the past half century. Prior to the 1960s, youth on the street were seen as delinquents who were there as a result of their own individual pathology and deviant nature (Appathurai 1987). This position shifted during the 1960s as the counter-culture movement saw an increased number of middle-class teens living on city streets. Factors related to the family and school were primary areas of concern in the literature on street-involved youth in the 1970s, while maltreatment of children became a paramount concern for research and service delivery during the 1980s and early 1990s (McCormack, Janus, and Burgess 1986). With the end of the twentieth century and the beginning of the twenty-first, structural factors now play an increasing role in our understanding of street-involved youth. The increase in HIV/AIDS (human immunodeficiency virus/acquired immunodeficiency syndrome), chronic poverty, inadequate housing, unemployment or underemployment, deinstitutionalization, and the challenged and overworked systems of child welfare all have a critical impact on street-involved youth in Canada (Worthington et al. 2008).

An ecological perspective has frequently been used as a theoretical framework for understanding the runaway and homeless phenomenon. The model described in this chapter was developed by Kufeldt and Burrows (1994), based on initial work by Bronfenbrenner (1974) and later expanded on by Garbarino (1982). Bronfenbrenner's influence was acknowledged in the authors' description of the ecological approach: "A child's development is influenced by a complex network of family, friends, school, community resources, and ultimately, by forces outside the child's immediate experience, such as government decisions and cultural or societal expectations" (Kufeldt and Burrows 1994, p. 13). This approach is useful for focusing the reader's attention on the interaction of the individual with different systems (e.g., school, peers, and child welfare) and within the predominant values, attitudes, and philosophies of society (see Figure 13.2).

Pathways to the Street—The Vulnerable Population

Young people become involved with street life in a variety of ways. A significant proportion of street-involved youth say that they initially left home as a result of family conflict, disruption, and maltreatment (Chen, Tyler, Whitbeck, and Hoyt 2004; Hyde 2005; McLean 2005). In addition, many youths leave home because they were thrown out or forced to leave, or because they sought further independence (McLean 2005; Public Health Agency of Canada 2006b). Other youths become street involved following an early exit from or aging out of the child welfare system (Lenz-Rashid 2006).

Family Experiences

A large percentage of street-involved youth report a history of child maltreatment at the hands of their caregivers. The Enhanced Surveillance of Canadian Street Youth (E-SYS) is an ongoing project to monitor behaviours, risk determinants, sexually transmitted infections (STIs), and related infections in the Canadian street youth population (Public Health Agency of Canada 2006b). The E-SYS reported that between 19 and 28 per cent of street-involved youth left home because of physical abuse, sexual abuse, and/or emotional abuse. In addition, 30 per cent reported experiencing neglect in their homes.

Other North American studies report that rates of maltreatment range from 12 to 50 per cent for sexual abuse, and 30 to 90 per cent for physical abuse (Adlaf and Zhanowicz 1999; Hyde 2005; Rotheram-Borus, Mahler, Koopman, and Langabeer 1996; Thrane, Hoyt, Whitbeck, and Yoder 2006; Worthington et al. 2008). The maltreatment experienced by street-involved youth is consistently reported to be chronic, extreme, and initiated at a young age (Cauce, Tyler, and Whitback 2004; Janus Archambault, Brown, and Welsh 1995; Tyler and Cauce 2002).

Worthington et al. (2008) found that 71 per cent of street-involved youth surveyed in Calgary reported at least one type of maltreatment while living at home, including physical abuse (43 per cent), sexual abuse (20 per cent), neglect (29 per cent), and emotional maltreatment (52 per cent). And abuse among street-involved youth is rarely a one-time occurrence.

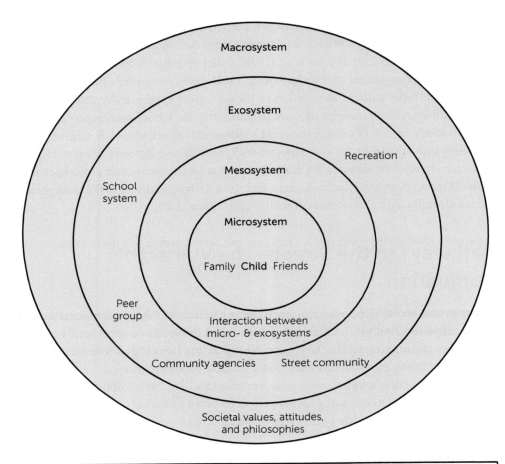

Microsystem	This is the immediate setting in which a person resides. For the street population, it can include family, school, child welfare placement, and the street culture itself.
Mesosystem	This represents the connections between the child's microsystems and exosystems. Risk and opportunity relate to the quality of connections and relationships and the congruencies of values within the microsystems.
Exosystem	Larger systems (school system, community agency) are exosystems in which policies and operations can enhance or detract from opportunities for homeless youth.
Macrosystem	This includes the culture and ideology of the society in which a person lives. The dilemma in leaving the street is the need to conform to predominant and straight culture without the means to incorporate and practise its values.

Figure 13.2   Ecological Framework

Source: Kufeldt and Burrows 1994, p. 14. Adapted from Bronfenbrenner 1974.

Of this group, 61 per cent reported that the maltreatment had consisted of multiple events during a period of more than six months, while an additional 31 per cent reported multiple events occurring within six months or less. Only 8 per cent reported that the maltreatment had been a single event. In addition, 54 per cent of surveyed street-involved youth reported having witnessed domestic violence between their parents (Worthington et al., 2008).

Children who experience maltreatment within their family may resort to running away from home as an alternative to the abuse or neglect. More than 11 per cent of children and teens who experienced substantiated maltreatment in Alberta in 2003 had a history of running away from home at the time of the child welfare investigation, and the percentage of teens (ages 12 to 15) was significantly higher (MacLaurin et al. 2006) (see Box 13.1).

Many children and youth coming out as lesbian, gay, bisexual, transsexual, transgender, queer or questioning (LGBTQ) experience heightened challenges within their families, and are overrepresented in homeless populations in North America. Estimates range from 20 to 40 per cent in homeless youth populations, and researchers suggest this may be conservative based on a reluctance to report (Abromovich, 2013; Coolhart and Brown, 2017; Maccio and Ferguson; 2016). LGBTQ youth highlight the role that family conflict and stress plays in leading to their exit to the street and contributes to this overrepresentation.

Child Welfare Experiences

Children and youth who have experienced maltreatment and family conflict frequently become involved with child welfare and are referred to child welfare care (MacLaurin and Bala 2004). Children in the care of child welfare (e.g., foster care, group homes, or treatment centres) are overrepresented in most street youth populations (Barker et al. 2014; Biehal and Wade 2000; Duval and Vincent 2009; Fitzgerald 1995; Kulik, Gaetz, Crowe, and Ford-James 2011; Min Park, Metraux, and Culhan 2005; Worthington et al. 2008). Worthington et al. (2008) reported that 62 per cent of street-involved youth surveyed in Calgary reported that their family had a history of child welfare involvement, and of this number 52 per cent had been placed in either foster or group care as a result of the involvement.

This overrepresentation may be a reflection of the number of youths who ran away from current child welfare care or of those youths who became homeless following emancipation from care (Lenz-Rashid 2006). Although less than 1 per cent of children in England were in foster care or group homes, more than 30 per cent of **runaways** reported as missing to the police were from care (Biehal and Wade 2000). This trend is also seen in Canada, with a high percentage of children reported missing to the police from institutional and foster care, and institutional care having the highest rate of repeat runners (Fisher 1989).

Child welfare agencies have the mandate to serve the transitional needs of youth effectively as they prepare for independence following their in-care placements. Research focusing on the health and housing outcomes of youth aging out of the child welfare system has identified that these young people are not consistently well served (Crosland, Joseph, Slattery, Hodges and Dunlap 2018; Lenz-Rashid 2006; Nicols 2013; Schelbe 2018). The percentage of youth emancipated from the care of child welfare who were described as homeless at the point of emancipation in the United States ranges from 25 to 66 per cent (Barth 1990; California Department of Social Services 2002; Courtney 2001).

There are significant differences noted for youths who enter street life from foster or group care compared to those youths who enter the streets from home (Biehal and Wade

runaways
Youths who run away from their family or child welfare placement, at least overnight, without parental or caretaker permission. They often leave as a result of family conflict or maltreatment.

2000; Rees 1993). Rees (1993) found that street-involved youth who had left child welfare placements were more likely to run repeatedly, more likely to run for longer periods of time, and more likely to be apprehended by police.

Children and youth who identify as LGBTQ and live in the care of child welfare contribute greatly to the disproportionate number of LGBTQ youth on the street, as discussed in the previous section (Abramovitch 2013; Dentlaff, Washburn, Carr, and Vogel 2018). Service providers within the child welfare field struggle to provide meaningful and engaging services that are appropriate for LGBTQ youth, as most policies and practice have been developed and tested with general populations (Maccio and Ferguson 2016).

Life on the Streets

Once youths make the transition from home to the street, they enter a new world with its own culture, norms, and rules. As Auerswald and Eyre (2002) point out, this initial experience of the street is characterized by feelings of loneliness, disorientation, and the need to survive. Their study suggests that youths find street mentors and become acculturated to the street, including the street's resources, economy, language, and drugs. Victimization on the street is extremely common among street-involved youth and can take the form of theft or robbery, sexual assault, physical assault, and assault with a weapon (Gaetz 2004). For minority groups like lesbian, gay, bisexual, trans, or questioning (LGBTQ) youth, the level of victimization can nearly double (Whitbeck, Chen, Hoyt, Tyler, and Johnson 2004). LGBTQ youth are clearly overrepresented in the street-involved population in Canada (Abramovich, A. 2013; Abramovich, I. 2012). Furthermore, the mortality rate for street-involved youth is about 11 times the expected rate for the general youth population (Boivin et al. 2005). Gaetz (2004) notes that a significant proportion of street-involved youth do not turn to anyone when they have experienced victimization on the street.

Social Support and Resilience

Street-involved youth develop social networks that can be a source of support (Bender et al. 2007; Johnson, Whitbeck, and Hoyt 2005). Nearly 80 per cent of youth have relationships that were formed prior to their time on the streets, and 66 per cent have friends from home, indicating that these youths still value the ties from their past. Furthermore, nearly one-third (31 per cent) of street-involved youth report family members as part of their social network, including siblings (Johnson et al. 2005). Weaker family ties are associated with youths who have externalizing behaviour problems; with gay, lesbian, and bisexual youths; and with those who experience caregiver abuse prior to leaving home (Johnson et al. 2005; Milburn et al. 2005). In a qualitative study by Kidd (2003), one-quarter of street-involved youth mentioned significant support from friends on the street who taught them the rules of street culture. Street acquaintances provide an element of family support for street-involved youth and are described as being there for personal, financial, and emotional support (Worthington et al., 2008). MacLaurin, Johansson, McDonald, and Soenen (2018) found that youth on the street grew to rely on their friends and that this was one factor that led to youth becoming re-involved with street life following an episode of stable housing.

Street-involved youth are resilient in a number of ways. MacDonald and Roebuck (2018) stress that young people experiencing homelessness act in ways that reflect significant resilience when facing the challenges and adversity of the street lifestyle. Kidd (2003) found that a large number of Canadian youth had a strong sense of confidence in their own abilities, of security in their own beliefs, and of self-worth. Other research supports these findings and indicates that youth have both resource-related strengths (e.g., knowledge of the street environment and streetwise skills) and self-improvement skills (e.g., making healthier choices and gaining emotional maturity). Beneficial coping mechanisms include having hope and goals for the future, having a sense of spirituality, having friends, having time alone to think, having positive thinking and humour, and having hobbies (Worthington et al. 2008). A major theme in Kidd's (2003) interviews with street-involved youth was their desire for more opportunities to increase their self-worth. These youths, despite their history and circumstances, continue to have a sense of hope for their future.

Risks Associated with Street Involvement

Substance Use and HIV Risk

Substance use is primarily used as a coping mechanism for life on the streets, stress, and early family abuse, but it can also be used for social or recreational purposes (Bender et al. 2012; Heerde and Hemphill 2014). Substance use is common among street-involved youth and includes the use of tobacco, alcohol, marijuana, hashish, crack cocaine, powder cocaine, heroin, lysergic acid diethylamide (LSD), mushrooms, crystal meth, speed, crank, ecstasy, and glue (Clatts, Goldsamt, Yi, and Gwadz 2005; Robert, Pauze, and Fournier 2005). The rate of substance use among street-involved youth varies by specific substance, with between 70 and 94 per cent of youth overall reporting the use of any substance (Worthington et al., 2008). Specific levels of reported substance use include alcohol (67 to 100 per cent), tobacco (96 per cent), and marijuana (43 to 93 per cent), although several other substances are also used by the majority of street-involved youth (Kulik et al. 2011; Thompson, Zittel-Palamara, and Maccio 2004; Tyler and Johnson 2006). Brands, Leslie, Catz-Biro, and Li (2005) found that substance use among street-involved youth is not only common but also tends to be extreme.

Most studies report rates of injection drug use among street-involved youth from 20 to 54 per cent (Clatts, Rees-Davis, Sotheran, and Atillasoy 1998; Leach, Wolitski, Goldbaum, Fishbein, and the AIDS Community Demonstration Projects 1997; Roy, Haley Leclerc, Cedras, and Boivin 2002). Furthermore, between one-quarter and three-quarters of youth who use injection drugs have shared drug-injection equipment (Gleghorn, Marx, Vittinghoff, and Katz 1998; Worthington et al. 2008).

Although some Canadian studies on street-involved youth have shown low risk of HIV infection through injection drug use, levels of injecting risk behaviours among street-involved youth require ongoing assessment. The majority of research shows that youth (defined as those under 30 years of age) who use injection drugs are at greater risk of HIV transmission than older users (Health Canada 2002b). This risk results from sharing contaminated needles, syringes, and other drug-use equipment and the tendency to engage in unsafe sex, often under the influence of drugs (Diaz, Conover, Edwards, Monterroso, and Susser 1998; Kral, Lorvick, and Edlin 1999; Marshall, Kerr, Qi, Montaner, and Wood 2010). Findings also indicate that youth who use injection drugs have a significantly higher rate of hepatitis C virus (HCV) (Boivin et al. 2005).

Physical and Mental Health Problems

Canadian research has consistently demonstrated that street-involved youth are a population with an overrepresentation of physical and mental health problems. It has been suggested that street-involved youth face barriers to exercising their rights and the opportunities of their citizenship (e.g., access to health care, to shelter, to mental health support) while having the same basic needs as all Canadians, and that they are one of the most disenfranchised groups in our society (Bassuk, Rubin, and Lauriat 1984; Miller, Miller, Hoffman, and Duggan 1980). A study of homeless Toronto **squeegee kids**, for example, suggests that the lives of this group of street-involved youth are characterized by a constant struggle to find safe, secure shelter, to generate income, and to find sufficient food (Dachner and Tarasuk 2002).

squeegee kids
A group of street-involved youth who are resourceful in attempting to develop and maintain a livelihood and means of survival by offering to clean windshields at major intersections.

Study findings indicate a higher prevalence of mental health problems for street-involved youth than for non-street-involved youth (Perlman, Willard, Herbers, Cutuli, and Eyrich-Garg 2014; Wong, Clark, and Marlotte 2014). Common mental health problems in this population include conduct and oppositional disorder, anxiety disorders, dissociative symptoms, and depression (Booth and Zhang 1997; Slesnick, Zhang and Brakenhoff 2017; Thompson et al. 2004; Tyler, Cauce, and Whitbeck 2004). However, Ayerst (1999) found that most street-involved youth felt less depressed and stressed on the street than when they were living at home. Street-involved youth are at a higher risk for attempted and completed suicide, and suicidal ideation often follows completed suicides of street friends (Clatts et al. 2005; Perlman et al. 2014; Wong et al. 2014; Yoder, Hoyt, and Whitbeck 1998). Documented rates of attempted suicide range from 25 to 46 per cent, with even higher rates noted for LGBTQ youth (Clatts et al. 2005; Kidd 2006; Whitbeck et al. 2004; Worthington et al., 2008). Mental health is a critical concern for all street-involved youth and specifically for select marginalized groups.

Given the lifestyle of street-involved youth, it is understandable that youth may not receive adequate health care and are frequently unable to obtain this care because of a lack of current health care coverage (e.g., some may not have access to a health care card) (Farrow, Deisher, Brown, Kulig, and Kipke 1992; Gaetz et al. 1999). Health concerns reported by street-involved youth include upper-respiratory-tract infections, skin disorders (including scabies and lice), gastrointestinal disorders, genitourinary disorders, and foot problems (e.g., fungus and blisters) (Dachner and Tarasuk 2002; Wright 1991). A higher percentage of street-involved youth with a current or previous history of living on the street reported physical health conditions than youth who had never lived on the street (Worthington et al. 2008). And chronic health concerns for street-involved youth may be twice as high as those for youth who are not street involved (Wright 1991). Additional health concerns are identified for street-involved youth who have children while they are living on the street (Pennbridge, MacKenzie, and Swofford 1991; Ray 1993). The literature highlights a relationship between the duration of street involvement and health outcomes for youth—the longer the duration, the greater the risk of tuberculosis, dental problems, viral and sexually transmitted diseases (STDs), HIV/AIDS, hepatitis B virus (HBV), and hepatitis C virus (HCV) (Kraus, Eberle, and Serge 2001).

Sexual Health—STIs and HIV Risk

According to findings from the Canadian E-SYS study (Enhanced Surveillance of Canadian Street Youth, initiated in 1998), street-involved youth are at high risk of contracting sexually transmitted infections (STIs) (Public Health Agency of Canada 2006a). Compared to the general youth population, street-involved youth included in the E-SYS study are 10 times more likely to have chlamydia, and 20 to 30 times more likely to have gonorrhea. Among youth included in the E-SYS study, between the years 1999 and 2003, approximately 2.3 per cent of street-involved youth had HBV, 3.6 to 4.5 per cent had HCV, and 14.2 to 18.8 per cent had herpes simplex virus-2 (HSV-2), associated with genital herpes.

Canadian and American incidence and prevalence data, in conjunction with surveillance data, reveal that street-involved youth are at very high risk of HIV infection (Boivin et al. 2005; DeMatteo et al. 1999; Hahn, Shafer, and Moss 1998; Kipke, Montgomery, Simon, and Iverson 1996; Larke 2001; Roy et al. 2001; Roy, Haley, Leclerc, Cedras, and Boivin 2002; Sullivan 1996). The number of new HIV cases in youth between the ages of 15 and 19 years has remained relatively constant since 1999; however, the proportion of females among this group is growing (Health Canada 2002a, 2002b). Sexual activity is likely to present a major risk for HIV transmission among street-involved youth. St Lawrence, Crosby, and O'Brannon (1999) found that the average age at first intercourse for street-involved youth is 12 years old, while the average number of times street-involved youth have sexual intercourse each week ranges from two to three times for casual sex, up to 13 times for paying sex (Public Health Agency of Canada 2006a). Studies report high percentages of youth with multiple sexual partners, and young men who have sex with men represent the most at-risk subgroup among street-involved youth, with an average of 45 lifetime partners (Booth and Zhang 1997; Public Health Agency of Canada 2006a; St Lawrence et al. 1999).

Although young people are generally aware of HIV risks, research on sexual risk behaviours shows that youth are among the least likely to employ safer sex precautions. A large percentage of street-involved youth do not use condoms to protect themselves from HIV or other sexually transmitted diseases, with a low of 10 per cent of female street-involved youth who consistently use condoms (Clatts et al. 1998; De Rosa, Montgomery, Hyde, Iverson, and Kipke 2001; Haley, Roy, Leclerc, Boudreau, and Boivin 2004b; Weber, Boivin, Blais, Haley, and Roy 2002).

Pregnancy is also common among street-involved youth. Studies report that 42 to 50 per cent of all female youth living on the street have been pregnant (Haley et al. 2004a; Weber et al. 2002; Worthington et al., 2008). Greene and Ringwalt (1998) examined the relationship between pregnancy in street-involved youth and street-involved youth's level of street involvement, and found that youth currently living on the street were most likely to become pregnant and to experience multiple pregnancies. There are significant risks for youth who experience a pregnancy while living on the street, including drug use, access to prenatal and medical services, financial resources, and infant health (Thompson, Bender, Lewis, and Watkins 2008); however, there is evidence that pregnancies among street-involved youth may provide motivation for some youth to establish more stable housing (Hathazi, Lankenau, Sanders, and Bloom 2009).

Involvement in Survival or Obligatory Sex

Survival or obligatory sex involves the bartering of sex for money or other necessities, such as food and shelter. Studies reveal that up to 25 per cent of street-involved youth have traded sex at some point in their lives and that females may be at higher risk for involvement (Clatts et al. 1998; Haley et al. 2004b; Public Health Agency of Canada 2006a; Weber et al. 2002; Worthington et al. 2008). Survival or obligatory sex may offer a way for street-involved youth to gain autonomy and independence while on the street. Many youth have left family or child welfare situations in a manner that does not allow their return, and survival or obligatory sex and eventual involvement in the sex trade is a way of establishing some immediate financial independence and autonomy from their former living situations (McIntyre 1999). Youth may emphasize that this involvement reflects strength and survival rather than victimhood which clearly calls for a reorientation of services for these youth (Ijadi-Maghsoodi, Bath, Cook, Textor, and Barnert 2018). Further work is needed in this area, however (Sapiro, Johnson, Postmus, and Simmel 2016). The importance of supportive adults cannot be underemphasized. Chisolm-Straker, Sze, Einbond, White, and Stoklosa (2018) found that youth who had been trafficked were similar in many ways to those who had not. However, the presence of a consistent and supportive adult playing a meaningful role in their life was a compelling protective factor against youth trafficking.

Street-involved youth may participate in unprotected sexual activity in order to receive a greater amount of money than that offered for protected sex or for a secure place to stay for the night (de Oliviera 1992; Slonim-Nevo, Ozawa, and Auslander 1991; Swart-Kruger and Richer 1997). Among Canadian street-involved youth involved in survival or obligatory sex, 44 per cent report not using a condom during their most recent obligatory sexual encounter (Public Health Agency of Canada 2006a; Swart-Kruger and Richer 1997).

Institutional Experiences of Street-Involved Youth

Education

For street-involved youth, education is a serious concern, as many of these youth may drop out of school or be expelled before finishing, or even reaching, high school (Semanchin-Jones, Bowen, and Ball 2018). Without education, young people have difficulty finding and maintaining a steady job, making it even more difficult for them to transition off the street. This population also experiences a higher rate of learning difficulties (Barwick and Siegal 1996; Thompson et al. 2004). One study reported that more than half of all street-involved youth display evidence of a reading disability; nearly 30 per cent display evidence of arithmetic/written work disability; and 20 per cent are classified as "normally achieving" (Barwick and Siegal 1996). School attendance declines as youth get older. Approximately 65 per cent of early-adolescent street-involved youth reported attending school within the past month, compared to 27 per cent of older-adolescent street-involved youth (Unger et al. 1998). Reasons for not attending school are complex, but Thompson, Zittel-Palamara, and Maccio (2004) determined that more than half of street-involved youth were either suspended or expelled from school. A survey of Calgary street-involved youth found that 69 per cent of respondents reported an incomplete high school education and 46 per cent reported having been kicked out of school (Worthington et al. 2008).

Child Welfare

A high percentage of street-involved youth have had previous child welfare experiences and foster-care placements (Clarke and Cooper 2000; Gaetz et al. 1999; Leslie and Hare 2000; Min Park et al. 2005; Nicols 2013). In 2003, 42 per cent of Canadian street-involved youth in the E-SYS study reported having been in foster care, and 47 per cent reported having been in group homes (Public Health Agency of Canada 2006b). In addition, between 12 and 38 per cent of youth transitioning out of foster care spend some time without a home shortly after discharge, either sleeping on the streets or in a homeless shelter (Cook 1994; Courtney 2001; Courtney and Dworsky 2006; Freundlich and Avery 2006). A number of studies have reported that youth with child welfare histories were two times more likely than other youth to be unable to pay their rent or utility bills and four times more likely to be evicted, and that, overall, youth transitioning out of care reported feeling poorly prepared for independent living (Courtney 2001; Leslie and Hare 2000; Reilly 2003).

Criminal Justice System

Extensive work by Baron has shown how crime is related to several factors in the lives of street-involved youth (Baron 2003, 2004, 2013; Baron and Hartnagel 1998, 2006). These factors include monetary dissatisfaction; unemployment; deviant/criminal peers; being a victim of robbery, violence, or theft; perception of blocked opportunities; drug/alcohol use; low self-control; and low self-esteem. All of these factors interact to increase the risk of crime involvement in street-involved youth. As can be seen, criminal involvement among street-involved youth is a complex interaction of numerous factors and cannot simply be explained as deviant behaviour (Gaetz, O'Grady, and Buccieri 2010; O'Grady, Gaetz, and Buccieri 2013).

Street-involved youth consistently report that selling drugs is a means of earning money while on the streets (Baron and Hartnagel 2006; Hagan and McCarthy 1997). A significant proportion of street-involved youth are involved in some form of gang activity while on the street (Yoder, Whitbeck, and Hoyt 2003), while violent crime such as assault is also commonly noted in Canadian and US studies (Baron and Hartnagel 2006; Gaetz 2004). Other criminal involvement includes shoplifting, theft, and property offences

Box 13.2 | Youth Justice in Action

Canada Failing Homeless Youth, Report Charges—Stress on Emergency Assistance, Not Prevention, Solves Little in the Long Run, Professor Says

Toronto Star, GTA, **Monday, 3 March 2014 by Leslie Ferenc**

Canada falls short of meeting the needs of homeless youth by treating them as adults and expecting shelter care to solve the problem, according to a new report. Many youth find themselves "languishing in a shelter for four or five years when they should be in school learning to be an adult with the supports they need . . . instead of rushing them to be adults, living in poverty and becoming chronically homeless adults," says report author Stephen Gaetz, a professor in York University's education faculty and director of the Homeless Hub (Canadian Homelessness Research Network). "By continuing to emphasize emergency supports, as important as they are, rather than prevention or rapid rehousing, our strategy is simply to manage the problem," he said. Gaetz is author of *Coming of Age: Reimagining the Response to Youth Homelessness in Canada*, which was released Monday.

The report looks at remedies used in Canada and countries such as the United Kingdom and Australia which address youth homelessness differently. "Youth homelessness is distinct from adult because of conditions . . . it's not just an age difference," he said, adding that they are thrust into adult roles before their time and the transition is often traumatic. For one, they don't have the resources and support they need to be independent. "They leave a home where they were dependent on the care of adults." Family conflict can also be a factor with youth fleeing difficulties at home, including abuse. They land in shelters and "suddenly, they find themselves having to behave as adults," said Gaetz.

While he acknowledged there will always be a need for emergency services, they are not the solution. "We need to refocus our efforts on preventing it from happening in the first place," he wrote in the report. "For those who can no longer stay at home we must develop a crisis response that allows them to rapidly move into housing in a safe and planned way, with the supports they need to help them transition to a healthy and fulfilling adulthood." The report recommends an integrated system of care that reconnects youth to their families if possible, offers outreach mental health and harm reduction programs as well as legal support for youth in conflict with the law. To meet the needs of youth means looking at what others are doing "so we can put together a framework for responding to youth homelessness differently," said Gaetz, adding it will also mean a shift in thinking.

Australia's Reconnect program targets youth 12–18 and their families. School social workers and teachers help identify at-risk or homeless youth. A series of programs and services such as assessment, counselling, and practical support are available to help young people work through their problems. A shelter diversion program in the UK offers youth a bed and support from a family in their neighbourhood, a place to chill while they resolve their problems. An integrated system of care includes housing and, if possible, family reunification. The report also cites the Infinity Project, run by the Boys and Girls Clubs of Calgary, which offers young people 16–24 permanent housing, leading to greater self-sufficiency. In Niagara Region, Youth Reconnect is a community-based shelter diversion program to help homeless and at-risk youth stay in their communities and in school. In Toronto, outreach and harm reduction programs at front-line agencies such as Eva's Satellite help meet service needs of diverse groups.

For Gaetz, it's a start, but he wants every community in Canada to make ending youth homelessness a

continued

priority. "Moreover, outside of the Province of Alberta which is readying its strategic response to youth homelessness, most higher levels of government across the country are largely silent on the issue," he said. "This means in most communities the response is fragmented and ad hoc, and the focus is on managing the problem rather than ending it through a coordinated response that shifts the focus to prevention and rehousing."

Reprinted with permission—Torstar Syndication Services.

The next step for Gaetz is to engage citizens, agencies, community groups, and all levels of government across the country to come to the table. "We are looking at developing a coalition model to support communities to end homelessness," he said. "It's not a cookie cutter response. Toronto's will be different from York Region's or Kenora's. I'm positive this can happen because there is a lot of momentum in Canada."

(Baron and Hartnagel 2006). A survey of Calgary street-involved youth found that 69 per cent of respondents reported that they had been charged with a crime at some point in their life, and of this group, 79 per cent were charged under the juvenile justice system, 48 per cent were charged under the adult system, and 75 per cent had spent time in jail or detention as a result of these charges (Worthington et al. 2008). Canadian research finds that street youth are generally more involved in crime than those who are housed, and the types of criminal activities ranged from shoplifting and consuming illegal drugs/alcohol in public to more serious concerns including assaults, robbery, and trafficking (O'Grady et al. 2013). It has been suggested that street-involved youth do not necessarily prefer to be delinquent or elect to become involved in criminal activities; rather, they become involved in response to the situational demands and challenges of living on the streets (Hagan and McCarthy 1997; O'Grady, et al. 2013). O'Grady and Green (2003) point out that the more disadvantaged a homeless person becomes, the more likely that person may opt to be involved in criminal activity. This is especially critical when appropriate avenues for earning are limited or criminalized.

During the late 1990s, there was a noted increase in the number of people involved in squeegee cleaning on the streets of many large Canadian cities. Squeegee cleaning, like panhandling, was an income-generating activity that was seen as the domain of street-involved youth and resulted in the term "squeegee kids" (O'Grady and Bright 2002). In 2000, the Safe Streets Act was enacted in Ontario, and it resulted in the criminalization of squeegee cleaning as a means of income generation (O'Grady et al., 2013; Schneiderman 2002). O'Grady and Greene (2003) question the rationale of this move, as research found that squeegee-cleaning street youth were less involved in criminal activity and reported lower levels of hard-drug use and lower levels of psychological distress than that reported by street youth who did not participate in squeegee cleaning (O'Grady, Bright, and Cohen 1998).

Street Services and Intervention Strategies

Street-involved youth do not take advantage of available services in all circumstances. McLean (2005) found that, in a sample of youth in Calgary without child welfare status, just over half reported knowing about or using community outreach services for homeless youth, and that they primarily heard about these services from their friends. Of those surveyed in this study who used shelters, 29 per cent said they experienced difficulty accessing the service, while 32 per cent said they had been turned away because they did not meet certain shelter criteria.

A San Francisco study that examined differential service use for street-involved youth at different stages of street involvement found that youth who were more entrenched in the street culture were less likely to access drug-related services while those attempting to leave the street were more likely to access medical services (Carlson et al. 2006). Regardless of the level of street involvement, virtually all street-involved youth in the study reported using at least one related service: 50 per cent used medical services, 45 per cent used outreach services, 21 per cent used drug-related services, and 7 per cent used shelters. This study demonstrated a high rate of service use overall but highlighted that the effectiveness of individual services truly differ for subpopulations (Carlson et al. 2006).

Worthington et al. (2008) report similar findings in Canada as use of specific services differed by type of street involvement. The three levels of street involvement included street-involved youth who were currently living on the street (Currently on Street); the second category included street-involved youth who were not currently living on the street but had a past history of living on the street (Not on Street—History); the third category included street-involved youth who were not currently living on the street and had no history of living on the street (Not on Street—No History). Youth currently living on the street reported higher use of shelters, drop-in centres, and outreach services, while street-involved youth who had not lived on the street reported higher use of alternative educational services (Worthington et al. 2008) (see Table 13.1).

The majority of street-involved youth speak very positively about the services available to them—specifically those services that are flexible, have employees with positive attitudes, offer a comfortable atmosphere, and provide a sense of safety and security (Worthington et al. 2008). A continued focus on high-quality assurance is needed, however, as street-involved youth continue to experience barriers to accessing timely and effective services. Karabanow (2004) provides an example of two Toronto-based shelters that have teamed with child welfare organizations. While these programs were originally designed to provide emergency housing and services to street-involved youth, they are now providing long-term care facilities for young people experiencing difficulty with child welfare services. Other barriers to services identified in the literature include inadequate program funding, unavailable programs and services, low salaries, insufficient and inexperienced staff, and government policy (Brooks, Milburn, Rotheram-Borus, and Witkin 2004; Worthington et al. 2008). According to Brooks et al. (2004), most of the issues identified by agencies as problem areas for street-involved youth are not well addressed by these agencies. Street-involved youth tend to respond best to service providers who are respectful, flexible, empathetic, supportive, encouraging, and empowering (Thompson, McManus, Lantry, Windsor, and Flynn 2006).

Effective service development is not a simple prescription for meeting the needs of street-involved youth. Given the diversity of street youth—as noted in the discussions of the life-cycle model of street involvement and the level of street involvement (Worthington et al. 2008), as well as the inherent risks associated with street involvement—there is

Table 13.1 Use of Street Services by Current Level of Street Involvement

Services Used in the Past Three Months (N=333)	Not on Street— No History		Not on Street—History		Currently on Street		Total	
	%	#	%	#	%	#	%	#
Food banks	22	14	38	43	33	50	32	107
Shelters*	19	12	32	36	72	111	48	159
Drop-in centres*	12	8	30	34	68	105	44	147
Medical clinics	35	23	45	51	40	61	41	135
Outreach services*	9	6	32	36	53	81	37	123
Financial aid	6	4	15	17	8	13	10	34
Employment services	23	15	21	24	29	44	25	83
Educational services	20	13	16	18	10	16	14	47
Counselling services*	15	10	26	30	10	16	17	56
No services used*	22	14	17	19	2	3	11	36
Total	Column totals not provided because participants could choose multiple responses							

Note: Based on a sample of 333 responses with information about use of street services and current street involvement.

* Significance level p ≤ 0.05.

Source: Worthington et al. 2008, p. 116.

a critical need to establish a continuum of services to meet the diverse needs of street-involved youth. Services are required to assist young people at different points in their life: before youth become regularly involved in the streets; during street involvement; during a transition from the street locale; and as a follow-up to street involvement (Kufeldt and Burrows 1994). Services at each of these points need to address the physical needs (e.g., food, clothing, and shelter) of young people involved in street life as well as needs related to their physical and mental health, education, and employment (see Table 13.2). Studies advocate a **youth-centric programming model** that allows youth to play a significant role in developing and evaluating programs and in which the agencies continue to be flexible in adapting to the changing needs of street-involved youth (Baer, Peterson, and Wells 2004; Whitmore and McKee 2001).

youth-centric programming model Youth play a significant role in developing and evaluating programs, and agencies continue to be flexible in adapting to the changing needs of street-involved youth.

Emerging research and advocacy are calling for a new response to street-involved youth and youth homelessness in Canada (Gaetz 2014; Raising the Roof 2009). Services at this point continue to focus on responding to crises and emergencies; however, a renewed emphasis on prevention services is required to reduce the growing numbers of street-involved youth. As well, a focus on supportive transitions and accommodations is required to support successful transitions to housing stability.

With these new and emerging practices for youth homelessness, there is a continuing call for a systematic and rigorous examination to determine what interventions work

Table 13.2	Continuum of Services for Homeless Youth: Stage of Homelessness and Type of Service Required			
	Before the Street	**On the Street**	**Transitional Services**	**Off the Street**
Accommodation	– Affordable housing	– Emergency housing – Place to go during the day		– Affordable housing
Protection	– Community outreach – Child welfare services	– Secure treatment – Safe, protected accommodation – Emergency child welfare placements		
Food	– Adequate family income	– Daily meals		– Adequate income
Clothing	– Adequate family income	– Clothing – Storage and laundry facilities		– Adequate income
Health and hygiene	– Accessible, affordable health care	– Walk-in or mobile medical services – Showers	– Accessible, affordable health care	– Accessible, affordable health care
Mental health	– Crisis intervention counselling and/or mental-health services	– Crisis intervention	– Supportive counselling	– Informal social supports
Substance abuse	– Information counselling and/or treatment	– Detoxification services	– Substance abuse treatment and follow-up	– Informal social supports
Education	– Drop-out prevention – Specialized programs	– Walk-in schooling	– Transitional school programs	– Regular schools – Adult upgrading
Income	– Adequate family income		– Social assistance	– Job
Employment	– Job or school		– Life skills training – Employment training – Job-finding help	– Job

Source: Kufeldt and Burrows 1994, p. 14. Used with permission of the University of Calgary.

best for what children and youth, and for what time frame. Recent work by the Canadian Homelessness and Research Network proposes the development of a hierarchy of evidence for promising practice research that will highlight the benefits of emerging work evidence for populations at risk (Canadian Homelessness Research Network 2013). One critical element of promising practice research will continue to be work focused on intervention research (McCay and Aiello 2013).

Box 13.3 | Youth Justice in Action

Need for Mental Health Support

Homeless Youth in Dire Need of Mental Health Support Finds Canadian Study
By Jayson MacLean

The mental health challenges faced by homeless youth in Canada were the subject of a recent study by researchers from three Ontario universities, who analyzed data from a nationwide youth homelessness survey to conclude that there's a "compelling need" for more mental health supports for homeless youth, finding mental health needs to be of particular concern for both homeless female youth and LGBTQ2S youth.

With an estimated 235,000 Canadians experiencing homelessness each year, Canada is currently in the midst of a homelessness crisis. A report last year by the UN Committee on Economic, Social and Cultural Rights criticized Canada for its "persistent housing crisis" and for government inaction on affordable housing and policies supportive of homeless rights. At the same time, social justice advocates say that the current housing crises in Toronto and Vancouver is putting too many Canadians at risk of ending up on the street.

For young Canadians, the challenges of homelessness are especially steep. Studies show that between 60 and 70 per cent of homeless youth report neglect, physical violence and/or sexual violence prior to becoming homeless. Difficulties in school, family problems, mental health challenges and criminal justice and child protection issues are also factors. Once on the street, suicide, drug abuse as well as mental and physical health problems become more prevalent and finding a secure path out of homelessness becomes difficult.

A new study from researchers at the University of Toronto, York University and the University of Guelph attempts to provide a more comprehensive understanding of the mental health issues faced by homeless youth, by drawing on data from the 2015 "Leaving Home" national youth homelessness survey. The study performed a cross-sectional analysis based on survey responses from 1103 youth and across a range of indicators including quality of life, psychiatric symptoms, substance abuse, suicide attempt history and resilience.

Overall, the researchers found that homeless youth were at high risk for mental health issues.

"At a general level, this is a high-risk population in marked distress," say the study's authors, whose research is published in the Canadian Journal of Psychiatry. "From an intervention perspective, this study provides clear and compelling evidence of a need for mental health support for these youth."

In particular, the study found that homeless female youth reported poorer mental health and higher suicide rate in comparison with cisgender males and that lesbian, gay, bisexual, transgender, queer and 2 spirit youth (LGBTQ2S) were at particular risk. "LGBTQ2S youth reported significantly lower quality of life, poorer mental health, a 70 per cent suicide attempt rate as compared with 39 per cent for straight and cisgender participants, and higher rates of substance abuse (66.5 per cent compared with 41.8 per cent)," say the study's authors.

The researchers found that Indigenous youth's reported quality of life was on average no different than non-Indigenous youth, although they did portray a higher suicide attempt rate and greater substance abuse.

Other factors that negatively affected quality of life for homeless youth included exposure to physical violence while on the street, sexual violence, having a history of child protection involvement and/

continued

or neglect. The study found that being in contact with at least one family member was associated with better quality of life, lower symptoms and a lower suicide attempt rate and that having someone who could help in an emergency was also associated with better quality of life.

Summary

Street-involved youth are a diverse, marginalized population that face multiple challenges and insufficient and fragmented support from institutions and services. Understanding the experience of street-involved youth and the risks associated with street involvement is critical to developing services to meet their needs at all stages of their involvement—from early contact with the street, during their extended time spent on the street, and following their decision to leave the street. Communities need to promote and support positive life choices among street-involved youth while respecting their independence. An increased focus on evidence-based intervention is required to better identify what can work best for what groups of this diverse population. Research has shown that while street-involved youth are at higher risk for a variety of issues related to survival, safety, and health, these youth possess resilience and a strong desire to develop a future for themselves. A male street-involved youth eloquently described this hope for the future during a study interview in Calgary: "It's not a dark road. I mean it's whatever I want to make of it. Wherever I want to go, I know I can get there. It's gonna take work, it's gonna take discipline, it'll take a lot of things, but it's not unreachable. So, I'm not hopeless" (Worthington et al. 2008, p. iii).

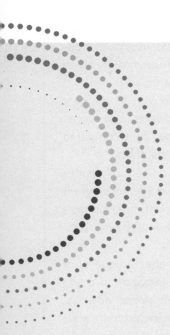

Key Terms

homeless youth
runaways
squeegee kids
street-involved youth

throwaways
underhoused
youth-centric programming model

Review Questions

1. Identify structural factors that may contribute to the involvement of youth in street life in Canada.

2. Identify and describe key factors that contribute to young people becoming involved on the street.

3. Why might typologies be useful in providing a framework for working with street-involved youth in Canada?

4. What kinds of risks are street-involved youth exposed to? Why?

Critical Thinking Questions

1. How would you propose getting an accurate count of the number of street-involved youth currently living in a major Canadian city?

2. What factors, if any, do you think would be important in developing a public awareness program for street-involved youth?

3. How would you counter the view that shelters and outreach services make it too easy for children to remain living on the street and that there is no incentive for them to get off the street?

4. Identify a group of street-involved youth (e.g., youth involved in survival or obligatory sex, or injection drug use). If you were designing a new program, what program components would be a priority for meeting their immediate and long-term needs? How would you know if the program was successful?

References

Abate, G. (2001, February 20). Squeegee ban violates Charter, lawyer argues. *Globe and Mail*, p. A23.

Abramovich, A. (2013). No fixed address: Young, queer and restless, In N.S. Gaetz, B., O'Grady, K. Buccieri, J. Karabanow, and A. Marsolais (Eds), *Youth homelessness in Canada: Implications for policy and practice* (pp. 387–404). Toronto: Canadian Homelessness Research Network Press.

Abramovich, I. (2012). No safe place to go: LGBTQ youth homelessness in Canada—Reviewing the literature. *Canadian Journal of Family and Youth, 4*(1), 29–51.

Adlaf, E.M., and Zdanowicz, Y.M. (1999). A cluster analytic study of substance abuse problems and mental health among street youths. *American Journal of Drug and Alcohol Abuse, 25*(4), 639–59.

Anonymous. (2010a, October 20). Guest comment: Why youth homelessness is an important social issue. *Victoria News*, p. 1.

Anonymous. (2010b, October 29). Scope of youth homelessness largely unknown. *Prince George Citizen*, p. 27.

Appathurai, C. (1987). *Runaway behaviour: A background paper.* Toronto: Ministry of Community and Social Services.

Auerswald, C.L., and Eyre, S.L. (2002). Youth homelessness in San Francisco: A life cycle approach. *Social Science and Medicine, 54*, 1497–512.

Ayerst, S.I. (1999). Depression and stress in street youth. *Adolescence, 34*(135), 567–85.

Baer, J.S., Peterson, P.L., and Wells, E.A. (2004). Rationale and design of a brief substance use intervention for homeless adolescents. *Addiction Research and Theory, 12*(4), 317–34.

Barker, B., Kerr, T., Taiaiake Alfred, G., Fortin, M., Nguyen, P., Wood, E., and DeBeck, K. (2014). High prevalence of exposure to the child welfare system among street-involved youth in a Canadian setting: Implications for policy and practice. *Public Health, 14*(197), 1–7

Baron, S.W. (2003). Self-control, social consequences, and criminal behavior: Street youth and the general theory of crime. *Journal of Research in Crime and Delinquency, 40*(4), 403–25.

Baron, S.W. (2004). General strain, street youth and crime: A test of Agnew's revised theory. *Criminology, 42*(2), 457–83.

Baron, S.W. (2013). Why street youth become involved in crime. In N.S. Gaetz, B. O'Grady, K. Buccieri, J. Karabanow, and A. Marsolais (Eds), *Youth homelessness in Canada: Implications for policy and practice* (pp. 353–68). Toronto: Canadian Homelessness Research Network Press.

Baron, S.W., and Hartnagel, T.F. (1998). Street youth and criminal violence. *Journal of Research in Crime and Delinquency, 35*(2), 166–89.

Baron, S.W., and Hartnagel, T.F. (2006). Street youth, strain theory, and crime. *Journal of Criminal Justice, 34*(2), 209–23.

Barth, R.P. (1990). On their own: The experiences of youth after foster care. *Child and Adolescent Social Work, 7*, 419–40.

Barwick, M.A., and Siegal, L.S. (1996). Learning difficulties in adolescent clients of a shelter for runaway and homeless street youths. *Journal of Research on Adolescence, 6*(4), 649–70.

Bassuk, E.L., Rubin, L., and Lauriat, A. (1984). Is homelessness a mental health problem? *American Journal of Psychiatry, 141*(12), 1546–50.

Bender, K., Thompson, S., Ferguson, K. Komlo, C., Taylor, C. and Yoder, J. (2012). Substance use and victimization:

Bender, K., Thompson, S., McManus, H., Lantry, J., and Flynn, P. (2007). Capacity for survival: Exploring strengths of homeless street youth. *Child Youth Care Forum, 36*, 25–42.

Street-involved youths' perspectives and service implications, *Children and Youth Services Review, 34*, 2392–9

Biehal, N., and Wade, J. (2000). Going missing from residential and foster care: Linking biographies and contexts. *British Journal of Social Work, 30*, 211–25.

Boivin, J.F., Roy, E., Haley, N., and Galbaud du Fort, G. (2005). The health of street youth: A Canadian perspective. *Canadian Journal of Public Health, 96*(6), 432–7.

Booth, R.E., and Zhang, Y. (1997). Conduct disorder and HIV risk behaviors among runaway and homeless adolescents. *Drug and Alcohol Dependence, 48*, 69–76.

Brands, B., Leslie, K., Catz-Biro, L., and Li, S. (2005). Heroin use and barriers to treatment in street-involved youth. *Addiction Research and Theory, 13*(5), 477–87.

Bronfenbrenner, U. (1974). Towards an experimental ecology of human development. *American Psychologist, 52*, 513–31.

Brooks, R.A., Milburn, N.G., Rotheram-Borus, M.J., and Witkin, A. (2004). The system-of-care for homeless youth: Perceptions of service providers. *Evaluation and Program Planning, 27*(4), 443–51.

Burt, M. (2001). *What will it take to end homelessness?* Washington: Urban Institute.

California Department of Social Services (CDSS). (2002). *Report on the survey of the housing needs of emancipated foster/probation youth.* Independent Living Program Policy Unit, Child and Youth Permanency Branch. Sacramento, CA: Author.

Canadian Homelessness Research Network. (2013). *What works and for whom? A hierarchy of evidence for promising practice research.* Toronto: Canadian Homelessness Research Network Press.

Carlson, J.L., Sugano, E., Millstein, S.G., and Auerswald, C.L. (2006). Service utilization and the life cycle of youth homelessness. *Journal of Adolescent Health, 38*, 624–7.

Cauce, A.M., Tyler, K.A., and Whitback, L.B. (2004). Maltreatment and victimization in homeless adolescents: Out of the frying pan and into the fire. *Prevention Researcher, 11*, 12–14.

Chen, X., Tyler, K.A., Whitbeck, L.B., and Hoyt, D.R. (2004). Early sexual abuse, street adversity, and drug use among female homeless and runaway adolescents in the Midwest. *Journal of Drug Issues, 34*(1), 1–21.

Chisolm-Straker, M., Sze, J., Einbond, J., White, J., and Stoklosa, H. (2018). A supportive adult may be the difference in homeless youth not being trafficked. *Children and Youth Services Review, 91*, 115–20

Clarke, M., and Cooper, M. (2000). *Homeless youth: Falling between the cracks.* Calgary: Youth Alternative Housing Committee.

Clatts, M., Goldsamt, L., Yi, H., and Gwadz, V. (2005). Homelessness and drug abuse among young men who have sex with men in New York City: A preliminary epidemiological trajectory. *Journal of Adolescence, 28*, 201–14.

Clatts, M., Rees-Davis, W., Sotheran, J.L., and Atillasoy, A. (1998). Correlates and distribution of HIV risk behaviours among homeless youth in New York City: Implications for prevention and policy. *Child Welfare, 77*(2), 195–207.

Community Action on Homelessness. (2009). *Halifax report card on homelessness 2009.* Halifax: Community Action on Homelessness.

Cook, R.J. (1994). Are we helping foster care youth prepare for their future? *Children and Youth Services Review, 16*(3/4), 213–29.

Coolhart, D., and Brown, M. (2017). The need for safe spaces: Exploring the experiences of homeless LGBTQ youth in shelters, *Children and Youth Services Review, 82*, 230–38.

Courtney, M.E. (2001). Foster youth transitions to adulthood: A longitudinal view of youth leaving care. *Child Welfare, 80*(6), 685–717.

Courtney, M.E., and Dworsky, A. (2006). Early outcomes for young adults transitioning from out-of-home care in the USA. *Child and Family Social Work, 11*, 209–19.

Crosland, K., Joseph, R., Slattery, L., Hodges, S., and Dunlap, G. (2018). Why youth run: Assessing run function to stabilize foster care placement. *Children and Youth Services Review, 85*, 35–42.

Cuthbertson, R. (2012, December 6). For homeless youth, "We're here to help you. Whoever you are." *Calgary Herald.* Retrieved from http://www.calgaryherald.com/life/ homeless+youth+here+help+whoever/7658219/story.html

Dachner, N., and Tarasuk, V. (2002). Homeless "squeegee kids": Food insecurity and daily survival. *Social Science and Medicine, 54*, 1039–49.

DeMatteo, D., Major, C., Block, B., Coates, R., Fearon, M., Goldberg, E.,...Read, S.E. (1999). Toronto street youth and HIV/AIDS: Prevalence, demographics and risks. *Journal of Adolescent Health, 25*, 356–66.

de Oliviera, W. (1992, July). *Street children and safe sex: Opportunities and barriers for changing behaviors.* Paper presented at the International Conference on AIDS VIII. Amsterdam, The Netherlands.

De Rosa, C.J., Montgomery, S.B., Hyde, J., Iverson, E., and Kipke, M. (2001). HIV risk behavior and HIV testing: A comparison of rates and associated factors among homeless and runaway adolescents in two cities. *AIDS Education and Prevention, 13*(2), 131–48.

Derworiz, C. (2010, April 5). "Plan within a plan" to end homelessness. *Calgary Herald*, p. A1.

Dettlaff, A., Washburn, M., Carr, L., and Vogel, A. (2018). *Lesbian, gay, and bisexual (LGB) youth within in welfare: Prevalence, risk and outcomes. Child Abuse and Neglect, 80*, 183–93.

Diaz, T., Conover, S., Edwards, V., Monterroso, E., and Susser, E. (1998, July). *Drug-using behaviors of young and recent initiate injection drug users in New York City: A unique opportunity for prevention of hiv*. Paper presented at the International Conference on AIDS XII, Geneva, Switzerland.

Duval, D.M., and Vincent, N. (2009). Affect regulation of homeless youth once in the child welfare system. *Child and Adolescent Social Work Journal, 26*, 155–73.

Farrow, J.A., Deisher, R.W., Brown, R., Kulig, J.W., and Kipke, M.D. (1992). Health and health needs of homeless and runaway youth. *Journal of Adolescent Health, 13*, 717–26.

Fisher, J. (1989). *Missing children research project*. Vol. 1: *Findings of the study—A focus on runaways* (No. 1989-07). Ottawa: Solicitor General of Canada.

Fitzgerald, M.D. (1995). Homeless youths and the child welfare system: Implications for policy and service. *Child Welfare, 74*(3), 717–31.

Freundlich, M., and Avery, R.J. (2006). Transitioning from congregate care: Preparation and outcomes. *Journal of Child and Family Studies, 15*, 507–18.

Gaetz, S. (2004). Safe streets for whom? Homeless youth, social exclusion, and criminal victimization. *Canadian Journal of Criminology and Criminal Justice, 46*(4), 423–55.

Gaetz, S. (2014). *Coming of age: Reimagining the response to youth homelessness in Canada*. Toronto: Canadian Homelessness Research Network Press.

Gaetz, S., O'Grady, B., and Buccieri, K. (2010). *Surviving crime and violence: Street youth and victimization in Toronto*. Toronto: JFCY and Homeless Hub.

Gaetz, S., O'Grady, B., Buccieri, K., Karabanow, J., and Marsolais, A. (2013). Introduction. In N.S. Gaetz, B., O'Grady, K. Buccieri, J. Karabanow, and A. Marsolais (Eds), *Youth homelessness in Canada: Implications for policy and practice* (pp. 1–14). Toronto: Canadian Homelessness Research Network Press.

Gaetz, S., O'Grady, B., and Vaillancourt, B. (1999). *Making money: The Shout Clinic report on homeless youth and employment*. Toronto: Central Toronto Community Health Centres.

Garbarino, J. (1982). *Children and families in the social environment*. New York: Aldine DeGruyter.

Gleghorn, A.A., Marx, R., Vittinghoff, E., and Katz, M.H. (1998). Association between drug use patterns and HIV risks among homeless, runaway, and street youth in northern California. *Drug and Alcohol Dependence, 51*(3), 219–27.

Goar, C. (2009, November 23). Street kids' toughness only skin deep. *Toronto Star*, p. A13.

Greene, J.M., and Ringwalt, C.L. (1998). Pregnancy among three national samples of runaway and homeless youth. *Journal of Adolescent Health, 23*(6), 370–7.

Grover, S. (2007). Homeless children and street involved children in Canada. In R.B. Howe and K. Covel (Eds), *Children's rights in Canada: A question of commitment* (pp. 343–72). Waterloo, ON: Wilfrid Laurier Press.

Hagan, J., and McCarthy, B. (1997). *Mean streets: Youth crime and homelessness*. Cambridge: Cambridge University Press.

Hahn, J., Shafer, K., and Moss, A.R. (1998, July). *High rate of HIV infection in homeless young injectors: Sex poses greatest risk*. Paper presented at the International Conference on AIDS XII, Geneva, Switzerland.

Haley, N., Roy, E., Leclerc, P., Boudreau, J-F., and Boivin, J-F. (2004a). Characteristics of adolescent street youth with a history of pregnancy. *Journal of Pediatric and Adolescent Gynecology, 17*(5), 313–20.

Haley, N., Roy, E., Leclerc, P., Boudreau, J-F., and Boivin, J-F. (2004b). HIV risk profile of male street youth involved in survival sex. *Sexually Transmitted Infections, 80*(6), 526–30.

Halifax Regional Municipality. (2005). *Homelessness in HRM: Portrait of streets and shelters*, vol. 2. Halifax: Halifax Regional Municipality, Planning and Development Services.

Hammer, H., Finkelhor, D., and Sedlak, A.J. (2002). *Runaway/thrownaway children: National estimates and characteristics*. Washington, DC: Office of Juvenile Justice and Delinquency Prevention.

Hathazi, D., Lankenau, S., Sanders, B., and Bloom, J. (2009). Pregnancy and sexual health among homeless young injection drug users. *Journal of Adolescence, 32*(2), 339–55.

Health Canada. (2002a). *HIV/AIDS Epi update: Prevalent HIV infections in Canada: Up to one-third may not be diagnosed*. Ottawa: Centre for Infectious Disease Prevention and Control.

Health Canada. (2002b). *HIV/AIDS Epi update: HIV and AIDS among youth in Canada*. Ottawa: Centre for Infectious Disease Prevention and Control.

Heerde, J., and Hemphill, S. (2014). A systematic review of associations between perpetration of physically violent behaviours and property offenses, victimization and use of substances among homeless youth, *Children and Youth Services Review, 44*, 265–77

Hyde, J. (2005). From home to street: Understanding young people's transitions into homelessness. *Journal of Adolescence, 28*, 171–83.

Ijadi-Maghsoodi, R. Bath, E., Cook, M., Textor, L., and Barnert, E. (2018). Commercially sexually exploited youths' health care experiences, barriers and recommendations: A qualitative analysis. *Child Abuse and Neglect, 76*, 334–41.

Janus, M.D., Archambault, F.X., Brown, S.W., and Welsh, L.A. (1995). Physical abuse in Canadian runaway adolescents. *Child Abuse and Neglect, 19*(4), 433–47.

Johnson, K.D., Whitbeck, L.B., and Hoyt, D.R. (2005). Predictors of social network composition among homeless and runaway adolescents. *Journal of Adolescence, 28*, 231–48.

Karabanow, J. (2004). Changing faces: The story of two Canadian street youth shelters. *International Journal of Social Welfare, 13*(4), 304–14.

Kidd, S.A. (2003). Street youth: Coping and interventions. *Child and Adolescent Social Work Journal, 20*(4), 235–61.

Kidd, S.A. (2006). Factors precipitating suicidality among homeless youth: A quantitative follow-up. *Youth and Society, 37*(4), 393–422.

Kipke, M., Montgomery, S., Simon, T., and Iverson, E. (1996, July). *Homeless youth: Variations in HIV risk according to peer group affiliation.* Paper presented at the International Journal on AIDS XI, Vancouver.

Kral, A.H., Lorvick, J., and Edlin, B.R. (1999, August). *Differences between young and old injection drug users in San Francisco* (Abstract 533). Paper presented at the National HIV Prevention Conference, Atlanta, GA.

Kraus, D., Eberle, M., and Serge, L. (2001). *Environmental scan on youth homelessness.* Ottawa: Canada Mortgage and Housing Corporation.

Kufeldt, K., and Burrows, B.A. (1994). *Issues affecting public policies and services for homeless youth.* Calgary: University of Calgary.

Kufeldt, K., and Nimmo, M. (1987). Youth on the street: Abuse and neglect in the Eighties. *Child Abuse and Neglect, 11*, 531–43.

Kulik, D., Gaetz, S., Crowe, C., and Ford-James, E. (2011). Homeless youth's overwhelming health burden: A review of the literature. *Paediatrics & Child Health, 16*(6), 43–7.

Larke, B. (2001). *HIV/AIDS surveillance.* Edmonton: Alberta Health, Disease Control and Prevention.

Leach, M.P., Wolitski, R.J., Goldbaum, G.M., Fishbein, M., and the AIDS Community Demonstration Projects. (1997). HIV risk and sources of information among urban street youth. *Psychology, Health and Medicine, 2*(2), 119–34.

Lenz-Rashid, S. (2006). Employment experiences of homeless young adults: Are they different for youth with a history of foster care? *Children and Youth Services Review, 28*, 236–59.

Leslie, B., and Hare, F. (2000). *Improving the outcomes for youth in transition from care.* Toronto: Working Group of the Children's Aid Society of Toronto, Covenant House, and Ryerson University Research Project.

McCarter, B. (2010, November 18). Growing up on streets trumps dysfunctional home life; Family dynamics—not drugs or alcohol—is the main reason why thousands of teens choose to run away from home. *Vancouver Sun,* p. A17.

McCay, E., and Aiello, A. (2013). The need for early mental health intervention to strengthen resilience in street-involved youth. In S. Gaetz, B. O'Grady, K. Buccieri, J. Karabanow, and A. Marsolais (Eds), *Youth homelessness in Canada: Implications for policy and practice* (pp. 229–42). Toronto: Canadian Homelessness Research Network Press.

Maccio, E. and Ferguson, K. (2016). Services to LGBTQ runaway and homeless youth: Gaps and recommendations. *Children and Youth Services Review, 63*, 47–57.

McCormack, A., Janus, M.D., and Burgess, A.W. (1986). Runaway youths and sexual victimization: Gender differences in an adolescent runaway population. *Child Abuse and Neglect, 10*, 387–95.

MacDonald, S. & Roebuck, B. (2018). *Staying alive while living the life: Adversity, strength, and resilience in the lives of homeless youth.* Winnipeg, MB: Fernwood.

McIntyre, S. (1999). The youngest profession—the oldest profession: A study of sex work. In C. Bagley and K. Mallick (Eds), *Child sexual abuse and adult offenders: New theory and research* (pp. 159–92). Aldershot, UK: Ashgate.

MacLaurin, B., and Bala, N. (2004). Children in care. In N. Bala, M.K. Zapf, R.J. Williams, R. Vogl, and J.P. Hornick (Eds), *Canadian child welfare law* (pp. 111–38). Toronto: Thompson Educational.

MacLaurin, B., Johansson, B., McDonald, M., and Soenen, D. (2018). Recurrence of street-involvement: Exploring the experiences of Calgary youth. *Wood's Home Journal Evidence to Practice, 2*(1), 13–21.

MacLaurin, B., Trocmé, N., Fallon, B., McCormack, M., Pitman, L., Forest, N., . . . Perrault, E. (2006). *Alberta incidence study of reported child abuse and neglect—2003 (AIS-2003), Major findings report.* Calgary: University of Calgary, Faculty of Social Work.

McLean, L. (2005). *Seeking sanctuary: An exploration of the realities of youth homelessness in Calgary—2005.* Calgary: Broadview Applied Research Group.

Marshall, B.D.L., Kerr, T., Qi, J., Montaner, J.S.G., and Wood, E. (2010). Public injecting and HIV risk behaviour among street-involved youth. *Drug and Alcohol Dependence, 110*, 254–8.

Milburn, N.G., Rotheram-Borus, M.J., Batterham, P., Brumback, B., Rosenthal, D., and Mallett, S. (2005). Predictors of close family relationships over one year among homeless young people. *Journal of Adolescence, 28*, 263–79.

Miller, D., Miller, D., Hoffman, F., and Duggan, R. (1980). *Runaways—illegal aliens in their own land: Implications for practice.* Westport: Praeger.

Min Park, J., Metraux, S., and Culhane, D.P. (2005). Childhood out-of-home placement and dynamics of public shelter utilization among young homeless adults. *Children and Youth Services Review, 27*(5), 533–46.

National Alliance to End Homelessness (NAEH). (2012) *An emerging framework for ending unaccompanied youth homelessness*. Washington: National Alliance to End Homelessness, Retrieved from https://endhomelessness.org/resource/an-emerging-framework-for-ending-unaccompanied-youth-homelessness/

Nichols, N. (2013). Nobody signs out of care: Exploring institutional links between child protection services and homelessness, In N.S. Gaetz, B., O'Grady, K. Buccieri, J. Karabanow, and A. Marsolais (Eds), *Youth Homelessness in Canada: Implications for policy and practice* (pp. 75–94). Toronto: Canadian Homelessness Research Network Press.

Nova Scotia Housing and Homelessness Network. (2012). *Halifax report card on homelessness in 2012*. Halifax: Nova Scotia Housing and Homelessness Network.

O'Grady, B., and Bright, R. (2002). Squeezed to the point of exclusion: The case of Toronto squeegee cleaners. In J. Hermer and J. Mosher (Eds), *Disorderly people: Law and politics of exclusion in Ontario* (pp. 79–90). Halifax: Fernwood.

O'Grady, B., Bright, R., and Cohen, E. (1998). Sub-employment and street youths: An analysis of the impact of squeegee cleaning on homeless youths. *Security Journal, 11*, 315–23.

O'Grady, B., Gaetz, S., and Buccieri, K. (2013). Policing street youth in Toronto, In S. Gaetz, B., O'Grady, K. Buccieri, J. Karabanow, and A. Marsolais, (Eds), *Youth homelessness in Canada: Implications for policy and practice* (pp. 335–52). Toronto: Canadian Homelessness Research Network Press.

O'Grady, B., and Greene, C. (2003). A social and economic impact study of the Ontario Safe Streets Act on Toronto squeegee workers. *Online Journal of Justice Studies 1*(1). Retrieved from http://web.archive.org/web/20060113223626/ojjs.icaap.org/issues/1.1/ogrady-greene.html

Pennbridge, J., MacKenzie, R.G., and Swofford, A. (1991). Risk profile of homeless pregnant adolescents and youth. *Journal of Adolescent Health, 12*, 534–8.

Peressini, T., McDonald, L., and Hulchanski, D. (1995). *Estimating homelessness: Towards a methodology for counting the homeless in Canada—Background report*. Toronto: Centre for Applied Social Research.

Perlman, S., Willard, J., Herbers, J., Cutuli, J., and Eyrich-Garg, K. (2014). Youth homelessness: Prevalence and mental health correlates. *Journal of the Society for Social Work and Research, 5*(3), 361–77.

Public Health Agency of Canada. (2006a). *Sexually transmitted infections in Canadian street youth: Findings from enhanced surveillance of Canadian street youth, 1999–2003* (No. HP5-14/2006). Ottawa: Minister of Health.

Public Health Agency of Canada. (2006b). *Street youth in Canada: Findings from enhanced surveillance of Canadian street youth, 1999–2003* (No. HP5-15/2006). Ottawa: Minister of Health.

Radford, J.L., King, A.J.C., and Warren, W.K. (1989). *Street youth and aids*. Ottawa: Health and Welfare Canada.

Raising the Roof. (2009). *Youth homelessness in Canada: The Road to Solutions*. Toronto: Raising the Roof Organization.

Ray, J. (1993). Survival methods of young street mothers. *Child and Adolescent Social Work Journal, 10*(3), 189–205.

Rees, G. (1993). *Hidden truths: Young people's experiences of running away*. London: Children's Society.

Reilly, T. (2003). Transition from care: Status and outcomes of youth who age out of foster care. *Child Welfare, 82*(6), 727–46.

Robert, M., Pauze, R., and Fournier, L. (2005). Factors associated with homelessness of adolescents under supervision of the youth protection system. *Journal of Adolescence, 28*, 215–30.

Rotheram-Borus, M.J., Mahler, K.A., Koopman, C., and Langabeer, K. (1996). Sexual abuse history and associated multiple risk behaviour in adolescent runaways. *American Journal of Orthopsychiatry, 66*(3), 390–400.

Roy, E., Haley, N., Leclerc, P., Boivin, J.F., Cedras, L., and Vincelette, J. (2001). Risk factors for hepatitis C virus infection among street youths. *Canadian Medical Association Journal, 165*(5), 557–60.

Roy, E., Haley, N., Leclerc, P., Cedras, L., and Boivin, J.F. (2002). Drug injection among street youth: The first time. *Addiction, 97*(8), 1003–10.

Sapiro, B., Johnson, L., Postmus, J., and Simmel, C. (2016). Supporting youth involved in domestic minor sex trafficking: Divergent perspectives on youth agency, *Child Abuse and Neglect, 58*, 99–110.

Schelbe, L. (2018). Struggles, successes, and setbacks: Youth aging out of child welfare in a subsidized housing program, *Children and Youth Services Review, 89*, 298–308.

Schneiderman, D. (2002). The constitutional disorder of the Safe Streets Act: A federalism analysis. In J. Hermer and J. Mosher (Eds), *Disorderly people: Law and politics of exclusion in Ontario* (pp. 79–90). Halifax: Fernwood.

Semanchin-Jones, A., Bowen, E., and Ball, A. (2018). School definitely failed me: Identifying opportunities to impact educational outcomes for homeless and child welfare-involved youth. *Children and Youth Services Review, 91*, 66–76.

Seven Cities on Housing and Homelessness. (2018). *2018 Alberta point-in-time homeless count technical report*. Calgary: Turner Strategies

Slesnick, N., Zhang, J., and Brakenhoff, B. (2017). Personal control and service connection as paths to improved mental health and exiting homelessness among severely marginalized homeless youth, *Children and Youth Services Review, 73*, 121–7

Slonim-Nevo, V., Ozawa, M.N., and Auslander, W.F. (1991). Knowledge, attitudes and behaviors related to AIDS among youth in residential centers: Results from an exploratory study. *Journal of Adolescence, 14*(1), 17–33.

St Lawrence, J.S., Crosby, R.A., and O'Brannon III, R. (1999). Adolescent risk for HIV infection: Comparison of four high risk samples. *Journal of HIV/AIDS Prevention and Education for Adolescents and Children, 3*(3), 63–86.

Sullivan, T.R. (1996). The challenges of HIV prevention among high-risk adolescents. *Health and Social Work, 21*(1), 58–65.

Swart-Kruger, J., and Richer, L.M. (1997). AIDS-related knowledge, attitudes and behaviour among South African street youth: Reflections on power, sexuality and the autonomous self. *Social Science and Medicine, 45*(6), 957–67.

Thompson, S., Bender, K., Lewis, C., and Watkins, R. (2008). Runaway and pregnant: Risk factors associated with pregnancy in a national sample of runaway/homeless female adolescents. *Journal of Adolescent Health, 43*(2), 125–32.

Thompson, S.J., McManus, H., Lantry, J., Windsor, L., and Flynn, P. (2006). Insights from the street: Perceptions of services and providers by homeless young adults. *Evaluation and Program Planning, 29*, 34–43.

Thompson, S.J., Zittel-Palamara, K.M., and Maccio, E.M. (2004). Runaway youth utilizing crisis shelter services: Predictors of presenting problems. *Child and Youth Care Forum, 33*(6), 387–404.

Thrane, L.E., Hoyt, D.R., Whitbeck, L.B., and Yoder, K.A. (2006). Impact of family abuse on running away, deviance, and street victimization among homeless rural and urban youth. *Child Abuse and Neglect, 30*, 1117–28.

Toro, P., Lesperance, T., and Braciszewski, J. (2011, September). *The heterogeneity of homeless youth in America: Examining typologies.* Homeless Research Institute, National Alliance to End Homelessness. Retrieved from https://b.3cdn.net/naeh/29187fa2fa05e03e4a_ysm6b8861.pdf

Tutty, L., Bradshaw, C., Waegemakers-Schiff, J., Worthington, C., MacLaurin, B., Hewson, J., . . . McLeod, H. (2010). *Risks and assets for homelessness prevention: A literature review for the Calgary homeless foundation.* Calgary: University of Calgary.

Tyler, K.A., and Cauce, A.M. (2002). Perpetrators of early physical and sexual abuse among homeless and runaway adolescents. *Child Abuse and Neglect, 26*, 1261–74.

Tyler, K.A. Cauce, A.M., and Whitbeck, L.B. (2004). Family risk factors and prevalence of dissociative symptoms among homeless and runaway youth. *Child Abuse and Neglect, 28* 355–66.

Tyler, K.A., and Johnson, K.A. (2006). Pathways in and out of substance use among homeless-emerging adults. *Journal of Adolescent Research, 21*(2), 133–57.

Unger, J.B., Simon, T.R., Newman, T.L., Montgomery, S.B., Kipke, M.D., and Albornoz, M. (1998). Early adolescent street youth: An overlooked population with unique problems and service needs. *Journal of Early Adolescence, 18*(4), 325–48.

Weber, A.E., Boivin, J.F., Blais, L., Haley, N., and Roy, E. (2002). HIV risk profile and prostitution among female street youths. *Journal of Urban Health, 79*(4), 525–35.

Whitbeck, L.B., Chen, X., Hoyt, D.R., Tyler, K.A., and Johnson, K.D. (2004). Mental disorder, subsistence strategies, and victimization among gay, lesbian, and bisexual homeless and runaway adolescents. *Journal of Sex Research, 41*(4), 329–42.

Whitmore, E., and McKee, C. (2001). Six street youth who could . . . In P. Reasor and H. Bradbury (Eds), *Handbook of action research: Participative inquiry and practice* (pp. 396–402). London: Sage.

Wong, C., Clark, L., and Marlotte, L. (2014). The impact of specific and complex trauma on the mental health of homeless youth. *Journal of Interpersonal Violence, 31*(5), 831–54.

Worthington, C., MacLaurin, B., Huffey, N., Dittmann, D., Kitt, O., Patten, S., and Leech, J. (2008). *Calgary, youth, health and the street—Final report.* Calgary: University of Calgary.

Wright, J.D. (1991). Health and the homeless teenager: Evidence from the National Health Care for the Homeless Program. *Journal of Health and Social Policy, 2*(4), 15–35.

Yoder, K.A., Hoyt, D.R., and Whitbeck, L.B. (1998). Suicidal behaviour among homeless and runaway adolescents. *Journal of Youth and Adolescence, 27*(6), 753–71.

Yoder, K.A., Whitbeck, L.B., and Hoyt, D.R. (2003). Gang involvement and membership among homeless and runaway youth. *Youth and Society, 34*(4), 441–67.

Youth Involvement in Systems of Sex Work and Strategies of Intervention

Kelly Gorkoff, Anne Miller, Chloe Shepherd, and Courtenay Bolton

14

Overview

This chapter offers an overview of the complex topic of young people involved in systems of sex work and sexual exploitation. It reviews and critically assesses the legal and governmental regulation of youth, including special legislative responses aimed at assisting youth. The chapter also addresses the lived experience of youth who are involved in the sex trade. In addition, we review terminology, social structural factors shaping sex work and youths engagement therein, and the health and safety risks that accompany sex work involvement for youth.

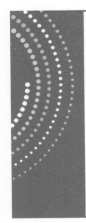

Key Objectives

After reading this chapter, you should be able to:

- Understand the different terminology used to describe young people involved in sex work and sexual exploitation.
- Understand the social structural conditions that define sex work and sexual exploitation.
- Identify the policy regulations for young people involved in sex work and sexual exploitation.
- Understand the experiences of youth involved in the sex trade.
- Identify the needs of young people and programming responses to these needs.

Introduction

Making sense of young people involved in systems of sex work is not easy, as the role of sex work in society is deeply stigmatized and precarious. Sex work has been variously thought of and given different names and roles in the social landscape, from "the world's oldest profession" to "survival sex" to the abhorrent "exploitation," "trafficking," and abuse of women and men. For many years, prostitution was deemed a moral crime but was generally tolerated as something that happens with some degree of regularity and normalcy. And although we have special criminal legislation regulating sex work and such work has never been fully accepted, it has also never been fully rejected.

Initially, adults involved in the sex trade were thought to be independent choice makers, and although prostitution itself was never illegal in Canada, communicating for the purposes of prostitution was illegal. This changed with the landmark Bedford decision in 2013 (*Canada v. Bedford 2013*), when it was decided that the existing laws violated the security-of-person provision ensured by section 7 of Canada's Charter of Rights and Freedoms. After this decision, the federal government passed Bill C-36, legislating that individuals communicating and performing the commercial exchange of sex were no longer criminalized. Instead, following the **Nordic model**, only the clients who purchase sexual services are penalized criminally. The Bedford decision and subsequent legislative changes have not directly impacted youth, as young people are not governed under the same provisions as adults. However, some have argued that the new legislation has resulted in youth, particularly young men involved in the sex trade, being more hidden than they were under previous legislation (McIntyre and Miller 2016).

The issue of youth involved in systems of sex work—referred to henceforth as the **sexual exploitation trade** (SET)—gained prominence in the 1980s with the Badgley Report (1985) and has since evolved as understanding and terminology has shifted. Badgley suggested that "youth prostitution is the sexual abuse of a young person rather than a case of delinquency by a youth" (Badgley 1985, p. 4). This paradigm remains dominant today. The term *youth sex work* is used synonymously with **sexual exploitation** as developing young people are seen to have less objective choice in sex trade involvement than adults. In response, legislation is used as a way to rescue and protect a vulnerable population from

Nordic model
An approach to legislating sex trade activities that criminalizes the demand side (the buying of sex) and third-party profit from prostitution without imposing punishment for selling sex.

sexual exploitation trade (SET)
A term for the systems of sex work and the sex trade industry.

sexual exploitation
The abuse, particularly of children and youth, through the exchange of sexual activity for money, drugs, and/or basic needs.

harm rather than regulate an economic activity. Generally speaking, children/youth have special protections under Canadian law and are immune from prosecution and criminalization for any crimes, including those related to the SET. There is also significant overlap with **child welfare** legislation, and many provinces have adopted specialized legislative initiatives to address the sexual exploitation of young people in Canada.

Painting a Picture—Commercialized Sexual Labour and Exploitation

What is sex work and how is it different from exploitation? What does it look like, how does it happen, and what do we know about it? What motivates people to become involved, especially young people? In many ways, it is difficult to separate the emotion and feelings involved in the commercial sexual exchanges from public morality, moral conceptions of childhood and sex, and all the politics therein. There are conflicting and diverse accounts of definitions, terminology, and conceptualizations of young people's engagement in the commercial exchange of sex. Media accounts, movies and television shows, government reports, and research findings all use slightly different lenses to frame and understand sex work. In the following section, we will talk about terminology and the social factors that shape the concept of sex work/exploitation, as well as ideas about causation.

A History of Terminology: What's in a Name?

The words and phrases we use to make sense of a social problem give it meaning. Foucault (1978) refers to this as "discourse," and argues that it is both an instrument and an effect of power. He says it is in discourse that power and knowledge are joined together and that when discourse is used, so is power. The terminology used to define an issue is therefore important to consider, as it impacts what gets revealed and what gets concealed based on the power exerted through discourse.

To provide a snapshot of the ways in which Canadian media shapes terminology regarding sex-trade-involved youth, Hilario, Saewyc, Matthews, Rivers, Hirakta, and Miller (2013) analyzed 853 Canadian newspaper articles from 1989 to 2008 and found that

> Sexually exploited adolescents were commonly described as *children* or the more casual or patronizing, *kids* in nearly half the articles (46.2%); as *youth or young* in 42.5% and as underage in 7.4%. They were described less commonly as *victims* (in 21.3%) although just 16.5% of the articles explicitly used the term *exploited or exploitation* to describe them as victims. However, they were also labelled as *workers* in 13.8% of the stories while the word *prostitute(s)* was explicitly mentioned in 33.2% of the stories. In some articles, they even used slang terms for sex workers such as *hooker*, although this was less common after 2000. (p. 9)

This passage suggests that the ways in which youth involved in the SET are discussed and described in Canadian media are greatly varied. It is also important to note that

child welfare
In Canada, this term is used to describe a set of government and private services intended to protect children and encourage family stability. The main purpose of these services is to safeguard children from abuse and neglect. One of the primary activities of the child welfare agencies is the investigation of allegations of abuse and neglect.

although there are a number of terms used by the media to discuss youth sex work, there are also a number of terms which are often not mentioned. For example, few Canadian media stories have accurately portrayed sexual exploitation as a crime against children and youth (Hilario et al. 2013, p. 101), and while 93 per cent of articles mentioned girls as victims of exploitation, fewer than 30 per cent mentioned boys.

When it comes to the ways in which Canadian scholars have been shaping youth sex work terminology, the definitions are often just as diverse. Most commonly, theories refer to youth engaged in the sex industry as *sexually exploited youth* as opposed to *prostitutes* or *sex workers*. According to Kidd and Liborio (2011) this may be due to a perceived need to not legitimize what should be regarded as victimization or abuse. Others choose to utilize the terms *commercial sexual exploitation* or *sex trade involved youth*. In this way, the scholarly literature diverges significantly from what has been provided by the news media, as there is a far greater emphasis on exploitation and victimhood in the scholarly community. Gorkoff (2011) claims that young people involved in prostitution are most often studied as victims of sexual exploitation and abuse or as deviant and "at risk." The resulting dialogue is one of victimization by social circumstance—including neglectful families, poor socialization, and improper schooling—or by predatory sex offenders. Since 1990, youth involved in the SET have been almost exclusively defined via risk factors for SET involvement, such as dropping out of school, running away from home, and a history with child welfare agencies (Biehal and Wade 1990; Brannigan and Van Brunschot 1997; Hagan and McCarthy 1997; Heerde, Scholes-Balog, and Hemphill 2015; Kidd 2006; Kidd and Liborio 2011). Vaughan (2000) claims that while this is not specifically problematic, it shifts focus away from the systemic and structural causes (i.e., social class and race and other spaces of vulnerability) of youth sexual exploitation. Emphasizing individual responsibility and individualized risk-management strategies burdens youth with becoming responsible for managing their own risk, which is a daunting and problematic task (see also Mann, Senn, Girard, and Ackbar 2007). Many times, this focus on individual risk factors lacks a social justice perspective.

The issue of young people in systems of exploitive sex work took the global stage beginning in the late 1990s and continuing into the 2000s. Saunders (2005) examines how, during that period, the language used to describe child/youth prostitution changed from an identity—*a youth prostitute*—to an acronym—CSEC, *the commercial sexual exploitation of children*. This term developed as a result of coalitions, working groups, and international non-governmental organizations (NGOs) that were curiously similar to the purity and philanthropic movements at the turn of the century. As a predominant group in the early 2000s, Save the Children Canada noted in an important project titled *Out of the Shadows and into the Light*,

> The term child or youth prostitute can no longer be used. These children and youth are sexually exploited and any language or reference to them must reflect that belief. We declare that the commercial exploitation of children and youth is a form of child abuse and slavery. (Bramly, Tubman, Pearson, and Kingsley 2001, p. 8)

The dominant terminology has now increasingly included the term *trafficking*. Bruckert and Parent (2004) and Benoit, Ouellet, Jansson, Magnus, and Smith (2017) express concern about how the term is used as a catch-all to refer to *all* youth involved in systems of sex work and exploitation. They and other authors caution that examining the issue in this way conflates and distorts the reality of those involved in systems of sexual exploitation and supports reactive, not proactive solutions (Lowman 2013, 2016). Further, the term *trafficking* supports the notion of a blameless "perfect victim." When compared to the lived experiences of those in the SET, the majority of individuals do not meet the standard of trafficking set out in legislation, which often restricts the assistance they are able to receive (Berlatsky 2015; Davies 2015). Generally speaking, Davies (2015) argues that in the new discourse we are encouraged to vilify villains and rescue victims, which she claims oversimplifies complex issues and forces a "pro and con structure" onto complex moral and political questions (p. 79).

Social Structural Factors Shaping the SET for Youth

In the sex work literature, initiation into the sex trade is often thought to occur through predisposing factors rooted deep in the structure of society, including childhood disadvantage, poverty, abuse, and neglect (Benoit et al. 2017). The definition of sexual exploitation is best conceptualized on a continuum. It ranges from sexual slavery to **survival sex** (see Box 14.1) to the more bourgeois styles of sex trade, like escort services, where both

> **survival sex**
> The exchange of sexual services for food, shelter, and other necessities, or for money to purchase food/shelter/necessities.

Box 14.1 | Youth Justice in Action

Survival Sex and Surviving

In most of the research reviewed in this chapter, young people consider their involvement in the sex trade not as a choice but rather as a means of survival. Surviving means having the necessities of life, including food, shelter, and safety. It is clear that some youth are more in need of providing for their own survival because they do not have support from others, such as family. There are a myriad of reasons why youth engage in sex for survival. The majority of research reviewed indicates that the SET is initially viewed by youth as a short-term method for having basic needs met. Lack of employable skills and marginalization increase the likelihood of engaging in the exchange of sex for money or other necessities longer term. While the term *survival sex* is often associated with vulnerability and victimhood, it can also be used to emphasize agency and active control over one's situation. For example, Ferris (2008)

challenges us to think about survival sex as akin to a streetfighter whose daily struggles to survive illustrate the pervasive effects of racism and misogyny. Therefore, in addition to thinking of survival sex as a form of victimization, we can think about it, as the name implies, as a solution for survivors trapped in traumatic and dreadful situations.

Critical Thinking Question

Given the discussion above about survival sex work, what should this mean for those who want to end "sexual exploitation" or intervene with youth involved in survival sex? What policy recommendations best fit this contention?

adults are consenting, albeit in a way that is shaped by their gender, sexuality, occupation, ethnicity, socio-economic status, and cultural values (Lowman 2000). Primarily due to municipal regulation, youth are less often found in off-street sex work such as escort services or exotic dancing, meaning they primarily work on the street, online, or in non-regulated off-street work such as gang houses, trick pads, or drug houses.

How Many and Who?

Partly due to differing definitions and partly due to the underground nature of sex trade involvement and its associated stigma, there are no concrete reliable statistics that reflect the number of youth involved in, and exploited through, prostitution. Goldenberg et al. (2014) report that 20 to 40 per cent of sex workers initiate sex work as adolescents. A landmark study in Vancouver estimated that on any given night there were 30 to 40 youth working the street and the average age of entry was 16.3 for girls and 15.6 for males (McCarthy 1995). An outreach program in Saskatoon suggested that 93 children under the age of 18 were on the street on any given night (Thibodeau 1996). The Manitoba government reported that the average age of entry is 13 to 14 (Manitoba Family Services and Housing 2008) and Benoit et al. (2017) found that the average age of entry is 24, with 29 per cent of their research sample engaging in sex work prior to the age of 19. McIntyre's (2002, 2005, 2009) research on males involved in the SET found that 73 per cent of her sample entered the sex trade before age 18. The federal government reports the average age of entry as between 16 and 20 (Cool 2004).

Gender
Research consistently finds that more girls than boys are exploited through prostitution. Benoit and Shaver (2006) report that males make up 10 to 25 per cent of the trade, but research on boys is more difficult to locate. In a review of the literature, Dennis (2008) finds that "the teenage boy sex-worker is subject to redoubled invisibility, his gender and his age causing him to virtually vanish from scholarly scrutiny" (p. 21). In Canada, this gap is partly filled by the important work of Susan McIntyre (see Box 14.2)

Indigenous Peoples and the SET
In the same way that Indigenous individuals are overrepresented in Canada's correctional systems, they are also estimated to be overrepresented in the SET (Sethi 2007). Due to the marginalized location of Indigenous people in Canadian society and the history of colonization and the combined effects of poverty, racial discrimination, and cultural losses, it is argued Indigenous women and girls are the most vulnerable to exploitation (Farley, Lynne, and Cotton 2005). While exact numbers are not possible to obtain, a 2005 study by Farley and Lynne found that 52 per cent of their 100 street-based Vancouver sex-worker study participants were Indigenous, while approximately 1.7 per cent of Vancouver's general population were Indigenous. This is a significant overrepresentation. McIntyre (2009) found that 61 per cent of the 157 youths interviewed identified themselves as Indigenous. Indigenous young men are at an alarmingly high risk of entering the SET and the criminal justice system. According to reports by Save the Children, Indigenous women account

Box 14.2 | Youth Justice in Action

McIntyre's *Under the Radar*

In Susan McIntyre's 1999 and 2002 research on sexual exploitation, she found that the issue of sexual exploitation had focused primarily on the female perspective. It was for this reason that the study *Under the Radar: The Sexual Exploitation of Young Men in Western Canada* was launched in the provinces of Alberta, British Columbia, Saskatchewan, and Manitoba. A total of 157 young men currently or formerly involved in the sex trade in the four Western provinces of Canada were interviewed. One key finding was that 61 per cent of the 157 young men interviewed identified as Indigenous. Thirty-five per cent of all the respondents indicated that they had completed high school, while 10 per cent had completed either college- or university-level programs. On the other hand, 15 per cent of the total number of respondents indicated they had only completed grade school. Over 83 per cent of the young men

had the experience of being runaways, throwaways, or both. Seventy-five per cent of respondents in all four Western provinces identified themselves as having been sexually abused prior to their involvement with the sex trade, and 79 per cent reported having a background of involvement with the police. In summary, this population is characterized by several risk factors, such as a history of abuse, criminal activity, community disorder, and running away and/or being thrown away.

Critical Thinking Question
Why do you think boys have been less often studied as involved in the SET? Why might that be concerning? How much do you think "gender" matters to those involved in the SET?

---

for up to 70 per cent of visible street-based survival sex work in Canadian cities (Chettiar, Shannon, Wood, Zhang, and Kerr 2010).

Additionally, Farley et al. (2005) report that First Nations women involved in the SET, when compared with non-First Nations women with the same involvement, report higher rates of violence within their lives before and after initiation into prostitution. Research has shown that as a result of policing, youth and Indigenous females are significantly more likely than their older and non-Indigenous counterparts to be pushed to working in isolated and potentially unsafe areas away from health and support services (Chettiar et al. 2010). Indigenous girls and women are also more likely to be trafficked for sexual exploitation in Canada, which may be due to their lower socio-economic status, isolation, drug abuse, and gang involvement (Hilario et al. 2013, p. 96). As Lynne (1998) argued 20 years ago,

Historical patriarchal and capitalist relations subjugated First Nations women collectively. This collective sexual oppression based on gender, created our inferiority as a class of people to both First Nations men and non-First Nations men. The sexual domination of First Nations women has remained unabated to the present-day due to patriarchy's stronghold. Thus, it has had and continues to have, profound and prolonged injurious consequences in First Nations women's lives. When sexual oppression is intersected by racism, and capitalism, the wounding worsens. (p. 2)

According to Hunt (2013), poor quality of life is prevalent in many Indigenous communities, which can contribute to the level of choice Indigenous people can exercise about whether or not to engage in sex work. For instance, those in Northern and isolated communities who lack transportation may exchange sex for a ride into a nearby town. Some argue that these conditions have led Indigenous women—as well as men and transgender people—to enter sex work without a real choice (Fletcher 2013).

Davies (2015) adds that none of the theoretical and philosophical positions used to understand the SET do justice to the historical and contemporary role of sexual commerce and violence in settler colonialism. Centuries of economic disruption, the Indian Act and the reservation system, environmental racism and the horrors of the residential school system make Indigenous communities and individuals especially vulnerable to all sorts of exploitation. Further, Davies suggests that using a victimization lens to understand sex work—as is done in the Nordic model and the discourse predominating in the youth sex trade—can result in assimilation policy as such a lens does not consider or address the systemic and social exploitation that Indigenous people continue to face in Canada. This model, while appropriate in Nordic countries, does not work in a settler colonial society. When law reduces systemic causes of exploitation to individualized instances of criminal action, broader forms of marginalization are obscured. Hunt (2014) argues that more government regulation can impede Indigenous women, two-spirited people, and youth from claiming or reclaiming their sexual agency, and may advance ongoing processes of shame and degradation with respect to Indigenous identity (see also JJ 2013).

Sexuality

Other academics have noted the link between sex work involvement and sexual minority status (Frederick 2014; Lyons, Kerr, Duff, Feng, and Shannon 2014; Marshall, Shannon, Kerr, Zhang, and Wood 2010). To elaborate, LGBTQ youth are often considered to be a particularly vulnerable group within an already vulnerable group of homeless young people (Frederick 2014). Homeless sexual minority youth are also overrepresented among homeless youth, and it has been suggested that this is due to LGBTQ youth leaving home due to their parents' disapproval of their sexuality (Frederick 2014). Once on the street, LGBTQ youth often turn to survival sex in order to provide for themselves and meet their basic subsistence needs (Frederick 2014). Over 10 per cent of homeless female youth and 50 per cent of homeless sexual minority male youth reported exchanging sex for money or basic needs (Marshall et al. 2010). Lyons et al. (2014) found that lesbian and bisexual youth often face a dual stigma associated with both their sexual minority status and their involvement in the sex industry. This stigma can lead to mental health issues, drug abuse, and a heightened risk of victimization. Researchers have highlighted the importance of increased support for homeless and SET-involved LGBTQ youth, as their intersectional experiences often require more sensitive and diverse programming (Marshall et al. 2010).

While female sex workers experience a range of sexual identities, Dennis (2008) found that they are almost always assumed to be heterosexual and to usually engage in heterosexual activities. On the other hand, articles exploring male sex work always consider sexual orientation and identity in relation to sexual exploitation (Redwood 2013). The terms **gay for pay** and **straight for pay** refer to two experiences of those involved in the SET.

To Choose or Not to Choose: Literature on Causation

The question of choice, or choosing to involve oneself in sex work activities, can be misleading. Much of the Canadian literature that considers youth involvement in sex work is concerned with why and how young people enter the sex industry. It has examined child sexual abuse as a precursor to prostitution and considered issues of homelessness and running away as causes of involvement.

A number of researchers have claimed that sex trade initiation among youth may be the result of early childhood abuse or other early traumatic experiences (Brannigan and Van Brunschot 2002; Stoltz et al. 2007; Weber, Boivin, Blais, Haley, and Roy 2004; Wender, Wilson, Macphail, Orchard, and Farr 2014). In their research sample, Stoltz et al. (2007) found a high prevalence of abuse, an independent relationship between childhood emotional abuse and youth sex work involvement, and strong associations between sexual abuse and later sex work involvement. Tutty and Nixon (2003) report that of 54 female sex workers interviewed in their study, 61 per cent had some experience of sexual victimization in their childhood (p. 30). McIntyre (2009) reports that 75 per cent of her male respondents in all four Western provinces identified themselves as having been sexually abused prior to their involvement with the sex trade and 85 per cent had a history of physical abuse.

According to proponents of this perspective, childhood experiences often continue to shape people's behaviours, decisions, and identities throughout adulthood, and childhood experiences are profoundly impacted by familial context (Wender et al. 2014). It is therefore argued that if children are sexually abused, they will be taught to view themselves as sexually degraded, and will be more susceptible to sex trade involvement (Van Brunschot and Brannigan 2002).

This data is debated and contradicted by other studies that find there is no difference in levels of sexual abuse experiences among youth-sex-trade-involved youth and the population at large (Benoit et al. 2017). In particular, given that one in three women experience sexual assault in their childhood, the causal link between childhood experiences and experience in the SET should be read with caution. Though much of the research regarding sex work initiation has cited childhood abuse as a potential precursor for sex trade involvement—the link may not be direct (Weber et al. 2004). The causal nature of the link between trauma and experiences in the SET intersects with numerous factors, such as running away, a lack of viable alternatives for youth generally, and a failure of the child welfare system (Gorkoff and Waters 2003; Benoit et al. 2018; Benoit et al. 2017; Estes 2001). Thus, although a connection between abuse and SET involvement does exist, many researchers are cautious to come to any definitive conclusions without also considering other social and structural factors (Weber et al. 2004, p. 592).

gay for pay
A person who is heterosexual but who, in order to survive, will work in the SET as a homosexual. In McIntyre's *Under the Radar* study (2005), respondents reported that customers often found the perceived opportunity to alter a young man's heterosexual orientation very attractive.

straight for pay
A person who is homosexual but who, in order to survive, will work in the SET as a heterosexual.

What is overwhelmingly agreed upon in the literature, and confirmed in almost every study, are the economic factors that draw young people to the sex industry (Gorkoff and Runner 2003; Hein 2011; Kingsley and Mark 2000; McIntyre and Miller 2016; Sanders, Connelly, and King 2016; Tutty and Nixon 2003). Acquiring money is the number one motivating factor for becoming involved and for staying involved in the SET (Kidd and Liborio 2011). Many youth turn to sex work for survival as it is often the only available option for young people in positions of poverty. The reality for many youth who have been forced onto the street is a reliance on sex work in order to sustain themselves. Frederick (2014) claims that, given their limited mainstream employment prospects, homeless youth typically rely on a range of subsistence strategies to meet their needs—including employment (both formal and informal)—which often includes sex work in conjunction with other strategies. From this perspective, participation in SET results out of necessity due to homeless young people's low human capital and inadequate access to necessary public services (Frederick 2014). The three most commonly cited uses of money obtained through sex trade were for survival (food and shelter), drugs and alcohol, and the pursuit of what some thought would be a glamourous lifestyle (Tutty and Nixon 2003). In Benoit et al.'s 2017 research, participants identified three overlapping structural and agentic reasons for entry into the SET: critical life events, desire or need for money, and personal appeal of the work.

Davies (2015) reports that many sex-trade-involved youth come from families where street-based networks are common and pathways into sex trade work are easily accessible (e.g., marginalized and/or homeless families). Tutty and Nixon (2003) found that about one-third of the women in their sample had family members who were regularly street involved, and when their child was in need of money, the sex trade was a normalized path to obtaining it. This challenges the media's sensationalized idea of the pimp who coerces youth into involvement in the sex trade, as most research agrees that pathways of entry into the SET are laid by those already known by the individual. There is also considerable slippage between the idea of a pimp and a boyfriend, and research suggests that in circumstances where couples are on social assistance, the women often engage in sex work to make ends meet for the couple (Seshia 2005). Kidd and Liborio (2011) suggest that SET experiences are a function of the socio-cultural context from which they originate. In their qualitative study of young Canadians, pathways to sex work were facilitated through partners, friends, older sex workers, and sometimes pimps.

Once youth are on the street, drug use is often a motivating factor for them to get or stay involved in the SET, and researchers have found that the use of drugs more than two times per week increased the risk of initiation into prostitution by 2.7 times (Weber et al. 2004). Tutty and Nixon (2003) found that about half the women in their research used cocaine, solvents, and heroin on a regular basis, whereas the rest used marijuana and alcohol (p. 39). Substance abuse can thus be seen as being both a pathway to sexual exploitation and a coping mechanism for the trauma of sexual exploitation (Saewyc et al. 2008). Sustaining an addiction is also often a reason for continuing in the SET and a significant barrier to exiting from it (Seshia 2005).

Upon analyzing the economic cost benefit to estimate the lifelong effects for individuals who entered the sex industry as youths, DeRiviere (2006) found that sex workers retain only a small portion of their earnings after feeding drug addictions and other third parties. Further, after exiting the sex industry, former sex workers often face major challenges in rejoining the mainstream labour market (DeRiviere 2006). DeRiviere's findings suggest that after tallying the total personal benefits and costs, the costs of SET involvement far exceed the benefits over an individual's lifetime, and given this fact, policy-makers should direct their attention to counteracting the conditions of vulnerability that bring youth into the sex industry in the first place.

In examining the literature on reasons for SET entry, it is clear there is no one simple linear pathway. Vulnerability, trauma, substance use, poverty, and marginalization combine and compound to produce circumstances where SET involvement becomes more likely. As Lowman (1987) claimed over thirty years ago,

> Once we transcend a phenomenal level of analysis to consider the context of a youth's choice to sell sexual services, it becomes obvious that the choice must be located in the "wider origins of the deviant act," particularly the marginal position of youth in the labour force, and the patriarchal power structures both inside and outside the family. (p. 111)

Some literature examines larger socio-economic issues that create favourable conditions for youth sexual exploitation (Dauda 2010; Davies 2015; Gorkoff 2011). The context of sexuality, the sexualization of youthful bodies, and inequitable attitudes about male and female social roles contribute to a set of circumstances where sexual exploitation can occur, while also contributing to who is most vulnerable. This wider social construction of youth and sexuality also plays a role in creating demand. Examining the disenfranchisement of youth from institutional decision-making and labour market employment, the failure of social services to assist street youth, and the lack of a political will to enable families to provide quality care for their children is therefore imperative for understanding this issue. A lack of appropriate job opportunities and housing for youth combines with sexual demand for young people to make the sex trade appear a viable source of income and independence.

Life in the SET

While there is very little research that gives voice to young people's experiences in the SET, the existing literature reveals some consistent themes and experiences. Researching this population can be quite difficult because they often avoid authority figures and are difficult to find/contact. In addition, research ethics approval can be difficult to obtain because young people are considered a vulnerable population. What is presented below is a snapshot of those studies that were able to secure approval and connect with this particularly difficult group. The primary themes related to youth experiences in the SET that will be discussed are health; fatigue and hunger; sexually transmitted infections; identity and well-being; and violence. It is important to note that there is very little research on youth's participation with the online sex industry. We touch on this research in Box 14.3.

Box 14.3 | Youth Justice in Action

Going Online—the Digital Turn in the SET

Increasingly, the market for sex is moving online. From apps like "Grindr" that may introduce young men into "sugar daddy relationships" after plausible hookups, to sites that facilitate the selling of sex, the sexual exploitation of young people may be becoming even more invisible as their services move online. Online sex work is typically referred to as part of "off-street" sex work. Holger-Ambrose, Langmade, Edinburgh, and Saewyc (2013) suggest that most people involved in the SET use the Internet to sell sex. However, the extent of the involvement of young people in online work is unknown, representing a significant gap in the research.

From the buyer side, digital spaces provide greater anonymity, reducing the perceived stigma of buying sex. From the seller side, Minichiello, Scott, and Callandar (2013) suggest that the Internet is popular not only because of reduced stigma but also because of decreased probability of arrest and increased control over marketing and client selection. Sanders et al. (2016) suggest that the online medium gives individuals control over their working conditions, prices, clientele, and services sold. However, they also find that harassment and blackmail is significant within these new technologies.

Critical Thinking Question

Given the gap in knowledge about this significant area, how would you suggest a researcher should go about finding out the extent of this issue? What would be good methods for understanding the landscape of Internet work?

Impacts of Involvement in the SET: Fatigue, Homelessness, and Precarious Living Situations

absolute homelessness
A term used to refer to experiences of living on the street or in emergency shelters. *Relative homelessness* refers to experiences of being housed but at risk of losing housing or living in substandard housing. *Hidden or concealed homelessness* refers to living without a place of one's own (e.g., living in a car, with family or friends [couch surfing], or in a long-term institution).

Being on the run, homeless, or in precarious living circumstances can have a significant effect on individuals' health. Benoit and Millar (2001) found that, of the sex workers they surveyed, 36.6 per cent reported having significant sleep disturbances, 13 per cent had or were experiencing chronic fatigue-related disorders, and 12 per cent had eating disorders. Fifty per cent of the participants in Downe's (2003) study talked about vague ill-health and generalized fatigue due to SET involvement. Participants in both studies talked about the need for a safe place to sleep and take a break from pressures such as ill-health, violence, exploitation, and chronic drug use. Securing a place to sleep often goes hand in hand with accessing food, shelter, clothes, and showers. Some sex workers have reported using shelters, staying with family, or exchanging sexual services for a hotel room.

McIntyre (2009) reports that 64 per cent of her respondents had stayed in shelters. For many, this was the only option available to them. Entrance into, and continuation within, the SET often results in a distinct lack of options. Miller et al. (2011) found that 69 per cent of youth sex workers reported **absolute homelessness**, which was almost twice the rate of the adult sex worker population.

Sexually Transmitted Infections

A more extensive area of inquiry in the youth sex trade literature is the health risks and repercussions of sex work involvement. Farley et al.'s 2005 research with SET-involved individuals showed participants scoring exceptionally high on the "Chronic Health Problems" questionnaire, indicating that health problems continue and get worse the longer one is involved with the SET. Many researchers are especially concerned with the ways in which young sex workers are disproportionately vulnerable to HIV infection (Goldenberg et al. 2014; Lyons et al. 2014; Marshall et al. 2010; Mehradabi et al. 2008; Miller et al. 2011; Spittal et al. 2003; Weber et al. 2002). According to research conducted by Goldenberg et al. (2014), certain individual biological factors increase the risk of HIV transmission, such as the large areas of cervical ectopy and trauma to an immature genital tract experienced by younger women and girls during intercourse. Drug use, and especially injection drug use, is also understood to greatly increase the likelihood of HIV infection among youth involved in the SET (Weber, Boivin, Blais, Haley, and Roy 2002). Drug use may also contribute to increased likelihood of HIV infection by disinhibiting sexual behaviour, resulting in reduced condom and other safe sex negotiations (Weber et al. 2002).

Many researchers have discussed the link between sexual minority status and a host of unique health challenges. According to Marshall et al. (2010), not only are sexual minority youth more likely to engage in survival sex than their heterosexual counterparts, but they also demonstrate elevated HIV risk behaviour. To elaborate, research has shown that lesbian/bisexual sex workers are significantly more likely to inject drugs, to report inconsistent condom use with regular clients, to solicit clients in street-based venues (rather than formal sex work establishments), and to report incarceration and homelessness (Lyons et al. 2014). In addition, homophobia and non-acceptance are consistently found to have a significant psychological impact on young people and are strongly believed to be a cause of the particularly high rates of mental health problems and substance use among LGBTQ youth in the SET (Frederick 2014).

Despite these elevated health risks, young sex workers often face severely restricted access to health care services. Research conducted by Goldenberg et al. (2016) has cited the unequal access and retention in antiretroviral therapy for people living with HIV as a public health and human rights issue of paramount concern. According to their research, female sex workers experience a greatly elevated HIV burden in both concentrated and generalized HIV epidemics, as well as a multitude of structural barriers to HIV prevention and care, including high levels of violence, stigma, criminalization, and mobility. This means that despite the heavy HIV burden among sex workers, they are often excluded from accessing voluntary, confidential, and non-coercive health services, including HIV prevention, treatment, care, and support (Deering, Shoveller, Tyndall, Montaner, and Shannon 2011). This is especially true for young sex workers, as they often possess less human capital and health-related knowledge. O'Doherty (2011) suggests that criminalization and the quasi-legal status of sex work limits access to protective health services and therefore attaches a higher priority to punishment than public health.

Identity and Well-Being

The ability to have some semblance of control over one's life is strongly associated with a healthy identity and well-being. For marginalized and SET-involved youth, control is something that is lacking in their day-to-day experiences. When this is paired with the stigma associated with sex work, feeling good about oneself is often difficult (Hannem and Tigchelaar 2016). The majority of the young men in McIntyre and Miller's (2016) study reported that they did not enjoy working in the SET. They felt victimized or traumatized in the SET and consistently spoke about how they felt "awful, full of shame," as well as sick, dirty, drained, and burned out. Many participants in the study spoke about how they felt compromised, strange, or immoral about what they were doing. Downe and Mika's (2003) participants report similar negative emotions about themselves and suggest that it is a constant struggle to maintain one's self-sufficiency and mental health within the SET. In both studies, participants discussed disassociating psychologically from their working and living conditions.

Kidd's (2006) research on street youth and those in the SET suggests that many youth within it feel trapped. Kidd further exposes common experiences of loneliness, worthlessness, and negative memories. Of the 208 participants involved in Kidd's study, the majority experienced feelings related to **suicidality**. The degree of sex trade involvement was found to be related to feeling trapped and to suicide attempts.

Both Downe and Mika (2003) and MacIntyre and Miller (2016) found that youth involved in the SET linked their involvement to their identity and social group (particularly while on the street and/or homeless). Through their involvement in the SET, youth said they found camaraderie and a level of acceptance they had not previously known or that had been missing from their lives. These youth suggested that exploitation was a small price to pay for a sense of community and belonging. Social networks can provide a strong source of support for those who are sexually exploited (Agustin 2005, 2008). Kennedy et al.'s (2017) research with 130 street-involved youth in Canada found that most participants were embedded in supportive social relations on the street. Youth reported that these street-based social ties, while sometimes short-term, provided consistent deep and immediate social support in a diversity of areas.

Violence

Violence takes many forms for those in the SET. Being victimized by clients is the most predominate fear of those involved. Twenty-nine per cent of McIntyre's (2009) respondents indicated that their greatest fear was a "**bad date**," and 80 per cent had experienced one at some point. The threat of being beaten, raped, or attacked with a weapon was the most prominent fear reported by respondents in all four Western provinces. Women involved in the SET describe violence as an everyday occurrence (Nixon, Tutty, Downe, Gorkoff, and Ursel 2002). Over half of the women in Nixon et al.'s study reported experiencing violence from bad dates, including being stabbed or cut, raped, forced to engage in degrading sexual acts, kidnapped, beaten with objects, and having a gun held to their head. Many women discuss being hospitalized and experiencing serious injuries due to violence experienced in the SET (Tutty and Nixon 2003).

suicidality
The contemplation of taking one's own life.

bad date
An episode of harm enacted upon a sex worker by a client, including assault, sexual assault, incidents of theft, refusal of payment, threats, rudeness, time wasting, harassment, aggressive behaviour, etc. Bad dates that include physical assault can lead to harm so profound a sex worker dies.

Stigma and violence from the general public and police is also discussed in the literature (Comack and Seshia 2010; Davies 2015; Dennis 2008). See Box 14.4 for a more detailed discussion of stigma and the SET. Bruckert and Hannem (2013a, 2013b) argue that the stigma of the sex trade is reproduced in media, neighbourhood associations, and police services. From these perspectives, sex workers are believed to pose a risk to society, to be dirty vectors of disease, to be immoral and to threaten family values, and to be drug addicts and a disruptive presence in neighbourhoods. Bruckert and Hannem (2013) suggest that these forms of "common knowledge" get reproduced in judicial reasoning and encapsulated in judicial-legal discourse. It is hardly surprising that one of the challenges sex workers face in trying to maintain their personal safety is their reluctance to call the police due to fear of arrest or violence from the police (McIntyre 2009).

Marginalized groups overwhelmingly report a lack of confidence when dealing with police (O'Grady 2007). Sex workers specifically report a wide range of negative experiences

Box 14.4 | Youth Justice in Action

Stigma

The term *stigma* was used by sociologist Erving Goffman (1963) to define a social trait that shames and dishonours an individual or a group. There are several dimensions of stigma, such as stereotyping, labelling, status loss, and discrimination, and these are readily seen in a variety of discourses regarding the SET. Stigmas are typically regarded as having a negative impact on self-concept and identity formation (Corrigan and Miller 2004; Link and Phelan 2006; Scambler 2009). Benoit et al. (2015a, 2015b, 2017, 2018) argue that stigma is a fundamental determinant of behaviour, well-being, and health. Use of derogatory terms such as *whore, slut* and the like, which are often attached to the SET, have a significant negative impact on the well-being of sex workers and help to sustain social, political, and economic aspects of social inequality. Benoit, McCarthy, and Jansson (2015a) demonstrated strong associations between depression and sex work, and between discrimination and depression. Bruckert and Hannem (2013) extend the idea of stigma to the assumptions made in criminal and regulatory law, including child welfare acts and specialized legislation. They call this

"structural stigma" in reference to the reproduction of risk and immortality occurring as the result of enacting legislation that is inherently othering and moralizing.

An interesting variety of stigma is *courtesy stigma*, or *stigma by association*, which involves the public disapproval of associating with stigmatized persons. Phillips and Benoit (2013) found this to be a discernible feature of the everyday reality of people who work with sex workers, who experienced inconsistent social support from family and friends regarding their work activities, as well as feelings of being treated poorly by professionals in other service organizations and by the public at large (Phillips, Benoit, Hallgrimsdottir, and Vallance 2012).

Critical Thinking Question
Of the types of stigma discussed above, do you think they all have similar impacts or do you think one type may have more significant effects than other types?

with police (Benoit et al. 2016), from not having information about bad dates taken seriously (Bowen and Shannon 2009), to experiencing ticketing and arrests (Lewis, Shaver, and Maticka-Tyndale 2013). This lack of positive police attention is often attributed to stigma and discrimination. Halter (2010) examined how youth involved in the SET were perceived by police attention and found that in 60 per cent of the cases, youth were considered victims of sexual exploitation, while in the other 40 per cent, they were viewed as offenders. Based on these numbers, Halter suggests that a potential ideological transition is occurring, wherein officers are beginning to see youth more often as workers and victims than as offenders.

Regulatory Framework: How to Govern the SET?

How to govern the sex trade industry has been widely debated with respect to adult sex trade involvement, let alone youth sexual exploitation. Historically, age was not relevant and all prostitutes were regarded as immoral and profane (Backhouse 1985, 1991). This perspective gave way, in the mid-twentieth century, to the consideration of child/youth prostitution as a form of delinquency, and early juvenile justice policy in Canada criminalized female sexual behaviour, with girls often being prosecuted for moral offences (i.e., real or suspected sexual behaviour) (Busby 2003). This approach changed in the 1980s when a victimization discourse gained prominence and became the dominant dialogue underpinning systems of regulation.

Within the theoretical literature on sex work, there are many sides to the regulation debate. Generally, the "anti-sex-work" feminist perspective holds that the existence of prostitution is the expression of male domination through which women, and more generally sex, are commodified and exploited. Debates from this perspective frame sex work in the discourse of victimization and exploitation (Dworkin 1989; MacKinnon 1987). Within this perspective, since prostitution is viewed as a part of overall gender inequality, there is a push to eradicate prostitution. Therefore, these critics argue, legislation should seek to criminalize the buying of sex with the recognition that those who are selling sex are victims.

The other side of the debate—loosely termed "pro-sex-work feminism"—argues that women must redefine their experience with sex and embrace all definitions and elements of sexual expression. Rather than always victimizing women, prostitution is seen in certain historical times and places to empower women financially and socially, as well as personally and politically, allowing women to interpret sex for themselves (McElroy 1997). For pro-sex-work feminist authors like Vanwesenbeeck (2001), sex work, in principle, is considered legitimate work, and should be regulated the same way as other workplaces.

It is important to note that neither perspective focuses directly on the experience of youth. Youth and adult sex work is traditionally separated in both research and theory, with the issue of youth sex work primarily addressed through the lens of other street youth or child abuse, and analysis focused on the exploitative and abusive nature of youth sex work. This paradigm is the basis for most forms of regulation. Others argue that it may be counter-productive to separate the study and regulation of adult and youth sex work as the processes of SET involvement and life circumstances of those involved do not differ significantly. Advocacy groups such as COYOTE (Call Off Your Old Tired Ethics) and CORP

(Canadian Organization for Prostitute Rights) suggest that separating youth from adults in the regulation of sex work is ineffective because, in doing so, the contextual nature of the SET is lost. These groups argue that the circumstances that bring youth and adults to the SET and keep them there are more similar than different.

The recent change in Canadian criminal legislation, with the passing of Bill C-36 in late 2014, has realigned and adopted the victimization paradigm on prostitution discussed above, rejecting the view that sex work can be empowering and continuing to legislate youth and adult involvement in the SET separately.

Legislation: Official Regulatory Regimes and Ideology

Youth involved in the SET in Canada are governed by at least two sets of legislation: the federal Criminal Code and provincial child welfare acts. The Badgley Report in 1985 provided a landmark set of recommendations that changed the regulation of what the report's authors called "adolescent prostitution." The committee recommended legislation that would make the sexual procurement of youth an indictable offence and controversially also recommended criminalizing youth sex workers so that social intervention could be possible (Badgley 1985). The latter recommendation was not accepted; however, in 1988, Bill C-15 was introduced as new legislation to criminalize the sexual procurement of youth. Bill C-15 also included measures to protect victims of child sexual abuse, raise the number of prosecutions of child sexual abuse, and increase the severity of sentences, seeking to improve the conditions for child victims and witnesses (Hornick and Bolitho 1992).

The bill included the addition of sections 212(2) and (3)—which addressed living on the avails of a young prostitute under the age of 18—and was amended to make it easier to arrest pimps while also increasing the maximum penalty for prostituting a young person from 10 to 14 years. Section 212(4) criminalized obtaining or attempting to obtain the sexual services of someone under the age of 18. There were also special witness protection programs added, as well as a host of interdisciplinary protocols for child welfare and police departments across the country, including the establishment of special Crown attorneys. While welcomed, the legislation was critiqued as ineffective on the grounds that it was unenforceable (Daum 1996, 1998; Daum and Dion 1996), and the government reacted by introducing Bill C-27, which added section 212(5), making it illegal to purchase the sexual services of someone who is under age 18 or who the offender believes to be under the age of 18.

Nevertheless, the legislative changes did not result in a significant increase in arrests or in effectively addressing the problem of youth involvement in the SET. This failure prompted numerous reports and critiques from provincial and territorial governments, NGOs, and international groups, all suggesting changes to child welfare acts to increase punitive responses from police and courts. Today in Canada, various legislative strategies are used to protect children exploited through prostitution, including federal legislation; general provincial child protection legislation (often called a child and family services act or a child welfare act); and special legislative initiatives, such as Alberta's Protection of Sexually Exploited Children Act (PSECA), British Columbia's Secure Care Act, and the Manitoba Strategy Responding to Children and Youth At Risk of, or Survivors of, Sexual Exploitation (known as the Manitoba Strategy).

Provincially, most of these legislative initiatives include a controversial strategy known as **protective confinement** or **involuntary coercive holding**, permitting police and/or social workers to apprehend anyone under the age of 18 who is involved in prostitution, either after obtaining a court order, or—in emergency situations—without such an order (Busby 2003, p. 106). While confined, youth can be assessed, which often includes tests for drug and alcohol use, sexually transmitted infections, HIV, and pregnancy, as well as mental health assessments and the prescription of anti-psychotic medication.

In Manitoba, after the death of Tracia Owen—a 14-year-old girl who spent most of her life in the care of child welfare, foster homes, and group homes and who hanged herself after using drugs purchased with money from her participation in the SET—there was public outrage over the inability of the existing legislative strategy to prevent such a death. In 2008, a 57-page inquest into Tracia's death became the new guiding document to provide services to youth involved in the SET in Manitoba. See Box 14.5 for more information about the Manitoba Strategy.

There is a clear legislative trend in Canada toward addressing the issue of youth involved in the SET via an approach that includes the confinement/coercive holding of youth as a method of risk management paired with punitive measures for those who purchase sex from children/youth. However, it is unclear if these responses produce positive outcomes for youth. Comte (2014) cautions against the criminalization of all activity in the SET. She argues that punitive programs aimed at protecting youth can end up repressing those involved and have a set of unintended consequences including negative effects on the health and safety of youth. Some of these effects include a youth being forced into unsafe and isolated areas to avoid police and child welfare attention, client refusal of safe sex practices, violence, and increased police attention (Socias et al. 2015, p. 967). Further, while youth are meant to have special protections under Canadian law, Bittle (2002, 2013) has claimed that the special care acts are actually unduly harsh governmental measures that serve only to control where and how sex work business is conducted and, in the process, drive young SET-involved individuals further from real help.

After analyzing several cases, Grover (2002) found that the Canadian justice system has been failing to provide ongoing services to street youth involved in the system, depriving such children of their section 7 Charter right to security, liberty, and life. Further, Mann et al. (2007) found that intervention and "partnering" practices across schools, child protection services, student welfare, and other services designed to alleviate youth risk may in fact propel youth toward criminal activities (p. 44). These researchers are among many who have argued that youth already engaged in the SET are not being properly protected and that those services meant to protect youth may actually be pushing them toward sex work engagement.

Program Variation: From Mandated Government to Non-judgmental NGOs

There are three primary types of services for youth involved in the SET in Canada: mandated services, specialized legislation, and non-governmental services. Mandated services are those services that provincial child welfare agents are mandated to provide to children

Box 14.5 | Youth Justice in Action

The Manitoba Strategy

In 2002, in response to legislation enacted in other provinces, the Government of Manitoba issued the Manitoba Strategy Responding to Children and Youth at Risk of, or Survivors of, Sexual Exploitation (known as the Manitoba Strategy). The strategy was launched through Healthy Child Manitoba—a newly formed agency to support children, separate from Child and Family Services. The implementation committee was led by Manitoba Family Services and Housing, and included numerous partner departments and expert-based agencies. The agencies took the lead on specific initiatives of the strategy, and approximately $10 million per year in funding was distributed among 18 different agencies, some offering similar services but each having different mandates. Some of the agencies were private, some were public, and some were quasi-public. Funding was contingent on adhering to specific parameters of service as well as program outcomes specified in the strategy. Some agencies partnered with existing strategies, leveraging $42 million in funding from the Aboriginal Justice Inquiry-Child Welfare Initiative in 2000.

There were three phases of the strategy—the first from 2004 to 2008, the second from 2008 to 2011, and the third from 2011 to the present (2019 at the time of writing). The overall focus of the strategy was prevention and increasing awareness of the issue of the sexual exploitation of youth through programming run by non-judgmental, child-centred, developmentally and culturally appropriate, creative, experiential people who could respond non-coercively under the rubric of harm reduction. This approach changed in 2008 when the strategy was modified based on a 57-page inquest titled *Tracia's Trust*, following the death of Tracia Owen (Manitoba Family Services and Housing 2008). Although the inquest acknowledged that poverty, class, racism,

social isolation, and marginalization contributed to Tracia's death, and despite testimony from youth involved in the SET indicating that the two most important programs available to them were Street Connections (a harm reduction van that gave practical advice about how to "work the street") and a drop-in centre at Sage House, as well as testimony from Tracia's father highlighting the connection between addictions and suicide on the family's home reserve, legislators made the conscious decision to focus on sexual exploitation as their primary concern, and the Manitoba Strategy took a punitive turn. The strategy turned its attention to offenders and the surveillance of youth "at risk."

Examples of this shift include Manitoba's Sexual Exploitation and Trafficking Act (2013), which focuses on the prosecution of those who purchase sex from individuals under the age of 18. Funds were also allocated toward "John schools" and the Child and Family Services Act was revised to include the ability for a youth care worker to obtain a protection order against clients. This was accompanied by a change in the Youth Drug Stabilization Act to include the involuntary confinement of youth who are causing serious self-harm, including via drugs and participation in the SET. Further, Manitoba established StreetReach, a risk assessment database modelled after the Dallas High Risk Victims Task Force, to identify high-risk runaways and empower police to apprehend them by allowing for ubiquitous surveillance of youth "at risk."

Critical Thinking Question

How do you think youth may respond to the measures outlined in Tracia's Trust? Why do you think this?

deemed to be in need of protection, which can include in-home treatment, supervision orders, temporary care, and Crown wardship. Special legislative initiatives, such as those discussed above, are increasingly being used to specifically target youth in the SET. They are meant to overcome some of the inadequacies in traditional child welfare models, which typically focus on generalized protocols. Non-governmental services include services provided to youth by NGOs. These services can be directly or indirectly focused on youth in the SET. Generally speaking, the methods used by NGOs stress non-state involvement and harm reduction. These organizations often act as advocates for marginalized youth.

Involvement in child welfare agencies is highly reported among those involved in the SET. It is estimated that over 200,000 children and youth are involved with child protection authorities annually in Canada (Trocmé et al. 2005). Mulcahy and Trocmé (2010) found that on any day in Canada there are up to 65,000 children and youth residing in or out of home care, with 67,000 in out-of-home care in 2007. A high number of youth engaged in the SET have a history of child welfare involvement in their families of origin (Benoit et al. 2017; Clark and Cooper 2000; Leslie and Hare 2000; Raychaba 1993). McIntyre and Miller (2016) report that just over half of the SET-involved young men interviewed in their research had experienced some degree of intervention through government-legislated child welfare authorities (p. 393). Schleirich (2004) reveals a similar pattern, with 63 per cent of sexually exploited youth having had some experience with child welfare systems and 77.8 per cent having been in agency care and/or in foster/group homes for years. Gorkoff and Waters (2003) report that 63 per cent of the SET-involved youth in their research had some type of child welfare involvement. The literature also reveals many youth have negative experiences while involved with child welfare interventions, including depersonalized care, rigid routines, neglect, judgmental caregivers, unrealistic financial assistance, and physical victimization (Gorkoff and Waters 2003).

There are some similarities and some differences with respect to official government child welfare mandates and specialized initiatives. In their study of service providers, Gorkoff and Waters (2003) found that there was mixed reaction to legislative responses to youth involved in the SET. Some providers agreed that special legislation gave them more power to apprehend and protect those in harm's way, while others thought this legislation wasn't significantly different and that it might have a negative effect on future programming.

Programming offered by NGOs often fills a significant need beyond that addressed by government intervention. NGOs tend to avoid protectionist strategies, instead providing responsive programming addressing youth needs or preventative programming. NGOs often provide programs such as clean needle exchanges, street kits (including condoms and bad date sheets), and a variety of other non-judgmental programs (Holger-Ambrose et al. 2013). Gorkoff and Waters (2003) found that although the majority of non-governmental programs had the same mandate as the government (i.e., protection of youth from abuse and transition off the street), they used different methods for reaching their goals. NGO programs tend to focus on relationship building, enabling the autonomy of youth, and non-judgmental counselling, and programs are often facilitated by people

Box 14.6 | Youth Justice in Action

RESET Society, Calgary

One example of an effective NGO program offering supports for young women seeking to exit the SET is RESET Society in Calgary (formerly Servants Anonymous Society). RESET began in 1989 when the program founder opened her home to women wanting to leave the sex trade. Today, RESET Society is a registered non-profit organization that operates 24 hours a day, year-round. RESET's stated mission is "To provide comprehensive individualized support and safe housing to women and girls age 16 and over exiting sexual exploitation and sex trafficking so that they may transform their lives."

Programming at RESET supports women and girls exiting the SET by providing a proven and trauma-informed three-phase continuum of services. The three phases are designed to holistically support participants in their journey from SET exit and stabilization, to healing, capacity building, and life-skills development, through to transitioning into independence and empowerment.

Phase One (i-EXIT) is a rapid exit program providing immediate safe housing and supports for exit from sexual exploitation and the risks inherently linked with it. Exiting sexual exploitation often includes high-risk violent situations, crisis, and fear. i-EXIT creates a safe, supportive, and stable housing environment for the first step in exiting.

After initial safety and stabilization is established in Phase One, participants move on to Phase Two (EXIT—Exploitation intervention and transition). EXIT includes 9 to 12 months of comprehensive, individualized, wraparound life skills and trauma recovery programming in tandem with 24/7 supportive housing.

Phase Three of RESET programming includes an individually tailored combination of employment skills development, along with training, support in returning to school or advancing in education, long-term support in the community, and housing search support for accessing independent, safe, community-based, affordable, and long-term housing. The transition from Phase Two to Phase Three includes some overlap to enable successful transitions. Participants are encouraged to build a network of natural supports in the community, including connecting with peer mentors who are accessible to participants on an individualized basis. Community support outreach is provided on an ongoing, individualized basis and a 24/7 crisis line is also available for any woman currently or formerly involved in the program.

Understanding that it can take multiple attempts to exit the SET before the exit is permanent, RESET allows participants to return to the program as many times as they need.

Critical Thinking Question

What do you think is most beneficial about a program like RESET? Given what you have read throughout the chapter, what makes it successful? What might be problematic about the program?

---

who have had experiences in the SET. Seshia (2005) claims this is very important, given that successful exits from the SET often involve role modelling and support provided by survivors of similar experiences (p. 26). (See Box 14.6 for a description of a successful NGO program.) Research has shown that programs that offer peer support, that are positive and non-shaming, and that work with youth to meet their basic needs of income and housing are more likely to be successful, and youth feel more comfortable going to these agencies for help (Bittle 2013; Bruckert and Hannem 2013; Gorkoff and Waters 2003; Hannem and Tigchelaar 2016; Seshia 2005).

Regulating the SET for Youth: Protection or Punishment?

In the process of examining the legislative and program landscape for youth involved in the SET, we can propose a few things. As Smandych (2001) claims, in the last 100 years we have witnessed an escalation of systems of regulation to control the lives of young people. These include everything from compulsory education, to juvenile delinquency legislation, the establishment of provincial ministries of youth, and numerous governmental and non-governmental programs. To that list we can add the host of programs developed to combat the involvement of youth in the SET. These programs tend to focus on a victimization paradigm to support new authoritarian governing strategies, such as secure care in the name of protection. Bittle (2013) claims that these victimization discourses that are part of most current governmental responses display characteristics of neo-liberal forms of governance, including responsibilization; networks of helping complexes; prudentialism; and "normalization," which casts the net of surveillance and social control of youth quite wide.

Although appearing as protection, these victimization-focused discourses and policies have a disciplinary and social control function wherein youth are pushed to "normal" standards of behaviour and the material conditions that lead to sexual exploitation remain unchallenged (Gorkoff 2011). Through many governmental policies and programs, the agency of youth gets stripped away as they are cast as victims of circumstance and poor socialization and viewed as incapable choice makers who need to be disciplined and protected at the same time. Phoenix (2002, 2007) argues that, by casting young people as victims, this approach leads to the specificities of individuals' lives being subsumed by the notion of their victimhood, thus erasing the social and material uniqueness of being a young person involved in society. It renders silent all the relevant issues of sex work such as health and safety, stigma, and working conditions because the "victim" label has supremacy. Further, such a victim-focused approach leaves unexamined the material context in which the "decision" to be involved in SET is made—particularly the factors of race, class, gender, and ability to earn a living wage (Davies 2015). Programs that focus on relationship building and forging connections between individuals tend to have greater success in supporting youth involved in the SET (Holger-Ambrose et al. 2013), although the road to this success is ever winding.

Summary

The overview presented in this chapter is meant to provide insights into the research conducted on young people involved in the SET. Understanding terminology and discourse is important, since shifts in law and social policy are not simply reactions to knowledge but are grounded in discourse. As contested definitions of behaviour acquire a new legitimacy, institutions such as law and social welfare take on these definitions and discourses authoritatively, giving them power and constituting their form. For our purposes, juxtaposing the terminology with the lived realities of young people on the street provides us with some contradictory themes, but it also gives us the power to question official discourse and move toward policy that is reflective of the needs of young people involved in the SET.

Key Terms

absolute homelessness

bad date

child welfare

gay for pay

Nordic model

protective confinement or involuntary coercive holding

sexual exploitation

sexual exploitation trade (SET)

straight for pay

suicidality

survival sex

Review Questions

1. What is discourse and why is it important to understanding the terminology used to understand youth sex trade involvement?

2. What are the factors that lead young people into the SET?

3. How is the SET impacted by race?

4. How might the risk factors for young men differ from those of young women in the SET?

Critical Thinking Questions

1. Why do you think there is a lack of research on youth involved in the SET, and how would you suggest researchers study it?

2. What impact do you think government legislation can have on the issue of sexual exploitation in Canada?

3. If you could write legislation, what elements would it have?

4. What would you do to ensure that young people don't have to engage in survival sex?

5. What do you think is most dangerous about the SET?

References

Agustin, L.M. (2005). Helping women who sell sex: The construction of benevolent identities. *Rhizomes, 10.*

Agustin, L.M. (2008). Sex and the limits of enlightenment: The irrationality of legal regimes to control prostitution. *Sexuality Research & Social Policy, 5*(4), 73–86.

Backhouse, C. (1985). Nineteenth-century Canadian prostitution law: Reflection of a discriminatory society. *Social History, 53,* 387–423.

Backhouse, C. (1991). *Petticoats and prejudice: Women and law in nineteenth century Canada.* Toronto: Women's Press.

Badgley, R. (Chairman) (1985). *Sexual offences against children: Volume 1: Report of the Committee on Sexual Offences against Children and Youths*: Ottawa: Ministry of Supply and Services; Library of Parliament.

Benoit, C., Jansson, M., Smith, M., and Flagg, J. (2018). Prostitution stigma and its effect on the working conditions, personal lives, and health of sex workers. *Journal of Sex Research, 55*(4–5), 457–71.

Benoit, C., McCarthy, B., and Jansson, M. (2015a). Occupational stigma and mental health: Discrimination and depression among front-line service workers. *Canadian Public Policy, 41*(Issue supplement 2), S61–S69.

Benoit, C., McCarthy, B., and Jansson, M. (2015b). Stigma, sex work, and substance use: A comparative analysis. *Sociology of Health and Illness, 37*(3), 437–51.

Benoit, C., and Millar, A., (2001). *Dispelling myths and understanding realities: Working conditions, health status, and exiting experiences of sex workers*. Victoria, BC: Prostitutes Empowerment, Education and Resources Society (PEERS).

Benoit, C., Ouellet, N., Jansson, M., Magnus, S., and Smith, M. (2017). Would you think about doing sex for money? Structure and agency in deciding to sell sex in Canada. *Work, Employment and Society, 31*(5), 731–47.

Benoit, C., and Shaver, F. (2006). Critical issues and new directions in sex work. *Canadian Review of Sociology and Anthropology, 43*(3), 243–52.

Benoit, V., Smith, M., Jansson, M., Magnus, S., Ouellet, N., Atchison, C., . . . Shaver, F. (2016). Lack of confidence in police creates a blue ceiling for sex workers safety. *Canadian Public Policy, 42*(4), 456–68.

Berlatsky, N. (2015, October 30). "Human trafficking" has become a meaningless term. *New Republic*. Retrieved from https://newrepublic.com/article/123302/human-trafficking-has-become-meaningless-term

Biehal, N., and Wade, J. (1999). Taking a chance? The risk associated with going missing from substitute care. *Child Abuse Review 8*(6), 366–76.

Bittle, S. (2013). Still punishing to "protect": Youth prostitution law and policy reform. In E. van der Meulen, E.M. Durisin, and V. Love (Eds), *Selling sex: Experience, advocacy, and research on sex work in Canada* (pp. 279–98). Vancouver: UBC Press.

Bittle, S. (2002). When protection is punishment: Neo-liberalism and secure care approaches to youth prostitution. *Canadian Journal of Criminology, 44*(3) 317–350.

Bowen, R., and Shannon, E. (2009). *Human trafficking, sex work safety and the 2010 games: Assessments and recommendations*. Vancouver: Sex Industry Worker Safety Action Group.

Bramly, L., Tubman, M., Pearson, L., and Kingsley, C. (2001). *Out from the shadows: International summit on sexually exploited youth—final report*. Vancouver: Save the Children Canada.

Brannigan, A., and Van Brunschot, E.G. (1997). Youthful prostitution and child sexual trauma. *International Journal of Law and Psychiatry, 20*(3), 337–54.

Brannigan, A., and Van Brunschot, E.G. (2002). Childhood maltreatment and subsequent conduct disorders: The case of female street prostitutes. *International Journal of Law and Psychiatry, 25*(3), 219–34.

Bruckert, C., and Hannem, S. (2013a). Rethinking the prostitution debates: Transcending structural stigma in systemic responses to sex work. *Canadian Journal of Law and Society, 28*(1), 43–63.

Bruckert, C., and Hannem, S. (2013b). To serve and protect: Structural stigma, social profiling and the abuse of police power in Ottawa. In E. van der Meulen, E.M. Durisin, and V. Love (Eds), *Selling sex: Experience, advocacy, and research on sex work in Canada* (pp. 297–313). Vancouver: UBC Press.

Bruckert, C., and Parent, C. (2004). *Organized crime and human trafficking in Canada: Tracing perceptions and discourses*. Ottawa: Research and Evaluation Branch, Royal Canadian Mounted Police.

Busby, K. (2003). The protective confinement of girls involved in prostitution: Potential problems in current regimes. In K. Gorkoff, and J. Runner (Eds), *Being heard: The experiences of young women in prostitution* (pp. 103–25). Winnipeg: Fernwood.

Canada v. Bedford, 2013, SCC 72.

Chettiar, J., Shannon, K., Wood, E., Zhang, R., and Kerr, T. (2010). Survival sex work involvement among street-involved youth who use drugs in a Canadian setting. *Journal of Public Health, 32*(3), 322–7.

Clarke, M., and Cooper, M. (2000). Homeless youth: Falling between the cracks an investigation of youth homelessness in Calgary. Calgary: The Calgary Foundation and The Community Mobilization Program of the National Strategy on Community Safety and Crime Prevention.

Comack, E., and Seshia, M. (2010). Bad dates and street hassles: Violence in the Winnipeg street sex trade. *Canadian Journal of Criminology and Criminal Justice, 52*(2), 203–14

Comte, J. (2014). Decriminalization of sex work: Feminist discourses in light of research. *Sexuality & Culture, 18*(1), 196–217.

Cool, J. (2004). *Prostitution in Canada: An overview*. Ottawa: Library of Parliament.

Corrigan, P., and Miller, F.E. (2004). Shame, blame and contamination: A review of the impact of mental illness stigma on family members. *Journal of Mental Health, 13,* 537–48.

Dauda, C. (2010). Childhood, age of consent and moral regulation in Canada and the UK. *Contemporary Politics, 16*(3), 227–47.

Daum, K. (1996). *Position paper on law 212(4): A time for action.* Vancouver: Downtown Eastside Youth Activities Society.

Daum, K. (1998). *The sequel: A time for action 2.* Vancouver: Downtown Eastside Youth Activities Society.

Daum, K., and Dion, A. (1996). *You are not alone: A support guide for parent and caregivers of sexually exploited children.* Vancouver: Downtown Eastside Youth Activities Society.

Davies, J.M. (2015). The criminalization of sexual commerce in Canada: Context and concepts for critical analysis. *The Canadian Journal of Human Sexuality, 24*(2), 78–91.

Deering, K.N., Shoveller, J., Tyndall, M.W., Montaner, J.S., and Shannon, K. (2011). The street cost of drugs and drug use patterns: Relationships with sex work income in an urban Canadian setting. *Drug and Alcohol Dependence, 118,* 2–3.

Dennis J. (2008). Women are victims, men make choices: The invisibility of men and boys in the global sex-trade. *Gender Issues, 25,* 11–25.

DeRiviere, L. (2006). A human capital methodology for estimating the lifelong personal costs of young women leaving the sex trade. *Feminist Economics, 12*(3), 367–402.

Downe, P. (2003). I don't know what the hell it is, but it sounds nasty. Health issues for girls working the streets. In K. Gorkoff and J. Runner (Eds), *Being heard: The experiences of young women in prostitution* (pp. 86–102). Winnipeg: Fernwood.

Downe, P., and Mika, A. (2003). The people we think we are: The social identities of girls involved in prostitution. In K. Gorkoff, and J. Runner (Eds), *Being heard: The experiences of young women in prostitution* (pp. 46–68). Winnipeg: Fernwood.

Dworkin, A. (1989). *Pornography: Men possessing women.* New York: Penguin

Estes, R., and Weiner, N.A. (2001). *The commercial sexual exploitation of children in the US, Canada, and Mexico.* Retrieved from https://abolitionistmom.org/wp-content/uploads/2014/05/Complete_CSEC_0estes-weiner.pdf

Farley, M., and Lynne, J. (2005). Prostitution of Indigenous women: Sex inequality and the colonization of Canada's First Nations women. *Fourth World Journal, 6*(1), 1–29.

Farley, M., Lynne, J., and Cotton, A. (2005). Prostitution in Vancouver: Violence and the colonization of First Nations women. *Transcultural Psychiatry, 42*(2), 242–71.

Ferris, S. (2008). Working from the violent centre: Survival sex work and urban Aboriginality in Maria Campbell's Halfbreed. *English Studies in Canada, 34*(4) 123–45.

Fletcher, T. (2013). Trans sex-workers: Negotiating sex, gender, and non-normative desire. In E. van der Meulen, E. Durisin, and V. Love (Eds), *Selling sex: Experience, advocacy, and research on sex work in Canada* (pp. 65–73). Vancouver: UBC Press.

Foucault, M. (1978). *The history of sexuality: Volume 1—An introduction.* (R. Hurley, Trans.). New York: Pantheon.

Frederick, T. (2014). Diversity at the margins: The interconnections between homelessness, sex work, mental health, and substance use in the lives of sexual minority homeless young people. In D. Peterson and V.R. Panfil (Eds), *Handbook of LGBT communities, crime and justice* (pp. 473–501). New York: Springer.

Glowatski, K., Jones, N.A. and Carleton, N.R. (2017). Bridging police and communities through relationship: The importance of a theoretical foundation for restorative policing. *Restorative Justice,* 5:2, 267–292, DOI: 10.1080/20504721.2017.1343416

Goffman, E. (1963). *Stigma: Notes on the management of spoiled identity.* New York: Simon & Schuster.

Goldenberg, S.M., Chettiar, J., Nguyen, P., Dobrer, S., Montaner, J., and Shannon, K. (2016). Complexities of short-term mobility for sex work and migration among sex workers: Violence and sexual risks, barriers to care, and enhanced social and economic opportunities. *Journal of Urban Health: Bulletin of the New York Academy of Medicine, 91*(4), 736–51.

Goldenberg, S.M., Chettiar, J., Simo, A., Silverman, J.G., Strathdee, S.A., Montaner, J.S., and Shannon, K. (2014). Early sex work initiation independently elevates odds of HIV infection and police arrest among adult sex workers in a Canadian setting. *Journal of Acquired Immune Deficiency Syndromes, 65*(1), 122–8.

Gorkoff, K. (2011). Othering or protecting? The discursive practice of saving youth prostitutes. *Annual Review of Interdisciplinary Justice Research, 2,* 5–34.

Gorkoff, K., and Runner, J. (2003). Introduction: Children and youth exploited through prostitution. In K. Gorkoff and J. Runner (Eds), *Being heard: The experiences of young women in prostitution* (pp. 12–28). Winnipeg: Fernwood.

Gorkoff, K., and Waters, M. (2003). Balancing safety, respect and choice in programs for young women involved in prostitution. In K. Gorkoff and J. Runner (Eds), *Being heard: The experiences of young women in prostitution* (pp. 126–46). Winnipeg: Fernwood.

Grover, S. (2002). On meeting Canada's charter obligations to street youth. *International Journal of Children's Rights, 10*(4), 313–44.

Hagan, J., and McCarthy, B., (1997). *Mean streets: Youth crime and homelessness.* Boston: Cambridge University Press.

Halter, S. (2010). Factors that influence police conceptualizations of girls involved in prostitution in six US cities: Child sexual exploitation victims or delinquents? *Child Maltreatment, 15*(2), 152–60.

Hannem, S., and Tigchelaar, A. (2016). Doing it in public: Dilemmas of gatekeepers, images, and voice in public sociology on sex work. *Symbolic Interaction, 39*(4), 634–53.

Heerde, J.A., Scholes-Balog, K.E., and Hemphill, S.A. (2015). Associations between youth homelessness, sexual offenses, sexual victimization, and sexual risk behaviors: A systematic literature review. *Archives of Sexual Behavior, 44*(1), 181–212.

Hein, L. (2011). Survival strategies of male homeless adolescents. *Journal of American Psychiatric Nurses Association, 17*(4), 274–82.

Hilario, C., Saewyc, E.M., Matthews, J., Rivers, R., Hirakata, P., and Miller, B.B. (2013). Competing discourses about youth sexual exploitation in Canadian news media. *Canadian Journal of Human Sexuality, 22*(2), 95–105.

Holger-Ambrose, B., Langmade, C., Edinburgh, L.D., and Saewyc, E. (2013). The illusions and juxtapositions of commercial sexual exploitation among youth: Identifying effective street-outreach strategies. *Journal of Child Sexual Abuse, 22*(3), 326–40.

Hornick, J.P., and Bolitho, F. (1992). *A review of the implementation of the child sexual abuse legislation in selected sites.* Ottawa: Department of Justice Canada.

Hunt, S. (2013). Decolonizing sex work: Developing an intersectional Indigenous approach. In E. van der Meulen, E. Durisin, and V. Love (Eds), *Selling sex: Experience, advocacy, and research on sex work in Canada* (pp. 82–100). Vancouver: UBC Press.

JJ. (2013). We speak for ourselves: Anti-colonial and self-determined responses to young people involved in the sex trade. In E. van der Meulen, E. Durisin, and V. Love (Eds), *Selling sex: Experience, advocacy, and research on sex work in Canada* (pp. 74–81). Vancouver: UBC Press.

Kennedy, M.C., Jansson, M., Benoit, C., Magnuson, D., Scramstad, J., and Hallgrimsdottir, H. (2017). Social relationships and social support among street involved youth. *Journal of Youth Studies, 20*(10) 1328–45.

Kidd, S. (2006). Factors precipitating suicidality among homeless youth. *Youth & Society, 37*(4), 393–422.

Kidd, S., and Liborio, R. (2011). Sex trade involvement in São Paulo, Brazil and Toronto, Canada: Narratives of social exclusion and fragmented identities. *Youth & Society, 43*(3), 982–1009.

Kingsley, C., and Mark, M. (2000). *Sacred lives: Canadian Aboriginal children and youth speak out about sexual exploitation.* National Aboriginal Consultation Project. Vancouver: Save the Children Canada.

Leslie, B., and Hare, F. (2000). *Improving the outcomes for youth in transition from care.* Toronto: Working Group of the Children's Aid Society of Toronto, Covenant House, and Ryerson University Research project 1995–1999.

Lewis, J., Shaver, F.M., and Maticka-Tyndale, E. (2013). Going 'round again: The persistence of prostitution-related stigma. In E. van der Meulen, E. Durisin, and V. Love (Eds), *Selling sex: Experience, advocacy, and research on sex work in Canada* (pp. 198–208). Vancouver: UBC Press.

Link, B., and Phelan, J. (2006). Stigma and its public health implications. *The Lancet, 367*(9509), 528–9.

Lowman, J. (1987). Taking young prostitutes seriously. *Canadian Review of Sociology and Anthropology, 24*(1), 99–116.

Lowman, J. (2000). Violence and the outlaw status of (street) prostitution. *Violence Against Women, 6*(9), 987–1101.

Lowman, J. (2013). Crown expert-witness testimony in *Bedford v. Canada:* Evidence-based argument or victim-paradigm hyperbole? In E. van der Meulen, E. Durisin, and V. Love (Eds), *Selling sex: Experience, advocacy, and research on sex work in Canada* (pp. 230–50). Vancouver: UBC Press.

Lowman, J. (2016). *Tripping point: Brief to the Standing Committee on Justice and Human Rights on the Protection of Communities and Exploited Persons Act.* Retrieved from https://sencanada.ca/content/sen/committee/412/lcjc/briefs/c-36/sm_c-36_brief_john_lowman_e.pdf

Lynne, J. (1998). *Colonialism and sexual exploitation of Canada's First Nations women.* Retrieved from http://www.prostitutionresearch.com/Lynne%20colonialism%20and%20the%20sexual%20exploitation%20of%20canada%27s%20first%20nations%20women.pdf

Lyons, T., Kerr, T., Duff, P., Feng, C., and Shannon, K. (2014). Youth, violence and non-injection drug use: Nexus of vulnerabilities among lesbian and bisexual sex workers. *Aids Care, 26*(9), 1090–4.

McCarthy, B. (1995). *On the streets: Youth in Vancouver.* Vancouver: Research Evaluation and Statistics Branch, Ministry of Social Services.

McElroy, W. (1997). A feminist defense of pornography. *Free Inquiry, 17*(4), 14–17.

McIntyre, S. (1999). The youngest profession: The oldest oppression: A study of sex work. In C. Badgley and K. Mallick (Eds), *Child sexual abuse and adult offenders: New theory and research.* Aldershot, UK: Ashgate.

McIntyre, S. (2002). *Strolling away.* Ottawa: Research and Statistics Division, Department of Justice Canada.

McIntyre, S. (2005). *Under the radar: The sexual exploitation of young men.* Calgary: Hindsight Group.

McIntyre, S. (2009). *Under the radar: The sexual exploitation of young men—Western Canadian Edition.* Calgary: Hindsight Group.

McIntyre, S., and Miller, A. (2016). Under the radar: The sexual exploitation of young men in Western Canada. In J. Winterdyk and R. Smandych (Eds), *Youth at risk and youth justice* (pp. 378–406). Toronto: Oxford University Press.

MacKinnon, C. (1987). *Feminism unmodified: Discourses on life and law.* Cambridge, MA: Harvard University Press.

Manitoba Family Services and Housing. (2008). *Tracia's trust: Front-line voices—Manitobans working together to end child sexual exploitation.* Winnipeg: Manitoba Family Services and Housing.

Mann, R.M., Senn, C.Y., Girard, A., and Ackbar, S. (2007). Community-based interventions for at-risk youth in Ontario under Canada's youth criminal justice act: A case study of a "runaway" girl. *Canadian Journal of Criminology & Criminal Justice, 49*(1), 37–74.

Marshall, B.D., Shannon, K., Kerr, T., Zhang, R., and Wood, E. (2010). Survival sex work and increased HIV risk among sexual minority street-involved youth. *Journal of Acquired Immune Deficiency Syndromes, 53*(5), 661–4.

Mehrabadi, A., Craib, K.J.P., Patterson, K., Adam, W., Moniruzzaman, A., Ward-Burkitt, B., . . . Spittal, P.M. (2008). The Cedar Project: A comparison of HIV-related vulnerabilities amongst young Aboriginal women surviving drug use and sex work in two Canadian cities. *International Journal of Drug Policy, 19*(2), 159–68.

Miller, C.L., Fielden, S.J., Tyndall, M.W., Zhang, R., Gibson, K., and Shannon, K. (2011). Individual and structural vulnerability among female youth who exchange sex for survival. *Journal of Adolescent Health, 49*(1), 36–41.

Minichiello, V., Scott, J., and Callander, D. (2013). New pleasures and old dangers: Reinventing male sex work. *Journal of Sex Research, 50*(3–4), 263–75.

Mulcahy, M., and Trocmé, N. (2010). *CEWC information sheet #78: Children and youth in out-of-home care in Canada*. Montreal: Centre for Research on Children and Families, McGill University.

Nixon, K., Tutty, L., Downe, P., Gorkoff, K., and Ursel, J. (2002). The everyday occurrence: Violence in the lives of girls exploited through prostitution. *Violence Against Women Journal, 8*(9), 1016–43.

O'Grady, W. (2007). *Crime in Canadian context: Debates and controversies*. Toronto: Oxford University Press.

Phillips, R., and Benoit, C. (2013). Exploring stigma by association among front-line care providers serving sex workers. *Health Care Policy, 9*(Special Issue), 139–51.

Phillips, R., Benoit, C., Hallgrimsdottir, H., and Vallance, K. (2012). Courtesy stigma: A hidden health concern among front-line service providers to sex workers. *Sociology of Health and Illness, 34*(5), 681–96.

Phoenix, J. (2002). In the name of protection: Youth prostitution reforms in England and Wales. *Critical Social Policy, 22*(2), 353–75.

Phoenix, J. (2007). Governing prostitution: New formations, old agendas. *Canadian Journal of Law and Society, 22*(2), 73–94.

Raychaba, B. (1993). *"Pain . . . lots of pain": Family violence and abuse in the lives of young people in care*. Ottawa: National Youth in Care Network.

Redwood, R. (2013). Myths and realities of male sex work: A personal perspective. In E. van der Meulen, E. Durisin, and V. Love (Eds), *Selling sex: Experience, advocacy, and research on sex work in Canada* (pp. 45–57). Vancouver: UBC Press.

Saewyc, E.M., Solsvig, W., and Edinburgh, L. (2008). The Hmong youth task force: Evaluation of a coalition to address the sexual exploitation of young runaways. *Public Health Nursing, 25*(1), 69–76.

Sanders, T., Connelly, L., and King, L.J. (2016). On our own terms: The working conditions of internet-based sex workers in the UK. *Sociological Research Online, 21*(4), 1–14.

Saunders, P. (2005). Identity to acronym: How child prostitution became CSEC. In E. Berstein, and L. Schaffener (Eds), *Regulating sex: The politics of intimacy and identity* (pp. 167–88). New York: Routledge.

Scambler, G. (2009). Health-related stigma. *Sociology of Health and Illness, 31*(3), 441–55.

Schleirich, W. (2004). Manitoba's strategy: Responding to children and youth involved in sexual exploitation. *Envision: The Manitoba Journal of Child Welfare, 3*(1), 1–20.

Seshia, M. (2005). *The unheard of speak out: Street sexual exploitation in Winnipeg*. Ottawa: Canadian Centre for Policy Alternatives.

Sethi, A. (2007). Domestic sex trafficking of Aboriginal girls in Canada: Issues and implications. *First Peoples Child and Family Review, 3*(3), 57–71.

Smandych, R. (2001). Accounting for changes in Canadian youth justice: From the invention to the disappearance of childhood. In R. Smandych (Ed.), *Youth justice: History, legislation and reform* (pp. 4–23). Toronto: Harcourt.

Socías, M., Deering, K., Horton, M., Nguyen, P., Montaner, J., and Shannon, K. (2015). Social and structural factors shaping high rates of incarceration among sex workers in a Canadian setting. *Journal of Urban, 92*(5), 966–79.

Spittal, P.M., Bruneau, J., Craib, K.J., Miller, C., Lamothe, F., Weber, A.E., . . . Schechter, M.T. (2003). Surviving the sex trade: A comparison of HIV risk behaviours among street-involved women in two Canadian cities who inject drugs. *Aids Care, 15*(2), 187–95.

Stoltz, J.A., Shannon, K., Kerr, T., Zhang, R., Montaner, J.S., and Wood, E. (2007). Associations between childhood maltreatment and sex work in a cohort of drug-using youth. *Social Science and Medicine, 65*(6), 1214–21.

Thibodeau, P. (1996). EGADZ year-end report. Saskatoon: Downtown Youth Centre.

Trocmé, N., Fallon, B., MacLaurin, B., Daciuk, J., Felstiner, C., Black, T., . . . Cloutier, R. (2005). Canadian incidence study of reported child abuse and neglect—2003: Major findings: Ottawa: Minister of Public Works and Government Services Canada.

Tutty, L., and Nixon, K. (2003). Selling sex? It's really like selling your soul. Vulnerability to the experience of exploitation through child prostitution. In K. Gorkoff and J. Runner (Eds), *Being heard: The experiences of young women in prostitution* (pp. 29–45). Winnipeg: Fernwood.

Vanwesenbeeck, I. (2001). Another decade of social scientific work on sex work: A review of research 1990–2000. *Annual Review of Sex Research, 12*, 242–89.

Vaughan, B. (2000). The government of youth: Disorder and dependence? *Social and Legal Studies, 9*(3), 347–66.

Weber, A.E., Boivin, J.F., Blais, L., Haley, N., and Roy, E. (2002). HIV risk profile and prostitution among female street youths. *Journal of Urban Health, 79*(4), 525–35.

Weber, A.E., Boivin, J.F., Blais, L., Haley, N., and Roy, E. (2004). Predictors of initiation into prostitution among female street youths. *Journal of Urban Health, 81*(4), 584–95.

Wender, C., Wilson, C., Macphail, S., Orchard, T., and Farr, S. (2014). Expanding the scope of inquiry: Exploring accounts of childhood and family life among sex workers in London, Ontario. *Canadian Journal of Human Sexuality, 23*(1), 9–18.

Part IV

Keeping Young Persons out of the System
Exploring Progressive Approaches to Youth Crime and Justice

To this point in the book, we have studied the history of youth justice in Canada, considered the impact and evolution of youth justice legislation, provided an examination of youth crime, and discussed some key types of youth crime and problems. In this concluding section, we include two chapters that explore some unique, if not promising, approaches to dealing with youth crime and youth problems.

In Chapter 15, Louis-Georges Cournoyer, Jacques Dionne, Michèle Goyette, Pierre Hamel, and Marie-Michèle Dumas provide a comprehensive overview of Quebec's unique approach to keeping young offenders out of the justice system. While many textbooks have given passing attention to the Quebec experience, this chapter represents one of the few detailed accouns of how and why Quebec has adopted a social welfare, psycho-educational approach toward dealing with youth at risk. Rather than focus on the gravity of the offence, Quebec has instead focused on the needs of young persons. While still operating within the parameters of the Youth Criminal Justice Act (YCJA), Quebec has managed to forge a model of juvenile justice that shows promise, and that is gaining full acceptance—indeed, a model that should serve as an example of what might be possible for Canada as a whole. The reader, we hope, will be inspired to debate and explore the potential of the Quebec model.

The final chapter, Chapter 16, authored by Brenda Morrison, Muhammad (Asad) Asadullah, and Colleen Pawlychka, focuses on juvenile justice and the development of restorative justice in Canada. Although the authors draw on a wide range of material in their discussion, they rely on the situation in British Columbia to ground their overview of the growth of and barriers to restorative justice. Restorative justice (RJ) is widely seen to represent a viable and robust alternative to conventional youth justice practices. Since the Youth Criminal Justice Act has legal provisions for the application of RJ, it is appropriate that, 17 years after its enactment (in 2003), its relative merits be examined. Morrison, Asadullah, and Pawlychka begin by providing a broad overview of the youth justice system in Canada, arguing that despite legislative reforms, young offenders are still mainly subject to "a system of social control." They note that although the YCJA does not specifically reference RJ, it does open the door to the development of RJ initiatives. The authors discuss the intersection of three primary practices of RJ. They provide a clear description of how several different models of RJ can be applied, and have been applied, in different strategic justice contexts. These strategic initiatives are also examined with a critical lens that helps to identify theoretical and practical issues that should be addressed if RJ is to become more mainstream. The chapter concludes with RJ recommendations from the 2018 federal report *Transforming Canada's Criminal Justice System* and a call for Canadians to harness the capacity to renew the promise of restorative justice by engaging in praxis locally, provincially, nationally, and internationally.

Although this textbook has endeavoured to cover a broad range of themes and issues, the information included here is in no respect the definitive word. Instead, we sincerely hope that the material presented will further stimulate your thinking as well as your desire to become involved in the quest to better understand and address youth crime, youth justice, and/or their related problems through one or more of the intervention, prevention, or control strategies discussed.

Keeping Youth Out of Jail
Quebec's Experience

*Louis-Georges Cournoyer, Jacques Dionne,
Michèle Goyette, Pierre Hamel, and
Marie-Michèle Dumas*

15

Overview

This chapter presents an overview of some key moments in the history of the efforts to rehabilitate young offenders in Quebec—key moments that have served to lay the foundation for how young offenders are dealt with in Quebec today. The chapter describes the evolution of Quebec's legislative youth justice framework as well as the evolution of the province's various intervention strategies, and focuses particularly on the views of rehabilitation in the province that led to the actual structure of services offered to youth offenders. Together, these elements are intended to help explain why most of the Quebec population is opposed to some of the fundamental principles of the Youth Criminal Justice Act (YCJA). A recent study on the impact of the YCJA confirmed these apprehensions (Lafortune et al. 2015). The chapter also provides insight into how and why Quebec's focus has shifted away from the gravity of the offence to try instead to address the needs and capacity of young persons who are recognized as "at-risk" youth and how this approach had been addressed since the application of the YCJA.

Key Objectives

After reading this chapter, you should be able to:

- Define the logic behind the assertion "the right measure at the right time."
- Identify the key moments in the history of the rehabilitation of youth offenders in Quebec that determined the way such rehabilitation is organized today.
- Identify the values that guide offenders' rehabilitation in Quebec.
- Understand the reasons why Quebec opposed the YCJA.
- Understand how the needs and capacity are addressed inside the parameters of the YCJA

Introduction

The Province of Quebec has a unique socio-political context in Canada. It is the only province to have French as the only official language. Under the provincial political system, Quebec also has a unique organization of public services (e.g., finance, justice, health, education). In addition, Quebec has maintained the Napoleonic Civil Code that it inherited from France, although in terms of criminal justice, the Canadian Criminal Code applies. This distinction goes back to the founding of Canada as the union of Upper and Lower Canada and has in some ways influenced the conceptualization of law as applied to youth offenders, as will be discussed in this chapter.

The Quebec Intervention Model for Young Offenders: The Right Measure at the Right Time

differential intervention
An approach arguing that, based on the identification of the type of delinquency associated with the behaviours of young offenders, interventions must then be tailored to meet young offenders' treatment needs and the level of risk they pose to society (risk of recidivism). It considers that people do not come in one-size-fits-all packages and therefore refrains from applying the same approach to each person involved in a class, program, or other forms of group-based change process.

Before 1950, in Quebec, as in the rest of Canada and some other Western countries, young offenders found themselves in adult prisons (Foucault 1984; Parizeau 1976). It was several decades before the incarceration of minors ended in Quebec. This chapter describes the evolution of this process from various perspectives over the past 100+ years. The changes made to the judicial system during this period were accompanied by new concepts of intervention and more extensive criminological, psychological, and psycho-educational research. The dynamic relationship between research and intervention has also played a major role in defining a **differential intervention** approach that has become more explicit and is now recognized as the basis of the Quebec intervention model used. We will describe the past and current organization of services for youth offenders in Quebec and the difficulties associated with the implementation of the Youth Criminal Justice Act (YCJA) in the province.

The Evolution of Quebec's Legislative Framework

In 1857, Canada adopted the Act for the Speedier Trial and Punishment of Juvenile Offenders to avoid long imprisonments before trial proceedings. It was at that time that the government decided to play a role in the protection of minors who had committed an offence (see Chapter 1 in this textbook for further discussion). Between 1868 and 1925, more than 80,000 poor children were sent from England to Canada without families, some of them with delinquency issues. They were initially placed in asylums before being integrated into Canadian families as farm labourers or domestic servants. To protect these abandoned children from delinquency, in 1869 Quebec adopted two laws that established institutions to take charge of these children: the Industrial Schools Act, which ensured housing and education for children under 14 years old who had been abandoned or were not being properly taken care of; and the Reform School Act, which aimed to rehabilitate offenders under 16 years of age. Prisons were, at that time, overflowing with minors. This system remained in place until 1892, when a change in law obliged municipalities to pay for half of the cost for youth offenders placed in industrial and reform schools. Unfortunately, municipalities avoided paying these new costs, and once again, youth offenders were sent to adult courts and prisons (Joyal 2000).

In 1908, the adoption of the Juvenile Delinquents Act (JDA) marked a societal shift toward juvenile offenders. As described in Chapter 1, this law was based on a paternalistic philosophy whereby minors were no longer seen as criminals but as poorly raised and, therefore, not to be held responsible for their actions (see Platt 1977). Like abused and neglected children, delinquent children were victims of their environment and deemed to need care, encouragement, and supervision. Intervention centred on helping these young people instead of reprimanding them for their delinquent behaviour. Constituting major social progress, this 1908 law conferred a special legal status on youth who had committed offences. Distinct tribunals and legal procedures for young offenders allowed them to receive help and remain with their family instead of being systematically incarcerated and/or treated like adults. Judges were now expected to act with reasonable and due care when it came to judicial proceedings involving young offenders.

By the beginning of the twentieth century in Quebec, religious institutions cared for abandoned children free of charge. The intention was to morally and physically "save" these children. Children were placed in big halls and dormitories, their basic needs were provided for, and they received minimal instruction. In 1951, Quebec passed the School Act of Youth Protection, a law that abolished reform and industrial schools. This new Act instituted youth protection schools and the court of social welfare, and judges were expected to hear the youth's situation. The spirit of this law favoured the substitution of the state for parents when the child needed protection. The tribunal responsible for administering this law was the same one responsible for the federal JDA. With the Act, however, the rules of law were minimal, since the legislation did not acknowledge the notion of rights for young people. The procedures in the court of social welfare were very basic, and the judge was expected to act with reasonable and due care. The principles of the Act were aligned with those of the federal law in effect at the time—the 1908 JDA. The procedures applied by the judge could be a concrete implementation of the state as the *parens patriae*.

In 1977, Quebec adopted the Youth Protection Act (YPA), which came into effect in January 1979. Adopting this Act was a major step that influenced the course of intervening with young offenders. In addition to dealing with children in need of protection, this law also dealt with young persons charged with an offence under the Criminal Code or under provincial or municipal laws. Provisions were included that defined voluntary measures that could be offered to young offenders as an alternative to judicial proceedings and were deemed to be in their best interest. These provisions allowed the youth protection director to propose a voluntary measure, refer the matter to court, or close the case. This process was invalidated with the Supreme Court of Canada declaring in 1981 that criminal law, including procedures, is a federal jurisdiction (*Procureur général du Québec c. Lechasseur et autres* [1981] 2 R.C.S. 253). However, the effect of this incursion of provincial legislation on federal jurisdiction has been to introduce recourse for young offenders outside of judicial procedures. This legislation affirms the notion of the "precedence of social intervention over court intervention," which constitutes an important milestone for differential intervention.

It was at this time that the Quebec National Assembly held the Charbonneau Special Parliamentary Commission addressing youth protection. Considering the Supreme Court's decision and the enactment of the Young Offenders Act (YOA) in 1982, the commission proposed the adoption of an alternative measures program that balanced social and judicial obligations. In this program, the first step consists of an examination of the evidence by the solicitor followed by the youth protection director deciding which regime is applicable, either by proposing alternative measures to the youth or by recommending to the solicitor that charges be pressed against the offending youth. The Charbonneau Commission also recommended that the youth protection director be made provincial director under the YOA, thereby giving the youth protection network responsibility over the rehabilitation services provided to young offenders. Hence, the notion of precedence of social intervention was reaffirmed with the adoption of the YOA. As soon as the Act came into effect in 1984, Quebec adopted its Alternative Measures Program (Charbonneau Commission, part II). As detailed in Chapter 3, the YOA considered that youths were able to assume responsibility for their actions, but it also insisted on protecting society. At the same time, the YOA emphasized the principle of considering adolescents' special needs in treating delinquency (see s. 3(1)(c)).

The nature and gravity of the offence are not the only elements considered when imposing a judicial decision: a juvenile's needs and circumstances must also be considered when explaining his or her behaviour. Inspired by Quebec's experience using extrajudicial measures, the YOA instituted the Alternative Measures Program (AMP), which allowed Quebec and other jurisdictions of Canada to elaborate on and implement these measures. Quebec rapidly adopted a decree to institutionalize this option. Under the AMP, the prosecutor was expected to evaluate the evidence and determine if an offence had been committed. If such was the case, for most offences each jurisdiction was obliged to transfer the young offender to the director of Youth Protection Services (YPS) for assessment and to determine how best to apply the program options. For some offences or specific situations, the prosecutor had the discretion whether to refer the offender to the director of YPS or to proceed directly with legal proceedings.

The methods of intervention used with young offenders and the place the non-judicial measures occupy are the result of the experience and thinking of the 1960s and 1970s (to be discussed later in this chapter). In 1984, Quebec became one of the first provinces to take advantage of these provisions by adopting the decree "the Alternative Measures Program" as a program outside of the court that was part of the YOA. Since 1984, the directors of YPS have been designated provincial directors according to the YOA and, consequently, have responsibility to oversee the Alternative Measures Program. And since 2003, the provincial directors have the same responsibilities under the new YCJA. In the same manner, the rehabilitation centres responsible for youth protection were designated detention centres for young offenders with custodial sentences. All custody measures in Quebec consist of a rehabilitation program that allows a series of systematic and intensive interventions and uses the most appropriate techniques to redirect the juvenile delinquent. In every rehabilitation centre, only trained professionals intervene, not the keepers or guardians. Since its application, a number of juveniles have benefited yearly from alternative measures. For example, in 2016, 4346 teens were given extrajudicial sanctions (Institut national d'excellence en santé et en services sociaux 2016).

In **extrajudicial programs**, the assessment carried out by the provincial director must examine certain key factors: the offence committed as well as who is responsible for the offence; the character of the offender and of his/her family; and the social environment. This allows the director to identify not only the nature of the action but also its meaning and significance for the young person, as well as the risk to society. This program is still in effect and has been extended under the YCJA as the Extrajudicial Sanctions Program.

extrajudicial programs Measures that are designed to hold youth responsible for their actions without the creation of a criminal record. They are generally applied to youth who are not engaged in a serious delinquent trajectory.

When implementing the YCJA, the provincial directors confirmed their support for a differential approach to the intervention option. A differential intervention is based on identifying the type of delinquency associated with the young offender's behaviours. The distinction here is between a "common" young offender and a "distinctive" young offender—a distinction that is fundamental to intervening with young offenders (Le Blanc 1983). To do so, one must take into consideration the young offender's conduct and personality and undertake a psychosocial evaluation. Such an assessment aims to identify the right measure at the right time for the right person.

The right measure at the right time is based on the offence for which the adolescent must assume responsibility according to his capacity to do so. The measure must be determined within the limits of the gravity of the offence. Within these limits, the aim is to protect and reaffirm reprobation for the offence while favouring education and rehabilitation measures; it also targets the needs and rights of victims. This measure takes into consideration the adolescent's entire situation to be influenced through tailor made decisions and measures that consider specific needs.

. . . This measure is the result of an equilibrium that is difficult to reach among the following concerns: taking proper, fair, moderated and personalized decisions and measures; the need to take into consideration the gravity of the offence and the reprobation of society; and the importance of intervening at the right moment. The choice and application of such measures are clearly challenging.[1]

In accordance with the YCJA, prosecution in youth court and the imposition of specific sentences should be limited to adolescents in situations (1) where the criminal conduct is an indication of a "distinctive delinquency" (Le Blanc and Fréchette 1989); (2) where there are risks for public security; or (3) where the offences are serious. Serious interventions ordered by the court are designed for juveniles with important developmental deficiencies. These measures consider both the young people's actions and the meaning these actions have for the young offender. This approach depends on the differential evaluation of each situation, considering the young offender's specific needs, especially in terms of rehabilitation and social reintegration. The intervention model in Quebec for young offenders is based on a differential evaluation before any intervention measures are taken. This approach was the result of extensive dialogue among judges, prosecutors, lawyers, and psychosocial professionals, following the YOA's implementation. This was evident in Judge Jasmin's 1995 report and has been supported since the 1970s by experts from both the judicial and social systems who have agreed to value prevention and rehabilitation.

Because of this judicial evolution, there have been profound and dynamic transformations in the way interventions are designed, whether the youth offenders are in open custody, in secure custody, or in the community, or whether alternative measures are being used.

The Evolution of Interventions

Transformation of Open-Custody Interventions

Beginning in the 1950s, during the creation of the court for "social welfare," uprisings against youth imprisonment and large repressive institutions intensified. At the same time, groups of professionals began setting up pilot experiments in rehabilitation, like that of **Boscoville** (Rumilly 1978), which will be discussed below (see Box 15.1). Educators and other professionals took young offenders out of prisons and integrated them into newly designed rehabilitation programs, considered as alternatives to adult prisons and reform schools.

Boscoville became the new rehabilitative project for young delinquents in Montreal and had an important influence on the evolution of rehabilitation throughout the rest of Quebec. In the larger institutions at the time, there were 200 to 300 young people along with only a few staff who were members of the church and had no specific training (Ménard 2003). On the other hand, at Boscoville, there were only about 75 teens. They were divided into small groups of 12 to 15, and they lived in cottages like family homes. There were no guardians, only educators who lived with the youth and led this innovative program, which included academics, sports, art, and social activities. The intention of the program was to contribute to the youths' re-education. This approach was inspired by innovations from European specialized educators (see Capul and Lemay 1996) after the Second World War and by the Americans Redl and Wineman (1951). Boscoville was

Boscoville
A unique program introduced in the 1950s in Quebec that was based on a social welfare and psycho-educative model and that introduced elements in its program designed to teach delinquent youth the necessary skills, values, and attitudes that would allow them to develop a sense of social responsibility.

Box 15.1 | Youth Justice in Action

Elements of the Boscoville Program

- Rehabilitation centre for delinquent teens ages 14 to 18 years
- Initiated as a summer camp toward the end of the 1940s
- Six groups of 15 adolescents in duplex-style apartments
- Staffed by trained educators who specialized in psycho-education (undergraduate- or master's-level education)
- Known as the birthplace of the psycho-educational treatment model and of psycho-education as a profession
- Program composed of activities addressing adolescent development, including academics, arts and crafts (theatre, ceramics, etc.), sports, group meetings; democratic means of engaging youths in collective arrangements, decisions, and individualized treatment; all activities aimed at achieving rehabilitation

Results of an evaluation conducted by Le Blanc (1983) showed that compared to similar programs, Boscoville resulted in lower recidivism rates than most other programs reviewed. For example, one year after attending the program, the adolescents who participated in the program had a 65 per cent rate of non-recidivism and showed significant improvement in their social functioning.

Critical Thinking Questions

What key elements of young offender programs can be identified in the Boscoville experience? How can/might these elements be linked to actual evidence-based practices?

---

structured as systematic action research that led to a theoretical concept of rehabilitation (Guindon 1970) as well as to a method of intervention (Gendreau 1978).

The program at Boscoville contributed to psycho-education, one of its areas of specialty being the rehabilitation of troubled youth. The **psycho-educative model** was unique to Quebec. This profession was created based on several assumptions. The first assumption was that "love" was not enough for working with youth. Contrary to what is believed in some religious environments, this model proposed that the worker must be relatively competent in certain areas. Therefore, educators working with young offenders in the program had to develop specific competencies to intervene effectively (e.g., everyday life skills, the capacity to plan and direct rehabilitative activities, knowledge of normal and abnormal adolescent development, the ability to perform educational clinical evaluations and to conduct educational monitoring interviews). The second assumption was that re-education of young offenders must be integrated into every activity throughout the day and shared with the psycho-educator so that these youths would have a chance to change and take responsibility for their development. Intense interactions between the young offenders and the educator were crucial for effective rehabilitation. This concept was new at the time, and there was resistance from both those who defended a more conservative concept—by limiting worker competencies and incorporating a dose of religious idealism and physical force—and those who were passionate about new therapeutic approaches.

psycho-educative model Developed in Quebec, this model followed the Boscoville experience and is now recognized as a profession specializing in the intervention of troubled youth.

For the latter, it was important to offer competent workers who could use psychotherapy with young people. Unfortunately, psychotherapy failed with these young persons (Trieschman, Brendtro, and Whittaker 1969).

Training for special educators working with young offenders and other troubled youth began to take shape with a program first developed at the University of Montreal. Today, five Quebec universities offer a bachelor's and master's degree in this area, and three of them dispense a doctorate in psycho-education (i.e., Université de Montréal, Université de Sherbrooke, and Université du Québec à Trois-Rivières).

Since 2000, psycho-education has been recognized and structured by a professional organization. The model used for the psycho-educative intervention has been the subject of both qualitative and quantitative research (see Szabo and Le Blanc 1994). This research was conducted over a 10-year period and evaluated the effects of programs used in open custody. Le Blanc (1983) showed that the Boscoville process, in using the psycho-educative intervention model, was able to create a positive social atmosphere. In other words, the social situation is a countervailing force on the negative effects of the delinquent subculture, and it is often created in environments where young offenders are housed. The results of the study also showed that 68 per cent of the youths who participated in the program were not involved in any recidivist activity for up to one year. These results are among the most significant reported in the literature on intervention programs for young offenders. The research also showed how effective rehabilitation programs can be in comparison to the absence of specific interventions and to strict detention. In fact, only 10 per cent of young offenders who appeared before a youth court and were placed in detention centres without rehabilitation programs did not recidivate within the year following the end of their sentence compared to the 68 per cent from the program who did not.

Another important contributor to the differential perspective for treating youth is the Philippe-Pinel Institute (see Box 15.2), which is a psychiatric penitentiary hospital with a special unit for teens with mental health problems associated with their delinquency. In the 1960s, some judges and political authorities made it possible for young offenders who had committed homicide to be integrated into the rehabilitation program. This practice made it clear that it was possible to re-educate even these young offenders in open custody with intervention programs adapted to their needs and societal expectations. Approximately 10 young offenders participated in this experiment throughout the 1960s. Most youths convicted of murder took part in Boscoville's internal program for three to five years, followed by two to three years of support in the community while they were being reintegrated into society. Both social adaptation and non-recidivism proved to be a success (Boisvert, Bisaillon, and Adam 1988; Ducharme 1999).

Research at the Philippe-Pinel Institute showed how important the differential intervention concept is when attempts were made to rehabilitate young offenders. Clearly, the intervention model used at Boscoville had many positive effects for some teen delinquents. According to Le Blanc (1983), the program was more effective with youth offenders presenting neurotic disorders (e.g., anxiety) than with highly criminalized teens presenting psychopathic disorders. However, it was not effective enough for certain types of offenders. This convinced researchers of the need to create a new generation of intervention programming whereby the type of program would match the type of young offender. This

Box 15.2 | Youth Justice in Action

The Philippe-Pinel Institute

Established in 1970, the Philippe-Pinel Institute is

1. A forensic psychiatric hospital.
2. A leading-edge evaluation and treatment facility for forensic psychiatry. Multidisciplinary teams treat patients suffering from severe mental health disorders who pose threats to society. These teams apply treatment programs designed to address specific mental health disorders among adults. The facility also houses a special unit for adolescents that is dedicated to offering forensic evaluation and rehabilitation beyond the capacity of youth centres.
3. A research centre studying mental health disorders with the purpose of enhancing evaluation and treatment methods. For instance, since the 1970s, the Philippe-Pinel Institute's team and its associated researchers have produced numerous studies and reports on prisoners and mental health problems, as well as on the characteristics, treatment, and personalities of sexual abusers, murderers, and other types of aggressors.

Critical Thinking Questions

What are the main motives for referring youth offenders to a forensic psychiatric hospital? Why is it important to be able to evaluate and assess young persons suspected of needing such services?

---

differential perspective has prevailed in many innovative attempts since the early 1990s (see Cournoyer and Dionne 2007; Le Blanc, Dionne, Grégoire, Proulx, and Trudeau-Le Blanc 1998). The results of the various studies on the psycho-educative model applied at Boscoville convinced many authorities that rehabilitation with rigorous and well-implemented programs is necessary. Like Boscoville, institutions were interested in applying the best practices developed elsewhere. For example, inspired by Boscoville, many tried using the Interpersonal Maturity Levels Theory for young offenders for the first time as a model of differential intervention. This typology, developed in the United States (Sullivan, Grant, and Grant 1957) was used to assess different levels of maturity that are associated with modes of reaction and for which a specific intervention can be put in place. This was the groundwork for the first attempts at differential intervention (see Warren 1966). Early in the 1970s, researchers became involved with intervention centres and contributed to their development and implementation in Quebec. Other factors and events, including the evolution of secure-custody interventions, were also partly responsible for improving the service delivery system for young offenders in Quebec.

The Transformation of Secure-Custody Intervention

By the mid-1970s, Montreal had a detention centre with a structure like that of a prison, called le Centre Berthelet. In 1975, a riot broke out and many young offenders were injured, and the buildings were ransacked and set on fire. The riot attracted considerable media attention and prompted an important reorganization of the centre. This reorganization had an enormous influence on how other secure-custody centres in the province operated. Although change and reform were gradual, the process leading up to change provided new knowledge about the conditions necessary to support rehabilitative efforts within a secure-custody centre.

Even though Martinson (1974) and some of his supporters believed that "nothing works" with offenders, Boscoville and other programs contradicted that view and confirmed that rehabilitation was possible in open custody. For high-recidivism-risk teens requiring secure custody, however, rehabilitation was still thought to be impossible. Besides initiatives such as that by Agee (1979) in the United States, few attempts at rehabilitation have been recorded in such environments. After the Berthelet riot, a new team of directors took over the centre. They changed its name to Cité des Prairies and concentrated restructuring efforts on putting in place a rehabilitation program that could satisfy the needs of youth offenders as well as the need for public protection. The main guidelines were as follows:

1. *To take the necessary means to find competent and well-trained employees.* The hiring process for the management, educators, and security staff was rigorous. The selection was completed through a continuous training mechanism for all the staff. This exhaustive process of changing the organizational culture favoured rehabilitation over physical control and confinement.

2. *To implement programs with activities intent on socializing the clientele and inspired by intervention methods proven to be effective.* This second principle led to the implementation of a program with academic, sport, and art activities that emphasized rehabilitation. The program included an individual clinical support process for each young offender that consisted of a thorough psychosocial assessment, an individualized intervention plan, regular educative sessions, as well as meetings with the family/guardians. In addition, a series of activities supported a harmonious social reinsertion for each youth.

3. *To establish an adequate equilibrium between dynamic and static security.* Secure-custody institutions are preoccupied with static security—that is, the physical control of the incarcerated person—comprising different dimensions such as the height of the walls, locks on doors, the use of surveillance cameras, and the presence of security guards. **Dynamic security** is ensured by the relational dimension within the institution. In a secure-custody rehabilitation centre, dynamic security is achieved by the constant presence of educators and the bonds built between the youths and the educators. As a result, the quality of the social climate is improved among peers, which in turn contributes to the security of the institution. While the new centre was being reorganized, tensions ran high for several months between the security staff and the educators, who were securing their relationships with the youths to ensure the dynamic security. This tension demanded efforts and dialogue to resolve conflicts between the two parties and to find a new equilibrium between rehabilitation practices and the necessity of a certain level of physical control (Le Blanc 1991).

dynamic security
Security that is ensured by the relational dimension. It is achieved by the constant presence of educators and the bonds built between the youths and them. As a result, the quality of the social climate is improved among peers, who in turn contribute to the security of the institution.

After a few years of difficult teamwork, the concept materialized and transformed the centre, which had a major influence on new centres that were being implemented or on existing ones that were being reorganized in the province. The Cité des Prairies was transformed into a secure-custody centre for young offenders. It was the first demonstration of the feasibility of modifying the marginalized and delinquent subculture known to prevail in prisons and detention centres and transforming it into a pro-social subculture that valued rehabilitation and was able to counter the iatrogenic effects felt in secure-custody establishments.

Unfortunately, it was not possible to evaluate the results on a large scale as was done at Boscoville (Borgo 1987). However, researchers have observed positive effects of this reorganization on the organizational culture as well as a change in behaviour among the clientele (Le Blanc et al. 1998).

The Evolution of Community Intervention

Since the early 1960s in Quebec, there has been enormous progress in community follow-up methods whether the offender is on probation or under an extrajudicial measure. In the past, the justice department took care of the intervention while the youth offenders were on probation, and there was no difference between services for adults or for young offenders. Probation officers were responsible for a great number of cases (approximately 100 per caseworker), which did not encourage meaningful intervention. Interventions were intermittent in their effectiveness. The transfer of juvenile probation services to the Ministry of Health and Social Services (Ministère de la Santé et des Services sociaux du Québec) in 1976 marked a turning point in the philosophy and means of intervention. From then on, juveniles on probation received intensive services based on supervision, monitoring, and guidance as well as help and counselling. The YOA brought about an important expansion in the development of clinical interventions during probation, and there was an awareness of the "right measures at the right time." Youth centres invested in training for their staff, notably on evaluation tools (e.g., the Jesness Inventory, which is a short 55-question survey that measures a number of different asocial tendencies); on intervention models, such as reality therapy (Glasser 1990); on the rational emotive approach (Ellis and Dryden 1997); or on the implementation of the Interpersonal Maturity Theory (Sullivan et al. 1957; Warren 1966, 1969).

The 1990s began with different intensive probation experiments in Quebec. Results from research projects carried out in the United States (Armstrong and Altshuler 1991) and Great Britain made this possible. The first documented experiment for which there was a formal evaluation was done by Quebec's Youth Centre (Piché and Fréchette 1995). Others in Montérégie, Estrie, and Montreal followed.

Research conducted in Ontario and elsewhere in Canada on the risk-need-responsivity model for offender assessment and rehabilitation (Andrews and Bonta 1998), as well as some experiments on intensive supervision in probation and parole (Armstrong and Altshuler 1991; Gendreau, Goggin, and Fulton 2000), inspired studies of intensive probation follow-ups with treatment for offenders presenting moderate to high risks of recidivism (Cournoyer and Dionne 2007). The research showed that the program significantly lowered the risks of criminal recidivism of the youths. In fact, 76 per cent of those who participated in the program had not recidivated one year after they completed the program. This study led to the implementation in 2009 of a new pilot program of intensive differential follow-up (SID or "suivi intensif différencié") for youths associated with gangs in Montreal, which has been under evaluation since 2011 (see http://www.securitepublique.gc.ca/cnt/rsrcs/pblctns/prgrm-sv-ntsf/index-fra.aspx).

In addition to the efforts made to improve rehabilitation methods in institutions and to the rigorous community follow-up for moderate to high-risk offenders, there was also an opportunity to create community interventions with lower-risk offenders. These represented the first steps in creating **alternative justice agencies**.

The alternative justice measures were significantly influenced by one of the first projects, called Projet Intervention Jeunesse de Montréal (Montreal's Youth Intervention Project), which was carried out from 1977 to 1979. The project's aim was to help young offenders avoid the judiciary process by offering alternative solutions: community work, direct reconciliation with the victim, paying for damages, or participation in measures that would improve social aptitudes. These options were proposed as alternative measures to prosecution, particularly because of the implementation of Chapter 40 of the Act of Youth Protection from 1979 to 1984 in Quebec. In some ways, as described earlier in the chapter, it is possible to say that the Alternative Measures Program, elaborated in 1984 within the framework of the YOA, has its roots in these projects.

The Evolution of Criminological Research

Another important factor in keeping young offenders out of Quebec prisons was the dynamics of the research in criminology, psychology, psycho-education, social work, and, at times, psychiatry (see Szabo and Le Blanc 2004). These studies shed light on youth characteristics, their evolution, and the characteristics of institutions for minors and the effects of their intervention programs (Le Blanc et al. 1998).

As mentioned earlier, open-custody research, conducted by Le Blanc (1983), and the study of the trajectories of 400 criminalized delinquents done by Le Blanc and Fréchette (1989) helped distinguish between "common" delinquency and "distinctive" delinquency. These notions are the basis for the differential intervention model used in many Quebec youth centres. According to these authors, common delinquency is committed by many teens and represents an epiphenomenon that is part of the developmental process in teens. The results of the studies show that most youth commit an infraction in the process of exploring their social environment without their actions being due to important personal, family, or social deficits (see also Chapters 9 and 10 in this textbook). Even though common delinquency is not usually a serious or repetitive commission of delinquent gestures, some acts are serious or repetitive. Intervention involving education, awareness, and the repairing of damages can provoke feelings of responsibility if one is dealing with "conventional" teens who have the necessary acquired knowledge and experience for adequate social development. Considering the potential most teens have for social adaptation, even without intervention, this type of delinquency usually disappears by itself (Le Blanc and Fréchette 1989). Using youth court with this type of delinquency appears unnecessary and even abusive.

alternative justice agencies Quebec-based agencies that are responsible for the application of the extrajudicial programs for youth, who are referred either by the police or by the provincial director, in accordance with the YCJA. Measures can include information and awareness programs on shoplifting, drugs, and law reinforcement as well as mediation or damage repair for the victim or, if that is not possible, damage repairs through community service.

The second category of delinquency deals with crimes that are more repetitive and that become a lifestyle that continues to more advanced stages. This includes about 5 per cent of youth. Making the distinction between the transition of young offenders exhibiting a typical personality development process and real criminal activities that appear at the same age is essential for intervention. Therefore, adolescent young offenders demand an approach that is focused on their needs during their personal and social development phase. This type of delinquency described in studies done by Fréchette and Le Blanc (1987), is qualified as "distinctive" delinquency. It is distinctive because of the important personality deficits identified in these young offenders and is characterized by a behavioural state in which the offensive gestures appear early, persist, are abundant, and are serious. Even though this type of offending is present in only a limited number of teens, it still represents an important part of offences committed by young persons. The behaviour associated with this type of delinquency is diverse and includes serious offences.

Differential intervention is based on identifying the type of young offender by the behavioural, social, and psychological course that the young person takes. Making a distinction between common and distinctive delinquency is fundamental to the intervention measures taken with young offenders. One does this by considering the delinquent conduct and the teen's personality and by confirming one's conclusion based on a psychosocial assessment. As previously mentioned, this evaluation aims to match the right intervention, at the right moment, with the right person.

Today's Services for Young Offenders

Over the past 50-odd years in Quebec, services for young offenders have been under the responsibility of Health and Social Services. Youth rehabilitation centres, social service centres, and youth protection centres joined forces in 1993. At the same time, 16 youth centres were created throughout the province of Quebec. These centres, under the YPA, the YCJA, the Act Respecting Health Services and Social Services (Loi sur le système de santé et les services sociaux), and the Civil Code of Quebec, offer juveniles and their parents psychosocial services and rehabilitation. In each of the youth centres, a director of youth protection (DYP), named according to the Youth Protection Act Quebec, is responsible for receiving reports concerning a child who may have his or her security or development compromised because of physical or sexual abuse, neglect, psychological cruelty, abandonment, or serious behavioural problems. The DYP is also responsible for evaluating the reports and proposing either voluntary measures or court measures to address and ameliorate the situation, as indicated previously in this chapter. When the YOA came into effect in Quebec in 1984, the duties accorded to the provincial director (PD) under the Act were devolved to the DYPs of the province. This disposition was maintained under the YCJA. Therefore, the PD is responsible for applying many aspects of the YCJA. To do so, she or he delegates authority to several people. These delegated individuals work, for the most part, in one of the 16 youth centres in the province.

In addition to the youth centres, Quebec provides a network of community centres. These centres are under the authority of the Ministry of Health and Social Services of Quebec and are mainly concerned with how teens become reconciled with their victims or the community for their wrongdoings. Known as alternative justice agencies, they are united in a provincial organization and are the first to collaborate with the youth centres in applying the YCJA. Centres can be found throughout Quebec, and they all offer the same types of services. Services offered for extrajudicial sanctions are determined by an agreement between the alternative justice agencies and the youth centres that standardize the underlying philosophy for intervention and how the roles are assigned.

Quebec is a vast province composed of different regions, each with its own characteristics. No matter where the adolescent lives, however, he or she will receive roughly the same service with the same rehabilitation perspective. The PD, under an organization that was named the Quebec Youth Centres Association, which has now been abolished after a governmental structure reorganisation in Quebec, and after enforcement of the YCJA, reaffirmed several statements of principles that guide staff working with youth throughout the province. The following section will briefly describe the steps for applying the Act by specifying each clinical position supported by the PDs and Quebec's YCJA working group. This group produced a reference manual guiding the application of the YCJA in youth centres (Hamel and Paradis 2004; Ministère de la Santé et des Services sociaux du Québec 2016) that is based on the scientific literature and on the values derived from the evolving services.

Extrajudicial Measures

Police Measures

The YCJA introduced a preliminary step that was referred to as "exchange measures." Under the Act, it was considered that a certain number of youths who committed offences could benefit from measures applied directly by the police. Besides the possibility of laying charges, the police could decide not to apply any measure, to give a warning, or to direct the adolescent to a community centre where measures would be taken. The interministerial committee of the YCJA in Quebec prepared a framework for these measures before implementing the law. The framework anticipates the type of offence and the measures that are necessary according to the severity of the offence, to traces of the offences left in the youth's police file (Centre Renseignement Policier Québec), and to the role each partner plays in applying measures (i.e., police officers, prosecutors, alternative justice agencies, and provincial director). The framework also includes allowances for regional committees under the authority of the PD who follows its progress. The alternative justice agencies take care of some of the measures for teens referred by the police. Most of these measures are information and awareness programs on shoplifting, drugs, law reinforcement, and so on. Though nonparticipation has no consequences, since 2003 young offenders in Quebec have participated in significant numbers.

Extrajudicial Sanctions

As mentioned in the previous section, extrajudicial measures define some offences for which the young offender can be held liable for criminal and penal prosecution. All other offences are referred to the PD for evaluation and implementation of the possible extrajudicial sanctions. Every youth centre has staff dedicated to this task. Staff members meet the adolescent and the parents for a brief evaluation of the circumstances surrounding the offence, the adolescent's situation, and his or her personal and social functioning. If possible, the provincial director's delegate proposes a measure to the youth. The outline of the agreement between alternative justice agencies and youth centres anticipates that before the delegate carries out the evaluation, the alternative justice agency contacts the victim. That way, when meeting with the adolescent, the delegate has the victim's point of view regarding the damage and can consider measures to address the damage that are suitable for the youth. The agreement in question also provides for a hierarchy of measures: the first measure allows some damage repair for the victim, but if that is not possible, repairing the damage in terms of the community would be considered. While the responsibility for evaluation and orientation resides with the professionals at the youth centres, the alternative justice agency sets the conditions so that the adolescent can carry out the measures.

During the evaluation process, the youth delegate must determine whether the youth is considered normal in terms of social and psychological development (i.e., determine if the youth is manifesting common delinquency) (Fréchette and Le Blanc 1987) and whether applying an extrajudicial measure appears enough to assist the young person. If the evaluation of the situation surrounding the minor (e.g., prior offences, behaviour, and social and psychological difficulties) leads the delegate to believe that she or he is getting into distinctive delinquency (Fréchette and Le Blanc 1987), the delegate can choose to return the case to the prosecutor and legal action may then be taken with measures geared toward establishing a structure and path that will discourage delinquency.

This program has been in place since 1984, and recent annual statistics collected by the PD between 2003 and 2008 indicate that approximately 93 per cent of young offenders with extrajudicial sanctions have successfully carried out the measures imposed (Ministry of Health and Social Services 2008). In 2016, 95 per cent of young offenders with extrajudicial sanctions successfully carried out the measures imposed (Institut national d'excellence en santé et en services sociaux 2016). Although these results are encouraging, further studies on young offenders returning to the justice system are needed to get a better sense of what these numbers mean. However, since the YCJA came into effect, the program has been used much less. The number of evaluations/orientations done by the PD dropped from 11,914 in 2002 to 7455 in 2007 (Association des centres jeunesse du Québec 2004, 2008). In the annual PD report of 2013/14, it is reported that 5156 evaluations/orientations were done (Association des centres jeunesse du Québec 2014). In the annual PD report of 2015/16, it is reported that 4372 evaluations/orientations were done (Institut national d'excellence en santé et en services sociaux 2016). This drop might be a result of the fact that many prospective cases included provisions dictated by the police. This introduces at least two problems: first, the decisions taken by police are not based on psychosocial assessments or on the risk of recidivism; and second, the decisions generally do not consider the victim's opinion or measures aimed at repairing damages.

As noted in an impact evaluation of the YCJA in Quebec (Lafortune et al. 2015), the seriousness of the offence and the number of previous contacts with the police are important predictors of the decision to use an extrajudicial measure. Some other factors that have not been initially anticipated in the framework and the conditions of the application—such as the location of the crime, the time it was committed, and the age and ethnic appearance of the adolescent—are also identified as significant predictors.

The Role of Social Proceedings in Provisional Detention: The Liaison Services in Place and Supervision before Sentencing

Youth Centres in many parts of Quebec have implemented liaison mechanisms with the judicial services. In most regions, a youth delegate must liaise with the prosecutor and with youth centre services. The delegate handles the evaluations requested by the prosecutor, the reports demanded by the court, and the rulings involving the PD. These services allow the exchanges to run more efficiently and effectively. The judicial system is thus ensured that requests sent to the PD arrive quickly and that rulings are applied the day they come into effect.

As well as conducting the liaison service, most youth centres, under Health and Social Services, implement voluntary services for adolescents and their parents before the adolescents go to court. For example, when a young person is released, support and concrete help are offered to both the parents and the adolescent. In particular, in cases of family violence, where the family is in crisis and requires immediate help, youth centres provide educative support or temporarily lodge the adolescent in another environment. Whether the program is referred to as "rapid intervention for delinquency" (*intervention rapide en délinquance*) or "follow-up programs before sentencing" (*programme de suivi avant peine*), it allows for rapid intervention and often prevents further deterioration of a potentially explosive family situation (Duret 2004).

The Pre-sentence Reports

The Youth Tribunal can request a pre-sentence report if more clarification of the case is required before making a ruling. If necessary, the court asks the PD to file the pre-sentence report. As well as answering the judge's questions to assist in the ruling, the report will trace the young person's differential profile and suggest measures according to his or her needs and the perceived risk of recidivism. To further the goals of the differential intervention perspective, youth centres train their staff to use clinical tools that allow them to establish the youth's profile and situation so that they can suggest the measures most likely to positively affect recidivism and rehabilitation. The pre-sentence report deals with the elements related to the present and history of the adolescent's delinquency, including early manifestations of delinquent episodes, aggravation, polymorphism, and persistence. The report will also determine whether the offence(s) are premeditated and organized, whether the youth is alone or involved in some type of organized group, and so forth. In addition to mentioning the behavioural variables, the report will also provide information about the youth's social history, including family history, school records, working experiences, leisure activities, friends, and present and past social life, to assess the youth's social capacities as a basis for intervention. Finally, the psychological profile will be informed by observations made during interviews, through information given by the parents, or through psychometric testing. The tools most often used in Quebec are the Jesness Personality Inventory, a research version of the Youth Level of Service-Case Management Inventory (Hoge and Andrews 1994), and the Crimino-Metric Grid (Piché and Fréchette 1995). These tools allow a better assessment of the youth's risk level and criminal capacity, as well as help to identify potential protective factors (i.e., his or her social capacity).

In Quebec, a pre-sentence report is always accompanied by a series of recommendations made by the youth delegate. The recommendations typically include measures thought to have a real impact on recidivism and on the youth's ability to reintegrate back into society.

Sentence Follow-Ups

Whether the pre-sentence measures involve follow-up in the community or in custody, clinical intervention undertaken by the PD is systematic. Before examining specific aspects of each measure, the PD will examine the general characteristics of the clinical intervention for the young offender in youth centres.

A Planned Intervention

The Quebec legislation on Health and Social Services mandates participation in developing an intervention plan for anyone who receives services from any Health and Social Services organization. No client subject to the YCJA is exempt from this intervention plan. The plan must be signed by the young person and his or her parent(s) or guardian and is subject to review every six months.

Community intervention necessarily requires the young offender to respect various conditions. There is a need for clinical and legal conditions. The youth must participate in the clinical structure, which includes pro-social activities as well as activities that help him or her learn new skills. The youth offender's family is also integrated into the intervention. The aim is to help parents and guardians take control over the family structure and learn to resolve conflict. Intervention plans are also prepared if the young offender is in custody. In such cases, the intervention plan clarifies the work that the youth must undertake while in custody as well as the responsibilities of the youth delegate in contact with the parent(s) or guardian(s). Intervention of this kind is re-adaptive, not repressive, and continues to protect society.

An Individualized Intervention: The Differential Approach

A well-judged intervention is based on an extensive assessment that measures the criminal risks as well as the adolescent's personal and social strengths and weaknesses. Such an intervention will be modulated to fit the adolescent's specific characteristics, and the intensity of the support, supervision, and control will vary depending on the type of offender.

A Specialized Intervention

Whether follow-up is in the community or in custody, intervention with young offenders is completed by a psychosocial or rehabilitation professional. Criminologists, social workers, psycho-educators, and special educators may work with the young offender in youth centres. Throughout their career, qualified staff members receive training on evaluation tools and intervention approaches or models. The intervention is, therefore, very specialized and structured according to rigorous practice standards.

Follow-Up in the Community

Several provisions in the YCJA (Chapters 102 to 109) allow for a follow-up in the community through a court order. The most commonly used provision is probation. According to the Quebec guide on juvenile probation (Piché 2006), probation is defined as "a judicial measure of re-socialization which at the same time guarantees public protection and endeavours to establish personal social functionality of the youth offender . . . while ensuring structure and assistance . . . so he can learn to adjust to the requirements of life in society" (p. 26). Probation, therefore, unites control and support to facilitate the development of the skills the young offender needs to enhance his or her social capacity while controlling the temptation to engage in criminal activity.

Probation follow-up normally consists of interventions that impose conditions to control the adolescent and of clinical measures such as addressing social obligations—going to school, work, and participating in structured leisure activities or clinical group activities. Intervention will also offer support and assistance, since it aims to help the teen's efforts toward social integration. Probation can consist of regular group and individual meetings at a local probation office. The nature of the follow-up depends on the young offender's identified needs and criminal risk. For example, in Montreal, a tool is available that helps make decisions about the intensity of the services needed; services can go from one meeting every two weeks for regular probation to at least three direct interventions a week for those following an intensive differential program (Laporte 2005).

In addition to providing support for the youth, the delegate also offers support to the parents or guardians. This "wraparound" service is designed to defuse conflicts between the parents and their child.

When appropriate, the surrounding community will also be involved in the intervention. Whether it is at school, at work, or during leisure activities, the delegate will mobilize surrounding resources to collaborate in restructuring and supporting the adolescent. Indeed, some measures embedded in the YCJA (e.g., Chapter 42) imply a follow-up in the community. Examples include the obligation to participate in an intensive program offering support and supervision; deferred custody and supervision; and post-custody supervision. The intervention method and the objectives of these measures are the same as in probation but are intensified because those adolescents subjected to these measures generally have a higher criminal risk.

Only a few regions in Quebec (e.g., Quebec City and Montérégie) have developed support and supervision programs approved by the PD. Although there is a lack of approval for these programs in other regions, all youth centres can offer intense follow-up in the community. The organization and resources of these services, however, vary from one region to another. In Montreal, for example, intervention cells consisting of several members who work together allow them to do a more intensive intervention in a community follow-up program.

Placements under Custody

Every youth centre has a few units reserved for youths held in provisional detention or in secure custody. Adolescents placed in open custody are placed in resources that are, in many regions, dedicated to teens who present serious behavioural problems, such as those under the Youth Protection Act.

The young offenders placed in secure custody are confined to a physical space that they cannot leave without permission. Youths placed in secure custody are subject to having to participate in a rehabilitation program that aims to increase their awareness and to make changes to their modes of thinking and behaving. Often based on a psycho-educative model, the program consists of a variety of elements that create equilibrium between different mediums and, therefore, allows the adolescent to develop skills in many different areas. Schooling is mandatory, whether it is an academic program or is in preparation for integration into the labour force. Participating in activities to complete social and personal development is also mandatory: sports, artistic expression, and activities to develop social competencies. Every moment of the day is employed to facilitate rehabilitation.

In addition, there are also group clinical activities aimed at teaching social skills, anger management, problem-solving, moral reasoning, and empathy development. The program also touches on the issue of drug consumption through group or individual activities.

Quebec's Guidelines for Youth Offenders' Rehabilitation

In Quebec, the PDs recommend differential intervention at each level of intervention. The introduction of Bill C-7 in penal law for adolescents provoked uproar in the province. Quebec was for the most part opposed to the federal government's wish to modify the foundations of the YOA. An important coalition of professionals from the justice department, social and community services, universities, and professional associations like the Quebec Bar manifested their opposition to the bill. Particularly, representatives from both the justice department and the social networks who work daily with young offenders were concerned about the impact this new bill could have. Principles like "sentencing" were introduced, inspired by rules that had usually been applied only to adults, thus facilitating the subjection of teens to adult sentencing. Specifically, introducing the idea that the sentence should be proportionate to the gravity of the offence as a guiding principle in determining the sentence was in total opposition to the approach used in Quebec (Trépanier 2004). As was indicated earlier, Quebec's approach encouraged an assessment of the situation that the adolescent was living in, including the offence, its gravity, and the circumstances of its perpetration, but also the psychosocial and developmental aspects of the adolescent.

In Quebec, it was agreed that the YOA was excellent and the foundations of its principles should be maintained (Trépanier 2004). If there were problems, they were most likely related to its enforcement. A few amendments would have been enough to correct it. In reaction to Bill C-7, the Quebec government requested that the Quebec Court of Appeal pronounce on the legality of certain aspects of the bill. Thus, on 5 September 2001, the Quebec government adopted Decree 1021-2001 concerning an amendment to the Court of Appeal to relate to Bill C-7 and its penal justice for adolescents. This decree asked the court to examine questions related to the bill's conformity to the United Nations agreement on children's rights, to the international pact of civil and political rights, and to rights guaranteed by clause 7 and paragraph 15(1) of the Canadian Charter of Rights and Freedoms.

On 31 March 2003, the Quebec Court of Appeal pronounced its verdict. To answer the questions of the decree, it ruled that the clauses on sentencing proposed with articles 38 to 82 did indeed infringe on the rights guaranteed by clause 7 and paragraph 15(1) of the Canadian Charter of Rights and Freedoms. This ruling was based on the rules of presumption, which would send juveniles to the penal justice system as adults at the age of 14. This was also true for the presumption of exceptions to confidential information when an adolescent is subjected to adult sentencing or to presumption related to this type of sentencing. The Supreme Court also declared that presuming an adult sentence in the ruling of *R. v. D.B.*, 2008 CSC 25 was unconstitutional.

Even though these rulings declared certain dispositions on subjecting adolescents to adult sentencing unconstitutional in Quebec, those involved in intervention remained concerned. The dispositions targeted a minority of the youth involved with the penal justice system, but for the majority, the dispositions of the YCJA applied completely. For example, the priority given by the YCJA to the principle of sentence proportionality and the criteria limiting the recourse for custody go against the principle of the right measure at the right time, which, in turn, imposes a series of measures based only on the nature of the offence and its gravity and accords little importance to the adolescent's needs or criminal risk (see Chapters 3 and 4 of this text for further discussion). The effect of this approach delays the social service and judicial systems' ability to apply the right measure at the right time. The right measures applied too late in the lives of teens are less likely to result in positive change. According to many Quebec youth workers, the YCJA has limited the application of differential intervention principles on youths that present an ongoing pattern of criminality when they are not accused of a violent crime (Lafortune et al. 2015). When the severity of the act is the only focus, many perpetrators of persistent non-violent crimes may evolve into delinquency with a sense of impunity (Lafortune et al. 2015).

A major research project on the impact of the YCJA has confirmed those doubts in many respects (Lafortune et al. 2015). Although a relation between the severity of the offence and the intensity of supervision provided is observed, extrajudicial sanctions are globally the first type of measures imposed, whatever the nature of the crime. Youth workers in the same study noted that clienteles' profile in custody has increased in severity over time: While there are fewer youths in their services, young offenders now have a more serious profile, with a significant antecedent history with both the YPA and the YCJA, and they often present various mental disorders (Lafortune et al. 2015). It is to be noted that the duration of the placement in custody itself has also seen a significant decline of 31 per cent over the years, decreasing from 166 days to 114 days (Lafortune et al. 2015). Consequently, youth workers are often under the impression that their influence on the rehabilitation of the youths is limited, especially when young offenders are approaching adulthood (Lafortune et al. 2015).

A new law known as the Safe Streets and Communities Act made important changes to the YCJA in 2012 (Correctional Service Canada 2012). This revision of the YCJA considers many initial criticisms of the Act. Putting an emphasis on public protection, it includes special dispositions aimed at violent and repeat offenders so that, for example, they can be detained in custody before their trial. It also states that a full pattern of history should be considered when addressing the differential assessment of youth offenders' needs. The necessity for the police to keep records of extrajudicial measures for the identification of the criminal engagement of the youths is also a new disposition of the law.

As mentioned previously, when the YCJA came into effect, the values and principles at the base of the Quebec intervention model were confirmed, and these guided interventions with young offenders during the application of legal proceedings. The PDs recommended a clinical approach based on the differential assessment of each adolescent. The implementation of the YCJA in Quebec was based on two premises:

- The established Quebec young offender intervention model should be preserved.
- Advantage should be taken of all possibilities offered by the YCJA to preserve the psychosocial and rehabilitation interventions.

The PDs recommended that interventions with young offenders rely on the values and the clinical vision of the following principles:

- The young person is a developing individual who has not reached full maturity and thus has different needs from adults. The intervention must correspond to this state of development.
- The characteristics of each young person's situation must be considered to provide the right service at the right time. For this, it is important that professionals working with the youth have the required skills. Young offenders need interventions with diversified approaches, methods, and resources. This principle highlights the need to adapt intervention to the nature and amplitude of the problem without a predetermined schedule.
- Rapid intervention is necessary, since the notion of time for an adolescent is significantly different from the adult's, particularly because changes happen rapidly during this phase of development. In the case of distinctive delinquency, pinpointing it early can be a turning point. It is necessary to intervene before the delinquent behaviour becomes entrenched.
- Parental involvement in intervention is essential. It must be sought out, valued, and supported throughout the intervention.
- The victims must be considered and the impact of the offence on them must be kept in mind. The young offender must be made aware of his or her actions and the damage caused. If appropriate, a process to repair damages must be proposed.
- Success of social intervention requires partners with the specific resources needed to confront the needs of the adolescent.

PDs consider the differential assessment of the young offender to determine services and to promote a differential approach during all phases of the intervention process. The assessment relies on the adolescent's delinquent trajectory and on his or her evolution in different areas of life. The assessment situates the risk of recidivism and identifies factors responsible for delinquency and its persistence. The differential assessment also helps determine the intensity and objective of the needed intervention in order both to protect the public and to resolve the adolescent's problems related to recidivism risk factors. Throughout the intervention, assessment must be continuous so that the intervention can be adjusted to the adolescent's evolution. This individualized approach allows the adolescent's needs to be prioritized during the intervention. To help reach targeted objectives, a choice of resources is established. As described earlier, Quebec has a network of community organizations with specialized staff who can offer young offenders a variety of quality services.

The differential assessment of young offenders is the foundation of all phases of intervention in delinquency: extrajudicial sanction programs, pre-sentence reports, community follow-up, custody and supervision in the community, reviews, and so on. As well, PDs support the use of a variety of clinical tools that contribute to systemizing data collection according to validated instruments and evaluating certain personality dimensions less accessible during interviews. Objectives of differential assessment include the following:

- to determine the adolescent's level of involvement in delinquency;
- to identify the factors contributing to delinquency;
- to determine the risk of recidivism;
- to assess the adolescent's resources and his or her capacity to benefit from available resources and services, as well as from those of his or her family;
- to identify the most appropriate services to prevent recidivism using supervision, monitoring, guidance, help, and counselling; and
- to establish intervention objectives.

Efforts to elaborate on principles that guide intervention for young offenders and to implement the necessary resources were spread out over the past 30-odd years and provided Quebec with a justice system and a system of intervention and rehabilitation that is recognized for its flexibility and efficiency.

The intervention model for young offenders and their families that is applied in Quebec youth centres can be summarized as follows:

- It is a differentiated intervention.
- It is based on a differential assessment of the young offender's situation.
- It is supported by known theories and validated clinical tools.
- It favours alternatives to judicial measures and prioritizes mediation with victims for adolescents presenting "common" delinquency.
- It uses the most appropriate measures within the judicial system of the YCJA to satisfy specific needs of adolescents with "distinctive" delinquency.
- It involves parents as well as the collaboration of community resources.
- It considers the victims' interests.

Summary

In 2011/12, next to Manitoba, Quebec had the second-lowest custody rate (9 per cent versus 10 per cent respectively) of young offenders in Canada (Dauvergne 2013). As a result, there have been a few inquiries as to how and why Quebec has maintained one of the lowest custody rates and what (if any) the implications have been. Without comparing the evolution of the youth offender systems in other provinces to that of Quebec, it appears that many answers to these questions can be found in Quebec's unique cultural, social, and political history related to the evolution of approaches to young offenders. Most of what is presented in this chapter is intended to help provide insight into the opposition in Quebec to the YCJA when it was submitted, as well as to the amendment proposed in Bill C-4. There was also opposition to the YCJA elsewhere in Canada, especially from the Canadian Criminal Justice Association (1998).

From a historical standpoint, one of the first elements presented in this chapter was the implementation of modalities to take charge of youth offenders that were distinct from those for adults, in recognition of their different needs. In terms of Quebec, the JDA was another important moment regarding the history of the youth offender system (Dubois and Trépanier 1999). In the 1950s, a series of initiatives in Quebec demonstrated that it is possible to implement effective rehabilitation programs for youth offenders being held in open custody (Le Blanc 1983). The opening of the Philippe-Pinel Institute enabled the creation of specialized assessment and treatment programs for young offenders who presented with severe mental disorders. Throughout the 1970s, four events had a major impact on improving rehabilitation services for youth offenders in Quebec: (1) initiatives that tested alternative measures for young offenders; (2) the major reorganization of all social services; (3) the creation of social service centres; and (4) the Youth Protection Act of Quebec. Under the YPA, youth protection directors were appointed, and later, in the 1980s, they were mandated under the YOA. All these events were significant in the development of today's services and today's philosophy behind the care of young offenders in Quebec.

Following the experiment in Boscoville, it became clear that one unique method of rehabilitation was not enough for all youth offenders. Research demonstrated the need to develop a differential perspective. As noted in the Jasmin II Report (Ministère de la Justice 1995), a consensus of all actors of the judicial and social service systems stated that it is possible to implement effective interventions that respect youth rights and offer the right measure at the right time. Assessments were recognized as fundamental in determining the best measures for young offenders. In addition to the provision of assistance to less serious types of young offenders, it became evident that there was a need to develop specialized programs for high-risk offenders. Programs involving intensive probation with treatment were then tested for youth offenders (offenders who would have normally been placed in custody) who were receptive to the intervention and who had families to support them and participate in the rehabilitation process.

Because of the YCJA's emphasis on the gravity of the offence and because the Act does not consider the youth's needs, recourse to such a differential approach became almost impossible. For example, for professionals, it appeared it was no longer possible to direct young offenders who had committed serious offences to intensive follow-up programs in the community. The overall rigidity of the YCJA was one of the main reasons for Quebec's opposition to the Act. Specifically, it has been recognized for some time now that the offence for which a young person is arrested is rarely a realistic reflection of his or her criminal capacity or of his or her prior offences (Le Blanc 1986). With its recent modifications, some new dispositions of the YCJA might facilitate the use of a differential intervention, especially with violent and repeat offenders. The question remains as to if those youths will receive the right measure at the right time or if they will be identified only after engaging in a serious criminal trajectory?

The development of psycho-education and criminology as professions also contributed to the improvement of practices and influenced the move toward the rehabilitation of young offenders in Quebec. The training given to the personnel working with youth offenders during the 1960s and 1970s was particularly important; indeed, most youth workers today have a university education in their field.

The principles associated with the rehabilitation of young offenders in Quebec have been supported by meta-analyses (see Lipsey 2009). The "Quebec model" has also been supported by the research work of Canadian experts in the field. For example, Andrews and Bonta (2003) have documented the necessity of choosing the best measure when considering offenders' risk of recidivism, their criminogenic needs, and the most effective approach for treatment given their characteristics. Supported by research and reinforced by the historical evolution of measures for youth offenders in the province of Quebec, provincial directors, clinicians, researchers, politicians, and a large part of the Quebec population have opposed, and still firmly oppose, the YCJA, which, for them, gives too much importance to the gravity of the offence to the detriment of the adolescents' needs and capacity.

But is the position of Quebec different from that of the rest of Canada? Although it can be argued that the applications of the Quebec ideal intervention model differ from one region to another in Quebec province, after many years under the YCJA, professionals from different regions of Quebec converge in their opinion that the YCJA restrained their capacity to apply the right measure at the right time with youth offenders.

Key Terms

alternative justice agencies	dynamic security
Boscoville	extrajudicial programs
differential intervention	psycho-educative model

Review Questions

1. Explain why the expression "the right measure at the right time for the right person" is particular to Quebec.

2. Identify five measures applied in Quebec under the YCJA that exemplify the principle "the right measure at the right time for the right person."

3. How do you understand Quebec's opposition to the YCJA?

4. How does psycho-education apply to young offenders' rehabilitation?

5. Name seven characteristics of the intervention model used by Quebec's youth centres.

Critical Thinking Questions

1. After comparing this chapter to others in the book, do you have any information that demonstrates that Quebec's rehabilitation model is different from that of other provinces?

2. How do you explain the difference in custody rates between Quebec and the rest of Canada?

3. After reading this chapter, do you consider that the precedence of social intervention over court intervention is justified?

4. Explain how the meta-analyses of the past decades on offenders' rehabilitation can justify Quebec's position toward the rehabilitation of youth offenders.

Endnote

1. Unofficial translation from excerpts of Ministère de la Justice et Ministère de la Santé et des Services sociaux du Québec (1995). *Les jeunes contrevenants: Au nom . . . et au-delà de la loi.* Rapport du groupe de travail chargé d'étudier l'application de la lois sur les jeunes contrevenant au Québec (Rapport Jasmin II) [Youth offenders: In the name . . . and beyond the law. Report of the Working Group on the Application of the Youth Offenders Act in Quebec (Jasmin II Report)], pp. 36–7.

References

Agee, V.L. (1979). *Treatment of the violent incorrigible adolescent.* Lexington, MA: Lexington Books.

Andrews, D.A., and Bonta, J. (1998). *The psychology of criminal conduct* (2nd ed.). Cincinnati, OH: Anderson.

Andrews, D.A., and Bonta, J. (2003). *The psychology of criminal conduct* (3rd ed.). Cincinnati, OH: Anderson.

Armstrong, T.L., and Altshuler, P.M. (1991). *Intensive interventions with high-risks youths: Promising approaches in juvenile probation and parole.* Monsey, NY: Criminal Justice Press.

Association des centres jeunesse du Québec. (2004). *Bilan des directeurs de la protection de la jeunesse/directeurs provinciaux* [Results from directors of youth protection/provincial directors]. Retrieved from http://observatoiremaltraitance.ca/Documents/Bilan%20DPJ_DP%202004.pdf

Association des centres jeunesse du Québec. (2008). *Au nom de la loi, la bonne mesure au bon moment: Bilan des directeurs de la protection de la jeunesse/directeurs provinciaux* [In the name of the law, the right measure at the right time: Results from directors of youth protection/provincial directors]. Retrieved from http://observatoiremaltraitance.ca/Documents/Bilan%20DPJ_DP%202008.pdf

Association des centres jeunesse du Québec. (2014). *Avec l'energie du premier jour: Bilan des directeurs de la protection de la jeunesse/directeurs provinciaux* [With the energy of the first day: Results from directors of youth protection/provincial directors]. Retrieved from https://ciusss-ouestmtl.gouv.qc.ca/fileadmin/ciusss_oim/Votre_CIUSSS/Documentation/Bilans_DPJ/bilan_dpj_2014.pdf

Boisvert, Y., Bisaillon, C., and Adam, J. (1988). *Les jeunes auteurs d'homicide: Rétrospective et prospective: L'expérience de Boscoville* [Young murderers: Retrospective and prospective: The Boscoville experience]. Montreal: Les Cahiers de Boscoville.

Borgo, J. (1987). Treating the violent offender. In J.M. MacLatchie (Ed.), *Insights into violence in contemporary Canadian society* (pp. 298–304). Ottawa: John Howard Society of Canada.

Canadian Criminal Justice Association. (1998). *Comments of the Canadian Criminal Justice Association on strategy for the renewal of youth justice.* Ottawa: Author.

Capul, M., and Lemay, M. (1996). *De l'éducation spécialisée [Of special education].* Paris: Érès.

Correctional Service Canada. (2012). *Bill C-10: Safe streets and communities act.* Retrieved from http://www.csc-scc.gc.ca/victims/003006-1002-eng.shtml

Cournoyer, L.G., and Dionne, J. (2007). Efficacité du programme de probation intensive du centre jeunesse de Montréal-Institut Universitaire: La récidive officielle. *Criminologie, 40*(1), 155–83.

Dauvergne, M. (2013). Youth court statistics in Canada, 2011/12. *Juristat.* Statistics Canada. Retrieved from http://www.statcan.gc.ca/pub/85-002-x/2013001/article/11803-eng.htm?fpv=2693

Dubois, P., and Trépanier, J. (1999). L'adoption de la loi sur les jeunes délinquants de 1908. Étude comparée des quotidiens Montréalais et Torontois [Adoption of the Young Offenders Act of 1908. Comparative study of Montreal and Toronto daily newspapers]. *Revue d'histoire de l'Amérique française, 52*(3), 345–81.

Ducharme, J. (1999). *Saute d'abord! Un parcours de trente-cinq ans en psychoéducation [Jump first! A thirty-five-year course in psychoeducation].* Montreal: Sciences et Culture.

Duret, A. (2004). LSJPA: La mobilisation du jeune et de ses parents dans le continuum de services aux jeunes contrevenants: Deuxième partie: Le projet intervention rapide en délinquance (Mobilization of the youth and the parents in the continuum of services to youth offenders: The rapid intervention project for delinquency). *Défi jeunesse, 10*(2), 8–13.

Ellis, A., and Dryden, W. (1997). *The practice of rational emotive behavior therapy.* New York: Springer.

Foucault, P. (1984). *Aider . . . malgré tout: Essai sur l'historique des centres de réadaptation au Québec* [To help . . . nonetheless: An essay on the history of rehabilitation centers in Quebec]. Montreal: Les Éditions des centres d'accueil du Québec.

Fréchette, M., and Le Blanc, M. (1987). *Délinquances et délinquants* [Delinquency and delinquents]. Chicoutimi, QC: Gaëtan Morin.

Gendreau, G. (1978). *L'intervention psychoéducative: Solution ou défi? [Psychoeducative intervention: Solution or challenge?].* Paris: Éditions Fleurus.

Gendreau, P., Goggin, C., and Fulton, B. (2000). Intensive supervision in probation and parole. In C.R. Hollin (Ed.), *Handbook of offender assessment and treatment* (pp. 195–204). Chichester, UK: John Wiley.

Glasser, W. (1990). *Reality therapy: A new approach to psychiatry.* New York: Harper & Row.

Guindon, J. (1970). *Les étapes de la rééducation des jeunes délinquants et des autres [The stages of the re-education of juvenile delinquents and others].* Paris: Fleurus.

Hamel, P., and Paradis, R. (2004). *L'application de la loi sur le système de justice pénale pour les adolescents dans les centres jeunesse: Manuel de référence* [Reference manual guiding the application of the Youth Criminal Justice Act in youth centres]. Quebec: Ministère de la santé et des services sociaux du Québec, Gouvernement du Québec.

Hoge, R.D., and Andrews, D.A. (1994). *The youth level of service/Case management inventory and manual.* Ottawa: Department of Psychology, Carleton University.

Institut national d'excellence en santé et en services sociaux. (2016). *Les mauvais traitements psychologiques: Bilan des directeurs de la protection de la jeunesse/directeurs provinciaux* [Psychological abuse: Results from directors of youth protection/provincial directors]. Retrieved from https://www.inesss.qc.ca/fileadmin/doc/INESSS/Services Sociaux/Bilan_DPJ/INESSS_Bilan_DPJ_Mauvais_traitements_psycho_2016.pdf

Joyal, R. (2000). *L'évolution de la protection de l'enfance au Québec: Des origines à nos jours [The evolution of child protection in Quebec: From origins to today].* Sainte-Foy, QC: Presses de l'Université du Québec.

Lafortune, D., Royer, M.N., Rossi, C., Turcotte, M.E., Boivin, R., Cousineau, M.M., . . . Laurier, C. (2015). *La loi sur le système de justice pénale pour les adolescents sept ans plus tard: portrait des jeunes, des trajectoires et des pratiques* [The Youth Criminal Justice Act seven years later: A portrait of youth, trajectories and practices]. Report from Fonds Québecois de la recherche sur la société et la culture. Retrieved from http://www.frqsc.gouv.qc.ca/fr/la-recherche/la-recherche-en-vedette/histoire/la-loi-sur-le-systeme-de-justice-penale-pour-les-adolescents-sept-ans-plus-tard-portrait-des-jeunes-des-trajectoires-et-des-pratiques-b6rcqhb51455717921176

Laporte, C. (2005). *Suivi intensif différencié dans la communauté* [Differentiated intensive follow-up in the community] (Unpublished manuscript). Montreal: Centre d'expertise sur la délinquance des jeunes et les difficultés du comportement, Centre jeunesse de Montréal–Institut universitaire.

Le Blanc, M. (1983). *Boscoville: La rééducation évaluée* [Boscoville: Rehabilitation evaluated]. Montreal: HMH.

Le Blanc, M. (1986). Pour une approche intégrative de la conduite délinquante des adolescents. *Criminologie, 19*(2), 73–96.

LeBlanc, M. (1991). Juvenile justice in Quebec: The anatomy of legislative and administrative changes and their impact on dispositions. In J. Junger-Tas, L. Boendermaker, and P.H. van der Laan (Eds), *The future of the juvenile justice systems.* Leuven, Belgium: Acco.

Le Blanc, M., Dionne, J., Grégoire, J., Proulx, J., and Trudeau-Le Blanc, P. (1998). *Intervenir autrement: Un modèle différentiel pour les adolescents en difficulté [To intervene differently: A differential intervention model for youth in difficulty]*. Montreal: Les Presses de l'Université de Montréal.

Le Blanc, M., and Fréchette, M. (1989). *Male criminal activity from childhood through youth: Multilevel and developmental perspectives*. New York: Springer-Verlag.

Lipsey, M.W. (2009). The primary factors that characterize effective interventions with juvenile offenders: A meta-analytic overview. *Victims & Offenders*, 4(2), 124–47.

Martinson, R. (1974). What works? Questions and answers about prison reform. *Public Interest*, 35, 22–54.

Ménard, S. (2003). *Des enfants sous surveillance: La rééducation des jeunes délinquants au Québec (1840–1950)* [Children under supervision: Rehabilitation of young offenders in Quebec (1840–1950)]. Montreal: VLB Éditeur.

Ministère de la Justice et Ministère de la Santé et des Services Sociaux du Québec. (1995). *Les jeunes contrevenants: Au nom . . . et au-delà de la loi. Rapport du groupe chargé d'étudier l'application de la loi sur les jeunes contrevenants au Québec (Rapport Jasmin II)* [Youth offenders: In the name . . . and beyond the law. Report of the Working Group on the Application of the Youth Offenders Act in Quebec (Jasmin II Report)]. Quebec: Gouvernement du Québec.

Ministère de la Santé et des Services Sociaux du Québec. (2016). *L'application de la loi sur le système de justice pénale pour les adolescents dans les centres jeunesse: Manuel de référence* [Reference manual guiding the application of the Youth Criminal Justice Act in youth centres]. Retrieved from http://publications.msss.gouv.qc.ca/msss/document-001008/?&txt=LSJPA&msss_valpub&date=DESC

Ministry of Health and Social Services. (2008). *Statistical annual report of youth centers* (AS-480 forms) (unpublished manuscript). Quebec: Gouvernement du Québec.

Parizeau, A. (1976). Le droit des mineurs et l'emprisonnement des jeunes au Québec. *Criminologie*, 9(1–2), 118–47.

Piché, J.-P. (2006). *L'encadrement des jeunes contrevenants dans la communauté: Guide d'intervention en matière de probation juvénile.* [The follow-up of youth offenders in the community: Intervention guide for juvenile probation]. Quebec: Ministère de la Santé et des Services Sociaux, Gouvernement du Québec.

Piché, J-P., and Fréchette, M. (1995). *Mesure probatoire intensive pour adolescents contrevenants: Application et efficacité* [Intensive probation for youth offenders: Implementation and effectiveness]. Quebec: Les Centres jeunesse de Québec.

Platt, A.M. (1977). *The child savers: The invention of delinquency*. Chicago: University of Chicago Press.

Redl, F., and Wineman, D. (1951). *Children who hate*. New York: Free Press.

Rumilly, R. (1978). *Boscoville*. Montreal: Éditions Fides.

Sullivan, C., Grant, M.Q., and Grant, J.D. (1957). The development of interpersonal maturity: Applications to delinquency. *Psychiatry*, 20(4), 373–95.

Szabo, D., and Le Blanc, M. (1994). *Traité de criminologie empirique [Workbook on empirical criminology]*. Montreal: Les Presses de l'Université de Montréal.

Szabo, D., and Le Blanc, M. (2004). *Traité de criminologie empirique [Workbook on empirical criminology]* (2nd ed.). Montreal: Les Presses de l'Université de Montréal.

Trépanier, J. (2004). What did Quebec not want? Opposition to the adoption of the Youth Criminal Justice Act in Quebec. *Canadian Journal of Criminology and Criminal Justice*, 46(3), 276–300.

Trieschman, A.E., Brendtro, L.K., and Whittaker, J.K. (1969). *The other 23 hours: Child-care work with emotionally disturbed children in a therapeutic milieu*. Piscataway, NJ: Transaction.

Warren, M.Q. (1966). *Interpersonal maturity level classification: Juvenile diagnosis and treatment for low, middle and high maturity delinquents*. Sacramento, CA: Youth Authority.

Warren, M.Q. (1969). The case for differential treatment of delinquents. *Annals of the American Academy of Political and Social Science*, 381, 47–59.

Juvenile Justice and Restorative Justice in British Columbia
Learning through the Lens of Community Praxis

Brenda Morrison, Muhammad (Asad) Asadullah, and Colleen Pawlychka

16

Overview

This chapter focuses on the development of restorative justice in British Columbia within a wider theoretical and institutional analysis of justice reforms in British Columbia as well as nationally and internationally. The chapter begins with broad reflections on juvenile justice policy, practice, and outcomes, suggesting that despite various legislative reforms, recommendations, and mandates, the juvenile justice system remains focused on state-based social control through mechanisms that continue to marginalize vulnerable populations. The theory and practice of restorative justice widens the humanistic and relational lens of justice, moving from a state-based social control to community-based social engagement. The chapter reflects on provincial policy that by and large operationalizes restorative justice as a police diversion measure away from the state-based system, rather than as integrative collaborative systems that respond to individual and community needs. These reflections suggest that holistic reform within the Canadian juvenile justice system has yet to come, as the justice system has yet to systemically embrace theoretical and evidence-based research that situates restorative justice within responsive collaborative regulatory practices that meaningfully engage communities.

Key Objectives

After reading this chapter, you should be able to:

- Describe specific legislative changes to juvenile justice related to restorative justice.
- Describe the development of restorative justice in British Columbia.
- Contextualize these developments in the context of state- and community-driven policy.
- Provide a case study of effective community engagement (e.g., Roca).
- Provide a comparative case of why Canada, once at the forefront of restorative justice, now falls behind other countries.

Introduction

Over 30 years have passed since *Taking Responsibility,* a 1988 report authored by a House of Commons Justice Committee (the Daubney Committee), recommended the use and evaluation of restorative justice in Canada. The report stated that the "Committee found the evidence it heard across the country about the principles of restorative justice compelling," and recommended that governments at all levels support the expansion and evaluation of RJ programs at all stages of the criminal justice process (Daubney 2010). In particular, Recommendation 19 supported the expansion and evaluation by the federal government, preferably in conjunction with provincial/territorial governments, of **victim–offender reconciliation programs (VORP)** at all stages of the Canadian criminal justice process that (a) provide substantial support to victims through effective victim services, and (b) encourage a high degree of community participation. In 1990, the United Nations Minimum Standards Rules for Non-Custodial Measures (i.e., the "Tokyo Rules"), essentially echoed this Recommendation through Rule 2.4, which called for greater use of alternatives (i.e., community-based measures), and complemented Rule 5 of the 1985 United Nations Standard Minimum Rules for the Administration of Juvenile Justice (i.e., the "Beijing Rules") (Winterdyk 2015).

In 1996, Canada became the first country in the world to include restorative justice, through the provision of reparations to victims and communities, as a legitimate option within the Criminal Code (see section 718.2 (e)). Canada has a strong legacy in the

victim–offender reconciliation programs (VORP)
A process through which a trained mediator(s), who could be a community-based volunteer, brings offenders and victims in a criminal event together to achieve a resolution that is satisfactory to both parties (Community Justice Initiatives 2011; see also Stutzman Amstutz 2009).

restorative justice (RJ)
Restorative justice is "a justice that puts its energy into the future, not into what is past. It focuses on what needs to be healed, what needs to be repaired, what needs to be learned in the wake of a crime. It looks at what needs to be strengthened if such things are not to happen again" (Sharpe 1998).

development and expansion of **restorative justice** (RJ) principles, programs, and practices; yet such programs and practices currently remain at the margins of the Canadian justice system, compared to developments in other countries. This chapter explores the history of the development of RJ as it relates to juvenile justice, using developments in British Columbia as a case study.

Sharpe (1998) offers five touchstones of restorative justice: invite full participation and consensus; heal what has been broken; seek full and direct accountability; reunite what has been divided; and strengthen the community, to prevent further harms.

Changing Lenses: "Crime" and "Reparation"

Contemporary RJ grew from the juxtaposing of state-based justice, wherein the primary focus is determination of guilt, and punishment, of the offender, with community-based justice, wherein repairing the harm of those most affected—victim, community, offender—widens the network of responsiveness. In other words, it signals a paradigm shift from the state responding to crime, to individuals, community, and the state responding to harm. From a rule-of-law perspective, crime is legally defined as a breach of a state-based criminal law (i.e., criminal code), that codifies negative/harmful behaviours that erode social order and formal negative/punitive sanctions. Conversely, an RJ perspective views crime as a violation of people and relationships, creating obligations to repair harm to victims and communities (Zehr 1990). This shift is characterized as a shift from guilt and punishment to responsibility and healing (see Sharpe 1998; Gavrielides and Artinopoulou 2013, pp. 344–8).

Juvenile Justice Legislation: From Social Control to "Off Ramps"

Canada has come a long way since the Juvenile Delinquents Act (JDA) of 1908, wherein youth, being understood as misguided through improper upbringing by their family, were charged with juvenile delinquency rather than criminal behaviour (Green and Healy 2003; Tustin and Lutes 2010; see also Chapter 1 in this textbook). As responsibility was placed with family, and not the youth, the focus of sentencing was on rehabilitation, re-education, and guidance, with the state providing a familial decision-making role. Similarly, during this same time period, Indigenous children became wards of the state to rehabilitate and reeducate them, and so to "kill the Indian" in the child (see Oudshoorn 2015, p. 28). Over 150,000 Indigenous children and youth attended residential schools. The traumatic and devastating effects of residential schools have led to disproportional representation of Indigenous peoples in our criminal justice system (CJS) (see Monchalin 2016). Indigenous children were also taken from their families in what is known as the "Sixties Scoop," as "it was common practice in [British Columbia] in the mid-sixties to 'scoop' from their mothers on reserves almost all newly born children." Within a decade, the proportion of children in care rose from 1 per cent to 35 per cent, due to the generational trauma of residential schools, resulting in the loss of culturally specific parenting skills, knowledge, and family ties (Indigenous Foundations 2009).

The Young Offenders Act (YOA) replaced the JDA *in 1984, with the focus shifting to rights and procedural justice through a formalization of due process.* The Act bridged youth justice with that of adults by referring to youth as offenders rather than delinquents; by having youth represented by counsel in court proceedings; by holding public court hearings; and by increasing the use of custody (Winterdyk 2015).

The use of custody increased until 1999, when Anne McLellan, then Canada's minister of justice, declared that we "incarcerate youth at a rate of four times that of adults and twice that of many US states" (in Green and Healy 2003, p. 32). Canada's youth incarceration rate at that time was the highest in the Western world (Winterdyk 2015).

In response to rising youth custody rates, the Youth Criminal Justice Act (YCJA) was implemented in 2003, as a middle ground between the JDA and the YOA (see Chapter 3). With this Act, the influence of RJ theory and practice begins to be recognized in the legislative direction:

> The YCJA introduced significant reforms to address concerns about how the youth justice system had evolved under [previous legislation] . . . the overuse of courts and incarceration in less serious cases, disparity and unfairness in sentencing, a lack of effective reintegration of young people released from custody, and the need to better take into account the interests of victims. (Government of Canada, Department of Justice 2002, p. 1)

The Act recognizes the following:
- Society has a responsibility to address developmental challenges and needs of young persons in order to guide them into adulthood.
- Communities and families should work in partnership through multidisciplinary approaches to address crime prevention by addressing its underlying causes, providing guidance and support to young persons, particularly vulnerable youth.
- Information regarding youth justice, crime, and measures taken to address youth crime should be publicly available.
- Young persons have rights and freedoms, including those set out in the United Nations Convention on the Rights of the Child, in the Canadian Charter of Rights and Freedoms, and the Canadian Bill of Rights.
- The youth criminal justice system should command respect and take into account the interests of victims.
- The youth criminal justice system should foster responsibility and ensure accountability through meaningful consequences and effective rehabilitation and reintegration.
- The youth criminal justice system should reserve its most serious interventions for the most serious crimes and reduce overreliance on incarceration.

These general principles, outlined in the preamble of the Act, reflect the principles of RJ. For instance, the YCJA aims to prevent crime by addressing underlying circumstances of offending behaviours and by emphasizing rehabilitation and reintegration of young persons into society, with specific consideration for the reduced level of maturity and greater level of dependency of young persons on adults. Consequences resulting from crime are to be meaningful to the young person, and must promote accountability while being fair and proportionate to the crime. The YCJA also makes specific provisions for young persons to be heard and involved in the processes that lead to decision-making. Finally, section 3(1) of the Act emphasizes that measures taken against young persons should

(c) (i) Reinforce respect for societal values;

(ii) Encourage the repair of harm done to victims and the community;

(iii) Be meaningful for the individual young person given his or her needs and level of development and, where appropriate, involve the parents, the extended family, the community and social or other agencies in the young person's rehabilitation and reintegration; and

(iv) Respect gender, ethnic, cultural and linguistic differences and respond to the needs of aboriginal young persons and of young persons with special requirements. (Department of Justice Canada 2002)

While the YCJA makes no direct reference to RJ, there is general agreement that the Act "does seem to open the door to the development of initiatives generally associated with restorative justice" (Charbonneau 2005, p. 75). For example, numerous extrajudicial measures form an essential first response to youth crime rather than a possible alternative to court as was the case under the YOA. That is, the Act requires that police and Crown attorneys consider extrajudicial measures, including informal warnings, police or Crown cautions, police referrals to community programs or agencies, referrals to pre-charge screening programs or youth justice committees, or conferences (Tustin and Lutes 2010; see also Chapters 3 and 4 in this textbook).

Two primary methods of allowing for RJ initiatives are the inclusion of victims and communities in the process and the authorization of RJ conferences. Under section 5, the YCJA directs (in part) that extrajudicial measures must:

• encourage acknowledgement and reparation of harm to the victim and community;

• encourage families (including extended families) of young persons, as well as the community, to become involved in the design and implementation of those measures; and

• provide an opportunity for victims to participate in decisions related to the measures selected and to receive reparation.

family group conferencing
". . . a process of collaborative planning in situations where decisions need to be made for children or youth. It is a formal meeting where members of a child or youth's immediate family come together with extended kin and members" (British Columbia Ministry of Children and Family Development 2005, p. 2).

The YCJA authorizes the use of conferences by a youth justice court judge, the provincial director, a police officer, a justice of the peace, a prosecutor or youth worker, or a youth justice committee. Defined in the YCJA, section 2(1), as "a group of persons who are convened to give advice in accordance with section 19," conferences refer to various types of processes in which affected or interested parties come together to formulate plans to "address the circumstances and needs involved" (Department of Justice Canada 2002, p. 6) and may take the form of **family group conferencing**, youth justice committees, community accountability panels, sentencing circles and inter-agency case conferences" (Department of Justice Canada 2002, p. 6). The inclusion of conferences in the YCJA and the broad nature of their mandate allow for some RJ initiatives through the inclusion of victims in the process of reparation of harm, and through the healing of young persons and communities.

With the requirement that extrajudicial measures, including RJ initiatives, be considered, there has been a decline in young persons charged by police, "with a 30 per cent rate of youths cleared otherwise" since implementation of the YCJA. This indicates some measure of success in the YCJA (see also Chapter 3 in this textbook for additional data in support of this argument). However, use of these extrajudicial measures is not mandatory; rather, police and Crown attorneys need only *consider* such measures in order to satisfy legislative requirements. Therefore, it is important to examine not only the reduction in charges but also the primary factors that play a role in the police and Crown attorney's decision-making regarding whether to divert these youth, and where they should be diverted to. A study of policing and RJ in Saskatchewan (Glowatski, Jones, and Carleton 2017) concluded that a broader shift than restorative policing is required beyond police diversion and participation in the restorative justice process:

> Police officers need to engage in more restorative justice practices (not to be read as synonymous with restorative policing), to foster better understandings of restorative justice, and to understand that justice is first and foremost about relationships. Restorative policing requires officers to go beyond partaking in restorative justice processes by shifting how they approach their entire praxis. The officers must also extend their focus beyond the mandate of community policing to include becoming community-builders who are aware of, and contributing to, all matters of concern in their community. (p. 289)

Overall, the YCJA has decreased youth incarceration, with data from British Columbia mirroring the national data: the rate of youth charged by police has decreased (by 27 per cent between 2012 and 2016) along with the total correctional rate (by 11 per cent between 2015/16 and 2016/17). Yet the aggregate data masks a disturbing trend for Indigenous youth, who continue to be overrepresented in the justice system at increasing rates (Malakieh 2018). Indigenous youth represent 8 per cent of the Canadian youth population yet account for 46 per cent of admission to correctional services. In British Columbia, over the past decade (2006/7 to 2016/17), the rate of admissions of youth into custody rose from 34 per cent to 44 per cent for Indigenous males, and 32 per cent to 60 per cent for Indigenous females. Despite legislative changes that have influenced RJ initiatives, particularly within BC, evidence suggests that these legislative changes alone are not enough for vulnerable youth (Representative for Children and Youth [RCY] 2014a, 2014b). In fact, reports find that "it is still not possible to say with certainty whether things are getting better for BC's vulnerable children and youth" (RCY 2014a, p. 5). These trends are consistent with the MacDonald Laurier Institute's (Perrin and Audas 2018) report card on the CJS, in which BC dropped from a "C+" to a "D" for the proportion of Indigenous persons in total custodial admission. The report card further noted, "the province also has one of the most disproportionately high levels of Indigenous incarceration anywhere in Canada" (p. 35). In 2016, BC ranked eighth out of the 13 provinces and territories, and in 2017, BC dropped to tenth place. Overall, the report indicated that

Confidence in the police, justice system, and courts in BC is below average. Victims in the province receive one of the lowest proportions of restitution orders in Canada. BC has a relatively high average daily cost per inmate, and relatively more police officers per capita than elsewhere in Canada. (p. 34)

RJ can be responsive to these concerns, which includes being more responsive to needs of vulnerable populations and being more responsive to victims, including the payment of restitution and increased satisfaction in the justice system (Braithwaite 2016).

The Development of Restorative Justice in BC: The Intersection of Three Practices

Victim—Offender Reconciliation Programs

The evolution processes of youth and adult RJ initiatives in BC are intertwined; as such, the development of both systems will be described. The RJ movement in Canada traces its emergence within the CJS to a landmark 1974 juvenile justice case in Elmira, Ontario, where two young men destroyed the property of 22 victims. The courageous and insightful decisions and actions of Mark Yantzi, a Mennonite probation officer, and Judge Gordon McConnell set a precedent for a new response to juvenile justice in Canada. Officer Yantzi, with the support of Dave Worth of Mennonite Central Committee, recommended in his pre-sentence report that the offending juveniles be ordered to knock on the doors of their victims, apologize for their crimes, listen to what the victims had to say, determine the amount of restitution, and ask for forgiveness. Judge McConnell saw no legal precedence to order these actions by the juveniles. Officer Yantzi, weighing the benefits offered by the court with those of a face-to-face meeting with the victims, spoke with the juveniles, convincing them that volunteering to perform these acts of restoration would allow the judge to include them as part of a probation order. The youths volunteered. Russ Kelly (2010), one of those two young men, stated,

> On that day, my life changed forever as I managed to overcome the challenges of a punitive society and turn my life around. Meeting my victims taught me a valuable lesson in humanity and I never damaged anyone's property after that. . . ." (para. 3)

This landmark case marked the beginning of Kitchener's victim—offender reconciliation program (VORP) and became a foundational program for community justice initiatives (CJI) in Kitchener-Waterloo, Ontario (Peachey 1989). As interest grew within Mennonite communities, the program spread west across Canada to Langley, BC.

David Gustafson, a pioneer of RJ in BC, received the province's first VORP referral in 1982, with the Langley Mennonite Fellowship offering funding support for the program. In 1985, after being awarded an alternative measures contract with BC's Ministry of the Attorney General, the Fraser Valley Community Justice Initiatives (FVCJI) was formed to operate VORP and other related programming for both juveniles and adults (Gustafson 2004). In 2002, provincial funding was cut for adult cases, limiting the program to juveniles. Despite these cutbacks, FVCJI's annual report demonstrates the effectiveness of VORP on youth's accountability to the community. FVCJI's funding for juvenile programs from the Ministry of Children and Family Development ended on 31 July 2004, and with this cut came the end of VORP—but not the end of FVCJI, who now work in partnership with the Correctional Service of Canada to deliver a post-sentence victim–offender mediation (VOM) process for serious crime. Since 1992, of the 246 offenders who participated in VOM, 89 per cent have not committed a new offence.

While BC, along with other provinces, has yet to carry out a comprehensive review of RJ for juveniles, the Nova Scotia Restorative Justice (NSRJ) program, in which referrals can be made at any stage of the criminal justice process for a wide range of offences, has been reviewed. Clairmont and Kim (2013) observed,

> Its strengths organizationally are many—province-wide programming; secure, substantial, long-term government funding generous for a small so-called have not province; collaboration with local non-profit agencies who deliver the service while the provincial NSRJ management provides coordination, protocols and training. . . . It has also partnered with, and contributed significantly to the success of, the province-wide Aboriginal RJ program. Its impact, measured in terms of conventional CJS evaluation concerns, has been impressive—less recidivism than in similar court-processed cases; high levels of satisfaction among all categories of participants in the RJ sessions (offenders, victims, supporters, police attendees and others); and diversion of roughly 33% of all cases of youth arrest from the court processing stream. (p. 389)

Clairmont and Waters's (2015) formative assessment of the NSRJ concluded that "Within a decade of its launching, the NSRJ had become institutionalized in the Nova Scotia Criminal Justice System (CJS). [Alternative measures] had essentially been a police-referred program, significant but marginal to the CJS, but RJ went well beyond the police gatekeepers for youth diversion not only in receiving many referrals post-charge and pre- and post-sentence but also in its impact on CJS culture and even the negotiation strategies between prosecutor and defence counsel" (pp. 18–19).

Developments in Canada have also influenced youth justice in the United States. A recent evaluation in Alameda County, California, of a community-based RJ program found that RJ reduced recidivism, reduced costs to the system, eased pressure on an overburdened court system to focus resources where they are most needed, increased victim satisfaction, alleviated symptoms of post-traumatic stress associated with victimization, helped strengthen family and community ties, and had the potential to reduce racial and ethnic disparities within the criminal legal system (Baliga, Henry, and Valentine 2017). No national survey has been conducted in Canada. Other than the meta-analysis carried out by the Department of Justice (Latimer, Dowden, and Muise 2001), there has been little effort to collect systemic data, from mapping existing programs to process- and outcome-based evaluations, across this country.

Sentencing/Peacemaking Circles

The harsh realities of the criminal justice system for Indigenous peoples in Canada began to be more fully recognized in the late 1980s and early 1990s—specifically, their disproportionate representation within the CJS (see Dickson-Gilmore and La Prairie 2005; Monchalin 2016). Recognizing the need for a shift in judicial practice, Yukon Territorial Court Judge Barry Stuart adjourned the case of *R. v. Moses* (1992)—in which the defendant pled guilty to carrying a baseball bat with the intention of assaulting a police officer—and convened the first sentencing circle, drawing on traditional Indigenous practice in the Yukon Territory (see Benevides 1994; Stuart 1996).

Sentencing circles have since been used in many Indigenous communities throughout Canada, drawing on local Indigenous traditions and values. The sentencing circle itself, however, is not a traditional practice of Indigenous peoples in Canada; rather, it is a creation of the existing system, introduced within Indigenous communities primarily by the judiciary serving these communities (Crnkovich 1995, p. 2). These practices are based on three guiding premises: (1) a criminal offence represents a breach of relationship between the offender and the victim/community; (2) the well-being of the community is dependent on healing these breaches; and (3) the community is the best resource to address these breaches. A sentencing circle, as it was originally conceived, is a community-directed process that partners with the criminal justice system in an effort to build consensus on a sentencing plan. Sentencing circles include a wide range of community members in the process: victims, victim supporters, offenders, offender supporters, judge, prosecutor, defence counsel, police, and court workers. Initially, judges were the primary facilitators of circle hearings and this evolved into Elders and community members co-facilitating the circles (Pranis, Stuart, and Wedge 2003; Stuart 1996, 1997).

The Supreme Court of Canada supported the use of sentencing circles in 1999 in the case of *R. v. Gladue* ". . . as an approach to remedying crime in which it is understood that all things are interrelated and that crime disrupts the harmony which existed prior to its occurrence, or at least which it is felt should exist . . . [and in which the] appropriateness of a particular sanction is largely determined by the needs of the victim, and the community, as well as the offender" (p. 690). The Gladue case encouraged the use of alternatives to incarceration and, in endeavouring to remedy the adverse background cultural impact factors and overrepresentation of Indigenous people in Canadian prisons, recognized that restorative approaches resonated with traditional Indigenous ways of dealing with conflict. Consequently, the Gladue decision was legislated in the Criminal Code amendment (section 718.2(e)), in which the sentencing principle states that "all available sanctions other than imprisonment that are reasonable in the circumstances should be considered for all offenders, with particular attention to the circumstances of aboriginal offenders" (Elliott and Gordon 2013).

Sentencing/peacemaking circles are recognized within the Indigenous Justice Program (IJP) strategy (previously known as the Aboriginal Justice Strategy [AJS]). This program is cost-shared federally, supporting approximately 31 programs in British Columbia. The program supports the use of traditional justice in Indigenous communities, which may or may not include the use of peacekeeping circles. For example, the Vancouver

sentencing/peacemaking circle
A process that brings together individuals who wish to engage in conflict resolution, healing, support, and/or decision-making. It provides a space for offenders to acknowledge responsibility for their behaviour and invites community members to participate in the decision-making and/or sentencing.

Aboriginal Transformative Justice Services Society (VATJSS) provides prevention, diversion, alternative measures, and housing services to Indigenous people in the city of Vancouver. This program's main objectives are to offer a community-based process focusing on repairing relationships among those affected by crime—i.e., the victim, the offender, their families, and the community—and to empower individuals to formulate appropriate responses and strategies to deal with the crime and participate directly in processes that affect the community's overall well-being. To accomplish these objectives, the VATJSS creates a community council forum—comprised of volunteers, an Elder, the victim, the offender, and their support people—to discuss the offence, its effects, and the causes of the behaviour that led to the offence. At the forum's conclusion, a healing plan is developed with the goal of making amends and reintegrating the offender into the community.

An evaluation of the VATJSS (Palys 2014) complemented a national 2010/11 evaluation (Department of Justice Canada 2011) that found reduced recidivism, cost savings, and community development and recommended that the federal government should

- make a long-term commitment to Indigenous justice in Canada;
- allow for variation in program funding;
- negotiate a new generation of protocol agreements involving the VATJSS;
- base new protocol agreements on the notion of default Indigenous jurisdiction; and
- provide funding adequate to the task.

A 2016 federal evaluation of the AJS found "a number of barriers to the achievement of anticipated AJS outcomes." It noted further,

> The fact that a majority of Indigenous communities do not receive AJS support means that large numbers of Indigenous people who are in conflict with the law are involved with the [mainstream justice system], which is unable to respond effectively to their particular needs, and may in fact be perpetuating the problem of overrepresentation. The evaluation also found a number of factors in AJS-supported communities that limit access to effective alternative programming. One is that the community-based justice programs rely heavily on referrals from police and Crown to enable offenders to take advantage of their programs, and referrals vary greatly from community to community. (Department of Justice Canada 2016, p. iv)

A more recent study of the IJP, focusing on victim impact across five Indigenous communities, found that

> Most of the cases that used a RJ process resulted in victims and survivors feeling heard and respected. In some cases, victims and survivors reported feeling relief from fear and anxiety, while in more serious cases victims and survivors felt that they could at least start to address these feelings. In addition, most victims and survivors felt considerable satisfaction with the plans developed through the RJ process. (Evans, McDonald, and Gill 2018, p. 31)

The Provincial Court of British Columbia also responded to the needs of Indigenous communities, by establishing First Nations Courts (FNCs) in New Westminster (2006), North Vancouver (2012), Kamloops (2013), and Duncan (2013). In the same vein as RJ, the FNCs seek to acknowledge and repair the harm done to victims and the community, creating space for victim participation. As Dandurand and Vogt (2017) note, these courts "generally adopt a restorative justice approach to sentencing, preferring a non-adversarial and non-retributive approach to justice that focuses on healing, holding the offender accountable, and reintegrating the offender into the community to achieve better justice outcomes" (p. 3).

Dandurand and Vogt conclude that, as with other RJ initiatives in British Columbia, "the data currently available on the FNCs are still limited. There is very little information being systematically collected on the cases referred to and dealt with by these courts" (p. 22). As Johnson (2014) observes in her review of FNCs in Canada,

> The work of FNCs and the people that labour within them cannot be viewed in isolation from the web of Indigenous healing supports, additional infrastructure and operating funds that are required to support and make sustainable change. Nor can one FNC process be expected to address all the colonizing issues that Indigenous peoples experience and underlie a lack of well-being and behaviours that bring people into contact with Canada's justice system. (p. 11)

For the Canadian justice system to be relevant, effective, and collaborative with Indigenous communities, additional resources and action will be necessary, and this will need to take the form of development in close collaboration with diverse Indigenous communities across the province.

Family Group Conferencing

Another internationally recognized form of RJ is family group conferencing (FGC). Developed in New Zealand, and legislated through the Children, Young Persons and Their Families Act in 1989 as a youth justice mechanism, this legislation includes police warnings, police youth diversion, and FCG (MacRae and Zehr 2004). Rather than being diverted from court to RJ (as is the case in BC), young offenders in New Zealand are directed from RJ to court when an FGC, alone, is not deemed appropriate. In New Zealand, youth court is typically reserved for very serious offences. The mandate of an FGC is to (a) build understanding of the consequence of the crime, allowing young offenders to hear the full impact of the crime, and (b) develop a reparative plan. An important step in New Zealand's FGC is private family time between these two stages. This process is widely held to be derived from traditional Maori practice. For example, the *Handbook of Restorative Justice Programs* (United Nations 2006) describes FGC as ". . . based on the centuries old sanctioning and dispute resolution traditions of the Maori, the New Zealand aboriginal group," noting that "The model is now also widely used in modified form as a police-initiated diversion approach in South Australia, South Africa, Ireland, Lesotho, as well as cities in Minnesota, Pennsylvania, and Montana" (p. 20).

Neither Canada nor British Columbia is mentioned here, even though the *Handbook* was written by two Canadian researchers from BC. Nevertheless, what appears most important is the Maori influence on the change of legislation, as Shannon Pakura (2005) states: "Regarding the origins of this development, let me emphasize that the law changed primarily because Maori were dissatisfied with the way professionals made decisions about them. Maori were distressed about the impact on them of these decisions and were no longer prepared to tolerate legal or professional systems that gave little weight to Maori customs, values and beliefs" (p. 2).

While there are historical connections of FGC with the Maori people in New Zealand, the more recent relationship between the Indigenous peoples of New Zealand and FGC has been deeply criticized (Cunneen and Tauri 2016). In particular, the inclusion of family group decision-making within a Western system of common law falls out of step with the larger cultural context of traditional Maori life and, as such, has not served to create more just responses from the CJS for the Indigenous people of New Zealand. Indeed it has been argued that extracting certain elements of Maori traditional justice out of a broader system of Maori justice leads to "selective and ahistorical claims . . . about indigenous social control conforming with the principles of restorative justice, while conveniently ignoring others" (Cunneen 2007, p. 43).

A more recent study of FGC and justice reforms in New Zealand (Moyle and Tauri 2016) observes,

> The success of these reforms is not evident when reviewing the 2010–2014 statistics on admissions to youth justice residences. Over this time, data shows a significant increase in admissions to residence for Maori and Pacifica [Indigenous] young people and children, while the number of Pakeha [non-Indigenous] youth admissions decreased. Since these reforms, Maori have gone from half to more than two-thirds of the total young people and children in youth justice residences. (CYF Practice Centre 2014, p. 100)

The researchers conclude,

> Simply put, for the FGC forum to work as a culturally responsive, empowering, and whanau-inclusive process for Maori participants, it must be delivered by (or at the very least reflect the needs and cultural contexts of) the communities within which it is practiced. For any intervention to be effective for whanau (i.e., the FGC), Maori need to be involved in its development and delivery—from identification of community needs to designing and directly delivering those programs themselves. They also need to be involved at all stages of program development, change, and local program evaluation. (p. 101)

Finally, when youth are diverted away from RJ for serious crime in New Zealand, they are often characterized as young adults and sentenced in adult court. As Cleland (2016) argues, "The result is harsh treatment of some extremely vulnerable young people, which breaches New Zealand's international obligations. That harsh treatment is particularly problematic, given its hugely disproportionate effect on Māori youth" (p. 377).

Despite these criticisms, adaptations of the New Zealand FGC are widely used internationally, and in the early 1990s FGC jumped the Tasman Sea from New Zealand to Australia.

In some Australian states, private family group time remained part of the FGC process, while in others it was omitted. For example, the scripted Wagga Wagga model of an FGC does not include private family time; instead, all participants (victims, offenders, and their respective communities of care) remain together throughout the process as the emphasis is on the *encounter* between the parties affected by the harm (see McDonald, Thorsborne, Moore, Hyndman, and O'Connell 1995). This adapted model was brought to BC in the late 1990s and was adopted by the Royal Canadian Mounted Police (RCMP) as a diversion process from court (see Chatterjee and Elliott 2003). While sometimes known as an FGC, this scripted model has also been called a **community justice forum** and a community conference. For example, in 1998, Corporal James Cooley of the RCMP "E" Division was trained and began facilitating *community justice forums* and mentoring other individuals interested in RJ. In 2003, he became RCMP "E" Division's RJ program director. Despite a diverse range of BC communities and schools being served, no systematic data is readily available.

The BC Ministry of Children and Family Development (MCFD) (2010), which has the provincial government mandate for youth justice, started to use the FGC shortly after the implementation of the YCJA. At any given time, the MCFD has five to eight conference specialists who work on both youth-justice and child-protection cases. Probation officers also facilitate the FGC. Referrals for restorative conferencing are based on voluntary participation and on a judge's order and can be requested by a probation officer, Crown counsel, or defence counsel. There is no readily available data on the extent of use or the outcomes achieved by this program at the provincial level.

The most rigorous testing of the adapted FGC (the scripted version, with no private family time) was conducted in Australia and England through the ongoing reintegrative shaming experiments (RISE), using randomized control trials (Strang 2017; Strang, Sherman, Mayo-Wilson, Woods, and Ariel 2013). Sherman and Strang (2007) conclude,

> In general, RJ seems to reduce crime more effectively with more, rather than less, serious crimes [and] RJ works better with crimes involving personal victims than with crimes without them. [The findings] suggest that it works with violent crimes more consistently than with property crimes. . . . These findings run counter to conventional wisdom, and could become the basis for substantial inroads in demarcating when it is "in the public interest" to seek RJ rather than CJ [criminal justice].
>
> Victims also benefit through increased satisfaction in the outcome and feelings of safety, and decreased likelihood of revenge. They are more likely to receive an apology and reduce their post-traumatic stress symptoms. (p. 8)

This level of research and development has yet to be carried out in Canada.

British Columbia's Justice Reforms

An understanding of how different forms of RJ have developed in BC must be framed within the context of strategic justice reforms that have been initiated. A news release on 13 November 1996, from BC's Ministry of the Attorney General expressed the ministry's

---

community justice forum
A safe, controlled environment in which the offender, the victim, and their families or supporters are brought together under the guidance of a trained facilitator. Together, using a scripted dialogue process, the participants discuss the offence and how they have all been affected, and jointly develop a plan to correct what has occurred.

initial intention to adopt an RJ approach to criminal justice. This was followed by the release of a number of documents, including *Strategic Reforms of British Columbia's Justice System* (April 1997), *Restorative Justice Framework* (January 1998), and the *Community Accountability Programs Information Package* (1998, 2004).

The overall policy shift reflected in these reforms and framework was stated by the then attorney general, Ujjal Dosanjh, as a belief "British Columbia is placing more emphasis on a restorative justice approach that focuses on repairing harm caused by criminal acts and restoring balance to communities" (British Columbia Ministry of Attorney General, 1998, para. 2). At that time, the RJ portfolio was located within the Community Programs Division of the attorney general's office. In 2001/02, the Ministry of the Attorney General was split into the Ministry of Public Safety and Solicitor General (Community Safety and Crime Prevention) and the Ministry of the Attorney General. The RJ portfolio moved to the office of the Ministry of Public Safety and Solicitor General, and the 2004 version of Community Accountability Programs Information Package was produced there. This information package specifies the scope of community accountability programs (CAP): they must be volunteer based; adhere to the ministry's Framework for Restorative Justice; demonstrate community and criminal justice support, including victim's organizations; and accept referrals for category 3 and 4 offences only (i.e., for less serious offending, e.g., mischief and property crime).

The *Directory of Restorative Justice Programs* (2010) lists 49 community-based RJ groups, many of which are in the greater Vancouver area and Vancouver Island, as well as in the Central Interior, east to the Rockies (e.g., Invermere), and as far north as Fort Nelson. Most of these programs take police diversion cases for first-time offenders; a few take referrals from Crown counsel; and others take referrals from schools and the community at large. These community-based groups could use any one of the models of RJ described above, as well as other forms (e.g., other forms of circles and community panels/boards/conferencing).

While there is little written on these community-based programs in BC, Dhami and Joy (2007) offer a rare overview of the challenges in establishing volunteer-run, community-based RJ programs. A community-based program in Victoria is used as a case study, and the paper concludes that

> As RJ programs are associated with the criminal justice system and its programs and processes, there is danger that rather than altering the state's way of doing business, these programs will themselves be co-opted and diluted by the pull of retributive and punitive practices. One of the greatest challenges will be to ensure that volunteer-run, community-based RJ programs, with their personal and humanizing appeal for participants at all levels, do not become so routine and formal that they lose their flexibility, their vitality, and eventually their effectiveness. (p. 20)

It is difficult to know whether or not this concern has efficacy, as there is little time for reflective practice and development within small community-based programs. Indeed, only a handful of CAPS have been evaluated, including the one in Abbotsford (Squires

2010), Communities Embracing Restorative Action in Coquitlam (Roberts and Couch 2009), and North Shore Restorative Justice (Roberts 2010).

Looking back over this past decade of reforms and development in BC, it is clear that there has been a notable amount of growth. But what marks the substance of that growth? For example, one of the early community-based programs, FVCJI, lost its funding to the MCFD. This program enjoyed a much more substantial and sustainable community-based juvenile justice role in the province compared to the current CAPs, particularly in relation to funding and referrals. Despite the challenges, a few of these community programs have been creative in carrying out evaluations through partnering with their local universities. In contrast, provincial government programs are much better funded but have yet to be evaluated. Thus, in terms of fulfilling at least one recommendation (19) of the House of Commons Standing Committee on Justice, BC has failed to step up to what was needed at the time, and what is still needed: systemic support, development, funding, and evaluation. In other words, BC lacks the research and development that was recommended over 30 years ago. Hence, both in practice and evaluation, RJ remains a marginal practice on the fringes of the CJS in BC.

Chris Cunneen and Carolyn Hoyle (2010) point out that even in Australia, where they do have a diverse level of evaluation, RJ lacks praxis. According to these authors, despite "clearly articulated legislative and administrative procedures for the use of conferences," as well as the development of RJ practices for youth, RJ remains a "peripheral add-on to the main workings of the criminal justice system," with minimal police or court referrals (p. 184). In fact, Cunneen and Hoyle point out that "police prefer traditional forms of intervention, referring only to 2–4% of youth to conferences, and that for every one young person appearing in a restorative justice conference, about 15 appear in court" (p. 185).

Cunneen and Hoyle (2010) conclude that the RJ movement does not actively engage in research development of current RJ practices within the context of the broader justice system, and that to move beyond the margins of the justice system, there needs to be a constantly reflexive, dialectical relationship between RJ theory and practice. They argue that RJ "lacks an analysis of its own significant shortcomings; it lacks an analysis of political power and social power; it lacks a transformative politics" (p. 186). In particular, Cunneen and Hoyle argue that, reduced to a marginal normative theory, RJ has failed Indigenous youth in Australia.

Based on the evidence to date, these claims also ring true for BC and for Canada, particularly for Indigenous peoples. There has been no consistent support for investing in praxis, particularly praxis that engages community- and state-based policy, programs, and practice. There is no good reason, other than political will, that RJ practice should remain relegated to a marginal normative theory when its theoretical roots span both normative and explanatory theory (see Braithwaite 2002a, 2002b; Gavrielides and Artinopoulou 2013 for an overview) and when there are community groups willing to engage in research and development—that is, engage in praxis.

Roca—The Praxis of Engagement

While the development of peacekeeping circles in BC has lacked praxis, this is not the case in Chelsea, Massachusetts, where the use of peacemaking circles as an organizational strategy has made a significant impact on a community-based organization called Roca.

This outcome-driven organization has a clearly defined goal: to help disengaged and disenfranchised young people, ages 14 to 24, move out of violence and poverty. Their mission is clear: disrupt the cycle of incarceration and poverty by helping young people transform their lives. Roca (2010) states that, through its work, "Young people will leave the streets and gangs to take responsibility for their actions and have jobs. Young immigrant mothers will raise their children in safety and will be recognized for their contributions to society. Our communities will have the ability to keep young people out of harm's way and in turn, thrive through their participation and leadership" (p. 3). Roca (2010) describes its peacemaking circle strategy as a method that

> teaches young people and families an alternative communication method that allows them to deal with extremely painful and difficult issues, how to manage their own healing process, and how to make agreements that promote safety so they can live in a healthy way. Circles are effective for identifying real issues and seeking appropriate solutions when there are conflict situations, when there is a need for healing or understanding, or a desire to reach consensus. (p. 5)

Mentored by the Tagish Tlingit people in the Yukon, and the development of peacemaking circles (Pranis, Stuart, and Wedge 2003), Roca (2010) finds that "Circles bring people together in a way that creates trust, respect, intimacy, good will, belonging, generosity, mutuality and reciprocity. The process is never about changing others, but, rather, is an invitation to change oneself and one's relationship with the community" (p. 8). Roca uses circle processes in a variety of ways with and without young people, internally and externally, often partnering with other agencies, groups, and community members.

Building on its peacemaking circle strategy is Roca's **engaged institutions (EI) strategy**. This strategy recognizes that a range of institutions are important and influential to the economic, social, and emotional well-being of a young person, including schools, local government, agencies, and organizations. Roca therefore creates a strong community base of partnerships with these institutions and organizations. Wheeler (2006) articulates the purpose and outcomes of the engaged institutions strategy as being to "ensure that the systems and institutions contribute to young people's self-sufficiency and help them to be out of harm's way" (p. 44). As a community-based organization, Roca seeks to (1) increase institutions' ability to understand and be more responsive to youth needs; (2) be accountable for services they provide; and (3) understand the impact they have on young people's lives. The processes of engaging institutions mirror those used to engage young people:

engaged institutions (EI) strategy
A program strategy that incorporates a range of institutions important and influential to the economic, social, and emotional well-being of a young person, including schools, local government, agencies, and organizations.

> The EI strategy was born as Roca realized that its core values of belonging, generosity, competence and independence needed to be lived not only among staff members and participants of the organization, but in its relationships with other public and private agencies in its locality. (Wheeler 2006, p. 2)

The data to date are promising. In the 2017 financial year, Roca actively served 854 high-risk young males through its intervention model. While most programs struggle with serving and retaining this population, 78 per cent of Roca's target population were retained, indicating that the program does not lose these young people. Of the young men retained for 24 months or longer by the end of the financial year, 84 per cent had no new arrests and 80 per cent retained employment for at least 90 days (Roca 2018).

In January 2014, Roca and the Commonwealth of Massachusetts launched the ground-breaking Juvenile Justice Pay for Success Project, and Roca has been chosen as the primary service provider for the five-year pilot phase of the program, which includes rigorous evaluation. Through its commitment to youth, Roca is building the foundation of a rich evidence base of innovation and change at the individual, community, and institutional level.

When Roca was founded in 1988, many thought that, like other non-profits that serve vulnerable communities, the program was destined to fail. Yet, three decades later, tens of thousands of youth and young adults have been served by Roca's high-risk youth intervention model. Roca has grown into a solid community-based organization, succeeding where others have failed. Roca invites change and accountability at an organizational level to model the change and accountability they invite in the young people they serve:

> Roca's job is to help young men and women get off the streets, stay out of jail, get good jobs, and create a better future for themselves. We believe that when we ask high-risk young people to make difficult changes in their own lives—to put down guns, to stop selling drugs, to show up at work on time, and become responsible adults—we too must have the courage to do things differently. We have learned that the only way forward is to focus on what works, to let go of what doesn't, and to hold ourselves to accountable to the highest standards possible. (Roca 2014)

This strategic model is based on a philosophy of social engagement with people, programming, institutions, and data; relentless outreach; transformational relationships; stage-based programming; engaged institutions; and performance-based management. This is a significant shift in praxis, moving from a paradigm of social control to one of social engagement (Morrison 2010). The city of Chelsea's city manager adds that "the real story is larger than that. Roca's work, their success with individuals, their bringing together community partners to work together for common goals all make Chelsea a much stronger community" (Lesley University 2011, para. 10). As Molly Baldwin, the founder of Roca, concludes,

> We know of no other community-based, non-mandated authority driving to outcomes and tracking efforts at this level. . . . In turn, we hope this will aid in others learning from what we have learned in the field. . . . Our penal system—the primary provider of "services" to the young people we work most with—isn't effective and it's dangerous and expensive. We've gone a long way to showing there are better ways—and we want to bring it further. (as cited in Lesley University 2011, para. 13)

Roca is a prime example of a thriving and sustainable community-based partner with the state-based criminal justice system. At the level of the state, the mantra of justice is "order and control"; at the level of community, the mantra can be, as exemplified by Roca, "engagement and transformation." This resonates with Zehr's (1990) suggestion that the government can bring order, but only the community can bring peace.

State and Community Collaboration: The Importance of Non-governmental Organizations (NGOs)

Over two decades ago at a conference in Nova Scotia, John Braithwaite (1996) put forward a strong argument for the importance of NGOs engaging in deliberative problem-solving and RJ to reinvest in community and democracy:

> The lived experience of modern democracy is alienation. The feeling is that elites run things, that we do not have a say in any meaningful sense. . . . Once citizens learn to be actively responsible as opposed to learning to rely totally on protection by a state that enforces passive responsibility, they will become active in social movement politics. NGOs offer the second great avenue for revitalizing meaningful forms of citizen participation in a democracy. . . . NGO influence can feed back into restorative justice conferences as advocacy of making the personal political, by invoking the possibility of agitating for structural change. The most important way this happens is when the justice of the people puts pressure on the justice of the law to change. (p. 9)

The importance of NGOs to driving active responsibility through participatory deliberation has continued to be an emergent factor of Braithwaite's current work on responsive regulation (2006, 2011, 2017; see also Drahos 2017). This resonates with Christie's (1977) seminal paper "Conflict as Property," in which he argues the need to address a range of problems inherent in state-based justice:

> This loss is first and foremost a loss in *opportunities for norm-clarification*. It is a loss of pedagogical possibilities. It is a loss of opportunities for a continuous discussion of what represents the law of the land. How wrong was the thief, how right was the victim? Lawyers are, as we say, trained into agreement on what is relevant in a case. But that means a trained incapacity in letting the parties decide what *they* think is relevant. (p. 8)

Community-based NGOs have more capacity to evoke the experience of civil society and meaningful deliberation when the core of RJ for juveniles is community-based rather than state-based. When considered in the context of NGOs' experience in BC, Christie's point is even more salient in that the state has now stolen the conflict, and the deliberative process, back from the community. In seeking state-based social control of RJ, the state has failed to deliver justice to communities and an evidence base to support its practice. Roca, as a community-based NGO, has delivered on this front by being true to its mission statement of engaging hope for a sustainable future to young people, and a means for those young people to live out of harm's way. Roca has captured the essence of Braithwaite's (2002b) work by coupling RJ with responsive regulation through two levers of change that work hand in hand: programming and institutional engagement. The program's fundamental premise is that individual change is best leveraged through responsive regulation at a community level.

The practice of RJ, coupled with responsive regulation, enables communities to tap into the rich ecologies of individual lives by creating safe spaces to dialogue through storytelling and listening. Communities cut across institutional domains of social control, being responsive to individual needs in ways that broaden the scope for crime prevention and community safety (see Morrison 2010).

Developing community-based civic capacity is good for the state, too, as communities have a capacity for problem-solving that is often thwarted by leaders at a state level, resulting in process paralysis (Briggs 2008). The role of mediating institutions, at the level of community, has long been argued for in public policy. For example, Berger and Neuhaus (1977) argue that community-based institutions serve as alternate mechanisms to provide for social welfare, allowing the public to continue to respond to major social problems without creating the sense of alienation characteristic of the state. Fundamental questions arise, then, in implementing RJ for juveniles, such as: What is the proper role of government in RJ? How can the government empower community-based NGOs while maintaining its need for order? These are bold questions that require bold governance and policy direction.

Justice Reform: Responding and Engaging with Communities in Criminal Justice

Almost thirty years after Canada's development of *Taking Responsibility* in response to concerns raised in the House of Commons, the federal mandate letter from the prime minister to the minister of justice called for the increased use of restorative justice to reduce the disproportionate representation of Indigenous peoples in our CJS (Government of Canada, Department of Justice 2015). Following provincial and territorial consultation, a federal report, *Transforming Canada's Criminal Justice System* (2018), suggested the following improvements:

- Integrate **restorative justice into the mainstream justice system**. Re-draft the *Criminal Code's* Purpose and Principles of Sentencing to include restorative justice principles.
- **Inform and educate the public** about restorative justice and its principles.
- Apply **restorative justice earlier and to more serious cases**.
  - Look into ending the moratorium on restorative justice for domestic violence and sexual assault cases. Research shows that restorative justice works best in relationship breakdowns.
  - Presently, restorative justice is often used for very low-risk cases that wouldn't head to court anyway. The *Criminal Code* would have to mandate any change in practice.

- **Fund and administer restorative justice** initiatives well and use data to track results.
  - Training is imperative to successful results.

Restorative justice should not be seen as a cheaper alternative to the mainstream system. The process is often resource intensive, but participants said that research and evaluation have shown both victims and offenders report higher levels of satisfaction, as well as lower rates of reoffending. (pp. 10–13; boldfacing in original)

The call to increase the support for restorative justice is also in the mandate letter from the premier of British Columbia to the minister of public safety and solicitor general. This follows provincial developments in February 2012, when the BC government launched a Justice Reform Initiative, beginning with the Ministries of Attorney General and Solicitor General re-merging within the Ministry of Justice, and the launch of a Green Paper: *Modernizing British Columbia's Justice System* (British Columbia Ministry of Justice 2012). Following extensive consultation, *A Criminal Justice System for the 21st Century* (Cowper 2012) recommended a broad suite of changes, including the development of a province-wide crime reduction plan. In June 2013, the parliamentary secretary for crime reduction, MLA Dr. Darrel Plecas, was appointed and convened a **blue ribbon panel** of experts to study crime reduction. Following extensive consultation with all levels of government, NGOs, community foundations, and universities, *Getting Serious about Crime Reduction* (British Columbia Ministry of Justice 2014) was released in December 2014, offering six major recommendations, including making greater use of restorative justice (see Recommendation #3 and Appendix F in the report). Following Cowper's (2012) recommendation, the blue ribbon panel reiterated that the government should develop a province-wide plan for diversion, including restorative justice, along with education, quality assurance and control, performance measures, reporting, and evaluation. The panel heard strong support for effective diversion mechanisms and a recommendation that the government work in collaboration with the Union of British Columbia Municipalities to develop province-wide standards to govern the implementation and management of diversion and RJ programs. The hope is that the government will have the courage and conviction to take these recommendations seriously, engaging with community and measuring what works, to develop a responsive evidence-based system of accountability and support at all levels: individual, community, and government.

Commenting on the blue ribbon panel's report, the BC parliamentary secretary for crime reduction observed,

> In recent years, no jurisdiction in the western world has done a better job reducing crime than British Columbia. The panel's recommendations focus on prolific offender management, treatment, *restorative justice*, "designing-out" environments that encourage opportunistic criminals, and other, proven approaches to build on this success and further our efforts to make B.C. Canada's safest province. (British Columbia Ministry of Justice 2014; emphasis added)

This provincial report was echoed by the Canadian Bar Association (BC Branch) in 2017, who recommended implementing a funding model for community-based restorative

blue ribbon panel
An independent group of experts and remarkable people appointed to investigate, study, or analyze a given question.

justice organizations, development of common standards and training requirements across BC, and professional development for all stakeholders in the justice system.

Summary

This chapter has called for a shift from state-based social control to collaborative community-based social engagement as a practical approach to serving vulnerable youth in conflict with the law. The evidence that has emerged from this analysis suggests that Judge Stuart's (2007) reflections on his experience of RJ in Canada still ring true: "Canada's role in the development of RJ is as an exporter. We invent it, and others develop it in a fuller capacity" (n.p.). One of the common adages in the field of RJ is to create opportunities to learn from our mistakes. Canada has the opportunity, and the capacity, to learn from the international experiment in RJ to which it has so proudly contributed. Moreover, Canada has the capacity to renew the promise of RJ as a domestic import. The lesson learned is that we must engage in praxis locally, provincially, nationally, and internationally—as is being done by the European Forum for Restorative Justice. We must import as much as we export, and develop the sustainable capacity of collaborative community engagement. For government and community, this will take the same courage and compassion of those early pioneers: from Judge Barry Stuart, to probation officer Mark Yantzi, to members of communities and NGOs like Dave Worth, and indeed to the young people themselves, such as Russ Kelley. It is in the hands of all of us that the promise of RJ resides. Independent of its contribution to the criminal justice system, restorative justice strengthens communities, honouring the inherent dignity and worth of young people both today and tomorrow.

> Where, after all, do universal human rights begin? In small places, close to home—so close and so small that they cannot be seen on any map of the world. Yet they *are* the world of the individual person: The neighborhood he lives in; the school or college he attends; the factory, farm or office where he works. Such are the places where every man, woman, and child seeks equal justice, equal opportunity, equal dignity without discrimination. Unless these rights have meaning there, they have little meaning anywhere. Without concerted citizen action to uphold them close to home, we shall look in vain for progress in the larger world. (Eleanor Roosevelt, "In Your Hands" 1958)

Key Terms

blue ribbon panel

community justice forum

engaged institutions (EI) strategy

family group conferencing

peacemaking circles

restorative justice (RJ)

sentencing circles

victim–offender reconciliation programs (VORP)

Review Questions

1. What is a diversionary process, and what are possible avenues (or points of referral) for other restorative justice opportunities within the criminal justice system?

2. Discuss Christie's (1977) argument that state-based justice results in a "trained incapacity" (p. 8) for decision-making and norm clarification.

3. What is VORP, and how has it contributed to the history of restorative justice in Canada?

4. What is Roca? What is Roca's primary vision and how are peacemaking circles important to Roca in achieving its vision?

5. What is *Taking Responsibility*? When was it developed, and what, in particular, did Recommendation 19 contribute to youth justice in Canada?

Critical Thinking Questions

1. Consider the impact of data collection on development and implementation of restorative justice programs for youth.

2. Discuss the potential to meet the provisions of the YCJA that require addressing youth's developmental challenges and needs as they grow into adulthood, through restorative justice processes as opposed to traditional criminal justice processes.

3. Do you think it is more effective for justice officials (police, Crown prosecutors, etc.) to make decisions about diversion to restorative justice on a case-by-case basis, or do you think a system-wide directive such as that in New Zealand where *all* youth experience restorative justice as a first approach is more effective? Why or why not?

4. What are the future directions and possibilities for RJ in Canada?

5. RJ tends to use the terms *harm*, *conflict*, and *dispute* instead of *crime* in its discourse. How and why might such terminology impact our conceptualization of crime/conflict?

References

Baliga, S., Henry, S., and Valentine, G. (2017). Restorative community conferencing: A study of Community Works West's restorative justice youth diversion program in Alameda County. *Impact/Justice*. Retrieved from http://impactjustice.org/wp-content/uploads/2017/07/CWW-Report_Final_6.14.17_electronic.pdf

Benevides, H.J. (1994). *R. v. Moses* and sentencing circles: A case comment. *Dalhousie Journal of Legal Studies, 3*, 241–50.

Berger, P., and Neuhaus, R. (1977). *To empower people: The role of mediating structures in public policy*. Washington, DC: American Enterprise Institute.

Braithwaite, J. (1996). Restorative justice and a better future. *Dalhousie Review, 76*(1), 9–32. Reprinted in E. McLaughlin, R. Fergusson, G. Hughes, and L. Westmorland (Eds) (2003). *Restorative justice: Critical issues*. London: Sage.

Braithwaite, J. (2002a). *Restorative justice and responsive regulation*. New York: Oxford University Press.

Braithwaite, J. (2002b). Setting standards for restorative justice. *British Journal of Criminology, 42*(3), 563–77.

Braithwaite, J. (2006). Accountability and responsibility through restorative justice. In M.D. Dowdle (Ed.), *Public accountability, designs, dilemmas and experiences* (pp. 33–51). Cambridge, UK: Cambridge University Press.

Braithwaite, J. (2011). The essence of responsive regulation, *UBC Law Review, 44*(3), 475–520.

Braithwaite, J. (2016). *Restorative justice and responsive regulation: The question of evidence*. RegNet Working Paper No. 51, School of Regulation and Global Governance (RegNet).

Braithwaite, J. (2017). Types of responsiveness. In P. Drahos (Ed), *Regulatory theory: Foundations and applications* (pp. 117–32). Canberra: ANU Press.

Briggs, X.S. (2008). *Democracy as problem solving: Civic capacity in communities across the globe*. Cambridge, MA: MIT Press.

British Columbia Ministry of Attorney General. (1998). *Parksville gets funding for innovative justice program* [News release]. Retrieved from https://archive.news.gov.bc.ca/releases/archive/pre2001/1998/980507b.asp

British Columbia Ministry of Children and Family Development. (2005). *Family group conference reference guide*. British Columbia. Retrieved from www.mcf.gov.bc.ca/child_protection/pdf/fgc_guide_internet.pdf

British Columbia Ministry of Children and Family Development. (2004). *Best practice approaches: Child protection and violence against women*. Victoria, BC: Author.

British Columbia Ministry of Justice. (2012). *Modernizing British Columbia's justice system*. British Columbia. Retrieved from https://www2.gov.bc.ca/assets/gov/law-crime-and-justice/about-bc-justice-system/justice-reform-initiatives/justicesystemreviewgreenpaper.pdf

British Columbia Ministry of Justice. (2014, December 18). *Crime reduction and corrections safety reports released* [News release]. Retrieved from https://archive.news.gov.bc.ca/releases/news_releases_2013-2017/2014JAG0348-001911.htm

Canadian Bar Association (BC Branch). (2017). Restorative justice: Recommended action. One-page document held at SFU Centre for Restorative Justice.

Charbonneau, S. (2005). The Canadian Youth Criminal Justice Act 2003: A step forward for advocates of restorative justice. In E. Elliot and R.M. Gordon (Eds), *New directions in restorative justice: Issues, practice, evaluation* (pp. 75–86). Cullompton, UK: Willan.

Chatterjee, J., and Elliott, L. (2003). Restorative policing in Canada: The Royal Canadian Mounted Police, community justice forums, and the Youth Criminal Justice Act. *Police Practice and Research, 4*(4), 1.

Christie, N. (1977). Conflict as property. *British Journal of Criminology, 17*(1), 1–14.

Clairmont, D., and Kim, E. (2013). Getting past the gatekeepers: The reception of restorative justice in the Nova Scotia criminal justice system. *Dalhousie Law Journal, 36*(2), 359–92.

Clairmont, D., and Waters, K. (2015). *The Nova Scotia restorative justice program: Assessment of current status and future directions*. Halifax: Dalhousie University.

Cleland, A. (2016). Portrait of the accused as a young man: New Zealand's harsh treatment of young people who commit serious crimes. *Round Table, 105*(4), 377–87.

Community Justice Initiatives. (2011). Victim offender mediation program. Retrieved from www.cjibc.org/victim_reconciliation

Cowper, G. (Chair). (2012, August 27). *A criminal justice system for the 21st century: Final report to the Minister of Justice and Attorney General Honourable Shirley Bond*. BC Justice Reform Initiative, British Columbia.

Crnkovich, M. (1995). Report on sentencing circles in Nunavik. In Pauktuutit Women's Association (Ed), *Inuit women and justice: Progress report no. 1*.

Cunneen, C. (2007). Reviving restorative justice traditions. In J. Johnstone and D. Van Ness (Eds), *The handbook of restorative justice*. Cullommpton, UK: Willan.

Cunneen, C., and Hoyle, C. (2010). *Debating restorative justice*. Oxford: Hart.

Cunneen, C., and Tauri, J. (2016). *Indigenous criminology*. Bristol, UK: Policy Press.

Dandurand, Y., and Vogt, A. (2017). *Documenting the experiences and the successes of First Nations courts in British Columbia*. Report presented to the Office of the Chief Judge of the Provincial Court of British Columbia and the Legal Services Society of British Columbia, June 25. Vancouver: International Centre for Criminal Law Reform and Criminal Justice Policy.

Daubney, D. (2010, November). *The role the 1987–88 justice committee of the House of Commons played in encouraging the use of restorative justice in Canada*. Paper presented at Restorative Justice Week 2010, Canada.

Department of Justice Canada, Criminal Justice System Review. (2018). *Transforming Canada's criminal justice system: A report on Provincial and Territorial stakeholder consultations*. Ottawa: Minister of Justice and Attorney General of Canada. Retrieved from http://www.justice.gc.ca/eng/rp-pr/other-autre/tcjs-tsjp/WWH_EN.pdf

Department of Justice Canada. (2016, December). *Evaluation of the Aboriginal Justice Strategy*. Retrieved from http://www.justice.gc.ca/eng/rp-pr/cp-pm/eval/rep-rap/2016/ajs-sja/ajs-sja.pdf

Department of Justice Canada. (2011, November). *Aboriginal Justice Strategy evaluation: Final report*. Retrieved from https://www.justice.gc.ca/eng/rp-pr/cp-pm/eval/rep-rap/11/ajs-sja/ajs-sja.pdf

Department of Justice Canada. (2002). *The Youth Criminal Justice Act: Summary and background*. Ottawa: Minister of Justice and Attorney General of Canada. Retrieved from https://www.justice.gc.ca/eng/cj-jp/yj-jj/tools-outils/back-hist.html

Dhami, M.K., and Joy, P. (2007). Challenges to establishing volunteer run community-based restorative justice programs. *Contemporary Justice Review, 10*, 9–22.

Dickson-Gilmore, J., and La Prairie, C. (2005). *Will the circle be unbroken?: Aboriginal communities, restorative justice and the challenges of conflict and change.* Toronto: University of Toronto Press.

Drahos, P. (Ed) (2017). *Regulatory theory: Foundations and applications.* Canberra: ANU Press.

Elliot, E., and Gordon, R. (Eds). (2013). *New directions in restorative justice: Issues, practices and evaluations.* Cullommpton, UK: Willan.

Evans, J., McDonald, S., and Gill, R. (2018). Restorative justice: The experience of victims and survivors. *Victims of Crime Research Digest No. 11*, 27–32. Department of Justice Canada.

Gavrielides, T., and Artinopoulou, V. (2013). *Reconstructing restorative justice philosophy.* Furnham, UK: Ashgate.

Green, R., and Healy, K.F. (2003). *Tough on kids: Rethinking approaches to youth justice.* Saskatoon, SK: Purich.

Gustafson, D. (2004). Is restorative justice taking too few, or too many risks? In H. Zehr and B. Toews (Eds), *Critical issues in restorative justice* (pp. 299–309). Monsey, NY, and Cullompton, UK: Criminal Justice Press and Willan.

Indigenous Foundations. (2009). *The Indian Act.* Retrieved from https://indigenousfoundations.arts.ubc.ca/the_indian_act/

Johnson, S. (2014). Developing First Nations courts in Canada: Elders as foundational to Indigenous therapeutic jurisprudence +. *Journal of Indigenous Social Development, 3*(2), 1–14.

Kelly, R. (2010, November). *The Elmira case . . . and beyond!* Paper presented at Restorative Justice Week 2010, Canada. Retrieved from www.csc-scc.gc.ca/text/rj/rj2010/kit/3-eng.shtml

Latimer, J., Dowden, C., and Muise, D. (2001). *The effectiveness of restorative justice practices: A meta-analysis.* Ottawa: Department of Justice, Research and Statistics Division.

Lesley University. (2011). *Roca, driving positive outcomes for the most at-risk youth.* Retrieved from https://web.archive.org/web/20110724162742/http://news.lesley.edu/2011/01/roca-driving-positive-outcomes-for-the-most-at-risk-youth.shtml

Malakieh, J. (2018). Adult and youth correctional statistics in Canada, 2016/2017. *Juristat.* Statistics Canada Catalogue No. 85-002-X ISSN 1209-6393. Retrieved from https://www150.statcan.gc.ca/n1/pub/85-002-x/2018001/article/54972-eng.htm

McDonald, J., Thorsborne, M., Moore, D., Hyndman, M., and O'Connell, T. (1995). *Real justice training manual: Coordinating family group conferences.* Pipersville, PA: Piper's Press.

MacRae, A., and Zehr, H. (2004). *The little book of family group conferences: A hopeful approach when youth cause harm.* Intercourse, PA: Good Books.

Monchalin, L. (2016). *The colonial problem: An Indigenous perspective on crime and injustice in Canada.* Toronto: University of Toronto Press.

Morrison, B.E. (2010, November 16). *From social control to social engagement: Enabling the time and place to talk through restorative justice and responsive regulation.* Paper presented at the American Society of Criminology Annual Meeting, San Francisco, California.

Moyle, P., and Tauri, J. (2016). Maori, family group conferencing, and the mystifications of restorative justice. In *The future of restorative justice?* Special Issue of *Victims and Offenders, 11*, 87–106.

Oudshoorn, J. (2015). *Trauma-informed youth justice in Canada: A new framework toward a kinder future.* Toronto: Canadian Scholars' Press.

Pakura, S. (2005, March). *The family group conference 14-year journey: Celebrating the successes, learning the lessons, embracing the challenges.* Symposium conducted at the American Humane Association's Family Group Decision Making Conference and Skills-Building Institute, Pennsylvania.

Palys, T. (2014, June 11). *A programme evaluation of Vancouver Aboriginal Transformative Justice Services Society (vatjss).* Retrieved from https://www.sfu.ca/~palys/VATJSEvaluation-2014.pdf

Peachey, D.E. (1989). The Kitchener experiment. In M. Wright and B. Galaway (Eds), *Mediation and criminal justice: Victims, offenders and community* (pp. 14–26). London: Sage.

Perrin, B., and Audas, R. (2018, March). *Report card on the criminal justice system #2.* Ottawa: Macdonald Laurier Institute. Retrieved from https://macdonaldlaurier.ca/files/pdf/MLI_JusticeReportCard_Final_web2.pdf

Pranis, K., Stuart, B., and Wedge, M. (2003). *Peacemaking circles: From crime to community.* St Paul, MN: Living Justice Press.

Representative for Children and Youth (BC). (2014a, October 9). *Not fully invested: A follow-up report on the Representative's past recommendations to help vulnerable children in BC.* British Columbia.

Representative for Children and Youth (BC). (2014b). *Who Cares? BC Children with complex medical, psychological and developmental needs and their families deserve better.* British Columbia.

Roberts, M.L. (2010). *Evaluating evaluation: An investigation into the purpose and practice of evaluation in restorative justice based programs.* Paper presented as thesis defence at Simon Fraser University, School of Criminology.

Roberts, M., and Couch, L. (2009). CERA *program evaluation report.* Coquitlam, BC: CERA.

Roca. (2010). *In the streets and in their lives* [Annual report]. Chelsea, MA: Author.

Roca. (2014). *Less jail; more future* [Annual report]. Chelsea, MA: Author.

Roca. (2017, October 10). Fiscal year 2017: High risk young men performance benchmarks and outcomes report. Retrieved from https://rocainc.org/wp-content/uploads/2016/09/FY17-Young-Mens-Outcomes-Report.pdf

Roca. (2018). *Roca 30. Relentless. Proving change is possible* [Annual report]. Chelsea, MA: Author.

Roosevelt, E. (1958). *In your hands: A guide for community action.* New York: United Nations.

Sharpe, S. (1998). *Restorative justice: A vision for healing and change.* Edmonton: Mediation and Restorative Justice Centre.

Sherman, L.W., and Strang, H. (2007). *Restorative justice: The evidence.* London: The Smith Institute.

Squires, C. (2010, April 30/May 1). *Program evaluation for RJ programs.* Paper presented at "Building Restorative Justice in BC": A Working Conference for Advocates and Practitioners, Abbotsford, BC, Canada.

Strang, H. (2017). Experiments in restorative justice. In P. Drahos (Ed), *Regulatory theory: Foundations and applications* (pp. 483–98). Canberra: ANU Press.

Strang, H., Sherman, L., Mayo-Wilson, E., Woods, D., and Ariel, B. (2013). *Restorative justice conferencing (RJC): Using face-to-face meetings of offenders and victims: Effects on offender recidivism and victim satisfaction. A systematic review.* Campbell Systematic Reviews. Oslo, Norway: Campbell Collaboration.

Stuart, B. (1996). Circle sentencing in Yukon Territory, Canada: A partnership of the community and the criminal justice system. *International Journal of Comparative and Applied Criminal Justice, 20*(1 & 2), 291–309.

Stuart, B. (1997). *Building community justice partnerships: Community peacemaking circles.* Ottawa: Department of Justice Canada.

Stuart, B. (2007). *Balanced and restorative justice for juveniles: a framework for juvenile justice in the 21st century.* Washington, DC: Office of Juvenile Justice and Delinquency Prevention.

Stutzman Amstutz, L. (2009). *The little book of victim offender conferencing: Bringing victims and offenders together in dialogue.* PA: Good Books.

Tustin, L., and Lutes, R.E. (2010). *A guide to the Youth Criminal Justice Act.* Toronto: Butterworths.

United Nations. (2006). *Handbook on restorative justice programs: Criminal justice handbook series.* Vienna: United Nations Office on Drugs and Crime.

Van Ness, D.W., and Strong, K.H. (2006). *Restoring justice: An introduction to restorative justice* (3rd ed.). Cincinnati: Matthew Bender & Company.

Wheeler, W. (2006, February 7). *Encircling institutions: Surrounding youth in crisis with mutual engagement and trust.* Takoma Park, MD: Innovation Center for Community and Youth Development. Retrieved from https://www.academyforchange.org/wp-content/uploads/2012/08/EncirclingInstitutions.pdf

Winterdyk, J. (Ed.). (2015). *Juvenile justice: International perspectives, model and trends.* Boca Raton, FL: CRC Press.

Zehr, H. (1990). *Changing lenses: A new focus for crime and justice.* Scottsdale, PA: Herald Press.

Statutes Cited

Criminal Code, RS, c. C-46 (1985). Retrieved from http://laws.justice.gc.ca/en/C-46/index.html

Juvenile Delinquents Act, SC c. 40. (1908). Retrieved from http://www.justice.gc.ca/eng/pi/icg-gci/jj2-jm2/sec02.html

R. v. Gladue, 1 SCR 688 (1999). Retrieved from http://www.indigenousbar.ca/cases/gladue.htm

R. v. Moses, 71 CCC 347 (1992). Retrieved from http://www.usask.ca/nativelaw/factums/view.php?id=124

Young Offenders Act, SC c. Y-1 (1985). Retrieved from http://laws-lois.justice.gc.ca/P DF/Y-1.pdf

Youth Criminal Justice Act, SC c. 1 (2002). Retrieved from http://www.justice.gc.ca/en g/pi/yj-jj/ycja-lsjpa/ycja-lsjpa.html

Glossary

absolute homelessness A term used to talk about experiences of living on the street or in emergency shelters. *Relative homelessness* is used to refer to experiences of being housed but at risk of losing housing or living in substandard housing. *Hidden or concealed homelessness* refers to living without a place of one's own (e.g., living in a car, with family or friends [couch surfing] or living in a long-term institution).

abstainers Youth who do not offend because of negative personality characteristics, social and biological maturation consistent with each other, and a lack of exposure to criminal peers.

access period The designated time frame during which a young person's youth record is active or disclosable and can be shared among relevant individuals attached to the young person as outlined in the YCJA (e.g., the youth, his/her parents, defence counsel, Crown counsel, detention centre, or correctional facility director).

accountability The YCJA includes provisions intended to ensure meaningful consequences for young people for their actions, with the intent of making clear that they are being held accountable for wrongdoing.

activity spaces The broad areas that encompass the locations where individuals conduct their daily regular activities, and the routes between these locations.

acute developmental crises Rapidly appearing moments of diminished mental health associated with stress of transitioning through stages of life. Youth are particularly prone to these stressors as they attempt to navigate the challenges of young adulthood. While these events are often very distressing, they are generally short-term and they respond well to treatment.

administrative offences Offences against the administration of justice— that is, violations of court-ordered behavioural requirements, such as complying with a curfew, attending mandated programs, and following through on all manner of bail conditions and probation orders.

adolescence A term popularized by child development expert G. Stanley Hall to refer to the stage of life during which a person progresses, both biologically and emotionally, from being a child to being an adult.

adolescence-limited offenders Individuals who begin their offending in, and restrict their offending to, adolescence.

adulteration The dismantling of a distinct system of criminal justice for youth and the re-merging with systems of justice for adults.

alternative justice agencies Quebec-based agencies responsible for the application of the extrajudicial programs for youth to which youth are referred either by the police or by the provincial director under the YCJA. Measures can include information and awareness programs on shoplifting, drugs, and law reinforcement as well as mediation or damage repair for the victim or, if that is not possible, damage repair through community service.

anti-social potential An individual's probability of undertaking criminal and other anti-social behaviours.

"at-risk" youth Young people who are "at risk" of offending or being victimized due to various social, family, and/or personal factors.

bad date An episode of harm enacted upon a sex worker by a client, including assault, sexual assault, incidents of theft, refusal of payment, threats, rudeness, time wasting, harassment, aggressive behaviour, etc. Bad dates that include physical assault can lead to harm so profound a sex worker dies.

bail surety A promise made by someone connected to the youth to pay the court money if the young person who was released on bail fails to return to court on the subsequent court date.

best interests of the child doctrine The approach in which the interests of a young person are paramount in decision-making regarding his or her experience in the criminal justice system.

bifurcated youth justice system Literally, a two-pronged justice system, meaning that it provides avenues for diverting first-time and less serious young offenders out of the system while at the same time making possible more punitive forms of punishment for more serious offenders.

binge drinking Heavy alcohol consumption over a short period for the purpose of becoming intoxicated. Generally, the concept is operationalized as the consumption of five or more drinks on one occasion (four or more for females).

biopsychosocial model An approach that addresses interdependent and bidirectional biological, psychological, and social risk factors related to the development of behavioural problems that are implicated in females' involvement with the justice system.

blue ribbon panel An independent group of experts and remarkable people appointed to investigate, study, or analyze a given question.

Boscoville A unique program introduced in the 1950s in Quebec that was based on a social welfare and psycho-educative model and that introduced elements in its program designed to teach delinquent youth the necessary skills, values, and attitudes that would allow them to develop a sense of social responsibility.

child welfare In Canada, this term is used to describe a set of government and private services intended to protect children and encourage family stability. The main purpose of these services is to safeguard children from abuse and neglect. Hence, one of the primary activities of the child welfare agencies is the investigation of allegations of abuse and neglect.

coercion A personal or an impersonal force that compels or frightens individuals to behave in a certain way.

colonization Refers to historical and ongoing processes that began with the arrival of Europeans to the country and that include attempts to dominate and assimilate Indigenous peoples.

community justice forum A safe, controlled environment in which the offender, the victim, and their families or supporters are brought together under the guidance of a trained facilitator. Together, using a scripted dialogue process, they discuss the offence and how they have all been affected, and jointly develop a plan to correct what has occurred.

co-morbidity Two or more independent and coexisting medical conditions.

context analysis Analyzing media content for themes such as sensationalism or distortion.

control balance The degree of control that individuals perceive they have over their environment relative to the degree of control they perceive their environment has over them.

convergence When a current issue is framed in terms of its relation to a previous one.

Crime Severity Index (CSI) Developed and introduced by Statistics Canada, the CSI uses a weighting system to measure (youth) offences according to their seriousness. Although introduced in 2009, CSI data are available back to 1998.

crime templates Guidelines for behavioural decisions regarding crime that people derive from their regular activities, offending experiences, and knowledge.

criminalization The process whereby individuals are assigned the label of "criminal."

criminogenic Situations or environments that cause or exacerbate criminal behaviours. These can even include institutions or programs that have been designed to reduce such behaviours.

critical criminology Scholarship on crime and justice that seeks to examine and alter inequalities, marginalization, and social exclusion.

critical discourse analysis An approach in sociolinguistics that links discourse with political structure.

crossover youth Young people, also referred to as "dually involved" or "multisystem" youth, who have had contact with the child welfare system and who also become involved in the youth justice system.

cultivation hypothesis The hypothesis that the media inundate the public with ideas about crime.

cumulative continuity A developmental model that outlines how crime in adolescence has negative consequences for future life chances in areas such as education, relationships, and employment, and increases the likelihood that criminal behaviour will continue into adulthood. These in turn undermine further life chances, escalating the probability of continued, persistent criminal behaviour.

custodial sanctions Under the Youth Criminal Justice Act, the sentencing of a young person to custody.

dark figure of crime Refers to incidents of crime or delinquency that go undetected or unreported by the police.

deconstruction Process that involves opening up words to their hidden or closed-off possibilities in an attempt to reveal what is going on behind language.

dependence A condition that occurs when an individual feels that use of a substance is necessary for normal daily functioning or when substance use leads to tolerance. Abruptly stopping use may lead to symptoms of withdrawal.

dial-a-dopers Individuals, often youth or young adults, who are given one or more cellphones by a criminal organization and deliver drugs to specific locations when customers wanting drugs call the phone to place an order.

differential intervention Based on the identification of the type of delinquency associated with the behaviours of young offenders, the interventions must then be tailored to meet young offenders' treatment needs and the level of risk they pose to society (risk of recidivism). Takes into account that people do not come in one-size-fits-all packages and therefore refrains from applying the same approach to each person involved in a class, program, or other form of group-based change process.

diminished criminal responsibility The general view that individuals who are not adults should not be held fully responsible for their criminal behaviour.

diminished moral blameworthiness Canada's approach to youth justice assumes that young people have not reached the same level of moral and social development as an adult.

disposition For young offenders, this is the equivalent of sentencing for adults. Under the YCJA, a disposition should in theory be more rehabilitative and/or restorative than retributive.

disproportionate minority contact A term describing the consistent overrepresentation of persons from certain ethnic minority backgrounds in police-citizen contacts, relative to representation in the population. In particular, young men from black, Indigenous, and Latino backgrounds have been found to be overrepresented in these statistics.

disrupted social control Events or life circumstances that weaken or destroy the relationships, attachments, and activities that provide barriers to engaging in criminal activities.

diversion Responses to transgressions that aim to keep involved parties out of the justice system. Under the YCJA, this includes extrajudicial measures and extrajudicial sanctions.

doli incapax A legal doctrine that literally translated means "incapable of doing harm" and refers to the English common-law presumption that children between 7 and 14 years of age could not be prosecuted for committing criminal offences, unless this presumption was contested by the Crown.

drug recognition expert (DRE) evaluation A standardized procedure performed by a trained drug recognition expert—involving visual cues, vital signs, questioning, and the provision of bodily fluids by the potentially impaired driver—that is used for determining impairment by drugs or by a drug in combination with alcohol.

dynamic risk factors Risk factors that are changeable; they are factors that may also contribute to criminal behaviour but can be modified through targeted interventions and/or treatment.

dynamic security Security that is ensured by the relational dimension. It is achieved by the constant presence of educators and the bonds built between the youths and them. As a result, the quality of the social climate is improved among peers, who in turn contribute to the security of the institution.

early starters Youth who exhibit anti-social behaviour in preschool years, have early arrest and chronic offending in adolescence, and become adult career offenders.

engaged institutions strategy A program strategy that incorporates a range of institutions important and influential to the economic, social, and emotional well-being of a young person, including schools, local government, agencies, and organizations.

ethnography A form of participatory research that involves immersion in the field of study. Because it allows for rich and descriptive findings on areas that are often hidden from view, ethnographic research is fundamental to cultural criminology.

extrajudicial programs Measures that are designed to hold youth responsible for their actions without the creation of a criminal record. They are generally applied to youth who are not engaged in a serious delinquent trajectory.

extrajudicial sanctions Under the YCJA, relatively formal diversion programs that have been authorized by the provincial authorities.

family group conferencing ". . . a process of collaborative planning in situations where decisions need to be made for children or youth. It is a formal meeting where members of a child or youth's immediate family come together with extended kin and members" (BC Ministry of Children and Family Development 2005, p. 2)

fear-based communication Messages used to frighten youth away from experimentation with substances by emphasizing the potential negative effects of use.

fetal alcohol spectrum disorder (FASD) Refers to a medical diagnosis of fetal alcohol syndrome (FAS), partial fetal alcohol syndrome (pFAS), alcohol neurodevelopmental disorder (ARND), and alcohol-related birth defects (ARBD), all of which refer to some degree of permanent central nervous system damage to a fetus as a result of maternal alcohol consumption during pregnancy.

folk devils   Any group that is perceived to pose a threat to the traditional values and institutions of society.

frame analysis   Analyzing media content to see how crime and criminals are depicted.

gay for pay   Label for a person who is heterosexual but who, in order to survive, will work in the SET as a homosexual. In McIntyre's "Under the Radar" study, respondents reported that customers often found the perceived opportunity to alter a young man's heterosexual orientation very attractive.

gender gap   Acknowledges the persistent and well-documented difference in the arrest rates for males and females, with males consistently committing significantly more crime than females.

gender role theories   Those explanations of delinquent and criminal behaviour that focus on the role that gender plays in the lives and behaviours of both females and males.

gender-sensitive responses   Responses that recognize that the pathways to criminal involvement and the needs of female offenders are different from those of male offenders. Such approaches include risk assessments, treatments, and supervision.

harm-reduction strategies   Any policy or program that is designed to reduce the level of harm associated with substance use without requiring the cessation of use.

homeless youth   Youths who have either left or have been urged to leave home with the full knowledge or approval of legal guardians. They have no alternative home in which to live.

hospitality   An unrestrained welcome to a stranger. It calls for open spaces that welcome the other as he or she arrives.

"hot spots" policing   A strategy of identifying the specific areas, usually in urban settings where crime has been shown to be concentrated. Through hot spots policing, the police are able to focus their resources on areas most likely to experience criminal activity.

ideological flexibility   Situation where the portrayal of persons is ambiguous—for example, a young offender is portrayed as both villain and victim.

indeterminate sentences   Sentences of incarceration that have no fixed expiration date, which means that a person can be held in custody until he or she is deemed by correctional officials either to be rehabilitated or to no longer pose a threat to society.

Indigenous   A term that includes individuals who identify as First Nations, Métis, or Inuit.

Indo-Canadian/South Asian   The term *Indo-Canadian* is widely used to refer to people of Indian heritage who are living in Canada as first-generation or second-generation immigrants. *South Asian* is an official term for visible minority group that includes "people who reported an ancestry that originates in South Asia including those reporting their origin as at least one of Bangladeshi, Bengali, East Indian, Goan, Gujarati, Kashmiri, Pakistani, Punjabi, Nepali, Sinhalese, Sri Lankan, Tamil, or South Asian" (Lindsay, 2001, p. 8). Both terms are used interchangeably in the media and official reports to describe gangs' members from this ethnic origin.

informal social control   The control over people's behaviour that develops as a result of relationships and attachments to significant others and investments in conventional activities that could be damaged by engagement in illegal activities.

intersectionality   Refers to a movement away from thinking categorically and toward thinking about the connections and crossroads between social facets. Intersectional thinking and theorizing recognizes the multiple, changing, and often overlapping dimensions, demographics, roles, and identities of criminals, victims, other individuals, and collectives.

jurisprudence   Literally translates as "practical wisdom about the law" and describes the process by which past legal interpretations of policy or law inform present applications.

just deserts   A legal philosophy that gives primacy to retributive punishments over deterrence or rehabilitation.

justice (Derrida)   For Derrida, justice is a messianic promise of a more just future "to come."

juvenile courts   Specialized courts first created in the late nineteenth century to apply juvenile justice laws in the care of dependent and delinquent children.

juvenile delinquency   The legal term that came into popular use in the nineteenth century to describe violations of the law by persons who had not reached the legal age of adulthood.

Juvenile Delinquents Act (JDA)   Canada's first juvenile delinquency legislation, enacted in 1908 and in force until 1984.

labelling   The stigmatization of a young person as deviant.

late starters   Youth who begin offending in adolescence with transient rather than chronic patterns of criminal behaviour that dissipate upon entry into adulthood.

life-course persistent offender   A person who begins their offending in early childhood, and continues to engage in offending through adolescence and adulthood.

life-course turning points   Events such as marriage/divorce or employment/unemployment that serve to direct an individual's developmental criminal career path toward either desistance or onset.

long-term anti-social potential   The probability of a person engaging in a criminal or anti-social act that develops as a result of life events, socialization, strain, anti-social models, and impulsiveness.

low self-control   A trait made up of impulsivity, short-sightedness, risk-taking, physicality, insensitivity, and low frustration tolerance, which leaves individuals less able to refrain from activities that provide short-term pleasure or gain.

marginalization   The partial exclusion of certain groups from mainstream society who routinely suffer as the result of gross inequalities.

method of administration   The path by which a drug or other substance is brought into contact with the body. Common methods include smoking, ingestion, injection, and intranasal inhalation.

mitigating factors   Information presented to the courts in relation to the facts of the case and the accused that may result in a lesser charge or sentence if he or she is found guilty. Conversely, aggravating factors are facts presented to the court surrounding the offence or offender's circumstances that may aggravate or increase the severity of the offence.

moral actions   Actions steered by moral rules that outline what behaviours are allowed or disallowed in particular circumstances.

moral panic   Exaggerated fears about social problems, including youth deviance, partly generated by the media.

multiple marginality   The combined disadvantages, marginalization, and powerlessness that racialized youth face, which often result in street socialization and gang involvement.

net narrowing   A phenomenon that occurs when youth who have been diverted from the criminal justice system struggle to access adequate resources.

net widening   A process whereby, in the attempt to divert individuals away from the criminal justice system, certain policies result instead in a greater number of individuals being formally processed.

Nordic model   An approach to legislating sex trade activities that criminalizes the demand-side (the buying of sex) and third-party profit from prostitution without punishment for selling sex.

not criminally responsible on account of mental disorder (NCRMD) Based on the Criminal Code's definition, a mental disorder is viewed as a "disease of the mind." For an individual to be found NCRMD, there must be a mental abnormality (not caused by voluntary intoxication, temporary mental conditions, or uncontrollable urges) causing significant impairment to preclude the individual's understanding of their behaviour.

official data The Canadian Centre for Justice Statistics, a branch of Statistics Canada, collects offender and offence data from the police, courts, and corrections for administrative purposes. The centre produces regular reports that are readily available to the public.

order-maintenance strategies Policing tactics designed to regulate the use of public spaces and to address signs of "disorder." Order-maintenance objectives have been associated with aggressive policing strategies that target high-crime areas through proactive arrests for minor crimes.

outcast spaces More than geographical locations at the social margins, outcast spaces are contexts characterized by exclusion, vulnerability, precarious resources, and barriers to belonging and community where youth are more likely to experience harm than healing, disregard than care.

parens patriae The legal doctrine that the state has a duty to assume the role of a substitute parent in the case of delinquent or dependent children who do not have parents who are able to adequately control or care for them.

parent The YCJA defines a parent as any person who has a legal duty to provide for a young person, or any person who has custody or control of a young person otherwise.

peacemaking criminology A theoretical approach that emphasizes non-violent punishment and stresses alternative criminal justice approaches, including restoring the offender to the community, rather than deterrence and retribution.

police legitimacy The extent to which individuals find the police to be legitimate has been linked to number of law-related behaviours, including compliance with the police and obeying the law. Legitimacy has been found to be predicated on the extent to which the police are seen to be acting in a fair or just manner consistent with the tenets of procedural justice.

populism Appealing to or aiming at what are popular concerns among the public. In the context of criminal justice, this may include tough-on-crime-style legislation, or policy.

power (Foucault) Rather than as a quantity held or possessed by the state, Foucault understood power to be relational, positive, and exercised.

power-control theory Refers to John Hagan and colleagues' 1989 integrated (conflict and social control theories) and feminist-informed explanation of the role of gender socialization in crime distributions.

pre-charge diversion The diverting of young offenders from the formal youth criminal justice system before they are charged with an offence by the police under the Criminal Code.

preliminary inquiry Occurs before the case proceeds to trial and is a hearing in which the judge can determine if there is sufficient evidence to proceed to trial.

pre-sentence report Report prepared by a probation officer or youth centre councillor in Quebec; these written documents present the youth court with detailed information on the young person.

pre-trial detention/remand custody The detention of a young person who has been charged with a Criminal Code offence in a youth custody facility as the youth awaits their trial/next court date.

proactive police work Enforcement activities that are police initiated rather than in response to a call for service.

procedural justice Based primarily on the work of Tyler (1990), procedural justice contends that evaluations of the fairness of police treatment and the fairness of the process by which the police commit their duties are more important in determining evaluations of the police than the fairness of the outcome of the situation.

proportionality An expectation that the severity of sanctions given for an unlawful act align with the level of harm that the act inflicts. Justice-involved youth in Canada are subject to a qualified version of proportionality that considers their diminished blameworthiness.

protective confinement or involuntary coercive holding A type of detention to protect a person from harm, either from outside sources or from themselves.

protective factors Circumstances and experiences that buffer young people's involvement in behaviours that would be damaging to themselves and to others.

psycho-educative model Developed in Quebec, this model followed the Boscoville experience and is now recognized as a profession specializing in the intervention of troubled youths.

psychosis A symptom of mental illness involving a substantial alteration to an individual's personality and a loss of contact with objective reality.

punishable young offender A term coined by Bryan Hogeveen (2005) to describe the discursive construction of some young offenders as "troublesome" and therefore requiring punishment in order to make them accountable for their criminal acts.

punitive turn thesis The argument that in recent decades the criminal justice systems of many Western countries have become more punishment oriented, with longer prison sentences and higher rates of incarceration.

radicalization A primary focus on the post-9/11 security discourse has been the issue of radicalization, whereby persons holding moderate beliefs are converted to extreme social, political, and religious beliefs that justify and compel violence. The focus of this concern has been young black and brown men from Arab and Muslim backgrounds living in Western nations.

racialized A term that denotes that race is not a biological construct but a social construct that is socially constructed and ascribed to persons on the basis of differential power relations in society.

racial profiling The increased surveillance of certain racial groups or culturally distinct neighbourhoods by the police that cannot be explained by such groups' actual increased involvement in criminal activities.

recidivism Repetition of criminal and/or delinquent behaviour. Recidivism can be measured through official sources or through self-report surveys.

reciprocal relationship The process where two causal factors influence each other.

reformable young offender A term coined by Bryan Hogeveen (2005) to describe the discursive construction of some young offenders as "troubled" and therefore needing intervention in the hope they can be rehabilitated.

rehabilitation A fundamental concept of the Youth Criminal Justice Act that holds that a young person can be reformed or changed as a result of appropriate treatment programs.

reintegration The introduction of the young person back into the community as a productive member of society.

resiliency   The ability of children and youth to develop positive self-esteem and self-efficacy despite facing crisis, challenges, or adversity.

restorative justice (RJ)   A process whereby all the parties with a stake in an offence resolve collectively how to deal with the aftermath of the offence and its implications for the future.

risk   The calculated probability of an event or a circumstance. Risks are calculated and managed through class, gender, age, and race categories.

risk assessment tools   Instruments used to assess the multitude of risk and protective factors that have been and/or are present in young people's lives that can influence the likelihood of recidivism. Youths are rated as low, medium, or high risk, and individualized interventions are developed based on these risk assessment outcomes.

risk society   This refers to a break with modernity into an emerging societal form characterized by the production of risks and of tools for their management. In contrast to the view that social problems are to be solved, issues in the risk society (e.g., crime) are risks to be managed.

runaways   Youths who run away from their family or child welfare placement, at least overnight, without parental or caretaker permission. They often leave as a result of family conflict or maltreatment.

screening tools   Instruments used to identify at-risk youth and assist in their referrals to appropriate programs and services.

Sebastien's Law   In 2010, the federal government introduced Bill C-4 as a measure to get tough on repeat young offenders. The bill was subsequently amended to become part of the Omnibus Crime Bill, passed in 2012. Section 3(1)(a) of the YCJA was subsequently slightly amended to read "protect the public," which encompasses the spirit of Sebastien's Law. The namesake of the law is 19-year-old Sebastien Lacasse, who was beaten and stabbed to death at a 2004 house party in Quebec by a 17-year-old. The incident prompted the courts to consider adult sentences for youth 14 or older found guilty of serious crimes like murder and aggravated assault.

secure custody   A form of custody under the Youth Criminal Justice Act whereby youth are removed from a community and confined to an institution.

self-report (SR) survey   A social-science questionnaire survey designed to ask respondents to report on their involvement in criminal or delinquent activities.

sentencing/peacemaking circles   A process that brings together individuals who wish to engage in conflict resolution, healing, support, and/or decision-making. It provides a space for offenders to acknowledge responsibility for their behaviour and invites community members to participate in the decision-making and/or sentencing.

sexual exploitation   The abuse, particularly of children and youth, through the exchange of sexual activity for money, drugs, and/or basic needs.

sexual exploitation trade (SET)   A term for the systems of sex work and the sex trade industry.

short-term anti-social potential   The probability of engaging in offending that is influenced by factors limited in time including intoxication, peers, and negative emotions.

situated choice   The choices individuals make to become involved in certain relationships, be they work or personal, that are situated under certain structural and historical conditions and that can influence future behaviour.

social bonds   The degree to which individuals, through socialization, have connections to people and institutions in a society and believe in the rules of the society. These connections serve as restraints against criminal opportunities and behaviour.

social constructionism   An approach that sees social problems as constructed in the media.

social desirability effects   Biases in research caused by respondents' desire to provide what they feel is the socially acceptable response or "what the researcher wants to hear."

social ecology of crime   Approach that focuses on the impact of human interactions with the lived environment on crime causation and victimization. Crime has been found to be concentrated in areas with high levels of socio-economic disadvantage and disorder. These areas are thus also prone to high levels of police supervision.

squeegee kids   A group of street-involved youth who are resourceful in attempting to develop and maintain a livelihood and means of survival by offering to clean windshields at major intersections.

static risk factors   Risk factors that are unchangeable; they include those traits that may contribute to an offender's offending and recidivism and cannot be altered through rehabilitation programming.

status offences   Behaviours that are considered delinquent or criminal only because the person who engages in the behaviour is not yet an adult. Examples include truancy (skipping school), underage drinking, and promiscuous sexual behaviour.

stigma   An attitude of disapproval, discredit, or shame directed towards an individual, or group of individuals, based on a particular behaviour or attribute.

strains   Experiences or situations that individuals perceive as being negative, creating a negative emotional reaction that provides the possible incentive for using crime as a coping mechanism.

"street checks" or "carding"   A common policing tactic involving police-initiated stops against persons in situations that typically do not involve an arrest. During these encounters, the police collect personal information from those stopped, which is later entered into a police database.

street interrogations   A tactic whereby persons are proactively stopped and questioned by police. Critics have alleged that these stops disproportionately target youth from racialized backgrounds and constitute a form of racial profiling as they are typically not predicated on involvement with criminal behaviour.

street-involved youth   Youths 25 years of age or younger who do not have a safe home or are underhoused; who have been forced to leave their family of origin; who have run away from their home without the consent of their parents or guardian or who left foster- or group-care placements; or who are not living on the street but who experiment and engage in street-involved activities and identify with street culture and street peer groupings.

substance abuse   Characterized by a pattern of recurrent use of a substance where at least one of the following occurs: failure to fulfill roles in major life areas, use in physically dangerous situations, recurrent alcohol- or drug-related problems and continued use despite this use contributing to social or interpersonal problems.

suicidality   Refers to the contemplation of taking one's own life.

surveillance   The direct or indirect observation of conduct, which is intended to produce a desired outcome (i.e., conformity).

survival sex   Involves the exchange of sexual services for food, shelter, and other necessities or for money to purchase food/shelter/necessities.

systemic racism   Critical racist theorists contend that racism is reflected in a variety of areas of social life including public policies, institutional practices, economic systems, and cultural representations. Systemic racism serves to perpetuate the political and economic dominance of whites in society over all other groups.

throwaways   Youths who are asked, or encouraged, to leave home by their parents/guardians, with the purpose of ending parental responsibility for the well-being of the youths.

trace   The silent elements that provide words with their essential meaning (see Spivak 1976) and that underlie all language.

trajectories   Paths or avenues of development throughout the lifespan. These are long-term patterns of behaviour that often consist of marriage, parenthood, employment, and involvement in criminal activities.

trauma   Experience that is psychologically painful, distressful, or shocking (such as suffering sexual abuse or witnessing serious violence) and that often results in long-term mental or physical problems (such as depression, anxiety, or insomnia). Also, the community-level and individual-level damage, pain, and suffering of Indigenous peoples—physically, spiritually, emotionally, and psychically—as a result of the historical and current processes of colonization.

trauma-informed approach   An approach to practice that incorporates an understanding of how experiences of acute and complex trauma shape the lives, identities, and perspectives of the people we respond to throughout the human services and the legal system. Trauma-informed practice requires us to implement steps that avoid re-traumatizing individuals and support wellness, recovery, and resilience (Randall and Haskell 2013).

triangulation   A research methods technique that involves using more than one source of criminological data to assess the validity of what is being observed. For example, this technique can include combining official crime data with self-report data to obtain a clearer picture of crime or delinquency facts.

underhoused   Youth who are underhoused live in housing that is temporary in nature and inadequate for space, that does not meet safety or health thresholds or has high risk for eviction.

unfit to stand trial (UST)   Description of an individual who is not fully capable of instructing counsel or understanding the nature and consequences of their trial.

unofficial data   Refers to data that are collected and usually published by private or independent researchers or research facilities. The primary data-collection techniques are self-report surveys and victimization surveys. Unofficial data are often used to enrich official data.

values   A collective conception of what is considered proper, desirable, and good—or improper, undesirable, and bad—in a culture.

victimization   The experience of being a victim, which can be linked to future criminalization.

victimization survey   A social-science questionnaire survey designed to measure the experiences of respondents as victims of crime(s).

victim–offender reconciliation programs (VORP)   A process through which a trained mediator, often a volunteer, brings offenders and victims in a criminal event together to achieve a resolution that is satisfactory to both parties (Community Justice Initiatives Association 2011; see also Stutzman Amstutz 2009).

visible minority   An official term for persons, other than Indigenous peoples, who are non-Caucasian in race or non-white in colour.

Young Offenders Act (YOA)   The federal legislation that replaced the Juvenile Delinquents Act from 1984 to 2003.

young person   The YCJA defines a young person as someone who is at least 12 years old but younger than 18 at the time an offence is committed.

youth-centric programming model   Youth play a significant role in developing and evaluating programs, and agencies continue to be flexible in adapting to the changing needs of street-involved youth.

Youth Criminal Justice Act (YCJA)   The federal legislation enacted in 2002 to replace the Young Offenders Act and which came into effect on 1 April 2003.

youth criminal justice systems   A term often used today as a substitute for *juvenile courts*. Critical criminologists argue that it signifies a shift toward treating young offenders more like adult offenders.

youth engagement   The meaningful participation and sustained involvement of a young person in an activity that has a focus outside of him- or herself. Full engagement consists of a behavioural component, an affective component, and a cognitive component.

youth justice   A separate and distinct criminal justice system that explicitly meets the unique needs of young people.

youth justice court   The court in which young people charged with an offence created by Parliament—usually under the Criminal Code or the Controlled Drugs and Substances Act—appear in order to enter a plea and then to have their trial or be sentenced.

Index

Note: Page references followed by a "*t*" indicate table; "*f*" indicate figure; "*b*" indicate box